THE ECONOMICS OF PUBLIC LAW

ECONOMISTS OF THE TWENTIETH CENTURY

General Editors: David Colander, *Christian A. Johnson Distinguished Professor of Economics, Middlebury College, Vermont, USA* and Mark Blaug, *Professor Emeritus, University of London, UK, Professor Emeritus, University of Buckingham, UK and Visiting Professor, University of Amsterdam, The Netherlands*

This innovative series comprises specially invited collections of articles and papers by economists whose work has made an important contribution to economics in the late twentieth century.

The proliferation of new journals and the ever-increasing number of new articles make it difficult for even the most assiduous economist to keep track of all the important recent advances. By focusing on those economists whose work is generally recognized to be at the forefront of the discipline, the series will be an essential reference point for the different specialisms included.

A list of published and future titles in this series is printed at the end of this volume.

The Economics of Public Law

The Collected Economic Essays of Richard A. Posner,
Volume Three

Richard A. Posner

*Judge, United States Court of Appeals for the Seventh Circuit, and
Senior Lecturer, University of Chicago Law School, USA*

Edited by

Francesco Parisi

*Professor of Law and Co-Director, J.M. Buchanan Center for
Political Economy, Program in Economics and the Law,
George Mason University, USA*

ECONOMISTS OF THE TWENTIETH CENTURY

Edward Elgar
Cheltenham, UK • Northampton, MA, USA

Published by
Edward Elgar Publishing Limited
Glensanda House
Montpellier Parade
Cheltenham
Glos GL50 1UA
UK

Edward Elgar Publishing, Inc.
136 West Street
Suite 202
Northampton
Massachusetts 01060
USA

A catalogue record for this book
is available from the British Library

ISBN 1 85898 643 5

Printed and bound in Great Britain by MPG Books Ltd, Bodmin, Cornwall

Contents

Acknowledgements

The publishers wish to thank the following who have kindly given permission for the use of copyright material.

Cardozo School of Law for article: 'Hegel and Employment at Will: A Comment', *Cardozo Law Review*, **10**, 1989, pp. 1625–36.

Columbia University in the City of New York for article: 'An Economic Theory of the Criminal Law', *Columbia Law Review*, **85** (6), October 1985, pp. 1193–231.

George Washington University for article: 'The Constitution as an Economic Document', *George Washington Law Review*, **56** (1), November 1987, pp. 4–38.

Georgetown University Law Center for article: 'Optimal Sentences for White-collar Criminals', *American Criminal Law Review*, **17** (4), Spring 1980, pp. 409–18.

Law and Society Association for article: 'Comment on Donohue', *Law and Society Review*, **22** (5), 1988, pp. 927–9.

New York University Press for article: 'Comment on "On the Economic Theory of Crime"', *Criminal Justice: Nomos 27*, edited by J. Roland Pennock and John W. Chapman, New York University Press, 1985, pp. 310–12.

RAND for articles: 'Theories of Economic Regulation', *Bell Journal of Economics and Management Science*, **5** (2), Autumn 1974, pp. 335–58; 'Taxation by Regulation', *Bell Journal of Economics and Management Science*, **2** (22), 1971, pp. 22–50; and 'The Appropriate Scope of Regulation in the Cable Television Industry', *Bell Journal of Economics and Management Science*, (3), 1972, pp. 98–129.

University of Chicago Law School for articles: 'Economics, Politics and the Reading of Statutes and the Constitution', *University of Chicago Law Review*, **49** (2), Spring 1982, pp. 263–91; 'Some Economics of Labor Law', *University of Chicago Law Review*, **51** (4), Fall 1984, pp. 988–1011; 'An Economic Analysis of Sex Discrimination Laws', *University of Chicago Law Review*, **56** (4), Fall 1989, pp. 1311–35; 'The Independent Judiciary in an Interest-group Perspective' with William M. Landes, *Journal of Law and Economics*, **18** (3), December 1975, pp. 875–901; 'A Statistical Study of Antitrust Enforcement', *Journal of Law and Economics*, **13** (2), October 1970, pp. 365–419; and 'The Costs of Enforcing Legal Rights', *East European Constitutional Review*, Summer 1995, pp. 71–83.

University of Chicago Press for article: 'The Social Costs of Monopoly and Regulation', *Journal of Political Economy*, **83** (4), August 1975, pp. 807–27.

University of Pennsylvania Law School for article: 'The Efficiency and the Efficacy of Title VII', *University of Pennsylvania Law Review*, **136** (2), December 1987, pp. 513–21.

Every effort has been made to trace all the copyright holders but if any have been inadvertently overlooked the publishers will be pleased to make the necessary arrangements at the first opportunity.

The editor gratefully acknowledges Ben Depoorter for his valuable comments and assistance during the production of this book.

Introduction

Richard Posner's contribution to the field of law and economics is remarkable for its broad horizon, which extends from the examination of fundamental methodological questions to the formulation of theories of legal evolution, and beyond that to the study of substantive, procedural, and constitutional doctrines. Richard Posner has written 30 books and more than 300 articles and review essays, establishing a record that most likely will never be challenged as the most productive and influential scholar in the law and economics community.

Posner's extensive academic *oeuvre* is also most notable in light of his 1981 appointment as a judge of the United States Court of Appeals for the Seventh Circuit. He has been extremely prolific on the bench: his 50 or more signed opinions per year have placed him first among his peers (Landes et al., 1998). This record-breaking productivity makes his judicial views influential across the United States, as, according to recent statistics, he ranks first among all Federal Courts of Appeal judges for the weight his opinions carry outside of his judicial circuit (ibid.).

In spite of his most successful judicial career and administrative responsibilities as Chief Judge, Richard Posner's academic production has in many ways surpassed the expectations engendered by the quantity of his published opinions. A recent study of the most frequently cited, and therefore influential, legal scholars ranked him as number one; in fact he surpassed the cumulative citations (1956 to date) of jurisprudential giants such as Roscoe Pound and Oliver Wendell Holmes, Jr. Furthermore, he has a substantial lead, with approximately twice as many citations as his closest competitors (Shapiro, 2000).

During the last three decades, Posner has carried out his admirable intellectual mission, continually tackling new areas of law from an economic perspective. While much of Posner's work on the economics of private law is an application of his well-known efficiency hypothesis of the common law, several of the papers presented in this volume demonstrate how Posner extends his analysis to the economics of constitutional law and legislation, criminal law, labor law, employment discrimination and antitrust regulation.

In spite of the increased acceptance and popularity of economic legal analysis in the field of private law, legal scholars have continued to cast a skeptical eye on the application of economics to public law; they believe that public law operates in a separate sphere from social science, maintaining that explanation of human behavior in society, however well researched, gives very little insight into the ways in which public law functions. In spite of such intellectual resistance, Posner successfully utilizes the analytical tools of microeconomics and public choice theory to examine important public law issues and provides valuable illustrations of how political economy can be used to understand the legal dimension of the state. Posner's work on the economics of public law is a critical component of the interaction between the new law and economics movement and public choice theory, and exemplifies the parallel influence that these two important intellectual movements have had on the current understanding of legal institutions. Within the law and economics community, Posner contributed to this important methodological revolution, focussing on the economic analysis of legal issues and offering a new perspective on the best ways for law to serve both democratic society and the free market. Put in historical perspective, Posner's contribution to the theory of public law is at least as important as his contribution to the study of core private law issues, such as his seminal papers on the economics of contracts, of torts, and the methodology of economic analysis. Posner is careful to impress upon his readers that the public law, even constitutional law, can hardly be separated from other areas of study when it comes to applying the principles of economics.

During the last three decades, Richard Posner has provided innovative contributions to the development of an overarching economic theory of law, with applications that include traditional legal subjects as well as unorthodox legal issues. This collection of essays showcases Posner's contribution to the economics of public law. While this is a relatively narrow sample of Posner's views in the field, the editor hopes it will provide valuable methodological insights into how economic principles can be used to analyse public law.

Richard Posner's writings in public law extend well beyond the papers selected for this collection, and his academic production continues to influence legal thought and leave a positive imprint on judicial decision-making. Posner's earliest academic writings include several examples of his developing economic theory of regulation, with papers dating from the late 1960s focussing on antitrust and economic regulation. Examples include Posner (1969a) on the question of the optimal regulation of natural monopoly; Posner (1969b) on the Federal Trade Commission; Posner's (1970) statistical study of antitrust enforcement; Posner (1971) outlining a theory of taxation by regulation; Posner (1972) on the appropriate scope of regulation in the cable television industry; Posner (1974a) considering theories of economic regulation; Posner's (1974b) casebook on the law and economics of antitrust law; and Posner (1975) on the social costs of monopoly and other regulation. After the first years, Posner only occasionally returned to the study of antitrust law, with Posner and Easterbrook (1980), *Antitrust: Cases, Economic Notes, and Other Materials*; and Posner (1999) on the effects of deregulation on competition in the United States.

During later years, Posner's work is most representative of his leading contribution to the establishment of the new law and economics movement, as it covers a wide array of subjects and applies economics to areas that are unrelated to explicit market realities. Among the several contributions to the field of constitutional law and legislation, we should indeed remember Posner (1982a) on the economics of politics and the reading of statutes and constitutions; Posner (1987b) developing a theory of the Constitution as an economic document; Posner (1998) on the speech market and legacy of Schenck. Worthy of mention also are Posner (1981) with an important volume on the economics of justice, containing several points of interest related to public law; and Posner's (1987a) methodological paper on the justice of economics.

Within the field of public law, Posner's work on the economics of criminal law is also noteworthy. Starting in the early 1980s, Posner (1980d) develops an economic theory of criminal sanctions, with a specific application to determining the optimal sentences for white-collar criminals. Posner (1985a) describes an economic theory of the criminal law; Posner (1985b) comments on the economic theory of crime; and, most recently, Philipson and Posner (1996) discourses on the economic epidemiology of crime.

Other areas of public law tackled by Richard Posner include the economics of labor law and employment discrimination. The main papers in this field include Posner (1984) on the economics of labor law; Posner (1989a) with a comment on Hegel and employment at will; Posner (1989b) with an economic analysis of sex discrimination laws; and Posner (1987c), on employment discrimination and the efficiency and efficacy of Title VII.

Among other topics related to the subject of the present volume, Posner's papers considering topics of political economy and his work on the economics of judicial administration are worthy of mention. Of more general interest are Posner (1995) on the costs of enforcing legal rights; Posner (1996) on the cost of rights, with applications to Central and Eastern Europe in addition to the United States; and, most recently, Posner (1997b) on the theme of equality, wealth, and political stability. Posner has written much about the judiciary and its role in the formation of legal rules, using economic analysis to help explain the incentives of judges, the effects of various judicial procedures, and the way in which these factors affect the laws as they are made and applied. A sampling of his work in the area includes Posner (1973), developing an economic theory of legal procedure and judicial administration; Ehrlich and Posner (1974), an economic analysis of legal rulemaking; Landes and Posner (1975), an interest group theory of the judiciary; Langbein and Posner (1976), a public choice analysis of the judiciary from an interest group perspective; Posner (1982b), an economic theory of federal jurisdiction; Posner (1988), engaged in a debate with Gordon Tullock; Posner (1994), on judges' incentives and judicial decision-making as a maximization process. Several of these papers were included in previous volumes of Posner's collected work.

Posner's economics of legislation and constitutional law

Legislative intent and competing theories of interpretation form one of the oldest and most complex conundrums in the theory of legislation. Posner attempts to show how economics can explain how judges perhaps should, and in fact do, interpret legislative provisions. As Posner suggests, this endeavor should interest anyone who realizes that interpretation is an intrinsic part of an economic theory of legislation, because the meaning of statutes is not fixed until interpreted.

Posner's theories of legislation and statutory interpretation

Posner (1982a) discusses recent theories on legislation: public interest theory, which holds that legislation cures market failures; interest group theory, which holds that organized interest groups procure laws in a way that is amorally redistributive; and legislative process theory, which concentrates on the structure of the legislative process itself, such as bicameralism. According to Posner, an economic approach to legislation requires a fourfold taxonomy, since public interest and interest group theories are really polar opposites on a continuum. Posner describes the first of the two middle categories as legislation that meets the public interest by furthering a widely held belief, such as just distribution of wealth through progressive taxation. The second category encompasses narrow interest group, or 'public sentiment', legislation, which, unlike public interest laws, cannot be explained on economic grounds due to insufficient knowledge about relevant costs and benefits. Posner cites laws against pornography as an example.

Posner discusses the implications of these categories of legislation for statutory interpretation, considering why judges take into account only the intent, but not the motives, of the drafters. By not looking at motive, judges avoid revealing interest group pressures behind the statute, but at the same time they cannot divine what influenced the drafters, or identify the 'real' context and political pressures if the statute represents a compromise. This lack of inquiry limits the ability of interest groups to deceive potential opponents by using language that can only be understood with reference to the group's basic objectives. As a result, looking only to intent as expressed in public documents, but not the underlying motives which prompted the legislation, may therefore limit interest group power. Since courts cannot tell which statutes are in the public interest and which serve an interest group, they do not extrapolate from the intent behind one statute to illuminate another for fear that this exercise might corrupt the process of statutory interpretation and/or sacrifice the public interest. Posner's conclusions on this point have laid the foundation for several later contributions to the economic theory of legislative interpretation.

In considering what role legislative history should have in statutory interpretation, Posner assumes that legislators vote not just on a bill's language, but also assent to the political bargain struck by the bill's sponsors. Since the terms of the legislative horse-trading are found in the committee reports and floor comments of the sponsors, but not in minority opinions or in post-enactment expressions of legislative intent, only the former should be considered in statutory interpretation.

Posner also considers whether a statute should be the basis for implied rights of action in private tort cases; the answer depends on whether one thinks that the statute is public interest or interest group legislation. If the first, it probably reflects the optimal standard of care based on analytical tools the legislature has, but courts do not possess, and so economics would suggest implied rights of action. If the statute is interest group legislation, however, the lack of a private remedy probably reflects the group's general low level of influence or may be the consequence of a legislative compromise. Finally, Posner observes that the choice of theoretical explanation for a given statute is not binary, a fact which may explain the apparent inconsistencies of courts' action in their interpretation.

Posner then considers the rule of lenity in constructing criminal statutes. Economic analysis suggests that lenience is a response to the problem of overdeterrence. Since the outer boundaries of criminal statutes are uncertain, people steer well clear of its terms, resulting in social costs because of beneficial conduct forgone. A narrow interpretation solves this drafting problem, and thus appears sensible from an economic viewpoint.

The economics of legislative and constitutional interpretation
After his discussion of statutory interpretation, Posner (1982a) considers how the economic analysis affects constitutional interpretation, arguing for looser construction of constitutional provisions than of statutes. The framers may have made amendment to the Constitution difficult because it could radically change the nature of the article

in question; nevertheless, they still may have wanted loose interpretation by courts, which otherwise could only make minor changes if too constrained by constitutional text and the history. Second, implementing the intent of language drafted hundreds of years ago through strict interpretation is probably beyond the ability of courts' time and resources. Interestingly, Posner therefore suggests that courts should only act upon historical research which conclusively discredits recognized interpretations of constitutional intent when it would not disrupt accepted public policy.

Posner argues further that invalidating legislation on the ground that it is not rationally related to a proper legislative purpose makes little sense. No one argues that interest groups should not influence the legislative process, but a serious and neutrally applied rationality review would by definition invalidate interest group legislation since their self-interest would probably not meet standards of rational benefit for the whole community.

Strict scrutiny review of statutes fares better under Posner's analysis. If a statute abridges a fundamental right, Posner does not object to the strict scrutiny standard, except to suggest that it may be too lax. On the other hand, strict scrutiny of 'public sentiment' statutes, such as laws regulating sex, interferes with their serious consideration because such laws cannot be justified on utilitarian grounds: their benefits are hard to measure even if they clearly exceed the costs. Since the 'clear and convincing' reasons that would uphold a statute reviewed with strict scrutiny are usually utilitarian, public sentiment statutes frequently fail the test. This is the case even if they could also qualify as public interest statutes according to Posner's taxonomy as described above.

Finally, Posner considers the economics of the doctrine of nondelegation, arguing that transfer of legislative, judicial, and executive power to specialized agencies may have an economic justification. For example, the cost of legislative action increases as a function of the body's size (diseconomies of scale); legislatures cannot conveniently increase output by adding members. Indeed, the cost of securing a majority agreement goes up with the number of members at the nonlinear rate of $n\,(n-1)]/2$, a pace that may outweigh any benefits of expanding legislative participation. According to Posner, parallel arguments justify the delegation of judicial and executive power as well, since the growth of the bureaucracies supporting these functions has the same detrimental effect on economic efficiency.

In concluding, Posner notes that courts' interpretation of newer statutes is more in keeping with economic principles than that of the Constitution and older statutes. Posner explains this discrepancy by noting that courts have little to gain by misinterpreting a modern statute, because the legislature can easily nullify their action. On the other hand, the difficulty in amending the Constitution, and the ambiguity of that document and older statutes, mean that judges have greater leeway because any political force with an interest in nullifying the court's interpretation no longer exists.

Social contract and the economics of constitutionalism
In addition to looking to legislation passed according to the rules of our republic, Posner (1982a) examines the Constitution itself and asserts that principles of economics are key tools in understanding how to maximize its protections and integrity of its framework. Building on the philosophy of John Locke, who greatly influenced the

Constitution's drafters, Posner begins by describing the Constitution as a social contract. Just as with contract law, a particular constitutional provision should not be enforced, or held to its strict language, when understood to be impracticable, unduly burdensome, or against public policy. Within this framework, Posner uses economic analysis to revisit doctrines of constitutional law that allow constitutions to operate as instruments that best serve citizens.

In a subsequent paper, Posner (1987b) touches on different topics related to the Constitution that can be studied using economics. He considers constitutionalism, discussing the economics of having a governing document that, somewhat like a contract, requires a supermajority to change any standard or rule it contains. He examines the economics of the governmental structure of separation of powers and federalism and also provides an economic critique of specific constitutional doctrines that do not pass economic efficiency muster. Other provisions of the Constitution, he argues, that are implicitly economic because they, and the interpretive doctrines that have grown up around them, lend themselves to economic analysis. He then discusses proposals to constitutionalize *laissez-faire*, that is interpret (reinterpret) the Constitution as a general guarantor of individual economic autonomy and free markets. He points out the critical tension between *laissez-faire* and democratic political theory and practice (the latter considered as in public choice), and objecting to making the Constitution a charter for *laissez-faire* ideals.

Posner also examines the current double standard in judicial decision-making, which liberally extends constitutional protection to personal freedoms, but does not do so to economic liberties despite the fact that the Constitution contains provisions that ought to protect both. He considers the macroeconomic effects of the Constitution, discussing the role it has played in creating the United States' wealth. He comments that provisions such as the commerce clause (among others) have had a positive economic effect as they prevent one state from being able to impose the costs associated with maintaining its commercial well-being upon another (externalities). Furthermore, Posner suggests that federalism may be the most important contribution of constitutionalism to economic growth. Finally, Posner considers the economics of constitutional interpretation. He shows why it is efficient first to interpret the Constitution's text, context, and background and then to decide cases according to law as gleaned from that process (as well as according to principles such as judicial restraint and *stare decisis*), rather than to follow judges' views of appropriate public policy.

The independent judiciary and interest group politics

One key feature of most constitutional systems of the Western legal tradition is the principle of separation of powers, with particular importance placed on an independent judiciary to ensure the fair adjudication of law. Landes and Posner (1975) examine the effect of the independent judiciary on lobbying, the *de jure* system of interest group purchase of legislative policy. Economic analysis of the role of the courts shows how an independent judiciary can make viable a governmental process that emphasizes interest group participation in policy formation. By enforcing laws validly passed, even in a previous legislative session, the judiciary ensures integrity in the constitutional process by imposing prohibitive costs on public interest purchase of judicial decisions.

The authors work from the perspective of interest group analysis, pointing out that interest groups will not purchase policy programs if they cannot assume that desired policy will last. In the absence of an enforceable contract, some other power must provide that guarantee. In the first instance, the high transaction costs associated with the cumbersome process of enacting legislation supply stability. Accordingly, if courts, which must enforce legislation, were agents of the Congress in session, the legislature could cheaply arrange a de facto repeal by asking its courts to rewrite legislation by taking advantage of interpretive leeway. If, on the other hand, the judiciary is independent and interprets legislation in accordance with enacting Congress' intent, it then supports, rather than interferes with, purchase of legislation by interest groups. However, the independent judiciary may also impose costs by declaring the law unconstitutional or interpreting it in a way that reduces gains to the group that paid for the law.

The authors acknowledge that the judiciary might not be truly independent. After all, in the US legal system Congress does have powers, such as appropriations of funds, creation of new judgeships, and rewriting jurisdiction by which they might compel judicial acquiescence. However, self-interested judges can increase their independence by rendering predictable decisions in accord with the original meaning of the statute. This increases the value of the judiciary to the current legislature because its members know that the courts will enforce the contracts they make. According to the authors, the structure of the judiciary – life tenure, rules against *ex parte* contact, and impeachment for accepting bribes – also prevents interest groups from influencing judges directly. Landes and Posner support these conclusions with a formal economic model.

Landes and Posner (1975) further explore the positive implications of the economic theory of the judiciary. First, they consider the case of 'dependent' judiciaries, such as those established in specialized agencies, making a consistent finding that such entities are established when the chance of judicial nullification of political and legislative bargains is high. Mild judicial review allows the agencies to keep the terms of a particular legislative deal, but since that review is not wholly effective, administrative adjudication becomes far less consistent over time, as would be expected from a dependent judiciary that is not protected from shifts in political emphasis.

The authors further consider the effect the economic system of legislation coupled with an independent judiciary has on the form of interest group legislation. Building upon public choice models of rent-seeking, the authors suggest that interest groups purchase legislation that does not require substantial annual appropriations. Legislative rents that require yearly congressional funding are quickly dissipated as it would be necessary to lobby each new Congress to support the program, the costs of which eat into the net present value of the legislation for its intended beneficiaries. Since the judiciary cannot help to enforce new annual appropriations, interest groups tend not to purchase such legislation.

The authors also consider the role of the independent judiciary in enforcing the Constitution, which, in their view, has two purposes in this context. First, it establishes ground rules for a system of interest group politics enforced by the independent judiciary. Second, the Constitution confers specific protective legislation on powerful interest groups willing to purchase such a provision in their favor. For example, broad interpretation of the First Amendment is a form of protective legislation purchased by publishers as an interest group. The Constitution's purpose, supported by the independent judiciary, is to protect groups powerful enough to obtain a constitutional provision or a special interest legislation in their favor.

The authors conclude that the independent judiciary is an essential element in the observed struggle among interest groups, which is a major component of political practice. Although the judiciary is a critical player in this process, it itself is not 'political', but rather is above politics because it fulfills its role by enforcing the legislative deals of earlier legislatures, not because it has special wisdom, integrity, morality, or commitment to principle.

The costs of enforcing legal rights
In analysing the Constitution, Posner (1995) considers guaranteed individual rights and liberties as another example of the usefulness of economics in policymaking. In the course of this examination, he points out that sometimes the cost of enforcing individual freedom, especially if done in an inefficient manner through a poorly developed system, often outweighs the benefits of doing so. Therefore, Posner asserts that societies, especially young democracies, must carefully evaluate the freedoms they choose to protect in light of the cost they will impose on society as a whole. In this context, Posner brings his knowledge of the history and practice of the Anglo-American legal system, his experience as a federal judge, and the theoretical model of cost–benefit analysis to the question of enforcing legal rights in the formerly communist states of Central and Eastern Europe.

Posner begins by defining rights as claims or entitlements enforceable through courts or some other centrally provided system. Next, he distinguishes positive liberties, such as the right to demand a service from government, from negative liberties, such as the right to be free from interference in carrying out individual activities. Though it is clear that negative rights are cheaper to protect than positive ones, still they require the public provision of an enforcement system, although the cost is generally justified. Looking at the US experience, Posner suggests that, despite the costs of enforcement (less than 1 percent of US GNP at the time of writing), the benefit to cost ratio is clearly more than one.

Accordingly, Posner identifies two reasons why more countries committed to free markets and democratic government do not have an effective public system of rights enforcement. First, a small, inexpensive enforcement mechanism remains so only by sacrificing procedure, creating the possibility that the small enforcement agencies and judicial bodies become so powerful that they abuse their authority by impinging upon negative liberties. As an example, Posner describes the change in both the UK and America from limited enforcement of a few rights for defendants, to greater enforcement of more rights, such as those offered by the Sixth Amendment, a system made possible by a high level of material wealth and therefore one which might not be appropriate for every society.

Posner also notes that overextension may interfere with the purchase of an effective system of rights enforcement. First, reallocation of resources from a system of positive to negative rights enforcement might be difficult because of the logic of public choice and the fact that negative rights enforcement imposes new costs in addition to those lingering from the old positive system. Second, many negative liberties, such as antitrust laws and laws against fraud, are vague enough to allow for manipulation that interfere with efficiency and some negative liberties, Posner concludes, may be more valuable to a poor society than others.

Accordingly, Posner goes on to consider five rights from the perspective of their cost and benefit, such as the prevention of brutal police tactics used on pretrial detainees. This right is enforced in the US by an exclusionary rule, tort remedies against the police, *Miranda* warnings, and police professionalism, costly mechanisms which may not be worth the benefit in other countries. For instance, such protection requires a well-paid and educated police force, and if talents that might be more valuable for other urgent tasks such as entrepreneurship or public health are devoted to this area, the net effect will be negative. Stated another way, measures that prevent coercive interrogation may undermine negative liberties (noninterference in one's business) because criminal enforcement is more costly and less effective as its costs rise.

Posner concludes that, regardless of the rights one chooses to enforce, countries with resource shortages ought to set priorities based on an awareness that enforceable rights are not costless or even cheap. A sophisticated analysis considers not only which rights to enforce, but how much to spend on each to maximize social benefit at modest cost. Work in that direction would be valuable for both the United States and for the nations of Central and Eastern Europe.

Posner's economics of criminal law

An important component of Posner's contribution to law and economics relates to his economic theory of wrongful behavior. Following our presentation of selected papers on the economics of tort law in the previous volume of Posner's collected writings, we shall now turn to a brief selection of his work exploring the economics of criminal law. While many of his critics are quick to differentiate criminal law from other areas more easily illuminated by economic principles, Posner asserts that even the criminal mind is responsive to changes in costs and benefits. Criminal activity is proscribed, he asserts, because it is economically inefficient and impedes the free functioning of the market. The design of criminal legislation and the policy choices concerning the prosecution of criminal behavior should be guided by economic principles and the need to foster the essential conditions for the functioning of a free market economy.

As part of his analysis, Posner asserts that economic theory should be accepted as much in criminal law as in other areas of law. Posner (1985b) expressed surprise at Professor Klevorick's theory of why the economic analysis of crime, unlike that of torts, has not entered the legal mainstream: economic analysis of crime is incomplete because it presupposes a political theory that is not yet in place, according to Klevorick. Posner responds that many critics of the economic analysis of torts say the same thing about tort law, thus the criticism does not distinguish between the analysis of crime and torts. He then notes that no legal theory in any field of law must be fully-fledged before it can be accepted into the mainstream. Economic theory must first be developed by law professors, who cannot rely on lawyers and judges for economic originality. Therefore the problem with the economic theory of criminal law is not that it is incomplete or lacks rigorous philosophical foundation (which he admits it is and does), but that it has not been adequately pursued despite the full promise of the opportunities in the field. Posner concludes that it would be shameful to defer this research pending the development of a political theory of rights commanding wide agreement.

Posner's economic theory of the criminal law

Posner (1985a) sets out to show that the substantive provisions of the criminal law, like those of tort and the common law in general, can be given economic meaning and be shown to promote efficiency. Posner (p. 1195) summarizes his analysis in his introduction by making the following three points:

(a) criminal law's major purpose 'is to prevent people from bypassing the system of voluntary, compensated exchange' that functions when transaction costs are low, thereby making the market more efficient;

(b) tort law will not sufficiently deter these attempts to bypass the market because optimal damages will frequently exceed the offender's ability to pay, and thus public enforcement and nonmonetary sanctions are necessary for effective deterrence;

(c) the costliness of these sanctions coupled with the 'worthless character of most of the sanctioned conduct' explains why, for example, the criminal law punishes unsuccessful crimes. Doing so raises the expected cost of completed crimes, which makes them less likely to be committed, and at the same time economizes costly punishments for completed crimes.

Throughout his analysis, Posner unveils critical economic principles which form the underlying structure of existing criminal law; these important concepts have now entered the core of any modern course in criminal law and constitute essential aspects of any law and economics curriculum.

Regarding the economics of theft, Posner shows that stealing is almost always a pure coercive transfer of wealth that is not part of any productive act. The optimally deterrent damages, when adjusted upward to discourage market bypassing, will often exceed the tortfeasor's ability to pay. This is because the amount must also take into consideration the nonlinear relationship between the risk of death that might result either inadvertently or deliberately from the felony itself, and compensation for bearing that risk, and the need to offset concealment efforts. Therefore theft requires public, nonmonetary enforcement and sanction, such as prison. (Posner also touches on his theory explaining why tort and criminal law constituted a unified system of remedies in primitive societies.)

Law and economics analysis concludes that the pursuit of absolute deterrence (that is, what economists would call corner solutions) is rarely desirable in the law. Posner argues that this principle applies even to situations of outright criminal behavior, noting that the severity of sanctions must be limited to avoid inducing innocent people to forgo socially desirable activities which are at the borderline of criminal activity. Absolute deterrence for smaller crimes would eliminate marginal deterrence (the incentive to substitute lesser crimes for more serious offenses) and thereby create external effects on disincentives for more serious violations of the law.

Referring to substantive provisions of the criminal law, Posner notes that much of the emphasis on prevention (especially in common law) can be explained by the fact that very little criminal activity can be justified in terms of social cost. Thus, for example, more severe punishment of repeat offenders is justified because the (expensive) prison time yields a greater reduction in future crime than for first-time offenders who might not violate the law again once released. Similarly, criminal law punishes attempted crimes because the action itself signals the person's higher propensity to break the law. Thus punishment has a higher-than-average marginal impact on prevention of future offenses: someone who attempts one robbery will probably try again, so imprisonment prevents future robberies. Yet attempts are not punished as severely as completed crimes; this differentiation denotes a system of two-stage sanctions aimed at maintaining optimal incentives during the criminal's decision-making process. Individuals who have begun, but not yet completed, a criminal undertaking have an incentive to stop before accomplishing the felony in order to avoid the full criminal penalty. Lower penalties for failed attempts to break the law further reduce the costs of erroneous convictions, given the greater evidentiary uncertainty likely to characterize such cases.

Posner also offers economic explanations of punishment for conspiracy; aiding and abetting; and he defends entrapment, provided that it only assists people in committing a crime they would otherwise commit (for example, sales of drugs to undercover police), making it preventive and, thus, legal. On the other hand, entrapment that induces people to commit a crime that they would not otherwise consider does not serve any prophylactic purpose and the accused should be able to avail themselves of the defense of entrapment in that instance.

Posner further discusses the economic rationale for requiring criminal intent, concluding that it can help demarcate real coercive transfers from accidental transfers with similar externally observable characteristics. Considering criminal intent also helps distinguish between crimes with different probabilities of apprehension and conviction as well as between situations with different likelihoods of effective deterrence. According to Posner, the insanity defense should be limited to those so mentally ill as to render the forward-looking and deterrent function of the criminal laws meaningless. In situations where the threat of criminal sanction provides no effective deterrence and where incapacitation might not be socially valuable, or could be achieved at less cost, no rationale would unconditionally support the imposition of the full criminal sanction.

The listing of Posner's contributions to the economics of criminal law continues with the economic analysis of nonmonetary sanctions such as afflictive punishments, primarily the death penalty and imprisonment; it further includes a comparative analysis of recklessness, negligence, strict liability, and necessity in torts and criminal law.

Optimal choice of sentences and penalties

While criminal liability is a key part of Posner's discussion, he also gives insight into criminal sentencing. As a means to achieve the optimal efficiency in sentencing, Posner emphasizes that the law needs to be more sensitive to the benefits of trading prison terms for paid fines as a way of discharging criminal liability.

Posner elaborates an economic theory of optimal sentencing, which links the nature of the most appropriate penalty (fines versus imprisonment) to the kind of crime, as opposed to giving sole consideration to the gravity of the criminal behavior. In this respect, Posner builds on the traditional wisdom of criminal law theory, introducing a novel paradigm in the thesis (1980d) that white-collar crime is better punished by fine than by imprisonment. These nonviolent offenses are most often committed by either well-to-do individuals or by associations, such as corporations. In essence, Posner argues that the cost of collecting fines from those who can pay them is cheaper than imprisonment and, so long as the monetary penalties are high enough to provide the most effective deterrence, the benefit is the same. Taking into account all the factors that make imprisonment a disutility might make it difficult to calculate optimal fines, but the equivalent of a short prison term (the norm in white-collar crime) can be determined by simply finding an appropriate rate of exchange between time imprisoned and dollars fined. Alternatively, the design of optimal sanctions could bypass this kind of conversion, by computing the most desirable penalties directly as a function of the existing incentives to commit the crime. While this approach might fall outside the orthodoxy of modern criminal law theory, it is not novel in the Western legal tradition. Several cases of wrongful behavior, such as theft, that would nowadays be considered as crimes, were once treated as wrongs deserving a monetary sanction, with restitution being a multiple of the value of the thing or money stolen. This factor was linked to the likelihood of detection and successful conviction and to the need to maintain a sufficiently high expected penalty for the action. The boundaries between torts and crimes, as well as the optimal scope of alternative criminal sanctions, have been relatively fluid throughout legal history, and Posner provides us with a valid economic framework to revisit this important legal question.

Posner responds to the criticism that a system that imprisons the poor and fines the rich discriminates against the former by showing that so long as the penalty is set at the level of optimal deterrence, there is no discrimination in either form of punishment. Instead, a nondiscriminatory system would either raise the fine progressively with the offender's wealth, or limit the prison term as the offender's wealth rises. The substitution of fines for imprisonment only discriminates where the fines are trivial when compared to the appropriate deterrent for the crime. So long as the criminal can pay the fine, the cost/benefit analysis leads to the conclusion that society is better off with monetary sanction than imprisonment, albeit with a fine more severe than those meted out today.

Labor law and employment discrimination

In addition to constitutional law, statutory construction, and criminal law, Posner's use of economics is also helpful in analysing regulatory law, of which labor law is an important part due to its critical impact on both the market economy and on the social well-being of the workforce. The proper understanding of economic incentives, and the parties' responsiveness to regulations promulgated by governmental agencies, is critical; Posner deftly guides the reader through some counterintuitive paradoxes to reach that comprehension. With the aid of economic analysis and public choice theory, Posner unveils some of the unintended consequences of economic regulation, providing a valuable framework for the evaluation of other areas of regulatory law.

Posner on the economics of labor law

Posner (1984) considers the economics of labor law, narrowly defined as the regulation conducted under the authority of the National Labor Relations Act governing collective bargaining by unions. He begins with a thumbnail sketch of US labor law beginning with the generally anti-union common law that the National Labor Relations Act (NLRA) transformed into generally pro-union federal labor law. Eschewing any attempt to summarize all the relevant statutory provisions and interpretive doctrines, Posner conveys the essential features of the National Labor Relations Board's (NLRB) regulation through a description of an effort to organize labor in a typical small industrial plant. His rendition covers union authorization; protection from being fired for employees who seek to organize; forbidding of 'yellow dog' contracts (no-strike contracts between employers and individual employees as opposed to those between employers and unions); defining of bargaining units; forced payment of dues to successfully organized unions; striking, hiring of replacements; rehiring of union members after a strike; and the enforceability of collective-bargaining contracts.

Posner further provides an illustrative discussion of unions as labor cartels and the NLRA as a means to promote this control. Large numbers of competitors or potential entrants into the market, which is the case with most labor markets, makes it very difficult to establish a cartel. Posner suggests that efforts to create labor cartels would fail without government assistance because of competition, free-rider, and defector problems. The NLRA provides the necessary support to counteract the natural course of the labor market in a variety of ways.

First, by stopping employers from firing employee organizers it prevents competition between employees willing to work for the competitive wage and those devoted to organized rent-seeking in the hope of a higher unionized wage.

Second, by forcing payment of dues the NLRA increases union wealth which can be devoted to effective organization and representation, and prevents employees from free-riding on the union's efforts. The provisions that require rehiring of strikers also prevent this because those who do not strike know they will eventually have to work next to those who did; similarly, peaceful picketing provisions discourage free-riding and defecting by identifying workers who do not participate in the strike, just like published rate tariffs enable competitors to detect cheating in other cartels.

Seniority rules, which require that the employer lay off the youngest employees first, also support unionization and thus cartelization. Senior employees have the greatest loyalty to, and derive the greatest benefits from, the union. In contrast, workers hired during a period of expansion might have less than average union loyalty, just as might be the case with younger workers. Accordingly, the union benefits whenever the senior employees are retained and the younger workers are let go because it avoids substitution of loyal workers for nonloyal ones when the employer rehires.

Posner explains why an administrative agency, not the courts, enforces the NLRA. If the act was a means for the federal government to invert common law labor law and support cartelization, Congress could rationally fear that federal and state judges, who had fashioned the common law, might resist its dilution and interpret the act accordingly. Even if judges would use the cartelization policy as an interpretive guide, the act, and amendments to it, interfere because they promote cartelization in an equivocal way. For example, the prohibition against the destruction of tangible assets weakens union power (as opposed to intangible assets such as consumer goodwill that unions may destroy during a strike). Similarly, but more ambiguously, Posner notes that requiring 30 percent of workers to authorize a union before an election will be ordered might weaken unions.

Race discrimination and the efficiency of Title VII

Title VII, administered by the Equal Employment Opportunity Commission (EEOC) is a large part of modern labor law. While Posner concedes that Title VII might have great social benefit, he refutes the argument of some contemporary legal scholars that it has economic justification. In an exchange with one of these proponents, Professor Donohue, Posner (1987c) contradicts his (1987) contention that forbidding employment discrimination on the basis of race may be a socially efficient intervention in labor markets.

Donohue (1986) builds on the idea that racial discrimination creates a transaction cost measured by the majority group's aversion to association with minorities. In this way Donohue implicitly accepts the logic of Nobel prize economist Gary Becker, when suggesting that lowering the transaction cost should give nondiscriminatory firms a competitive benefit, thereby providing an incentive to be inclusive that will erode the effects of discrimination over time. But Donohue then argues that an anti-discrimination law would accelerate this process and thus maximize business profit.

Posner's critique starts by pointing out that Donohue's analysis fails to consider the costs of administering the suits that Title VII generates, which would effectively counteract any gains from lowered transaction costs. He then continues that Title VII imposes substantial expenses in addition to administrative ones: for bigots, the cost of associating with minorities is real and will not be reduced by a law against the discrimination. Second, forcing the pace of adoption of nondiscriminatory policies that would be reached in the long run might distort the path to the new equilibrium, just as scrapping old technology the moment a superior one is developed may not produce optimal results. Third, discriminating between groups may be the least costly method of setting the optimum wage in the face of high information costs, thus forcing the employer to pay everyone equally may be inefficient. Posner recognizes that many of these economic arguments led to inequitable conclusions. Conversely, imposing a de facto tax on ethnic majorities by forcing association with members of ethnic minorities may be justifiable based on societal norms of equality. However, these points do show that Donohue's conclusion that Title VII is wealth maximizing is not justified.

Posner also argues that Title VII may not be effective: its administrative costs are an economic dead weight and the law itself is neither efficient nor equitable. It may be ineffective, according to Posner, because it forces nondiscriminatory employers to pay some workers more than their marginal value product (that is, more than the wage employees could secure in a world with perfect information) because of high information costs stemming from the fact that some personal characteristics (for example, honesty) are not easily observable or verifiable by the employer. This informational asymmetry provides an incentive to employ fewer members of those minority groups that are statistically less talented or have lower performance averages. Although it is easy to enforce the requirement of equal pay for equal work, it is hard to monitor discriminatory hiring and firing practices, as one must show, for example, disparate treatment. Since most workers do not have perfect performance records, and most employers will not admit to discriminatory hiring and firing practices, and are careful not to leave a paper trail, proving unequal treatment is difficult and costly. A second way to prevail on a claim is to show the discriminatory impact of a nonracial screening device like an aptitude test, by comparing the percentage of minorities employed to the percentage of that group in the labor pool the firm draws from. This method will force firms away, on the margin, from areas with a high percentage of less desirable minorities, and thus will cause lower employment. In the aggregate, therefore, increases in minority wages will be offset by the reduced number of minorities employed overall, with a potential downward spiral effect on the well-being of those groups. Accordingly, Posner concludes that the arguments defending Title VII on strictly economic grounds – as opposed to grounds of social equity or moral grounds – are unpersuasive.

Posner on the economics of sex discrimination laws

After an examination of the economic properties of the laws and doctrines relating to sex discrimination in employment (1989b), Posner wonders if existing laws prohibiting gender discrimination might do more harm to women than good. Although he cannot calculate either the efficiency or distributive effects of these laws and doctrines because of lack of adequate data, Posner argues for a plausible hypothesis that sex discrimination law has not increased, and may even have reduced, the aggregate welfare of women. This conclusion is supported by four general considerations: the variety of practices that fall under the label of sex discrimination; the distributed complexities arising from interdependent positive utilities (that is, the presence of positive external effects in the well-being of members of the opposite sex) and joint consumption between men and women, pervasive conflicts between different groups of women; and the substantial, and probably growing, costs of administering the sex discrimination laws.

Posner builds his analysis on a few general assumptions. He assumes that both men and women are rational in the usual economic sense; that women will invest less on average than men in development of human capital (because they will spend less time in the workforce); that the propensity of women to take time out of the labor force for child rearing is determined more by nature than by culture; and finally, that men's and women's utility functions are interdependent (that is, that an increase in the well-being of one group indirectly increases the well-being of the other).

Next Posner defines sex discrimination in the terms of Title VII, namely as treating a woman differently from a man because of her gender, and then considers the hypothetical causes of discrimination by employers, listing them in descending order of invidiousness. He includes misogyny; physical or psychological aggression; ignorance about the average working woman; monopsony (employers able to discriminate because married women have higher relocation costs than men); conduit of discrimination (employer as a proxy discriminator for other discriminatory employees); statistical discrimination resulting from information costs of distinguishing particular female employees from average female employees; and situations where differentiation between women are prohibitively costly. Only three of these causes (monopsony, aggression against women, and ignorance of average qualities) can be classified as market failures, however, leading Posner to conclude that sex discrimination theoretically cannot be a substantial source of economic inefficiency.

Ignorance about average ability is no longer prevalent, monopsony seems to have little effect on employment decisions, and harassment is largely self-correcting. Accordingly, Posner notes that the costs of administration may be a deadweight cost economically, and sex discrimination laws may thus not serve the public interest.

Freedom of contract and employment at will
In addition to studying modern statutes such as Title VII, Posner also looks at the common law rules relating to labor law. A key issue in many employment contracts relates to employment at will provisions. Posner (1989a) joins a debate between Professors Epstein and Cornell on this delicate issue, arguing in favor of a statutory system that would delineate the rights of employees, in the absence of bargained-for provisions. Cornell (1989) uses Hegelian logic to confute Epstein's (1984) position, and suggests that employment at will should be abandoned for a statutory system that specifies certain grounds which may not be used as a basis for discharging an employee.

While Posner believes that individualism, the basis of Epstein's ethical view on employment at will, is a social construct rather than a presocial norm, he does not believe that such distinction undermines Epstein's case in favor of employment at will. Cornell uses Hegelian notions of personality through relations with the external world and reciprocal symmetry in personal interaction in his case against Epstein, but Posner shows that these arguments cannot support Cornell's position. As Posner points out, union workers have no greater sense of personality than others, and reciprocal symmetry would require employees to give employers a valid reason for quitting, something that appears contrary to current social conceptions of individual freedom. In essence, both men's arguments require the freedom to contract that employment at will fosters. Posner also considers the costs that a 'just-cause' or 'rational-cause' firing principle would impose. Consumers would be harmed because costs would be passed on to them in part. Workers would be disadvantaged as well, because an employer would pay less to offset being limited in his/her ability to let a worker go. Not mandating a 'just cause' system would not mean its abolition, however: those workers who value it more than higher wages would bargain for it. Those who do not value such protection, on the other hand, would not be forced to purchase such privilege as part of their employment package.

More importantly, employment at will may be regarded as a valuable tool for reducing employers' information costs, thereby decreasing the value of, and reliance on, relatively cheap statistical data. It would also reduce the use of observable ethnic, racial, and gender characteristics as a proxy for unobservable workers' quality. Consequently, just-cause protection would increase unemployment because it would make hiring and firing more costly. Interestingly, Posner notes that such a burden would fall disproportionately on the marginal workers, women, nonwhites, and the handicapped whose interests just-cause advocates seek to protect.

Posner on economic regulation and antitrust
Richard Posner's early academic writings include several notable illustrations of his developing theory of economic regulation, including several papers, starting in the late 1960s, with a specific focus on antitrust. His work parallels that of other public choice theorists who were developing economic theories of regulation. Posner

contributes to this area of economics by offering valuable insight into the functioning of existing laws while assessing the respective merits of competing economic theories in explaining actual cases of economic regulation.

Competing theories of economic regulation

Posner (1974a) considers the ability of 'public interest' and 'capture' theory of economic regulation to explain why the government regulates the economy as it does. He starts with public interest theory, which suggests that markets left alone would run inefficiently or inequitably, but that such failure can be avoided by relatively costless government regulation. He undermines this basic hypothesis by showing that the industries which are regulated are not necessarily prone to market failure, and also by demonstrating that government regulation is neither costless nor dependably effective for controlling market behavior.

Posner further considers a variation on the basic public interest theory, which suggests that the regulation itself is sound, but that inefficient administration, which can be remedied, causes the failures. He offers three reasons why this reformulation is unsatisfactory. First, it fails to account for the paradoxical evidence that the groups who campaigned for the enactment of the regulatory scheme frequently desire its socially undesirable results. Second, there is little to indicate mismanagement by regulatory agencies. Available data are consistent with the view that agencies are rather reasonably efficient at fulfilling the enacting legislature's goals, which may, in fact, be deliberately inefficient or inequitable. Third, no compelling theory has been proposed that explains why agencies are inherently less efficient than other organizations, with the possible exception of the partially persuasive argument that they are like private firms with monopolies.

Posner is a little more convinced by a further refinement of public interest theory, which suggests that government regulation fails to promote the public interest because the problems it attempts to address are intractable. Although it is unclear why legislatures assign such tasks to agencies in the first place, the economics of law-making bodies may provide an explanation: their efforts require political consensus, meaning that increasing output is difficult because growth in the size of a legislature does not create a comparable increase in productivity. Instead, bargaining costs rise rapidly with an increase in the number of parties. In spite of this helpful analysis, public interest theory fails to offer a persuasive model for how a perception of public interest is translated through behavior into legislative action. Finally, Posner thinks that the inquiries suggested here do not discriminate adequately between this version of public interest theory and some capture theories of regulation, which are described below.

Posner looks at variations on the theory of capture, beginning with a challenge to Marxist and progressive (muckrakers) assertions that small-business or nonbusiness groups often 'capture', and so benefit from, regulation. Next, he considers the political science theory that regulated industries capture the agencies that regulate them, but dismisses it as unsatisfactory for two reasons. First, it does not explain why the regulated industry is necessarily the one that is able to influence, or capture, the regulating agency, rather than, for example, customers of that industry, who clearly also have an interest in regulation. Second, even in cases when one can say that the efforts of regulated industries to promote their interests are more concentrated than those of consumers' groups, the theory does not adequately explain why certain industries gain the upper hand when a single agency regulates separate industries with conflicting interests. Third, the capture theory is counterfactual because regulatory agencies frequently promote the interests of customer groups, not those of regulated firms.

Finally, Posner considers the economic theory of regulation directly, finding it to be based on two simple insights. First, economic regulation gives valuable benefits to particular individuals or groups, so that it can be viewed as a product whose allocation is governed by the laws of supply and demand. Second, the theory of cartels can help theorists determine the relevant demand and supply curves.

Among the more interesting conclusions that follow from this view of regulation is Posner's explanation of why industries, which lack the characteristics allowing for successful cartelization, frequently purchase regulation. He suggests that the high costs of cartelization for these industries simply make the purchase of public regulation cheaper.

Testing competing theories of regulation
Posner (1974a) also examines some weaknesses in the economic theory of regulation, as it was formulated at the time of his paper: the primary fault being that it only offered plausible explanations for the regulations in force. For cases where groups had not purchased regulation, it merely provided a list of criteria relevant to predicting whether an industry would obtain favorable legislation, which was not coherent enough to yield unambiguous, and thus testable, hypotheses.

In addition, Posner considers the empirical evidence bearing on the economic theory of regulation, beginning with neglected procedural data from the process itself of creating regulations. Economic theory suggests that a struggle between interest groups produces regulation, with the corollary that the means chosen should achieve the ends efficiently. Posner discusses how delegation to a regulatory agency facilitates interest group purchase of regulation most efficiently. Otherwise, groups would have to do so through the courts (the legislature being unable to produce it), which would be inefficient and costly since the judicial system is designed in part to withstand interest group pressure. Therefore administrative agencies provide evidence that supports the interest group theory.

Nevertheless, even on this point, Posner (1974a) analyses the weakness of the economic theory of regulation. Although several case studies unambiguously show that much regulation benefits interest groups, such research nevertheless fails to contradict the theory that interest groups influence regulation. In short, the theory needs to be developed further to acquire predictive force, forecasting which groups would obtain future regulations rather than simply explain past instances of regulations as benefitting some interest group. Other weaknesses of current economic theories of regulation include inability to explain maximum price regulation or the possibility that some regulations might address a mixture of public interest and interest group purposes. In addition, the theories cannot clarify the precise economic effects of a given regulation or the prevalence of the public interest rhetoric that accompanies debates about the legislation and which frames the policies themselves.

While Posner offers tentative explanations for all of these (for example, by suggesting that the high cost of determining the actual quality of legislation explains the public interest rhetoric), he is forced to conclude that neither public interest theory nor political interest group theory yet has substantial empirical support. Nor can either theory generate hypotheses sufficiently precise to be verified convincingly. Posner's challenge has influenced heavily the subsequent evolution of public choice models of regulation. Later contributions to the economic theory of regulation have indeed formulated testable propositions, spelling out the relevant variables that influence the effectiveness of legislative and regulatory rent-seeking efforts, and laying out the theoretical foundations for an empirical testing of such theories.

Taxation by regulation
In one of his early papers, Posner (1971) identifies a peculiar form of special interest regulation, namely the wealth transfer to special classes of the buying public at the expense of other consumers, which he analogizes to a form of taxation by regulation.

Posner shows that standard capture theories of regulation (with the usual transfers from consumers to regulated industries) cannot explain public utility and common carrier regulations, which in many cases subsidize some consumers, usually at the cost of others. This result would be unthinkable in a competitive market, where a firm would simply not supply a service to consumers unwilling to pay at least the marginal cost. Nor does this phenomenon make sense from the view of capture theories of regulation, in which a firm dominates agency regulators, since in many cases the company neither benefits directly or indirectly, nor would it use such a pricing and cross-subsidy strategy if it held a monopolistic position in the absence of regulatory constraints.

Accordingly, Posner suggests that regulation is an exertion of state power akin to a kind of excise tax that burdens purchasers of certain goods or services, with the result that some members of the public support a service which the market would otherwise provide at a reduced level or not at all. Posner illustrates his theory with various case studies, including the international telegraph industry, which insulated itself from competition, despite strong opposition, only because it had long subsidized some customers at the expense of others. Those who benefitted would be injured by free entry into the industry, and thus allied themselves with the telegraph industry in seeking the Federal Communications Commission's protection.

Beyond explaining the phenomenon of internal subsidization, Posner shows how this view of regulation as a method of taxation or public finance consistently explains many other features of government controls and regulated industries that are otherwise poorly elucidated by the mainstream views. Posner discusses regulatory authority over entry into regulated markets; mandatory review of new construction; the duty of the regulated firm to provide service and limitations on stopping that activity; competitive market structures (which are also regulated); and the remarkable fact that regulated industries produce services, including those related to provision of infrastructure.

Next, Posner compares internal subsidization through regulation with other methods of public finance. First, he responds to critics who argue that delegating taxing authority to agencies offends the organizational principles of our government or who argue that internal subsidization distorts the allocation of resources. Posner responds that delegation of authority is not unusual and is done whenever practical, and continues that while internal subsidization may cause a misallocation of resources, it should be compared to other methods of taxation that do the same. Almost every viable levy has distortive effects and in an ideal scheme of public finance the level of aberrations for different forms of taxation should be equalized at the margin.

Posner also considers other attributes of regulation as a method of public finance, such as the 'equitable' or distributive effects; difficulty and expense of enforcement; low public scrutiny and responsible review; manageability of regulation; and private demand for taxation by regulation. In contrast with these disadvantages, Posner notes several advantages: namely, lower administrative expense; ability to work within legislative capacity; protection of expectations; and the 'justice' of forcing customers of a given industry to subsidize the service they enjoy instead of passing on that cost to the taxpaying public at large.

Given the positive and negative features of taxation by regulation, Posner suggests two modest reforms. First, when maintenance of an internal subsidy is at issue before an agency, the pertinent amount and costs, as well as the identity of the payers and beneficiaries, should be placed on the public record. Second, Posner suggests that consideration be given to the most efficient method of attaining the ends of internal subsidization.

The social costs of monopoly and regulation

In a well-known paper published in the *Journal of Political Economy*, Posner (1975) examines the properties of both public and private monopolies, suggesting that their social cost is higher than scholars generally believe. In this paper, which parallels similar formulations derived from literature describing the tendency of noncompetitive markets to encourage behavior that erodes the economic rent derived from the market activity, Posner further argues that regulatory monopolies are costlier than their private counterparts.

Posner discusses why the social cost of a monopoly is even greater than the consumer surplus lost to those who forgo purchase because of the monopoly price. According to Posner, the monopolist's surplus should not be treated as a mere transfer from consumers who purchase at the monopoly price to monopolists, but should rather be treated as a social cost. This proposition may appear counterintuitive to any scholar trained in industrial organization, yet it anticipates a very important result of public choice and rent-seeking theory. Posner assumes that in the case of regulatory monopolies, potential monopolists compete to purchase the control of the market, and thus allocate resources to purchasing the monopoly that equal their expected profits (economic rent). The eventual monopolists' surplus (technically a mere transfer from consumers to producers) instead becomes a deadweight loss with no socially valuable contribution because all of their revenues are dissipated in competing to secure, and preserve for themselves, the benefit of the regulatory protection.

Accordingly, Posner develops models that allow him to calculate the ratio between the deadweight loss of purchases that consumers who are priced out of the market forgo and the 'transferred' loss that monopolists reallocate to purchasing, and keeping, the monopoly. After estimating these ratios, Posner calculates the total social cost of monopoly in relation to the traditionally identified deadweight losses, concluding that the total social cost of monopoly equals the sum of the direct deadweight loss plus the monopolist's surplus (or wealth transfer from consumers), which he predicts will be entirely dissipated in the rent-seeking competition.

Later contributions to the rent-seeking literature have offered game-theory models that would suggest that, under simplified assumptions of symmetry, rational firms will not dissipate the entire value of the rent. Nevertheless, under plausible premises about elasticity of demand, the direct deadweight loss is only a small fraction of the total social cost of monopoly. Posner's suggestions that (1) social costs have been underestimated and that (2) they are higher in regulatory than in private monopolies, continue to stand as a fundamental insight at the intersection of industrial organization, public choice theory, and law and economics.

Comparing the social costs of monopoly by regulation and private monopoly, Posner concludes that the former has a higher social cost. He assumes that supracompetitive pricing is easier to maintain when a regulatory agency aids the monopolist. On a macro level, the social cost of regulatory monopoly is considerable, because the industries that purchase it account for 17 percent of the nation's GNP. Posner argues that private monopoly is less costly: although about 20 percent of the industries, which account for 30 percent of the nation's GNP, are in that category, private monopolies tend to be constrained by antitrust laws, and so are unlikely to be as effective in raising prices as regulatory monopolies. The total social cost of private monopolies would thus be lower because of the less dramatic deadweight losses and rent dissipation observable in this category of firms. Though he recognizes that these estimates do not include the relative costs of regulation and antitrust enforcement, he thinks that these factors, if added to the balance, would most likely play against the regulated sector.

Posner also considers (1) why monopolies do not have pervasive distributive effects, (2) why courts should not recognize economies of scale arguments as a defense in merger cases, (3) why antitrust law should continue to concern itself with practices that are merely methods of price discrimination, (4) why the theory of the second best (economy) does not weaken arguments for antitrust enforcement, (5) why there is a positive correlation between concentration (and cartel) and use of advertising, (6) why firms with monopolies could not use their profits to discharge 'social responsibilities' without jeopardizing solvency, (7) ways in which transformation of all the profits from monopoly into social costs can be avoided, and (8) whether economic analysis can help decide whether excise taxation is less costly than income taxation.

Posner's statistical study on antitrust enforcement

Posner (1970), a statistical study of antitrust enforcement since the enactment of the Sherman Act in 1890, has three main purposes: (1) to show by example that collection and analysis of statistical data is fruitful and practical; (2) to set forth the statistics succinctly and explore their implications for issues of antitrust policy; (3) to identify gaps and deficiencies in the existing statistical sources and suggest methods for their improvement. In the process, Posner considers statistics quantifying the number of cases filed, the length of the proceedings, the record of success of antitrust claimants, the use of various civil and criminal remedies, the pattern of violations alleged, and the industries involved.

Beyond the methodological implications of his study, Posner's statistical analysis argues in an interesting way that antitrust enforcement is not closely related to political party. At first glance, the data seem to support the hypothesis that politics explains antitrust enforcement because the percentage of antitrust cases which Democrats brought significantly exceeded their expected quota relative to the amount of time they held the White House. However, a refined view of the statistics shows that this interpretation of the data is inaccurate. Republican control of the White House was mostly during the earlier part of the century, a time when neither party enforced antitrust vigorously. When the period is broken into two parts, the statistics show that both parties brought very close to their share of cases; eliminating periods of recession does not change the results. In addition, about one quarter of all antitrust cases were initiated in years preceding presidential elections, a time when one would expect disproportional increases or decreases in enforcement activity if antitrust enforcement were politically relevant. Finally, Posner shows that 'landmark' cases were also not brought disproportionately by one party or the other.

Finally, Posner considers how more complete and systematic reporting could improve the available statistics, offering several reasons why the government should invest in research to produce accurate data. He notes that better statistics would allow (1) a rational allocation of enforcement duties among responsible parties, (2) the ability to evaluate which programs within an agency have the highest payoffs, and (3) identification of areas where existing resources or authority are inadequate.

The appropriate scope of regulation
Posner (1972) addresses the difficult problem of defining the optimal scope and level of regulation, using the cable television industry as an example. Posner considers the major policy choices related to federal, state, and local regulations of the cable industry and concludes that the economics of the industry can only justify limited regulation. Finally, he proposes a federal statute that would carefully define the roles of the different levels of government in crafting an efficient regulatory scheme.

Posner looks at the effects of the regulations in force for the cable industry, showing, as is typical, that regulation provides an internal subsidy by forcing some customers to pay more so that the industry can provide services that the market would not otherwise produce (sufficiently or at all). As he notes, the effects of such taxation by regulation are slower growth, slower upgrade of old technology, and cumbersome administrative control on entry into the market. Furthermore, the effects of regulation are not equitable because the internal subsidy is likely to be regressive. For example, the government subsidizes 'public' television, primarily watched by 'highbrow' viewers, at the expense of the vast majority of television viewers who prefer network programming.

Posner then considers the effects of the regulation on the content of cable programming, concluding that minimal regulation of pay per view channels probably fosters diversity because it reduces producer reliance on advertising, which requires very high numbers of viewers to be efficient. With pay per view, small audiences with strong preferences can buy programs that would otherwise not be made. Further, because of the economics of the cable industry, greater diversity probably will not adversely affect current broadcast programming and so comes at little negative cost.

Posner further considers the possible effects of local cable monopolies, discussing why regulation of price might lead to reduced quality. If the regulated monopolist cannot recoup the rent-seeking expenditures through pricing, rational monopolistic behavior will lead the firm to maximize its profit by reducing production costs and thus lowering output and service quality. Next, Posner considers the possibility that monopolists might get nonpecuniary satisfaction out of broadcasting programs that support their political views or social agenda. He concludes, however, that this is unlikely unless the same person owns cable, broadcast television, and newspaper outlets. In that case the local news market would be monopolized, since outside stations carried by the cable company would not cover local matters.

In examining the nature and magnitude of monopoly in the cable industry, Posner considers the hypothesis that it is characterized by diminishing marginal costs, offering an opportunity for natural monopoly like other network industries. He responds by asking how contracting, rather than regulation, would constrain such monopoly. In this case of natural monopoly, wealth transfers are the main risk, not deadweight loss. Even in the event of an unregulated natural monopoly, output is unlikely to be reduced, because the monopolist can price discriminate, leading to a wealth transfer as perfect price discrimination leads to the capture of the entire surplus. Posner also considers the alternative hypothesis that the monopoly is not natural, but created by municipal franchising, noting that the high profits of the cable industry might be caused by either natural or technical (franchised) monopoly. Finally, he considers alternative approaches to solving the monopoly problem, including approaches such as contracting, franchising, and rate regulation, concluding that all the alternatives are fraught with substantial difficulties and so a period of experimentation is in order.

Posner also considers whether there are reasons to protect the broadcast television industry from inroads by the cable industry but can find little reason to do so, arguing that protection would harm program copyright holders and lower-income purchasers of cable television services without much accompanying benefit.

Finally, Posner considers the future of cable television regulation, opining that taxation by regulation at the municipal level, public utility controls at the state level, and limitation on content and competition against broadcast television at the federal level are all likely. Furthermore, these possibilities are not mutually exclusive, although taken together they are distinctly unattractive because of the cost and accompanying slow growth. Accordingly, Posner offers an outline of a statute defining appropriate roles and policies for federal, state, and local government.

Conclusion

This volume completes a three-volume set of Richard Posner's collected economic papers. The extent of Posner's production and the steady expansion of his scholarship into new areas of law and economics has made the task of selecting representative articles all the more difficult. These volumes, while considering only a very small sample of Posner's vast opus, will, the editor hopes, illustrate the breadth of his contribution to the field of law and economics.

In this volume, Richard Posner introduces a depth of reason into several areas of public law by applying the analytical power of economic analysis in the study of constitutional law, legislation, and economic theories of regulation. Posner's papers show that the analytical methods of the new law and economics movement are immensely valuable in understanding the proper domain – as well as the limits and implicit costs – of legal intervention. As for other areas of the law, Posner's papers on the economics of public law unveil intriguing paradoxes and convincingly show the value of economics in the context of alternative ideological conceptions of law.

Posner's work is of critical importance in pushing the boundaries of our under-standing of the effects of regulation, providing scholars and policymakers with a renewed awareness of the simple, yet fundamental, interrelationship between the direct effects, and the indirect consequences, of law on individual behavior. Posner's economic papers expose the unintended consequences of legal intervention, revealing that the chosen rules may not necessarily produce the desired effects and that the traditional debate over normative issues often ignores the underlying economic nature of human action.

In his work on the economics of public law, Posner challenges several well-known propositions from other areas of economics, including industrial organization and public choice theory. His work challenges the prevailing wisdom in the economics profession with evidence and theoretical results developed within the law and economics tradition, testing the leading economic theories of regulation and revisiting the previously settled issue of the social cost of monopoly. In later papers, he challenges traditional conceptions of employment discrimination, and crime and punishment. In each of these areas Posner leaves an indelible mark, with contributions that are commendable for their intellectual rigor and appealing simplicity.

Posner's contribution to the field of law and economics should be singled out for the novel application of economics to areas that were traditionally thought to be out of the reach of the discipline. The growing influence of Posner's writings in the judicial profession, and in the legal and economic academic world, underscores the relevance and importance of his work and the growing maturity of the new law and economics movement. Posner provides seminal contributions to the development of an overarching economic theory of law and, most importantly, has opened new areas of research for present and future generations of jurists and economists alike.

References

Cornell, Drucilla (1989), 'Dialogic reciprocity and the critique of employment at will', 10 *Cardozo Law Review* 1575.

Donohue, John J. III (1986), 'Is Title VII efficient?', 134 *University of Pennsylvania Law Review* 1411.

Donohue, John J. III (1988), 'Law and economics: the road not taken', 22 *Law and Society Review* 903.

Ehrlich, Isaac and Richard A. Posner (1974), 'An Economic Analysis of Legal Rule-making', *Journal of Legal Studies* 257–86.

Epstein, Richard (1984), 'In defense of the contract at will', 51 *University of Chicago Law Review* 947.

Landes, William M. and Richard A. Posner (1975), 'The independent judiciary in an interest-group perspective', 18 *Journal of Law and Economics* 875–901.

Landes, William M., Lawrence Lessig and Michael E. Solimine (1998), 'Judicial Influence: A Citation Analysis of Federal Courts of Appeals Judges', **27** (2) *Journal of Legal Studies* 271.

Langbein, John H. and Richard A. Posner (1976), 'Market Funds and Trust-investment Law', *American Bar Foundation Research Journal* 1.

Philipson, Tomas J. and Richard A. Posner (1996), 'The economic epidemiology of crime', 39 *Journal of Law and Economics* 405.

Posner, Eric A. and Richard A. Posner (1998), 'The demand for human cloning', in *Clones and Clones: Facts and Fantasies about Human Cloning* 233 (Martha C. Nussbaum and Cass R. Sunstein eds).

Posner, Eric A. and Richard A. Posner (1999), 'The demand for human cloning', 27 *Hofstra Law Review* 579.

Posner, Richard A. (1969a), 'Natural monopoly and its regulation', 21 *Stanford Law Review* 518.

Posner, Richard A. (1969b), 'The Federal Trade Commission', 37 *University of Chicago Law Review* 47.

Posner, Richard A. (1970), 'A statistical study of antitrust enforcement', 13 *Journal of Law and Economics* 365.

Posner, Richard A. (1971), 'Taxation by regulation', 2 *Bell Journal of Economics and Management Science* 22.

Posner, Richard A. (1972), 'The appropriate scope of regulation in the cable television industry', 3 *Bell Journal of Economics and Management Science* 98.

Posner, Richard A. (1973), 'An Economic Approach to Legal Procedure and Judicial Administration', 2 *Journal of Legal Studies* 399.

Posner, Richard A. (1974a), 'Theories of economic regulation', 5 *Bell Journal of Economics and Management Science* 155.

Posner, Richard A. (1974b), *Antitrust: Cases, Economic Notes, and Other Materials*, St. Paul, MN, West Publishing, 1974.

Posner, Richard A. (1975), 'The social costs of monopoly and regulation', 83 *Journal of Political Economy* 897.

Posner, Richard A. (1976), *Antitrust Law: An Economic Perspective*, Chicago: University of Chicago Press.

Posner, Richard A. (1980a), 'A theory of primitive society, with special reference to law', 23 *Journal of Law and Economics* 1.

Posner, Richard A. (1980b), 'Anthropology and economics', 88 *Journal of Political Economy* 608.

Posner, Richard A. (1980c), 'Retribution and related concepts of punishment', 9 *Journal of Legal Studies* 71.

Posner, Richard A. (1980d), 'Optimal sentences for white-collar criminals', 17 *American Criminal Law Review* 409.

Posner, Richard A. (1981), *The Economics of Justice*, Cambridge, MA: Harvard University Press.

Posner, Richard A. (1982), 'Economics, politics, and the reading of statutes and the Constitution', 49 *University of Chicago Law Review* 263.

Posner, Richard A. (1982b), 'Toward an Economic Theory of Federal Jurisdiction', 6 *Harvard Journal of Law and Public Policy* 41.

Posner, Richard A. (1984), 'Some economics of labor law', 51 *University of Chicago Law Review* 988.

Posner, Richard A. (1985a), 'An economic theory of the criminal law', 85 *Columbia Law Review* 1193.

Posner, Richard A. (1985b), 'Comment on "On the economic theory of crime"', in *Criminal Justice: Nomos 27*, at 310 (J. Roland Pennock and John W. Chapman eds).

Posner, Richard A. (1987a), 'The justice of economics', 1987–1 *Economia delle Scelte Pubbliche* 15.

Posner, Richard A. (1987b), "The Constitution as an economic document', 56 *George Washington Law Review* 4.

Posner, Richard A. (1987c), 'The efficiency and the efficacy of Title VII', 136 *University of Pennsylvania Law Review* 513.

Posner, Richard A. (1988), 'Comment: Responding to Gordon Tullock', 2 *Research in Law and Policy Studies* 29–33.

Posner, Richard A. (1989a), 'Hegel and employment at will: a comment', 10 *Cardozo Law Review* 1625.

Posner, Richard A. (1989b), 'An economic analysis of sex discrimination laws', 56 *University of Chicago Law Review* 1311.

Posner, Richard A. (1994), 'What Do Judges and Justices Maximize? (The Same Thing Everybody Else Does)', 3 *Supreme Court Economic Review* 1.

Posner, Richard A. (1995), 'An economic perspective on basic rights: the costs of enforcing legal rights', 4 *Eastern European Constitutional Review* 71.

Posner, Richard A. (1996), 'The cost of rights: implications for Central and Eastern Europe – and for the United States', 32 *Tulsa Law Journal* 1.

Posner, Richard A. (1997a), 'The economic approach to homosexuality', in *Sex, Preference, and Family: Essays on Law and Nature* 173 (David M. Estlund and Martha C. Nussbaum eds).

Posner, Richard A. (1997b), 'Equality, wealth, and political stability', 13 *Journal of Law, Economics, and Organization* 344.

Posner, Richard A. (1998), 'The speech market and the legacy of Schenck' (unpublished manuscript).

Posner, Richard A. (1999), 'The effects of deregulation on competition: the experience of the United States', 23 *Fordham International Law Journal* 7.

Posner, Richard A. and Frank H. Easterbrook (1980), *Antitrust: Cases, Economic Notes, and Other Materials*, 2nd edn, St. Paul, MN, West Publishing.

Shapiro, Fred R. (2000), 'The Most-Cited Legal Scholars', 29 *Journal of Legal Studies* 409.

PART I

LEGISLATION AND CONSTITUTIONAL LAW

VOLUME 49   NUMBER 2   SPRING 1982

Economics, Politics, and the Reading of Statutes and the Constitution

Richard A. Posner†

Economists have in recent years begun to study the causes and effects of legislation, and the elements of a positive economic theory of legislation are now in place.[1] Such a theory would appear to have implications for how judges do, and perhaps for how they should, interpret legislative provisions, both statutory and constitutional. But to date these implications have not been explored

---

† Judge, United States Court of Appeals for the Seventh Circuit; Senior Lecturer, University of Chicago Law School. The research assistance of Edward Wahl is gratefully acknowledged, as are the helpful comments of David Currie, Frank Easterbrook, Gerald Gunther, Frank Michelman, George Stigler, and Cass Sunstein on a previous draft. This article was conceived and largely written during the lengthy gestation of my appointment to the Seventh Circuit—a period in which the issues discussed in the article assumed a greater than merely academic significance to me. I hasten to add, however, that the views expressed are wholly personal and in no way official.

[1] The seminal paper, breaking with the older, predominantly normative tradition, is Stigler, *The Theory of Economic Regulation*, 2 BELL J. ECON. & MGMT. SCI. 3 (1971). For efforts at systematization of Stigler's insights, see Peltzman, *Toward a More General Theory of Regulation*, 19 J.L. & ECON. 211 (1976), and G. Becker, A Theory of Political Behavior (Sept. 1981) (Working Paper No. 006-1, Center for the Study of the Economy and the State, University of Chicago) (extensive and up-to-date bibliography); for review essays, see Jordan, *Producer Protection, Prior Market Structure and the Effects of Government Regulation*, 15 J.L. & ECON. 151 (1972), and Posner, *Theories of Economic Regulation*, 5 BELL J. ECON. & MGMT. SCI. 335 (1974).

263

systematically. There are only brief discussions in the literature on the economic analysis of law,[2] and none, as far as I know, in the traditional legal literature on statutory and constitutional interpretation.[3] This article is a start toward filling the gap. The attempt should be of interest not only to students of the economic analysis of law, as well as to theorists and practitioners of statutory construction, but also to economists of the political process. That the economist takes statutes to be complete when enacted is striking to a lawyer, who realizes that the meaning of a statute is not fixed until the courts have interpreted the statute. Judicial interpretation of statutes is thus an intrinsic part of a complete economic theory of legislation, though whether an important part remains to be seen.

It is easy to see how a new view of legislation might require changes, perhaps radical ones, in how courts interpret legislation. It is more difficult to see how the new view might explain what the courts have been doing all along—but my greater interest is in this, the positive question. I believe that the apparent discordance between an economic view of legislation, which emphasizes the efforts of interest groups to redistribute wealth in their favor, and a traditional legal view, which requires the court to divine and effectuate the public interest goal of legislation, is not real; that courts have generally been realistic about legislation; and that the legal tradition in interpreting statutes becomes more, rather than less, intelligible when an economic view of legislation is adopted.

I.   THE ECONOMIC APPROACH TO LEGISLATION

There is now an extensive economic literature on the determi-

---

[2] *See* R. POSNER, ECONOMIC ANALYSIS OF LAW 408-15, 495-96 (2d ed. 1977); Landes & Posner, *The Independent Judiciary in an Interest-Group Perspective*, 18 J.L. & ECON. 875 (1975).

[3] The lawyers' neglect of the economic theory of legislation is a bit surprising, because though many lawyers find economic concepts alien and repulsive, the most distinctive element in this particular theory—the emphasis placed on the procurement of protective legislation by interest groups—has been a part of the political science literature at least since the discussion of "factions" in THE FEDERALIST No. 10 (J. Madison). *See also* A. BENTLEY, THE PROCESS OF GOVERNMENT (1908); D. TRUMAN, THE GOVERNMENTAL PROCESS (1951). In fairness, however, I should point out that Professor Gerald Gunther's proposal for more stringent constitutional review of state economic legislation, *see infra* notes 64-66 and accompanying text, reflects an awareness of the role of interest groups in procuring legislation. *See also infra* note 63. The lawyers' literature on how to read a statute is well represented by H. HART & A. SACKS, THE LEGAL PROCESS 1144-1417 (tent. ed. 1958), and F. FRANKFURTER, *Some Reflections on the Reading of Statutes*, in OF LAW AND MEN 44 (P. Elman ed. 1956).

nants of legislation. At least three major theories can be discerned in the literature, though they can, I shall argue, be treated as elements of a single theory.

A. Public Interest Theory

The "public interest" theory, which is the oldest of the three, is well represented in the writings of such economists as Baumol[4] and Pigou.[5] It conceives both the ideal and the actual function of legislation to be to increase economic welfare by correcting market failures such as crime and pollution. Some laws designed to transfer wealth from rich to poor also can be fitted into the theory. Free-rider problems might thwart private efforts to bring about the level of transfers from rich to poor that the rich would prefer; to that extent public wealth redistribution is a public good no different in kind from protection against crime or pollution.

There is little, if any, tension between the economist's public interest theory and the traditional lawyer's view of legislation.[6] The lawyer's view is also that legislation is designed to protect the public interest, implicitly defined in utilitarian terms. If this were the only economic theory of legislation, this article would not be worth writing.

B. Interest Group Theory

The "interest group" theory asserts that legislation is a good demanded and supplied much as other goods, so that legislative protection flows to those groups that derive the greatest value from it, regardless of overall social welfare, whether "welfare" is defined as wealth, utility, or some other version of equity or justice.[7] An

---

[4] *E.g.,* W. BAUMOL, WELFARE ECONOMICS AND THE THEORY OF THE STATE (2d ed. 1965).

[5] A. PIGOU, THE ECONOMICS OF WELFARE (4th ed. 1932).

[6] The traditional view is soon to celebrate its four-hundredth anniversary. *See* Heydon's Case, 76 Eng. Rep. 637, 638 (Ex. 1584), where the court said that the essential steps in interpreting a statute are to ascertain "[w]hat was the mischief and defect for which the common law did not provide," "[w]hat remedy the Parliament hath resolved and appointed to cure the disease of the Commonwealth," and "[t]he true reason of the remedy; and then the office of all the Judges is always to make such construction as shall suppress the mischief, and advance the remedy." But not every statute that a court is called upon to interpret is intended to correct a mischief; the intent may have been simply to redistribute wealth from a less to a more powerful segment of the community. For a modern statement of the theory of legislation implicit in Heydon's Case, see H. HART & A. SACKS, *supra* note 3, at 1410-17.

[7] *See, e.g.,* J. BUCHANAN & G. TULLOCK, THE CALCULUS OF CONSENT (1962); A. DOWNS, AN ECONOMIC THEORY OF DEMOCRACY (1957); W. RIKER, THE THEORY OF POLITICAL COALI-

important determinant of the net benefit of legislative protection to a group, and the primary focus of this literature, is the cost of organizing effective political action. That cost increases as group membership becomes larger and the group less cohesive. The size of the group also bears on the benefits of legislative protection. As the group becomes larger, the benefits to each member are likely to become smaller, and hence the individual's incentive to contribute to the group's endeavor will be weakened. Should the group try to overcome this problem by seeking so large a redistribution that all members would benefit substantially, the redistribution will be much more costly to those outside the group who will be taxed to defray its cost, and this will increase resistance to the group's objective. From an analysis of such factors, the literature concludes that effective interest groups are usually small and directed toward a single issue. The benefits of a redistribution in their favor are concentrated, the costs of organizing the group are small, and the costs of the redistribution are so widely diffused that nobody has much incentive to oppose it.

The properties that make legislative redistributions feasible have nothing to do with the public interest, whether defined in efficiency or equity terms. If anything, they tend to make legislation systematically perverse from a public interest standpoint by fostering the redistribution of wealth from large groups, including the public as a whole, to small ones. From a normative standpoint, therefore, the interest group theory is pessimistic concerning the purpose and effects of legislation, while the public interest theory is optimistic. It is not surprising that the public interest theory flourished in the period when most people favored an expansion of government action, and the interest group theory in the period of disillusionment with big government that began in the 1970's.

The interest group theory, incidentally, has had some distinguished judicial adherents—suggesting that judges may be more realistic about legislation than legal scholars. Holmes said in an early essay:

> The struggle for life, undoubtedly, is constantly putting the interests of men at variance with those of the lower animals. And the struggle does not stop in the ascending scale with the monkeys, but is equally the law of human existence. Outside of legislation this is undeniable. It is mitigated by sympathy,

---

TIONS 3-31 (1962); G. STIGLER, THE CITIZEN AND THE STATE (1975).

prudence, and all the social and moral qualities. But in the last resort a man rightly prefers his own interest to that of his neighbors. And this is as true in legislation as in any other form of corporate action. All that can be expected from modern improvements is that legislation should easily and quickly, yet not too quickly, modify itself in accordance with the will of the *de facto* supreme power in the community, and that the spread of an educated sympathy should reduce the sacrifice of minorities to a minimum. But whatever body may possess the supreme power for the moment is certain to have interests inconsistent with others which have competed unsuccessfully. The more powerful interests must be more or less reflected in legislation; which, like every other device of man or beast, must tend in the long run to aid the survival of the fittest. . . . [I]t is no sufficient condemnation of legislation that it favors one class at the expense of another; for much or all legislation does that. . . . The fact is that legislation . . . is necessarily made a means by which a body, having the power, put burdens which are disagreeable to them on the shoulders of somebody else.[8]

Holmes's belief in social Darwinism, evident from the quoted passage, makes him an ancestor of the modern economic theory of legislation as the outcome of a struggle between interest groups. The affinity between economic theory and the theory of biological evolution has often been remarked;[9] social Darwinism, applied to the legislative process, connects them.

   Justice Black's opinion for the Court in *Eastern Railroad Presidents Conference v. Noerr Motor Freight, Inc.*[10] is another noteworthy example of judicial realism about statutes. The Court in that case held that the Sherman Act[11] does not prevent collective action to obtain legislation that would hurt competitors.[12]

---

   [8] O.W. HOLMES, *Herbert Spencer: Legislation and Empiricism*, in JUSTICE OLIVER WENDELL HOLMES: HIS BOOK NOTICES AND UNCOLLECTED LETTERS AND PAPERS 104, 107-09 (H. Shriver ed. 1936). Although the essay was written before Holmes became a judge, it describes accurately the attitude that he brought as a judge to the task of determining the constitutionality of legislation.
   [9] For a systematic treatment, see Becker, *Altruism, Egoism, and Genetic Fitness: Economics and Sociobiology*, 14 J. ECON. LIT. 817 (1976).
   [10] 365 U.S. 127 (1961).
   [11] 15 U.S.C. §§ 1-7 (1976).
   [12] 365 U.S. at 136. The defendants in that case had engaged a public relations firm to conduct a publicity campaign designed to foster the adoption and retention of laws harmful to the trucking business.

Black, whose realism about legislation was rooted not in theory, but in his experience as a United States Senator, stated for the Court:

> The right of the people to inform their representatives in government of their desires with respect to the passage or enforcement of laws cannot properly be made to depend upon their intent in doing so. It is neither unusual nor illegal for people to seek action on laws in the hope that they may bring about an advantage to themselves and a disadvantage to their competitors.[13]

By the Court's holding, he said, "we have restored what appears to be the true nature of the case—a 'no-holds-barred fight' between two industries both of which are seeking control of a profitable source of income."[14] In another case,[15] Black rejected the concept of "rationality review"—a rejection clearly implied, as we shall see below, by the interest group approach.[16]

C. Legislative Process Theory

The public interest and interest group theories are theories about the content of legislation, the former predicting that it will be efficient (always bearing in mind that efficiency may require some public redistribution of wealth), the latter that it will be amorally redistributive. Some economists, however, have focused on the legislative process itself rather than on the content of the legislation that results.[17] They have sought to explain, for example, why different sized majorities are required for different types of legislation, why legislatures are frequently bicameral, why there is increasing delegation of legislative authority to administrative

---

[13] *Id.* at 139.

[14] *Id.* at 144 (footnote omitted).

[15] Ferguson v. Skrupa, 372 U.S. 726, 731-32 (1963).

[16] *See infra* notes 63-66 and accompanying text. Examples of judicial realism in relation to statutes could be multiplied, but I will give just one more, from Learned Hand. In discussing statutes that made an employer liable to any employee injured as a result of the employer's failure to take the precautions specified in the statutes, Hand stated: "Such statutes are partial; they upset the freedom of contract, and for ulterior purposes put the two contesting sides at unequal advantage; they should be construed, not as theorems of Euclid, but with some imagination of the purposes which lie behind them." Lehigh Valley Coal Co. v. Yensavage, 218 F. 547, 553 (2d Cir. 1914).

[17] The seminal works are J. Buchanan & G. Tullock, *supra* note 7; A. Downs, *supra* note 7.

agencies, and what effects such delegation is likely to have.[18]

D. A Four-Fold Typology

There is no incompatibility between either the public interest or interest group theory, on the one hand, and the various theories of legislative process, on the other. Less obviously, there is no necessary incompatibility between the public interest and interest group theories. The public interest theory is mainly concerned with identifying market failures that could, in principle, be rectified by legislation, and its proponents would hardly be willing to shoulder the burden of establishing what proportion of legislation actually enacted is of this character. The interest group theory does not deny the possibility that a large group—perhaps the whole society—occasionally might procure legislation on its own behalf. If the benefits to the individual members of a large group are great enough and the costs to nonmembers small enough (there may be few or even no nonmembers), the legislation will be enacted. There will be free-rider problems, but they need not be insurmountable under the postulated conditions. Laws against murder illustrate this point.

I conclude that the public interest and interest group theories are, at least in some mixture, complementary rather than antagonistic. It should be possible, therefore, to classify statutes between those that advance the public interest and those that advance instead the interest of some (narrow) interest group. A number of statutes clearly belong in one group or another—the basic criminal laws, the original antitrust law,[19] and the provision of a court system, in the public interest category; the tobacco subsidy, the Interstate Commerce Act,[20] and the regulation of taxicabs,[21] in the interest group category.

But these are just polar cases. There are many intermediate

---

[18] On voting majorities, see A. Downs, *supra* note 7, at 51-74. On bicameralism, see J. Buchanan & G. Tullock, *supra* note 7, at 233-48. On delegation, see Ehrlich & Posner, *An Economic Analysis of Legal Rulemaking*, 3 J. Legal Stud. 257, 279-80 (1974).

[19] Sherman Antitrust Act, ch. 647, 26 Stat. 209 (1890) (current version at 15 U.S.C. §§ 1-7 (1976)).

[20] Interstate Commerce Act of 1887, ch. 104, 24 Stat. 379 (current version in scattered sections of 49 U.S.C. (1976)); *see* Hilton, *The Consistency of the Interstate Commerce Act*, 9 J.L. & Econ. 87 (1966).

[21] *See, e.g.*, Ill. Rev. Stat. ch. 24, § 11-42-6 (1979) (authorizing municipalities to license taxicabs); Kitch, Isaacson & Kasper, *The Regulation of Taxicabs in Chicago*, 14 J.L. & Econ. 285 (1971); *cf.* R. Posner, *supra* note 2, at 267-68 (economic argument that public utility regulations are "interest group" statutes).

cases, and to fit these into the eclectic theory we need a richer categorization than the public interest/interest group dichotomy. I suggest a four-fold typology, with the economically defined public interest theory and the narrow interest group theory as categories at opposite extremes, and two new intermediate categories: a public interest category defined in terms other than economic, and a "public sentiment" category.[22]

1. *Public Interest, Economically Defined.* This category is limited to legislation that corrects market failures such as crime and pollution, though as mentioned earlier certain redistributions could be included because they correct failures in the market for charitable giving.[23] Important examples of laws that serve the public interest economically defined are the provisions of the Constitution that establish the separation of powers and freedom of political speech and thereby protect society against a particularly costly form of monopoly—a monopoly of political power.

2. *Public Interest in Other Senses.* Whatever one's own conception of the public interest may be, it seems inappropriate to dismiss *a priori* any other conception that is widely shared. For example, if the progressive income tax can be justified in terms of benefits received, it is in category (1) above; but even if it cannot be justified in those terms, it would still be public interest legislation if justifiable in terms of some widely held concept of the just distribution of wealth. This example also illustrates the equivocal nature of my classification. Many economists regard the progressive income tax either as a means of maximizing utility[24]—which, depending on one's precise view of the meaning of "economic efficiency,"[25] could be part of either category (1) or category (2)—or alternatively as a means of soaking the rich[26]—which would put it

---

[22] This typology of legislation (broadly defined to include the Constitution) ignores the question of effectiveness, an issue that still dominates the economic analysis of legislation. A fascinating literature, beginning with Stigler & Friedland, *What Can Regulators Regulate? The Case of Electricity*, 5 J.L. & ECON. 1 (1962), has questioned the effectiveness of a variety of statutes, especially those relating to securities, health, and safety. *See, e.g.*, Peltzman, *An Evaluation of Consumer Protection Legislation: The 1962 Drug Amendments*, 81 J. POL. ECON. 1049 (1973); Sands, *How Effective is Safety Legislation?*, 11 J.L. & ECON. 165 (1968). The finding of these studies that statutes frequently miscarry is strictly empirical and does not explain why ineffectual legislation is enacted. The issue is therefore tangential to this article, which focuses on the determinants of legislation, but it does have some relevance to my analysis. *See infra* notes 38-39 and accompanying text.

[23] *See supra* p. 265.

[24] *See, e.g.*, A. LERNER, THE ECONOMICS OF CONTROL 228-40 (1944).

[25] *See* R. POSNER, THE ECONOMICS OF JUSTICE 48-87 (1981).

[26] *See, e.g.*, M. FRIEDMAN, CAPITALISM AND FREEDOM 161-76 (1962); F. HAYEK, THE CON-

into category (4) below (interest group legislation).

3. *Public Sentiment.* Much legislation cannot be justified or explained on economic grounds, but perhaps only because not enough is known about the relevant costs and benefits. Legislation forbidding the sale of pornography is an example. Such legislation seems at first glance to be an interference with freedom of contract that reduces efficiency, just as a usury law does. But despite the loose use of the term "special interests" in recent political discussion to describe people who feel strongly about an issue, the supporters of laws against pornography do not have the characteristics that make for an effective interest group. And the possible external effects of pornography (on the crime rate, relations within the family, even perhaps population) may, though they have never been quantified, justify the laws and explain the intense hostility that many people feel toward pornography.

Laws based on public sentiment rather than on either an objective weighing of demonstrable pros and cons or on cartel-like pressures for redistributing wealth resemble public interest legislation in that their support seems both broadly based and not motivated by narrow self-interest. But they cannot readily be defended on economic grounds given our existing and deficient knowledge of their effects. They have largely been ignored by economists but their importance in the legislative output requires that they not be ignored in this article.

4. *Narrow Interest Group Legislation.* Most recent economic analyses of legislation have focused on statutes that appear to promote the narrow self-interest of a particular industry or a group of firms within an industry. Yet what has occurred is less a change than a sharpening of focus, for the change in professional opinion about the economic nature of legislation has resulted largely from a reevaluation of statutes, such as the Interstate Commerce Act[27] and the Civil Aeronautics Act of 1938,[28] that were once regarded as legitimate responses to deficiencies or excesses of competition. The interest group theorists have had their greatest success, as one would expect, in explaining legislation applicable to a particular industry, such as the laws regulating the various transportation

---

STITUTION OF LIBERTY 306-23 (1960).

[27] Interstate Commerce Act of 1887, ch. 104, 24 Stat. 379 (current version in scattered sections of 49 U.S.C. (1976)).

[28] Ch. 601, 52 Stat. 973 (current version at 49 U.S.C. §§ 1301-1552 (1976 & Supp. III 1979)).

and utility industries, occupational licensure laws, and industry-specific tax and subsidy schemes. They have been less successful in explaining economy-wide legislation such as the antitrust laws and health and safety regulations. Some of these laws may, of course, be public interest laws; others may not be. In any event, the boundary between narrow interest group legislation and public interest legislation is indistinct.

II. IMPLICATIONS OF THE ECONOMIC ANALYSIS OF LEGISLATION FOR STATUTORY INTERPRETATION

A. Motive *vs.* Intent

I begin with a principle that may seem to belong to constitutional rather than to statutory interpretation: in reviewing a statute, courts are to look to the intent but not to the motive of the enacting legislature. This principle is usually invoked in constitutional cases, where the issue is whether a statute should be invalidated because of the motive behind its enactment.[29] But it also defines the scope of judicial inquiry into the meaning of a statute in cases where the statute is assumed to be valid and only its application is in dispute. Courts look to the language of the statute, to the legislative history,[30] and to other evidence of legislative intent, but they do not speculate on the motives of the legislators in enacting the statute.[31] They do not, in short, conduct the kind of economic or political science inquiry that might reveal the pattern of interest group pressures behind the statute.

This limitation is of extraordinary interest given the theme of this article. At first glance it may seem diametrically opposed to a realistic view of the political process and may seem to place the judiciary in opposition to the legislative will, even when there is no issue of constitutionality. In fact it is merely inevitable. Courts do not have the research tools that they would need to discover the motives behind legislation. Nor can they just presume the presence of an interest group somewhere behind the scenes. Many statutes

---

[29] The usual answer is "no." *See, e.g.,* Palmer v. Thompson, 403 U.S. 217, 224-25 (1971). The extensive scholarly literature on this issue is well represented by Brest, *Palmer v. Thompson: An Approach to the Problem of Unconstitutional Legislative Motive,* 1971 SUP. CT. REV. 95; Ely, *Legislative and Administrative Motivation in Constitutional Law,* 79 YALE L.J. 1205 (1970); and *Legislative Motivation,* 15 SAN DIEGO L. REV. 925 (1978).

[30] For possible limitations, see *infra* notes 35-36 and accompanying text.

[31] *See, e.g.,* United States v. O'Brien, 391 U.S. 367, 383-85 (1968); McCray v. United States, 195 U.S. 27, 56 (1904); Fletcher v. Peck, 10 U.S. (6 Cranch) 87, 130 (1810).

really are enacted in the public interest; in those statutes, the actual and the ostensible purposes coincide. Moreover, even where it is obvious that a particular statute was procured by some particular interest group—the National Labor Relations Act[32] by the labor movement, for example—it will not be clear, at least without an inquiry that is beyond the judicial competence to undertake, how completely the group prevailed upon Congress to do its will. The statute as ultimately enacted may represent a compromise with other groups; if so, the "real" legislative purpose may be unclear.

Therefore, if the legislature wants to indicate the lines of political pressure along which the law should be interpreted, it has to say so explicitly, either in the statute or in the legislative history materials to which courts have ready access. No matter how faithfully judges wish to carry out the will of Congress, they are limited to public materials in divining that will.

This limitation on judicial capacity imposes a further limitation on the operation of interest group politics that is wholly distinct from the limitations that the Constitution may or may not place on that operation. To the extent that legislators use Aesopian language to deceive potential opponents of the interest groups behind legislation, they may fool the courts as well and thereby limit the political power of those interest groups.

This limitation can be reconciled with a normative theory of democratic politics along the following lines. The theory assumes an informed electorate. Although interest groups can take advantage of the limited incentives that voters have to inform themselves concerning public issues, the interposition of a judiciary that, in interpreting legislation, is limited to public materials offsets to some extent the distortions that voter ignorance introduces into the operation of a democratic political system. This is not an argument for free-wheeling statutory interpretation. The point is simply that, however conscientiously the judge tries to follow the legislature's will, he will be limited to the statutory text and to other public materials; he will not ask which interest group got how much of what it wanted from the legislature.

---

[32] Ch. 372, 49 Stat. 449 (1935) (current version at 29 U.S.C. §§ 151-169 (1976 & Supp. III 1979)).

B.   Reasoning from One Statute to Another

In piecing out the meaning of a statute, courts do not use the intent behind one statute to illuminate the intent behind another; that is, they do not treat statutes in the same way that a common law court treats prior cases—as precedents whose reasoning may illuminate the issues in a case.[33] This seeming myopia has been criticized,[34] but makes good sense once a realistic view of the legislative process is taken. If some statutes—and the courts will have trouble knowing which ones—reflect the pressures of narrow interest groups rather than any coherent view of the public interest, it is perilous for courts to use one statute to illuminate the meaning of another. There is no assurance that the particular constellation of political pressures that produced the first statute was also at play when the second was adopted. And because the first may have been purely the product of pressure and not of a sincere search for the public good, the first cannot serve as a dependable *reason* for interpreting the second in a particular way.

C.   Legislative History

The approach taken in this article casts light on two recurrent issues in the use of legislative history to interpret statutes. The first is whether it is proper to use legislative history at all, and if so, which parts of that history to use.[35] Because legislators vote on the statutory language rather than on the legislative history, they cannot be presumed to have assented to all that has been said, either in the committee reports or on the floor, about a bill that becomes law.

This matters, however, only if one holds the unrealistic view that each enacted bill reflects the convictions of a majority of legislators voting for it. If instead it is assumed that some unknown fraction of all bills are passed at the behest of politically powerful interest groups, it is not so clear that each member of the legislative majority behind a particular bill has studied the details of the

---

[33] This rule is subject to a narrow exception for statutes *in pari materia. See, e.g.,* Erlenbaugh v. United States, 409 U.S. 239, 243-45 (1972); United States v. Stewart, 311 U.S. 60, 64-65 (1940).

[34] *See* Landis, *Statutes and the Sources of Law,* in HARVARD LEGAL ESSAYS 213 (R. Pound ed. 1934).

[35] For controversy over these questions, compare Radin, *Statutory Interpretation,* 43 HARV. L. REV. 863 (1930) with Dickerson, *Statutory Interpretation: A Peek Into the Mind and Will of a Legislature,* 50 IND. L.J. 206 (1975).

bill he voted for. It may be more realistic to assume that he assented to the deal struck by the sponsors of the bill. The terms of the deal presumably are stated accurately in the committee reports and in the floor comments of the sponsors (otherwise the sponsors will have difficulty striking deals in the future), though not necessarily by opponents of the bill, who may take the floor or write minority opinions in committees to create a specious legislative history that they hope will influence judicial interpretation of the statute.

This picture is especially persuasive if we assume a considerable amount of "log rolling"—that is, vote trading—in the legislative process. Log rolling implies that legislators often vote without regard to their personal convictions. This process makes it unrealistic to demand that each legislator assent only to those aspects of statutory meaning that are fixed in the language of the bill, divorced from the intentions of its sponsors as reflected in their statements in the committee reports and on the floor.

My analysis is also germane to the question what weight to give post-enactment expressions of legislative intent. The answer it suggests, which is also the traditional answer,[36] is that such expressions should be given little or no weight. The deal is struck when the statute is enacted. If courts paid attention to subsequent expressions of legislative intent not embodied in any statute, they would be unraveling the deal that had been made; they would be breaking rather than enforcing the legislative contract. Nor, if one takes seriously the interest group theory of politics, can subsequent expressions of legislative understanding be treated simply as impartial interpretations of the law; they are as likely to be a gambit in the practice of interest group politics.

D.   Implied Rights of Action

A statute often will provide for criminal or other public remedies for its violation but not say whether private individuals can bring damage or injunctive actions to enforce it. The present analysis may shed some light on whether a private right of action can be "implied" in a statute that is silent on private remedies, a ques-

---

[36] *See, e.g.*, Oscar Mayer & Co. v. Evans, 441 U.S. 750, 758 (1979); United States v. Wise, 370 U.S. 405, 411 (1962). For a striking exception to the conventional approach, consider the recent practice of the California courts in receiving courtroom testimony on legislative intent from legislators, discussed in Comment, *Statutory Interpretation in California: Individual Testimony as an Extrinsic Aid*, 15 U.S.F.L. Rev. 241 (1981).

tion that has become controversial in recent years.[37]

The question has an antecedent in the interplay between the standard of care in negligence cases and criminal safety statutes. Suppose a legislature passes a statute forbidding people to drive automobiles faster than fifty-five miles per hour, and someone violates the statute, injuring another as a result. If the victim of the accident sues the injurer, may violation of the statute be used as evidence, perhaps conclusive, of the injurer's negligence? The answer could depend on one's theory of legislation. The public interest theory implies that a legislative pronouncement on safety should be given great weight: the legislature was honestly trying to determine an optimal safety standard, and it has tools not available to courts for making such determinations.[38] The interest group approach implies, to the contrary, that there is no presumption that a legislative safety standard represents a sincere effort at optimal safety, so courts should give it no more weight in private cases than the legislature prescribed. Under this view, if there is no evidence that the legislature wanted the standard used in private cases, courts should not use it. The recurrent finding in the economic literature that legislated safety standards are perverse or ineffectual, quite apart from whether they serve some group's special interest, reinforces this conclusion.[39]

The choice between theories of legislation has implications for four specific issues regarding the use of legislated standards in tort cases, and for one issue regarding an implied private right of action to enforce a statute that does not explicitly provide for such a remedy.

1. *Legislative Intent.* As already suggested, if the interest group view is taken the only question for a court asked to use a

---

[37] For analysis, see Stewart & Sunstein, *Public Programs and Private Rights*, 95 HARV. L. REV. 1193 (1982). The Supreme Court has in a short period swung from enthusiasm for implied rights of action to hostility. For example, compare Bivens v. Six Unknown Named Agents of Fed. Bureau of Narcotics, 403 U.S. 388 (1971) (private cause of action for money damages available under fourth amendment for warrantless search) and J.I. Case Co. v. Borak, 377 U.S. 426 (1964) (private cause of action available under section 27 of the Securities Exchange Act of 1934) with Kissinger v. Reporters Comm. for Freedom of the Press, 445 U.S. 136 (1980) (neither Freedom of Information Act, Federal Records Act of 1950, nor Records Disposal Act confer private right of action) and Touche Ross & Co. v. Redington, 442 U.S. 560 (1979) (no private cause of action available under section 17(a) of the Securities Exchange Act of 1934).

[38] This seems to be the thrust of Ezra Ripley Thayer's influential analysis of the impact of statutes on the standard of care in negligence cases. *See* Thayer, *Public Wrong and Private Action*, 27 HARV. L. REV. 317, 321-23 (1914).

[39] *See supra* note 22.

statutory standard in a private case is whether the legislature intended to require such use. The issue of legislative intent does not arise under the public interest view, where the only question is whether the legislative standard is pertinent to the issues in the case. The test most often used by tort courts—whether the plaintiff claiming the benefit of the statute was one of the people whom the legislature was trying to protect[40]—seems to come to the same thing: an inquiry into the relevance of the standard to the case at hand.

2. *Technical Invalidity.* Suppose a statute containing a safety or health standard is enacted but later is invalidated because of some technical defect in the enactment process. Should the statute nonetheless be given weight by a court in a private action involving the subject matter of the statute? Again the answer depends on one's theory of the legislative process. The public interest theory implies that the defective statute should be given effect unless the defect raises a doubt whether the statute really reflects the deliberate choice of the legislature;[41] a purely technical defect does not nullify the information content of the statute. Under the interest group view of legislation, however, there is no presumption that a statute has any such content. The courts bow to the legislative determination only as a matter of power; if the legislation is defectively enacted, it is not an authentic exercise of legislative power and therefore should not influence, let alone bind, the courts.[42]

3. *Federal Standards in State Courts.* If a state court is asked in a private tort action to derive the applicable standard of care from a federal safety statute, the choice between theories of

---

[40] W. PROSSER, HANDBOOK OF THE LAW OF TORTS § 36, at 192-95 (4th ed. 1971). *See, e.g.,* Fitzwater v. Sunset Empire, Inc., 263 Or. 276, 502 P.2d 214 (1972) (snow-clearing ordinance creates duty in favor of the municipality only); Akers v. Chicago, St. P., M. & O. Ry., 58 Minn. 540, 60 N.W. 669 (1894) (railroad yard safety statute not designed to protect trespassers).

[41] *See* Clinkscales v. Carver, 22 Cal. 2d 72, 136 P.2d 777 (1943) (technical invalidity does not affect applicability of legislative standard); W. PROSSER, *supra* note 40, § 36, at 191-92.

[42] The same result should follow in the courts' use of health or safety standards enacted by the legislature after the commission of a tortious act. Under the public interest theory, courts should give the standard effect because it embodies the legislature's judgment of the proper standard of reasonable care. *See* Fall v. ESSO Standard Oil Co., 297 F.2d 411 (5th Cir. 1961) (subsequently enacted statute prohibiting sale or possession of switchblade knives used to demonstrate that a switchblade knife is a dangerous weapon). Under the interest group approach, however, the standard reflects legislative power only and should be given no effect, for that power had not been exercised at the time of the tortious conduct.

legislation may again be decisive. Courts that adopt the public interest view presumably should use any pertinent federal standards, because the standards can be assumed to provide information on whether the defendant was negligent. But under the interest group approach, courts have no reason to pay any attention to federal statutes, unless the statutes bind state courts by preempting any inconsistent state determinations on issues within their scope.

4. *Tortious Acts Outside the Legislative Purpose.* In *Gorris v. Scott,*[43] the defendant violated a statute that required animals to be penned on shipboard. The purpose of the statute was to prevent contagion; the plaintiff's animals were washed overboard, although they would not have been had the defendant penned them as the statute required. The court held that the defendant's violation of the statute did not make him liable. This is the usual result in such cases,[44] but viewed from a public interest standpoint is difficult to understand. If the defendant violated the statute, he acted wrongfully, and liability would have the salutary effect of increasing the incentives to observe the statutory command. But if the statute was just a favor to some interest group, adding sanctions for its violation via the tort law may upset the deal struck in the legislature by giving the interest group more than it could obtain in the political arena.

5. *Implying a Private Right of Action.* In deciding whether a statute creates a private cause of action for those injured by its violation, courts frequently ask whether the statute creates an adequate set of public remedies for its violation, so that implied private remedies are not needed to enforce it effectively. If courts find the statutory remedial scheme so incomplete or defective that private remedies are necessary to make it enforceable, they are more likely to imply a private remedy.[45] This result is defensible only under the public interest theory of legislation. The absence of ef-

---

[43] 9 L.R.-Ex. 125 (1874).

[44] *See* W. PROSSER, *supra* note 40, § 36, at 195.

[45] *See, e.g.,* J.I. Case Co. v. Borak, 377 U.S. 426 (1964) (private right of action implied under section 14(a) of the Securities Exchange Act of 1934); Breitwieser v. KMS Indus., Inc., 467 F.2d 1391 (5th Cir. 1972) (rejecting private right of action under the Fair Labor Standards Act), *cert. denied,* 410 U.S. 969 (1973). The Supreme Court has become hostile to implying private rights of action and may no longer be willing to do so even if the remedial scheme is defective. In fact, the Court currently is reluctant to recognize a private right of action unless Congress indicates that it intended to create one. *See, e.g.,* Touche Ross & Co. v. Redington, 442 U.S. 560, 568-78 (1979) (no private right of action found under section 17(a) of the Securities Exchange Act of 1934). Under the analysis in this article, this is the correct approach if the interest group theory of legislation is adopted.

fective remedies implies to the interest group theorist that the group that procured the legislation lacked the political muscle to get an effective statute, and it is not the business of the courts to give an interest group a benefit that was denied by the legislature. Under this view, to imply a private right of action is to intervene in the legislative struggle on the side of one interest group, overriding opposing groups that had managed to thwart the enactment of an effective statute. The issue is identical to that in *Gorris*.

The public interest and interest group theories of legislation have very different implications for the proper use of statutes in private cases. But as I argued in part I, we are not limited to a binary choice, and this gives rise to a puzzle: if the output of a legislature is a mixture of public interest and interest group statutes, together with others (based on "sentiment") that are difficult to classify into either group, and if, moreover, courts lack the research tools they need to classify statutes correctly, what is the judge to do when asked to rely on a statute in a private case as a source either of the standard of care or of the underlying right of action? As a matter of logic, it seems he cannot act at all without determining whether a statute is motivated by public interest or interest group considerations—a determination beyond his competence.

Because there is no easy way out of this dilemma, I am led to predict that courts will act with apparent inconsistency. Casual empiricism supports this prediction. Not only has the Supreme Court veered sharply in recent years in its attitude toward implying private rights of action,[46] but courts asked to use criminal statutes in tort cases have responded inconsistently. An example will show this.[47] By relying on criminal statutes to determine a standard of care without regard to the legislature's intentions regarding such a use, courts implicitly embrace the public interest theory of legislation. However, by refusing to use statutes for this purpose in cases not envisaged by the legislature, as in the *Gorris v. Scott* line

---

[46] *See supra* note 45.

[47] For other examples, see W. PROSSER, *supra* note 40, § 36, at 194-95. *Compare* Ross v. Hartman, 139 F.2d 14 (D.C. Cir. 1943) (statute requiring motor vehicles to be locked intended to protect against accidents involving car thieves), *cert. denied*, 321 U.S. 790 (1944) *and* Heiting v. Chicago, R.I. & P. Ry., 252 Ill. 466, 96 N.E. 842 (1911) (railway fencing statute intended to protect children) *with* Kiste v. Red Cab, Inc., 122 Ind. App. 587, 106 N.E.2d 395 (1952) (ignition key statute not intended to protect against car accidents involving the intervening negligence of thieves) *and* Di Caprio v. New York Cent. R.R., 231 N.Y. 94, 131 N.E. 746 (1921) (railway fencing statute not intended to protect children).

of cases,[48] courts shrink from a full embrace of the public interest approach. Judicial uncertainty regarding the use of statutes in private cases is well illustrated by a federal district court decision holding both that (1) the sternness of the remedies prescribed for violations of the Occupational Safety and Health Act ("OSHA")[49] precludes implying a private right of action[50] and that (2) a state court would not rely on OSHA as a source of the standard of care in a tort suit.[51] If my analysis is correct, the first holding implies adoption of the public interest view of legislation and the second implies its rejection.[52]

E.   The Construction of Criminal Statutes

Although the canons of statutory construction have received well-merited criticism on grounds of fatuity and inconsistency,[53] the "rule of lenity,"[54] under which courts construe criminal statutes more narrowly than those that provide only civil remedies, usually escapes criticism as long as unnatural constructions are avoided. Economic analysis suggests the following explanation. Every statute overdeters to a certain extent, because its bounds are uncertain and fear of inadvertent liability causes some people to steer well clear of those bounds. The harsher the sanctions for violation, the greater the overdeterrence and the resulting costs in socially beneficial conduct forgone. Overdeterrence can be reduced by careful specification of the statutory limits. If a statute is intended to be specific, courts should not construe it broadly.

This assumes that the legislature is sensitive to the costs of overdeterrence—in other words, that it wants considerations of efficiency to guide judicial interpretation of its product. Not all criminal statutes can be interpreted in this light, but I assume most can

---

[48] See *supra* notes 43-44 and accompanying text.
[49] 29 U.S.C. §§ 651-678 (1976).
[50] Otto v. Specialties, Inc., 386 F. Supp. 1240, 1242-43 (N.D. Miss. 1974).
[51] *Id.* at 1244-45 (applying Mississippi law).
[52] For a very different view of why courts apply statutory norms in common law adjudication, stressing moral factors, see Michelman, *Norms and Normativity in the Economic Theory of Law*, 62 MINN. L. REV. 1015, 1016-27 (1978).
[53] For good treatments, see Friendly, *Mr. Justice Frankfurter and the Reading of Statutes*, in FELIX FRANKFURTER: THE JUDGE 30 (W. Mendelson ed. 1964), *reprinted in* H. FRIENDLY, BENCHMARKS 196 (1967); K. LLEWELLYN, THE COMMON LAW TRADITION: DECIDING APPEALS 521 (1960).
[54] *See, e.g.,* Dunn v. United States, 442 U.S. 100, 112 (1979); United States v. Wiltberger, 18 U.S. (5 Wheat.) 76, 95-96 (1820); Hall, *Strict or Liberal Construction of Penal Statutes*, 48 HARV. L. REV. 748 (1935).

be. If this assumption is true, then the courts' inability to distinguish on a statute-by-statute basis between public interest and interest group motivations for legislation implies that they should treat all criminal statutes as public interest statutes and assume that the legislature would want the statute interpreted narrowly.

A statute can underdeter as well as it can overdeter, and if overdeterrence is the characteristic vice of broad construction, underdeterrence is the characteristic vice of narrow construction. But the costs are not symmetrical. The harsher the sanction for a violation of law, the higher the cost-justified level of care in drafting. Careful drafting avoids both underdeterrence and overdeterrence. If the legislature can be assumed to draft criminal statutes more carefully than civil statutes, then courts should construe criminal statutes more narrowly than they construe civil statutes—and they do.

Not all criminal sanctions are more severe than civil sanctions. The antitrust laws illustrate this point. The maximum criminal fine that can be imposed on a corporation for violating the Sherman Act is one million dollars,[55] but trebling of civil damages[56] makes two-thirds of every private damages judgment for violation of the Sherman Act penal. Thus there is no limit to the amount a corporation might be forced to pay in a civil suit under the Sherman Act. The question of when civil penalties should be equated with criminal sanctions and therefore be governed by stricter procedural safeguards is beyond the scope of the present inquiry.[57] But I do think that a statute that provides for civil penalties comparable in severity to typical criminal sanctions should be interpreted as narrowly as a criminal statute covering the same subject matter. In antitrust cases, therefore, treble damages should be awarded only where there would be criminal liability. I do not contend that the rule of narrow construction that I am proposing for statutes that impose civil penalties is constitutionally required; thus the suggested reform would require amending the antitrust

---

[55] 15 U.S.C. §§ 1-2 (1976).

[56] *Id.* § 15.

[57] The Supreme Court's jurisprudence in this area approaches complete deference to congressional labeling. *See* United States v. Ward, 448 U.S. 242, 248-51 (1980) (deference to congressional decision that penalty under the Federal Water Pollution Control Act was civil); Atlas Roofing Co. v. Occupational Safety and Health Review Comm'n, 430 U.S. 442, 449-50 (1977) (deference to congressional decision that OSHA administrative proceedings are not subject to the seventh amendment). *See generally* Charney, *The Need for Constitutional Protections for Defendants in Civil Penalty Cases*, 59 CORNELL L. REV. 478 (1974).

laws, which now entitle any plaintiff who proves actual damages to a trebling of them.

III. IMPLICATIONS FOR CONSTITUTIONAL INTERPRETATION

A. Strict or Loose?

There is great debate today, as always, over how strictly constitutional provisions should be construed. I do not want to enter the debate;[58] it is enough for my purposes to observe that virtually everyone who writes on the question thinks that constitutional provisions should not be construed as strictly as statutory provisions. I want to consider whether there are any economic reasons supporting looser construction of constitutional provisions, without worrying how much looser that construction is or should be.

I once thought the most powerful reason for looser construction of constitutional provisions was the cost of amending the Constitution relative to that of amending a statute. But this reasoning is superficial; it merely invites the courts to amend the Constitution through loose construction. There is a better reason for construing the Constitution less strictly than statutes. The Framers made it difficult to amend the Constitution because an easy amendment policy would create instability in the nation's fundamental institutions.[59] But this does not mean they necessarily rejected liberal construction of constitutional provisions by the courts (or would have done so if the question had been put to them), for construction is unlikely to change the nature of the instrument as radically as amendment. Text and history provide some check on construction (though in some eras precious little), but none at all on amendment. This argument resembles my earlier view but is more persuasive because it derives not from the Constitution's amendment clause but from a contrast between what courts can do to an instrument through construction and what a constitutional convention or a legislature can do through amendment.

There is another reason for construing the Constitution less strictly than statutes, though if this reason is operative the term

---

[58] I do point the reader to two excellent and brief defenses of the tradition of judicial self-restraint that are easily overlooked: P. DEVLIN, *The Judge as Lawmaker*, in THE JUDGE 1 (1979); L. HAND, *How Far is a Judge Free in Rendering a Decision*, in THE SPIRIT OF LIBERTY 103 (I. Dilliard 3d ed. 1960).

[59] *See* Dellinger, *The Recurring Question of the "Limited" Constitutional Convention*, 88 YALE L.J. 1623, 1625 (1979).

"loose" may be a misnomer. It is extraordinarily difficult to ascertain the intent of a document drafted two hundred years ago or, as in the case of the fourteenth amendment, even one hundred years ago. The cultural, political, and even linguistic setting is so altered that reconstructing the intent behind the constitutional provisions becomes a task of historical research. Judges do not have the time or the training to do such difficult research; even when it is done by competent legal historians it often yields highly uncertain results. If the intended meaning of a provision is difficult to recover because of the passage of time, any construction of the provision (except one that denies it any contemporary application at all) will seem "loose" to opponents of that construction. It would be more accurate to say that uncertainty over intended meaning increases the variance of defensible interpretations around the (unascertainable) true meaning, for the court is as likely to undershoot as to overshoot the mark.

Although we tend to think of the problem of unrecoverable meaning as one peculiarly of constitutional interpretation, the point is not limited to the Constitution. It applies to any very old statute, such as the Sherman Act,[60] enacted in 1890 and not significantly amended since. There is as much warrant for departing from the literal meaning of the Sherman Act as for departing from the literal meaning of the fourteenth amendment.

If historical research should yield an unambiguous answer regarding the meaning of a particular constitutional provision, the question would arise whether a court interpreting the provision today should feel bound by the historical understanding. If, but only if, a contrary meaning is well established in precedent, I would answer "no." Legal principles that have been well settled for a century or more should not exist at the sufferance of historians, so that a piece of brilliant historiography could change the public policy of the nation at a stroke. This conclusion, related to the policies that underlie stare decisis and statutes of limitations, does not necessarily flout the intent of the Framers. They were practical men rather than ideologues; they probably would not have wanted the country to pay a big price for correcting mistakes in interpretation many years after such mistakes had been made and after the country had adapted to them.

The disruption of established institutions is a less acute prob-

---

[60] Ch. 647, 26 Stat. 209 (1890) (current version at 15 U.S.C. §§ 1-7 (1976)).

lem in the case of old statutes. If legislative history of the Sherman Act turned up conclusively proving that the Act was intended to protect competitors rather than consumers, so that ninety years of judicial construction were unsound, Congress could restore the judicial interpretation with the stroke of a pen. It could not do the same thing if the American Historical Society certified that the due process clause of the fourteenth amendment had not been intended to place any substantive limitations on state action.

I am advocating a more limited role for historical research with regard to constitutional provisions that have a long-settled construction than with regard to equally old statutes, but the argument also reinforces in a different way the case for looser construction of constitutional than of statutory provisions. If constitutional provisions are characteristically old and hence difficult to interpret, constitutional adjudication is inescapably more difficult than statutory construction because the courts lack the usual assistance of an intelligible text and a meaningful legislative history. Thus we can expect the incidence of error in constitutional adjudication to be higher than in statutory adjudication. We must therefore decide which kind of error is more costly: the erroneous denial of the legislative will expressed in a statute (or in administrative or executive action thereunder) invalidated on constitutional grounds, or the erroneous denial of a constitutional right. I believe that the erroneous invalidation of a statute is generally more costly, especially if interest group legislation is only a fraction of all legislation. It must generally be better to thwart the desires of a small group seeking to get from the courts what, by definition, it was unable to get from the political branches than to thwart the will of the majority, even if not every statute embodies the will of the majority.

Because I am speaking only of cases where the meaning of the Constitution is unclear, my conclusion does not place the minority at the mercy of the majority and thereby deny the very concept of a constitutional right. If someone has a clear constitutional right, it must be enforced. But if a court cannot honestly determine whether such a right exists, the right should be denied; doubts should be resolved against the claimant.[61]

This conclusion may hold even if most statutes are assumed to be the product of interest group pressures. Such legislation reflects

---

[61] This was urged in Thayer, *The Origin and Scope of the American Doctrine of Constitutional Law*, 7 HARV. L. REV. 129, 144 (1893).

and expresses the dominant power in the community, and it is the counsel of prudence for courts to yield to the dominant power when to do so does not deny a clear constitutional right. Prudence—call it, if you will, timidity in the face of superior power—is an acceptable tie-breaker where, by hypothesis, courts' interpretive tools yield no clear answer to a claim of constitutional right.[62]

In short, all other arguments aside, the utilitarian notions that underlie most versions of welfare economics, coupled with considerations of political prudence frankly imported from outside economics, indicate that, in general, constitutional rights should be narrowly construed but constitutional powers broadly construed. The qualification "in general" is important, though, because if the meaning of a constitutional provision is clear, the problem of construction does not arise.

B. Rationality Review

I have explained elsewhere why I think the interest group theory of legislation shows the fallacy of invalidating legislation on the ground that it is not rationally related to a proper legislative purpose.[63] Because no one seems to think it improper for interest groups to influence the legislative process, it cannot be right to invalidate legislation just because it was procured by an interest group. Yet that would be the effect of rationality review if it were taken seriously and applied neutrally, for legislation passed on behalf of an interest group typically will flunk any test of rationality other than pure self-interest. It is a different matter if such legislation infringes people's express constitutional rights. But that is not the issue where legislation is invalidated merely as irrational, for there is no express constitutional right not to be disadvantaged by the characteristic operation of the political process.

Responding to the problem of interest groups that use voter ignorance to subvert the ideal operation of the democratic system,[64] Professor Gerald Gunther has proposed that legislation not reasonably related to the legislators' stated end be held to violate the equal protection clause of the fourteenth amendment.[65] The

---

[62] This was Holmes's position. *See supra* note 8 and accompanying text.

[63] *See* R. POSNER, *supra* note 2, at 495-96; Linde, *Due Process of Lawmaking*, 55 NEB. L. REV. 197 (1976). For a criticism of my analysis, see Michelman, *Politics and Values or What's Really Wrong with Rationality Review?*, 13 CREIGHTON L. REV. 487, 503-06 (1979).

[64] See *supra* p. 273.

[65] Gunther, *The Supreme Court, 1971 Term—Foreword: In Search of Evolving Doc-*

legislature would be forced to state its actual purpose clearly and so give more information to the electorate. Gunther's proposal is appealing; and though, as he is well aware, it cannot be derived from the text, history, or purpose of the fourteenth amendment, perhaps it is too late in the day to return to the original understanding of the amendment. I have a different point to make: that if my analysis is correct, Gunther's proposal may be redundant. To repeat an earlier point,[66] if the judiciary is constrained to interpret statutes in accordance with their stated rather than true ends, the ability of interest groups to manipulate an ignorant electorate is automatically limited. No doubt there are cases where the stated objective is so incongruous compared with the actual statutory directive (for example, requiring the licensing of shoe salesmen to limit the spread of athlete's foot) that Gunther's principle would require invalidating the legislation, whereas mere interpretation would allow attainment of the interest group's desires. But a case so transparent to a court may also be transparent to the electorate or its representatives, while if the lack of reasonable connection between means and stated end is not so transparent, the judges are apt to be fooled along with the voters. No doubt there is a middle ground of cases that would be affected by his proposal; the question is how large it would be—it may be small.

C. Strict Scrutiny

In recent years the Supreme Court has declared that statutes infringing "fundamental rights" are valid only if they survive "strict scrutiny" of the justifications offered for them.[67] There can be no objection to this standard—except perhaps that it is too lax[68]—if the fundamental right in question has firm constitutional roots, as does, for example, the right not to be discriminated against on racial grounds. But when the concept of fundamental rights is expanded to take in a host of interests with no specific constitutional provenance, and when, moreover, most of those interests involve sex or its consequences,[69] the practical effect of the

---

trine on a Changing Court: A Model for a Newer Equal Protection, 86 HARV. L. REV. 1, 20-21, 23 (1972).

[66] *See supra* notes 29-32 and accompanying text.

[67] In addition to the cases cited *infra* note 69, see Shapiro v. Thompson, 394 U.S. 618 (1969) (right to travel); Harper v. Virginia Bd. of Elections, 383 U.S. 663 (1966) (right to vote).

[68] *See* R. POSNER, *supra* note 25, at 375-76.

[69] *See, e.g.,* Zablocki v. Redhail, 434 U.S. 374 (1978) (right of father with prior child

strict scrutiny standard is to prevent serious consideration of any possible justifications for the challenged statute.

Laws regulating sex fall into the class of statutes that I call "public sentiment" statutes,[70] for they rest on public feeling rather than on a utilitarian or economic calculus. A strict scrutiny standard asks the state to furnish clear and convincing reasons for the statute; and whatever may be the status of utilitarianism among contemporary philosophers, the reasons that strike judges as clear and convincing are usually utilitarian reasons.[71] To show that a statute confers a great enough benefit to justify infringing a "fundamental" right requires a showing that the statute promotes a compelling state interest, which in practice means the greatest good of the greatest number. But it is the nature of public sentiment statutes that they are not susceptible of utilitarian justification—and most of the fundamental rights created by the Supreme Court in recent years are rights against constraints imposed by public sentiment statutes on personal behavior.[72]

Indeed, despite all the efforts to ground the fundamental rights approach in antiutilitarian thought, it is difficult to resist the impression that the approach is utilitarianism run wild. Courts perceive the claims of the woman seeking an abortion or of the teen-aged girl seeking the joys of sex unthreatened by pregnancy as claims to happiness not offset by any happiness claim on the other side, with the result that the statutes restricting abortions or denying teenagers access to contraceptives flunk an elementary Benthamite test. So strong is the utilitarian hold over the judicial imagination that even in an area not governed by a strict scrutiny standard—sex discrimination[73]—the Court prefers a specious utilitarian justification to a frank acknowledgment that a challenged statute rests on public sentiment. For example, in the recent

---

support obligations to marry without court approval); Carey v. Population Servs. Int'l, 431 U.S. 678 (1977) (distribution of contraceptives to minors under 16); Roe v. Wade, 410 U.S. 113 (1973) (right to abortion); Weber v. Aetna Casualty & Sur. Co., 406 U.S. 164 (1972) (right of dependent, unacknowledged, illegitimate child to recover under worker's compensation law for death of father); Stanley v. Illinois, 405 U.S. 645 (1972) (right of unwed father to child custody); Eisenstadt v. Baird, 405 U.S. 438 (1972) (use of contraceptives by unmarried people); Stanley v. Georgia, 394 U.S. 557 (1969) (right to private possession of obscene material); Griswold v. Connecticut, 381 U.S. 479 (1965) (use of contraceptives by married people).

[70] *See supra* notes 19-20 and accompanying text.

[71] For a recent example, see Kaplan, Book Review, 95 Harv. L. Rev. 528, 533 (1981).

[72] *See* cases cited *supra* note 69.

[73] *See* Craig v. Boren, 429 U.S. 190 (1976) (intermediate scrutiny).

Michael M. case,[74] where a young man challenged the constitutionality of his conviction for statutory rape on the ground that the statute did not punish females, the Court upheld the conviction on unconvincing deterrent grounds.[75] The statutory distinction obviously rested on conventional views regarding the male and female roles in sexual activity rather than on any view that excusing females from liability would have a greater deterrent effect than would making them liable as well as males.

It may seem odd for me to be criticizing the use of a utilitarian calculus to guide constitutional adjudication. But whether or not the fourteenth amendment adopts the felicific calculus, there is a pitfall in using the calculus where only the costs of regulation, and not its benefits, can be measured.[76] The costs of statutes that limit personal freedom are patent, whether or not they can actually be quantified; the benefits are unmeasurable, yet they may still exceed the costs.

D. Delegation

There has been renewed interest lately in the doctrine of nondelegation, which holds that the powers granted to the separate branches of government in the Constitution are not delegable to other branches.[77] If there is such a principle, it has characteristically been honored in the breach, notably in the creation of independent administrative agencies. These agencies exercise legislative authority without being part of Congress; judicial authority, without complying with the requirements of article III; and executive authority, without being subordinate to the executive.[78] But I think there is an economic argument, though not necessarily a con-

---

[74] Michael M. v. Superior Court, 450 U.S. 464 (1981).

[75] *Id.* at 469-73 (statute justified by legitimate state interest in preventing teenage pregnancy).

[76] This is a frequent criticism of cost-benefit analysis in environmental regulation. *See, e.g.,* Anderson, *The National Environmental Policy Act,* in FEDERAL ENVIRONMENTAL LAW 301-03 (E. Dolgin & T. Guilbert eds. 1974); Hammond, *Convention and Limitation in Benefit-Cost Analysis,* 6 NAT. RESOURCES J. 195, 203-10 (1966).

[77] *See, e.g.,* Industrial Union Dept. v. American Petroleum Inst., 448 U.S. 607, 672-76 (1980) (Rehnquist, J., concurring); T. LOWI, THE END OF LIBERALISM 92-126 (2d ed. 1979); Gewirtz, *The Courts, Congress, and Executive Policy-Making: Notes on Three Doctrines,* LAW & CONTEMP. PROBS., Summer 1976, at 46, 49-65; Scalia, *Back to Basics: Making Law Without Making Rules,* REG., July/Aug. 1981, at 25.

[78] The President can neither remove members of independent agencies before their terms expire nor nullify their actions. *See* Wiener v. United States, 357 U.S. 349 (1958); Humphrey's Ex'r v. United States, 295 U.S. 602 (1935).

clusive one, to be made for the constitutionality of the independent agency. Like the argument for construing criminal statutes more narrowly than civil statutes,[79] it depends on a legislative process analysis rather than on a legislative substance analysis.

It is a peculiarity of legislatures committed to decision by majority vote that they cannot easily be enlarged to meet a greater demand for their output,[80] as an ordinary business enterprise or government department can be. Adding members to a legislature increases the costs of securing majority agreement and does so at an increasing rate. The formula for the number of separate communication links required to connect all members of a group of n members, $n(n-1)/2$, will give us a crude idea of the transaction costs involved in legislative production. If the legislature has 100 members, the number of separate links required for a majority is 1275. If the number of legislators is raised to 200, the number of required links rises to 5050—almost a four-fold increase, although the number of legislators has only doubled. In short, an expanding legislature encounters severe diseconomies of scale.

This point supplies a practical justification for the delegation of legislative authority to independent agencies. Parallel arguments are available to justify delegation to the agencies of judicial and executive power as well. There must be one Supreme Court, and it would lose its judicial character if its membership were increased very much, as it might have to be if the lower federal courts exercised the judicial power that has instead been vested (subject to only limited review) in the agencies. Expansion of the executive through a proliferation of subordinate officers reduces popular control of the executive branch, because the span of control of the only elected executive official, the President, is limited.

Accepting this justification is not tantamount to endorsing judicial amendment of the Constitution. There is no explicit principle of nondelegation in the Constitution. The Framers could not have foreseen the enormous growth of the nation and presumably did not want to limit the adaptability of the Constitution to remote future conditions, except insofar as they placed explicit limitations on such adaptation. Arguing for constitutional adaptability is different from asserting that courts are free to amend the Con-

---

[79] *See supra* notes 54-57 and accompanying text.

[80] I am speaking of the legislature's legislative output. Legislators have other functions besides the enactment of statutes, and these functions are unaffected by my analysis because they do not depend on majority agreement.

stitution by interpretation just because the Framers deliberately made amendment by any other route very difficult—a proposition that cannot withstand casual, let alone strict, scrutiny.

But if the suggested interpretation is not usurpative, it may still be wrong. The independent agency, with its combination of legislative, judicial, and executive powers, seems to violate the principle, fundamental in the Constitution's text and history, of the separation of powers. Specifically, the growth of the independent agency may well have placed more power in the hands of the legislature relative to the other branches than the Framers contemplated. Against this consideraton must be set the unreality of expecting the Supreme Court to attempt at this late date to dismantle the administrative state. In these equivocal circumstances, the economic argument outlined above should carry weight.

IV.   FITTING THE COURTS INTO THE THEORY

The economic theory of legislative and constitutional interpretation assumes that courts are simply agents of the enacting body. As Professor William Landes and I have argued elsewhere,[81] this assumption is not inconsistent with the tradition of judicial independence from political control, for independence is a precondition of the courts acting as agents of the enacting, rather than the current, legislature. Of course, independence from current political pressures does not guarantee that the courts will try to follow the will of the statutory or constitutional draftsmen rather than their own views of proper policy. The discredited canon of statutory construction that statutes in derogation of the common law are to be narrowly construed[82] is an example of judicial independence asserted to thwart the will of the enacting legislature, and my discussion of constitutional interpretation has revealed many discrepancies between contemporary judicial practice and what the economic theory of constitutional interpretation implies would be the correct practice. To complicate the issue further, courts seeking guidance on the meaning of a statute are limited to the text itself and the published legislative history, and this limitation, as we have seen, reduces the legislature's practical ability to get the courts, however willing they may be, to work its will.

---

[81] *See* Landes & Posner, *supra* note 2.
[82] *See, e.g.,* Pound, *Common Law and Legislation,* 21 HARV. L. REV. 383 (1908). Though discredited, the principle is not dead. *See, e.g.,* 3 J. SUTHERLAND, STATUTES AND STATUTORY CONSTRUCTION § 61 (C. Sands 4th ed. 1974).

Despite all this, a comparison of the analyses in this article of statutory and constitutional interpretation reveals a greater congruence of the former than of the latter with the economic theory of legislation. A possible reason for this difference is that if courts misinterpret a statute, the legislature can nullify their misinterpretation rather easily through an amending statute. Courts therefore have little to gain by setting their will against the legislature's. Thus a theory that correctly identifies the forces operating on the legislature should also predict the behavior of the courts in interpreting legislation. Courts have much more leeway in interpreting the Constitution, not only because the Constitution is so costly to amend, but also because its antiquity makes it unlikely that the same political forces that procured its enactment are still around to nullify departures from it.

By the same token we would expect, and we find, at least if the antitrust laws are a representative example, less responsible judicial interpretation of old than of recent statutes. This is not only because of the inherently greater difficulty of accurately interpreting the older laws; it also reflects the greater independence from legislative retribution that courts enjoy when they are interpreting very old statutes.

[2]

The Constitution as an
Economic Document

Richard A. Posner*

There was a time when an "economic" theory of the Constitution meant the theory, expounded years ago by Charles Beard, that the purpose of the Constitution was to redistribute wealth from the poorer segments of society to the upper class, to which the Framers belonged.[1] This was an extremely narrow view, both of economics (implicitly viewed by Beard as the unmasking of exploitation) and of the Constitution, and is now discredited.[2] Today when one thinks of how economics might be used to study the Constitution, no fewer than eight distinct (though overlapping) topics come to mind:

(1)   The economic theory of constitutionalism; that is, the economic properties, and likely consequences, of requiring a supermajority for some kinds of political change.

(2)   The economics of constitutional design — of the constitutive rules of a political system — and thus (a) of the separation of powers within the federal government and (b) of federalism (i.e., the overlapping sovereignty of the federal government and the states).

(3)   The economic effects (broadly defined) of specific constitutional doctrines, such as the exclusionary rule or the limitations

* Judge, United States Court of Appeals for the Seventh Circuit; Senior Lecturer, University of Chicago Law School. The research assistance of Nir Yarden and John Muller, and the exceptionally helpful comments of Gary Becker, Edward DuMont, Frank Easterbrook, David Friedman, Sanford Levinson, Fred McChesney, Charles Silver, George Stigler, and Cass Sunstein, are gratefully acknowledged.

1.   *See* C. BEARD, AN ECONOMIC INTERPRETATION OF THE CONSTITUTION OF THE UNITED STATES (1913).

2.   *See, e.g.*, F. McDONALD, WE THE PEOPLE: THE ECONOMIC ORIGINS OF THE CONSTITUTION (1958).

November 1987   Vol. 56   No. 1

4

that the Supreme Court has imposed in the name of the First Amendment on suits against the media for defamation, whether or not the doctrines themselves are founded on sound, or on any, economic principles.

(4)   The interpretation of constitutional provisions or doctrines that may have an implicit economic logic — for example, freedom of speech, when conceived of as a guarantor of a free market in ideas; the commerce clause, when conceived of as a guarantor of a national common market; and the takings clause, when conceived of as a guarantor of property rights.

(5)   Proposals to refashion constitutional law to make it a comprehensive protection of free markets, whether through reinterpretation of existing provisions or through new amendments, such as a balanced-budget amendment.

(6)   The problem of "dualism," by which I mean the paradox of the Supreme Court's being passionately committed to liberty in the personal sphere and almost indifferent to liberty in the economic sphere.

(7)   The relationship (if any) between the Constitution, as drafted and as interpreted, and the economic growth of the United States.

(8)   The extent to which judges should feel themselves free to use economic analysis as an overarching guide to constitutional interpretation (that is, beyond the limits of points (3) and (4)); in other words, the relationship between economics and interpretation.

I shall touch on each of these eight areas, though the touch will at times be light.

I.   The Economics of Constitutionalism

Words like "constitution" and "constitutionalism" have multiple rather than single meanings. They can refer to the principle of limited government, to the constitutive rules of government, to the most important rules — constitutive and otherwise — of government, and to legislation that cannot be revised by the ordinary legislative process. It is with the last of these meanings that I shall begin, for it is perhaps the most distinctive feature of the United States Constitution that it can be changed only by a supermajority. This feature raises the question — on which there is a substantial economic literature[3] — of what constitutive rules and what rights ought

---

3.   *See, e.g.,* G. BRENNAN & J. BUCHANAN, THE REASON OF RULES: CONSTITUTIONAL POLITICAL ECONOMY (1985); J. BUCHANAN & G. TULLOCK, THE CALCULUS OF CONSENT ch. 6 (1962) ("A Generalized Economic Theory of Constitutions"); Davidson, *The Limits of Constitutional Determinism,* in CONSTITUTIONAL ECONOMICS: CONTAINING THE ECONOMIC POWERS OF GOVERNMENT 61 (R. McKenzie ed. 1984); Macey, *Competing Economic Views of the Constitution,* 56 GEO. WASH. L. REV. 50 (1987); Rae, *Decision-Rules and Individual Values in Constitutional Choice,* 63 AM. POL. SCI. REV. 40 (1969).

to be placed beyond the power of a majority to correct. I shall take up that question after first examining a largely unexamined, but I think logically prior, economic problem inherent in the decision to have a written constitution that cannot be changed through the ordinary legislative process.[4] This is the problem of governance by rules over time.

The problem has been discussed extensively in relation to long-term contracts and (a substitute for long-term contracts, as we shall see) public-utility regulation. A contract cannot (in general) be lawfully revoked or modified without the unanimous consent of the parties. In this respect it is more like a constitution, which requires a supermajority to amend, than like a statute, which requires only a majority to amend and is therefore relatively easy to alter as changed circumstances may require. Like a constitution, but unlike a statute, a contract establishes a rule that is difficult to change yet is designed to govern the future.

The name given in the contract setting to governance by rules over time is "contingent contracting" — contracting with reference to contingencies that may never occur.[5] The cost of anticipating and providing explicitly for all possible contingencies is very high; in the case of a contract designed to remain in force for the indefinite future and govern a wide range of social interactions, it is for all practical purposes infinite. So, if some contingency arises, there may very well be no contractually specified response to it. What to do? One possibility is a supplementing interpretation by a court — an effort to supply the solution the parties might have been expected to supply if they had negotiated with reference to the contingency. The difficulty is that if the contingency occurs many years after the contract was made, a court may find it impossible to figure out what the parties would have decided to do about the contingency had they foreseen it and contracted with specific reference to it.

Another possibility is renegotiation by the parties. This solution may be reasonably satisfactory if the situation is one of bilateral monopoly, and thus mutual dependence, which creates pressure for a solution (while also, however, making negotiation costly).[6] But it has seemed inadequate where only one party to the contract is going to have a monopoly when the contingency occurs — for example, where a single firm (street railway, retail supplier of electricity, local telephone company, etc.) is going to confront a mass of unorganized consumers for the indefinite future. That essentially would be the situation in constitutional law if the Constitution just "ran out,"

---

4. If a constitution can be amended as easily as a statute can be amended, then functionally it *is* a statute, at least in a country like ours where, unlike in England, custom and tradition are not venerated.

5. *See* K. Arrow, Essays in the Theory of Risk-Bearing (1971); R. Posner, Economic Analysis of Law §§ 4.1, 13.7 (3d ed. 1986); O. Williamson, Markets and Hierarchies: Analysis and Antitrust Implications (1975); Williamson, *Franchise Bidding for Natural Monopolies — In General and with Respect to CATV*, 7 Bell J. Econ. 73 (1976).

6. *Cf.* Epstein, *In Defense of the Contract at Will*, 51 U. Chi. L. Rev. 947 (1984).

in the sense of being deemed inoperative if problems not foreseen and provided for by the Framers arose, leaving the society's constitutional arrangements to a renegotiation between the government and the people.

Another possible solution — the regulatory solution of having a permanent agency act (in principle, though generally not in practice) as the consumers' representative — is approximated in the constitutional setting by the Supreme Court, which is designed to be independent, so far as possible, from the other branches of government. When viewed so, as a kind of regulatory protector of the citizenry, the Court cannot adopt a narrow interpretation of the constitutional text, because that text will not provide for all possible contingencies, especially ones that arise over a period of what is now two hundred years. On this view, the significance of the constitutional text as a constraint on courts is in setting broad outer bounds to the exercise of judicial discretion rather than in prescribing the actual rules of decision. As a realistic matter, this approach describes much of constitutional law; it is a body of judge-made law, constrained by the constitutional text but not derived from it or prescribed by it in a substantial sense.

The regulatory analogy is reinforced by consideration of the economic tradeoffs between rules and standards as methods of controlling behavior.[7] A rule is a precise directive that leaves little discretion to those charged with applying it; a standard provides some direction but delegates considerable discretion to those charged with applying it. A standard is more adaptable to changed circumstances than a rule and is therefore preferred when the indefinite future is being regulated. Public-utility statutes usually (but not always) contain broad standards such as "public convenience and necessity." The Constitution, too, contains many broadly worded provisions that invite or at least permit interpretation as standards — "freedom of speech," "respecting an establishment of religion," "general welfare," "necessary and proper," "due process," "cruel and unusual punishments," etc. — and many of its rule-like provisions have become either obsolete, irksome, or irrelevant (e.g., the right to bear arms, the right to jury trial in civil cases at law if the stakes exceed $20, the requirement that the President be native-born and at least thirty-five years old). The problem with a standard is that often its practical effect is to delegate the real policymaking authority to the persons who administer the standard — in the present setting, the judges. Because of this problem it may well be descriptively more accurate to view the Supreme Court as the

---

7. *See* Ehrlich & Posner, *An Economic Analysis of Legal Rulemaking.* 3 J. LEGAL STUD. 257 (1974).

(constrained) agent of the present generation than as the agent of
the Constitution's Framers, the latter view being unrealistic because
of an insurmountable agency-cost problem. The Framers are dead;
the "instructions" they left, the most important of which are in any
event (and inevitably) vague, are losing pertinence with every passing year; and the Framers' agents — if this is how the judges should
be viewed normatively — have weak incentives to be faithful agents.
Although, as Professor Landes and I have argued, an independent
judiciary is a necessary condition for enforcing legislative "deals"
(including the original "deal" embodied in the Constitution and Bill
of Rights) in accordance with their original tenor rather than current political preferences,[8] it is not a sufficient condition, because it
does not by itself create strong incentives for judges to carry out the
will of the Framers rather than their own will.

The question of judicial incentives is a baffling one because judicial employment, especially at the federal level, is hedged with restrictions designed to reduce, though they can never eliminate, the
role of self-interest in judicial decisionmaking. One is led to ask
such questions as: Why should minorities entrust their protection
to judges — what incentive has the judiciary, which is not likely to be
drawn predominantly from members of minority groups, to side
with those groups rather than the majority? Shouldn't minorities be
expected to do well in the legislative arena, where, as we know, special interest groups, invariably minority groups of some sort, generally do well? About all that can be said in our present and
inadequate state of knowledge of judicial incentives is that the strip-
ping away of the usual incentives to self-advancement makes it
somewhat more likely that judges will actually try to conform their
decisions to the law; so if the law contains protections for minorities,
those protections are more likely to be enforced by judges than by
legislators. More on this in Part VIII.

Although agency costs are the subject of an extensive economic
literature,[9] they have been ignored in economic writing about constitutionalism. Libertarian economists, and (a largely overlapping
group) members of the balanced-budget amendment school,[10] often
evince an unwarranted faith in the power of the written word to anticipate contingencies and constrain responses to them, making the
judges' role mechanical and their incentives an uninteresting question. Economists and other nonlawyers tend to exaggerate the ob-
jectivity of judicial decisions, i.e., the degree to which those
decisions are determined by nondiscretionary application of clear
and settled principles. Not so Richard Epstein, a lawyer who recognizes the slipperiness of legal text and wants the judges to make new

---

8. *See* Landes & Posner, *The Independent Judiciary in an Interest-Group Perspective*, 18 J.
Law & Econ. 875 (1975).

9. *See, e.g.,* Jensen & Meckling, *Theory of the Firm: Managerial Behavior, Agency Costs
and Ownership Structure*, 3 J. Fin. Econ. 305 (1976).

10. On which see, e.g., The Constitution and the Budget: Are Constitutional
Limits on Tax, Spending, and Budget Powers Desirable at the Federal Level? (W.S.
Moore & R. Penner eds. 1980).

constitutional law — aggressively designed to promote free markets — by freely interpreting the Constitution. More on his proposal in Part IV.

In analogizing the Constitution to a long-term contract, I do not mean to embrace the fallacy pointed out recently by Russell Hardin of supposing that constitutions rest on the same solidly consensual foundations as contracts between adequately informed adults.[11] Apart from the facts that the Constitution was not ratified by popular vote, that voters are often poorly informed and rarely unanimous, and that many who supported the Constitution did so because it seemed better than the Articles of Confederation rather than because it was their preferred set of arrangements, there is the elementary fact that the vast majority of people who have lived under the Constitution have never had a chance to vote, directly or indirectly, for or against it. Acquiescence is not necessarily consent. For some purposes the Constitution can be analogized to a contract, but it is not a contract.

Having considered the costs created by having rules or standards that are difficult to change — costs in inflexibility in the case of rules, agency costs in the case of standards — I am now prepared to consider when those costs are worth incurring and when therefore the supermajoritarian feature that principally distinguishes constitutions from other forms of legislation should be used to place a subject outside the ordinary political arena.

The easiest case is where inflexibility is unimportant because the required rule is by its nature arbitrary: e.g., two senators from each state. The harder but more important case is where allowing a topic to be the subject of ordinary majority-vote politics would invite very costly rent seeking. If the vote of a simple majority could change the basic form of government or expropriate the wealth of a minority, enormous resources might be devoted to seeking and resisting such legislation. In a sense, a supermajoritarian constitutional provision confines legislative discretion to matters that do not matter all that much; the stakes are not large enough to evoke a disproportionate expenditure of resources on redistributing wealth or utility.

A qualification should be noted: Resources deflected by the Constitution from investment in making fundamental changes or dispossessing minorities of their wealth will be redirected not only into commercial or other presumptively efficient private activity but also into efforts to obtain "ordinary" legislative redistributions. And this brings me to the difficult question that underlies the proposals for a balanced-budget amendment, whether there should be a general

---

11. R. Hardin, Why a Constitution? (1987) (copy on file in the offices of the *George Washington Law Review*).

constitutional prohibition of rent-seeking, or (in other words) purely redistributive, legislation.[12] A purely redistributive statute by definition does not increase the size of the social pie, but actually shrinks it because resources will be expended on obtaining and resisting the enactment of the statute. So there is an economic argument for outlawing such legislation, and it can be done only by constitutional provision. The counterargument (more on this later) is that courts cannot readily identify purely redistributive legislation, in part because much redistributive legislation may be defensible on efficiency grounds by reference to problems of social peace, free-rider problems, and so forth.

One may be led by this discussion to wonder how a constitution could ever come to contain substantial protections for disfavored minorities, such as criminal defendants or members of fringe religious sects; any minority powerful enough to obtain constitutional protection need hardly fear — one might think — adverse legislation. Three answers come to mind. First, persons who might fear one day becoming members of a disfavored minority might support constitutional protection for minorities even at the cost of extending protection to people they did not like. This does not explain how, for example, the equal protection clause—designed primarily though not exclusively for the protection of racial minorities and in particular blacks—got into the Constitution, but may explain why the clause is drafted in general terms: so that it can cover groups to which members of the majority might someday belong. Moreover (and this is my second point), the interests of minority and majority groups, or of minority groups that in the aggregate form a majority, may be so intertwined that there is majority (more precisely, supermajority) support for a constitutional provision because members of these groups fear that the balance of political power may someday shift against them. Third, special interest groups are not excluded from constitutional deliberation, and a minority group may have the political muscle to obtain a constitutional provision that a majority of voters do not want.

II.   The Constitutive Principles of the Constitution

Besides protecting rights, the Constitution establishes the basic constitutive rules of American government (some scholars would regard some of the rights, such as free speech, as constitutive also). I shall discuss these rules under two headings: "separation of powers" and "federalism."

A.   Separation of Powers[13]

I use this term loosely; I realize that the Framers rejected separa-

---

12. Macey, *supra* note 3, Epstein, and others think the Constitution was intended to do this, so that no amendment is necessary.

13. Silver, *Economic Theory of the Constitutional Separation of Powers*, 29 Pub. Choice 95 (1977), is a rare example of economic analysis of the separation of powers. On the

tion of powers in its purest form. The most striking example of this rejection is the provision giving the President a veto power over legislation; this makes him a part of the legislative process. The requirement of senatorial advice and consent brings the Senate into the executive process.

These are details, though not unimportant ones; by increasing the number of persons whose views must be taken seriously, the provisions on sharing power reduce the dangers of mistake and impetuosity. The essential point, however, is that the parceling out of legislative, executive, and judicial powers among different branches, with or without much overlap, increases the transaction costs of governing. Effective government requires the concurrence of all three branches. Hence, separation brings about a situation analogous to bilateral (or "trilateral") monopoly. Analogous — not identical. Because none of the branches is a profit maximizer, both the incentives to withhold agreement and the incentives to negotiate to a mutually beneficial solution are different than in the usual case of bilateral monopoly. But it seems a fair guess that the transaction costs of governing are indeed higher than they would be in a unitary system.

They are higher, moreover, for wealth-enhancing programs as well as for redistributive or exploitive ones. This makes unclear as a matter of theory whether the separation of powers results in a net improvement in social welfare compared to a system such as England's, where the executive and legislative powers are combined (in principle in the House of Commons, in practice in the Cabinet) and where the courts, though independent in much the same sense as our courts, do not have power to invalidate legislation. The question has not been examined empirically.

Another wrinkle is that separation of powers can lower as well as raise the costs of government, not only by increasing deliberation (the point I began this section with) but also by enabling a more efficient exploitation of the division of labor. If judges' tenure were subject to the vicissitudes of legislative politics, it would be difficult to attract able people to a career in judging; law would be even less stable than it is, because it would change with changes in the opinions or desires of powerful legislators; and the quality of justice meted out by dependent courts would be low in cases in which the legislature had an interest. It might even be difficult for the legislature to make the interest group "deals" that are such a staple of legislative activity. An independent judiciary is more likely to enforce such a deal according to its original terms than a judiciary that

---

history of the concept, see M.J.C. VILE, CONSTITUTIONALISM AND THE SEPARATION OF POWERS (1967).

bends with every breeze from Congress, and an interest group is more likely to make a deal if it has some confidence that it will obtain benefits that extend beyond the two-year term of the enacting Congress.[14]

Similarly, though less certainly, if Congress took upon itself the executive role, that role might be performed badly (as the Continental Congress discovered), because the effective execution of policy requires unity of command; I say "might" because this is a problem that most parliamentary systems have solved. And some observers believe that experience has demonstrated that courts are not well equipped to make and execute laws outside the scope of traditional judicial power — though that has not kept them from trying, others believe, with great success. The executive branch may be at a comparative disadvantage to the legislative branch in legislating and to the judicial branch in judging; yet this is not certain, either, because much of what the executive branch does is legislating (through the promulgation of regulations) and judging (through administrative agencies and Article I courts).

Despite all these qualifications, I believe that the separation of powers is in part an effort to increase governmental efficiency by tailoring the institutional structure to particular governmental tasks. The consequence may be to offset the effect of separation in raising the transaction costs of government; so government may not be weaker, on balance, than under a system of concentrated powers. It is true that our government does not seem more efficient, in the sense of maximizing the wealth of society, than the governments of other countries at a similar stage of economic development (more on this later). But this may be because the effect of separation of powers in increasing transaction costs and thus reducing the scope (and presumably therefore enhancing the efficiency) of government is offset by its effect in reducing the costs (and thus facilitating the expansion) of government by enabling a more thorough division of labor than in a parliamentary system.

An additional consideration, however, is that the vesting of different governmental powers in different and independent branches places limits (in principle anyway — more on the actualities of the situation in Part VI) on the growth of government. The power of each branch to grow without experiencing a serious loss of control is inherently limited. Unless Congress relaxed the principle of majority rule, it could not accommodate greater legislative business by expanding the number of its members. On the contrary, the more members it had, the higher would be the cost (in communication and negotiation) of reaching agreement, in accordance with the formula for the number of links required to connect up all members of a set (here the set consisting of a majority of the members of each house of Congress): $n(n-1)/2$. Congress can do only so much by

---

14. *See* Landes & Posner, *supra* note 8; Crain & Tollison, *Constitutional Change in an Interest-Group Perspective*, 8 J. LEGAL STUD. 165 (1979).

hiring staff assistants and delegating responsibility to committees. It has done what it can, of course.

The same problem of inherent limitations of capacity (namely large diseconomies of scale) afflicts efforts to expand the decisional capacity of a court system by increasing the number of judges. The creation of intermediate courts is only a partial solution, because problems of delay and lack of coordination become more severe with every increase in the height or width of a judicial hierarchy, and because increases in the number, and reductions in the responsibility, of federal judges make it more difficult to recruit able people to be judges.

The executive branch, being in principle unitary and thus able in principle to impose a rigid hierarchy controlled by a single person, faces the fewest difficulties in expanding to accommodate a larger governmental function. But every enterprise encounters net diseconomies of scale eventually — and governments sooner than other enterprises because economies of scale in the provision of most governmental services are quickly exhausted. Hence, the effect of expanding the executive branch is to diminish control and coordination. Civil service rules further undermine the unity of the executive branch.

B. *Federalism*[15]

The system of power sharing between the federal government and the states — the system that has come to be called "federalism" — might seem to be just another aspect of the separation of powers. This is true in one sense but not another. It is true in the sense that decentralizing government, like creating specialized branches, may increase efficiency. Federalism enables the massive diseconomies of scale that would be encountered by any effort to govern so large, populous, and complex a society as ours from Washington, D.C., the way France is governed from Paris or England from London, to be avoided. It also encourages experimentation with different methods of providing governmental services and may foster the provision of services tailored to differing local conditions — although these are really just aspects of avoiding diseconomies of scale. Yet federalism does not substantially increase the transaction costs of governing, the way the separation of powers within the fed-

---

15. For previous discussions of the economics of federalism, see THE ECONOMICS OF FEDERALISM (B. Grewal, G. Brennan & R. Mathews eds. 1980); R. POSNER, *supra* note 5, ch. 26; R. POSNER, THE FEDERAL COURTS: CRISIS AND REFORM ch. 6 (1985); Easterbrook, *Antitrust and the Economics of Federalism*, 26 J.L. & ECON. 23 (1983); Hamlin, *The Political Economy of Constitutional Federalism*, 46 PUB. CHOICE 187 (1985); Rose-Ackerman, *Does Federalism Matter? Political Choice in a Federal Republic*, 89 J. POL. ECON. 152 (1981); G. Stigler, The Constitution and the Economy (May 8, 1987) (unpublished manuscript, copy on file at the *George Washington Law Review*).

eral government does, because, as we are about to see, the federal government can always override the states in matters within the scope of its authority. If the federal government could govern only with the concurrence of the state governments, we would have a federation, not a nation, and the transaction costs of governing would be exceedingly high. But of course federalism is not costless; one cost is a more complex legal system than if we had a unitary judiciary enforcing a uniform body of law.

The point I want to emphasize is the efficiency of parceling out governmental powers among competing (not merely independent) institutions. With regard to governmental powers exercised on the state level, or even more clearly on the local level, there is competition among governments to provide good service at low (tax) cost; those governments that do not will tend to lose residents to the others. (Such competition exists at the international level as well, but in severely attenuated form.) The competition is not perfect (what is?). Not only are there costs of relocation, but some taxable assets are immobile — land, for example. The Framers were therefore wise not to stop with creating a competitive structure. In the commerce clause they authorized Congress to regulate interstate and foreign commerce and thus to prevent states from imposing harmful externalities on other states and to internalize beneficial externalities; several other provisions also restrict the power of states to tax or otherwise burden interstate or foreign commerce. The due process and equal protection clauses of the Fourteenth Amendment provide some protection to owners of immobile resources, who without these federal protections might be at the mercy of state expropriation. Consistent with these observations I have tried to construct a theory of federal law in relation to the states that would define the federal government's mission as one of overcoming the externalities that a system of competing governments fosters.[16] But in my previous work I treated the sovereignty of the states (limited as that sovereignty has become as a result of successive amendments to and interpretations of the Constitution) as being irrelevant to economic analysis. It is not; it is what assures a genuine competition among states. If state and local governments merely were administrative conveniences decreed by the central government, they would be no obstacle to centralization, i.e., to monopoly government. To the extent they are independent of the central government they provide real, if today very limited, competitive alternatives for consumers of governmental services.

This point may seem inconsistent with my previous point that the federal government can override the states in any area within the capacious scope of its authority. There is indeed little if any constitutional impediment to the federal government's preempting a specific area of governance, but the structure of the Senate, as well as the states' quasi-sovereign status in the constitutional scheme, dis-

---

16. *See* R. Posner, The Federal Courts: Crisis and Reform ch. 6 (1985); *see also* Easterbrook, *supra* note 15.

courages a wholesale transfer of functions from the states to the federal bureaucracy. The federal system provides a more secure basis for decentralized government than a formally centralized system that the central government might (or might not) choose, for reasons of convenience, to decentralize administratively.

But like separation of powers in its economies-of-specialization aspect, decentralization is a two-edged sword. It makes government more efficient, but all this means is that it enables government to do more with a given amount of resources. The result may not be a smaller government with the same output of services but an equally large or larger government with a higher output of services — and the higher output may be inefficient because it may take the form of economically unwarranted interferences (redistributive or paternalistic) with free markets and personal liberty.

III. *The Economic Criticism of Specific Constitutional Doctrines*

Despite what I have said so far, I certainly do not believe that every provision of the Constitution is efficiency enhancing. An example of one that is not is the provision that the President must be at least thirty-five years old. This is rank paternalism. It is true that, for a variety of good economic reasons, voters lack good information about candidates; but the one fact a voter is well able to assess in evaluating a candidate's qualifications is the candidate's age. A more important example is the self-incrimination clause of the Fifth Amendment; no economic reason has ever been offered for why government should not be allowed to penalize a person who refuses to give testimony, merely because the testimony might show that the person has committed a crime. And in an age when constitutional tort suits are a reality, the exclusionary rule — an inefficient sanction for violations of the Fourth Amendment's prohibition against unreasonable searches and seizures — no longer has a persuasive economic justification.[17]

But a legal doctrine is not beyond the range of fruitful economic analysis just because the doctrine lacks a core of economic good sense, especially if, as is often the case, the doctrine has an implicit economic logic — only a bad one. The greatest triumphs of "law

---

17. These two examples, self-incrimination and the exclusionary rule, are discussed in Posner, *Excessive Sanctions for Governmental Misconduct in Criminal Cases*, 57 WASH. L. REV. 635 (1982); *see also* Posner, *Rethinking the Fourth Amendment*, 1981 SUP. CT. REV. 49. A caveat should be entered: Rules conferring broad tort immunities on public officials may, when combined with the Supreme Court's refusal to recognize respondeat superior (employer's vicarious liability) in constitutional tort suits, deprive the tort remedy of much of its practical utility. *See id.* at 64-68. I add — though it should not be necessary to do so (the qualification should be obvious) — that when I say there is no "economic" reason for a rule or practice or institution, I do not mean there is no reason, period. There may be good reasons that are not economic.

and economics" have come in demonstrating the economic senselessness of well-established legal doctrines in such fields as antitrust and corporation law. So when, as in the Supreme Court's efforts to defend more extensive regulation of broadcast than of print media by reference to the inherent "scarcity" of the electromagnetic spectrum,[18] the Court neglects greater scarcities that afflict the production of newspapers, or when it makes arbitrary distinctions between personal and economic rights (see Part V), its economic blunders should be pointed out — and maybe eventually the doctrines will be changed, just as many antitrust doctrines have been changed under the pressure (it seems) of careful economic thinking.

Here are two more examples of judge-made constitutional doctrines that seem to rest, in part anyway, on bad economic thinking. First, the presumption that due process of law in repossessing property obtained on credit requires a hearing before rather than after repossession is defended by asserting that property rights will be impaired without such a hearing. Second, the principle that legislation which seems irrational must therefore violate the due process or equal protection clauses is defended by reference to a model of the legislative process in which the characteristic product of the process is legislation that promotes the general welfare. In truth, requiring "predeprivation" hearings in credit-sale cases will just raise interest rates, to the detriment of the class ostensibly protected by additional procedural safeguards. And the interest group theory of politics — revived, refined, and expanded by economists[19] — suggests that it is quixotic to invalidate all legislation that is not welfare maximizing. The point is not that no legislation promotes the general welfare, but that the legislative process is a market in which legislation is in effect auctioned off to the highest bidders, and often these are compact interest groups scheming to transfer wealth to themselves from diffuse, uninformed, and for both reasons underrepresented groups, such as consumers and taxpayers. An unknown but possibly quite large fraction of legislation reduces the total wealth of society without making the distribution of that wealth any more "equitable" according to any defensible criterion of distributive justice. A consistent judicial commitment to good-faith "rationality review," designed to identify and invalidate "nakedly" redistributive legislation, would therefore portend an enormous increase in the already overextended role of the courts in our society, and might, indeed, require a return to the *Lochner* era (see Part V).

A more modest function of economic analysis in relation to noneconomic doctrines is to remind the courts that all legal doctrines have costs. By displaying those costs, whether analytically or quantitatively, the economist can place warranted pressure on the supporters of the doctrines to establish the existence of offsetting benefits. For example, the exclusionary rule leads to overdeter-

---

18. *See* Red Lion Broadcasting Co. v. FCC, 395 U.S. 367 (1969). For criticism, see R. POSNER, *supra* note 5, § 28.3, at 633-34.

19. *See* R. POSNER, *supra* note 5, §§ 24.4, 25.3.

rence of police searches. The resulting costs to the legal process, and to the community (in the form of a higher crime rate, because criminal investigations are made more cumbersome and uncertain), cannot easily be justified if there exists — and there does — an alternative sanction, the tort suit, which if properly configured would provide a deterrent more likely to approximate the optimum.[20]

IV. Implicitly Economic Constitutional Doctrines

A number of provisions of the Constitution seem to have an implicit economic logic. This is perhaps clearest with respect to the "negative" or "dormant" commerce clause, which is to say the interpretation of the commerce clause as forbidding states to erect barriers to interstate commerce unless Congress authorizes them. When so interpreted, the commerce clause becomes a charter of free trade — a subject of detailed economic analysis since Adam Smith — and, relatedly, an element of an efficient federalism. By preserving the sovereignty of the states the Framers of the Constitution created a danger that, like independent nations, states might be pressured by interest groups to establish trade barriers. This would be of no concern if competition among states were perfect, for that would imply that any consumer or supplier in a state who was harmed by such a barrier would move immediately and costlessly to another state; the trade barrier would be ineffective. But as mentioned earlier, interstate competition is not perfect; there are significant immobilities. If Wisconsin, say, forbids the importation of milk in order to protect its dairy farmers, the price of milk in Wisconsin will rise, and although Wisconsin consumers will be hurt, they may lack sufficient political "clout" (being a diffuse and unorganized group) to undo the prohibition, while the costs of relocating to another state may be too great for them to vote against the prohibition with their feet. The "negative" commerce clause is one device (and the privileges and immunities clause in Article IV is another — and one better grounded in the text and history of the Constitution[21]) for preventing states from abusing their "market power" and thus for ensuring that the federal principle is used to promote rather than retard interstate competition aimed at optimizing the cost and quality of governmental services.

The takings clause of the Fifth Amendment also seems founded on economic considerations — and so indeed does the Fourth Amendment (and not just the exclusionary rule that has been

---

20. See *supra* note 17.
21. See Eule, *Laying the Dormant Commerce Clause to Rest*, 91 YALE L.J. 425, 446-55 (1982). For further discussion of the economics of the negative commerce clause, see R. POSNER, *supra* note 5, §§ 26.3, 26.4, and references cited therein at 612-13.

grafted onto it by the courts). In forbidding only *unreasonable* searches and seizures, the Fourth Amendment requires courts to balance the costs, to privacy and property, of searches and seizures against the benefits in reducing the incidence of crime, and therefore to use an essentially economic calculus in applying the amendment to specific conduct. In so arguing, I do not mean to suggest that any time a legal doctrine requires judgments of more and less, as almost any doctrine that speaks in terms of reasonableness does, it is economic in character. All rational activity involves a balancing of pros and cons, and while economics is in its broadest sense the science of rational choice, it does not follow that every rational choice is in an interesting sense economic. Moreover, the things balanced might not be monetizable even in principle, or might be weighted in a manner remote from utilitarian or economic calculation. It is an empty form of economic analysis of law that is content to attach the economic label to every balancing test in law. However, as I have argued elsewhere in discussing the Fourth Amendment,[22] economics does more than identify the interests to be balanced. It teaches that the exclusionary rule leads to overdeterrence by creating a sanction that costs more to society than the social (not private) cost of an illegal search to the criminal defendant, and it teaches that, other things being equal, the graver the crime being investigated the lower should be the level of probable cause that the police need establish in order to be authorized to conduct a search. These are not truisms; they are nonobvious implications of economic analysis.

I even believe that the speech and religion clauses of the First Amendment can be interpreted to require that the government allow the operation of a free market in ideas and religion respectively, so that no regulation of these markets that cannot pass a strict efficiency test should be allowed to stand. Such an interpretation seems broadly consistent not only with the delphic text and equivocal background of these provisions, but with much, though not all, of the vast interpretive superstructures that have been erected on them.[23] Again, I am not suggesting that (for example) just because the courts balance the interest in a fair trial against the interest in freedom of the press in deciding what restrictions can be placed on news coverage of a trial, what they are doing is economics in an interesting sense. But I do think that economics is useful in explaining the situations in which censorship is allowed and not allowed, the differential treatment of commercial and noncommercial speech, and such interpretive concepts under the First Amendment's religion clauses as "neutrality" and "accommodation." But these are stories for another day.

I realize that in speaking of constitutional rights in economic terms I open myself up to the accusation that I am distorting the

---

22. *See supra* note 17.
23. *See* Posner, *Free Speech in an Economic Perspective*, 20 SUFFOLK U.L. REV. 1 (1986); Posner, *The Law and Economics Movement*, 77 AM. ECON. REV. PROC. 1, 7-12 (1987).

meaning of the word "right" by viewing it as instrumental rather than ultimate, a means rather than an end, a ground for resisting governmental action rather than an absolute barrier to it. But the truth is that the boundary of every constitutional right is drawn at the point of balance between conflicting social goals; no right is absolute. The reason that the Constitution's prohibitions of such practices as torture and slavery seem absolute is that the inevitable balancing act is built into the definition of the practice. "Torture" and "slavery" are not neutral, referential terms; they are the names of the forms of practices (coercing statements and involuntary servitude, respectively) that we abhor. We do not call the methods by which we permit confessions to be extracted against the better judgment of the suspect torture even though it is plain that there would be fewer confessions if all custodial interrogation were forbidden. And we do not call the forms of involuntary servitude that we condone slavery — whether that servitude takes the form of involuntary military service, compulsory labor by prison inmates and prisoners of war, school attendance under compulsory schooling laws, parents making their children perform household chores, dangerous or demeaning work that workers "agree" to do only under the compulsion of economic necessity, or adherence procured only by threat of monetary or injunctive sanctions to a long-term employment contract that has turned disadvantageous to the employee.

I claim, indeed, that both the prohibition against extracting evidence by torture (one meaning that has been given to the Fifth Amendment's self-incrimination clause) and the prohibition against slavery (the Thirteenth Amendment) can be given an economic grounding. A long history of using torture to extract evidence has shown that it is an inefficient method of criminal investigation and proof. It has very high error costs, creates much gratuitous suffering, and deflects law enforcers from devoting adequate resources to solving difficult crimes; it is sometimes easier to extract a confession from an innocent person by torture than to convict a guilty person. As for slavery, it is abundantly clear that involuntary slavery is the antithesis of the free market model that underlies most concepts of economic efficiency. And while in principle it might occasionally be efficient for a person to sell himself into slavery, at least temporarily (as in eighteenth-century contracts of indentured servitude), so unlikely is such a case today that it makes good sense to ban self-enslavement; the probability is overwhelming that a case ostensibly of self-enslavement would in fact be a case of enslavement by force or fraud.

Much could be said on each of the implicitly economic doctrines of constitutional law, but they have been considered in some detail elsewhere[24] and I shall therefore pass on to —

V.   *Proposals to Constitutionalize Laissez-Faire*

I refer to the proposals by legal scholars such as Bernard Siegan and Richard Epstein to interpret the Constitution as a general guarantor of free markets,[25] and by some economists to strengthen this aspect of our constitutional system by amending the Constitution: for example to require a balanced federal budget in the hope that this would reduce the role of government, and thus increase that of private markets, in the allocation of resources.[26] Obviously the merit of proposals to reinterpret the Constitution cannot be appraised on economic grounds alone, even if the purpose and substance of the reinterpretation are economic to the core; for, as I shall argue, the first task of interpretation is interpretation, rather than the choice of optimal policies. Yet much of the argument in support of such proposals is of course economic. And economics does not just suggest the desirability of using free markets to allocate resources; it also points out the illogical features in existing interpretations of the "economic" clauses of the Constitution. As Professor Epstein has stressed, to limit the takings clause to the physical seizure of private property and ignore completely the effects of regulation in diminishing or even destroying property values is problematic, because the consequences of the two types of seizure are often the same. True, there are also differences. Many more people are affected by a regulation than by a taking, and therefore the organizing of political resistance is more feasible.[27] And the costs of rendering compensation are greater the more people

---

24. *See* R. POSNER, *supra* note 5, pt. 7, and references cited therein.
25. *See, e.g.,* R. EPSTEIN, TAKINGS: PRIVATE PROPERTY AND THE POWER OF EMINENT DOMAIN (1985); B. SIEGAN, ECONOMIC LIBERTIES AND THE CONSTITUTION (1980); Epstein, *Toward a Revitalization of the Contract Clause,* 51 U. CHI. L. REV. 703 (1984); ECONOMIC LIBERTIES AND THE JUDICIARY (J. Dorn & H. Manne eds. 1987). I believe I was the first to suggest that the discredited "liberty of contract" doctrine could be given a solid economic foundation and as good a jurisprudential basis as the Supreme Court's aggressive modern decisions protecting civil liberties. *See* R. POSNER, ECONOMIC ANALYSIS OF LAW § 19.1 (1973). I have never believed, however, that such a restoration of the "*Lochner* era" (so named because of Oliver Wendell Holmes's magnificent dissent in Lochner v. New York, 198 U.S. 45, 74 (1905)) would be, on balance, sound constitutional law. Of course, the idea of using the Constitution as a bulwark against redistributive (collectivist, socialist) policies did not originate with me — it is the idea that underlay the cases of the *Lochner* era. Its leading modern proponent is Friedrich Hayek. *See, e.g.,* F. HAYEK, LAW, LEGISLATION AND LIBERTY (1973); *cf.* Backhaus, *Constitutional Guarantees and the Distribution of Power and Wealth,* 33 PUB. CHOICE 45 (1978); Radnitzky, *The Constitutional Protection of Liberty,* in HAYEK ON THE FABRIC OF HUMAN SOCIETY 17 (E. Butler & M. Pirie eds. 1987). For general debate and discussion, see essays and comments in CONSTITUTIONAL ECONOMICS, *supra* note 3; *Proceedings of the Conference on Takings of Property and the Constitution,* 41 U. MIAMI L. REV. 49 (1986).
26. Probably a forlorn hope: The government can tax and redistribute wealth effectively through regulation, at small budgetary cost. *See* Posner, *Taxation by Regulation,* 2 BELL J. ECON. & MGMT. SCI. 22 (1971).
27. This point is only superficially inconsistent with the proposition stated earlier that compact interest groups are more effective than diffuse ones. An interest group with one member is compact all right (say, the owner of a home that the government would like to take for an official residence), but is likely to be powerless. On the economics of interest group politics, see *infra* note 29.

the "taking" affects, holding constant the total value affected. But the differences must be brought into the analysis explicitly before the traditional distinction between physical takings and regulatory impairments can be validated on functional grounds.

Like any form of aggressive constitutionalism, whether left-wing or right-wing, the economic libertarian approach (whether it takes the form of reinterpretation of the existing Constitution, amendment, or both) diminishes the role of democracy — potentially dramatically. The approach does not entail merely a redirection of constitutional protection from so-called personal liberties to economic liberties, for the consistent libertarian believes as strongly in the former as in the latter. To him the "marketplace in ideas" is a reality and not a metaphor, and sexual freedom, provided it does not cause harm to third parties, is as worthy of constitutional protection as freedom to choose an occupation or decide how much rent to charge a tenant. What is envisaged therefore is a drastic curtailment, across the board, in the scope of permissible legislative, executive, and administrative action. Not only much "moral" regulation, but all redistributive measures, would be forbidden unless justifiable on efficiency grounds, as the basic criminal laws can be justified as measures against a crude but highly inefficient form of "rent seeking," or as the charitable deduction from income tax can be justified as a measure for overcoming the free-rider problem that depresses charitable giving below the optimal level.[28] The scope of democratic government would not quite be limited to the selection and oversight of persons administering a small number of relatively uncontroversial governmental functions, such as internal and external security, the prevention of (other) harmful externalities, and the encouragement of beneficial ones. But that is the direction in which the proposal tends. And as both the regulation of morals and the redistribution of wealth are commonplace activities of modern government (whether they should be is a separate question), there is tension between the economic approach on the one hand and democratic political theory — not to mention democratic political practice — on the other.

The tension illustrates how economic analysis challenges conventional pieties. If E.M. Forster was unable to give more than two cheers for democracy, the economic analyst is unlikely to be able to give more than one. The economist recognizes that government can do some things better than the free market can do but he has no reason to believe that democratic processes will keep government from exceeding the limits of optimal intervention. On the contrary, the acute free-rider problem of democratic voting (the benefits of

---

28. *See* R. POSNER, *supra* note 5, §§ 7.1, 17.8 at 469.

voting are too small to make it worthwhile to incur the considerable costs of becoming a well-informed voter) ensures that compact interest groups will be able to use the democratic process to redistribute wealth in their favor, often at great social cost.[29] So, for Proudhon's "property is theft," the economist is likely to substitute "government is theft." This insight provides the essential underpinning for proposals to constitutionalize laissez-faire.

To grasp the nature and extent of the tension between laissez-faire and democratic political or legal theory it is necessary to distinguish between two fundamental political conceptions that are sometimes confused: limited government and democratic government. The proponents of limited government want the government to be relatively powerless and, partly for this reason, are not much interested in how the people who run the government are chosen; their interest is in preserving a large sphere for private action free of governmental interference. The proponents of democratic government want to make sure that the government is in some sense in the hands of the people and are confident that if it is placed there it can be trusted to promote the general welfare, without having to be limited. Among economists, Bentham was the most emphatic advocate of the position that a democratic government, unimpeded by constitutional limitations, would indeed promote the general welfare. But of course modern economic libertarians do not believe this. They believe that unfettered democratic government leads to the special interest state. They are of the limited-government school, and it might almost be a detail whether the government being limited is democratic or monarchical.

In fact, economists have little to say about forms of government. Because our government is democratic, the economic criticisms of government have focused on democratic government. Economists have pointed out that because an individual's vote in a political election has little instrumental value (one vote is not going to change the outcome), voters have only weak incentives to become informed about the impact of public policy on them unless they can be molded into effective interest groups. The result is a strong bias in favor of legislation that favors such groups, regardless of the general will. This bias is an embarrassment to democratic theory, because, other things being equal, the smaller a group is the easier it will be for its members to organize an effective interest group, while the larger and more diffuse the group is that the interest group seeks to plunder, the harder it will be for the members of the victimized group to concert resistance. But as there is no reason to believe that monarchy or dictatorship or oligarchy or other nondemocratic forms of government are less susceptible to interest

---

29. *See* G. STIGLER, THE CITIZEN AND THE STATE: ESSAYS ON REGULATION (1975); Becker, *Public Policies, Pressure Groups, and Dead Weight Costs,* 28 J. PUB. ECON. 329 (1985); Becker, *A Theory of Competition Among Pressure Groups for Political Influence,* 98 Q.J. ECON. 371 (1983); Mueller & Murrell, *Interest Groups and the Size of Government,* 48 PUB. CHOICE 125 (1986); Stigler, *The Theory of Economic Regulation,* 2 BELL J. ECON. & MGMT. SCI. 3 (1971).

group pressures, the economic criticism may be a criticism of government rather than of democracy. And democracy does have important advantages over the other forms of government. It is the most risk-averse form (and most people are risk averse), and it solves better than any other the problem of arranging an orderly succession of government officials.

The more aggressive one's constitutionalism the more the risk-averse character of democratic government is compromised, however, as the locus of power shifts to a small, unelected, life-tenured committee — the Supreme Court. It is not possible to limit government *tout court*; it is only possible to tell one branch to limit the others. The branch with this fortunate assignment is part of limiting, not limited, government. A pragmatist must agree with Charles Evans Hughes that the Constitution is what the judges say it is; the practical effect of constitutionalizing laissez-faire would be to make the Justices even more powerful oligarchs than they are today.

This point can be made more concrete by noting that the line between efficient public policy (which the laissez-faire Constitution would permit) and purely redistributive policy (which it would forbid) is not clear in practice or even in theory. In particular, a good deal of compelled redistribution of wealth may be the cheapest method of preserving social peace and so may be cost-justified; plausible examples are pro-union legislation designed to head off labor violence, generous welfare allotments designed to head off riots in the slums, and make-work public employment designed to reduce the incidence of crime by enlarging the opportunities of potential criminals to obtain lawful income, thereby increasing the opportunity costs of crime. Moreover, some, perhaps much, "immoral" behavior between consenting adults may, like pollution, have third-party effects warranting regulation. Indeed, economists cannot even agree on what shall count as a third-party effect. If I am offended by your reading pornography, does this mean that you are imposing a cost on me and I am therefore entitled on strictly libertarian grounds to advocate a law against the sale of pornography even to consenting adults? Finally, voluntary democracies, such as condominium associations, use majority-voting principles that allow for some redistribution of wealth among members of the association.

Far from fixing clear limits to the welfare state the libertarian approach may, paradoxical though this must seem, lay a theoretical foundation for inferring a constitutional obligation to provide basic, and perhaps other, government services.[30] After all, the libertarian

---

30. This point is suggested in an unpublished paper by Professor Frank Michelman of Harvard Law School. F. Michelman, Remarks at the Annual Meeting of the American Political Science Association on "The Constitution, Property Rights, and the Welfare State" (Sept. 4, 1987) (available from Professor Michelman). On the general question of

approach, at least in the form pressed by its most ardent proponent among lawyers, Professor Epstein, is rooted in the political philosophy of Hobbes and Locke, and latterly of Robert Nozick, all of whom believe that the legitimacy of the state depends on our being able to say that people would give up the liberties they enjoy in the state of nature in exchange for the state's guarantees of internal and external security. The "nightwatchman state" is the consideration for the surrender of these liberties. What if the state fails to carry out its part of the social contract? What if, for example, it provides ineffectual police protection, a common situation in the United States today? Does not the social contract theory that underlies the libertarian approach to constitutional interpretation imply that the state has violated the Constitution (viewed in that approach as the embodiment and guarantor of the social contract)? But why stop with police protection? What about fire protection, public education, and even welfare — all services that the state provides in lieu of private services? To the extent that public provision of these services cannot be justified in laissez-faire terms, Epstein might reply that the Constitution forbids their provision, and hence the issue of their adequate provision does not arise. But as I said earlier, the boundaries of the nightwatchman state are uncertain, and a variety of services not envisaged by Hobbes and Locke, ranging from pollution control to public support of the arts, may be reconcilable with it. Does not the libertarian approach therefore open up vast possibilities for a most aggressive constitutionalism — one that does not just tell the state to leave people alone but tells it to allocate more resources to particular public uses? I fear so.

A final objection to libertarian proposals for reinterpreting the Constitution to make it a charter of laissez-faire is the cost of judicial decisionmaking. Courts have limited competence to make economic (as other) decisions; and once it is recognized that constitutional doctrines are not self-defining or self-enforcing, the risk of heavy error costs and heavy litigation costs in any ambitious expansion of constitutional regulation becomes apparent. Courts seem to do well in developing common law principles that allocate resources efficiently; whether they would do well in shifting the boundary between common law and statutory regulation is more doubtful. The courts may not be competent to oversee the return of the nation to laissez-faire principles, however desirable those principles are.

VI. *Personal Versus Economic Liberties: The Double Standard*

The recent upsurge of interest in remaking the Constitution into a charter of economic liberties has brought to the fore the fascinating issue of the contemporary dualism in constitutional interpretation.

"positive" as distinct from the more familiar "negative" constitutional liberties, see DeShaney v. Winnebago County Dep't of Social Servs., 812 F.2d 298 (7th Cir. 1987) (and cases cited therein); Currie, *Positive and Negative Constitutional Rights*, 53 U. CHI. L. REV. 864 (1986).

However, discussion of that issue is not new;[31] indeed, the dualism is not new. Between the 1890s and the late 1930s the Supreme Court was extremely solicitous of infringements of economic liberty but paid little attention to infringements of civil rights or civil liberties; since the 1950s the reverse has been true. No satisfactory explanation for this about-face has ever been offered — though if it is interpreted, as it can be in part, as a change from emphasizing efficiency to emphasizing distributive values, it is consistent with broader changes in the role of government over this interval. The reversal is not total, and indeed recent years have seen an epicyclical movement. The Supreme Court in the name of the First Amendment has partially deregulated commercial advertising, and in the process has gone far to deregulate the legal profession.[32] And in cutting back on some of the excesses of the "Warren Court" in the field of criminal and welfare rights the Court has sometimes employed a rough version of cost-benefit analysis.[33] Nevertheless the tendency to upgrade "personal" rights such as the right to an abortion, and to downgrade "economic" rights such as the right not to have one's property taken without just compensation, the right to occupational liberty, and the right to transact interstate business without discrimination by reason of being a nonresident, persists.[34]

Efforts to justify the contemporary dualism are no more convincing than efforts to explain it. Constitutional provisions protecting personal liberties are no more emphatic or more broadly worded than those protecting economic liberties. Article I, for example, flatly forbids the states to pass any "ex post facto Law," or any "Law impairing the Obligation of Contracts." The courts have rewritten the first of these provisions to put "criminal" before "ex post facto," and the second to put "unreasonably" before "impairing."[35] Imag-

---

31. *See* R. POSNER, *supra* note 25, § 19.1; Coase, *Advertising and Free Speech,* 6 J. LEGAL STUD. 1 (1977); Coase, *The Market for Goods and the Market for Ideas,* 64 AM. ECON. REV. PROC. 384 (1974); Director, *The Parity of the Economic Market Place,* 7 J.L. & ECON. 1 (1964); Lucas, *Constitutional Law and Economic Liberty,* 11 J.L. & ECON. 5 (1968); Mashaw, *Constitutional Deregulation: Notes Toward a Public, Public Law,* 54 TUL. L. REV. 849 (1980); McCloskey, *Economic Due Process and the Supreme Court: An Exhumation and Reburial,* 1962 SUP. CT. REV. 34.

32. *See* Coase, *Advertising and Free Speech, supra* note 31; Jackson & Jeffries, *Commercial Speech: Economic Due Process and the First Amendment,* 65 VA. L. REV. 1 (1979); McChesney, *Commercial Speech in the Professions: The Supreme Court's Unanswered Questions and Questionable Answers,* 134 U. PA. L. REV. 45 (1985).

33. *See, e.g.,* United States v. Leon, 468 U.S. 897, 906-08 (1984); Mathews v. Eldridge, 424 U.S. 319, 335 (1976). *See generally* Easterbrook, *Foreword: The Court and the Economic System,* 98 HARV. L. REV. 4 (1984).

34. *See, e.g.,* CTS Corp. v. Dynamics Corp. of Am., 107 S. Ct. 1637 (1987); Fisher v. City of Berkeley, 106 S. Ct. 1045 (1986); United States v. Locke, 471 U.S. 84 (1985); Hawaii Hous. Auth. v. Midkiff, 467 U.S. 229 (1984); Illinois Psychological Ass'n v. Falk, 818 F.2d 1337, 1341-42 (7th Cir. 1987) (discussing cases that distinguish "personal" from "economic" rights).

35. On the interpretation of the ex post facto clause, see Calder v. Bull, 1 U.S. (3

ine what a similar program of watering down clear constitutional language would have done to the First Amendment! And it is not true that the Framers thought that personal liberties were worthier of constitutional protection than economic liberties or that the competition of interest groups would somehow produce a social optimum.[36] Nor is it true that courts know more about the personal and social realm than about the economic realm, though they think they do — confusing the technical with the difficult, as if evaluating the consequences of a rent-control ordinance, which is a form of tax on landlords and the subject of a vast and convergent economic literature, were more difficult than evaluating a tax on newspapers or the ethical implications and social consequences of abortion on demand. It is not even true that racial and religious minorities, women, homosexuals, criminal defendants, advocates of unpopular causes, or other groups whose members make aggressive claims of civil rights and civil liberties necessarily have less political "clout," and therefore are more needful of judicial protection, than the victims of constitutionally dubious economic regulations. The victims of oppressive economic regulations are mainly consumers, marginal workers (predominantly female or nonwhite), poor tenants, and other people of average or low income who — and this is the most important point — are diffuse, inarticulate, unorganized, and therefore politically weak. That is *why* they are the victims of redistributive legislation.

Here, by the way, is a possibility for linking up the economic-libertarian approach to the Constitution with the more fashionable approach of John Ely, who argues that the grand design of the Constitution is to assure representation, if need be by judicial action, for persons and groups who are underrepresented in the ordinary political process.[37] He thinks that blacks, homosexuals, aliens, and adherents to unpopular religions or ideologies are typical examples of underrepresented groups; implicitly he believes that economic interests are well represented. But that is because he either is not familiar with or does not agree with interest group theories of the political process; maybe he also does not realize that corporations are not economic persons but merely conduits to persons (workers, shareholders, employees) who may not be wealthy or well organized. Only some economic interests are well represented — those that are espoused by effective interest groups (e.g., by farmers, retail druggists, physicians, and lawyers). The interests of consumers, taxpayers, marginal workers, victims of crime, and

---

Dall.) 269 (1798); on the interpretation of the contract clause, see cases cited in Chicago Bd. of Realtors v. City of Chicago, 819 F.2d 732, 742-44 (7th Cir. 1987). I am not suggesting that these decisions are incorrect; *Calder,* for example, relied on the understood meaning of "ex post facto Law" in 1787. But in dealing with personal liberties the courts typically do not rely on historical meanings, e.g., of religious establishment, freedom of the press, or cruel and unusual punishments.

36. *See* F. McDONALD, NOVUS ORDO SECLORUM: THE INTELLECTUAL ORIGINS OF THE CONSTITUTION ch. 4 (1985); Sunstein, *Interest Groups in American Public Law,* 38 STAN. L. REV. 29 (1985).

37. *See* J. ELY, DEMOCRACY AND DISTRUST: A THEORY OF JUDICIAL REVIEW (1980).

housewives are seriously underrepresented. And on the other side, the advocacy of personal liberties by "single-interest" groups is often potent politically even though not supported by a majority; it would be incorrect to think that blacks, or supporters or opponents of abortion, or for that matter opponents of teaching the theory of evolution, are not effective interest groups.

VII.   The Macroeconomic Effects of the Constitution

I now want to shift gears and consider the overall economic effects of the Constitution. Stated concretely, would the United States be less, more, or just as wealthy if, like England, we had no written constitution? Before taking a stab at this question I must revisit the ambiguity in the idea of a "constitution." Obviously, England has a constitution, in the sense of a set of basic governing arrangements; its parliamentary system is constitutional in this sense even though Parliament could change it without worrying about judicial review. One thing our Constitution did was to create a set of arrangements — the separation of powers system discussed earlier — that was (and is) different from that of England and most of the rest of the world. Another important structural feature is, of course, the federal system, with all its refinements, such as the commerce clause. In addition, the Constitution established a uniquely powerful judiciary to police adherence to these arrangements and enforce the various rights created by the Constitution and later by the Bill of Rights and other amendments. The original Constitution, together with all of its amendments and the interpretive glosses (often radical) that the Supreme Court and the other courts have placed on the written Constitution as it has been amended, is what I shall mean by "the Constitution" in asking what its effects on economic progress have been. A distinct and even more speculative question, which I shall not essay, is what the effects of the Constitution on progress would have been if the courts had adhered to its pristine terms or at least interpreted it with greater restraint than they have shown.

The reasons why some nations are wealthier than others are not well understood.[38] Obviously the difference depends in the long run largely on national differences in the rate of economic growth, but that just pushes the inquiry back a step, to the causes of those differences. We know in a general way that economic growth depends on such things as the rate of saving, the rate of investment, receptivity to technological change, changes in the composition of the work force (e.g., because of immigration or emigration), and changing attitudes toward work, but again this knowledge just pushes the inquiry back a step, to why some nations invest more

---

38. *See* THE POLITICAL ECONOMY OF GROWTH (D. Mueller ed. 1983).

than others, and so forth. The role of legal institutions in all this is obscure. It is highly plausible, however, that economic growth will be helped if the government protects property and contract rights through a system of impartial courts enforcing property, contract, tort, and basic criminal law against not only private but also public misconduct (e.g., expropriation). Such protections for economic freedom would seem to encourage hard work and investment for the future — yet even this is not certain, given Mancur Olson's "destabilization" hypothesis, which is that stable institutions foster interest groups and that war and other sudden shocks may set the stage for rapid economic growth by making it more difficult for interest groups to form.[39]

I shall put Olson's hypothesis aside and assume that effective protection of basic economic rights promotes economic growth. Although the basic protection of such rights is traditionally a function of state rather than federal law, the Constitution is not irrelevant to this function. As I mentioned earlier, the Constitution guarantees a limited sovereignty to the states and thereby increases the likelihood that governmental services, notably including the provision of a court system, police, etc., for the protection of basic property (including tort) and contract rights, will be provided efficiently. Given the federal concept — itself a force for efficiency, I have argued — the Constitution has then to make provision for preventing the federal system from degenerating into a loose confederation, riddled with externalities. The commerce clause and the privileges and immunities clause are devices to this end, as is the clause enabling Congress to issue patents and copyrights and the clause giving the federal government a monopoly of bankruptcy law in order to prevent debtors from fleeing to states where they might dominate the government and obtain forgiveness of their debts.

The Constitution has other economic effects. By placing the basic governmental arrangements beyond the power of the normal political process, the Constitution (in its structural aspect) has freed the people's energies for productive private activities.[40] Basic political questions have simply been removed from the agenda by making the fundamental arrangements too difficult to change. This illustrates a point too often ignored in discussions of rules: Rules can liberate as well as repress. The rules of contract law are another example of this point.

In addition, a government strong enough to maintain law and order, but too weak to launch and implement ambitious schemes of economic regulation or to engage in extensive redistribution, is probably the optimal government for economic growth. The Constitution as originally drafted would have kept the United States

---

39. *See* M. Olson, The Rise and Fall of Nations: Economic Growth, Stagflation, and Social Rigidities (1982); Olson, *The Political Economy of Comparative Growth Rates*, in The Political Economy of Growth, *supra* note 38, at 7.

40. *See* S. Holmes, Precommitment and Self-Rule, Constitutionalism and Democracy (J. Elster & A. Slagstad eds., forthcoming 1988).

Government on approximately this even keel, for reasons explained earlier; but judicial interpretations have, by authorizing a "Fourth Branch" of administrative agencies, by expansively construing congressional power over interstate and foreign commerce and congressional power to enact statutes that purportedly promote the general welfare, greatly strengthened the power of the federal government to regulate markets. As discussed earlier, the net impact of the separation of powers on the power of government is uncertain, because while in one respect it reduces that power by increasing the transaction costs within government, in another it increases that power by enabling government to exploit economies of specialization.

Some of the specific rights guaranteed by the Constitution may have had good effects from an economic standpoint. Plausible examples are the religion clauses of the First Amendment, which may have reduced the amount of religious strife in this country — strife antithetical to economic growth because it is destructive, time consuming, and rooted in nonmarket values; the speech and press clauses of the First Amendment, which promote scientific and technical progress by protecting the marketplace in ideas; the takings clause, which protects property rights (though incompletely); and the due process clauses, which forbid the federal government and the states to deprive persons of property without due process of law. The problem is that a glance around the civilized world suggests that a written constitution may not be necessary to secure these rights. Countries at the same level of development as the United States generally are free from serious religious strife, do not restrict the production or dissemination of scientific or technical ideas, and do not confiscate private property without compensation. The compensation is not always adequate — but neither is compensation under the "just compensation" clause of the Fifth Amendment as the clause has been interpreted.

Although the separation of powers envisaged two hundred years ago has been greatly relaxed, the structure of the federal government is still distinguishable, at least in table-of-organization terms, from that of the dominant form of government in other countries at our stage of development — the parliamentary system. In such a system the legislature is supreme. Judges may, and in most advanced nations do, enjoy independence similar to that of our federal judges, but they are not authorized to invalidate legislative acts. The executive is a member of, and serves at the pleasure of, the legislature. There are many variants of the standard arrangement. In England, by virtue of its highly disciplined parties, the Cabinet is supreme. France has a unique system of power sharing between the president and prime minister, and Germany has a constitutional court. But virtually no advanced country has a system that looks much like our system, even countries whose contemporary governmental structures were influenced by the United States as an occupying power after World War II. The Philippines, along with some South American nations — as well as, of course, all of our own states, with the partial exception of Nebraska, which has a unicameral legislature — has imitated the structure created by the Constitution, but minus its most distinctive and perhaps valuable feature — federalism; and whether with good results can only be conjectured.

It would be perilous to infer from the failure of the leading foreign countries to imitate our system of government that it must not be a good system. But there is no solid evidence that it is superior to a parliamentary system. Whether one tries to imagine what this country would have been like under such a system or to compare it with other countries, holding constant other determinants of wealth and freedom besides constitutional structure, it is hard to be confident that ours is a better — or even, having regard for output rather than input, for accomplishments rather than aspirations, a different — system. We are marginally less collectivist than most advanced countries but the margin is small and there are counterexamples, including Japan, which has a parliamentary system. Such a system might, to be sure, be expected to exhibit faster and wider swings of public policy than would a separated system, and with destabilizing effects. Casual comparison with England supports this conjecture, but most parliamentary systems do not seem to experience such swings and some experience fewer and narrower ones than we. Moreover, studies of England's surprising decline do not ascribe it to the parliamentary system.[41] And to the extent that a parliamentary system enables government to turn on a dime, this has its upside (corresponding to our system's downside), illustrated by the swift replacement of Chamberlain by Churchill in 1940 as compared with our inability to replace promptly such *fainéants* as Buchanan, Andrew Johnson, Wilson, Hoover, and Nixon. So far as size of government is concerned, when due regard is had for regulation as well as expenditures (regulation in effect shifts part of the cost of government from the taxpayer to the shareholders, employees, and consumers of the regulated firm), our government seems to be as large as that of most parliamentary systems and no more efficient.

I come back to my earlier suggestion that federalism may be the most important contribution of American constitutionalism to economic growth. So vast, complex, and heterogeneous is this nation that it is hard to imagine providing basic governmental services efficiently on a uniform, centralized, nationwide basis. Although the federal government is of higher quality than most state governments, it would not be of higher quality if it absorbed every function now performed by state government; this seems to be the lesson of social security. I expect that it would be of lower quality than what

---

41. *See* Brittan, *How British Is the British Sickness?*, 21 J.L. & ECON. 245 (1978).

the average of all the governments in this country now is, because the spur of competition would be missing.

Not only is the upside of our Constitution somewhat uncertain (despite the last point) from an economic standpoint, but there is a downside. By making American law more complicated than it would otherwise be, and by enhancing the prestige of lawyers, the Constitution may have contributed to an exaggerated concern with legality and legal rights in this country, a concern that is a drag on economic growth. In addition, the Constitution as interpreted has helped give us one of the world's most costly and least effective criminal justice systems. It has also (in the name of equal protection of the laws, freedom of speech, and religious freedom) interfered profoundly with the employment policies of American government at all levels, and this too may have been a source of social costs with little offsetting social benefit — though one cannot be confident of this, because principles of efficiency do not dominate public employment.

VIII.   Economics and Interpretation

The last question I shall consider, the role of economics in constitutional decisionmaking, is a question about the proper limits of adjudication. Merely because economics may have many insights to contribute to understanding constitutional questions (as I hope I have shown), it does not follow that a judge, at any level in the judicial hierarchy, is entitled to use these insights to resolve all such questions. Although this point is simple and should be obvious, it is sometimes misunderstood by critics of economic analysis of law and perhaps by some defenders, and there may be some utility therefore in repeating and amplifying it.

I am aware of the tension between this part of my paper and the earlier parts. Earlier I took the hard-nosed approach to judicial interpretation of the Constitution, emphasizing the absence of incentives for judges to act as honest agents, whether of the Framers or of the present generation. And in the absence of incentives what is the point of exhorting judges to conform to some preordained concept of the judicial role? For two hundred years now, the federal courts in general and the Supreme Court in particular have been "activist." Often they have pushed their own power just as far as the political system would permit (and that is far) and sometimes even farther. What ground is there for expecting any change?

One possible answer is that, with the usual spurs to self-interest ruled out by the terms and conditions of judicial employment, judges can be expected to be more than ordinarily concerned with reputation. If, therefore, the climate of professional opinion changes (as a result, perhaps, of articles such as this, though of course the impact of a single article is apt to be minuscule) and judicial activism is seen to be a vice rather than a virtue, we can (without straying from the economic model of human behavior) expect that more judges will forswear or at least reduce activism.

There are two fundamental normative approaches to constitutional adjudication. The first regards the Constitution as essentially an empty vessel into which the judge pours his own ideas of sound policy. No judge avows such an approach, but there are a fair number of judicial decisions that cannot be otherwise explained and there is a fair amount of implicit and explicit scholarly support for it. The age of the Constitution, the generality of many of its provisions, the rejection (indeed infeasibility) of strict construction of constitutional language, the absence of clear-cut "legislative history" for many of the Constitution's provisions, the tradition, the popularity, and the occasional pragmatic triumphs of judicial activism, the vast accumulation of constitutional precedents (many inconsistent and all subject, in principle, to reexamination by the Supreme Court), the political character of judicial appointments, the rise of interpretive skepticism — this medley of forces and conditions has created a situation in which a Supreme Court Justice can go in virtually any direction that his personal political philosophy moves him without appearing to violate his oath of office. A Justice who took up the invitation thus extended and believed that normative economics (say, the idea of wealth maximization that I have defended) provided the best orientation for public policy would feel himself free — at least insofar as he was able to persuade enough of his brethren to constitute a majority and able to avoid being overruled by constitutional amendment — to decide constitutional cases in such a way as to make constitutional law economically efficient. For such a Justice, economics would provide a virtually complete guide to adjudication.

The other fundamental approach to constitutional adjudication regards the judge as constrained, most of the time anyway, by the text, structure, and history of the Constitution, and by certain general jurisprudential principles such as judicial self-restraint and decision according to precedent (stare decisis), in deciding constitutional cases. Realistic practitioners of this approach recognize that the constraints are far from total; not every decision (to put it mildly) is dictated. Moreover, important constraints, such as the idea of judicial self-restraint, are themselves political principles, chosen by judges rather than prescribed in the constitutional text.[42] And I have stressed that a legislative text cast in general terms — establishing standards rather than rules — invariably delegates substantial discretionary authority to the judges. So text, structure, history, etc., provide starting points but often not ending points for decision. And therefore notions of economic efficiency might legitimately be used to resolve some, perhaps many, constitutional ques-

---

42. *See* R. Posner, *supra* note 16, ch. 7 ("Judicial Self-Restraint").

tions; I have given examples. But the *first* task of constitutional adjudication is interpretation of a written text.

Interpretation is a problem in epistemology rather than economics, though economics is not irrelevant. Economics helps identify the consequences of alternative interpretations, and consequences are an important element in interpretation. One reason that no one will interpret me literally if I say, "I'll eat my hat," is that it would be a painful and protracted experience actually to eat a hat. Also, many honestly interpretive decisions are influenced by judges' implicit economic views and might therefore change if the judges were economically literate and realized for example that usury laws do not help debtors and rent control laws do not help tenants. Moreover, the interest group theory of politics, a theory to which economics has made important contributions, has much to say about the nature of the legislative enactments that courts are called on to interpret. Nevertheless, the act of interpretation is not just a form of economic policy analysis.

The justifications for viewing the task of constitutional adjudication as interpretive rather than (purely) creative or wealth-maximizing have more to do with the theory and practice of politics than with economics. People who are not lawyers, and in fact most lawyers, believe that most courts, most of the time anyway, decide cases in accordance with law, viewed as a body of principles external to the policy preferences of the individual judges. The legitimacy, prestige, and ultimately the authority of the Supreme Court appear to derive in significant part from this belief. If Lincoln was correct that you can't fool all of the people all of the time, this belief had better be true if the Court is to have a bright future, free of debilitating political controversy and popular suspicion. And if this is correct then it would be a serious mistake for the Supreme Court or any other court implicitly or explicitly to embrace the view that constitutional law is merely the expression in legal decisions of judges' views of public policy. It makes no difference whether those views come from Friedrich Hayek or Friedrich Engels.

An economic point reinforces this conclusion. A body of constitutional law tied, albeit by a loose tether, to an unchanging text is likely to be more stable than a body of law that the judges make up as they go along, unless, as in the case of the common law, the values understood to shape their lawmaking are themselves stable. The stability of the constitutional framework has economic value; by reducing uncertainty it facilitates investment. Stability is not the only value served by law, which is why a rigid policy of stare decisis is not optimal; but it is a value and it therefore weighs on the side of a policy of constrained constitutional lawmaking.

Not only is the proper starting point in formulating the principles of constitutional law the text, structure, and history of the documents that make up the Constitution, and the interpretive principles (broadly conceived) that translate text, structure, and history into contemporary meaning, but sometimes the starting point is the ending point. The Constitution provides that no one is eligible to be President who has not reached the age of thirty-five. This provision is perfectly clear (not because the words are clear, but because the purpose is clear), so whether such a limitation on eligibility is economically efficient (it is not, as I said earlier) is irrelevant to the task of adjudication. Many other provisions of the Constitution, though of course not all of them, are also clear, at least tolerably so, and at least with regard to some of the questions about their meaning. It is reasonably clear for example that capital punishment today does not violate the Eighth Amendment's prohibition against cruel and unusual punishments. Not only is capital punishment presupposed by the due process clauses of the Fifth and Fourteenth Amendments[43] (the latter promulgated long after the Eighth Amendment); not only was it a common form of punishment throughout the period from the adoption of the Bill of Rights to the adoption of the Fourteenth Amendment; not only are there respectable retributive as well as utilitarian arguments for it; but it has been supported continuously by the vast majority of the people of the United States from the founding of the nation up to the present day, so that it cannot be dismissed as the product of a temporarily inflamed majority.[44] The only candid basis on which it could be held unconstitutional would be that it revolted a majority of Supreme Court Justices. The refusal of two Justices to accept its constitutionality in the face of overwhelming case law merely underscores the fact that the constitutionality of capital punishment is also supported by the principle of stare decisis. These Justices' steadfast opposition may do them credit as sensitive men of advanced ethical views, but it is difficult to ground in law.

There are, however, many issues of constitutional law to which the documents do not speak with clarity; and with every passing year the documents recede further into the past and speak to us with a fainter voice. Remember that the Framers faced the uncomfortable choice between drafting rules, which would obsolesce rapidly, and standards, which would endure but only because standards, by their very nature, delegate much of the actual policymaking function to the judges who apply the standards in circumstances that the Fram-

---

43. But this is the weakest argument for the constitutionality of capital punishment; by assuming that capital punishment would continue to be administered and therefore deciding to require procedural safeguards for its administration, the Framers were not necessarily deciding that it could never be deemed a cruel and unusual punishment.

44. I do not rely merely on the well-known public opinion polls on the death penalty. Polls are unreliable indices of public opinion for a variety of reasons, including the fact that the person polled is not being asked to pay the costs of whatever public policy is being asked about. Yet when the poll data are added to the evidence provided by the unbroken history of statutes in most states imposing the death penalty, there can be little doubt that the death penalty is and always has been "popular" with the vast majority of Americans.

ers did not foresee. This point must not be pressed too far. I do think it is important to insist that the Constitution is a communication from the adopters to the judges and that the judges' duty is to decode the communication as best they can.[45] But often this is difficult or even impossible, and then the judges must have recourse to "interpretive" principles that may actually be substitutes for interpretation in a narrow sense. The Framers both expected the Constitution to endure (this is apparent from the obstacles that they created to amending it) and must have known, being highly intelligent men and, many of them, experienced lawyers, that many of its most important provisions were unspecific and would become even less directive as time passed and social change threw up new and unforeseen problems within the general scope of the provisions. They left many important details to be filled in through the adjudicative process over which the Supreme Court was to preside.

Consider, by way of example, the clause in the First Amendment that forbids Congress to make any law respecting an establishment of religion. "[E]stablishment" is not defined. At the time the First Amendment was drafted and ratified there were established churches in some of the states and of course in England (as there is today). Although the principal purpose of the clause apparently was to confirm the federal government's lack of authority in matters religious,[46] unquestionably the clause by its terms forbids Congress to establish one of the Christian sects as the national church, as Massachusetts, for example, had established the Congregational Church as its state church. Can the clause be interpreted as going further and forbidding Congress to declare Christianity the official religion of the United States? The nation was overwhelmingly Christian in 1789; there were few Jews or acknowledged atheists, and virtually no Moslems; and there is some doubt whether the religion clauses were intended to protect *any* "infidel."[47] Today the country is vastly more diverse religiously, and an attempt to establish Christianity as the national religion would be enormously resented even in the unlikely event that it could command the assent of a majority of both houses of Congress and avoid or override a presidential veto. Does the concept of "establishment" have sufficient play in its joints that it can be interpreted to forbid the establishment of Christianity, not just the establishment of a particular sect? I think it does, when one considers the general terms in which the establishment clause is

45. I develop this view in Posner, *Legal Formalism, Legal Realism, and the Interpretation of Statutes and the Constitution*, 37 CASE W. RES. L. REV. 179 (1987). *Cf.* Powell, *The Original Understanding of Original Intent*, 98 HARV. L. REV. 885, 911 (1985).

46. *See* L. LEVY, THE ESTABLISHMENT CLAUSE: RELIGION AND THE FIRST AMENDMENT 84, ch. 5 (1986).

47. *See* Wallace v. Jafree, 472 U.S. 38, 52 & n.36 (1985).

written ("Congress shall make no law respecting an establishment of religion") and its underlying objective of keeping government from taking sides in religious controversies. But I reach this conclusion by interpreting the clause in a manner designed to fit its underlying purposes or principles to current conditions, irrespective of my notions of sound policy, or economically efficient policy, whereas I think that, however abhorrent one may personally find capital punishment, there is no persuasive interpretive route by which to invalidate it under the Constitution.

The task of constitutional interpretation is not exhausted by study of the text, context, and background of the Constitution, for it is influenced by certain large jurisprudential principles, of which the two most important are judicial self-restraint and stare decisis. As I have explained elsewhere,[48] judicial self-restraint, if it is to have any concrete meaning, cannot be equated to caution, prudence, moderation, or refusal to innovate. That would simply run it together with stare decisis. It properly means a disposition to limit the power of the courts (in the realm of federal constitutional law, the power of the federal courts and above all the Supreme Court) vis-a-vis the other organs of government — Congress, the President, the federal administrative agencies, and all branches of state government. It means pulling in the federal judicial horns. The federal courts are overextended today and may eventually find it difficult to maintain their effectiveness unless they learn to defer more to the other branches of government. But the force of the principle of self-restraint is necessarily limited. It cannot properly be used to override relatively clear constitutional directives; otherwise it would nullify the Constitution. It is usable only in very close cases. In my establishment clause hypothetical the restrained solution would be to allow Congress to establish Christianity as the nation's official religion; but I cannot believe it would be the correct solution; the arguments for interpreting the clause to forbid such a measure are powerful. The principle of judicial self-restraint is properly a tie-breaker.

The principle of stare decisis, so far as pertinent here, is that Justices of the Supreme Court should stand by the existing interpretations of the Constitution unless a powerful reason for departing from them is shown. Because it is so difficult to undo a constitutional decision by the amending process, a rigid adherence to precedent in this area would be unsound. This is provided one thinks that a later decision, informed as it is by experience not available to the authors of the earlier decision, is therefore more likely to be right than its predecessors. Either decision — the original, or the overruling — will, if wrong, be equally difficult to correct through the amending process. But the overruling decision is somewhat more likely to be correct than the overruled one, if only because the former will be based on more experience than the latter.

---

48. *See* R. POSNER, *supra* note 16, ch. 7.

The opposite extreme, which involves treating every constitutional question as being up for grabs however often it has been decided in the past, is also untenable. There are three related reasons for this conclusion. The first is that an area of law will never be settled if opponents of existing doctrines believe that a mere change in the membership of a court will wipe the slate clean and make every legal question one of first impression; and there is value in legal stability, as I said earlier.

Second, the idea of decision according to law, on which popular belief in the legitimacy of constitutional adjudication rests, is weakened if decisions are conceived of as having no binding effect on judges who did not actually vote for them. This suggests that a decision should not be overruled if (1) none of the judges who joined it originally has changed his mind and (2) no relevant circumstances have changed since the original decision, so that it is impossible to say that the original decision may have been correct when decided and has merely become obsolete. These grounds are roughly reciprocal. Usually, (2) will be available only if, through passage of time, few if any participants in the original decision are still on the court. And if (1) is available, chances are that not enough time has elapsed since the original decision for (2) to be.

Third, a decent respect for the possibility that one's own constitutional notions may be wrong should make a judge hesitate to set them up in opposition to the contrary views of many previous judges who have wrestled with the same question and come to a different answer.

There is an obvious tension between the idea of judicial self-restraint and the idea of decision according to precedent. If (the position we are in today) the body of judge-made constitutional law contains a high proportion of aggressive doctrines created during a long period in which judicial activism was in the ascendancy, to make self-restraint effective would require overruling a lot of cases and thereby damage the principle of stare decisis — which is also an important principle. There is no satisfactory general resolution of this tension.

The task of interpretation in light of general jurisprudential principles such as self-restraint and stare decisis is logically prior to the application of economic theory to constitutional adjudication. It would be irresponsible to approach the task of constitutional adjudication by asking how constitutional law can be made to conform to the dictates of economic efficiency, even if, as I believe, efficiency provides the best single guide to public policy in general and judicial doctrine (i.e., common law, state or federal) in particular. The limits of an economic approach to deciding constitutional cases are set by the Constitution interpreted in light of the principles I have discussed.

Yet within those limits much can be done with economics. Consider again whether capital punishment violates the Eighth Amendment. The case for such a conclusion would be strengthened if it turned out that capital punishment had no incremental deterrent effect over life imprisonment, for this would suggest that it was being imposed out of sheer bloodthirstiness. I do not think the case would be conclusive even so, for one man's bloodthirstiness is another's (Kant's, for example) just retribution. In any event the economic model of crime and punishment suggests, and there is some confirmation in empirical research by economists,[49] that capital punishment does have an incremental deterrent effect. So although the Eighth Amendment has no clear economic interpretation, economics may provide insight into questions that bear on the proper legal interpretation.

---

49. *See* D. Pyle, The Economics of Crime and Law Enforcement ch. 4 (1983) (citing studies).

[3]

THE INDEPENDENT JUDICIARY IN AN INTEREST-GROUP PERSPECTIVE*

WILLIAM M. LANDES and RICHARD A. POSNER

The University of Chicago Law School and National Bureau of Economic Research

INTRODUCTION

Economists, even those who are deeply interested in government and politics, have not examined critically the idea of a nonpolitical, or "independent," judiciary.[1] Most economists would doubtless agree with Professor Buchanan that the judiciary is, and should remain, a thing apart from the political process. The basic structure of constitutional democracy, in his words,

> involves a conceptual separation between (1) the constitution, which defines the rights of persons and groups to do things and defines the rules under which collective decisions are to be made, (2) the institutions of "the law," which adjudicate the conflicting claims made within this set of rights and rules, and (3) the collective decision-making process of the ordinary legislative variety, which presumably promotes "public good," but again within the rules laid down in the constitution.[2]

This conception of the law in general, and the Supreme Court in constitutional adjudication in particular, as standing apart from and limiting the scope and intrusiveness of the political process has been shared by most legal commentators[3] since at least the time of Alexander Hamilton.[4] A quite different conception has been proposed by political scientists writing in the tradition of interest-group analysis, notably Martin Shapiro.[5] He argues

---

* This study has been supported by a grant from the National Science Foundation to the National Bureau of Economic Research for research in law and economics. The paper is not an official Bureau publication since it has not yet undergone the full critical review accorded Bureau publications, including review by the Bureau's Board of Directors.

[1] We define an "independent" judiciary as one that does not make decisions on the basis of the sorts of political factors (for example, the electoral strength of the people affected by a decision) that would influence and in most cases control the decision were it to be made by a legislative body such as the U.S. Congress.

[2] James M. Buchanan, Good Economics—Bad Law, 60 Va. L. Rev. 451, 491 (1974). See also Frank H. Knight, Economic Theory and Nationalism, in The Ethics of Competition and Other Essays 277-79, 299 (1935); F. A. Hayek, The Constitution of Liberty, ch. 12 (1960).

[3] See, for example, Gerald Gunther, The Subtle Vices of the "Passive Virtues"—A Comment on Principle and Expediency in Judicial Review, 64 Colum. L. Rev. 1 (1964).

[4] See The Federalist No. 78.

[5] Martin Shapiro, Law and Politics in the Supreme Court: New Approaches to Political Jurisprudence (1964). Cf. Robert A. Dahl, Decision-Making in a Democracy: The Supreme

875

that, like other organs of government, the Supreme Court is the agent of interest groups—in Shapiro's view, interest groups not represented adequately by other governmental organs. We are not convinced by Shapiro's effort to transform the Court into a political body. In particular, his conception leaves unexplained why it is that the Supreme Court, viewed as a political organ, should be systematically responsive to the *least* politically influential segments of the society.

We believe that economic analysis may hold the key to reconciling the notion of an independent judiciary with a conception of the political-governmental process that emphasizes the importance of interest groups in the formlation of public policy. The reconciliation that we propose may seem at first paradoxical, for we grant that the judiciary is in an important sense independent of and dissimilar to the political branches of the government yet at the same time maintain that it is a necessary element in the successful functioning even of a government of interests and powers, as distinguished from a government that seeks to maximize some general notion of welfare or the public interest.

Article III of the U.S. Constitution provides for the appointment (rather than election) of federal judges, provides that they are to have life tenure, and forbids Congress to reduce their salaries while they are in office. These provisions, while they are as we shall see not airtight, were designed and have operated in practice to endow the federal judiciary with a substantial measure of independence from the wishes of Congress and the President. To a lesser degree, the same thing may be said of state and municipal judges, of judges in many other countries, and, for that matter, of judges at all levels, in America and elsewhere, long before Article III was conceived.

The existence of an independent judiciary seems inconsistent with—in fact profoundly threatening to—a political system in which public policy emerges from the struggle of interest groups to redistribute the wealth of the society in their favor, the view of the political process that underlies much of the recent economic work, as well as an older political-science literature, on the political system. The outcomes of the struggle can readily be nullified by unsympathetic judges—and why should judges be sympathetic to a process that simply ratifies political power rather than expresses principle? The Supreme Court's policy toward economic legislation during a period of roughly 50 years ending in the late 1930's[6] illustrates the power and proclivity of an independent judiciary to nullify the legislative results of interest-group politics.

Court as a National Policy-Maker, 5 J. Pub. Law 279, 294 (1957) (comparing Supreme Court to "a powerful committee chairman in Congress"). For a penetrating critique of the legal and political-science literature dealing with the relationship between the Supreme Court and politics see Jan G. Deutsch, Neutrality, Legitimacy, and the Supreme Court: Some Interactions Between Law and Political Science, 20 Stan. L. Rev. 169 (1968).

[6] See Robert G. McCloskey, Economic Due Process and the Supreme Court: An Exhumation and Reburial, 1962 Sup. Ct. Rev. 34.

We believe, however, that at a deeper level the independent judiciary is not only consistent with, but essential to, the interest-group theory of government. Part I of this paper explains our theory of the independent judiciary. Part II discusses several implications of the theory, relating to administrative regulation, the form of interest-group legislation, the tenure of judges, and constitutional adjudication. The appendix to this paper presents an empirical analysis of judicial independence using data on Acts of Congress that have been held unconstitutional by the Supreme Court.

I.   AN ECONOMIC THEORY OF THE INDEPENDENT JUDICIARY

A.   *Legislative "Deals" and Judicial Independence*

In the economists' version of the interest-group theory of government, legislation is supplied to groups or coalitions that outbid rival seekers of favorable legislation.[7] The price that the winning group bids is determined both by the value of legislative protection to the group's members and the group's ability to overcome the free-rider problems that plague coalitions. Payment takes the form of campaign contributions, votes, implicit promises of future favors, and sometimes outright bribes. In short, legislation is "sold" by the legislature and "bought" by the beneficiaries of the legislation.

Private sales, and other private contracts, carry legal sanctions for non-performance. Where the performances of the buyer and seller are not simultaneous, and the parties are not constrained to act in good faith by a desire to obtain similar business in the future, the legal sanctions are likely to be an important factor in the decision to enter into the transaction. But there are no legal sanctions for the failure of a legislature to carry out its "bargain" with an interest group. Suppose the airline industry obtains from Congress (as it did in 1938) legislation designed to foster monopoly pricing while preventing the entry of new competitors that such pricing would ordinarily attract. There is no legal mechanism analogous to a binding long-term contract by which the enacting Congress can prevent a subsequent Congress from amending the legislation in a way unfavorable to the airlines, or indeed from repealing it altogether. Yet both the enacting Congress and the airlines, in procuring the legislation, may have incurred substantial costs that would not prove worthwhile if the legislation were to be altered unfavorably or repealed within a few months or years. To be sure, congressional bad faith of this sort would reduce the present value of legislative protection to interest groups in the future, and hence the enacting Congressmen's welfare. Such a manifestation of congressional bad faith would, by reducing the value of legislative protection to interest groups, impose costs on the faithless Congressmen: the "price" they could demand for enacting such legislation

---

[7] See George J. Stigler, The Theory of Economic Regulation, 2 Bell J. Econ. & Management Sci. 3 (1971), and, for a general review of the literature, Richard A. Posner, Theories of Economic Regulation, 5 Bell J. Econ. & Management Sci. 335 (1974).

would be lower. For many individual Congressmen, however, especially those who did not expect to remain in Congress for long, the benefits from repudiating a previous Congress' "deal" might outweigh the costs. And even if the good faith of the majority of Congressmen were assured, it would be insufficient to guarantee legislative stability in any case where the initial vote enacting the legislation was not one-sided. If the vote was close, the defection of only a few Congressmen, as a result of retirement or defeat at the polls, from the winning coalition might lead to a repeal in the next session of Congress, since the newly elected Congressmen would have no commitments to honor the "deals" of their predecessors.[8]

The element of stability or continuity necessary to enable interest-group politics to operate in the legislative arena is supplied, in the first instance, by the procedural rules of the legislature, and in the second instance by the existence of an independent judiciary. The most significant of the procedural rules is the requirement that legislation (including amending or repealing legislation) must be enacted by a majority of the legislators voting. This requirement makes legislative enactment a difficult and time-consuming process because of the transaction costs involved in getting agreement among a large number of individuals.[9] Consequently, once a statute is passed, it is unlikely, given the press of other legislative business, to be substantially altered or repealed in the immediate future. Other characteristics of the legislative process also create resistance to both the speedy enactment of new laws and the repeal of old ones: bicameralism, the committee system, and filibusters are important examples. Consider the tradition (now beginning to erode) of appointing committee chairmen on the basis of seniority. The use of seniority tends to channel chairmanships to holders of "safe" congressional seats—Congressmen whose tenure can be expected to be long and who are therefore more likely to honor the commitments made by Congress.[10]

The impediments to legislation have the effect of endowing legislation,

[8] Presumably, the new Congressmen could be "bought" by the group that had obtained favorable legislation from their predecessors. But this is simply an example of having to pay twice for a single good. We consider later the alternative possibility of paying for favorable legislation on an installment basis.

[9] On the costs of legislative enactment see Isaac Ehrlich & Richard A. Posner, An Economic Analysis of Legal Rulemaking, 3 J. Leg. Studies 257, 267 (1974).

[10] At the beginning of the 93rd Congress (January 1973) the average Senate Committee chairman had been a member of Congress for 20 (continuous) years. The corresponding figure for the House of Representatives was 26.4. A partially offsetting factor is that when seniority is the basis of selection, chairmanships tend to be awarded to older members, who may not have a long period of continued service ahead of them. Thus, two of the 17 Senate committees in 1973 (and six of the 21 House committees) had new chairmen. The chairmen of the remaining 15 Senate committees had been chairmen an average of 6.1 (continuous) years; the average was the same for the House chairmen. Note that the maximum tenure of a chairman in 1973 would have been 18 continuous years since there had been a democratic majority in Congress since 1955. The source of these statistics is 3 Congressional Quarterly Service, Congress and the Nation: A Review of Government and Politics 1969-1972, at 52a-55a.

once it is enacted, with a measure of durability. The result is to increase the value of and hence the demand for legislation. But there is an offsetting effect: by increasing negotiation costs and uncertainty the impediments reduce the productivity of expenditures on obtaining legislation in the first place. However, under plausible assumptions the increase in the value of legislation will exceed the increase in its cost, since a modest increase in the cost of enacting legislation could multiply many-fold the length of the period in which the legislation was expected to remain in force.

Legislation is not self-enforcing, however. If the people subject to a law refuse to obey it, recourse to the courts is necessary to enforce the law. A judiciary that was subservient to the current membership of the legislature could nullify legislation enacted in a previous session of the legislature. Suppose that Congress in year one "sells" the dairy industry a heavy tax on margarine, but the next year the producers of margarine offer Congress generous inducements to remove the tax. Congress is unlikely to respond to this demand by enacting repealing legislation, due to the impediments to swift legislative action that we have discussed. But if the judges are the perfect agents of the current Congress, they will refuse to enforce the margarine tax, and the effect will be the same as legislative repeal. Although outright refusal to enforce a law is an extreme example, the limits of human foresight, the ambiguities of language, and the high cost of legislative deliberation combine to assure that most legislation will be enacted in a seriously incomplete form, with many areas of uncertainty left to be resolved by the courts. Insofar as judges are merely agents of the current legislature, they will utilize their considerable interpretive leeway to rewrite the legislation in conformity with the views of the current rather than the enacting legislature and they will thereby impair the "contract" between the enacting legislature and the group that procured the legislation.

If we assume that an independent judiciary would, in contrast, interpret and apply legislation in accordance with the original legislative understanding[11] (an assumption examined shortly) it follows that an independent judiciary facilitates rather than, as conventionally believed, limits the practice of interest-group politics. To be sure, like the constitutive rules of the legislative process, the independent judiciary increases the cost of enacting legislation in the first place. Being independent, the judges may (directly or indirectly) refuse to enforce legislation that they do not like and this possibility reduces the value of legislation to the group seeking it. But that is a necessary price to pay for a system in which interest groups will have incentives to invest in legislation that yields them benefits over an extended period of time.

[11] This does not imply literal-minded or otherwise inflexible interpretation of the legislation. On the contrary, judicial interpretations that enable a law to survive the vicissitudes of unforeseen technical or economic changes that might effectively nullify the law were it not interpreted flexibly are perfectly consistent with the idea of an independent judiciary.

B. *A Formal Model*

Before examining certain objections to the analysis, it will be helpful to present a more formal version of it. Let d_0d_1 in Figure I represent the demand curve of various groups for special-interest legislation (such as protective tariffs, import quotas, or minimum rate regulation) under the assumption that the benefits from such legislation will be limited to a single period, namely the term of the enacting legislature. The demand curve is negatively sloped because some groups will obtain greater benefits from protective legislation and accordingly will offer a higher price. S_0S_1 is the marginal cost curve of the legislature, viewed as the seller of special-interest legislation. The legislature's costs include the costs of drafting legislation (primarily the opportunity costs of the time spent by legislators in attending committee meetings, roll calls, etc.) and other expenses.[12] The market for special-interest legislation will clear at point E_0 in Figure I, where L_0 units of legislation are produced. At E_0 all the gains from trade between interest groups and legislators will be fully exploited under the (restrictive) assumption that legislation is sold only for a single period. The dollar benefits after deducting the costs of writing the legislation will equal the area $d_0E_0S_0$, and are distributed between legislators and groups obtaining legislation, the simplest assumption being that the benefits received by legislators are proportional to the area $d_0E_0S_0$.[13]

Now let the gains from special-interest legislation extend beyond the period of the enacting legislature. To simplify, assume that the legislation will never be repealed and that the group benefited by it expects to obtain constant profits per period from the legislation. Then the maximum price the group will pay to obtain the legislation will equal the present value of those profits. In terms of Figure I, the relevant demand curve is now D_0d_1, which is a vertical multiple of the single-period demand curve.[14] Assuming

[12] The analysis does not depend on the shape of the marginal cost curve (assumed in Figure I to be horizontal) or on the assumption that there are positive costs of selling legislation.

[13] Our assumption that the market clears when gains from trade are fully exploited rules out a monopoly *output*, which would be less than L_0. But it does not imply that legislators are perfectly discriminating monopolists (in which event they would cover their costs and receive in addition the entire area $d_0E_0S_0$; a competitive market in the sale of legislation is possible. Such a market would also clear at E_0 but the area $d_0E_0S_0$ would be received by purchasers, contrary to our assumption that legislators receive part of $d_0E_0S_0$. (If marginal costs in Figure I were rising, legislators would receive an amount in excess of their costs even in the purely competitive case.) An additional question is whether the benefits in Figure I will be competed away by expenditures to obtain legislative seats or expenditures on lawyers, lobbyists, etc.

Since the results we obtain in this paper are unaffected by which assumption we make (that is, monopoly, perfect price discrimination, competition with and without rents, gross benefits versus net benefits), we do not pursue these questions any further.

[14] When legislation lasts for more than one period, the demand curve faced by the current (enacting) legislature will also depend on the amount of legislation sold earlier. Previous legislatures will have already exploited many attractive opportunities that the current legislature cannot resell again. Thus D_0d_1 in Figure I will be a vertical multiple of a single-period curve that is lower than d_0d_1 since the latter was constructed on the assumption that legislation lasted

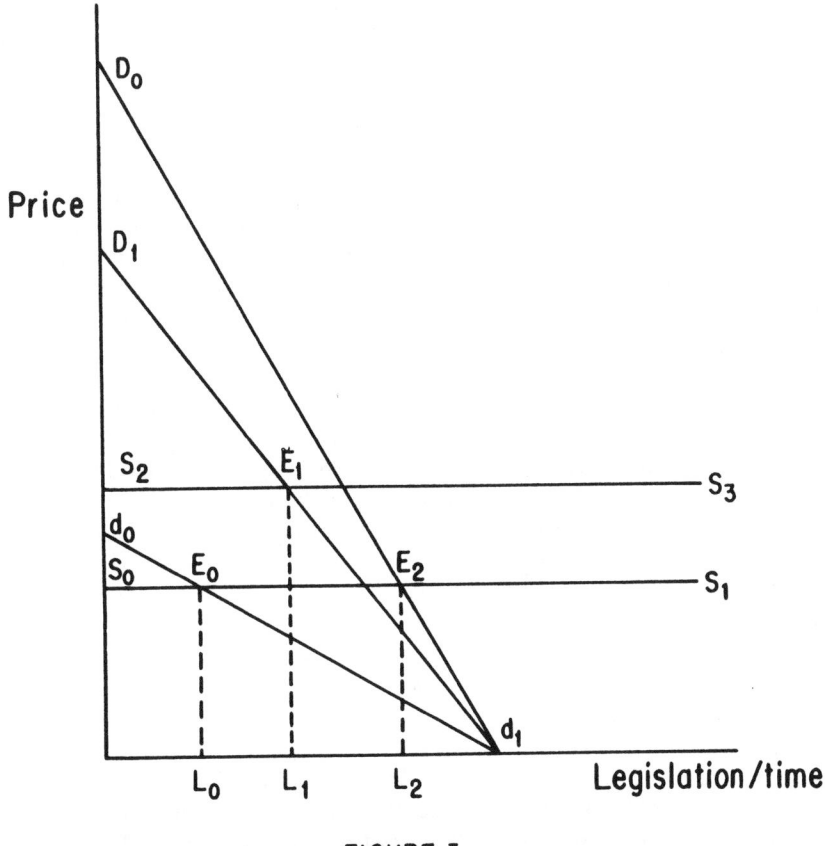

FIGURE I

for the moment that it costs no more to enact permanent than single-period legislation and that legislative "deals" can be permanently enforced at zero cost, the new equilibrium position will be at E_2. This differs from the single-period model in two important respects. First, there is more special-interest legislation (L_2 compared to L_0), since some legislation that was not profitable to enact when the return was received for only one period is now profitable.[15] (Indeed, if $d_0 d_1$ were everywhere below the marginal cost

---

only a single period (implying that the current legislature was not encumbered by past deals). In the subsequent analysis, which compares $D_0 d_1$ to $d_0 d_1$, we assume (contrary to the initial exposition) that both demand curves are constructed on the assumption that multi-period deals were possible in the past and that some of these deals extend into the term of the current legislature.

[15] This conclusion depends critically on the modification in the model (see *supra* note 14) whereby $d_0 d_1$ allows for multi-period deals in the past. If $d_0 d_1$ did not, then it is possible that the current legislature would face a multi-period demand curve that was lower than $d_0 d_1$, causing the multi-period quantity of legislation to fall short of the single-period quantity. In the

curve, there would have been no special-interest legislation at all in the single-period model.) Second, since the discounted benefits of the legislation as measured by the area $D_0E_2S_0$ exceed the single-period benefits, the "take" of the enacting legislature, which we assume to be proportional to the benefits of the legislation to the group procuring it, increases when legislation extends beyond one period.

Thus, the legislature has powerful incentives to devise methods of increasing the permanency of legislation.[16] As we have seen, there are two complementary methods of doing this. The first involves establishing procedures for the enactment of legislation that increase the cost of repealing it; the second, the creation of an independent judiciary to enforce legislation in accordance with the intentions of the enacting legislature. In terms of Figure I, the effect of the internal procedures is to shift the marginal cost curve upwards to S_2S_3 while at the same time shifting the demand curve to the right of d_0d_1. Internal procedures will presumably be added until the additional benefits of the legislature from increasing the demand for legislation are just equal to the additional costs of the procedures.

If, however, the judges served at the pleasure of the legislators, their decisions would presumably be in perfect harmony with the current legislature's wishes, and we would be back to the single-period model with demand curve d_0d_1 no matter how cumbersome were the internal procedures of the legislature. It is no answer that interest groups would simply pay for legislation on the installment plan—a sum each period in exchange for the continuation of the original "deal." The enacting legislature would still have an incentive to produce only L_0 units of legislation since it would not be compensated for additional units. As noted earlier, the legislature might find it unprofitable to "sell" any legislation at all unless the future benefits of the legislation could be capitalized and received by the enacting legisla-

---

limit, if all profitable deals had been exploited by the time the current legislature was elected, and technological and demand changes did not yield new opportunities, the current legislature would not be able to make any multi-period (or for that matter single-period) deals. In comparison, if past and present deals are limited to a single period, the current legislature might find many profitable single-period deals available. Even if D_0d_1 were lower than d_0d_1 as originally derived, the total stock of special-interest legislation existing at a moment in time would still be greater if multi-period deals were permitted. The time distribution of these deals would differ, however, as most would have been arranged by earlier legislatures with few deals remaining for the current legislature to make. In that event, the main beneficiaries of multi-period deals would be past legislators.

Thus, our model provides an explanation for the original formation of an independent judiciary since early legislatures, not encumbered by past deals, would favor an institution—the independent judiciary—that fostered the making of long-term contracts. It is also consistent with the current legislature's favoring an independent judiciary; provided that one takes past legislative deals as given and generally beyond the reach of current legislatures, the current legislature would also benefit from being able to make multi-period deals compared to being restricted to single-period ones.

[16] We consider in Part IIB, *infra,* the question why optimum special-interest legislation does not take the form of a single lump sum that is paid to the interest group by the legislature in the first period.

ture. Finally, even if the costs of producing the legislation were zero, so that the number of "deals" was independent of whether or not the enacting legislature could appropriate future benefits, the legislature would still have a strong incentive to build durability into its legislation in order to capture some of those future benefits.

If the judiciary is independent,[17] it can be expected, for reasons explained in the next subpart, to enforce existing statutes in accordance with the intent of the enacting legislature. But while the combination of high legislative costs of repeal and an independent judiciary thus turns out to be an ingenious device for promoting the sale of long-term special-interest legislation, independence is not without its costs. The judiciary may decide not to enforce the deal worked out by the legislature. It may declare the law unconstitutional or interpret it in a manner that reduces the gains from the law to the group intended to benefit from it, since most sitting judges, having been appointed in an earlier period, will "owe" nothing to the enacting legislature.

The cost of independence is shown in Figure I by the demand curve D_1d_1, which is lower than D_0d_1. The difference between the two curves is due to the positive probability in each future period that the returns from the special-interest legislation will not be forthcoming because of adverse judicial rulings. These expectations will be incorporated into the maximum price that groups are willing to pay for favorable legislation. Since judicial nullification of legislation has in fact been relatively infrequent,[18] it seems reasonable to assume that D_1d_1 will lie substantially above d_0d_1, the single-period demand curve. This is illustrated in Table 1, which shows the ratio of the multi-period to the single-period maximum price for several hypothetical values of the probability of judicial nullification, the number of time periods, and the interest rate. We assume that the single-period returns occur with certainty (since in the single-period model, it will be recalled, the judiciary is assumed to be the perfect agent of the enacting legislature), while the multi-period returns are subject to the risk of nullification in each period.[19] If, for example, a 10 per cent interest rate and a

[17] See note 1 *supra*.

[18] For example, between 1789 and 1972 the Supreme Court held only 97 acts of Congress unconstitutional. This figure provides, of course, only a crude measure of judicial nullification and hence of the "unreliability" of the federal courts, since they exclude both unfavorable interpretations (which may be made by the lower courts as well as by the Supreme Court) that stop short of declaring a statute unconstitutional and statutes that are never enacted in the first place because prior judicial rulings indicate a high probability that they will be invalidated. See the appendix to this article for a further discussion of, and attempt to measure, the effect of the Court's power to nullify legislation on the costs of an independent judiciary.

[19] The single-period and multi-period expected maximum prices are respectively:

$$Z_1 = \frac{R}{(1 + i)}$$
$$Z_2 = \frac{Rp}{(1 + i - p)} \left(1 - \frac{p^T}{(1 + i)^T}\right),$$

TABLE 1

THE RATIO OF MULTI-PERIOD TO SINGLE-PERIOD RETURNS

	Interest Rates					
	.05		.10		.20	
			T			
$(1 - p)$	∞	10	∞	10	∞	10
.10	9.5	5.7	5.0	4.3	3.6	3.4
.20	4.0	3.6	2.9	2.8	2.4	2.4
.30	2.3	2.3	1.9	1.9	1.7	1.7

$(1 - p)$ = profitability of judicial nullification.

T = number of time periods.

20 per cent probability of nullification per period are assumed, the present value of the legislative returns (and hence the maximum price the interest group is willing to pay for favorable legislation) is between 2.8 and 2.9 times greater in the multi-period (10 or more periods) than in the single-period model. Overall, the multi-period to single-period ratios range from 1.7 to 9.5 in Table 1, the ratio being greater the lower the probability of nullification, the lower the interest rate, and the greater the number of time periods. These calculations indicate that there are substantially higher benefits from multi-period deals even when the probabilities of nullification are themselves substantial. In fact, in order for the single-period price to equal the multi-period price and thus for $d_o d_1$ to equal $D_1 d_1$ in Figure I, the probability of nullification would have to be between .45 and .50 in each period.[20]

The equilibrium sale of legislation, which incorporates both the costs of the self-imposed rules on the legislative process and the expected "tax" resulting from the independence of the judiciary, occurs at E_1 in Figure I, where L_1 units of legislation are produced, yielding benefits equal to $D_1 E_1 S_2$ which are divided between the interest groups and the legislature. Even assuming that these benefits are greater than the area $d_o E_o S_o$, this solution is a second-best one. The benefits would be greater if the long-term commitments of the current legislature could be enforced at zero cost. With this possibility excluded, the independent judiciary serves the function of

where R is the return per period from the special-interest legislation, i is the interest rate, $(1 - p)$ is the probability of judicial nullification of the legislation, and T is the number of time periods. R, i and p are assumed constant per period. A constant p implies an increasing probability that future returns will not be forthcoming since p^t (where t = 1, . . . , T)—the present probability that the returns will be received in any future period t—is a decreasing function of t. The assumption that p is constant is probably incorrect. The importance of precedent in judicial decision-making is likely to produce probabilities (p) in periods 2, . . . , T that are close to one provided that the legislation is upheld in its initial test in the first period. This implies that the calculations in Table 1 understate the multi-period to single-period ratios.

[20] This is calculated by setting Z_1 equal to Z_2, fixing i and T within the range given by Table 1, and solving for p.

permitting some capitalization of future returns into the pockets of the current legislature.

C. *A Closer Look at the Concept of Judicial "Independence"*

The reader may be troubled by the assumption that the "independent" judiciary is really independent of interest-group political pressures, by our failure to present an explicit theory of judicial behavior, and by the existence of alternative theories of the independence of the judiciary.

It is of course unrealistic to suppose the judiciary wholly independent of the current desires of the political branches. The legislature could refuse to appropriate funds to pay the judges' salaries; the executive could refuse to enforce judicial decrees. Short of outright confrontation, there are various methods by which the political branches can impose costs on the judiciary, such as budgetary harassment,[21] tinkering with the courts' jurisdiction, and altering the composition of the judiciary by the creation of many new judgeships. Yet such devices have been resorted to infrequently, even in periods of intense hostility to judicial rulings. The reason, we conjecture, is the high costs of the available methods of harassment in relation to the benefits sought. The current legislature may want judicial interpretations that gut some existing laws, but if it tries to procure them by forms of coercion that impair the functioning of the judiciary across the board, it will impose costs on all who use the courts, including various politically effective groups and indeed the beneficiaries of whatever legislation the current legislature has enacted.

At the same time, the fact that the legislative and executive branches do have means of coercing the judiciary helps to explain why the self-interest of independent judges is promoted by enforcing legislation according to its original tenor. If courts are not valued highly, the imposition by the current legislature of coercive measures that impair the courts' effective functioning will not be perceived as highly costly, and such measures will therefore be imposed more often. The value (both social and private) of courts is a function in major part of the predictability of their decisions, and decision according to the original meaning of a statute rather than according to the ever-shifting preferences of successive legislatures is probably an important source of that predictability, in part because such a decision is based on materials (for example, the congressional debates) available to all to study and base predictions of judicial behavior on. In short, the ability of courts to maintain their independence from the political branches may depend at least in part on their willingness to enforce the "contracts" of earlier legislatures according to the original understanding of the "contract."

There is, to be sure, the possibility that although the judiciary is independent of the political branches, interest groups will intervene directly

---

[21] Refusing to raise judges' salaries in the face of inflation, refusing to make adequate appropriations for supporting personnel, etc.

with judges to undo the results of an earlier legislative process. However, the methods of imparting independence from the political branches of government also serve to reduce the possibility of direct or indirect bribery of the judges by interest groups. Life tenure—in circumstances where the job holder intends to remain in the job for the remainder of his active life—[22] reduces the likelihood of an important (because difficult to detect) form of bribery that consists of dangling prospects of future employment before the bribe-taker. Life tenure also increases the expected penalty for bribery, assuming dismissal is a major sanction for bribery.[23] Other rules of the judicial process also operate to reduce the operation of interest groups in the judicial arena, notably the rules limiting *ex parte* contacts with judges and denying legal standing to groups, as distinct from the individuals or firms immediately affected, in a narrow legal sense, by the legislation in question.

Not only is the assumption of independence plausible, but the judiciary in fact commonly behaves as if it were independent of the wishes of the current legislature.[24] Yet, if so, what *does* determine the outcome of judicial decisions? As mentioned, there are constraints, imposed by the legislative and executive branches, that set the outer limits on judicial autonomy, but they leave a broad area in which judicial behavior cannot be explained by refer-

[22] De facto life tenure or an approximation of it is the rule for the overwhelming majority of Supreme Court Justices. Of the 94 former Justices, 55 died in office or within one year of leaving office, and 24 more died within 10 years of leaving office after having retired at an average age of 71. The remaining 15, several of whom are still living, left the Court at an average age of 61. (See 1975 World Almanac and Book of Facts 770.) We have also compiled data on the turnover rate every two years since 1885 of all federal court judges. Turnover data can be used to estimate average tenure on the job, provided that a period is selected in which the number of judges remains approximately constant. Unfortunately, the latter condition is rarely met as the number of federal court judges (including retired but still sitting judges) has risen from 74 in 1885 to 635 in 1975. However, the increase was relatively modest (297 to 348) from 1949 to 1965, and the average two-year turnover rate in the period was .0787 which converts into an average tenure on the bench per judge of 25.4 years (2/.0787). Moreover, most of the turnover has come from deaths (particularly of retired but still sitting judges) rather than from resignations. Therefore, our assumption that a federal judicial appointment is generally a terminal job is consistent with the evidence on Supreme Court and other federal court judges.

[23] Cf. Gary S. Becker & George J. Stigler, Law Enforcement, Malfeasance, and Compensation of Enforcers, 3 J. Leg. Studies 1 (1974).

[24] For example, in 1911 the Supreme Court, in Dr. Miles Medical Co. v. John D. Parke & Sons Co., 220 U.S. 373, held that the Sherman Act forbade resale price maintenance. Powerful pressures for exempting resale price maintenance from the Act eventuated in the passage of the Miller-Tydings Act of 1937 and the McGuire Act of 1952 which created such an exemption for states enacting Fair Trade laws. The enactment of the Miller-Tydings and McGuire Acts would have been unnecessary if the Court had responded to the rising political pressure for resale price maintenance by reinterpreting the Sherman Act to permit the practice. The Court's steadfastness in interpreting the Act in accordance with what it believed (correctly or not) to be the original understanding of the framers rather than the desires of the current legislators is a good, but not a rare, example of judicial independence.

Other examples from the trade-regulation field are the enactment of the original Clayton Act; the Robinson-Patman Amendments thereto; the 1938 Wheeler-Lea amendments to the Federal Trade Commission Act; the Celler-Kefauver Antimerger Act; and the Bank Merger Act of 1966. All resulted from congressional dissatisfaction with judicial interpretation of previously enacted statutes. Numerous examples from other federal statutory fields could also be cited.

ence to those constraints. Within this area, the development of an economic theory of judicial behavior is hampered by the studied efforts of society to divorce judicial rewards from the outcome of judicial decisions. A possibility is that judicial decision-making should be viewed as a consumption activity from the judge's standpoint. He decides in a certain way not because it will get him something else but because he derives personal satisfaction from preferring one party to the lawsuit over the other or one policy over another, a form of satisfaction that individuals routinely seek in a variety of areas. However, to develop this or any other theory of judicial behavior would carry us far beyond the scope of this paper, and is we believe unnecessary to it.

It remains to consider alternative explanations for the existence of the independent judiciary to the one proposed here. The commonest explanation is that an independent judiciary is necessary to enforce the Constitution against the legislative and executive branches of government. This is unconvincing. The English judiciary is also independent but English judges probably lack—and certainly do not exercise—the power to invalidate acts of Parliament. In most other societies as well, the judiciary has considerable independence (save in politically very sensitive areas, mainly involving internal security) yet no power to invalidate legislative action.

Another possible explanation is that an independent judiciary minimizes the costs of legal procedure. Life tenure reduces turnover and thereby imparts greater predictability to judicial decision-making. The longer a judge is on the bench, the easier it becomes to predict his decisions in many different kinds of cases. Also, long tenure imparts valuable experience to a judge and thereby increases his efficiency. Finally, as just mentioned, long tenure reduces the danger of bribery—a danger that exists quite independently of the existence of interest groups. What these points overlook, however, is that while long judicial service may be socially desirable, granting life tenure and a guaranteed salary is not an efficient method of optimizing the length of judicial service. (Observe that legislators are not employed on any such basis, though most of the arguments just noted apply to them also.) A more efficient method would be to pay high salaries contingent on satisfactory performance. This would avoid the disincentive effects of divorcing tenure and compensation from performance and would be clearly preferable to the life-tenure system—were it not for the exigencies of an interest-group system of government.

II. Positive Implications of the Economic Theory of the Independent Judiciary

A. *Administrative Regulation*

Administrative agencies such as the Interstate Commerce Commission and the Civil Aeronautics Board are examples of what we may call the "dependent" judiciary. Congress, lacking the time to regulate railroad rates in detail, establishes an Interstate Commerce Commission to do so. The Commission has some indicia of independence but many fewer than the federal courts; in particular, its members serve for limited terms and turn-over is in fact quite rapid. Furthermore, the fact that it has a much more specialized jurisdiction than the federal courts facilitates congressional sur-veillance and direction through the appropriations process in a way that would be infeasible with respect to the courts.

The analysis in Part I of this paper suggests three propositions concern-ing administrative regulation which seem consistent with at least casual observation:

1. Administrative agencies will be established most frequently when the probability of *de facto* judicial nullification of legislation is high (for exam-ple, during the New Deal, when the courts were hostile to federal economic regulations[25]). This is because the ability of courts to nullify legislation, especially by adverse factfinding in enforcement proceedings, can be cur-tailed by consigning the factfinding function to an administrative agency, which will tend to be more subservient to the legislature.

2. The legislature will, however, preserve judicial review of administra-tive determinations[26] in order to assure that the agency, in its eagerness to serve the current legislature, will not stray too far from the terms of the legislative "deal" establishing the regulatory program that the agency ad-ministers.

3. Since, however, judicial review cannot be expected to be wholly ef-fective, we expect—and find—that administrative adjudication is far less consistent over time than judicial. (A related point is that precedent plays a smaller role in administrative than in judicial decision-making.) This fol-lows directly from the relatively dependent character of administrative judging.

B. *The Form of Interest Group Legislation*

We have thus far treated the legislative act as complete at the time of enactment—all of the benefits of the legislation are assumed to flow with-out subsequent legislative action. Yet some legislation is ineffective without substantial annual appropriations by the legislature, either to pay a periodic subsidy or to defray the expenses of a public agency charged with enforcing the statute. Legislation incomplete in this sense at the time of enactment is much less valuable to its beneficiaries than legislation that is complete when enacted; in the first case, the beneficiaries may have to

---

[25] See, for example, United States v. Butler, 297 U.S. 1 (1935); Schechter Corp. v. United States, 295 U.S. 495 (1935); Hopkins Savings Ass'n v. Cleary, 296 U.S. 315 (1935).

[26] For an alternative explanation, mainly relevant to judicial review of administrative factfindings, see Richard A. Posner, An Economic Approach to Legal Procedure and Judicial Administration, 2 J. Leg. Studies 399, 416-17 (1973).

"buy" the legislation anew every year. In terms of our formal model, we are in effect back at the single-period demand curve in Figure I. In order to enable the enacting legislature to appropriate part of the future benefits, we would expect—and we find—that interest-group legislation is typically cast in a form that avoids the necessity for substantial annual appropriations. Legislation setting up regulatory agencies that use power over rates and entry to redistribute wealth is an important example: the annual budgets of these agencies are very small in relation to the redistributions that they effect.[27] Not only is regulation used much more often than direct subsidization to benefit interest groups, but when direct subsidies are used their funding is often made independent of further legislative action by the device of the earmarked tax, as in the interstate-highway and social-security programs.

The problem of legislation that requires substantial annual appropriations to maintain its effectiveness is forcefully illustrated by the experience with Prohibition. The supporters of Prohibition were able to obtain a constitutional amendment, normally as we shall see[28] a particularly durable form of interest-group legislation. However, unlike many other forms of regulation, prohibiting the sale of alcoholic beverages required a massive law-enforcement effort. This is strikingly illustrated in Table 2, which shows how Prohibition cases came to dominate the dockets of the federal courts. Of course subsequent Congresses could have appropriated the sums necessary to increase the number of federal judges, prosecutors, customs inspectors, etc. to levels at which Prohibition would have been effectively enforced, but they were unwilling to do so. The result was that the constitutional amendment was effectively nullified, and it was repealed in 1933 after having been in effect for only 13 years. Constitutional amendments that do not require substantial annual appropriations to enforce (*e.g.*, the First Amendment) have proved a good deal more durable.[29]

An alternative to both annual subsidies and regulatory legislation would be the payment of a single lump sum to the interest group in the first period, a sum equal to the discounted present value of the annual subsidies or regulatory protection. Here, it would seem, the transaction would be complete in the first period and there would be no need to have any enforcement mechanism. However, if legislative enactment were a cheap and speedy process or the judges were the agents of the legislators, the interest group that had obtained the lump-sum payment would have no protection

---

[27] Some sense of the disproportion can be obtained by comparing the agency budgets listed in George J. Stigler, The Process of Economic Regulation, 17 Antitrust Bull. 207 (1972), with the estimates (admittedly rather crude) of the transfers involved in regulation presented in Richard A. Posner, The Social Costs of Monopoly and Regulation, 83 J. Pol. Econ. 807, 818 (1975).

[28] In Part IID, *infra*.

[29] An apparent counterexample is the just-compensation provision of the Fifth Amendment, which to be effective requires a substantial annual appropriation by Congress to defray the expense of the government's eminent-domain proceedings.

TABLE 2
FEDERAL JUDICIAL CASELOAD—NATIONAL PROHIBITION ACT

Fiscal Years	Prohibition Civil Cases		Prohibition Criminal Cases	
	Terminated (Annual average)	Per cent of total Civil Terminations	Terminated (Annual average)	Per cent of total Criminal Terminations
1920	92	1.6	5,095	14.8
1921	622	9.8	21,297	45.0
1922	1,537	18.8	28,743	54.1
1923-1928	6,997	42.3	47,495	61.3
1929-1933	12,952	50.2	59,821	67.7
1934	5,279	32.0	19,043	41.8

Source: U.S. Att'y Gen'l, Annual Reports.

against the legislature's taxing away the entire payment in the second period, either by the levying of a special tax or by the courts' adopting a discriminatory interpretation of existing tax laws unequally.

C. *The Determinants of Judicial Tenure*

The value of judicial independence is a function of the number of periods over which the returns from special-interest legislation accrue. Since an independent judiciary is, as we have seen, a source of costs as well as benefits to the legislature, we would expect the judiciary to be less independent the shorter the expected duration of special-interest legislation. This may explain certain differences that one observes in the selection and tenure of judges at the federal, state, and local levels of government. As we progress down this ladder, we find in general shorter terms for judges and greater reliance on election rather than appointment as the method of selecting judges. This diminishing judicial independence is consistent with the fact that, the more confined or local is the jurisdiction of a legislature, the less scope it will have for enacting protective legislation.[30] There is more competition for residents among cities and towns than among states, and among states than among countries, because from the resident's standpoint different cities are better substitutes for one another than different states, and different states better substitutes than different countries. Citizen mobility limits the effectiveness of schemes of redistributing wealth from one group to another at the state and local levels. Also, the regulation of a product or service is less effective the more limited the jurisdiction of the regulatory authority, because the providers are more mobile within a more limited area.

Thus it is hardly surprising that many federal regulatory schemes, such as railroad regulation, arose from the debris of state regulatory attempts and that much state regulation came about as a result of failures of regulation at the municipal level. But this means that the importance of an independent judiciary to the practice of interest-group politics declines as we move from regulation that is less local to regulation that is more local. The interest groups will not seek durable compacts from state and local legislatures anyway, so why should the political branches pay the price of an independent judiciary?

Another situation in which the independent judiciary will be less valuable to the political system is where legislators, despite having to stand for reelection every few years, in fact enjoy a long enough tenure in office for interest groups to be willing to accept long-term commitments from them. In this situation, an independent judiciary may not be very attractive to the legislature; its value as an enforcement agency will be slight and may well be

[30] See George J. Stigler, The Tenable Range of Functions of Local Government, in Staff of Jt. Econ. Comm., Federal Expenditure Policy for Economic Growth 213 (Jt. Comm. Print 1967).

outweighed by its costs in potential nullification of legislative compacts. Short of eliminating the independence of the judiciary, the political branches can limit the consequences of that independence either (1) by expanding the size of the judiciary so as to be able to appoint a substantial number of new judges whose policy views will be compatible with those of the current legislature, or (2) by filling vacancies as they arise with older judges, whose expected terms of office will be short (shorter, perhaps, than those of the legislators). If this analysis is correct, one would expect an inverse relationship between legislative tenure and judicial tenure. That is, the longer the tenure of the legislators, the greater will be judicial turnover, presumably brought about by election of judges or by appointment of older people to the bench.[31]

D. *The Constitution and the Independent Judiciary*

Earlier we rejected the suggestion that the existence of an independent judiciary is best explained in terms of its role in enforcing the Constitution. Nonetheless, the role of the courts in enforcing constitutional provisions is an important one on which the analysis in this paper casts some light. We have argued that the existence of an independent judiciary and the constitutive rules of legislative bodies (such as the requirement of a majority vote to enact legislation) are methods of imparting durability to an initial legislative judgment protecting some group. A constitutional right is simply another device for doing the same thing. Since such a right is much more difficult to retract than a statutory right—the procedures for constitutional amendment being so costly and time-consuming—a constitutional provision confers more durable protection than is possible by ordinary legislative action. But enforcement by an independent judiciary remains necessary. Otherwise the constitutional provision would be continuously reinterpreted to accord with the preferences of the current legislators.

In the view proposed here, the Constitution has two purposes. One is to establish the ground rules for a system of interest-group politics; Article III is to be understood in this light. The second is to confer protective legislation of a peculiarly durable kind on those specially effective interest groups that are able and willing to incur the costs necessary to obtain a constitutional provision in their favor.[32]

Such a view has important implications for a number of constitutional controversies; we shall mention three here.

---

[31] Older judges have an additional advantage from the legislators' standpoint: their views are likely to be better known, and hence their behavior as judges is likely to be more predictable. On the other hand, older judges will be less susceptible to legislative or executive "bribery" in the form of promotion to higher office.

[32] We do not, however, suggest that the protected groups are necessarily those urged by Charles A. Beard in his controversial book, An Economic Interpretation of the Constitution of the United States (1913). The details of Beard's analysis have been sharply criticized. See Robert E. Brown, Charles Beard and the Constitution (1956).

1. It is sometimes suggested that the protection of freedom of speech and of the press by the First Amendment should be limited to political expression, on the theory that the purpose of the First Amendment is to protect the electoral process by which members of Congress and the President are selected.[33] However, a broader view of the scope of the First Amendment may be quite consistent with the approach taken here, for it would be congenial to that approach to view the First Amendment as a form of protective legislation extracted by an interest group consisting of publishers, journalists, pamphleteers, and others who derive pecuniary and nonpecuniary income from publication and advocacy of various sorts.[34]

2. The question has sometimes been raised whether it is not a perversion of constitutional principle to invoke a constitutional provision on behalf of a majority rather than a minority group, as in cases challenging "reverse" discrimination (for example, preferring blacks to whites) or—a more clear-cut example—cases challenging schemes of legislative malapportionment that have been adopted by popular referendum. From the standpoint of interest group analysis adopted in this paper, it is a detail whether the group comprises more or less than half of the voting population. Indeed, because a large group will often be politically less effective than a small one, due to the higher costs of collective action to the large group, such a group may benefit substantially from obtaining constitutional protection against legislative regulation—though by the same token it may find it difficult to obtain such protection in the first place.

More broadly, our interest-group analysis casts doubt on the conventional view of constitutional lawyers that the Constitution is designed to protect the powerless, unrepresented elements of society. In a view of the governmental process as one in which the courts and Constitution play an integral role in a system of interest-group politics, the Constitution can more accurately be described as designed to protect groups sufficiently powerful to obtain constitutional protection for their interests.[35] This of course does not explain why the "Warren Court" interpreted the Constitution as conferring extraordinary rights on the common criminal. There is considerable doubt whether the framers of the Constitution and its amendments intended to create these rights, and perhaps this episode is best understood as an example of judicial independence. But we do not pretend to have developed a complete theory of the Supreme Court's behavior.

3. There is a long-standing debate over the question whether the Supreme

[33] See Robert H. Bork, Neutral Principles and Some First Amendment Problems, 47 Ind. L.J. 1 (1971).

[34] It may seem paradoxical to view as protectionist legislation that forbids regulation rather than limits entry. But whether a group will seek regulation or freedom from regulation depends on whether it anticipates friendly or unfriendly regulation. The "gun lobby" is another example of an interest group aggressively seeking nonregulation.

[35] Of course, as just mentioned, a group that feels vulnerable to legislative politics may on that account have a greater demand for constitutional protection.

Court should use the due process and equal protection clauses of the Constitution to strike down legislation that, even though it does not infringe upon a specific constitutional right such as freedom of speech, is unreasonable as judged by some general criterion of social welfare or public interest. It should not, and will not, if the view suggested here—that the Court's role is to enforce the specific interests protected by the Constitution rather than to act as a general brake on legislation promoting "factions"[36] (special interests)—is correct. And, in general, the Court has not acted as a general brake on special-interest legislation, as the growth of the welfare state attests. The view that the Court's function is to promote or assure the consistency of the legislative product with the public interest,[37] besides placing an enormous cloud over legislative activity in general, implies that the Court and the Constitution are outside of the structure of interest-group politics, whereas we have tried to show that they are integral elements of that structure.

CONCLUSION

This paper has sketched an approach to the question of the independent judiciary that enables a seeming anomaly in the older political-science and newer economic theory of the political process as a struggle among interest groups to be incorporated as an essential element of that theory. Our analysis has certain positive implications with respect to the structure of government that seem consistent with observed reality. It also has, as we have just seen, normative implications with respect to constitutional interpretation.

A striking element of our approach is that although we view the independent judiciary as an essential component in a system of interest-group politics, we do not view the judiciary as itself "political" in the sense suggested by Martin Shapiro[38] and other debunkers of the idea of a genuinely independent judiciary. Our view of how the courts operate is closer to that of the legal commentators who extol the courts as "above" politics.[39] Where we differ from these commentators is in not venerating the courts as repositories of some special wisdom, integrity, morality, or commitment to principle. In our view the courts do not enforce the moral law or ideals of neutrality, justice, or fairness; they enforce the "deals" made by effective interest groups with earlier legislatures.[40] Of course, since the judges are independent, an appeal to principles may be effective courtroom or law-review advocacy.

---

[36] See note 3 *supra*; The Federalist, No. 10.

[37] A view strongly implied in Gerald Gunther, The Supreme Court 1971 Term—Foreword: In Search of Evolving Doctrine on a Changing Court: A Model for a Newer Equal Protection, 86 Harv. L. Rev. 1, 20-21, 23 (1972), discussed critically in Richard A. Posner, The DeFunis Case and the Constitutionality of Preferential Treatment of Racial Minorities, 1974 Sup. Ct. Rev. 1, 29.

[38] See text at note 4 *supra*.

[39] See, for example, Gerald Gunther, *supra* note 3.

[40] This is not to say that all legislation is inconsistent with efficiency or some other general

APPENDIX

Some Empirical Tests of Judicial Independence

We have argued in this paper that an independent judiciary imposes expected costs on the sale of legislation. The possibility that the judiciary will not enforce the deals worked out by the legislature reduces the expected value of legislation, which in turn reduces the benefits to the groups procuring the legislation and the payments to the enacting legislators. Thus, the degree to which the courts overturn legislative deals is of critical importance in evaluating the usefulness of the hypothesis that an independent judiciary fosters interest group politics. If the courts were sufficiently unreliable, the expected benefits from the sale of multi-period legislation, made possible by judicial independence, would not offset the costs of the legislative deals that were frustrated by the courts. And if this were the case, one would have to search further for an explanation of judicial independence.

The question of judicial unreliability or the costs of independence is amenable to empirical analysis although what follows must be viewed as a crude and preliminary attempt. We focus on a single measure of unreliability—the number of acts of Congress that have been held unconstitutional by the Supreme Court. Nullification is an extreme example of judicial unreliability, and for this reason is likely to be deficient as an overall measure of the costs of judicial independence.[41] Nevertheless, it is the only measure that is readily available, and the development of a more suitable measure is beyond the scope of this paper.

Ninety-seven acts of Congress were held unconstitutional in whole or in part in the period 1789-1972, or an average of about one per term of Congress.[42] Figure II indicates, however, that there has been a great deal of variability over time in the number of Supreme Court nullifications per term of Congress. Only two acts were nullified in the 1789-1864 period while 11 were nullified in the next 15 years. Three peaks in nullification activity are observable: 1920-1924 (11 nullifications in the 66th-68th Congresses); 1935-1936 (10 nullifications in the 74th Congress); and 1963-1972 (25 nullifications in the 88th-92nd Congresses). Between the latter two peaks, the number of nullifications diminished sharply (5 nullifications in the 1937-1962 period).

---

welfare norm. Our point is rather that the judicial attitude implied by our analysis is one of indifference to the ethical content of the legislative or constitutional provisions that the court is being asked to enforce.

[41] These deficiencies include the following: (1) Nullification fails to account for judicial interpretations of statutes that stop short of nullification but nevertheless significantly reduce the value of the legislative deals. Further, if lower-court rulings gut the law in question, a Supreme Court bent on nullification may accomplish this purpose simply by not granting certiorari. Thus, observed nullifications may be an alternative to unfavorable lower-court rulings, and present a biased picture of overall judicial unreliability. (2) If nullification of a *particular* law can be anticipated, legislators and groups are likely to be deterred from enacting that law in the first place, thereby saving the costs of enactment. Observed nullifications, therefore, will fail to account for the number of laws that are not enacted because of anticipated nullification. (3) If nullification merely delays for a short period of time the passage of a similar law that is acceptable to the Court (whose composition may change in the interval), the costs of observed nullifications may actually be less than the costs of continuous unfavorable interpretations that stop short of nullification.

[42] See The Constitution of the U.S. of America, Analysis and Interpretation 1597-1619, at S125-S126. We have excluded one act from our enumeration, involving legal-tender clauses, that was declared unconstitutional in 1870 in a case overruled in 1871.

FIGURE II

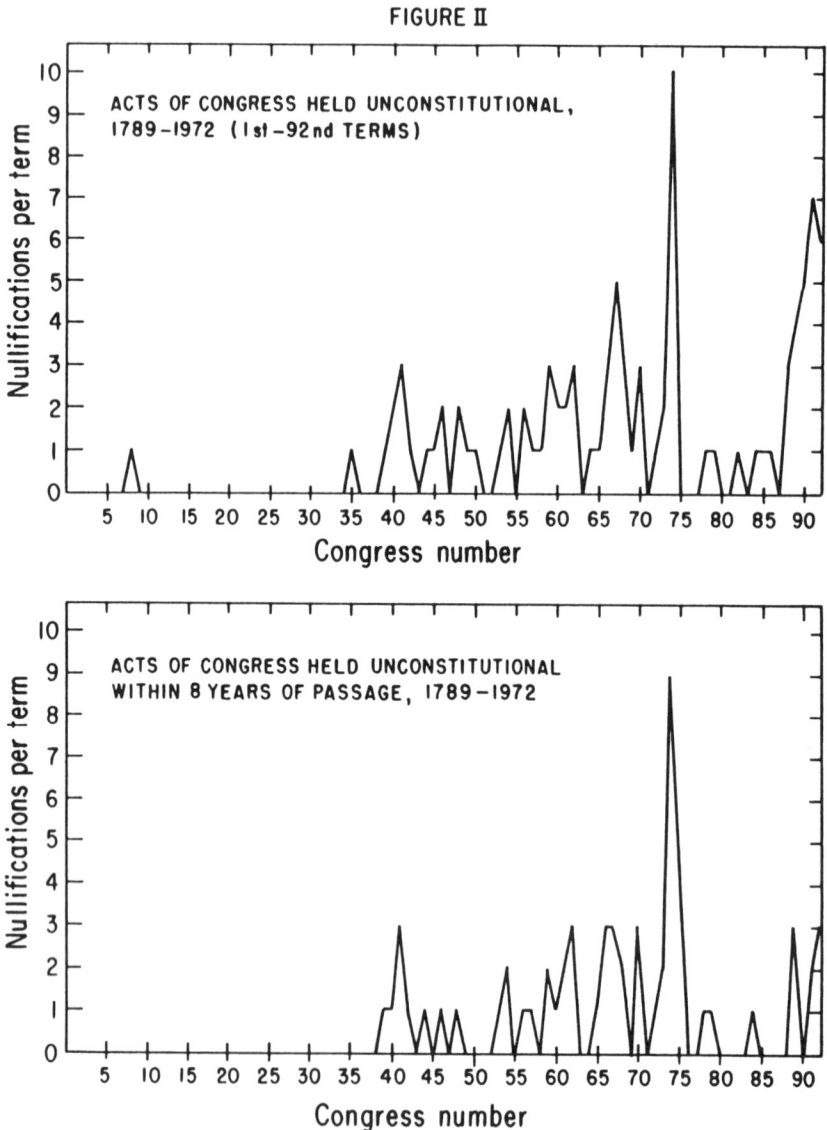

What are the overall costs imposed by nullifications on the political process whereby legislation is bought and sold? Two inferences from the data lead us to believe that these costs are minimal. First, in comparison to the total number of public bills enacted by Congress, the number of nullifications is insignificant: 97 nullifications out of a total of more than 38,000 acts suggests an average probability of nullification per act of about .0026. Even in the peak nullification period, 1935-1936, only nine out of the 1,526 statutes enacted between 1933 and 1936 were declared unconstitutional.[43] Probabilities of such a small magnitude would seem unlikely to deter significantly the enactment of special-interest legislation.[44] Second, the nullification data take no account of the time span between passage of a statute and its nullification. A Supreme Court that in 1970 nullified a provision of a statute passed 61 years earlier would not be imposing substantial costs (discounted back to 1909) on the groups that originally procured the statute.[45] Legislation that lasts 61 years is of sufficient durability to allow the full benefits of the deal to have been captured by the groups involved. So long a lag between passage and nullification is atypical, however. Thirty-eight acts were nullified within four years of their enactment, 58 within eight years, and 76 within 12 years. Only seven acts were more than 25 years old at the time of their nullification.[46] However, even an act that lasts eight or ten years has sufficient durability to enable the bulk of the present value of its benefits to be appropriated.[47] If we restrict the sample to acts nullified within eight years of passage (because these are likely to have imposed the largest costs on the groups procuring the acts), not only does the number of nullifications fall by 40 per cent (from 97 to 58) but the time pattern of nullification changes in one interesting respect. The recent period, 1963-1973, is no longer a period of peak nullification activity (see Figure II). Of the 27 nullifications in this period, only nine took place within eight years of enactment.[48]

Multiple regression analysis can be used to estimate the influence that various factors have had on the frequency of Supreme Court nullifications and on the time lag between enactment and nullification of an act. The variables included in the regression analysis are as follows:

N_t : number of nullifications per congressional term.

N_t^8 : number of nullifications per term of acts passed within last eight years.

N_t^{16} : number of nullifications per term of acts passed within last 16 years.

LAG_j : number of years between enactment and nullification for each of the j nullifications ($j = 1, \ldots, 95$) between 1789 and 1972.

AGE_t : average age of the Supreme Court judges at the end of each congressional term.

TEN_t : average tenure of the Supreme Court judges at the end of each congressional term.

[43] The one additional nullification during 1935-1936 was of a statute enacted in 1926.

[44] We emphasize that this inference is limited by the absence of data on unfavorable judicial interpretations of statutes which may be positively correlated with nullifications and vastly greater than the number of nullifications in any period.

[45] Act of Feb. 9, 1909, § 2, 35 Stat. 614, as amended.

[46] The frequency distribution of the time between passage and nullification for the 97 acts is as follows:

				Time (years)			
	≤4	5-8	9-12	13-16	17-25	26-50	>50
Number	38	20	12	13	7	5	2

[47] See Table 1 supra.

[48] Sixteen of the remaining 18 nullifications in this period were of acts passed between 1946 and 1956, with an average lag between enactment and nullification of 15.7 years. The two other nullifications, which took place in 1970 and 1973, were of 1909 and 1960 acts respectively.

BILL$_t^i$: number of public bills passed by Congress within the last i years. Note that i = 8 when the dependent variable is N_t^8 and i = 16 when the dependent variable is either N_t or N_t^{16}.

PAR$_t$: dummy variable that takes the value 1 if the political party of the President and the majority party of both the House and Senate are the same, and 0 if the President's party is different from the majority party of either the House and Senate.

DIS$_j$: number of dissenting votes in the Supreme Court for each of the j nullifications.

t : identity of Congress (t runs from 1st to 92nd Congress).

Multiple regression equations were estimated on the three dependent variables, N_t^8, N_t^{16}, and N_t, over the period 1789-1972. The specification of the N_t^8 regression is of the following form:

$$N_t^8 = \alpha + \beta_1 AGE_t + \beta_2 TEN_t + \beta_3 PAR_t + \beta_4 BILL_t^8 + u. \qquad (1)$$

The N_t^{16} and N_t specifications are identical to (1) except that BILL$_t^{16}$ replaces BILL$_t^8$. The model of legal decision making that underlies the above equation is basically a variant of the economist's theorem that when the costs rise from engaging in certain behavior or the gains fall, the frequency of such behavior declines. Accordingly, AGE is expected to have a positive effect on the rate of nullifications. Older judges, with fewer active years ahead, will be less susceptible to legislative or executive "bribery" in the form of promotions to higher office and are more likely to view their present position as a terminal one. Hence older judges will exercise their greater "independence" by nullifying more acts. The effect of the TEN variable is less certain than AGE. We expect that recently appointed judges will be more indebted to the current legislature and executive, and hence will be less likely to nullify the acts of their benefactors, but on the other hand, judges with less tenure will be less indebted to more distant Congresses. Hence TEN should have a positive effect on nullifications only if the nullification variable is restricted to acts that have been nullified within, for example, eight years of passage.[49] PAR is included in the regression analysis to test the hypothesis that the court is less likely to demonstrate independence and hence nullify laws the less conflict there is between the executive and Congress. A crude measure of this conflict is whether the President's party is the same as the majority party of Congress. Thus we expect a negative sign on the PAR variable. Since the dependent variable is the number of nullifications while the model generates hypotheses on nullification propensities, we have included the number of bills passed (BILL^i) as an independent variable in the regression. Thus, holding BILL^i constant implies that variations in nullifications reflect differences in the nullification propensities of the Court.

[49] Since shorter tenure may have a positive effect on nullification of older laws (for example, laws that are more than eight years old at the time of nullification), the effect of TEN on all nullifications per term (N_t) is uncertain.

[50] The period 1789-1972 spans the 1st-92nd Congresses. However, the first observation in equation 3.1 is the 5th Congress (to allow for the passage of bills over the preceding eight years) and hence 3.1 contains 88 observations. Similarly, in equation 3.2 the first observation is the 9th Congress, and the regression contains 84 observations. When all nullifications is the dependent variable, the BILL variable is computed for bills passed over the last 16 years, and thus the first observation in 3.3 is also the 9th Congress.

Table 3 presents the regression results on three nullification variables—N_t^8 (acts 8 years old or less), N_t^{16} (acts 16 years old or less), and N_t (all acts). Equations 3.1-3.3 are for the period 1789-1972,[50] and equations 3.4-3.6 are for a narrower set of observations, the 39th-92nd Congresses.[51]

Overall the regression results are inconclusive. The age variable behaves as predicted but is statistically significant only in the equations that include the full set of observations. In contrast, the tenure variable is insignificant when all observations are included but significant in the N_t^{16} and N_t regressions that are estimated on the 39th-92nd terms. And the positive and significant effect of tenure in equations 3.5 and 3.6 compared to its insignificant effect in 3.4 is contrary to the prediction that the strongest positive impact of tenure should be observed in the N_t^8 regressions.[52]

One difficulty in estimating the separate effect of AGE and TEN in the same regression is that the two variables are highly correlated. This is particularly true in the regressions limited to the 39th-92nd Congressional terms where the correlation between AGE and TEN is .70. When TEN is excluded from equations 3.4-3.6, the AGE variable becomes highly significant. And similarly, when AGE is excluded from 3.4-3.6, the significance of TEN improves.[53] Of the two remaining variables in the regression analysis, PAR is insignificant in all six regressions while BILL[1] is significant in two of the six. In sum, except for the AGE variables the results of the regression analysis yield little support for a theory of legal decision-making that hypothesizes that the observed degree of judicial independence is a function of the

[51] Since there were only two nullifications during the first 38 Congresses, the narrower sample excludes at least 36 observations (depending on whether N_t^8, N_t^{16}, or N_t is the dependent variable) where the dependent variable takes a zero value. The large number of zero-valued dependent variables, particularly in the regressions that include the early Congresses, suggests that ordinary least squares is not the most appropriate statistical technique. We have not, however, made use of an alternative procedure (for example, tobit analysis).

[52] An additional implication of the analysis is that the likelihood of nullification of older acts will decline with increases in tenure. This can be tested directly by employing $N_t - N_t^8$ as the dependent variable. The regression coefficients and t-values of TEN are .074 (2.237) for the 9th-92nd terms and .218 (2.556) for the 39th-92nd terms, which is contrary to our expectation. Note that our definition of "older" acts (nine years or older) is arbitrary. Nevertheless, similar results are observed if 13 years is the cut-off point for older acts.

[53] The regression coefficients and (t-values) of AGE and TEN when the other is excluded from equations 3.4-3.6 are as follows:

	AGE	TEN
N^8	.180	.235
	(2.910)	(2.527)
N^{16}	.234	.398
	(3.263)	(3.890)
N	.285	.461
	(3.788)	(4.275)

We observed that AGE was insignificant in equations 3.4-3.6 when TEN was also entered but here the t-value on AGE always exceeds 2.91 when TEN is excluded. TEN, which was insignificant in 3.4 when AGE was entered, is also highly significant in the above table. The effects of deleting either AGE or TEN in equations 3.1-3.3 are less dramatic because the correlation coefficient between the two variables drops to .41 on the full set of observations (1st-92nd Congressional terms). Nevertheless, TEN becomes significant in the N^{16} and N regressions when AGE is deleted.

TABLE 3
REGRESSION COEFFICIENTS AND T-VALUES ON NULLIFICATION VARIABLES

Equation Number	Dependent Variable	n	α	AGE	TEN	PAR	BILL[1]	DIS	t	N	R²	D.W.
3.1	N⁸	88	-5.483 (2.777)	.094 (2.627)	-.008 (.160)	.185 (.621)	.0002 (1.005)				.19	1.943
3.2	N¹⁶	84	-6.208 (2.587)	.090 (2.111)	.063 (1.092)	.065 (.184)	.0003 (2.724)				.27	1.747
3.3	N	84	-7.849 (3.075)	.116 (2.560)	.072 (1.174)	.107 (.287)	.0003 (2.757)				.31	1.439
3.4	N⁸	54	-8.442 (1.732)	.135 (1.545)	.096 (.746)	.141 (.328)	-.0006 (.220)				.15	2.075
3.5	N¹⁶	54	-7.717 (1.416)	.089 (.916)	.306 (2.128)	-.047 (.098)	.0001 (.842)				.26	1.927
3.6	N	54	-10.340 (1.816)	.130 (1.277)	.327 (2.173)	-.076 (.152)	.0001 (.901)				.31	1.633
3.7	Ln LAG	95	4.829 (1.796)	-.075 (1.652)	.141 (2.262)	-.114 (.518)		-.033 (.470)	.014 (2.073)	-.143 (2.616)	.17	

Notes: (1) t-values are in parentheses. (2) n = number of observations in regression equation. (3) R² = coefficient of determination. (4) D.W. = Durbin-Watson statistic. Note that in equations 3.1–3.6 we would not reject the null hypothesis at the .95 confidence level that the error terms are serially independent. The null hypothesis, however is accepted only in equations 3.1, 3.4 and 3.5. (a) N, LAG, DIS—The Constitution of the U.S. of America, Analysis and Interpretation, 1597-1669, 5125-5126 (1973, 1974). (b) AGE, TEN—The 1975 World Almanac & Book of Facts at 770.

costs and benefits to the judiciary of exercising independence. It would be premature, however, to abandon the theory since our measures of costs and benefits (age, tenure, political party of executive and Congress) and our measure of independence (nullifications) are highly imperfect.

Our second empirical test is an analysis of the determinants of the time lag (LAG) between the passage of a bill and its nullification. Here each of the 95 acts nullified between 1789 and 1972 is an observation in the regression analysis. The regression specification is

$$\ln \text{LAG}_j = \alpha + \beta_1 \text{AGE}_j + \beta_2 \text{TEN}_j + \beta_3 \text{PAR}_j + \beta_4 \text{DIS}_j + \beta_5 t + \beta_6 N_t + u \quad (2)$$

where the LAG variable is in logarithmic form.[54] Based on the theory outlined earlier, we would expect both AGE and TEN to have negative effect on the LAG variable. Since the nullification of older acts is less costly to long-term legislative deals (because most of the present value of benefits are still being received by groups procuring the act), the younger the judges are, the more susceptible they will be to legislative and executive "bribery" and pressure and the less likely they will be to nullify recent congressional acts. Similarly, as average tenure diminishes the Court will be more indebted to recent Congresses and less to past Congresses, making the Court less likely to nullify acts of the former and more likely to nullify acts of the latter. We expect PAR to have a positive effect on LAG because the greater the conflict between the executive and legislature, as measured by PAR, the less effective the two branches will be in bringing joint pressure on the Court not to nullify recent acts. We have no strong a priori predictions on the three remaining variables, DIS, t and N_t, in equation (2). N tests whether there is a systematic effect on the time lag when more acts are nullified per term; t tests whether there has been a trend over time in the age of acts nullified; and DIS tests whether the degree of conflict within the Court (as measured by the number of dissenting votes) varies with the age of the act nullified.

Equation 3.7 of Table 3 presents the LAG regression. AGE behaves as predicted—younger judges are less likely to nullify more recent acts—though its effect is only marginally significant. TEN is significant but its effect is contrary to our prediction. PAR and DIS are not significant. Both the t and N variables are highly significant. Here we find that the more recent the Congress, the greater the average age of the acts nullified; and the more acts nullified per term, the less is the average age of the acts nullified.[55]

[54] The following example illustrates how the data for each observation are constructed. During the term of the 57th Congress (1901-1902) one act was nullified (1901). The act was 3 years old and there were 4 dissenting votes on the Court. Hence LAG equals 3 and DIS equals 4. The values of AGE, TEN, PAR, and N of this observation are their values at the end of the 57th Congress. Note that if more than one act is nullified during a given Congressional term, then each of these acts is a separate observation in the regression. The LAG and DIS values would be act specific while the values assigned to the remaining variables, which are Congress specific, would be identical.

[55] The t and N results, however, do not appear very robust. Ten acts were nullified during the term of the 74th Congress (1935-1936) and the average age of each act was 2.3 years. This compares to an average age of 10.8 years for the other 85 acts nullified. If we add a dummy variable to equation 3.7 (which takes the value 1 if the observation is from the 74th Congress and 0 otherwise), then both t and N become insignificant though their signs are unchanged.

[4]

Feature: An Economic Perspective on Basic Rights

The Costs of Enforcing Legal Rights
Richard A. Posner

I am not an expert on the formerly communist states of Central and Eastern Europe. What I bring to this conference is a theoretical model (cost-benefit analysis) of general applicability to problems in social ordering, some knowledge of the history and practice of rights enforcement in the Anglo-American legal culture, and my experience as a federal judge involved in such enforcement.

The organizers of this conference asked the participants to concentrate on five specific rights, and I will discuss each of these but only after discussing the general issue of rights and their enforcement. I will not discuss the bearing of the European convention on human rights, which, I understand, nations must sign, submitting to the jurisdiction of the court of human rights in Strasbourg, in order to be accepted as members of the European Union.

I. I take "right" to mean simply a claim or entitlement normally enforceable through courts or equivalent agencies; and I assume—more controversially, but consistently with taking an economic approach to the issue—that rights are instruments for promoting social welfare rather than things of value in themselves. This is not to deny the existence of moral rights[1], or even to treat them, in defiance as it were of Kant, as mere instruments. It is obvious that the law does not enforce all moral rights, but only a subset; and the selection of the subset is decisively influenced by instrumental considerations.

Isaiah Berlin distinguished in a famous essay between positive and negative liberties. I offer a version of that distinction to help frame my analysis. A positive liberty is a right to demand a service from the government. A negative liberty is a right not to be interfered with by the government, or, more broadly, by anyone. Positive liberties are associated with the modern welfare state, negative liberties—most compendiously expressed in Brandeis's famous phrase as "the right to be let alone"—with classical liberalism. Negative liberties are less of a burden on the public fisc. Indeed they are often assumed, especially in theoretical analyses, to be costless, unless one is discussing national defense. Consider the basic right of property: if I own a good, say my automobile, you (private person or government official) cannot take it without my consent. To make my property right meaningful, about all that is—or at least that seems—necessary is a simple registration system for automobile titles, a criminal penalty severe enough to deter theft, and appropriate remedies against governmental takings. Not only do the costs of negative liberties seem slight, but the benefits are immense, rights being the cornerstone of a system of free markets and democratic political governance. Positive liberties are more costly, and their benefits often elusive. Many positive liberties, such as financial assistance to the poor, public education, and publicly subsidized health care, are largely redistributive in purpose and effect rather than directly productive of valuable output[2] and they may affect incentives in a way that reduces productivity.

But on further reflection the distinction between negative and positive liberties blurs. Every negative liberty, especially when the term is understood to include liberty from private as well as public aggression or expropriation, can be seen to imply a corresponding positive liberty. The rights of property and of personal safety, which are negative liberties enforced by criminal and tort laws, imply a public machinery of rights protection and enforcement, a machinery that includes police, prosecutors, judges, and even publicly employed or subsidized lawyers for criminal defendants who cannot afford to hire their own lawyer. This implied right to government protection may or may not be legally enforceable (usually not, because it would require budgetary and administrative decisions that courts are poorly equipped to make), but without it the negative liberties may be largely ineffectual. It is true that much rights protection and enforcement is carried on privately rather than publicly; the role of arbitrators, mediators, and private lawyers and police is particularly important. But, with all due respect for the ingenious and forcefully articulated views of "anarcho-capitalists" such as David Friedman, it is difficult to believe that the negative liberties could be made meaningful without intervention by the public sector.

The costs of the positive liberties have been studied extensively, but little is known about the costs of protecting and enforcing negative liberties in any society. The reasons for this ignorance are numerous:

First, the costs of law enforcement, adjudication, and the private legal profession are not broken down in existing sources of data according to the rights enforced. For example, today in the United States a large part—but no one is sure how large a part—of the total resources devoted to criminal law enforcement is aimed at suppressing the traffic in illegal drugs; and this suppression makes no obvious contribution to securing the negative liberties. Even in principle, it is difficult to allocate the costs of law enforcement across rights enforced, because many of their costs are joint; the same judges, police, prosecutors, and private lawyers enforce them.

Second, it is not clear what rights ought to be counted as part of the sphere of negative liberties. Consider the right, found in the Fifth Amendment to the U.S. Constitution, not to be compelled to be a witness against oneself. Is this a negative liberty, or an impediment to the enforcement of the negative rights of potential victims of crime?

Third (and related to the preceding point), some rights straddle the line between negative and positive. The right to counsel and the right to abortion are examples. For an affluent person, both rights are negative: they are rights against the government's interfering with the hiring of a lawyer and of an abortion doctor respectively. But for a poor person, these have to be positive liberties, because without public assistance the poor person cannot hire a lawyer or purchase an abortion.

Fourth, many of the costs of rights are not public budgetary costs at all. They are such things as erroneous convictions and acquittals, police brutality and other abuses of power by rights enforcers, and, above all, private nonlegal expenditures on rights protection and enforcement, including such mundane but cumulatively expensive items as locks and car alarms.[3]

Fifth, rights are a preoccupation mainly of wealthy countries, in which the purely budgetary costs of enforcing rights are not a significant factor.

Finally, there is a good deal of rights fetishism. We romanticize rights. We—and I am speaking now of almost the entire Western legal and political community—even sacralize them. The religious feelings of secular moderns have been displaced onto various aspects of "civic religion," including the protection and enforcement of rights. Rights are treated as Platonic forms, universalized and eternalized. They are treated (in the famous expression of Ronald Dworkin's) as trumps, rather than as tools of government and hence as subject to the usual tradeoffs. Who talks of the cost of a Platonic form?

All this said, it is pretty obvious that the benefit-cost ratio of the public and private machinery for the protection and enforcement of the basic negative liberties is much higher than one. A suggestive although far from definitive statistic is that the total public expenditures on the administration of justice in the United States—expenditures on police, the courts, prosecutors, public defenders, and prison administration—are only $61 billion a year,[4] which is less than one percent of the Gross National Product. So the question arises: why do any countries committed to the principle of free markets and democratic government *not* have effective systems for the protection and enforcement of the liberties that undergird a democratic free-market system?

II. Poverty cannot be the answer, or at least the complete answer. Few countries outside of sub-Saharan Africa cannot afford the relative handful of minimally honest and competent judges, lawyers, prosecutors, and police that is necessary to operate a legal system whose only job is to protect and enforce the fundamental rights to property, contract, and personal safety. Two other answers are more plausible. The first is the paradox of power. A government need not be large, but it must be strong, in order to protect and enforce rights, but strong government is a threat to those rights. Second, legal systems have become encumbered with so many functions besides the protection and enforcement of the essential negative liberties that they have become extremely costly, and some nations cannot afford the cost. In these nations the legal system is asked to do too much and fails at everything, including the protection of negative liberties.

A. An effective system of property and personal rights requires an apparatus for deterring crime, especially acquisitive crime. Not just theft, robbery, embezzling, the forging of wills, certain types of fraud, and other familiar acquisitive crimes, but also bribing officials, including judges, police, and officials in charge of registering titles to real or personal property, must be prevented, or, more precisely, must be kept within tolerable bounds.[5] It is pretty easy to think up ways of maximizing deterrence: impose savage punishments, deny procedural rights to persons accused of crime, require citizens to carry identification papers, pay informers generously, place judges under the control of prosecutors (or dispense with judges altogether), and allow the police a free hand to use brutal methods in investigating crime. Some of

these measures might be countereffective, but as a package modeled on military discipline culminating in the drumhead court-martial it would be an effective method of minimizing the crime rate and thus maximizing the protection of rights, provided that the judges, police, and other administrators of the criminal justice system acted competently and in good faith. That is the rub. The criminal justice system that I have sketched would be so powerful that it would be a threat to negative liberties. Innocent people would find themselves caught in police dragnets, arrested and detained on suspicion of crime, eavesdropped and informed on, occasionally even convicted.

To check these dangers it is necessary either to alter the incentives of law enforcers or to create countervailing rights, or to do both—and the countervailing rights may alter incentives. This process is visible in the history of English criminal procedure in the eighteenth century. By the beginning of that century (in fact earlier) very severe punishments for crime were in place, but there were no police forces, and the right of law enforcement officers to enter a person's home was severely limited ("a man's home is his castle"). These two features of the criminal justice system must have greatly undermined the protection of rights yet have seemed justified by the danger of abuse of power if the reins of the law enforcement authorities were loosened. Early in the eighteenth century judges were given secure tenure, emancipating them from control by the prosecutorial authority (the king and his ministers). Yet by the end of the century there were still no police forces and there was still no general right to search a person's home. At the same time there was no right of appeal by criminal defendants and they had no right to counsel either, so constraints on law enforcement were in effect offset by constraints on defendants. The state had limited power but defendants had limited rights. Criminal proceedings were short and cheap.

The criminal justice system of twentieth-century America furnishes parallel illustrations. By the beginning of the century there were large police forces, which frequently abused citizens. Prison conditions were often brutal. Indigent defendants often had no counsel, even though criminal proceedings were more complex than they had been in the eighteenth

Figure 1: Homicide Rate in United States per 100,000 Inhabitants, 1933–1990

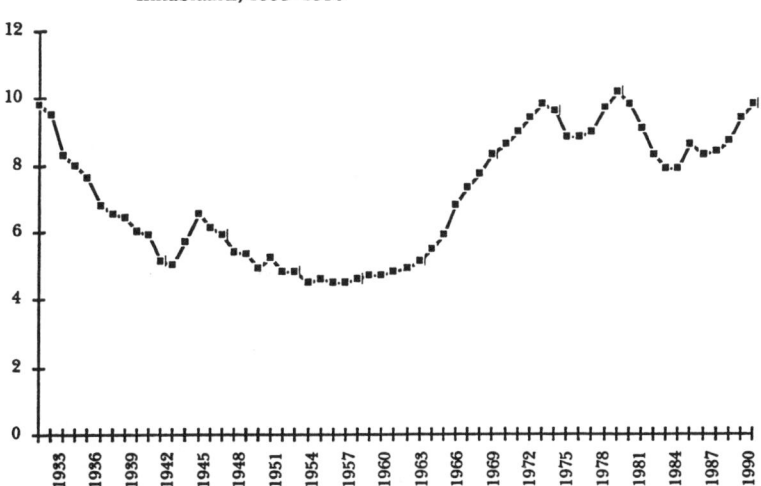

century. The Supreme Court, beginning in the 1930s but accelerating greatly in the 1960s, took the lead in seeking to rectify these conditions by creating countervailing rights, including the right to exclude illegally seized evidence from a criminal trial, the right to effective assistance of counsel in all criminal cases, the right to invoke federal habeas corpus to obtain review of state convictions by federal courts, and the right to bring tort suits complaining of police brutality and inhuman prison conditions.

The creation of these countervailing rights made the criminal justice system cumbersome, expensive, and probably less effective in deterring crime. As shown in Figure 1, a great upsurge in crime rates accompanied the "Warren Court's" adventurous rulings in criminal procedure, although the causality is deeply uncertain,[6] there is some evidence that these rulings did cause crime rates to rise.

Legislators responded by expanding pretrial detention, authorizing more use of wiretapping and other electronic surveillance, extending the length of sentences, reducing judicial discretion in respect of sentencing, hiring more educated police, increasing the scope of pretrial prevention (that is, reducing the right to release upon the posting of a bond), and appropriating more money for prisons and for prosecution. Expanding the rights of criminal defendants, while in one respect fostering negative liberties, in another and possibly more important respect had impaired them by undermining the protection of property and personal rights that were threatened by crime and imposing large indirect costs by making the criminal justice system more costly.[7]

These points are obscured by the historical origins of the rights of criminal defendants. The people who pressed for and obtained the rights of criminal defendants that were recognized first in English law and then in the American Bill of Rights were not poor people, let alone members of the criminal classes. They were businessmen, publishers, writers, and politicians. The rights they fought for were rights that a society needs in order to make property and political rights secure against abuse by government. In contrast, the rights that the "Warren Court" derived, by flexible interpretation, from the Constitution were rights that criminals, and members of an underclass or lumpenproletariat most likely to be mistaken for criminals by overzealous police or prosecutors, want or need. For the most part the enforcement of these rights undermines property rights and personal security by making the punishment of criminals less swift and certain.

The difference is illustrated by the changing meaning of the Sixth Amendment to the US Constitution, one clause of which entitles criminal defendants to the assistance of counsel. The original understanding was that the clause entitled criminal defendants to hire counsel if they could afford to. Only in the twentieth century has the amendment been understood in addition to entitle indigent criminal defendants to the assistance of counsel furnished at the government's expense. To speak with perhaps brutal exaggeration, the twentieth century has witnessed a shift in the legal system of the United States from protecting the rights of the propertied to protecting the rights of the unpropertied who covet the wealth of the propertied.

The rights that are recognized in the United States today are not rights *semper et ubique*. They are the culmination of a specific historical process and they are relative to a specific legal and political culture, one shaped by a high level of material wealth. They are not equally well adapted to every society. It is not even clear—this is an especially neglected point in discussions of civil liberties—that the amplitude of criminal rights recognized in the United States today reduces the net costs of erroneous convictions. There is a tug of war between the courts, which are primarily responsible for the creation (as by flexible interpretation of the Sixth Amendment and other constitutional provisions) of new rights, and the legislatures. Legislatures can neutralize the effect of a new court-created right either by reducing the funding for the defense of indigent criminal defendants, thus making it easier to convict them, or by increasing the severity of punishments,[8] with the consequence that even if fewer innocent people are convicted, those that are will serve longer sentences. The total suffering of the innocent will not be reduced, unless the courts invalidate statutes that impose severe punishments, or require generous compensation of lawyers for indigent criminal

defendants, and American courts have been unwilling to do either.

The leaders of the postcommunist societies of Central and Eastern Europe, like the leaders of the American Revolution, have, of course, a lively sense of the danger of governmental oppression of the respectable classes. That lively sense may lead to the creation of a costly system of rights invoked primarily by members of the criminal class, as has happened in the United States.

B. The other factor that I want to emphasize in the costs of protecting and enforcing rights is the overextension of the legal system. Suppose that at time t a nation is communistic. Its system of law enforcement will presumably be operating at or near its capacity to enforce the society's existing laws, many of which will be devoted to the enforcement of positive liberties. Suppose that at time $t+1$ the nation converts from communism to capitalism and it wishes to devote resources to the protection of negative liberties, which have greater importance in a system of free markets. Many of the old laws will remain intact, so it will not be possible simply to reallocate enforcement resources from positive to negative liberties. What is more, since the transition from communism to capitalism will often involve an initial drop in net public revenues and an initial increase in criminality because of the disappearance of the police state and the greater inequality of income and wealth in a capitalistic compared to a communistic system, the nation may be unable to maintain, let alone increase, the existing level of resources devoted to law enforcement.

Reallocation will be particularly difficult for two reasons. The first is that the benefits of effective enforcement of negative liberties, as distinct from positive ones, often are diffuse. This makes it difficult to marshal an effective interest group behind the enforcement of negative liberties. Second—a point I mentioned earlier—negative liberties are costs as well as benefits. The rights of criminal defendants are the clearest illustration of this point. Anything that strengthens those rights is apt, by doing so, to weaken the protection of property rights by reducing the expected punishment cost of theft and other acquisitive crimes. The *net* benefits of a wholesale reallocation of enforcement resources from positive to negative liberties may be small.

One implication of this analysis is that property rights are cheaper to protect than other negative liberties, and in particular the rights of criminal defendants. Expanding the rights of those defendants, or enforcing them more effectively, makes it more costly to protect property rights, but the reverse is not true; expanding property rights does not make it more costly to fight crime. Another implication is that deregulatory measures unrelated to the protection of rights—for example the removal of price controls, or of limits on an employer's right to fire a worker—will promote the protection of rights by freeing up resources of the legal system for that protection.

A further point is that the borderline between positive and negative liberties is hazy, and not only because of the economic links that I have stressed. In principle, for example, antitrust laws and laws against fraud protect free markets from distortion. But the practice is often different. Since concepts such as monopolization and misrepresentation (and especially "misleading omission") are vague, laws aimed at preventing or punishing these practices invite manipulation and expansion, and historically have often been used to punish efficient practices and express economic resentment. Antitrust laws and laws against any but the most flagrant forms of fraud appeared late in the development of Anglo-American law, implying that such laws are inessential to the achievement of a high level of prosperity. Nonwealthy countries should be cautious about adopting expansive prohibitions against these and other "economic" crimes, lest they deter aggressive but efficient economic activity.

III. If I am correct so far that negative liberties, especially when they take the form of rights for criminal suspects, defendants, and prisoners, may be costly for a nation that while not poor in the way that many African nations are poor is not wealthy the way the United States and Germany are, we should not be sanguine that these liberties are likely to be placed on a secure footing in the post-communist societies of Central and Eastern Europe any time soon. Nor is it clear that these societies *should* accord

a high priority to securing *all* the negative liberties. Perhaps those liberties differ greatly among themselves in their value to a poor society. I shall illustrate this point with reference to the five rights focused on during the conference.

A. The first is preventing brutal police tactics directed against pretrial detainees. These tactics generally center on the use of third-degree methods to extract incriminating or otherwise useful information (such as identifying confederates) from a suspect before he is formally charged. This abuse, formerly prevalent in the United States, has been curbed by a combination of the exclusionary rule (coerced confessions are not admissible in evidence), tort remedies against the police enforceable in federal court, the *Miranda* warnings, and increased levels of police training,[9] of police "professionalism," implying good salaries. This combination would be difficult to implement in a poor nation. A rule of evidence against coerced confessions requires that judges be willing at times to credit criminal defendants over police, since there rarely will be evidence of coercion other than the defendant's say-so. Even in the United States, and even more in nations that do not have a tradition of civil liberties and that have an inquisitorial rather than an adversarial system of justice, judges hesitate to side with lawbreakers against law enforcers. The effectiveness of the *Miranda* warnings likewise depends on the willingness of judges to disbelieve police testimony. Without such willingness, the police will not give the warnings but will merely testify that they did.[10] The provision of tort remedies against public officers implies, realistically, the indemnifying by the state of officers found liable. So the state must appropriate funds to compensate criminal defendants most of whom are in fact guilty of the crime to which they confessed, since most coerced confessions are truthful, though this depends in part on how much coercion is applied. Only in the last quarter century have tort suits provided a meaningful remedy to the victim of coercive interrogation in the United States.

The most effective method of reducing the role of coercion in the interrogation of suspects may simply be to pay police officers very well.[11] That will enable the hiring of educated and competent police, who being intelligent and competent will not need to rely so heavily on coercion to obtain evidence against suspects. And by making the job of a policeman more valuable, a high salary will make him more reluctant to jeopardize his job by engaging in misconduct. But it is difficult for a nonwealthy nation to pay its police high wages. Apart from the financial cost, the effect is to divert a disproportionate fraction of what is bound to be a smallish group of educated and able people from other urgent national tasks, such as entrepreneurship, administration, medicine and public health, and defense.

Probably the greatest cost of measures to prevent coercive interrogation is that it undermines negative liberties at the same time that it secures them. Much pious denial to the contrary, coercion, unless taken to the brutal extreme at which it will induce an innocent person to confess, is a cheap and effective method of criminal investigation. It is used routinely in situations in which the need for information is desperate. The idea that it brutalizes the interrogators and thus fosters abuses unrelated to interrogation appears to be unsubstantiated. The more that coercive interrogation is curtailed, the less secure are property and personal rights. This is an unpleasant tradeoff, yet any realistic regime operating in circumstances of poverty must face up to it. I abstract, as I said at the outset, from any constraints that the European convention on human rights may place on the freedom of a nation that wants to belong to the European Union to make such a tradeoff. And I emphasize that I am speaking of the relatively mild forms of coercion, such as protracted interrogation and false promises of leniency, that are unlikely to induce innocent people to confess.

B. The second right with which the conference is concerned is the right of patients in psychiatric hospitals not to be abused by the hospital staff. I take it that "abuse" is meant to comprehend neglect, which is the more serious problem. Instances of brutality toward patients are not unknown. But they are less common than in the parallel case of pretrial detention, since a hospital staff has less to gain from abusing a patient than the police have to gain from beating a confession out of a suspect. The problem of

neglect is largely one of resources and so cannot be solved simply by giving patients legally enforceable rights, especially since an individual suffering from a severe mental illness is an unlikely candidate to win a lawsuit. So here is another example of the merger of positive and negative liberties: the right to be decently treated in a psychiatric hospital depends as a practical matter on the allocation by society of adequate resources for psychiatric facilities. But like the rights of pretrial detainees, a right to decent treatment in psychiatric hospitals is two-edged. Suppose that a nation's budget for health care is essentially fixed. Increasing the resources devoted to psychiatric hospitals will reduce the resources available for other, and possibly as or more urgent, health-care needs. Once more a difficult tradeoff is inescapable.

A related problem, and one with a sinister resonance in the formerly communist nations, is that of improper commitment to mental institutions, or, what is closely related, that of failure to release a committed person when he has ceased to be a danger to himself or others. The difficulty, however, is that a generous construal of due process, designed to prevent improper commitment or retention, will also impede proper commitment and retention, resulting in more murders, other crimes, and suicides by the insane.

A similar tradeoff is required in the case of bail. Admitting criminal suspects to bail reduces the cost of jails and the costs to the innocent of being incarcerated mistakenly, but increases the amount of crime since many of the people released on bail are in fact criminals. As these examples illustrate, rights impose costs (not all of them monetary) as well as confer benefits. That, indeed, is the essential point that I make in this paper. It is a point that economists are not likely to ignore, but that lawyers, who reverence rights and are not professionally sensitive to cost, are likely to ignore. It illustrates the important role of economics in value clarification. By showing how much some much-desired good such as "rights" will cost in some other desired good forgone (all that the word "cost" means to an economist is what must be given up to obtain something desired), the economist forces society to decide how much it *really* values the good.

I have stated this as a normative point but it also has positive implications. The weak footing of rights in the ex-communist states is typically thought a legacy of the totalitarian past. It may instead be a matter of economics–of cost, not culture.

C. The third conference topic is the provision of competent lawyers for defendants in criminal cases. For affluent defendants, there should be no problem; the market will provide competent counsel. Most criminal defendants, however, certainly in the United States and presumably to an even greater degree in most other countries, are indigent. The direct costs of providing lawyers for indigent criminal lawyers are unlikely to be high. In the United States, Congress appropriates some $400 million a year for retaining or employing lawyers for indigent defendants in federal criminal cases.[12] Although only a small fraction of all criminal cases, federal cases are disproportionately complex, with the result that the total bill for the defense of the indigent, state and federal, is only $1.4 billion a year.[13] This is little more than $5 per American. Granted, the figure of $1.4 billion is an understatement. Some lawyers are pressured by judges to "volunteer" their services to indigent criminal defendants at below-market rates.[14] Others truly volunteer their services, but they do so either to obtain on-the-job training or as genuine charity, so in neither case is there a net cost to the volunteers. Nevertheless the total costs of defending the indigent are slight–and would be even slighter in a country with a lower crime rate[15] or with an inquisitorial rather than an adversarial system of criminal justice (since lawyers play a smaller role in an inquisitorial system)–were it not for indirect effects of the sort that I have mentioned. A represented defendant is more difficult to convict than an unrepresented one, so the provision of representation to indigent criminal defendants makes the criminal justice system more costly, and possibly less effective in deterring crime.

I say *possibly less effective* because a system of criminal justice in which innocent persons are frequently convicted may actually reduce the expected punishment cost of crime, since that cost is net of the expected punishment cost of not engaging in crime.[16] But it is not clear that denial of an automatic right to counsel in criminal cases would result in the frequent conviction of the innocent. When the crime rate is very high in relation to the resources allocated for prosecution, prosecutors will tend to select for prosecution only the strongest cases, and in general these will be the cases in which the defendant is least likely to be innocent. This selection effect will be weaker, however, in a nation that follows the German practice of mandatory prosecution rather than the U.S. practice of discretionary prosecution. It will also be weaker if the nation contains a disliked minority that has a high crime rate, such as gypsies in Hungary and Romania. It may be easier to convict an innocent member of that group than a guilty member of the majority. This was a serious problem in the southern states of the United States with respect to blacks as late as the 1950s and was an unacknowledged motive for the "Warren Court's" program of expanding the rights of criminal defendants.

Notice that if criminal law and procedure were so simplified that a person could defend himself without a lawyer's assistance, and if the resources allocated to prosecution were kept down so that prosecutors would be discouraged from pursuing (and were not required, by a principle of mandatory prosecution, to pursue) borderline cases, the overall costs of a criminal justice system might be extremely low yet the risk of convicting the innocent might also be low.

An extensive literature criticizes the current level at which the defense of indigent criminal defendants in the United States is funded as inadequate, noting the low quality of much of this representation.[17] I can confirm from my own experience as a judge that indigent defendants are generally rather poorly represented. But if we are to be hardheaded we must recognize that this is not entirely a bad thing. The lawyers who represent indigent criminal defendants are probably good enough to reduce the probability of convicting an innocent person to a very low level. If they were much better, either many guilty people would be acquitted or the state would have to devote much greater resources to the prosecution of criminal cases. Especially for a nonwealthy country (though possibly even for the United States), a "barebones" system for the defense of indigent criminal defendants may be optimal.

Here, though, is a complicating factor. If the law entitles a defendant to *effective* assistance of counsel, then paying lawyers too little to attract competent lawyers to defend indigent defendants may cost the system more in the long run by leading to retrials following a determination that the defendant's lawyer at his first trial was incompetent. But this observation is consistent with my suggestion that a nonwealthy nation may want to set a level of compensation generous enough to induce moderately, but not highly, competent lawyers to represent indigent criminal defendants.

A problem with the right to counsel that is unrelated to subsidization is that a wealthy defendant may be able to obtain an unjust acquittal by deploying a flock of pricey lawyers, overpowering a prosecutorial team that is underfunded. Poor countries often contain a number of very wealthy people—and have inadequate resources for prosecution.

Several participants in the conference emphasized the value of a criminal defendant's or suspect's lawyer as a witness to improper behavior by police or to substandard conditions in jails and prisons. This value is genuine but is largely independent of the lawyer's quality.

D. Delay in court is an old story, and a sad one; the slogan "justice delayed is justice denied" states an important truth. Remarkably, the enormous upsurge in case filings in the federal courts of the United States since 1960 has led to no increase in the court queue,[18] even though the increase in the number of judges has been much smaller than the increase in the number of cases. There are three reasons why the queue has not grown: Judges work harder; they delegate more of their work to nonjudges, such as law clerks;[19] and they have become more summary in their dispositions. These adaptations, though the last two have been widely criticized,[20] appear not to have lowered significantly the average quality of federal judicial output; and they may provide a model for other countries that encounter an upsurge in litigation.

A qualification is necessary, however. Court queues are to some extent self-limiting. The longer the queue, the greater the incentive to substitute arbitration or other nonjudicial methods of dispute resolution for the courts; there also may be greater pressure to settle the case rather than go to trial, though this is not certain.[21] Conversely, the shorter the queue, the

greater the demand for judicial services. The analogy is to adding lanes to a highway in order to relieve congestion. The resulting reduction in congestion will make the highway a more attractive travel route, drawing travelers from other roads and other modes of transportation. The net decrease in congestion may be slight. Similarly, a large investment in increasing judicial capacity in order to meet surging demand may have little effect on the court queue because the increase in capacity will attract people from other methods of dispute resolution into the courts.[22]

A judiciary is pretty cheap, even for a nonwealthy nation. The federal courts of the United States are generously funded. Federal judges are well paid (especially when their pensions are taken into account as of course they should be), and have large offices, large staffs, modern equipment, and tolerable although heavy workloads. Nevertheless, at a cost of only $2.3 billion, the federal courts in 1992 handled some 320,000 civil and criminal cases (not to mention an even larger number of bankruptcy filings),[23] which comes out to an average cost of less than $8000 per case. (Of course, these are only budgetary costs; the expense of lawyers is much more.) Court queues are short, except for civil jury trials in some of the larger cities; and the quality of the justice dispensed is certainly tolerable, and often distinguished.

E. The last specific right on which the conference has focused is the protection of health by public inspectors of restaurants and producers of food products. This example differs from the others in involving bureaucratic rather than judicial regulation. Here the danger of corruption is acute, because many inspectors are needed and they deal face-to-face with the managers of the establishments being inspected, which lowers the transaction costs of bribery. There are many techniques for dealing with the danger: Inspectors can be shifted about to avoid developing stable relationships with the establishments that they inspect. "Sting" tactics can be used to weed out dishonest inspectors (this is commonplace in the U.S. Postal Service). Severe punishments can be prescribed for both giving and accepting bribes. Standards of cleanliness can be set at minimum rather than optimum levels, so that it is easy for the establishments to satisfy them and therefore less urgent to bribe the inspectors to excuse noncompliance. Generous tort remedies can be provided for victims of food poisoning. The discretion of inspectors can be minimized, since it is easier to detect the violation of a rule than it is to detect an abuse of discretion. The sale of tainted food can be made a strict-liability crime (as has frequently been done in the United States), so that the seller's intent or even negligence need not be proved and his lack of evil intent and even his due care are not defenses. Employees of food establishments can be hired, or rewarded, as informers. The number of restaurants and other food producers can be limited, in order to generate monopoly profits for them and thus increase the cost of being forced to close by a food-poisoning incident.[24] The investigation of inspectors can be placed in a separate (and elite) agency from the inspectors themselves, to minimize fraternizing. And as in the case of the police, generous compensation, heavily backloaded, of inspectors can be used to increase the expected punishment costs of bribe-taking.

So many are the techniques for preventing the widespread corruption of food inspectors, and so obvious the social benefits from preventing lethal or epidemic diseases caused by bacteria in food,[25] that failure to prevent such corruption would be difficult to attribute to hardheaded economic tradeoffs such as the ones I have discussed in connection with other rights. I add that unless a society is completely disorganized, a food inspector is unlikely to accept a bribe to overlook a *lethal* danger, since if the danger materializes he is bound to be in very serious trouble.

We should not confine our consideration to lethal dangers, however. As Dr. van Rijckevorsel has emphasized in his paper for the conference,[26] nonlethal food poisoning is responsible for many days of lost work, as well as considerable suffering, and these costs may justify a substantial program of public food inspections. At the same time, it is important to bear in mind that if the standards to which food producers are required to adhere are set far above what is necessary to avoid serious food poisoning, corruption will be a great, perhaps an irresistible, temptation. We have known at least since George Orwell's *Down and Out in Paris and London* that the kitchens even of distinguished restaurants are often filthy, yet without

palpable harm being done to the clientele. And recent investigative reporting in the United States has revealed disgustingly unsanitary conditions in the processing of chickens, yet again seemingly with little danger to the public health. So it is possible that minimum standards of cleanliness, even when they are rather laxly enforced, in the production of food are adequate to protect the public health. In 1983, the most recent year for which I have the requisite data, the total cost, state and federal, of food inspection in the United States was only about $1 billion,[27] which again is only $4 per American; and perhaps that is enough, though I do not know enough about the subject to express a confident opinion.

The protection of the water supply is a more urgent task. The water supply is at once more vulnerable and more integrated; the same water sources are shared by far more people than share the same source of food. But the protection of the water supply is also much cheaper by virtue of its greater concentration.

I have mentioned corruption but the real dangers of corruption to a nation's prosperity lie elsewhere than in food inspection. When corruption, for example of tax collectors, drains off public revenues—and incidentally makes it difficult for the government to pay tax collectors wages generous enough to discourage them from accepting bribes—or when essential licenses to conduct business can be obtained only by bribing a sequence of officials, any one of whom can block the license, substantial macroeconomic consequences are possible.[28] The main solution to these problems is lower tax rates and less government regulation, which reduce the incentive to bribe public officials. The cost of this solution, political obstacles to one side, may actually be negative; reducing the size of government may stimulate output directly at the same time that it does so indirectly by reducing the amount of corruption. But that is a story for another day.

IV. I have said nothing about "culture" as a factor in the protection or enforcement of rights, except for a glancing reference to the U.S. civil liberties tradition. No doubt, despite my emphasis on the costs of rights, a nation's political and legal culture affects the extent to which rights are enforced, too. But as no one seems to know how to alter a culture, there is not much to be gained from dwelling on the point. This is not to say that cultures do not change; obviously they do. They change with wealth; history teaches that civil liberties are a superior good in the economist's sense, which is to say a good the demand for which grows with income. (This observation suggests that efforts to increase civil liberties without regard to their costs may impair those liberties in the long run.) My point is only that we do not know how to intervene directly to change a nation's political or legal culture. But within the limits imposed by a nation's existing culture there is much that can be done—and much that should *not* be done—if careful attention is paid to the economics of rights.

I have also not addressed, at least directly, the question of the *priority* that the protection and enforcement of rights should enjoy in a country that has a desperate shortage of resources. I believe that the protection of property rights and of basic political rights (including the right to vote and the freedom of the press—and both are checks on abuse of official power) is very important, but I do not myself attach similar importance to three of the five rights that were the focus of the conference. Apart from the points I made in discussing each of them, I note that as recently as thirty years ago, these three rights (protection from police brutality in pretrial detention, protection from custodial abuse in public psychiatric hospitals, and provision of a competent defense attorney to indigent criminal defendants) were not securely established in the United States, yet the United States was on the whole (granted, an important qualification) prosperous and free. The fourth right (reasonably prompt justice) and the fifth (effective food inspections) were securely established, and they are both important. But they are also, I believe, feasible even for a relatively poor country.

I am giving my personal view on the priority to be accorded these various rights. Other people, hav-

ing different values, may accord them a different priority. All that is important is that they proceed in full awareness that enforceable rights are not costless, or even cheap.

A more sophisticated analysis would consider not whether to recognize this right or that, but how much money to spend on each one. The fact that a right is relatively unimportant is not a good argument for spending nothing at all on it. Large social gains might be obtainable from very modest expenditures.[29] I glanced at this issue in discussing the right to assistance of counsel in a criminal case. I pointed out that a modest level of assistance might be sufficient to attract lawyers competent enough to obtain the acquittal of the innocent, whereas a higher level might, by attracting lawyers skillful enough to obtain the acquittal of many guilty defendants as well, on balance undermine rights, since criminals are rights infringers. I glanced at the issue again when I distinguished between levels of coercion in interrogation.

Obviously, however, much more work must be done before the optimal level of enforcing either particular rights or rights in general can be pinpointed, whether for the United States or for the nations of Central and Eastern Europe. This conference will have served its purpose if it has helped to launch and to guide this work.

Richard A. Posner is Chief Judge, United States Court of Appeals for the Seventh Circuit, and Senior Lecturer at the University of Chicago Law School. The author thanks David Friedman, Stephen Holmes, Dan Kahan, William Landes, Martha Nussbaum, Kim Scheppele, Stephen Schulhofer, and Cass Sunstein for helpful comments on an earlier draft of this paper and Kevin Cremin, Scott Gaille, Steven Neidhart, and Andrew Trask for valuable research assistance.

Notes:

1 I mean in their philosophical sense. I am not referring to the concept of "moral rights" as it is employed in European intellectual-property laws.

2 They may be indirectly productive. Public education, for example, may overcome the unwillingness or inability of parents to invest optimally in the human capital (earning capacity) of their children.

3 Aggregate private expenditures on preventing crime in the United States have been estimated to be in the area of $300 billion a year, Amy Kaslow, "The High Cost of Crime," *Christian Science Monitor*, May 9, 1994, p. 9, which far exceeds public expenditures, as we shall see. The importance of private self-protection against crime is emphasized in Tomas J. Philipson and Richard A. Posner, "Public

Health and the Natural Rate of Crime" (June 1995, unpublished).

4 U.S. Dept. of Justice, Bureau of Justice Statistics, *Justice Expenditure and Employment in the US*, 1988 xix (Aug. 1991, NCF-125619) (tab. F) (1988 statistics).

5 It obviously would not pay to try to extirpate crime completely. Expenditures on criminal law enforcement must not be carried to the point where the last dollar of expenditures buys less than a dollar's worth of benefits (however benefits are computed) in reduced criminal activity.

6 See Isaac Ehrlich and George D. Brower, "On the Issue of Causality in the Economic Model of Crime and Law Enforcement: Some Theoretical Considerations and Experimental Evidence," 77 *American Economic Review* 99 (May 1989). The source for Fgure 1 is Figure 2 in Philipson and Posner, note 3 above, at 21, which is based on National Crime Survey (NCS) data. The increase in the homicide rate understates the increase in the propensity to commit homicide and in the total costs of homicide and its prevention, since an increased risk of criminal behavior induces increased efforts at self-protection by the potential victims of crime, dampening the increase in the actual crime rate.

7 A clue is the enormous increase in the educational level of police in the United States. Between 1960 and 1970—the heyday of the "Warren Court"—the percentage of police with some college education rose from 20 to 31.8 percent. U.S. Dept. of Justice, National Institute of Law Enforcement and Criminal Justice, *The National Manpower Survey of the Criminal Justice System*, vol. 5: *Criminal Justice Education and Training* 138 (1978) (tab. IV-1). The increased complexity of criminal procedure required more educated police, since they are the front-line administrators of the criminal justice system and their legal mistakes make successful prosecution of criminals impossible.

8 In economic terms, the expected cost of punishment, a measure of deterrence, is EC = pS, where p is the probability of apprehension and conviction and S is the sentence. If a court-created right leads to a reduction in p for both innocent and guilty defendants (and that is the likeliest consequence, since a right that makes it more difficult to convict an innocent person will also make it more difficult to convict a guilty one), and the legislature wishes to maintain EC at its previous level, it can do so either by raising S through a law increasing the penalties for crime or by raising p through a reduction in funding for the defense of indigent defendants. Both have in fact been legislative responses in the United States to perceived judicial excesses in the protection of the rights of criminal defendants and to the increased crime rates that may be, in part, a consequence of that protection.

9 I mentioned the increased educational level of the police. See note 7 above. By 1974, the percentage of police with some college education had risen to 46.2 percent, compared to only 20 percent in 1960. U.S. Dept. of Justice, note 7 above, at 138 (tab. IV-1).

10 A requirement that all confessions be videotaped might alleviate this problem, though it would be an expensive requirement for a nonwealthy nation and might be ineffective, since the police might not begin the videotaping until they had coerced the suspect's agreement to confess. This of course is why requiring that a confession be signed is not a secure preventive of coerced confessions.

11 This compensation, as in the case of judges, should be "backloaded" to maximize the deterrent effect of the threat to fire the employee for misconduct. If the employee has generous pension benefits that are forfeited if he is fired for misconduct, then even in the last period of his employment, and even if the chance of his actually being detected (if he misbehaves) and fired is quite low, he will have a strong incentive to behave himself. See, for example, Gary S. Becker and George J. Stigler, "Law Enforcement, Malfeasance, and Compensation of Enforcers," 3 *Journal of Legal Studies* 1 (1974); Richard A. Ippolito, "The Implicit Pension Contract: Developments and New Directions," 22 *Journal of Human Resources* 441 (1987).

12 U.S. Dept. of Justice, note 4 above, at xix (tab. F).

13 Id.

14 This is a less efficient measure than using tax revenues to hire lawyers to represent the indigent,

since it interferes with the allocation of lawyer time in accordance with the principle of comparative advantage. A corporate lawyer might find himself assigned to defend a criminal, even though he had no experience in criminal law.

15 The United Kingdom, for example, with a population almost a fourth the size of the U.S. population, has only one-twentieth the number of jail and prison inmates. *A Digest of Information on the Criminal Justice System: Crime and Justice in England and Wales* 56 (Home Office Research and Statistical Department, Gordon C. Barclay ed. 1991).

16 In the limit, if the probability of being convicted were independent of guilt or innocence, the prospect of punishment would not provide any inducement to avoid committing crimes.

17 See Stephen J. Schulhofer and David D. Friedman, "Rethinking Indigent Defense: Promoting Effective Representation through Consumer Sovereignty and Freedom of Choice for All Criminal Defendants," 31 *American Criminal Law Review* 73 (1993), and references cited there.

18 See *Annual Report of the Director of the Administrative Office of the United States Courts*, various years.

19 Between 1960 and 1994, the percentage of federal judicial employees who were full-fledged ("Article III") judges fell from 10.1 percent to 3.2 percent.

20 As creating "assembly-line justice." I think it is wrong to denigrate the analogy of the assembly line, which marked a big advance over previous methods of production. On the resistance of the legal profession to modernization, see my book *Overcoming Law*, ch. 1 (1995).

21 See Richard A. Posner, *Economic Analysis of Law* 556-59 (4th ed. 1992).

22 Id. at 579.

23 The source for these statistics is, again, the *Annual Report of the Director of the Administrative Office of the United States Courts* for various years.

24 This is a parallel measure to "overpaying" police or inspectors in order to increase the penalty to them of being detected in misconduct and losing their jobs.

25 As suggested by the fact that in 1990 Mexico reported 6323 cases of cholera, the United States 6, and Canada 1. Donna U. Vogt, "NAFTA: Cross-Border Health and Food Safety Concerns," *Mexico Trade and Law Reporter*, Jan. 1993, pp. 24, 25 (tab. 1).

26 Jan L. A. van Rijckevorsel, "On Food Law and Its Enforcement" (June 16, 1995).

27 See William Patrick, *The Food and Drug Administration* 230-231 (1988).

28 The economics of corruption is the subject of an extensive literature well represented by Andrei Shleifer and Robert W. Vishny, "Corruption," 103 *Quarterly Journal of Economics* 599 (1993).

29 This is just the point in note 5 that expenditures on the protection and enforcement of rights should be guided by a comparison of *marginal* benefits and costs.

PART II

CRIMINAL LAW

COLUMBIA LAW REVIEW

VOL. 85   OCTOBER 1985   NO. 6

AN ECONOMIC THEORY OF THE CRIMINAL LAW

Richard A. Posner*

INTRODUCTION

The economic analysis of criminal law began on a very high plane in the eighteenth and early nineteenth centuries with the work of Beccaria and Bentham,[1] but its revival in modern times dates only from 1968, when Gary Becker's article on the economics of crime and punishment appeared.[2] Since then there has been an outpouring of economic work on criminal law, concentrated in the following areas: the optimal tradeoff between certainty and severity of punishment, the comparative economic properties of fines and imprisonment, the economics of law enforcement and criminal procedure, and above all the deterrent and preventive effects of criminal punishment (including capital punishment).[3] Notice, however, what is missing from this list: the substantive doctrines and concepts of criminal law, about which there has been little economic writing.[4] This is in striking contrast to the

---

* Judge, U.S. Court of Appeals for the Seventh Circuit; Senior Lecturer, University of Chicago Law School. I am grateful to Gary S. Becker, Isaac Ehrlich, George P. Fletcher, William M. Landes, Geoffrey P. Miller, Norval Morris, A. Mitchell Polinsky, Steven Shavell, Steven J. Shulhofer, A.W.B. Simpson, George J. Stigler, and participants in the Law and Economics Workshop and the Seminar on Rational Choice Methods in Social Sciences (both at the University of Chicago), for helpful comments on a previous draft of this Article, and to John H. Langbein for discussion of the subject matter of the Article. The Article was stimulated in part by critical remarks on the economic approach to criminal law made by George Fletcher at a conference held on November 16, 1984, on New Directions in Law and Economics, sponsored by Columbia Law School's Center for Law and Economic Studies.

1. See C. Beccaria, On Crimes and Punishments (H. Paolucci trans. 1963); J. Bentham, An Introduction to the Principles of Morals and Legislation, *in* 1 Works of Jeremy Bentham 1, 86–91 (J. Bowring ed. 1843); J. Bentham, Principles of Penal Law, *in* 1 Works of Jeremy Bentham, supra, at 365.

2. See Becker, Crime and Punishment: An Economic Approach, 76 J. Pol. Econ. 169 (1968).

3. For a comprehensive bibliography of research on the economics of crime and punishment to 1980, see The Economics of Crime 411–26 (R. Andreano & J. Siegfried eds. 1980); and for an excellent review of almost the entire literature, see D. Pyle, The Economics of Crime and Law Enforcement (1983).

There is also some interesting literature on the economics of organized crime. See, e.g., P. Reuter, Disorganized Crime: The Economics of the Visible Hand (1983); T. Schelling, Choice and Consequence: Perspectives of an Errant Economist chs. 7–8 (1984).

4. There is a short treatment of substantive issues of criminal law—the germ of this Article—in my economic analysis text. See R. Posner, Economic Analysis of Law ch. 7 (2d ed. 1977). Both Becker, supra note 2, and Stigler, The Optimum Enforcement of

situation with respect to tort law, though tort and criminal law are closely related. Tort notions seem to lend themselves to economic translation and elaboration—the Learned Hand formula for negligence being the most dramatic example[5]—while the concepts that dominate the substantive criminal law, such as attempt, conspiracy, entrapment, insanity, and premeditation, seem alien to the economist's way of thinking about problems. In particular, the pervasive emphasis placed in the criminal law on punishing harmless preparatory activity, on the mental state of the accused, and, related to both points, on the moral character rather than the consequences of behavior, suggests a decidedly noneconomic perspective.

But I think this is wrong, and that the substantive doctrines of the criminal law, as of the common law in general, can be given an economic meaning and can indeed be shown to promote efficiency.[6] That, at any rate, is the burden of this Article. I certainly do not want to be understood, however, as arguing that every rule of the criminal law is efficient, or that efficiency is or ought to be the only social value consid-

---

Laws, 78 J. Pol. Econ. 526 (1970), written in response to Becker, also touch on some substantive issues, and in so doing anticipate (by many years!) some of the analysis of substantive criminal law doctrine in this Article. A paper by Steven Shavell, originally written in 1980, contains many parallels to my own analysis. I had not read his paper before completing the first draft of mine, and although I have read it since and revised my own, I have made no changes based on his analysis. I have thus refrained from discussing the principles of causation in criminal law, a topic omitted from my original draft and one on which Shavell's paper contains a fascinating discussion. See Shavell, Criminal Law and the Optimal Use of Nonmonetary Sanctions as a Deterrent, 85 Colum. L. Rev. 1232 (1985).

Skepticism about the prospects for a positive economic theory of substantive criminal law is the leitmotif of the papers—all but mine, of course—in Nomos XXVII: Criminal Justice pt. IV (J. Pennock & J. Chapman eds. 1985). In the same vein, see Seidman, Soldiers, Martyrs, and Criminals: Utilitarian Theory and the Problem of Crime Control, 94 Yale L.J. 315 (1984). As I said in my paper in *Nomos*, "[t]he problem with the economic analysis of criminal law is not that it is incomplete or lacks rigorous philosophical foundations, though it is and does, but that the economic analysts have yet to tackle the principal concepts that trouble legal analysts of the field—such concepts as attempt, conspiracy, diminished responsibility, provocation, insanity, strict criminal liability, recklessness, compulsion or necessity, and premeditation." Posner, Comment on *On the Economic Theory of Crime*, in Nomos XXVII: Criminal Justice, at 310, 311 (J. Pennock & J. Chapman eds. 1984). This Article, like Shavell's, supra, is an effort to repair the omission.

5. See United States v. Carroll Towing Co., 159 F.2d 169 (2d Cir. 1947); see also R. Posner, Tort Law: Cases and Economic Analysis ch. 1 (1982) (discussing formula); Landes & Posner, The Positive Economic Theory of Tort Law, 15 Ga. L. Rev. 851, 884–85 (1981) (same).

The Hand formula of negligence is $B < PL$, where B is the burden of precaution, P is the probability of an accident if B is omitted, and L is the magnitude of the loss if the accident occurs. If $B < PL$, then B is cost-justified, and omitting B is negligent.

6. On the "efficiency theory" of the common law, see, e.g., R. Posner, supra note 4, pt. II; R. Posner, supra note 5; Landes & Posner, supra note 5. Although criminal law is no longer a pure common law field, most of its doctrines are of common law rather than statutory origin.

ered by legislatures and courts in creating and interpreting the rules of the criminal law.

My analysis can be summarized in the following propositions:

1. The major function of criminal law in a capitalist society is to prevent people from bypassing the system of voluntary, compensated exchange—the "market," explicit or implicit—in situations where, because transaction costs are low, the market is a more efficient method of allocating resources than forced exchange. Market bypassing in such situations is inefficient—in the sense in which economists equate efficiency with wealth maximization[7]—no matter how much utility it may confer on the offender.

2. Much of this market bypassing cannot be deterred by tort law—that is, by privately enforced damage suits. The optimal damages that would be required for deterrence would so frequently exceed the offender's ability to pay that public enforcement and nonmonetary sanctions such as imprisonment[8] are required.

3. Such sanctions are extremely costly for a variety of reasons, and this, together with the socially worthless character of most of the sanctioned conduct, has a number of implications for efficient criminal law doctrine, such as that unsuccessful attempts should be punished in order to economize on costlier punishments for completed crimes. The threat of punishing attempts, as we shall see, makes the completed crime more costly in an expected sense and therefore less likely to be committed. I contend that the main differences between substantive criminal law and substantive tort law can be derived from the differences in (1) the social costs of criminal and tort sanctions and (2) the social benefits of the underlying conduct regulated by these two bodies of law. I contend, in short, that most of the distinctive doctrines of the criminal law can be explained as if the objective of that law were to promote economic efficiency.

I. THE FUNCTION OF CRIMINAL LAW

A. *An Economic Typology of Crimes*

In this section I try to derive the basic criminal prohibitions from the concept of efficiency; I argue that what is forbidden is a class of inefficient acts. As this is a controversial endeavor I think it important to note that the rest of the Article does not depend on it—that it would be little affected if I took as given that society wants to prevent the acts that it calls murder, theft, rape, etc., and did not inquire why.

When transaction costs are low, the market is, virtually by definition, the most efficient method of allocating resources. Attempts to by-

---

7. See R. Posner, The Economics of Justice 66–107 (1981).

8. Even the fine, we shall see, is not a purely monetary sanction equivalent to tort damages.

pass the market will therefore be discouraged by a legal system bent on promoting efficiency. If I covet my neighbor's car, it is more efficient to force me to negotiate with my neighbor—to pay him his price—than it is to allow me to take his car subject to being required by a court to pay the neighbor whatever the court decides the car is worth. If I happen to have no money but want a car, it would be inefficient to let me just take a car. Indeed, unlike the first case, this transfer cannot possibly improve the allocation of resources—that is, it cannot move resources from a less to a more valuable employment—because value is a function of willingness to pay. Since I am unwilling (because unable—but it does not matter why) to pay my neighbor's price for the car, it follows that the car would be less valuable in an economic sense in my hands than in his.[9] Moreover, if I am allowed to take the car I will have an incentive to expend resources on taking it and my neighbor will have an incentive to expend resources on preventing it from being taken, and these expenditures considered as a whole, yield no social product.

In short, it is inefficient to allow pure coercive transfers of wealth—"pure" implying that the transfer is not an incident of a productive act. But this is an important qualification. The invention of a new product or process can also cause all sorts of wealth transfers that are involuntary from the standpoint of the losers, but invention increases, as well as transfers, wealth in a way that merely taking someone's wealth from him does not. Invention is not just a coercive or involuntary transfer, and it would be infeasible to force the inventor to identify and negotiate terms of compensation with all the losers.

The role of the criminal law in discouraging market bypassing is obscured by the fact that the market transaction that the criminal bypasses is usually not a transaction with his victim. If someone steals my car, normally it is not because he wants *that* car and would have bought it from me if the criminal law had deterred him from stealing it. He steals to get money to use in buying goods and services from other people. The market transaction that he bypasses is the exchange of his labor for money in a lawful occupation. But it is still market bypassing.

Although the market-bypassing approach provides a straightforward economic rationale for forbidding theft and other acquisitive crimes—such as burglary, robbery, fraud (false pretenses), embezzlement, extortion (by threat of violence), most kidnapping, some murder, some assault and battery, some rape—we must also consider "crimes of passion," which loom large in thinking about the criminal law and which may seem to have nothing to do with bypassing markets. Such crimes can be defined in economic terms as crimes motivated by inter-

---

9. The car might, of course, confer more utility (pleasure, satisfaction) on me than on my neighbor, but there is a difference between utility in a broad utilitarian sense and value in a (perhaps narrow) economic sense, where value is measured by willingness to pay for what is not yours already, or willingness to accept payment for what is yours. See R. Posner, supra note 7, at 66–67; infra text following note 10.

dependent negative utilities. An example is murdering someone because you hate him rather than because you want his money. These are not wealth transfers in any obvious sense and may seem to have nothing to do with bypassing the market. It might seem, therefore, that before we could pronounce such conduct inefficient we would have to compare the offender's utility with the victim's disutility.[10] We could not do this without exceeding the conventional limits of economics, which do not allow interpersonal comparisons of utilities, just as we could not describe a theft as efficient because the impecunious thief would derive greater pleasure from his act than the pain suffered by his wealthy victim.

Now as a matter of fact it is a pretty safe empirical guess that most such conduct does create net disutility. The whole idea is to inflict as much disutility on the victim as possible, and it is unlikely that every disutile experienced by the wretched victim confers an equal and opposite utile on the offender. Indeed, there would seem to be a fundamental asymmetry between the pleasure that one would obtain from killing another person who has sullied one's honor, and the victim's pain, broadly defined to include the disutility to him of losing his life. But I want to emphasize four other economic, rather than utilitarian, points:

1. Coercion arising from interdependent negative utilities cannot increase the wealth of society and therefore cannot be an efficient act. If A kills B because the resulting disutility to B confers utility on A, the wealth of the society is not increased even in the unlikely event that the total amount of human happiness is increased.

2. The dichotomy between acquisitive crimes and crimes of passion is overstated. Acquisitive crimes bypass explicit markets; crimes of passion often bypass implicit markets—for example, in friendship, love, respect—that are the subject of a growing economic literature illustrated by Becker's work on the family.[11] Less obviously, crimes of passion often bypass explicit markets too. The essential characteristic of a market, and the source of the ethical appeal of market systems, is that in a market people have to be compensated for parting with the things that have value to them, unless transaction costs are prohibitive. Someone who gets his satisfactions in life from beating up other people, without compensating them, rather than from engaging in trade with them is thus bypassing explicit markets. This point is obscured by the fact, noted earlier in the context of acquisitive crimes, that the victims of the crimes and the people that the aggressor would be trading with if he were not committing crimes are different people.

To sum up, one who spends his time brawling rather than working

---

10. This is a common criticism of attempts to apply economics to deliberate wrongdoing. See, e.g., Ellis, An Economic Theory of Intentional Torts: A Comment, 3 Int'l Rev. L. & Econ. 45 (1983).

11. See G. Becker, A Treatise on the Family (1981).

is bypassing an explicit market;[12] if he spent his time raping rather than dating women he would be bypassing an implicit market. The essential point in both cases is that he would not be deriving his satisfactions in life from acts that confer benefits on other people.

3. Allowing coercion would create incentives for potential victims to spend heavily on self-protection and for potential aggressors to spend heavily on overcoming the victims' self-protective efforts. All this spending would yield little if any net social product.

4. Some crimes of passion are costly and inefficient efforts at self-help. *A* slanders *B*, and *B*, instead of suing *A*, kills him. The suit would have given *B* almost the satisfaction that killing *A* did, and at far lower social cost.

It may clarify the analysis to consider two seemingly more problematic examples of the concept of crime as pure coercive transfer:

(1) *Counterfeiting.* This can be viewed as a form of theft by false pretenses, the false pretense being that the "payor" is actually paying. The victim is whoever has the money when it is discovered to be counterfeit. Even if the counterfeiting is never discovered so that no individual or firm suffers a loss, counterfeiting imposes a social cost measured by the resources consumed in counterfeiting and in trying to prevent counterfeiting and also by the social costs of the inflation caused by counterfeiting. An increase in the stock of currency will have an inflationary effect—a very considerable one if counterfeiting is not punished at all.

Actually, the counterfeiter whose counterfeiting is never discovered differs from the thief only in the number of his victims. Both take slices of the social pie without putting in anything in return, but the victims of the undiscovered counterfeiter are all those who pay higher prices as a result of the increase in the amount of currency in circulation.

All of this assumes that even if counterfeiting is not a crime, counterfeit money is not legal tender. If it is, there can be no individual victims of counterfeiting, but incentives to work and save will be totally undermined. Anyone who wants anything will simply print up some money and "buy" the thing he wants.

(2) *Rape.* Suppose a rapist derives extra pleasure from the coercive character of his act. Then there would be (it might seem) no market substitute for rape, suggesting that rape is not a pure coercive transfer and should not, on economic grounds, anyway, be punished criminally. But the argument would be weak:

(a) Because there are heavy penalties for rape, the rapes that take place—that have not been deterred—may indeed be weighted toward a form of rape for which there are no consensual substitutes; it does not

---

12. Professional boxing would be an example of a lawful market alternative to battery.

follow that the rape that is deterred is generally of this character.[13]

(b) Put differently, the prohibition against rape is to the marriage and sex "market" as the prohibition against theft is to explicit markets in goods and services.[14]

(c) Given the economist's definition of "value," even if the rapist cannot find a consensual substitute (and one such substitute, prostitution, is itself illegal), it does not follow that he values the rape more than the victim disvalues it. There is a difference between a coerced transaction that has no consensual substitute and one necessary to overcome the costs of consensual transactions; only the second can create wealth, and therefore be efficient. Indeed, what the argument boils down to is that some rape is motivated in part or whole by the negative interdependence of the parties' utilities, and this, as I have argued in connection with crimes of passion, is no reason for considering the act efficient.

(d) As with my earlier discussion of crimes of passion, it is important not to take too narrow a view of market alternatives. Supposing it to be true that some rapists would not get as much pleasure from consensual sex, it does not follow that there are no other avenues of satisfaction open to them. It may be that instead of furtively stalking women they can obtain satisfactions from productive activities, that is, activities in which other people are compensated and thus derive benefits. This is an additional reason to think that the total wealth of society would be increased if rape could be completely repressed at a reasonable cost.

All this may seem to be a hopelessly labored elucidation of the obvious, that rape is a bad thing; but I think it useful to point out that economic analysis need not break down in the face of such apparently noneconomic phenomena as rape.

All of the pure coercive transfers that I have discussed are intentional torts at common law; and the subset of intentional torts that consists of pure coercive transfers (not all intentional torts are such) represents the largest category of criminal acts. Let us call them category (1). There are, however, several other categories:

(2) Tax evasion, price-fixing, and other examples of nonproduc-

---

13. This is a general problem with inferring the character of criminal conduct from observations of actual criminals. Not only are the observations limited to the criminals who are caught, but, more importantly, they are by definition limited to criminals who are not deterred by what are rather heavy penalties even when discounted by the small probability of actually punishing most criminal acts. Observed criminal conduct must have more of a mad dog character than the deterred conduct would have if it were not deterred.

14. This is suggested by the high fraction of rapes—approaching 50% in some surveys—in which the rapist and the victim have a prior acquaintance. See McDermott, Rape Victimization in 26 Cities 51 (Law Enforcement Assistance Admin., U.S. Dep't of Justice (1979)) (Analytic Rep. SD-VAD-6, App. A).

tive wealth-shifting conduct made criminal by statute. In contrast, category (1) crimes were punishable at common law.

(3) Voluntary exchanges incidental to activities that the state has outlawed. Some examples are pimping and prostitution, engaging in deviant (but voluntary) sexual relations, selling pornography, selling babies for adoption, selling regulated transportation services at prices not listed in the carrier's published tariffs, and trafficking in narcotics.

(4) Certain menacing but nontortious preparatory acts such as unsuccessfully attempting or conspiring to murder someone where the victim is not injured and the elements of a tortious attempt are not present. They would not be present if, for example, the victim did not know of the attempt at the time it was made.

(5) Conduct that if allowed would thwart other forms of common law or statutory regulation. Examples are leaving the scene of an accident, bribing judges and other public officials, and fraudulently concealing assets from a judgment creditor.

(6) Blackmail, and certain other forms of private law enforcement when these are made criminal.

Categories (3) and (6) create obvious difficulties for a positive economic analysis of law. It is hard for an economist to understand why the voluntary exchange of valuable goods should be criminal. Such exchange, prima facie at least, promotes rather than reduces efficiency—whether it concerns hard-core or soft-core pornography, cocaine or cigarettes, common carriage or contract carriage. The qualification is important, however. Voluntary transactions may have such serious effects on third parties that when those effects are taken into account the transaction is not value-maximizing after all.[15]

Category (6) is mysterious because it might seem that blackmailers, vigilantes, and others who prey on criminals would be valued auxiliaries in the war on crime rather than criminals themselves. Informers *are* valued auxiliaries; why should not blackmailers be? Like informers they are private enforcers of the community's ethical norms, including those embodied in the criminal law. Although the question is too difficult to be done complete justice to here, I shall venture to suggest an answer, though not a complete one, as it is inapplicable to the punishment of one who blackmails with discreditable but not incriminating information.

A person who learns that someone else is a criminal could in a regime that allowed blackmail either sell the information to the police—police pay informers, sometimes handsomely—or sell secrecy to the criminal. By outlawing sale to the criminal, society reduces the price of information to the police (by removing a competitor from the buying side of the market) and at the same time raises expected punish-

---

15. Whether any or all of the examples I have given should be condemned on this ground is not a question examined in this Article.

ment costs to the criminal. For it is not true that the money the criminal pays the blackmailer is equal to the punishment costs he would undergo if he were convicted and sentenced for his crime. As we shall see, most criminals cannot pay optimal fines—and their ability to pay puts a ceiling on what the blackmailer can extract from them. It might seem, however, that if the criminal cannot bid on the information, informers will have lower incomes, so there will be less informing and expected punishment costs will decline. But the police can (in principle, at least) control the level of informing by the prices they pay informers; it is not necessary to admit the criminal into the market.

B. Why Isn't Tort Law Enough of a Social Control?

Although the major criminal prohibitions seem explicable as measures for discouraging inefficient behavior rather than for achieving moral objectives that economics may not be able to explain—the major exception being the prohibition of victimless crimes—this does not explain why there is a criminal law, given that there is a law of torts and that it predates criminal law.[16] An explanation of why the six categories of criminal activity have not and cannot be left to tort law leaps to mind for categories (3) and (4): no one is hurt, at least in any very direct sense. But the answer is superficial because society could allow whomever the law was intended to protect to sue for punitive damages. A better answer is that detection is difficult where there is no victim to report and testify against the wrongdoer. The answer is incomplete because, as we shall see, punitive damages can be adjusted upward to take account of the difficulty of detection. In principle, this device could take care of category (5) crimes as well. But as we shall also see, the higher the optimal level of punitive damages, the less likely they are to be collectable.

Another question about categories (3) and (4) is, why punish acts that do not hurt anybody? For category (3) the answer lies, as I have said, outside of economics, or at least outside the scope of this Article. For category (4) the answer is bound up with the question of why tort law is not adequate to deal with categories (1) and (2) (coerced transfers in violation of common law or statutory principles). The proper sanction for a pure coercive transfer is something greater than the law's estimate of the victim's loss—the extra something being designed to confine transfers to the market whenever market-transaction costs are not prohibitive.[17] We can be a little more precise: the extra something should be the difference between the victim's loss and the offender's gain, and then some. To understand this, assume first that the gain is greater than the loss: *B* has a jewel worth $1000 to him, but worth

---

16. See R. Posner, supra note 7, at 192, 203–04.
17. See Calabresi & Melamed, Property Rules, Liability Rules, and Inalienability: One View of the Cathedral, 85 Harv. L. Rev. 1089 (1972).

$10,000 to *A*, who steals it ("converts" it, in tort parlance). We want to channel transactions in jewelry into the market, and this requires that the coerced transfer be a losing proposition to *A*.[18] If *A* is risk neutral, if the probability of *B*'s getting and collecting a judgment against *A* is one (an important assumption, to be relaxed shortly), and if legal proceedings are costless, then making *A* liable for damages of only $1000 will not do the trick, and even making him pay $10,000 (restitution) will not quite do it, but will just make him indifferent between stealing and buying. We shall have to add something on, and make the damages, say, $11,000.

Of course, the jewel might be worth less to *A* (or to its ultimate purchaser from *A*) than to *B*, since *A* is not planning to pay for it. In that event a smaller fine would deter *A* given our assumption that the probability of punishment is one. If the jewel is worth only $500 to *A*, damages of $501 will be enough. But as we cannot determine subjective values, we shall want to base damages on the market value of the jewel (especially since if the subjective value is lower than market value, he can sell, and thus realize that value as his gain from the theft, less any expenses of sale), and then add on a hefty bonus to take account of the possibility that the thief may place a higher subjective value on the jewel than does the victim.

With regard to crimes of violence, such as murder, battery, and rape, which inflict nonpecuniary as well as or instead of pecuniary loss, it is not so easy to set a money value on the victim's loss, although tort law does of course make such estimates. Quite properly, they often are very high. For a crime that creates a substantial probability of death, the optimal damages may in fact be astronomical. This is clearest in the case where one person deliberately kills another. If the average person (someone not extraordinarily altruistic toward his heirs) were asked how much money he would demand to surrender his life on the spot, his answer would be that no finite offer would be high enough, since he would get no utility out of the money. For similar reasons, the average person would demand a very high price to incur a substantial risk of death even though he might demand only a small premium to take a small risk of death.[19] This nonlinearity suggests why tort law may be adequate for many small risks of death (for example, the risk of being killed in an automobile accident caused by negligence), but not for the large risks that are created by crimes of violence.

---

18. Of course, if we really knew the respective values to *A* and *B*, the superiority of market to coercive transactions would be less marked. It is precisely because subjective values are hard to determine except as revealed in markets that a market system is economically and ethically attractive. The example is therefore unrealistic—but its purpose is didactic rather than descriptive.

19. For good summaries of the literature on risk premia and the value of life, see Dardis, The Value of a Life: New Evidence from the Marketplace, 70 Am. Econ. Rev. 1077 (1980); Nichols, The Regulation of Airborne Benzene, *in* Incentives for Environmental Protection 145, 173–75 (T. Schelling ed. 1983).

Optimal tort deterrence of the pure coercive transfer would require even heavier punitive damages than suggested thus far, for we have ignored the problem of concealment. Being a byproduct of lawful public activities, accidents usually are difficult to conceal. But when the tortfeasor's whole object is to take something of value, he will naturally try to conceal what he is doing and will often succeed. Subject to qualifications not necessary to address here, the formula for deciding how large an award of damages (D) must be if the probability (p) that the tortfeasor will actually be caught and forced to pay the damages is less than one is

$$D = L/p \qquad\qquad (1)$$

where L is the harm caused by the tortfeasor in the case in which he is caught, and includes any adjustment to discourage bypassing the market by a coerced transfer. If $p = 1$, L and D are the same amount. But if, for example, $L = \$10,000$ and $p = .1$, meaning that nine times out of ten the tortfeasor escapes the clutches of the law, then D, the optimal penalty, is $\$100,000$. Only then is the expected penalty cost to the prospective tortfeasor (pD) equal to the harm of his act (L).

Once damages for the pure coercive transfer are adjusted upward to discourage efforts to bypass the market, to recognize the nonlinear relationship between risk of death and compensation for bearing that risk, and to offset concealment, it becomes apparent that the optimal damages will often be very great—greater, in many cases, than the tortfeasor's ability to pay. This is further true because bonding or compulsory insurance cannot be used to bring monetary incentives to bear on people who lack substantial liquid assets when those people are deliberate tortfeasors. It generally is impossible to buy insurance against intentional misconduct, because of the acute moral-hazard problem.[20] Also, coercive transfers are more attractive to the poor than to the rich, since the poor have only a limited ability to use the market as an alternative route to getting their wants satisfied. The problem, then, is not only that the optimal penalty for pure coercive or involuntary transfers is high relative to the average person's wealth, but also that it is extremely high relative to the wealth of the people most likely to consider attempting to bring about such transfers.

This has not always and everywhere been true. Primitive and ancient societies (including Anglo-Saxon England) have relied much more heavily than has our society on a form of tort damages (usually fixed in amount rather than assessed individually in each case)—"bloodwealth," "wergeld," "composition"—to control crime, apparently with some success. Among the things that make this approach feasible in such societies are the lack of personal privacy, which makes

---

20. The moral hazard is the danger that the insured will be induced by the fact that he has insurance to commit the act against which he has insured and thereby escape the costs of the act while reaping its benefits.

probabilities of apprehension and conviction high, and the principle of collective responsibility, which makes the offender's kinship group liable for his damages, thus enabling the society to set fines that exceed the individual's ability to pay.[21]

Three responses to the problem in our society of the infeasibility of primary reliance on fines to deter antisocial behavior are possible (enforcement responses—I exclude as beyond the scope of this Article such alternatives as reducing inequalities of wealth), and all are used. One is to impose disutility in nonmonetary forms, such as imprisonment or death. Another is to reduce the probability of concealment, and so lower D in equation (1), by maintaining a police force to investigate crimes.[22] A third response, which involves both the maintenance of a police force and the punishment of preparatory acts (category (4)), is to prevent criminal activity before it occurs. If, as seems a good guess but no more than that, economies of scale, coupled with the danger to political stability of encouraging the growth of private armies, make public policing more efficient than private, the state is in the enforcement picture (whether or not prosecution itself, as distinct from policing, is public or private) and thus has a claim to any monetary penalties imposed. Hence these penalties are paid to the state as fines rather than to the victims of crime as damages. The victims can seek damages if the crime is also a tort, whether common law or statutory. The optimality of this feature is discussed briefly in Part III.

In cases where tort remedies, including punitive damages, are an adequate deterrent because they do not strain the potential defendant's ability to pay, there is no need to invoke criminal penalties—penalties which, as we shall see in the next part, are costlier than civil penalties even when just a fine is imposed. In such cases, the misconduct probably will be deterred. If in a particular case it is not, even though the tort remedy is set at the correct level and there is no solvency problem to interfere with it, so that the tort remedy must actually be applied to maintain the credibility of the tort deterrent, there still is no social gain from using a criminal sanction.[23] Although in some cases, notably antitrust cases, affluent defendants are both prosecuted criminally and sued civilly, criminal sanctions generally are reserved, as theory predicts, for cases where the tort remedy bumps up against a solvency limitation.

This means that the criminal law is designed primarily for the

---

21. See R. Posner, supra note 7, at 197.

22. An alternative would be to pay bounties to private enforcers, but that involves technical difficulties discussed in Landes & Posner, The Private Enforcement of Law, 4 J. Legal Stud. 1 (1975).

23. Tort remedies do not operate with perfect efficacy. If they did, there would never be a litigated tort case. But the occasional, and inevitable, failures of the tort system do not in themselves provide a strong argument for criminal remedies. Those remedies are necessary for classes of cases where tort law is bound to fail, as where the defendants cannot pay tort damages and therefore are not deterred by the threat of being ordered to pay them.

nonaffluent; the affluent are kept in line, for the most part, by tort law. This may seem to be a left-wing kind of suggestion ("criminal law keeps the lid on the lower classes"),[24] but it is not. It is efficient to use different sanctions depending on an offender's wealth. The suggestion is not refuted by the fact that fines are a common criminal penalty. They are much lower than the corresponding tort damage judgments, and hence usable even against relatively nonaffluent offenders, for two reasons. The government invests resources in raising the probability of criminal punishment above that of a tort suit, which makes the optimal fine lower than the punitive damages that would be optimal in the absence of such an investment. Second, a fine is a more severe punishment than its dollar cost. Almost every criminal punishment imposes some non-pecuniary disutility in the form of a stigma, enhanced by such rules as forbidding a convicted criminal to vote. There is no corresponding stigma to a tort judgment.

II. OPTIMAL CRIMINAL PENALTIES

A. Limitations on Severity, with Special Reference to Fines

We have seen that the main thing the criminal law punishes is the pure coercive transfer, or, as it might better be described in a case of tax evasion or price-fixing, the pure involuntary transfer, of wealth or utility. In discussing what criminal penalties are optimal to deter such transfers, I shall assume that most potential criminals are sufficiently rational to be deterrable—an assumption that has the support of an extensive literature.[25]

We saw earlier that the sanction for a pure coercive transfer should be designed so that the criminal is made worse off by his act, but now a series of qualifications must be introduced. First, some criminal acts actually are wealth-maximizing. Suppose I lose my way in the woods and, as an alternative to starving, enter an unoccupied cabin and "steal" some food. Should the punishment be death, on the theory that

---

24. See, e.g., Carlen, Radical Criminology, Penal Politics and the Rule of Law, in Radical Issues in Criminology 7, 20–22 (P. Carlen & M. Collison eds. 1980).

25. See D. Pyle, supra note 3, ch. 3 (reviewing the literature). It should be noted, however, that most estimates of the elasticity of the crime rate to changes in either the probability of apprehension or conviction or the severity of punishment (changes in the former usually are found to have a greater deterrent effect than equivalent changes in the latter) are less than one. See id. at 39–58 for a review of the studies. Thus, increasing the average length of prison sentences by 10%—a large increase—would reduce the crime rate by less than 10%. Very large increases in the length of imprisonment would run into a serious discounting problem. See infra note 39 and accompanying text. Large increases in the probability of apprehension and conviction, on the other hand, would require heavy additional investments in police forces, prosecutors' offices, and courts. The costs of bringing the crime level down may help explain why the crime rate is so high, and why a high crime rate need not signify that the criminal justice system is inefficient.

This assumption of deterability is relaxed in Part III of this Article.

the crime saved my life, and therefore no lesser penalty would deter? Of course not. The problem is that while the law of theft generally punishes takings in settings of low transaction costs, in this example the costs of transacting with the absent owner of the cabin are prohibitive. One approach is to define theft so as to exclude such examples; the criminal law has a defense of necessity that probably would succeed in this example. But defenses make the law more complicated, and an alternative that sometimes will be superior is to employ a somewhat overinclusive definition of the crime but set the expected punishment cost at a level that will not deter the occasional crime that is value-maximizing.

There is a related but more important reason for putting a ceiling on criminal punishments such that not all crimes are deterred. If there is a risk either of accidental violation of the criminal law or of legal error, an expected penalty will induce innocent people to forgo socially desirable activities at the borderline of criminal activity. The effect is magnified if people are risk averse and penalties are severe. If, for example, the penalty for carelessly injuring someone in an automobile accident were death, people would drive too slowly, or not at all, to avoid an accidental violation or an erroneous conviction. True, if through the concept of intentionality and defenses such as necessity the category of criminal acts is limited to cases where, in Hand formula terms, there is a very great disparity between B and PL,[26] the risk of either accident or error will be slight and the legal system will be freer about setting heavy penalties.[27] But not totally free: if the consequences of error are enormous, even a very slight risk of error will generate costly avoidance measures. And, as there are costs of underinclusion if the requirements of proof of guilt are set very high, it may make sense to make proof easier but at the same time make the penalty less severe in order to reduce avoidance and error costs.

Once the expected punishment cost for the crime has been set, it becomes necessary to choose a combination of probability and severity of punishment that will bring that cost home to the would-be offender. Let us begin with fines. An expected punishment cost of $1000 can be imposed by combining a fine of $1000 with a probability of apprehension and conviction of one, a fine of $10,000 with a probability of .1, a fine of one million dollars with a probability of .001, etc. If the costs of collecting fines are assumed to be zero regardless of the size of the fine, the most efficient combination is a probability arbitrarily close to zero and a fine arbitrarily close to infinity.[28] For while the costs of apprehending and convicting criminals rise with the probability of apprehen-

---

26. See R. Posner, supra note 5; Landes & Posner, supra note 5.

27. See Landes & Posner, An Economic Theory of Intentional Torts, 1 Int'l Rev. L. & Econ. 127 (1981).

28. This is a major theme of Becker, supra note 2. He also notes many of the practical limitations of fines.

sion—higher probabilities imply more police, prosecutors, judges, defense attorneys, and so forth because more criminals are being apprehended and tried, than when the probability of apprehension is very low—the costs of collecting fines are by assumption zero regardless of their size. Thus, every increase in the size of the fine is costless, and every corresponding decrease in the probability of apprehension and conviction, designed to offset the increase in the fine and so maintain a constant expected punishment cost, reduces the costs of enforcement.

There are, however, many objections to assuming that the cost of collecting a fine is unrelated to its size:

(1) For criminals who are risk averse, an increase in the fine will not be a costless transfer payment.[29] In Becker's model,[30] the only cost of a fine is the cost of collecting it, because either the fine is not paid—the crime is deterred—or, if paid, it simply transfers an equal dollar amount from the criminal to the taxpayer. But for a risk-averse criminal, every reduction in the probability of apprehension and conviction, and corresponding increase in the fines imposed on those criminals who are apprehended and convicted, imposes a disutility not translated into extra revenue of the state. Thus, the real social cost of fines increases for risk-averse criminals as the fine increases. Nor is this effect offset by the effect on risk-preferring criminals, even if there are as many of them as there are risk-averse criminals. To the extent that a higher fine with lower probability of apprehension and conviction increases the utility of the risk preferrer, the fine has to be put up another notch to make sure that it deters—which makes it even more painful for the risk averse.

(2) The stigma effect of a fine (as of any criminal penalty), noted earlier, is not transferred either.

(3) The model implies punishment of different crimes by the same, severe fine. This uniformity, however, eliminates marginal deterrence—the incentive to substitute less for more serious crimes.[31] If robbery is punished as severely as murder, the robber might as well kill his victim to eliminate a witness. Thus, one cost of making the punishment of a crime more severe is that it reduces the criminal's incentive to substitute that crime for a more serious one. To put this differently, reducing the penalty for a lesser crime may reduce the incidence of a greater crime. If it were not for considerations of marginal deterrence, more serious crimes might not always be punishable by more severe penalties than less serious ones.

There is, however, a tradeoff between marginal deterrence and total deterrence, as shown in equation (2):

---

29. See Polinsky & Shavell, The Optimal Tradeoff Between the Probability and Magnitude of Fines, 69 Am. Econ. Rev. 880, 884–85 (1979).

30. See Becker, supra note 2.

31. See Stigler, supra note 4.

$$M_r = R(f_r) \times p_{m|r}(f_r) \tag{2}$$

M_r, the number of murders committed in the course of robberies, is a product of the number of robberies (R) and the probability that, given a robbery, a murder will occur ($p_{m|r}$). Both R and $p_{m|r}$ are functions of the penalty for robbery (f_r)—but R is a negative function, and $p_{m|r}$ a positive function. It is impossible to say a priori which dominates. If R were very sensitive to increases in the penalty, there might well be fewer murders—and of course many fewer robberies—if robbery were punishable by death.

In this example the greater and the lesser offense are complements rather than substitutes. Suppose we were speaking not of robberies and murders in the course of robberies, but of auto theft and bicycle theft. If the punishment for bicycle theft were raised to that of auto theft, there would be more auto theft. Moreover, even if all crimes were punished with the same severity, some marginal deterrence could be preserved by varying the probability of punishment with the severity of the crime: that is, by looking harder for the more serious criminal. Maybe, then, marginal deterrence should not be a very important factor in the design of a schedule of penalties.

(4) Limitations of solvency cause the cost of collecting fines to rise with the size of the fine—and for most criminal offenders to become prohibitive rather quickly. The solvency problem is so acute that the costs of collecting fines would often be prohibitive even if the probability of punishment were one and fines correspondingly much smaller than in the model. This explains the heavy reliance on nonpecuniary sanctions, of which imprisonment is the most common today. Imprisonment both reduces the criminal's future wealth, by impairing his lawful job prospects, and imposes disutility on people who cannot be made miserable enough by having their liquid wealth, or even their future wealth, confiscated.

(5) The solvency limitation is made all the more acute because a fine generally is considered uncollectable unless the criminal has liquid assets to pay it.[32] The liquidity problem may seem superficial and easily solved by requiring payment on the installment plan or by making the fine proportional to future earnings. But these are more costly forms of punishment than they seem, because by reducing the offender's net income from lawful activity, they increase his incentive to return to a life of crime.

(6) Very low probabilities are difficult to estimate accurately. Criminals might underestimate them or overestimate them, resulting in too little or too much deterrence.

---

32. However, the Sentencing Reform Act of 1984, Pub. L. No. 98-473, Title II, § 211, 98 Stat. 1837 (to be codified at 18 U.S.C. § 3551), and Criminal Fine Enforcement Act of 1984, Pub. L. No. 98-596, 98 Stat. 3134 (to be codified in scattered sections of 18 U.S.C.), not only greatly increase the fines for federal crimes but also greatly improve the methods for collecting them.

B. *Nonmonetary Sanctions*

1. *"Afflictive" Punishment, with Special Reference to Death.* — The fore-going analysis shows that there is a place in the criminal justice system, and a big one, for imprisonment; and perhaps for other nonmonetary criminal sanctions as well. Since the cost of murder to the victim approaches infinity, even very heavy fines will not provide sufficient deterrence of murder, and even life imprisonment may not impose costs on the murderer equal to those of the victim. It might seem, however, that the important thing is not that the punishment for murder equal the cost to the victim but that it be high enough to make the murder not pay—and surely imprisoning the murderer for the rest of his life or, if he is wealthy, confiscating his wealth would cost him more than the murder could possibly have gained him. But this analysis implicitly treats the probability of apprehension and conviction as one. If it is less than one, as of course it is, then the murderer will not be comparing the gain from the crime with the loss if he is caught and sentenced; he will be comparing it with the disutility of the sentence discounted by the probability that it will actually be imposed. Suppose, for example, that the loss to the murder victim is one hundred million dollars, the probability of punishing the murderer is .5, and the murderer's total wealth is one million dollars and will be confiscated upon conviction. Then his expected punishment cost when he is deciding whether to commit the crime is only $500,000—much less than his total wealth.

This analysis suggests incidentally that the much heavier punishment of crimes of violence than seemingly more serious white-collar crimes[33] is not, as so often thought, an example of class bias. Once it is

---

33. The following table will give some sense of the disparity:

Length of Sentence, in Months,
by Type of (Federal) Felony, 1981

Violent	
First-degree murder	180.3
Bank robbery	161.2
Assault	49.4
Rape	103.6
Kidnapping	250.9
Nonviolent	
Burglary	58.0
Bank larceny	68.6
Bank embezzlement	35.6
Tax fraud	38.0
SEC fraud	33.0
Counterfeiting	45.8
Drug offenses	55.5
Bribery	35.9
Antitrust	4.1

Source: Bureau of Justice Statistics, U.S. Dep't of Justice, Sourcebook of Criminal Justice Statistics 1982, at 464–67 (1982).

recognized that most people would demand astronomical sums to assume a substantial risk of death, it becomes apparent that even very large financial crimes are less serious than most crimes of violence. The same people who would accept quite modest sums to run very small risks of death would demand extremely large sums to run the substantial risks that many crimes of violence create, even when death does not ensue. This point holds even if the white-collar crime (say, violating a pollution regulation) creates a safety hazard, provided that the probability that the hazard will result in the death of any given person is low. Even if it were a virtual certainty that some people would die as a result of the crime, the aggregate disutility of many small risks of death may be much smaller than a single large risk of death to a particular person. This is the nonlinear relationship between utility and risk of death that I have stressed.[34]

By the same token the argument sketched above for capital punishment is not conclusive. Because the penalty is so severe, and irreversible, the cost of mistaken imposition is very high; therefore greater resources are invested in the litigation of a capital case. Indeed, if I am right in suggesting that the cost of death inflicted with a high probability (a reasonable description of capital punishment) is not just a linear extrapolation from less severe injuries, it is not surprising that the resources invested in the litigation of a capital case may, as one observes, greatly exceed those invested in litigation in cases where the maximum punishment is life imprisonment, even if there is no possibility of parole. The additional resources expended on the litigation of capital cases may not be justified if the added deterrent effect of capital punishment over long prison terms is small. But there is scientific evidence to support the layman's intuition that it is great.[35]

Capital punishment is also supported by considerations of marginal deterrence, which require as big a spread as possible between the punishments for the least and most serious crimes. If the maximum punishment for murder is life imprisonment, we may not want to make armed robbery also punishable by life imprisonment, for then armed

---

These figures include only persons sentenced to prison; in addition, the fraction of convicted defendants who are sentenced to prison is higher in the violent crime categories. See id.; see also Hagan & Nagel, White-Collar Crime, White-Collar Time: The Sentencing of White-Collar Offenders in the Southern District of New York, 20 Am. Crim. L. Rev. 259 (1982) (results of multiple regression analysis reveal generally more lenient sentences for white-collar offenders).

34. This point is overlooked in "radical" critiques of criminal law. See, e.g., S. Box, Power, Crime, and Mystification 9 (1983).

35. See, e.g., D. Pyle, supra note 3, ch. 4; Ehrlich, The Deterrent Effect of Capital Punishment: A Question of Life and Death, 65 Am. Econ. Rev. 397 (1975); Ehrlich & Gibbons, On the Measurement of the Deterrent Effect of Capital Punishment and the Theory of Deterrence, 6 J. Legal Stud. 35 (1977); Layson, Homicide and Deterrence: A Reexamination of the U.S. Time-Series Evidence (August 1984) (unpublished manuscript) (on file at the offices of the Columbia Law Review). The evidence has not gone unchallenged, of course. See D. Pyle, supra note 3, ch. 4, for discussion and references.

robbers would have no additional incentive not to murder their victims. But arguments based on marginal deterrence for a differentiated penalty structure are inconclusive, as we saw earlier, particularly when the greater offense is a complement of the lesser one, as is often the case with murder. Moreover, the argument does not lead inexorably to the conclusion that capital punishment should be the punishment for simple murder. For if it is, then we have the problem of marginally deterring the multiple murderer. Maybe capital punishment should be reserved for him, so that murderers have a disincentive to kill witnesses to the murder, though again the number of such complementary murders may be less if the initial murder is punished severely.

An important application of this principle is to prison murders. A prisoner who is serving a life sentence for murder and is not likely to be paroled has no disincentive not to kill in prison, unless prison murder is punishable by death. Considerations of complementarity might argue for making out-of-prison murders capital also, since reducing the number of murders and the fraction of murderers in prison would reduce the occasions for prison murder. What makes little sense is to have capital punishment for neither out-of-prison nor prison murders, so that the latter becomes close to a free good. This is the present situation in federal law. Notice that varying the probability of apprehension and conviction cannot preserve marginal deterrence in this situation. The probability of apprehension and conviction in the prison murder case is close to one; the problem is that for the murderer already fated to spend the rest of his life in prison, there is no incremental punishment from being convicted of murder again.

Of course there is no realistic method of preserving marginal deterrence for every crime, although medieval law tried. It is a reasonable conjecture (if no more than that) that because more medieval than modern people believed in an afterlife, because life was more brutal and painful, and because life expectancy was short, capital punishment was not so serious a punishment in those days as it is today. Furthermore, because society was poor, severe punishments were badly needed and law enforcement was inefficient, so that devoting much greater resources to catching criminals would not have been feasible or productive. In an effort to make capital punishment a more costly punishment to the criminal, especially gruesome methods of execution (for example, drawing and quartering)[36] were prescribed for especially heinous crimes, such as treason. Boiling in oil, considered more horrible than hanging or beheading, was used to punish murder by poisoning; since poisoners were especially difficult to apprehend in those times, a heavier punishment than that prescribed for ordinary murderers was (economically) indicated.

---

36. This punishment was still "on the books" in 18th century England. For the grisly details, see 4 W. Blackstone, Commentaries *92.

The hanging of horse thieves in the nineteenth century American West is another example of a penalty whose great severity reflects the low probability of punishment more than the high social cost of the crime. But the most famous example is the punishment of all serious (and some not so serious) crimes by death in pre-nineteenth century England,[37] when there was no organized police force and the probability of punishment was therefore very low for most crimes.[38]

Death is not the only modern form of "afflictive" punishment. Flogging is still used by many parents and, in attenuated form, in some schools. The economic objection to punishing by inflicting physical pain is not that it is disgusting or that people have different thresholds of pain that make it difficult to calibrate the severity of the punishment—imprisonment and death are subject to the same problem. The objection is that it may be a poor method of inflicting severe but not lethal punishment. Just to inflict a momentary excruciating pain with no aftereffects might be a trivial deterrent, especially for people who had never experienced such pain; while to inflict a level of pain that would be the equivalent of five years in prison would require measures so drastic that they might endanger the life, or destroy the physical or mental health, of the offender. For slight punishments, fines will do. Incidentally, I do not mean, by omission, to disparage noneconomic objections to "afflictive punishment." But this is an Article about economics.

The infliction of physical pain is not the only way in which the severity of punishment can be varied other than by varying the length of imprisonment. Size of prison cell, temperature, and quality of food could also be used as "amenity variables." It may seem very attractive from a cost-effectiveness standpoint to reduce the length of imprisonment but compensate by reducing the quality of the food served the prisoners; the costs of imprisonment to the state, but not to the prisoners, would be reduced. The problem is that this would make information about sanctions very costly, because there would be so many dimensions to evaluate. Time has the attractive characteristic of being one-dimensional, and differs from pain in that it has more variability. But as a matter of fact, society does vary the amenities of prison life for different criminals. Minimum security prisons are more comfortable than intermediate security prisons, and the latter are more comfortable than maximum security prisons. Assignments to these different tiers are related to the gravity of the crime, and in the direction one would predict.

2. *Imprisonment.* — If society must continue to rely heavily on imprisonment as a criminal sanction, there is an argument—subject to ca-

---

37. See, e.g., Langbein, Shaping the Eighteenth-Century Criminal Trial: A View from the Ryder Sources, 50 U. Chi. L. Rev. 1, 36–49 (1983).

38. Many capital sentences, however, were commuted to banishment to the colonies.

veats that should be familiar to the reader by now, based on risk aversion, overinclusion, avoidance and error costs, and (less clearly) marginal deterrence—for combining heavy prison terms for convicted criminals with low probabilities of apprehension and conviction. Consider the choice between combining a .1 probability of apprehension and conviction with a ten-year prison term and a .2 probability of apprehension and conviction with a five-year term. Under the second approach twice as many individuals are imprisoned but for only half as long, so the total costs of imprisonment to the government will be the same under the two approaches. But the costs of police, court officials, and the like will probably be lower under the first approach. The probability of apprehension and conviction, and hence the number of prosecutions, is only half as great. Although more resources will be devoted to a trial where the possible punishment is greater, these resources will be incurred in fewer trials because fewer people will be punished, and even if the total litigation resources are no lower, police and prosecution costs will clearly be much lower. And notice that this variant of our earlier model of high fines and trivial probabilities of apprehension and conviction corrects the most serious problem with that model—that is, solvency.

But isn't a system under which probabilities of punishment are low "unfair," because it creates ex post inequality among offenders? Many go scot-free; others serve longer prison sentences than they would if more offenders were caught. However, to object to this result is like saying that all lotteries are unfair because, ex post, they create wealth differences among the players. In an equally significant sense both the criminal justice system that creates low probabilities of apprehension and conviction and the lottery are fair so long as the ex ante costs and benefits are equalized among the participants. Nor is it correct that while real lotteries are voluntary the criminal justice "lottery" is not. The criminal justice is voluntary: you keep out of it by not committing crimes. Maybe, though, such a system of punishment is not sustainable in practice, because judges and jurors underestimate the benefits of what would seem, viewed in isolation, savagely cruel sentences. The prisoner who is to receive the sentence will be there in the dock, in person; the victims of the crimes for which he has not been prosecuted (because the fraction of crimes prosecuted is very low) will not be present—they will be statistics. I hesitate, though, to call this an economic argument; it could be stated in economic terms by reference to costs of information, but more analysis would be needed before this could be regarded as anything better than relabeling.

There is, however, another and more clearly economic problem with combining very long prison sentences with very low probabilities of apprehension and conviction. A prison term is lengthened, of course, by adding time on to the end of it. If the criminal has a significant discount rate, the added years may not create a substantial added disutility.[39] At a discount rate of ten percent, a ten-year prison term imposes a disutility only 6.1 times the disutility of a one-year sentence, and a twenty-year sentence increases this figure to only 8.5 times; the corresponding figures for a five percent discount rate are 7.7 and 12.5 times.

Discount rates may seem out of place in a discussion of nonmonetary utilities and disutilities, though imprisonment has a monetary dimension, because a prisoner will have a lower income in prison than on the outside. But the reason that interest (discount) rates are positive even when there is no risk of default and the expected rate of inflation is zero is that people prefer present to future consumption and so must be paid to defer consumption. A criminal, too, will value his future consumption, which imprisonment will reduce, less than his present consumption.

The discounting problem could be ameliorated by preventive detention, whereby the defendant in effect begins to serve his sentence before he is convicted, or sometimes before his appeal rights are exhausted.[40] The pros and cons of preventive detention involve issues of criminal procedure that would carry us beyond the scope of this Article, and here I merely note that the argument for preventive detention is stronger the graver the defendant's crime (and hence the longer the optimal length of imprisonment), regardless of whether the defendant is likely to commit a crime if he is released on bail pending trial.

The major lesson to be drawn from this part of the Article is that criminal sanctions are costly. A tort sanction is close to a costless transfer payment. A criminal sanction, even when it takes the form of a fine, and patently when it takes the form of imprisonment or death, is not. And yet it appears to be the optimal method of deterring most pure coercive transfers—which are therefore the central concern of the criminal law. These points will be seen to have important implications for substantive criminal doctrine.

III. Substantive Principles of Criminal Law

A. Preventing Crime: Herein of Multiple-Offender Laws, Attempt and Conspiracy, Aiding and Abetting, Entrapment

1. *Introduction.* — The theory of the criminal sanction presented in Parts I and II was purely one of deterrence. The state rations the demand for crime by setting a high price for it in the form of an expected cost of paying a fine or going to prison for committing a crime, but people are actually fined or imprisoned only to maintain the credibility of the deterrent system. This view leaves many important features of

---

39. See Block & Lind, An Economic Analysis of Crimes Punishable by Imprisonment, 4 J. Legal Stud. 479, 481 (1975).

40. Both devices are found in the Bail Reform Act of 1984, 18 U.S.C.A. §§ 3141–3150 (Supp. 1985).

the criminal justice system unexplained. One is that a repeat offender is usually punished more severely than a first offender even if the repeat offender served in full whatever sentences were imposed for the earlier crimes; another is that fines often are proportional to wealth. Consumers in competitive markets are not charged higher prices just because they are wealthier than other consumers or have bought the same product previously, and they certainly are not required to give back the thing they have bought if they have not consumed it yet, as a thief would be required to do. A similar puzzle is the punishment of the "inchoate" crimes, such as attempts and (unsuccessful) conspiracies. If the purpose of the criminal law is to make the criminal regard the full costs of his acts, why punish him when his conduct, because thwarted, imposes no costs? Another puzzle is that imprisonment is often thought to serve the additional value, besides deterrence, of preventing further criminal acts by the imprisoned criminal while he is in prison. Yet assuming that the criminal justice system maintains a proper schedule of prices for unlawful acts, why should anyone care that the criminal, if not imprisoned but punished with equivalent severity by some method that left him at large, might commit further criminal acts? Presumably he would do so only if the acts were socially (as well as privately) cost-justified.

A clue to the answers to these questions lies in the fact that the emphasis on preventing, rather than simply pricing, crime falls on the common law crimes—crimes whose essence is a coerced transfer in a setting of low transaction costs. Very little of the criminal activity in this category is socially cost-justified; examples such as the theft from the cabin under conditions of dire necessity are quite rare, and that example may be a noncrime by virtue of the defense of necessity. The high incidence of the common law crimes reflects not their social desirability, which is close to zero, but the costs of making punishment severe enough to achieve one hundred percent deterrence. If we therefore take as our admittedly exaggerted working hypothesis that but for the high cost of criminal sanctions the optimum level of criminal activity would be zero, we shall be driven to conclude that these sanctions are not really prices designed to ration the activity; the purpose so far as possible is to extirpate it.[41] The smaller the proportion of socially cost-justified crimes, the smaller are the social costs and the larger the potential social benefits of preventing them if prevention is possible at a reasonable cost. This point explains the emphasis in the criminal law on prevention, which would make no sense in a market setting or even an unintentional-tort setting. It explains why fines should be proportional to the criminal's wealth, quite apart from any notions of a just distribution of wealth,[42] and why a thief who is caught

---

41. This distinction is stressed in R. Posner, Economic Analysis of Law 357–59 (1972), and in Cooter, Prices and Sanctions, 84 Colum. L. Rev. 1523 (1984).

42. The principle of the diminishing marginal utility of income implies that a heav-

should be required to return what he has stolen in addition to whatever other punishment is meted out to him, even if the victim is not seeking restitution (maybe the victim is another thief!). It also shows that imprisonment is not so much more costly socially than fines as first appears. Imprisonment confers a social benefit that fines do not, by preventing the criminal from committing crimes (except in prison—an important exception today) during the term of his imprisonment.

2. *Multiple-Offender Laws.* — The practice, systematized in multiple-offender laws, of punishing repeat offenders more severely than first offenders illustrates the last point. The repeat offender has demonstrated by his behavior a propensity for committing crimes. Therefore, by imprisoning him for a longer time we can expect to prevent more crimes during his period of imprisonment than we would do if we imprisoned a first offender, whose propensities are harder to predict, for the same period. The same prison resources "buy" a greater reduction in crime. But if this were the only basis for the heavier punishment of repeat offenders, we would not observe the practice with crimes punishable mainly by fines, because fines have no preventive effect. There is more. The practice raises the price of crime to people who, judging by their past behavior, value crime more than other people do. If our object is to minimize the amount of crime, we must "charge" more to people who value that activity more. We could do this by uniformly increasing the punishment for the particular crime, but selective increases in the severity of punishment are less costly. Heavier punishment of repeat offenders may also be necessary because the stigmatizing effect of criminal punishment diminishes with successive punishments.[43]

An important qualification must be entered here. The effect of prevention in actually reducing crime depends on the elasticity of supply of offenders.[44] If it is very high, then the principal effect of taking one criminal out of circulation is, by making room for another, to attract a person into crime from a lawful occupation or to cause a part-

---

ier fine is necessary to impose the same disutility on a rich as on a poor person, assuming (perhaps dubiously) that the average rich and average poor person have the same marginal utility schedules, and are merely situated at different points on them.

43. Another reason for the practice of punishing recidivists more heavily is suggested in Rubinstein, Offenses that May Have Been Committed by Accident—An Optimal Correction Policy for Offenses that May Have Been Committed by Accident, in Applied Game Theory 406 (S. Brams, A. Schotter & G. Schwödiauer eds. 1979). The fact that the defendant has committed previous crimes makes us more confident that he really is guilty of the crime with which he currently is charged, and therefore the risk of error if a heavy sentence is imposed is less. There is merit to this point, but it overlooks the fact that a previous offender is easier to convict than a first offender, because if he takes the stand the prosecution can introduce his record of convictions to try to undermine his credibility.

44. This point is emphasized in Ehrlich, On the Usefulness of Controlling Individuals: An Economic Analysis of Rehabilitation, Incapacitation, and Deterrence, 71 Am. Econ. Rev. 307, 315–19 (1981).

time criminal to allocate more of his time to crime. With regard to "business-like" crimes such as trafficking in drugs, the elasticity of supply of offenders may be quite high. But with regard to crimes of violence, it is probably low, as most people in our society are quite averse to the personal risks involved in such crimes. This analysis implies that society will place more emphasis on preventing, relative to deterring, crimes of violence than acquisitive nonviolent crimes—an interesting question for further investigation.

Another point to notice about the greater punishment of repeat offenders may help to explain why the higher the percentage of young people in the population is the higher the crime rate is. Young people, as beginners in crime, are punished less severely, hence are less deterred and less incapacitated from committing crimes.

3. *Attempt and Conspiracy.* — Consider now the punishment of attempts. A man enters a bank, intending to rob it, but a guard spots him and seizes him before he can do any harm. The fact that he came so close to robbing it indicates that he is quite likely to try again unless restrained, so by putting him in prison we can probably prevent some robberies. This is one benefit of punishing attempts. Another is to increase the expected costs of bank robbery to the robber without making the punishment for bank robbery more severe, which would create all the problems discussed earlier. The robber cannot be certain that his attempt will succeed, and if it fails he will not merely forgo the gains from a successful robbery, but will incur additional (punishment) costs.

In equation (3), for example, the net expected income ($E(I)$) from some crime in a world without punishment for attempts is the difference between the expected gain from the crime, which is a product of the gain if the crime succeeds (G) and the probability of success (p_s), and the expected punishment cost ($p_p f$). If the attempt fails, there is no gain, but no punishment cost either.

$$E(I) = p_s G - p_p f \tag{3}$$

But now suppose an unsuccessful attempt is punished by penalty f_a, imposed with a probability p_{pa} (probability of punishment for an attempt). Now the prospective criminal's net expected gain falls.

$$E(I) = p_s G - p_p f - (1 - p_s) p_{pa} f_a \tag{4}$$

Punishing attempts is thus like maintaining a public police force. It is a way of increasing expected punishment cost without making the sanction for the completed crime more severe, and we have seen that the costs of criminal sanctions mount rapidly as the sanctions are made more severe.

The attempter in our example will not, however, be punished so severely as if he had actually robbed the bank. There are two economic reasons for this: to give offenders an incentive to change their minds at the last moment (a form of marginal deterrence), and to minimize the costs of error, since there is a higher probability that an attempter really is harmless than that a person punished for an actual robbery has really done nothing.

What if the defendant had simply said to a friend, who turned out to be a police informant, "I intend to rob that bank," but had taken no steps toward accomplishing his aim? This would not be a criminal attempt. The probability that such a person would actually rob a bank is much less than it would be if he were caught on the verge of doing so, so the social benefits from imprisoning him are much less; to put it differently, the expected costs of error are higher.

Sometimes attempts fail not because they are interrupted but because the attempter has made a mistake. He may have shot what he thought was a man sleeping in a bed but it turns out to be a pillow. Or he may have made a voodoo doll of his enemy and stabbed it repeatedly in the mistaken belief that this would kill the enemy. The question for the economist is whether the nature of the mistake makes it highly unlikely that the attempter will ever succeed. If no crime will be prevented by imprisoning him, there will be no social benefit of imprisonment but cost aplenty. The second hypothetical case is of this character. But while there is some authority for not punishing the first kind of attempt,[45] there is more for not punishing the second. The issue ought to be dangerousness, not whether the defendant mistook the end or the means.

The attempt that fails because of a mistake rather than because it is interrupted provides the strongest case for punishing an attempt less severely than the completed crime. If the punishment for attempted murder were the same as for murder, one who shot and missed (and was not caught immediately) might as well try again, for if he succeeds, he will be punished no more severely than for his unsuccessful attempt.

Conspiracies to commit criminal acts are punished whether or not they succeed. Where the conspiracy succeeds, punishing it as a separate crime makes the punishment for the underlying crime greater than if only one person had committed it and also confers certain procedural advantages on the prosecutor. The special treatment of conspiracies makes sense because they are (though only on average, of course) more dangerous than one-man crimes.[46] If they were more dangerous only

---

45. See R. Perkins & R. Boyce, Criminal Law 621 (3d ed. 1982), which incidentally is an excellent treatise on criminal law, as are G. Fletcher, Rethinking Criminal Law (1978); W. LaFave & A. Scott, Handbook on Criminal Law (1972); G. Williams, Textbook of Criminal Law (2d ed. 1983). On preparatory crimes, such as attempt and conspiracy, Schulhoffer, Harm and Punishment: A Critique of Emphasis on the Results of Conduct in the Criminal Law, 122 U. Pa. L. Rev. 1497 (1974), is a particularly good treatment. On the basic principles of criminal law, see H.L.A. Hart, Punishment and Responsibility: Essays in the Philosophy of Law (1968).

46. This explains why an illegal sale is not in law a conspiracy between the seller and the buyer, and why a bribe is not a conspiracy between the person paying and the person receiving the bribe. A crime *defined* as requiring the cooperation of two people need not be socially more costly than if it could be committed by one person. There is a

in the sense of committing more serious crimes, there would be no need for extra punishment; the punishment would be more severe anyway. But actually they are more dangerous in being able to commit more crimes (just as a firm can produce more goods or services than an individual) and perhaps do so more efficiently (in a private, not social, sense) by being able to take advantage of the division of labor—for example, by posting one member of the conspiracy as a sentinel, another to drive the getaway car, and another to fence the goods stolen. Although these advantages are offset to some extent by the fact that a conspiracy is more vulnerable to being detected because of the scale of its activities, that scale may also enable the conspiracy to avoid punishment through corruption of law enforcement officers. And some of the most serious crimes, such as insurrection, can be committed only by conspiracies. All this implies that the optimal punishment of conspiracies is indeed more severe than that of individuals.

A conspiracy that does not succeed is still punished. It is a form of attempt. The principal legal difference is that the conspiracy—which is to say the agreement to commit the crime—is punishable even if the conspirators do not get anywhere near the scene of the crime but are caught in the earliest preparatory stage. But again, if conspiracies are more dangerous than one-man crimes, the expected harm may be as great as in the case of the one-man attempt even if the probability of the completed crime is lower because the preparations are interrupted earlier.

4. *Aiding and Abetting.* — Related to the concept of conspiracy is the concept of aiding and abetting a crime. Consider the following cases:

(a) A witness fails to report a crime to the police.

(b) A merchant sells a fancy dress to a woman he knows to be a prostitute.

(c) A merchant sells a gun to a man who tells the merchant that he is planning to use it in a murder.

In all three cases there is an argument for imposing criminal liability: it will raise the expected costs of the (principal) criminal. In the first case, however, the avoidance costs will be very great; people who have information about crime but do not volunteer it at first will be scared to do so later. In the second case the benefits of criminal liability will be rather trivial, and this is only in part because the crime is pretty trivial (and victimless); in addition, the prostitute will incur little added cost by shopping at stores that don't know her occupation. In the third case the benefits in criminal liability seem substantial—and it is the only one where the law (occasionally) imposes such liability.[47]

---

curious analogy here to the differential treatment of "horizontal" and "vertical" agreements in antitrust law—the former being punished more harshly.

47. For an interesting discussion, see R. Perkins & R. Boyce, supra note 45, at 745–47. Under the increasingly popular formulation of the aiding and abetting offense that requires the aider and abettor to share the principal's purpose, rather than just have

5. *Entrapment.* — A concept closely related to attempt is entrapment, even though the former is a crime and the latter is a defense to a criminal prosecution. Conventional legal scholarship finds the concept ill-defined and enigmatic.[48] Maybe economics can make some sense out of it. Often the police solicit or assist a person to commit a crime. The most common form of this tactic is sending an undercover agent to buy narcotics from a drug dealer who is then prosecuted for an illegal sale. It may seem odd that the law should punish a harmless act, for obviously the sale of narcotics to an undercover agent, who then destroys the narcotics, harms no one. The only important thing, it might seem, would be to get the money used for the purchase back from the seller. But the rationale is again prevention. *This* act is harmless, but it is altogether likely that the dealer, unless prevented, will make illegal sales, and we arrest and convict him now becaue it is much cheaper to catch him in an arranged crime than in his ordinary criminal activities. The benefits of imprisonment are virtually as great, the costs of apprehension and conviction much lower.

This sort of "entrapment" is perfectly lawful. The defense of entrapment comes into play only if the entrapped person lacked a "criminal predisposition." This fusty legal term can be given the following economic meaning: the defendant would have committed the same crime, only in circumstances that would have made it harder for the police to catch him, if he had not fallen into the police trap. But suppose that instead of just simulating the target's normal criminal opportunities, the police go further and induce him to commit crimes that he would never commit in his ordinary environment. The police offer a poor man who has no criminal record one thousand dollars to steal a bicycle; he does so, and is arrested. The resources used to apprehend and convict the man of bicycle theft are socially wasted, because they do not prevent any crimes. Had it not been for the police offer, he would not have stolen a bicycle (only doing so at a time when they were not looking); the expected benefits of theft were negative to him. Nothing is achieved by the police conduct except deflecting scarce resources from genuine crime prevention, and a defense of entrapment will lie. Police inducements that merely affect the timing and not the level of criminal activity are socially productive; those that increase the crime level are not.

---

knowledge of that purpose, even the third case would not be actionable. But the better economic view, for which there is some legal support, would not require the sharing of the principal's purpose if the crime is very grave. See id. at 746; W. LaFave & A. Scott, supra note 45, at 509.

48. See, e.g., Seidman, The Supreme Court, Entrapment, and Our Criminal Justice Dilemma, 1981 Sup. Ct. Rev. 111. W. LaFave & A. Scott, supra note 45, at 372, suggests, rather unhelpfully, it seems to me, that entrapment is contrary to public policy because it is "reprehensible."

B. *Criminal Intent*

1. *In General.* — The subjective intentions, or state of mind, of the accused criminal are a pervasive consideration in the criminal law. This is puzzling to the economist: one can read many books on economics without encountering a reference to "intent." But in fact the concept of intent in criminal law serves three economic functions: identifying pure coercive tranfers, estimating the probability of apprehension and conviction, and determining whether the criminal sanction will be an effective (cost-justified) means of controlling undesirable conduct.

If I take from a restaurant an umbrella that I mistakenly think is mine, I am not a thief; if I know the umbrella is not mine and take it anyway, I am. The economic difference is that in the first case I would have to expend resources to avoid taking the umbrella and the probability of my taking the wrong umbrella is low, so the disparity between B and PL in Hand formula terms is not great, and the risk of overdeterrence through a criminal penalty is great. In the second case, where I expend resources in order to take someone else's umbrella (maybe I went to the restaurant for the sole purpose of stealing an umbrella), B is negative and P is high (one is more likely to bring about a harm if one wants to bring it about).[49] The problem is that the external acts involved in these two transactions are the same; only the state of mind with which they are done provides a clue to the difference in their economic character. I admit that this is not an entirely satisfactory explanation. Unless the criminal defendant confesses or makes damaging admissions, his state of mind has to be inferred from external acts; so why not infer the existence of a pure coercive transfer from those acts directly, without the intermediate step of hypostasizing criminal intent? Maybe criminal intent is just a locution that laymen use to describe a pure coercive transfer.

We must be careful to distinguish intent from awareness. Otherwise we could fall into the trap of thinking that the managers of a railroad are murderers because they know with a fair degree of confidence that their trains will run down a certain number of people at railroad crossings this year. They know, but they derive no benefit from killing. They only derive a benefit from saving the resources necessary to prevent the killing, and the benefit, social as well as private, may exceed the cost. Criminal intent is the intent to bring about a forbidden object by investing resources in its attainment.

Although the cost of trying criminal cases would be reduced by not bothering to draw a sharp line between the pure coercive transfer and the accident that it externally resembles, the result would be excessive criminal punishment, leading to all sorts of serious social costs from avoidance of lawful activity—checking umbrellas in a restaurant's cloakroom, for example. Yet sometimes the line wavers. A well-known

---

49. This is emphasized in Landes & Posner, supra note 27, at 132–33.

example is statutory rape. The girl may look sixteen (let us assume sixteen is the age of consent), but if she is younger, a reasonable mistake will not excuse the male. Another example is felony murder: if death occurs in the course of a felony through no fault of the felon's, still he is liable as a murderer. Again we do not care about deterring activity bordering on the activity that the basic criminal prohibition is aimed at. Because we do not count the avoidance of that activity as a social cost, it pays to reduce the costs of prosecution by eliminating the issue of intent (more precisely, *an* issue of intent). The male can avoid liability for statutory rape by keeping away from young girls, and the robber can avoid liability for felony murder by not robbing, or by not carrying a weapon. In effect we introduce a degree of strict liability into criminal law as into tort law when a change in activity level is an efficient method of avoiding a social cost.[50]

A related idea explains why a person who robs a federally insured bank, thereby violating federal as well as state law, is not excused from federal criminal liability just because he had no reason to know the bank was federally insured. He knew he was committing a crime, and it is but a detail that he did not know the full penal consequences—a detail offset by the savings in resource costs from not having to prove his knowledge of the bank's insured status. Conceivably, this analysis explains the punishment of "mercy killings," even in circumstances where it is likely that the killing averted more suffering than it created. Since it will often be difficult to distinguish the true mercy killing from the murder that is dressed up as a mercy killing, we cast the net of prohibition somewhat wider than the particular conduct we want to deter.[51]

The second function of intent in the criminal law is illustrated by the degrees of murder. First-degree murder requires premeditation. Second-degree murder requires a high degree of recklessness; a familiar example is that of the fleeing robber who shoots in the general direction of his pursuers and kills one. Voluntary manslaughter would be committed by one who killed "in the heat of passion," for example, under serious (but not adequate) provocation. The probability that the attempt to kill will succeed is clearly greater in the case of premeditated murder than in the other cases. In addition, the probability of apprehension and conviction is greater in the case of voluntary manslaughter than in the first two cases. The pattern of severity therefore appears to make economic sense. It would make even more sense if within the class of first-degree murders a distinction were made between the planned and the unplanned. Generally this is not done, but there is a hint of the distinction in many murder statutes that single out killing

---

50. For the tort analysis, see Shavell, Strict Liability versus Negligence, 9 J. Legal Stud. 1 (1980); see also Landes & Posner, supra note 5, at 871, 875–76, 905–12 (economic comparison of negligence and strict liability standards).

51. An alternative approach might be to require the mercy killer to prove beyond a reasonable doubt that it was a true mercy killing.

while "lying in wait" or by means of poison as examples of first-degree murders.[52] These are advance-planning murders, where not only is the probability of death maximized, but the probability of apprehension and conviction is minimized, as one who plans a murder in advance will also take steps to escape detection afterward.

There might seem to be another reason for punishing the impulsive crime less severely than the deliberated one: the impulsive crime is less deterrable; punishment is less efficacious, less worthwhile, and therefore society should buy less of it. But this analysis is incompelete. To begin with, the fact that a given increment of punishment will deter the impulsive criminal less than the deliberate one could actually point to heavier punishment for the former. Suppose that a twenty year sentence is enough to deter virtually all murderers for hire, but to achieve the same deterrence of impulsive murderers would require a sentence of thirty years if it were not for differences in the probability of apprehension and conviction. The additional sentence is costly, but if the cost is less than the benefits in additional deterrence it may still be a good investment. And we must not forget the incapacitative effect of imprisonment. The fact that certain criminals may not be deterrable argues for greater emphasis on their incapacitation, which implies long prison terms.

2. *Insanity.* — The conflict between deterrence and incapacitation as objectives of the criminal sanction is keenest in relation to the defense of insanity. If a person is insane in the sense either that he does not know that what he is doing is criminal (he kills a child, thinking it is a gerbil) or that he cannot control himself (supernatural voices command him to kill), the threat of criminal punishment will not deter him. So if the only purpose of the criminal sanction were deterrence, it would be doubtful that such people should be punished as criminals. The resources consumed in punishing them, including the disutility of the punishment to the "criminal" himself, would buy very little deterrence—not zero, though. The existence of an insanity defense attracts resources to proving and disproving it, and deterrence is impaired to the extent either that criminals succeed in faking insanity or that a reduction (for whatever reason) in the number of people punished reduces the deterrent signal that punishment emits.

Once the preventive or incapacitative goal is brought into play, however, an insanity defense is weaker. It increases the cost of the criminal process without reducing the need to incapacitate the defend-

---

52. See, e.g., 18 U.S.C. § 1111(a) (1982) (federal murder statute) ("Every murder perpetrated by poison, lying in wait, or any other kind of willful, deliberate, malicious, and premeditated killing; or committed in the perpetration of, or attempt to perpetrate, any arson[,] escape, murder, kidnapping, treason, espionage, sabotage,, [sic] rape, burglary, or robbery; or perpetrated from a premeditated design unlawfully and maliciously to effect the death of any human being other than him who is killed, is murder in the first degree.").

ant. However, part of the "kick" of criminal punishment comes from its stigmatizing effect, an effect enhanced by such sanctions as taking away a convicted felon's right to vote, but more deeply grounded in the sense that criminal punishment is reserved for serious wrongdoing— for what in economic terms is socially more costly conduct than is characteristically dealt with by tort law. Stigma has no incapacitative effect; it is therefore wasted on the undeterrable. Incapacitation will still be cost-effective if the expected costs inflicted by the insane person exceed the costs to society of incapacitating him, but there is no reason to brand him a criminal; civil commitment will therefore be preferable. An additional reason for incapacitating the criminally insane is to raise the costs of faking an insanity defense; the defendant will not get off scot-free even if the defense succeeds.

To say that criminal punishment should be reserved for people who are deterrable may seem inconsistent with my emphasis on the preventive function of criminal punishment, and with my remarks about strict liability in the criminal law. But there is no inconsistency. Because criminal sanctions are so costly, they have to be set at levels that do not deter everyone, but it does not follow that a person who is not deterred is not a wrongdoer. He is just someone for whom criminal activity is utility maximizing. As for strict liability, it *will* deter, by inducing a change in activity level.

By arguing that insanity should be a defense to criminal liability to the extent that it isolates a class of undeterrables, I necessarily reject the *Durham*[53] test of insanity, which requires only that the criminal act be shown to have been a product of the defendant's insanity. The test amounts to asking whether, but for being insane, the defendant would not have committed the act. Even if he would not have, this tells us very little about whether he could have been deterred by threat of punishment. If he could have been deterred, it is efficient to punish him. This incidentally is why it is no defense to a criminal charge that the defendant would not have committed the crime but for a bad upbringing, racial discrimination, or some other condition beyond his control. Provided the criminal act is socially undesirable, and the criminal deterrable by threat of punishment, it makes economic sense to punish him even if his incentive to commit the crime might have been reduced by some other measure, especially if the alternative measures would be very costly.

The relevant meaning of insanity, then, is that the defendant is so mentally diseased as to be undeterrable; the reason for requiring proof of mental disease, and not just proof of undeterrability, is to focus inquiry and to reduce the risk of a legal error in the defendant's favor. This seems the approximate meaning of the *M'Naghten*[54] rules as sup-

---

53. Durham v. United States, 214 F.2d 862 (D.C. Cir. 1954).
54. M'Naghten's Case, 8 Eng. Rep. 718 (1843).

plemented by the concept of "irresistible impulse."

If mental incapacity is self-induced, as where a person kills in a drunken fit, the law does not excuse the crime, but does reduce the severity of the punishment through the concept of diminished responsibility. The threat of punishment for acts committed while drunk reduces the incentive to become drunk in the first place. However, punishment is lightened in recognition of the fact that the drunk is less likely to succeed in doing harm than if he were sober and also is more likely to be apprehended and convicted.

Insanity is rarely recognized as a defense in tort law[55]—and in general the defendant's state of mind is much less likely to be considered an excuse or mitigation of civil than of criminal liability. Criminal sanctions, as I have emphasized, are more costly than tort sanctions, and this alters the tradeoff between the costs of factfinding and the costs of imposing a sanction on conduct outside the intended domain of the sanction. Thus, it is no defense to civil trespass that the trespasser did not know and could not at reasonable cost have found out that he was on the plaintiff's property,[56] but it is a defense to criminal trespass. Since the sanction for civil trespass is less severe, the costs of a difficult inquiry into the defendant's state of mind are less likely to produce an offsetting benefit in avoiding the costs of imposing a sanction on conduct that no one wants to deter—a trespass unavoidable in an economic sense—than where the sanction is criminal.

3. *The Costs of Information.* — It often is unclear whether a buyer of stolen goods knows they are stolen. The test of criminal liability is whether, suspecting they were stolen, the buyer "consciously avoided" acquiring the knowledge that would verify or dispel his suspicions. The test places on the buyer a legal duty, enforceable by criminal punishment, of investigating the provenance of the goods when the costs of investigation are extremely low.[57] Something similar may be at work in the hoary maxim, which still retains much vitality, that ignorance of the law is no defense to criminal liability. Because unclear criminal laws can impose substantial "steering clear" costs, these laws are generally rather clear, less by being clearly drafted than by being confined to a type of conduct that everyone knows is antisocial. The cost of acquiring knowledge of one's duties under criminal law is thus made extremely low.

C. Recklessness, Negligence, and Strict Liability Again

Focusing on one type of sanction cost, the "steering clear" cost, will help to explain why accidental conduct is much less likely than in-

---

55. See W. Keeton, D. Dobbs, R. Keeton & D. Owen, Prosser and Keeton on the Law of Torts 1072–75 (5th ed. 1984).

56. See id. at 74–75.

57. See J. Elster, Ulysses and the Sirens: Studies in Rationality and Irrationality 178 (1979).

tentional conduct to be made criminal. A characteristic of accidental conduct is that it cannot be avoided with certainty but can only be made less probable. To be absolutely certain of never hitting another car as a result of negligence, one must forgo driving altogether. Since criminal sanctions are severe, to attach them to accidental conduct would create incentives to avoid what may be a very broad zone of perfectly lawful activity in order to avoid the risk of criminal punishment.

But there are many exceptions to this generalization; here are the principal ones.

(1) There is an argument for criminal liability whenever B in the Hand formula is low relative to PL *and* where L is high. If B and PL are close together there is a substantial risk of erroneously imposing liability, and the social costs of that risk are greatly magnified when the liability is criminal. Even if B is much smaller than PL, if L is small there is no reason why the matter cannot be left to the tort system. But suppose both conditions are satisfied, as where by driving extremely carelessly one creates a substantial risk of killing someone. Granted, B will be larger and P smaller than if one is trying to kill someone, but that means only that the case for criminal liability is stronger in the intentional case. The reckless, or grossly negligent, case still fits the basic model for criminal liability, and one is therefore not surprised to find that reckless and grossly negligent life-endangering conduct is criminal.

Another example is killing in the honest but unreasonable belief that it is necessary in self-defense. This is a deliberate killing; hence both P and L are high. B is also high; the killer by definition fears for his own life. Nevertheless the gap between PL and B may well be substantial, which together with the fact that L is large would establish the conditions for criminal punishment of conduct that is in an important sense accidental. In the example, the crime would be manslaughter, not murder; the gap between PL and B is smaller than in the case put earlier of reckless killing that is punishable as second-degree murder.[58]

Consistent with this analysis, simple negligence, and gross negligence that does not endanger life, are rarely made criminal.[59]

(2) There are, of course, strict liability crimes—where neither intent nor even simple negligence is an element of the crime. The most important as a practical matter is driving above the speed limit. But

---

58. "Recklessness" is confusingly used in two distinct senses in criminal law: indifference to consequences (shooting into a crowded room for fun, not caring whether or not you hit anybody), and extreme carelessness. Reckless conduct in the first sense is assimilated to intentional conduct in accordance with my discussion of criminal intent and information costs; a reckless murderer in this sense would in most states be guilty of second-degree murder. Recklessness in the second sense is assimilated to gross negligence, and in a death case would make the defendant guilty of manslaughter. For a good discussion of the importance of the actor's state of mind in distinguishing these two senses of unintended murder, see Note, Defining Unintended Murder, 85 Colum. L. Rev. 786 (1985).

59. See W. LaFave & A. Scott, supra note 45, at 209–13.

except in extreme cases, where it becomes part of category (1) above, this is not a crime in a functional sense, as it is punished by a small and nonstigmatizing fine, the practical equivalent of tort damages.

The interesting question about the speeding offense, and about other strict liability crimes, such as selling liquor to a child and selling adulterated foods, is why it is thought necessary to supplement tort remedies with any sort of publicly enforced sanction. My answer draws on the analysis by Wittman and Shavell of ex ante versus ex post sanctions.[60] In the case of life-endangering conduct, a feature of virtually all strict liability crimes, the fixing of L in a tort suit (that is, after the accident has occurred) is difficult to do because it is difficult to estimate the value of a human life, and may be a futile act because the tortfeasor may lack the money to pay a large judgment. L, then, is both uncertain and large. The alternative to regulation through the tort system is to have the government step in and (ideally) make the speeder pay a fine equal to PL, in order to induce the taking of the right precautions (which is approximated by complying with the speed limit). PL, the expected cost of being endangered, can be estimated from studies of compensating wage differentials for dangerous work and personal investments in safety, and since PL will be a much smaller number than L, there is unlikely to be a solvency problem.[61]

Strict liability is a misnomer in this setting. The speed limit is a rough estimation of B, and so with the other regulatory rules the breaking of which establishes strict criminal liability. Because B and PL may be close together, costly criminal sanctions would not be optimal even though L is high, but much cheaper transfer payments to the government may be optimal.

(3) An important doctrine of strict liability in tort law is respondeat superior: the employer is liable regardless of his personal fault for torts committed by an employee within the scope of the employment. The basic justification for the doctrine is that employees rarely can pay substantial money judgments, and therefore tort liability will have little effect on their incentives. If the employer is liable, his incentives will be productively affected—he will take greater care in hiring, supervising, and where necessary, firing employees. Since the criminal law does not rely primarily on monetary sanctions, since imposing criminal sanctions on the employer would duplicate tort sanctions, and particularly since criminal sanctions can induce too much care because they are so heavy,

---

60. See Shavell, Liability for Harm Versus Regulation of Safety, 13 J. Legal Stud. 357 (1984); Wittman, Prior Regulation Versus Post Liability: The Choice Between Input and Output Monitoring, 6 J. Legal Stud. 193 (1977).

61. The analysis is not entirely satisfactory. If PL is known, L can be calculated, for purposes of figuring tort damages, and potential injurers can be made to insure (which is practical since we are speaking of accidental rather than intentional misconduct), thus solving the problem of insolvency.

it is no surprise that the criminal law has not adopted respondeat superior.

The major exception is the criminal liability of corporations.[62] If a crime at least ostensibly on the corporation's behalf is committed or condoned at the directorial or managerial level of the corporation, the corporation is criminally liable. This means that the shareholders will bear the burden of the fine. They are analogous to employers of the people who did the actual deed. Since a corporation can only be fined, since corporations are either risk neutral or if risk averse less so than individuals, and since there is little stigma to corporate punishment (a corporation can act only through individuals, and there is a constant turnover of these individuals), corporate criminal punishment is much less costly than individual punishment. So there is much less danger of causing the shareholders to be too careful in hiring, supervising, and terminating directors (and through the board of directors, the managing employees).

These circumstances make corporate criminal liability sensible. Assume to begin with that the corporation's managers are perfect agents of the shareholders, so that any revenue obtained from criminal activity inures to the shareholders. Then if the shareholders bear no responsibility for a manager's crime, they will have every incentive to hire managers willing to commit crimes on the corporation's behalf. Of course the shareholders will have to compensate the managers for the expected costs of criminal punishment, but, given the limitations on the severity of criminal sanctions emphasized earlier, they may be able to do this and still have an expected gain from corporate criminal activity.

Now assume that the managers are not perfect agents of the corporation—that in fact they use their corporate positions to facilitate criminal activity intended to enrich themselves. Even so, the corporation has supplied the facilities they are using, and its owners should be given incentives to select and supervise managers more carefully.[63]

The real puzzle about corporate criminal liability, it might seem, is why it has to be *criminal* liability. The entire rationale of the criminal law is that the optimal tort remedy is sometimes too large to be collectible, and how can that be a consideration with an entity that can only be subjected to monetary sanctions? But corporations are not infinitely solvent, and two of the fundamental techniques of criminal law are fully applicable even to an entity that cannot be punished other than by a

---

62. This subject is comprehensively surveyed in K. Brickey, Corporate Criminal Liabilty: A Treatise on the Criminal Liability of Corporations, Their Officers and Agents (1984); see also Metzger, Corporate Criminal Liability for Defective Products: Policies, Problems, and Prospects, 73 Geo. L.J. 1 (1984) (discussing whether the deficiencies of product liability law are so great as to warrant imposing criminal sanctions on corporations).

63. Notice the analogy to collective punishment in primitive societies. See supra note 21 and accompanying text.

nonstigmatizing fine: the use of public resources to raise the probability of punishment above what might be a very low level because of efforts taken to conceal criminal responsibility, and the punishment of preparatory activity in order to reduce the net expected gain from crime.

Since, however, corporate criminal punishment is purely monetary, it is not clear why the corporation should be entitled to the elaborate procedural safeguards of the criminal process. Those safeguards make economic sense only on the assumption that criminal punishments impose heavy social costs rather than merely transfer money from the criminal to the state.[64]

D. *The Defense of Necessity*

The famous case of *Regina v. Dudley and Stephens*[65] involved a murder trial of two men who, *in extremis* in a lifeboat, killed and ate one of their crew mates (the cabin boy). A defense of necessity was raised but rejected. In the modern law the defense of necessity, though still regarded with disfavor except when it takes the form of self-defense, will usually succeed if there is a very great disparity between the cost of the crime to the victim and the gain to the injurer. In our earlier example of "stealing" food from a cabin in the woods in order to maintain life, the "theft" probably would be excused. Notice also that, unlike the case of insanity—a fundamentally different type of defense—no incapacitative goal would be served by rejecting a defense of necessity; we do not *want* incapacitation in this case.

But change the example slightly: I am starving, and beg a crust of bread from a wealthy gourmand, who turns me down. If I go ahead and snatch the bread from his hand, I am guilty of theft, and cannot interpose a defense of necessity. The economic rationale for this hardhearted result (a good illustration of the difference between efficiency and utility as grounds of criminal punishment) is that, since transaction costs are low, my inability to negotiate a successful purchase of the bread shows that the bread is really worth more to the gourmand, in the strictly economic sense in which value is a function of willingness and hence ability to pay. But transaction costs were prohibitive in the cabin example.

In *Dudley and Stephens*, there was evidence that the cabin boy was near death anyway and that killing and eating him saved the lives of three men.[66] Yet we know that unless the victim knew he was too far gone to be saved, probably he would not have sold his life to the others at any price. Therefore the case seems similar to that of the starving

---

64. See R. Posner, Economic Analysis of Law 433–34 (2d ed. 1977).

65. 14 Q.B.D. 273 (1884).

66. The third was not charged because he had not participated in the killing. See id. at 274.

beggar. Yet something must be wrong. Even though transaction costs were not high in the usual sense in *Dudley and Stephens*, at some point the sacrifice of one person so that others will live must increase social welfare. If in advance of the voyage the members of the crew had agreed to sacrifice the weakest should that become necessary to save the others, there would be an economic argument for allowing the defense of necessity if the agreement had to be performed.

It is only one step beyond that to argue that if we are confident that the members of the crew would have made such an agreement if they had foreseen the contingency that materialized, the defense of necessity ought to have been recognized—always assuming that economic efficiency is to be the guidepost for criminal law doctrine. There actually is some legal support for the related idea that killing and eating a person in conditions of desperation will be excused if lots are drawn to determine who shall be the victim.[67] Compared to an ex ante agreement to sacrifice the weakest, the drawing of lots has the advantage of being both cheaper to administer and a better insurance scheme. An agreement to sacrifice the weakest will give whoever has the least robust constitution the least insurance protection. But drawing lots has the disadvantage that it may result in unnecessary sacrifices, as where the strongest man draws the short straw and is killed and eaten but the weakest dies anyway because he was too far gone to be saved.

CONCLUSION

If the analysis in this Article is sound, the criminal law, though generally considered the domain *par excellence* of moral rather than economic thinking in law, has an impressive economic logic. On reflection this conclusion (which can be reinforced by reference to the literature on the economics of criminal procedure)[68] is not weird as it sounds. Criminal acts are a source of enormous social costs that no society can ignore, and the modern criminal law is the product of a painstaking evolution powerfully influenced by the explicitly economic approach of Jeremy Bentham. Although judges and legislators do not often speak the language of economics, this Article suggests that they often do reason implicitly in economic terms, and that economic analysis is therefore helpful in explaining the basic structure of law, including the criminal law.

If this Article were not already so long, I would go on and compare the economic approach with its principal rival, the "moral" theory

---

67. See United States v. Holmes, 26 F. Cas. 360 (E.D. Pa. 1842) (No. 15,383); R. Perkins & R. Boyce, supra note 45, at 1056; cf. A. Simpson, Cannibalism and the Common Law 140, 145, 233–34 (1984).

68. See, e.g., Easterbrook, Criminal Procedure as a Market System, 12 J. Legal Stud. 289 (1983) (arguing that important aspects of criminal procedure—prosecutorial discretion, plea bargaining, and sentencing discretion—can be understood in economic terms).

of criminal law, which argues that the crminal law should only punish morally blameworthy conduct. Whatever the normative merits of this approach, I doubt that it is as good a positive theory of criminal law as the economic,[69] since in so many areas conduct is punished that is not blameworthy in the moral sense. But this is a topic for another day.

---

69. I am quite sure that the economic approach has more power than the approach of the radical criminologists. See supra text accompanying notes 24 and 34.

[6]

COMMENT ON "ON THE ECONOMIC THEORY OF CRIME"

RICHARD A. POSNER

The question Professor Klevorick poses at the outset of his paper is why the economic analysis of crime,[1] unlike the economic analysis of torts, has not entered into the mainstream of lawyers' thinking. The question is a somewhat surprising one for an economist to put, as it is a question about the sociology of legal education and practice rather than about economic analysis. But Professor Klevorick's answer is more surprising. It is that the economic analysis of crime is incomplete; it presupposes a political theory that (by implication) is not yet in place. This is a surprising answer, because most people think the economic analysis of tort law is also incomplete and in just the same sense—that it presupposes a political theory that has not yet been developed. If tort law decides that the farmer shall have to bear the costs of damage from locomotive sparks—that he has no "right" to prevent the railroad from causing such damage—it is making the same kind of judgment that it makes when it says that a woman does have a property right in her body, i.e., that rape is a crime.

While it would be very nice to have a complete economic theory of any field of law, it is hardly a prerequisite for entering the mainstream of legal theory. There is a much simpler answer to Professor Klevorick's question. It is that there has been very little applied work on the economics of criminal law—very

310

little attempt, that is to say, to apply the theory to the specific legal doctrines taught in a criminal law class or deployed in a judicial opinion in a criminal appeal. You are not entitled to expect economic originality from judges or practicing lawyers. The lead must be taken by Professor Klevorick and his law school colleagues.

I should add that I think the incompleteness that Professor Klevorick observes in the economic analysis of criminal law is of a rather peripheral character. The crime of buying votes or slaves is not likely to be in the forefront of attention either in a course on criminal law or in the practice of criminal law. While the prohibitions against paying workers less than the minimum wage are important, I believe they are rarely enforced by criminal sanctions. Some victimless crimes that Professor Klevorick does not mention, notably trafficking in narcotics, are very important, and raise questions for an economist because what is being punished are voluntary, and hence presumptively welfare-enhancing, transactions. But most such crimes are made so by legislation rather than by the common law; few economists believe any more that the characteristic product of legislation is welfare-enhancing in an economic sense. Most of the common law crimes are, as the economic analysts claim, attempts to bypass the market in settings of low transaction costs—theft in its myriad forms being the best example. Though in principle, as Professor Klevorick points out, the victim rather than the aggressor might be the "cheaper cost avoider," in Calabresi's terminology, it appears that the market-bypassing acts that have been made criminal are primarily those where the victim is never (or very rarely) the cheapest cost avoider. Other harmful acts are more likely to be governed by tort law, with its concepts of assumption of risk and contributory negligence that facilitate comparing the costs to potential injurer and to potential victim of avoiding injury.[2]

The problem with the economic analysis of criminal law is not that it is incomplete or lacks rigorous philosophical foundations, though it is and does, but that the economic analysts have yet to tackle the principal concepts that trouble legal analysts of the field—such concepts as attempt, conspiracy, diminished responsibility, provocation, insanity, strict criminal liability, recklessness, compulsion or necessity, and premeditation. Moreover, although I do not know whether Professor Klevorick would regard criminal procedure as a separate field (his citation of the Harris article and Isaac Ehrlich's work on capital punishment suggests he would not), the procedural aspects of criminal law are much more important in the practice of law than the substantive aspects. Yet apart from the debate over the deterrent effect of capital punishment, there has been very little economic analysis of criminal procedure, though a recent article by Professor Frank Easterbrook suggests that there are many promising applications of economics to criminal procedure.[3]

The economic analysis of criminal law is indeed full of promise. It offers exciting research opportunities for academic economists interested in law and academic lawyers interested in economics. It would be a shame to defer this research pending the development of a political theory of rights that commands wide agreement.

NOTES

1. For a brief and already rather outdated summary, see Richard A. Posner, *Economic Analysis of Law*, 2d ed., (Boston: Little, Brown, 1977), chap. 7. For an up-to-date bibliography see C.G. Veljanovski, *The New Law-and-Economics: A Research Review* (1982), pp. 83–87. Veljanovski mingles substantive criminal law and criminal procedure; I shall hold them separate till the end of this comment.
2. Professor William Landes and I have discussed this distinction in the context of intentional torts (many of which are also crimes). See William M. Landes and Richard A. Posner, "An Economic Theory of Intentional Torts," *Int 'l. Rev. L. & Econ.*, (1981): 127.
3. Frank H. Easterbrook, "Criminal Procedure as a Market System," *J. Legal Stud.* 12 (1983): 289. See also Posner, Economic Analysis of Law, chap. 21.

[7]

Optimal Sentences for White-Collar Criminals

RICHARD A. POSNER*

Those concerned by the growth of white-collar crime disagree over the choice of a fine or imprisonment as the more appropriate sentence. In this article, Professor Posner argues that a sufficiently large fine is an equally effective deterrent that is cheaper to administer and therefore socially preferable.

I have agreed to participate in this symposium because it gives me an opportunity to argue a favorite plank in the economist's platform for reforming the legal system, in a context in which the economic position can be simply but persuasively stated without elaborate argument and evidence. The plank is the substitution, whenever possible, of the fine (or civil penalty) for the prison sentence as the punishment for crime; the appealing context in which to argue the case for such substitution is the punishment of the white collar criminal.

The coiner of the term "white collar crime" defined it "as a crime committed by a person of respectability and high social status in the course of his occupation,"[1] but this is not a good definition. The terms "respectability" and "high social status" are ambiguous, and the definition arbitrarily excludes certain white-collar crimes, such as evasion of the personal income tax, which are not committed in the course of one's occupation. More important, it is not an apt definition from the standpoint of sentencing policy, which is the focus of this article.

I shall instead, for reasons that I hope will soon become clear, use the term white-collar crime to refer to the nonviolent crimes typically committed by either (1) well-to-do individuals or (2) associations, such as business corporations and labor unions, which are generally "well-to-do" compared to the common criminal. White-collar crime in the sense I use it is illustrated by the criminal offenses created by the securities laws, the labor laws, the antitrust laws, other regulatory statutes, and the income-tax laws. But not every offender under such laws is a white-collar criminal as I use the term. A waitress, for example, could commit a criminal violation of the tax laws by not reporting her tips as income; but because, as we shall see, the affluence of the offender is very important to the correct punishment for the offense, I would not describe *her* offense as a white-collar crime. Nor would a murder committed by a wealthy person—or by a criminal gang seeking to monopolize

---

* Lee and Brena Freeman Professor of Law, University of Chicago. B.A. 1959, Yale University; LL.B. 1962, Harvard University.

1. E. SUTHERLAND, WHITE COLLAR CRIME 9 (1961). *See also* H. PACKER, THE LIMITS OF THE CRIMINAL SANCTION 534 (1968). The term "white collar crime" is, of course, "not subject to any one clear definition." Edelhertz, *The Nature, Impact and Prosecution of White Collar Crime,* in WHITE COLLAR CRIMES: DEFENSE AND PROSECUTION 15, 16 (B. George, Jr. ed. 1971). Edelhertz argues that Sutherland's definition is too restrictive, and proposes the following: "an illegal act or series of illegal acts committed by nonphysical means and by concealment or guile, to obtain money or property, to avoid the payment or loss of money or property, or to obtain business or personal advantage." *Id.* at 16-17. Surely this is too broad—it includes, for example, espionage.

the garbage-collection business of a city, for example—be a white-collar crime; the reason, as again we shall see, is that the proper punishment for a crime of violence raises special questions. To summarize, white-collar crimes are those more likely to be committed by the affluent than by the poor criminal—crimes that involve fraud, monopoly, and breach of faith rather than violence. The white-collar criminal is the affluent perpetrator of those crimes.

The point I wish to argue in this article, an application of the economic analysis of crime and punishment pioneered by Gary Becker,[2] can now be stated simply: the white-collar criminal as I have defined him should be punished only by monetary penalties—by fines (where civil damages or penalties are inadequate or inappropriate)[3] rather than by imprisonment or other "afflictive" punishments (save as they may be necessary to coerce payment of the monetary penalty). In a social cost-benefit analysis of the choice between fining and imprisoning the white-collar criminal, the cost side of the analysis favors fining because, as we shall see, the cost of collecting a fine from one who can pay it (an important qualification) is lower than the cost of imprisonment. On the benefit side, there is no difference in principle between the sanctions. The fine for a white-collar crime can be set at whatever level imposes the same disutility on the defendant, and thus yield the same deterrence, as the prison sentence that would have been imposed instead. Hence, fining the affluent offender is preferable to imprisoning him from society's standpoint because it is less costly and no less efficacious.

The reason that the fine is the cheaper sanction is that, unlike imprisonment, it is a transfer payment. Because the dollars collected from the criminal as a fine show up on the benefit side of the social ledger, the net social cost is limited to the costs of collecting the fine.[4] A term of imprisonment, on the other hand, yields no comparable social revenue if we disregard the negligible, and nowadays usually zero, output of the prisoner. On the contrary, to the social costs of imprisonment must be added the considerable sums spent on maintaining prisoners. To be sure, for a middle-class offender, a short prison term might be the deterrent equivalent of a large fine. But it would not follow that the social costs of the short prison term were correspondingly low, because the greater one's income, the greater is the cost of imprisonment in lost earnings. As long as these are earnings in legitimate occupations, their loss is a social cost similar to the cost of the prison guards. The large fine avoids these costs.

I anticipate relatively little disagreement with the proposition that fines are cheaper to society than imprisonment when the offender can pay the fine. I expect great resistance, however, to the proposition that the social *benefits* of

---

2. *See* Becker, *Crime and Punishment: An Economic Approach*, 76 J. POL. ECON. 169 (1968); for a nontechnical discussion, see R. POSNER, ECONOMIC ANALYSIS OF LAW 164-72 (2d ed. 1977). Becker argues that the use of fines as punishment minimizes the social loss resulting from crime.

3. *See* text accompanying notes 24-27 *infra.*

4. The equation is imprecise because it fails to measure completely the disutility to the offender. If a defendant is risk averse—and assuming (realistically) that the probability of apprehension and conviction is less than one—a fine will impose greater disutility on offenders than the dollar amount of the fine, so that the transfer payment is less than the cost of the punishment. *See* Polinsky & Shavell, *The Optimal Trade-off Between Probability and Magnitude of Fines*, 69 AM. ECON. REV. 880 (1979). But the principle asserted in the text still holds, for in the case of imprisonment there is no transfer payment at all and it is therefore always more costly if the offender can pay the fine.

punishment are no greater when punishment takes the form of imprisonment than when it takes the form of a fine. It will be argued that there is no money equivalent to the pain of imprisonment, perhaps especially to the affluent, educated, "sensitive" person—the white-collar criminal—that would be within his power to pay. (The offender here is necessarily an individual: a corporation or other "artificial" person cannot, of course, be punished by imprisonment.) But whether this is so depends, in a theoretical analysis, on the gravity of the crime in relation to the probability of apprehension and conviction,[5] and, in a practical analysis, on the severity of the prison sentences actually imposed for white-collar crimes. As to the first, it is no doubt true that very few people would consider a fine of any size to be as severe a punishment as death, or imprisonment for life, or, perhaps, imprisonment for twenty years. Thus, if these are optimal punishments (putting aside the consideration that imprisonment is more costly to administer), it might indeed be difficult to find a monetary equivalent. Perhaps these are optimal punishments for some white-collar crimes. If so, my proposal to substitute fines for prison for white-collar criminals is in serious difficulty—but only in a rather academic sense. For whatever may be theoretically optimal, white-collar criminals, at least in this country, are not punished by death or long prison terms. Table 1 provides some data on the type and length of sentences for various federal crimes.[6] With the (surprising) exception of securities offenses, the prison sentences for white-collar crimes—when prison sentences are imposed on the perpetrators of such crimes[7]—barely exceed two years. Even this figure greatly exaggerates the actual time served behind bars, which is shortened by parole and time off for good behavior.

Perhaps, as I have suggested, these prison terms are too short given the gravity of the crimes and the difficulty of detecting them. That is a large question that I do not propose to investigate here. I shall instead treat the existing level of imprisonment for white-collar crime as part of the background of the analysis. Given that level, it is highly improbable that there is *no* fine equivalent to a prison sentence in the amount of disutility it imposes on the offender. An individual who has the boldness, the effrontery, to commit a crime—even of the white-collar variety—will have the capacity and inclination to consider realistic trade-offs between 90 days, or even a year or two, in one of the federal system's minimal security prisons and a hefty fine. If he would be deterred by the threat of such a prison sentence, he would be equally deterred by the threat of a $50,000 or $100,000 or $250,000 fine. (And fines could be indexed to prevent inflation from reducing their bite.)

---

5. *See* Becker, *supra* note 2, at 191-92. For further economic analysis of optimal punishment, see Ehrlich, *Participation in Illegal Activities: An Economic Analysis*, in ESSAYS IN THE ECONOMICS OF CRIME AND PUNISHMENT 68 (G. Becker & W. Landes ed. 1974); Ehrlich, *The Deterrent Effect of Criminal Law Enforcement*, 1 J. LEGAL STUD. 259 (1972).

6. Homicide and robbery are not white-collar crimes; they are included for the sake of comparison. Embezzlement is a mixed case—as indeed are virtually all of the other categories—because it fails to differentiate between the affluent and nonaffluent offender. As I have argued in the text, if a waitress evades federal income tax it might be optimal to imprison rather than fine her because the optimal fine (optimal in light not only of the amount evaded but also of the difficulty of detecting such evasions) might exceed her ability to pay.

7. The difference in Table 1 between the number imprisoned and fined and the total number sentenced is the number placed on probation.

Table 1

TYPE AND LENGTH OF FEDERAL PRISON SENTENCES, 1976

Nature of the Offense	Total Def's Sentenced	Number Imprisoned	Average Sentence of Imprisonment (months)	Number Fined Only
Total	40,112	18,478	47.2	3,198
Homicide, total	108	84	125.1	0
Robbery, total	2,286	2,031	134.3	0
Embezzlement, total	1,650	289	22.4	14
Fraud, total	3,691	1,234	22.7	222
Income Tax	1,157	340	15.4	68
Lending Institutions	390	121	18.4	12
Postal	938	404	31.1	37
Securities and Exchange	86	40	45.7	12
Federal Statutes, total	4,208	565	29.7	1,501
Antitrust	175	1	Not shown	137
Food and Drug Act	103	6	Not shown	78
Customs Laws	182	36	19.9	34
Motor Carrier Act	105	0	Not shown	97
Agricultural Acts	459	3.7	20.0	203
Migratory Bird Laws	894	17	Not shown	621
Postal (other than fraud, obscenity, and embezzlement)	1,003	150	7.6	32

Source: 1977 Sourcebook of Criminal Justice Statistics at pp. 552-53 (Table 5.22).

It should be noted also that the affluent offender presents interesting opportunities for society to exercise its ingenuity in the collection of fines. For example, a penalty that takes the form of barring the defendant from pursuing his occupation—a penalty frequently used by the SEC in dealing with securitites fraud and by state authorities in dealing with misconduct by lawyers—is the equivalent of a fine. The amount of the "fine" is simply the difference between the defendant's future income in the occupation from which he is barred and the income in his best alternative occupation, discounted to present value. This device offers a means of collecting a large fine from an individual who has a large earning capacity but little wealth. An alternative possibility is the collection of a large fine in periodic installments.' The availability of these devices enables one to contemplate realistically the possibility of levying very large fines in lieu of the present prison sentences for white-collar crimes.

If it is objected that the schedule of prison-fine equivalences cannot in fact be calculated, there are two replies. The first is that a nice calculation is not required; the prison sentences imposed in white-collar cases—or in any other cases for that matter—are not themselves the product of any nice calculation of the amount of disutility imposed by the sentence on the offender, but are only the roughest of guesses. The second and more interesting reply is that there are in fact methods, imperfect ones to be sure, of empirically tracing out the curve of indifference between fine and imprisonment. One incomplete method would be to calculate directly the costs of imprisonment to the prisoner (primarily in terms of income foregone by him); the other and, I think, more promising method would be to infer statistically the relative deterrent effect of fine and prison. Suppose that in one federal district the average fine for a federal white-collar offense is $1,000 and the average prison term 30 days, and in another district it is $800 and 40 days, and so forth. Then, by comparing the incidence of the offenses across districts, we should be able to infer the rate of exchange at which days in jail translate into dollars of fine with no loss of deterrence. (A study of state white-collar prosecutions, conducted along similar lines, might also be feasible.) Since no such study has been attempted, I cannot evaluate the difficulties it might encounter arising, for example, because the incidence of many white-collar crimes (*e.g.,* price-fixing conspiracies) is unknown, or the gravity of the crime may vary across districts or states, which affects the optimal sentence.[8] Such a study might not produce results entitled to great confidence. Nevertheless, supplemented by the intuition that guides judges today in devising fine-prison "packages" to impose on white-collar offenders, such a study should provide a close enough approximation of the actual fine-prison trade-off that we need not fear that by substituting fines for prison sentences in white-collar cases we would be drastically altering the expected punishment cost, and hence the level, of white-collar crime. The substitution could, of course, be made incrementally, one offense at a time, starting with the least important.

Professor Coffee, in his contribution to this symposium, offers three reasons why the threat of imprisonment is inherently greater than that of a fine.[9] One is that the optimal fine may exceed the offender's ability to pay.[10] While this is certainly possible, it is no reason to prefer imprisonment to fines in cases where offenders *can* pay the fines. All I am arguing in this paper is that fines are preferable to imprisonment where the fines are collectible.

---

8. Perhaps this problem could be solved by standardizing for income, which might be a reasonable proxy for the expected gains from the crime.

9. *See* Coffee, *Corporate Crime and Punishment: A Non-Chicago View of the Economics of Criminal Sanctions,* 17 AM. CRIM. L. REV. 419 (1980).

10. *Id.* at 434-36.

Second, Coffee, following Block and Lind,[11] argues that in order to be sure that an offender will pay whatever fine is levied, he must be threatened with a prison sentence that is more severe than the fine. If there is no difference in severity, the offender will be indifferent between the two forms of punishment. This point is correct but does not support Coffee's position. The purpose of imprisonment in Block and Lind's analysis is not to deter the offender but to coerce collection of the fine. The very premise of their proposal is thus the superior economic efficiency of fines to imprisonment as a method of punishment.

Third, Coffee erects an elaborate argument on Block and Lind's further point that offenders are risk preferrers with regard to imprisonment even if they are risk averters with regard to fines.[12] Coffee compares two probability distributions of punishment having the same mean, one a distribution of prison sentences and the other a distribution of fines, and argues that the latter distribution will be wider (*i.e.* more dispersed) because there is less difference among individuals in the disutility of imprisonment than in the disutility of fines. Coffee argues that, because the offender is a risk preferrer with regard to imprisonment, the relatively narrow dispersion of the probability distribution of imprisonment will make imprisonment a less attractive form of punishment than its fine equivalent. Of course, if people are risk averse with regard to fines, as Coffee himself had argued initially in his paper,[13] the greater dispersion of the probability distribution of fines would have a deterrent effect symmetrical to that of the narrower dispersion of the probability distribution of imprisonment. Yet Coffee retracts his earlier point and argues that offenders will also be risk preferring with regard to the fine distribution, because the opportunities to conceal assets are greater at the high end of the distribution. Therefore, he concludes, the narrower dispersion of the probability distribution of imprisonment is unequivocally less attractive to offenders.

Every step in Coffee's complicated argument can be questioned, but it is unnecessary to do so because the argument leads nowhere. If it is true, for whatever reason, that imprisonment is unpleasant relative to fines—because of a "stigma" effect,[14] or because prison guards are brutal, or because imprisonment interferes with an offender's predilection for taking risks more than fines do—this affects simply the exchange rate between dollars of fine and days of imprisonment and not the choice of which method of punishment to use. If we think that the term of imprisonment for a crime provides the correct amount of deterrence, then in computing the fine equivalent we will want to be sure that we take account of all of the factors that make imprisonment a source of disutility. The fine equivalent is still the cheaper punishment method, however, as long as the fine can be collected from the offender.

I turn now to what seems a separate, but is really the same, objection to substituting fines for imprisonment in white-collar crimes: namely, that a

---

11. *Id.* at 473-77; *see* Block & Lind, *Crime and Punishment Reconsidered,* 4 J. LEGAL STUD. 241, 244 (1975).

12. Coffee, *supra* note 9, at 430-33; *see* Block & Lind, *An Economic Analysis of Crimes Punishable by Imprisonment,* 4 J. LEGAL STUD. 479, 481 (1975).

13. *See* Coffee, *supra* note 9, at 430.

14. *See* text accompanying notes 23-26 *infra.*

system in which poor offenders were usually imprisoned and rich offenders usually fined would be a system that discriminated against poor people.[15] This argument is just a variant of the fallacy that imprisonment is inherently more punitive than fines. It gains some plausibility only from the ridiculous "rates of exchange" that used to be commonplace in crimes where the criminal had the option of paying a fine or going to jail, a practice that has been invalidated by the Supreme Court under the Equal Protection Clause of the fourteenth amendment.[16] The assumption behind this argument, however, is false. For every prison sentence there is some fine equivalent; if the fine is so large that it cannot be collected, then the offender should be imprisoned. How then are the rich favored under such a system?

A possible answer is that the rich could "buy" more crime under a fine system than under an imprisonment system. Suppose that the expected cost to society of a crime is $100, the probability of apprehension and conviction is 10 percent, and therefore the fine is set at $1,000 so that expected punishment cost will be equal to the expected social cost. A rich man would not be deterred from committing this crime as long as the expected benefits to him were greater than $1000. But now suppose that instead of a fine of $1000, a prison term of one month is imposed for this crime based on a study which shows that the disutility of a month in prison to an average person is $1,000. Since the disutility of imprisonment rises with income, this form of punishment will deter the rich man more than the poor one. Stated differently, a nominally uniform prison term has the effect of price discrimination based on income.

But this is not to say that a system of fines discriminates against the poor. It is rather that a *uniform* prison term discriminates against the rich compared with a *uniform* fine. If we want to discriminate against the rich through a fine system, that is easily done by progressively varying the fine with the offender's income.[17] If we want not to discriminate against the rich through an imprisonment system, we can make the length of the sentence inverse to the offender's income.[18] In either case the choice to discriminate is independent of the form of the punishment.[19]

---

15. The argument is made by Coffee, *supra* note 9, at 446-49.

16. The practice has been invalidated in those cases in which the defendant's indigency is a determining factor in his imprisonment. *See* Tate v. Short, 401 U.S. 395 (1971) (inability to pay fine resulting from traffic offense cannot justify imprisonment if affluent offender not subject to possible imprisonment); Williams v. Illinois, 399 U.S. 235 (1970) (defendant sentenced to fine and imprisonment may not be imprisoned for period greater than statutory maximum because of his inability to pay the fine). In *Williams*, the choice was a $500 fine or 100 days in jail. Putting aside all other costs to the individual of imprisonment, and ignoring taxes, someone who earned $5 a day was better off paying the fine than going to prison, and for an affluent offender there was no semblance of equivalence between the fine and the prison sentence. To take another example (though one not involving a choice by the offender and hence not implicating the constitutional issue decided in *Tate* and *Williams*), the Sherman Act until 1955 provided a maximum prison sentence of one year in jail and a maximum fine of only $5,000. Sherman Act, ch. 647, § 1, 26 Stat. 209 (1890), *as amended by* Act of July 7, 1955, ch. 281, 69 Stat. 282 (substituting $50,000 for $5,000). Today, these maxima are three years and $100,000, a more reasonable rate of exchange though still one unduly favorable to the fine. 15 U.S.C. § 1 (1976).

17. Varying the amount of the fine with the offender's income was first suggested by Jeremy Bentham. J. BENTHAM, THE THEORY OF LITIGATION 217 (Baxi ed., R. Hildreth trans. 1975) ("Pecuniary punishments should always be regulated by the fortune of the offender. The relative amount of the fine should be fixed, not its absolute amount . . . .").

18. *See* Becker, *supra* note 2, at 195.

19. Whether we want to discriminate against the rich in the penal system depends basically on whether

Professor Coffee is of course not alone in disregarding the "equivalence principle" developed above. It is commonly disregarded both in discussions of punishment for white-collar criminals, and in the assumption that only the threat of imprisonment will deter white-collar crime.[20] For example, a survey of merchants "revealed that they considered imprisonment [for black market violations] a far more effective penalty than any other government action, including fines."[21] Findings like these have led some criminologists to consider imprisonment and fines incommensurable sanctions. Yet in the same analysis we read that a company found to have committed black market violations involving 300,000 pounds of meat in a five-month period received a total fine of $1,500; the profit from the violations seems to have been at least $25,000.[22]

Where fines are trivial, it is natural to suppose that only substantial jail sentences will carry a "stigma" effect which adds to deterrence. Yet even if, improbably, imprisonment produced a stigma effect which no magnitude of fine could duplicate, only the rate of exchange between fine and imprisonment, and not the principle of equivalence, would be affected. The fine equivalent would then be higher than if a fine carried a stigma as well. But, in fact, the presence of stigma is an argument for fines rather than for prison sentences. Most students of the criminal process locate the source of the stigma in the fact of conviction rather than the form of the sentence.[23] The more punishment society obtains simply from the stigmatizing effect of conviction, the smaller the fine that must be imposed to produce the optimal severity of punishment; and the smaller the fine, the less likely it is to exceed the white-collar criminal's ability to pay.

The existence of a stigma of conviction[24] bears on the question, why, if a money sanction is adequate, is criminal punishment necessary at all? Why not rely entirely on money damages, as in a civil action? If the stigma arises either because the action is brought by the state and denominated as criminal, or because the higher standard of proof for criminal cases makes it less likely that a convicted defendant is really innocent, then it would be lost if civil penalties were substituted for criminal fines. Of course, the latter aspect of the stigma effect could be preserved simply by increasing the standard of proof in a civil penalty suit to the criminal level.

---

the optimal incidence of the criminal activity, costs of enforcement aside, is zero or greater than zero. If it is zero, then one possible system of punishment would be to levy a fine equal to the offender's total wealth. This, of course, may be viewed as discrimination against the rich because the fine would increase with the offender's wealth. If, however, the criminal activity is not totally devoid of social utility, so that its optimal incidence is not zero, then the object of punishment is not to deter as such but to make the offender internalize the social costs of his activity, and the case for discrimination is no longer established. For in this case we do not want to deprive society of the utility obtained from the criminal's act, but only to make sure that he pays the costs he imposes on others. *See* R. POSNER, *supra* note 2, at 166. Some would argue, of course, that the rich should be punished more severely than the poor in order to make the distribution of wealth more equal. Whatever the merits of greater equality of income in general, the criminal justice system seems a haphazard and inefficient device for redistributing income and wealth.

20. *See, e.g.,* Geis, *Criminal Penalties for Corporate Criminals,* 8 CRIM. L. BULL. 377 (1972).

21. M. CLINARD, THE BLACK MARKET—A STUDY OF WHITE COLLAR CRIME 244 (1969).

22. *Id.*

23. *See, e.g.,* Hart, *The Aims of the Criminal Law,* 23 LAW & CONTEMP. PROB. 401 (1958).

24. This stigma may be especially pronounced in the case of this "sensitive" white-collar criminal as contrasted with the rough, uneducated, and "insensitive" street criminal.

I am not entirely happy with this answer, however, and not only because I think the stigma or moral revulsion that attaches to certain conduct does so because of the nature of the conduct rather than the fact that it is labeled criminal or proceeded against by the criminal process.[25] The economic objection to relying on stigma for deterrence is that, like imprisonment, it is more costly to society than the pure fine (or civil penalty) because it does not yield any revenue. (Stigma, unlike a fine, imposes costs on the criminal with no corresponding gain to society.) Hence, it would seem more efficient to drop the criminal label, and any stigma attached to it, and offset any loss in disutility to the criminal by increasing the size of the civil penalty. In that way, the social revenue can be increased with no loss of deterrence.

In fact a good deal of punishment is meted out in civil penalty suits. The example with which I am most familiar is the treble-damage action in antitrust cases, in which two-thirds of every damage award is in effect a fine—often a much higher one than the statutory maximum for a criminal antitrust suit—albeit the fine is paid to the plaintiff rather than to the state. I am inclined to think that the civil penalty is superior to the criminal fine as a method of punishing white-collar criminals. Whether the penalty should be paid to a private plaintiff or to the state, however, should depend on the relative efficiency of private and public enforcement in particular contexts, an issue discussed elsewhere.[26]

But I am straying into the question of decriminalization. My subject is the sentencing of white-collar criminals, which assumes that some white-collar offenses should, or at least will, continue to be dealt with by the criminal process. If the criminal sanction is to be retained in this area, then, as I have argued in this article, fines should be substituted for prison sentences when the optimal fine is within the power of the offender to pay. In principle, this position could, and I think should, be extended beyond the white-collar domain to include the non-white-collar crimes that the affluent occasionally commit. The problem is that while some of these crimes, such as murder, are so serious that even the affluent cannot pay adequate fines, not all white-collar crimes are less serious than crimes of violence. Nevertheless, the most serious white-collar crimes are probably committed by corporations rather than by individuals. Within this corporate category, the gravity of the offense is probably more or less proportional to the size of the company, so solvency limitations should not preclude the imposition of very large fines for white-collar crime where such fines are optimal.

The reference to corporations brings me to the final point that I want to make in this article. It concerns the case for a different approach to crimes committed by individuals acting as agents of corporations or other associations rather than acting on their own behalf. There is an argument that I have

---

25. An intermediate position is that the fact of conviction has a moral effect which can, however, be impaired if the criminal label is attached to conduct that the community does not regard as morally reprehensible. *See* Kadish, *Some Observations on the Use of Criminal Sanctions in Enforcing Economic Regulations,* 30 U. CHI. L. REV. 423 (1963). The problem with this position is that it implies that the stigma derives from community opinion rather than from the denomination of conduct as criminal. If so, then logically there is no stigmatizing effect of conviction to be blunted.

26. *See* Landes & Posner, *The Private Enforcement of Law,* 4 J. LEGAL STUD. 1 (1975). In some cases, primarily where the probability of detection and punishment of a wrongful act is near unity without much investment in detection and punishment, such as breach of contract, the optimal "penalty" will be simple damages.

made elsewhere in the antitrust context for confining criminal (or civil-penalty) liability to the corporation, on the theory that if it is liable it will find adequate ways of imposing on its employees the costs to it of violating the law.[27] Of course, this assumes the existence of an adequate set of sanctions, capable of hurting the corporation for its violations of the law. Perhaps this is too quixotic an assumption or aspiration (outside of the antitrust context) to support so radical a proposal. I mention it only to make clear that the adoption of such a proposal would still leave a wide area in which one would want to retain criminal or civil-penalty sanctions for white-collar crime as I have defined it; for not all white-collar crimes are the work of corporations—and in the area of income tax, for example, not most. But wherever and for whatever reason it is decided to retain criminal sanctions for individual white-collar offenders, the movement should be toward the abolition of imprisonment and the substitution of fines—albeit fines more severe than those today meted out to such offenders.

---

27. *See* R. POSNER, ANTITRUST LAW: AN ECONOMIC PERSPECTIVE 225-26 (1976).

PART III

LABOR LAW AND EMPLOYMENT DISCRIMINATION

[8]

Some Economics of Labor Law

Richard A. Posner†

The law governing employment is of vast compass. Among the subjects it embraces are racial and sexual discrimination in employment, the liability of an employer ("master") for the torts of his employees ("servants"), the regulation of occupational health and safety, employees' rights under the pension-regulation law (ERISA), the emerging tort of wrongful discharge of an employee at will, and much else besides. But, to lawyers anyway, the most important subjéct in the law of employment, as measured by the number of cases, the density of legal doctrine, and other measures of legal activity, remains—even in a period of union decline—the regulation by the National Labor Relations Board of the process by which unions seek to bargain collectively on behalf of workers.[1] This regulation is conducted under the authority of the National Labor Relations Act,[2] which is the Wagner Act of 1935,[3] as amended, principally by the Taft-Hartley Act of 1947.[4] When I use the term "labor law" in this paper, I shall, unless otherwise indicated, be referring to this regulatory scheme, even though properly speaking it is just a part of a much larger field.

Whether defined broadly or, as I am doing, narrowly, labor law is as natural a field for the application of economics to law as one could imagine. It regulates explicit markets that have been a subject of continuous and fruitful economic study since Adam Smith's

† Judge, United States Court of Appeals for the Seventh Circuit; Senior Lecturer, University of Chicago Law School. This is the revised text of a paper given on April 27, 1984, àt the Symposium on the Conceptual Foundations of Labor Law, held at the University of Chicago Law School, sponsored jointly with the Social Philosophy and Policy Center of Bowling Green State University. The author is grateful to William Landes, Douglas Leslie, Michael Lindsay, Bernard Meltzer, Melvin Reder, Ronald Schy, George Stigler, and James Talent for many helpful comments on a previous draft of this paper.

[1] Regulation by the NLRB is subject to review by the federal courts of appeals, 29 U.S.C. § 160(e) (1982), and on writ of certiorari by the Supreme Court, 28 U.S.C. § 1254 (1982).

[2] 29 U.S.C. §§ 151-169 (1982).

[3] Pub. L. No. 74-198, 49 Stat. 449 (1935) (codified as amended at 29 U.S.C. §§ 151-169 (1982)).

[4] Labor-Management Relations Act, Pub. L. No. 80-101, 61 Stat. 136 (1947) (codified as amended at 29 U.S.C. §§ 141-197 (1982)).

988

day.[5] And though in recent years the focus of labor economics has shifted from unions to other phenomena of labor markets,[6] such as human capital and employment discrimination, there is a rich—and reviving—contemporary literature on the economics of unions.[7] Moreover, as I shall argue in this paper, a well-developed field of economic analysis outside of labor economics—the economic analysis of cartels—can yield to the student of the legal regulation of unionizing many insights.

Yet despite abundant opportunity, there has been relatively little writing in an economic vein about the particulars of labor law, especially—and especially surprisingly—of labor law as I am narrowly defining it.[8] There are, I conjecture (a word used advisedly), two reasons for this situation. The first is that because labor law is doctrinally complex (much more so than antitrust, the economists' favorite field of law), economists have not found it accessible in the way they have found antitrust law, and more recently

---

[5] For a summary of the economics of labor, see R. EHRENBERG & R. SMITH, MODERN LABOR ECONOMICS: THEORY AND PUBLIC POLICY (1982); *see also* THE ECONOMICS OF TRADE UNIONS: NEW DIRECTIONS (J. Rosa ed. 1984); F. MARSHALL, A. KING & V. BRIGGS, LABOR ECONOMICS: WAGES, EMPLOYMENT, AND TRADE UNIONISM (4th ed. 1980). A notable contribution, highly pertinent to the theme of this article, is MANCUR OLSON, THE LOGIC OF COLLECTIVE ACTION 66-97 (1965). The current periodical literature is well-illustrated by Lazear, *A Competitive Theory of Monopoly Unionism*, 73 AM. ECON. REV. 631 (1983).

[6] *See* Johnson, *Economic Analysis of Trade Unionism*, 65 AM. ECON. REV. PAPERS & PROC. 23 (May 1975).

[7] *See, e.g.*, NEW APPROACHES TO LABOR UNIONS (J. Reid ed.) (Research in Labor Economics Supp. 2, 1983); ALBERT REES, THE ECONOMICS OF TRADE UNIONS (2d rev. ed. 1977); sources cited *supra* notes 5-6.

[8] Some exceptions to this generalization should be noted. There is an economically informed literature on the application of the antitrust laws to the union activities that are not exempt from those laws. *See, e.g.*, Leslie, *Right to Control: A Study in Secondary Boycotts and Labor Antitrust*, 89 HARV. L. REV. 904 (1976); Meltzer, *Labor Unions, Collective Bargaining, and the Antitrust Laws,* 32 U. CHI. L. REV. 659 (1965). There is, of course, an extensive economic literature on the effects of laws regulating wages and hours, industrial health and safety, and employment discrimination. Wrongful discharge is a new area of labor law that has received interesting economic treatment recently. *See* Epstein, *In Defense of the Contract at Will*, 51 U. CHI. L. REV. 947 (1984); Harrison, *The "New" Terminable-at-Will Employment Contract: An Interest and Cost Incidence Analysis*, 69 IOWA L. REV. 327 (1984). But economic analyses of specific provisions of the National Labor Relations Act appear to be rare, although I do not pretend to have made a complete search of the literature. I have found a few brief analyses of such provisions by economists. *See* JACK HIRSHLEIFER, PRICE THEORY AND APPLICATIONS 380-82 (3d ed. 1984); Alchian, *Decision Sharing and Expropriable Specific Quasi-Rents: A Theory of* First National Maintenance Corporation v. NLRB, 1 S. CT. ECON. REV. 235 (1982). Some contributions of economically minded lawyers are cited *infra* notes 9 & 21. The legal community is not unaware of the economic literature on unions—quite the contrary. *See, e.g.*, BERNARD D. MELTZER, LABOR LAW: CASES, MATERIALS, AND PROBLEMS 37-94 (2d ed. 1977). But for the most part that literature has not yet been brought to bear on particular provisions of the NLRA.

tort law, accessible. The second reason is that because labor law is (as we shall see) founded on a policy that is the opposite of the policies of competition and economic efficiency that most economists support, the field is unlikely to attract, as a subject for teaching and scholarship, the lawyer who is deeply committed to economic analysis; it is likely to repel him. Of course, you don't have to agree with the normative premises of a field to find it a worthwhile subject for teaching and scholarship. But the fact is—I suppose it reflects the lawyer's training in advocacy—that it is rare for a law professor to make a sustained commitment to a field for whose premises he feels no sympathy at all.

Nevertheless, and somewhat ironically since unions have been in decline in the United States, England, and other countries in recent years, the last few months have seen the appearance of several interesting papers in which economic analysis is brought to bear (in very different ways) on specific problems of labor law in my narrow sense of the term.[9]

One task I have set myself in this paper is simply to make labor law less mysterious to economists, in the hope that they will be encouraged to overcome a natural resistance to immersion in complex legal doctrine. I shall begin therefore with a brief sketch of the American system of labor law and then propose a simple economic model of that system. My basic thesis will be that American labor law is best understood as a device for facilitating, though not to the maximum possible extent, the cartelization of the labor supply by unions. Lest this seem an impolitic (especially for a judge) condemnation of the union movement, I emphasize that I am using the word "cartelization" in a nonpejorative, technical sense: it is the cooperative endeavor of competing sellers to raise the prices of their goods or services (here labor services) above the level that would prevail under conditions of unregulated competition. I take no position on whether it is socially preferable for the price of labor to be determined on a competitive or on a cartelized basis. My analysis is positive, not normative.

---

[9] *See* Epstein, *A Common Law for Labor Relations: A Critique of the New Deal Labor Legislation*, 92 YALE L.J. 1357 (1983) [hereinafter cited as Epstein, *Common Law*]; Epstein, *Agency Costs, Employment Contracts, and Labor Values*, in THE AGENCY RELATIONSHIP (J. Pratt & R. Zeckhauser eds. forthcoming); Leslie, *Labor Bargaining Units*, 70 VA. L. REV. 353 (1984). Professor Epstein's papers sound themes very similar to those that I develop in this paper. It may be significant that neither of us is a specialist in labor law.

I. AMERICAN LABOR LAW

Professor Richard Epstein has conducted a very useful survey of the position of the common law with regard to labor unions.[10] Although that position is typically and not inaccurately described as "anti-union," Professor Epstein shows that it could just as well be called "pro-competitive," or, as some economic analysts of the common law would have it, "pro-efficiency."[11] At common law, labor unions were recognized for what they were: worker cartels designed to raise the price of labor above the competitive level.[12] Picketing, too, was recognized for what it was: an attempt to interfere, by means inherently intimidating, with contractual relationships between the picketed firm and its customers and suppliers, including new workers hired to replace the strikers.[13] So-called "yellow dog" contracts (under which workers agreed not to join unions during the term of their employment) were enforced on the assumption, congenial to classical economic thinking, that the worker was compensated for giving up his right to join a union.[14] If he was not *generously* compensated, that was nothing to worry about; compensation for not combining with other workers to create a labor monopoly is itself a form of monopoly rent.

It can of course be argued that this picture of an efficient common law of labor relations rests on unrealistic premises about the nature of labor markets, especially in the years prior to the revolution in labor law brought about by the Wagner Act in 1935. If many workers were ignorant of their alternative employment opportunities, wages would frequently have been below the competitive level. If many workers (especially, perhaps, older workers) would have incurred heavy costs by changing jobs, maybe because they had become specialized to a particular employer's methods or had developed close social and family ties to a particular community or region, employers would have monopsony power, and the workers might be paid less than a competitive wage.[15] If, as Adam Smith believed, conspiracies among employers to depress wages

---

[10] *See* Epstein, *Common Law, supra* note 9, at 1358-86.

[11] This finding provides additional support for the thesis, which I have expounded elsewhere, that the common law is on the whole efficiency-promoting. *See, e.g.,* RICHARD A. POSNER, ECONOMIC ANALYSIS OF LAW 25-191 (2d ed. 1977).

[12] *See* SELIG PERLMAN, A HISTORY OF TRADE UNIONISM IN THE UNITED STATES 147 (1922).

[13] *See, e.g.,* Vegelahn v. Guntner, 167 Mass. 92, 97-98, 44 N.E. 1077, 1081 (1896).

[14] *See generally* Epstein, *Common Law, supra* note 9, at 1370-75, 1382-85.

[15] This description is not wholly accurate; the situation would be one of bilateral monopoly since specialization would also tend to give the workers monopoly power.

were common,[16] this would be another source of monopsony power.

These conditions *may* have been common in the nineteenth and early twentieth centuries in this country, when there were low levels of worker education, a great deal of immigrant labor, a limited number of employers in some markets, no serious enforcement of antitrust laws against employer cartels, and some obstacles to labor mobility (though Americans have always moved around a lot).[17] But against all this must be set the facts that in the great era of immigration between the Civil War and the end of unrestricted immigration after World War I, America had a chronic labor shortage, which was the main reason for the great immigration; that wages were much higher in the United States than in the rest of the world; and that competition for workers must have been intense and should have limited the extent of monopsony power in labor markets.[18]

Even assuming that American labor markets were substantially distorted from the competitive norm in ways that unions might have alleviated,[19] by 1935 these distortions must have been largely in the past (they certainly have a quaint ring today). But whether economically justified or not, the Wagner Act brought about a revolution in the American law of labor relations. The common law was displaced by a system of federal regulation administered by a new agency, the National Labor Relations Board, and designed—as its sponsors and supporters made clear[20] and as is anyway obvious from the structure of the Act—to foster unionization. In the Taft-Hartley Act in 1947, Congress redressed the Wagner Act's tilt toward unions somewhat. Legislative and judicial

---

[16] ADAM SMITH, THE WEALTH OF NATIONS 66-67 (Mod. Lib. reprint 1937, E. Cannan ed. 1904) (1st ed. London 1776).

[17] *See generally* DON D. LESCOHIER, 3 HISTORY OF LABOR IN THE UNITED STATES, 1896-1932, at 15-47, 293-302 (1935).

[18] *Id.*

[19] But not cured: the negotiations between monopolistic unions and monopsonistic employers, a situation of classic bilateral monopoly, will result in fewer employees than under competition because both sides are trying to restrict the supply of labor. *Cf.* GEORGE J. STIGLER, THE THEORY OF PRICE 207-08 (3d ed. 1966).

[20] *See, e.g.*, 78 CONG. REC. 3443 (1934) (statement of Sen. Wagner); 78 CONG. REC. 3679 (1934) (address by Sen. Wagner); *Hearings on S. 2926: Hearings Before the Senate Comm. on Education and Labor*, 73d Cong., 2d Sess. 59 (1934) (statement of Dr. Sumner Slichter, Professor of Economics, Harvard Business School, and William Green, President, AFL); 79 CONG. REC. 267 (1935) (address by Donald Richberg, Executive Director, National Emergency Council); *Hearings on S. 1958: Hearings Before Senate Comm. on Education and Labor*, 74th Cong., 1st Sess. 151 (1935) (statement of Charlton Ogburn, counsel for AFL), *reprinted in* 1 NLRB LEGISLATIVE HISTORY OF THE NATIONAL LABOR RELATIONS ACT OF 1935, at 15, 20, 95-99, 1291-92, 1531 (1949).

innovation since 1947 has greatly expanded the scope of labor law, so that today, as I said at the outset, it extends beyond the regulation of union-organizing activities to embrace the internal governance of unions, racial and other discrimination in labor markets, the regulation of pension plans, and much else besides. But the core of modern labor law remains the NLRB's regulation, under the Wagner Act as amended by the Taft-Hartley Act, of unions' efforts to organize employees and bargain with the employers on their behalf.[21]

Rather than attempt to summarize the relevant statutory provisions and interpretive doctrines, I will try to convey the essential features of the NLRB's regulation through a description of the process of union organizing and bargaining as it might occur in a small industrial plant.[22] The process begins with an employee of a union ("business agent," he is usually called) approaching a friendly employee of the plant (sometimes the plant employee initiates the contact) and giving him union authorization cards to hand out to his fellow employees; when signed, these cards authorize the union to represent the employees who sign them.[23] The importance of union authorization cards lies in the fact that if a majority of the workers in the bargaining unit (of which more presently) sign them, the employer may decide to recognize the union as the workers' exclusive representative for collective bar-

---

[21] Two other statutes complete the core: the Norris-LaGuardia Act, 29 U.S.C. §§ 101-115 (1982), which among other things greatly restricts the authority of the federal courts to issue injunctions in labor cases, and the Railway Labor Act, 45 U.S.C. §§ 151-188 (1982), which imposes a form of compulsory arbitration on the railroad and airline industries. Compulsory arbitration is also a common legal regime for labor relations in the public sector, which is exempt from the federal labor laws and will not be discussed in this paper, in part because it is already the subject of a rich, and economically well-informed, literature. *See, e.g.,* H. WELLINGTON & R. WINTER, THE UNIONS AND THE CITIES (1971); Meltzer & Sunstein, *Public Employee Strikes, Executive Discretion, and the Air Traffic Controllers,* 50 U. CHI. L. REV. 731, 738-44 (1983). On the economics of compulsory arbitration, see Ashenfelter & Bloom, *Models of Arbitrator Behavior: Theory and Evidence,* 74 AM. ECON. REV. 111 (1984).

[22] The reader who wants greater detail and citations to cases is advised to begin with ROBERT A. GORMAN, BASIC TEXT ON LABOR LAW: UNIONIZATION AND COLLECTIVE BARGAINING (1976). This is a lucid, compact, and relatively nontechnical introduction to the field. No extensive knowledge of law is required to be able to read it with understanding and profit. Also very good and more up-to-date, though longer, is the two-volume THE DEVELOPING LABOR LAW (C. Morris 2d ed. 1983). For a brief, serviceable description of the federal labor statutes for nonlawyers, see F. MARSHALL, A. KING & V. BRIGGS, *supra* note 5, at 426-52.

[23] *See* R. GORMAN, *supra* note 22, at 41. The reason the business agent will work through one or more plant employees, rather than distribute the cards himself, is that the Board allows the employer to forbid union solicitation on his premises. The Board's position rests on the practical ground that a stranger's presence on the premises can disrupt work discipline and in some cases can be a hazard to the employees' safety.

gaining without the formality of a representation election.[24] More important, if at least thirty percent of the workers sign authorization cards and the employer refuses to recognize the union, the Board will order a representation election.[25]

The efforts of an employee to induce his fellows to sign union authorization cards would often, in the absence of legal protection or of successful concealment by the employee of his activities, be set at naught by the employer's firing him. This would be an example of rational predatory action.[26] It is true that the employer would impose a cost on himself by firing the worker, assuming that he was a satisfactory worker (and if he were not, he probably would have been fired already). But the cost would be small compared with the benefit to the employer of signaling to the remaining employees that if any one of them stepped forward to take the place of the fired employee as the union's organizer, he would be fired too. True, if the workers hung together and struck in support of the fired employee, the balance of costs would be altered and the employer might back down. But since the workers would be unorganized (for I am speaking of how an employer might try to thwart an organizational drive), a strike might be difficult to arrange: the workers would face classic free-rider problems. Those problems, however, should not be exaggerated. There were independent unions (as well as "company unions," which the Wagner Act forbade[27]) long before the Wagner Act was passed.[28] But the fraction of workers who were unionized rose very rapidly after the Act was passed, and this is some evidence that it was indeed difficult to organize workers without the protections that the Act extended to union-organizing efforts.

The key protections are in the sections of the Act that entitle employees to engage in concerted activities and that make it unlawful for the employer to interfere with those activities.[29] Firing an employee because he is trying to organize the plant presents a

---

[24] *See id.* at 230.

[25] *See* 29 C.F.R. § 101.18(a) (1983).

[26] For an alternative characterization, see *infra* notes 52-55 and accompanying text.

[27] *See* National Labor Relations Act § 8(a)(2), 29 U.S.C. § 158(a)(2) (1982).

[28] For an interesting, if dated, treatment of independent unions, see S. PERLMAN, *supra* note 12. Incidentally, chapter 7 contains some interesting discussion of common law attitudes toward labor unions.

[29] *See* National Labor Relations Act §§ 7-8, 29 U.S.C. §§ 157-58 (1982); *see also* Inter-Collegiate Press v. NLRB, 486 F.2d 837, 845 (8th Cir. 1973) ("Conduct having even a 'comparatively slight' impact on employee rights may be a violation of § 8(a)(3), unless the employer has established a legitimate and substantial business justification." (citation omitted)).

clear case of unlawful interference, as do much milder forms of retaliation—even something as trivial as not inviting the employee to
a company party.[30] The employer is thus denied the natural advantage that he would have, as one facing many, in fending off organizing activities. In addition, "yellow dog" contracts are forbidden by section 3 of the Norris-LaGuardia Act.[31]

Let us assume that the union organizer has gotten signatures
from thirty percent of the employees. The next step chronologi-
cally is the election campaign, but before getting to that I must
pause briefly to discuss the electoral unit, or the "bargaining unit"
as it is called. It is not a synonym for the firm, or even for the
plant. Rather, it is any group of employees that the Board decides
is sufficiently homogeneous, and sufficiently distinct from other
employees, to be allowed to form its own bargaining unit.[32]
Ordinarily, though not always, the unit will be limited to one plant
even if the firm owns other plants as well. Often there will be more
than one unit in the plant or facility. For example, a single hospital, whether or not part of a chain, might contain separate units for
doctors, for registered nurses, for nurses' aides and other maintenance employees, and perhaps for technical employees such as X-
ray technicians. The Board's discretion in determining the appropriate bargaining unit for a particular type of firm is broad, but
there are some restrictions on it; most important, the Taft-Hartley
Act denies protected status to supervisory employees, from fore-
men on up, unless their supervisory responsibilities are incidental
(e.g., a doctor supervising his secretary).[33]

Only one question is put to the electorate—the members of
the bargaining unit—in the representation election: whether to
make the union that is trying to organize the unit the exclusive
agent of the unit employees for purposes of bargaining with the
employer over wages and working conditions.[34] The outcome of the
election is determined by majority vote of the employees in the
unit, voting by secret ballot.[35] The election is preceded by a campaign that in some ways is like a political campaign. But it is
shorter, and the voting is on whether to unionize rather than on
candidates for office. Furthermore, the contending parties—union

---

[30] *See* NLRB v. Village IX, Inc., 723 F.2d 1360, 1366-67 (7th Cir. 1983).

[31] 29 U.S.C. § 103 (1982).

[32] *See* National Labor Relations Act § 9(b), 29 U.S.C § 159(b) (1982).

[33] *See id.* (as amended by Taft-Hartley Act) §§ 2(3), 2(11), 7, 29 U.S.C. §§ 152(3),
152(11), 157 (1982).

[34] *See id.* § 9(a), 29 U.S.C. § 159(a) (1982).

[35] *See id.* § 9(c)(1), 29 U.S.C. § 159(c)(1) (1982).

and employer—are more limited in what they are allowed to say than are candidates and supporters in political elections: not only must the employer refrain from firing union adherents or otherwise interfering with the union's campaign, but he may not threaten retaliation if the union wins or promise specific benefits if the union loses;[36] promises of benefits if the candidate wins are of course a staple of true political campaigns.

If the union loses a valid representation election, the Board will not direct another election for a year,[37] and then only if the union again gets at least thirty percent of the employees to sign union authorization cards.[38] If the union wins the election the consequences are more complicated. First, all the employees in the bargaining unit, whether or not they voted for the union and whether or not they want to belong to it, are forbidden to bargain individually with the employer;[39] the union is as much the exclusive bargaining representative of the dissenters as of the employees who voted for it. Second, all the employees, again regardless of their personal sympathies, must, if the collective-bargaining agreement between the employer and the union so provides (and it is a provision for which unions press very hard in negotiations), pay union dues and often must actually join the union.[40] Third, the employer must negotiate with the union in good faith for a collective-bargaining agreement that will specify the terms and conditions of employment of the members of the unit[41] for a specified period, usually one to three years.

But the employer is not required to yield to the union's demands even in part (which makes one wonder whether the duty to bargain in good faith has much bite), and often he will not. In that event the union may decide to call a strike in an effort to win at least partial agreement to its demands. If it does not call a strike, even though the employer has made no significant concessions to its demands, the union may lose the workers' support: they will see that they are getting nothing in exchange for union dues that are

---

[36] See NLRB v. Exchange Parts Co., 375 U.S. 405, 409 (1964) ("We have no doubt that [the NLRA] prohibits not only intrusive threats and promises but also conduct immediately favorable to employees which is undertaken with the express purpose of impinging upon their freedom of choice for or against unionization and is reasonably calculated to have that effect.").

[37] See National Labor Relations Act § 9(c)(3), 29 U.S.C. § 159(c)(3) (1982).

[38] See 29 C.F.R. § 101.18(a) (1983).

[39] See National Labor Relations Act § 9(a), 29 U.S.C. § 159(a) (1982).

[40] See NLRB v. General Motors Corp., 373 U.S. 734, 740-44 (1963).

[41] See National Labor Relations Act § 8(d), 29 U.S.C. § 158(d) (1982).

not trivial.

The economic function of the strike requires consideration at this point. It is related to the bilateral-monopoly character of labor-management negotiations. When a nonlabor market becomes cartelized, members of the cartel raise their price and, anticipating some substitution away from their product by consumers, reduce output, but not to zero. But if there were only one consumer for the cartel's product, he might say to the cartel, "I won't buy from you at the higher price," and they would then face the choice of either backing down or not selling to him. This happens occasionally in nonlabor markets, but in labor markets it happens often. The union deals with a single employer (or several employers bargaining as one in a multi-employer bargaining unit), who may be tempted to refuse to accept the union's demands (i.e., may threaten to buy nothing rather than come to terms), and then the union must either strike in order to enforce its terms or else back down. The union cannot just write off this "customer" as marginal, as a product monopolist often can when he raises his price; for each employer's work force will be represented by its own local union (often more than one), and if the union ignores the workers' interests they will vote the union out and the employer will be free to go his own way. Thus we have a classic example of bilateral monopoly: the union and employer can deal only with each other and a refusal to deal, by imposing costs on the other party, makes him more likely to come to terms. The strike imposes costs on both parties: on the employer, by forcing him to reduce or cease production, and on the workers, by stopping their wages. The balance of those costs will determine the ultimate settling point between the union's initial demand and the employer's initial offer.

Labor law affects these costs. For example, the Board allows the employer, if there is a strike, to hire replacements for the striking workers.[43] He is even allowed to offer the replacement workers permanent jobs—and to do so even if such an offer would not be necessary to induce them to work for him. It would never be necessary if the employer were permitted to pay a wage high enough to induce a replacement to work temporarily, without promise of a permanent job. But the employer is not permitted to pay replacement workers a higher wage than he paid the workers who have struck. This rule shifts the balance the other way; it limits the em-

---

[43] *See* NLRB v. Mackay Radio & Tel. Co., 304 U.S. 333, 345 (1938) ("Nor [is] it an unfair labor practice to replace the striking employes with others in an effort to carry on the business.").

ployer's ability to hire replacements, permanent or temporary.

Although, subject to this qualification, the employer may hire permanent replacements, he may not fire the striking workers who have been replaced.[43] True, unless the strike was provoked by an employer's unfair labor practice, the employer does not have to reinstate all of the strikers as soon as the strike ends or pay any of them their back wages. But when the strike is over, those strikers whose places have been filled by permanent replacements must be put at the head of the queue, to be reinstated as vacancies appear, and those strikers whose places have not been filled must be reinstated immediately.[44]

Attempts to defeat strikes by hiring replacement workers are less common than one might expect; more common is the use of supervisory personnel to replace the striking workers temporarily (hence the importance of the National Labor Relations Act's exclusion of such personnel from the Act's protections). The problem with using replacement workers is that in order to get to the workplace they will have to cross the picket line thrown up by the striking workers' union. Even though picketers are not legally privileged to use force to prevent the crossing of picket lines, whether by replacement workers or by customers or suppliers of the picketed establishment, there is often a latent threat of violence (which cannot, however, be used as a ground for firing or enjoining a picketer[45]), especially against replacement workers ("scabs"). And in pro-union communities the police may not have the desire or ability to control this threat effectively (though they may come down hard on any effort by the employer to hire "goons" to intimidate the picketers). Usually the picketing workers can at the very least identify the replacement workers, who may therefore fear eventual retaliation even if the picketing itself is completely peaceful. Their fear will be enhanced by the Act's provision forbidding the employer to fire striking workers. When the strikers eventually return to work, they will be working side-by-side with the permanent replacements, who may entertain fears for their own safety or at least for the continued congeniality of the workplace.

---

[43] 29 U.S.C. § 152(3) (1982) preserves the strikers' status as "employees" protected by the NLRA. See also NLRB v. Fleetwood Trailer Co., 389 U.S. 375, 378 (1967) ("[U]nless the employer who refuses to reinstate strikers can show that his action was due to 'legitimate and substantial business justifications,' he is guilty of an unfair labor practice." (citation omitted)).

[44] See NLRB v. Fleetwood Trailer Co., 389 U.S. 375, 379 (1967).

[45] See, e.g., Chevron U.S.A., Inc. v. NLRB, 672 F.2d 359, 360-61 (3d Cir. 1982); NLRB v. W.C. McQuaide, Inc., 552 F.2d 519, 527-28 (3d Cir. 1977).

If a collective-bargaining contract between union and employer is signed, with or without a strike, it will be judicially enforceable in accordance with a federal common law of collective-bargaining contracts.[46] Often such contracts contain no-strike clauses, and if such a clause is violated, the employer may be able to get an injunction against the strike and an award of damages against the union.[47] Whether or not there is a no-strike clause, a "wildcat" strike—a strike not authorized by the union—is not protected activity if it has a tendency to interfere with the union's role as exclusive bargaining representative;[48] and if a strike is unprotected, the employer can fire the wildcat strikers with impunity.

Unlike an elected public official, a union that is elected to be the collective-bargaining representative of some unit does not serve a fixed term. But upon a showing that the union probably has lost majority support the employer can file an election petition or can refuse to bargain with the union and thus force the union to file such a petition.[49] In such a case the Board will order a new election if at least one year has elapsed since the union was certified as the unit's bargaining representative.[50]

II.   UNIONS AS LABOR CARTELS

Cognoscenti of labor law will recognize the preceding discussion as but a crude thumbnail sketch of the law of collective bargaining. But it will serve to frame an inquiry into the economic logic of that law. My discussion will be illustrative rather than exhaustive: multi-employer bargaining, secondary boycotts, and antitrust restrictions on union activity are among the relevant topics that I have omitted in the interests of time and space.

If unionization is a means of cartelizing labor markets, the National Labor Relations Act, which even with the Taft-Hartley amendments plainly fosters unionization, is likewise a means to cartelize such markets. Economists have long treated unions as labor cartels,[51] though alternative explanations have been ad-

---

[46] Textile Workers Union v. Lincoln Mills, 353 U.S. 448, 456-57 (1957).

[47] Boys Mkts., Inc. v. Retail Clerks' Local 770, 398 U.S. 235, 252-54 (1970).

[48] *See* Emporium Capwell Co. v. Western Addition Community Org., 420 U.S. 50, 70-73 (1975) (unauthorized strike by minority employees to protest discrimination not protected by NLRA).

[49] *See* National Labor Relations Act § 9(e)(1), 29 U.S.C. § 159(e)(1) (1982).

[50] *See id.* § 9(e)(2), 29 U.S.C. § 159(e)(2), (1982).

[51] *See, e.g.,* J. HIRSCHLEIFER, *supra* note 8, at 380-82; G. STIGLER, *supra* note 19, at 268-70; Friedman, *Some Comments on the Significance of Labor Unions for Economic Policy,* in THE IMPACT OF THE UNION 204 (D. Wright ed. 1951); Lazear, *A Microeconomic Theory of*

vanced.[52] One is that the way in which unions benefit their members is not by reducing the supply of labor (and hence forcing up the price, i.e., wages), but by increasing the productivity of the work force.[53] This they are said to do in various ways. One is by providing a vehicle for collecting, and communicating to the employer, workers' complaints about wages and working conditions.[54] In the absence of such a vehicle, it is argued, workers might be afraid to voice their complaints, and the employer would learn of them only indirectly and belatedly, by observing a higher quit rate. Another example: unions invariably press for inclusion, in any collective-bargaining contracts that they negotiate, of a provision forbidding management to fire workers except for good cause, and requiring it, when it lays off workers because of an economic downturn, to lay them off in reverse order of seniority (i.e., juniors first). When such job security is lacking, as is usually the case in nonunion firms, the older, more experienced workers may—it is argued—be reluctant to share their know-how with the younger, newer employees, fearing that if they do the younger employees will then be competing for their jobs. As a result of this reluctance, productivity is thought to suffer.

Although some empirical support has been marshaled for this productivity-enhancement theory of unionization,[55] the theory is extremely hard to accept. It is inconsistent with the fundamental assumption of economics: that people, in this case employers, are rational profit or utility maximizers. Although this assumption may not hold true in all settings, the behavior of business employers towards their employees is one setting where it probably does.

Labor Unions, in NEW APPROACHES TO LABOR UNIONS, *supra* note 7, at 53; Machlup, *Monopolistic Wage Determinations as a Part of the General Problem of Monopoly,* in CHAMBER OF COMMERCE OF THE UNITED STATES, ECONOMIC INSTITUTE ON WAGE DETERMINATION AND THE ECONOMICS OF LIBERALISM 49 (1947); Reder, *Unionism, Wages, and Contract Enforcement,* in NEW APPROACHES TO LABOR UNIONS, *supra* note 7, at 27; Simons, *Some Reflections on Syndicalism,* 52 J. POL. ECON. 1, 6-9 (1944); Viner, *The Role of Costs in a System of Economic Liberalism,* in CHAMBER OF COMMERCE OF THE UNITED STATES, *supra,* at 15.

[53] *See, e.g.,* Brown & Medoff, *Trade Unions in the Production Process,* 86 J. POL. ECON. 355 (1978); Freeman, *Individual Mobility and Union Voice in the Labor Market,* 66 AM. ECON. REV. PAPERS & PROC. 361 (1976); Freeman & Medoff, *The Two Faces of Unionism,* 57 PUB. INTEREST 69 (1979); Lester, *Reflections on the "Labor Monopoly" Issue,* 55 J. POL. ECON. 513 (1947); and for an able summary, Leslie, *supra* note 9, at 910-20.

[53] *See, e.g.,* Brown & Medoff, *supra* note 52, at 356-59; Freeman, *supra* note 52, at 365.

[54] *See, e.g.,* Freeman, *supra* note 52, at 366 (unionism is a "market mechanism for imparting information, aggregating preferences, [and] altering authority relations"); *see also* Freeman & Medoff, *supra* note 52, at 70-74.

[55] *See* Brown & Medoff, *supra* note 52, at 362-69; Freeman & Medoff, *supra* note 52, at 78-87.

If granting his employees tenure will increase their productivity, the rational employer will do so, for this will reduce his costs of production. Even if the whole productivity gain is paid to the employee in the form of a higher wage, the employer will be better off. He will have lower total costs than his competitors and will therefore be able to expand his output relative to theirs and increase his profits. Even if only a single employer in a competitive industry tumbled to the advantages of granting tenure, competition would force the others to follow suit.[56] And so with encouraging workers to complain rather than waiting for them to quit: the rational employer will encourage them to complain, by cash rewards or whatever it takes, if worker turnover is costly to him.

The proposition that unions enhance productivity also flies in the face of massive, if unsystematic, evidence pointing to the opposite conclusion. Featherbedding seems a more common attribute of unionized than of nonunionized work forces (at least in the private sector); many industries that are heavily unionized are notable for their low productivity; and for every older worker whom job security encourages to share his know-how, casual observation suggests that there is at least one other older worker, and probably several, whom job security protects at the expense of a more efficient younger worker. Most important of all, for many generations now employers have expended substantial resources to prevent unionization of their plants—expenditures that would be irrational if it were true that unions enhanced labor productivity. Such *persistent* irrationality by American businessmen is very hard to credit, but it is a proposition entailed by the productivity-enhancement theory of unionization.

It seems far more plausible to assume that the intended and actual effect of unionization is to raise the price of labor above the competitive level, and to depress the supply of labor below the competitive level, in the unionized sector (about twenty percent of the American work force is unionized[57]). This view not only is commonsensical but explains a wide range of phenomena. It explains the support of unions for the minimum wage, which has the effect of raising the price of substitute nonunion labor, and for government regulation of workplace safety, which reduces competition from nonunion employers. It also explains the pattern of unioniza-

---

[56] These points are neglected by Freeman & Medoff, *supra* note 52, at 91-93, in their attempt to explain management opposition to independent unions.

[57] BUREAU OF THE CENSUS, U.S. DEPT. OF COMMERCE, STATISTICAL ABSTRACT OF THE UNITED STATES 408 (103d ed. 1982-1983).

tion in the American economy, which is about what one would predict from differences in the ability to cartelize the labor supply in different industries. Thus we predict that we will find, and do find, the most effective unions in industries where competition among employers is weak (often because of government regulation), the cost of the organized work force is a small part of the employer's total costs, and the employer produces a nonstorable commodity, so that a strike will impose heavy costs on him. Excellent examples of all three factors (all of which are different aspects of labor-supply inelasticity) are found in the airline pilots' union before the deregulation of the airline industry and in the railroad industry in its heyday, where unionization took hold long before government came directly to its aid. Finally, as we will now see, the cartel theory of unionization explains better than any alternative theory the dominant features of the regulation of labor relations by the National Labor Relations Board.

The theory of cartels[58] teaches that cartelization of a market is a very difficult, perhaps hopeless, endeavor if there are a large number of competitors. And that is the typical situation in labor markets. It is not only that the work force of all but the smallest employers will contain far more members than has been thought the limit for effective cartelization without government assistance (a critical qualification in the present context, obviously); in addition, the relevant market includes workers employed by other firms (or unemployed) who, for a slightly higher wage, would go to work for an employer facing a strike.

These workers are an important part of the relevant market. In the theory of cartels, potential entrants are important only when the number of firms actually selling in the market—a number corresponding in the labor market to the number of employees actually selling their services to the employer in question—is small. If the number of significant firms is large (the qualification being added to exclude the case where a few firms have most of the sales and there is an unimportant fringe of tiny firms), cartelization probably will fail because each firm can expand its output and will be irresistibly tempted to do so if others reduce their output. (If none could expand its output, then a reduction in output by even a single firm would push the market price above the competi-

---

[58] For a discussion of the theory of cartels, see RICHARD A. POSNER, ANTITRUST LAW: AN ECONOMIC PERSPECTIVE 39-77 (1976); GEORGE J. STIGLER, THE ORGANIZATION OF INDUSTRY 39-63 (1968); McGee, *Ocean Freight Rate Conferences and the American Merchant Marine*, 27 U. CHI. L. REV. 191, 196-201 (1960).

tive level because the market's total output would be smaller as a result of that reduction.) Now it is easier for a firm to expand its output than for an individual worker to do so. The firm can add to its work force or to its capital; the individual worker would have to work harder or work longer hours. Of course this is possible within limits, especially for a short time. And a short time may sometimes be good enough: since a strike is costly to the striking workers, keeping the firm operating for a short time may be sufficient to break the strike even if the firm is forced to contract its operations—provided it is not forced to shut down completely. But if the strikers have more staying power than this, their strike may be effective though far fewer than all the workers join it, for the remaining workers may not be able to take up the slack by working harder, or for longer hours, for as long as it would take to break the strike. The strike might last too long for nonstriking workers or supervisors to be able to keep the plant operating and too long for the employer to substitute capital inputs for the labor inputs no longer available to it. In either case the firm's ability to hire replacement workers from other employers or from the pool of unemployed workers could determine the success or failure of the strike.

The large number of potential competitors of the striking workers is such a large obstacle to cartelizing labor markets without governmental assistance that most union-organizing efforts probably would be ineffectual without such assistance, provided the government enforced against unions as against the rest of society the basic laws protecting rights of property, contract, and personal safety (so that unions could not use force or the threat of force to achieve their ends). We now have to consider how the National Labor Relations Act alleviates the large-number problem and in other ways fosters effective if incomplete cartelization of labor markets.

To begin with, through the concept of the employer unfair labor practice, the Act prevents the employer from engaging in the kind of rational predatory activity that, as I suggested earlier, could be used to defeat unionization in its incipient stage. Put differently (for those skeptical of the economic rationality of predatory behavior in any form), the Act prevents competition between two groups of workers: those willing to work for the competitive wage and those willing to devote time to (and take risks in the hope of) obtaining a higher wage through unionization. The employer is forbidden to substitute members of the former group for members of the latter; it is as if a consumer were forbidden to switch his patronage to price cutters.

Next, the Act increases the wealth of unions and thus helps them play their vital role as agents for organizing workers. The union's role corresponds to that of trade associations, exclusive sales agencies, the old railroad rate bureaus, and other institutions for organizing competitors in product markets, but the union is more essential because of the large number of competitors to be organized. The Act, as interpreted by the Board and the courts, helps unions in several ways. It forbids the employer during the union-organizing campaign to offer (or even promise) its workers the higher wages or better fringe benefits that the union has promised to press for. Such an offer, if accepted, would undermine the union by preventing it from recouping the expenses of organizing by collecting union dues. The Act protects unions from another form of free riding by forbidding workers, after the union has been certified as the exclusive bargaining representative, to negotiate separately with the employer and by empowering the union, without regard to the wishes of individual members, to negotiate a provision in the collective-bargaining contract requiring all members of the bargaining unit to pay union dues.[59] Such a provision prevents an individual worker from obtaining the benefits of unionization without paying his share of the costs. Without dues, unions could not function. Indeed, assuming that what unions seek to maximize is their dues income,[60] if there is competition between unions that income will be proportionate to the benefits that the union confers on the workers it represents. The union's income would in any case be much less if a worker could enjoy the benefits conferred by the union without paying any dues.

The devices for preventing free riding on a union's organizing and other activities are very far from being perfect. If an employer, in an effort to discourage a union from organizing his workers, pays a wage that is less than the union scale by a smaller margin than the union's dues—as he can do without violating the Act—both the workers and the employer will be better off than if the union or-

---

[59] The Taft-Hartley Act, however, allows the states to forbid "union security clauses," as they are called, see National Labor Relations Act (as amended by Taft-Hartley Act) § 14(b), 29 U.S.C. § 164(b) (1982), and a number of states, disproportionately southern, have taken up this option, see, e.g., ALA. CODE §§ 25-7-30 to -36 (1975); GA. CODE ANN. § 34-6-21 to -28 (1982); MISS. CODE ANN. § 71-1-47 (1972).

[60] There is great debate over just what it is that unions maximize. For a discussion of contending positions, see DONALD L. MARTIN, AN OWNERSHIP THEORY OF THE TRADE UNION 6-30 (1980). Dues maximization seems the natural assumption but is not essential to my analysis.

ganizes the workers. Yet it is only the threat of unionization that enables this benefit to be obtained, and the union receives no compensation for creating it. Furthermore, although every worker must pay union dues once the union has become the collective-bargaining agent for his unit and has negotiated a union security clause with the employer, the union cannot force the workers to honor a strike call[61] (unless they are union members—not just dues-payers—and have not quit the union before crossing the picket line[62]). Much like the fringe firm in a cartelized market, the individual worker may seek the best of both worlds by continuing to work during the strike while hoping that the union will succeed in wresting concessions from the employer so that after the strike the worker's wages will be higher as a result of it. If enough workers think this way, the strike will fail and all the workers may be worse off than if they had joined it. But this is the same phenomenon as occurs when a cartel of product sellers fails because of defections by members of the cartel who think they can have the best of all worlds by free riding. Such failures are common.

What limits the form of free riding that consists of refusing to honor a strike call is a practical sanction that has no counterpart in nonlabor markets. The worker who continues to work during the strike knows that once it is over he will be working side-by-side with the workers who struck (unless all of their places are filled by permanent replacements), and he may fear retaliation in forms difficult to detect and prevent. Even if the strikers have been permanently replaced, the workers who refused to honor the strike will know that the strikers may eventually come back to work because, as noted earlier, the Act puts the strikers at the head of the queue to be hired (technically, reinstated) when vacancies occur. The prospect of eventually finding oneself working side-by-side with the former strikers will not only increase the likelihood that a strike call will be honored by all; it will also, as I mentioned earlier, discourage some new workers from signing on as permanent replacements in the first place, especially since they cannot be paid a higher wage for doing so.

Genuinely peaceful picketing is thus the counterpart in the la-

---

[61] *See* NLRB v. Textile Workers Local 1029, 409 U.S. 213, 215-18 (1972).

[62] There is divided authority on a union's right to prevent an employee from resigning from the union during a strike. *Compare* Pattern Makers' League v. NLRB, 724 F.2d 57 (7th Cir. 1983) (allowing resignation), *cert. granted,* 53 U.S.L.W. 3235 (U.S. Oct. 1, 1984), *and* International Assoc. of Machinists, Local 1414, 270 N.L.R.B. Dec. No. 209 (June 22, 1984) (same), *with* Local 1327, Int'l Ass'n of Machinists v. NLRB, 725 F.2d 1212 (9th Cir. 1984) (prohibiting resignation).

bor setting of the practice (required, for example, in the rail and trucking industries by the Interstate Commerce Act) of pricing in accordance with published tariffs. The published tariff shores up a cartel by enabling competitors to detect cheating on the cartel price immediately. Picketing serves a similar function by enabling the striking workers, corresponding to the members of a cartel who observe the cartel price, to identify any member of the cartel (i.e., any fellow worker) who is cheating by continuing to work during the strike. In this analysis, picketing is not really an informative activity (setting aside the information that is implicit in any threat); it is an information-gathering activity.[63]

The cartel analogy may help explain why unions invariably insist that the collective-bargaining contract provide some form of job security. No doubt, part of the reason is merely to back up the law's prohibition of discrimination against union supporters,[64] but the theory of cartels suggests a further point. An important object of job-security provisions is to obtain preferential treatment for senior workers. Some workers laid off during a business downturn will find other jobs during the period of layoff and not return to their original employer, who will therefore be hiring replacements for them. And just by the workings of chance, these replacements may be less well disposed to the union than those who were laid off and later quit. So the union will want some criterion for the order of layoffs that will ensure so far as possible that those workers who are least likely to favor the union will be laid off first. These are the younger workers.

Much casual observation supports this proposition, but it also has a theoretical basis. Younger workers are more mobile than older ones. The older ones are more likely to have family obligations that make it difficult to relocate geographically, and their

---

[63] This has possible implications for the analysis of the first amendment rights of pickets, but I shall not attempt to develop those implications here.

[64] Besides overt discrimination, employers might find subtle ways of discouraging unionization. For example, workers must differ in their propensity to vote for unions, to go out on strike, and otherwise to engage in cartel-promoting behavior. Therefore, in the absence of contractual job protection, the employer, after discovering that a majority of his workers wanted a union, might discharge some of the workers at random. (I am now assuming that he would not try to discharge solely, or disproportionately, those whom he knew to be union adherents, because that would be clearly unlawful conduct.) His hope would be that the replacement workers might, simply by chance, contain a lower proportion of union supporters, so that he might eventually be able to get the union decertified. Of course this would be a sensible strategy only if the employer thought that union support among his existing work force was above average for his industry, location, etc. The strategy would violate the law, but would be more difficult to detect than the firing of just (or mainly) union supporters.

human capital may have become specialized to the particular job they are doing for their employer (assuming that the older worker, on average, has worked longer for this employer than has the younger worker). Many younger workers are temporary employees, trying out one job after another; some are teenagers working part-time and bound for very different careers. Being less mobile, the older workers are more at the mercy of the employer (like shareholders whose shares are not freely tradable) and therefore have more to gain even in the short run from unionization. They also are more likely to be around to enjoy the benefits that the union generates for the workers in exchange for dues (the collection of dues begins before any of those benefits are realized). True, the younger workers, if they do stick around, will enjoy those benefits longer. But the discount rate applied to benefits from unionization other than those that can be realized in the immediate future must be high, not because workers are short-sighted, but because the union may be decertified or the plant closed before the benefits are realized. An additional point is that, at least in jobs that require strength or stamina, older workers may be less productive than younger workers, with whom—but for union-negotiated seniority protection—the older workers would be competing.

If this analysis is right, then by requiring the younger workers to be laid off first, the union is less likely to lose union adherents than if layoffs were random with respect to age. Moreover, they would never be random. The employer not confined by a collective-bargaining agreement would want to lay off the least productive workers first. They are likely to be disproportionately older and in any event disproportionately pro-union, for it is the least productive employees (whatever the reason why they are least productive) who fare the worst if wages are determined on a competitive basis.

This analysis also explains why unions want employers to use seniority to determine the order of layoffs even though productivity might be maximized, to the mutual benefit of employer and employees, if the union allowed the employer to choose whom to lay off in return for the generous compensation of any older worker laid off. Even if senior workers were made whole, there would still be a disadvantage from the union's standpoint: some of those laid off would find other jobs and therefore not return to their original employer when the layoff ended, and they would be replaced by younger workers less likely to support the union. Finally, we should note that a seniority rule, by making the employer's work force less mobile (senior workers have more to lose from quitting), generates additional support for the union.

Another important factor facilitating or retarding the organization of a plant or other facility is the determination of the bargaining unit (the electoral unit for the representation election). In general, the larger the unit the better off the employer is, and the smaller the unit the better off the union is.[65] The larger the unit is—that is, the more employees it has—the more difficult it will be for the union to obtain the majority vote that it needs in order to be designated the exclusive bargaining representative for the unit. This is not only because it takes more resources in absolute terms to get more votes (a national political election is more costly than a local one), but also because the members of the unit are more likely to have divergent interests with respect to tradeoffs among wages, fringe benefits, job security, and workplace safety. This will make it difficult for the union to appeal to a majority and, even if it gets a majority, will make it difficult for the union to formulate a coherent set of demands and enforce those demands by an effective strike threat. This is much like the problem of fixing prices in a producers' cartel when the producers have dissimilar cost functions.

A potentially offsetting factor is that a strike by a small unit may not impose substantial costs on the employer, in which event the union and the workers will gain little (in dues and in wages, respectively) from a successful organizing campaign, even if it is cheap to conduct. But if the unit is small precisely because the workers who comprise it do a different type of work from the other workers in the plant (so that making them a part of a larger unit would result in a heterogeneous unit), it is quite possible that if they go out on strike the plant will have to close down; the work they do, not being duplicated elsewhere in the plant, may well be essential. In addition, a small unit may be large relative to the size of the plant or facility in question. Both points are illustrated by health-care facilities (mainly hospitals and nursing homes), where unions have made great strides since the NLRB's authority was extended to nonprofit health-care facilities in 1974.[66] A hospital may have a small number of employees overall, divided as I noted earlier into several units (doctors, registered nurses, etc.), and a strike by any unit might close the facility down. Since the employer cannot produce for inventory, it will incur very substantial costs from even a short strike. This is why the law requires that

---

[65] *See* R. GORMAN, *supra* note 22, at 67-68.

[66] *See* Health Care Institutions Amendments Act, Pub. L. No. 93-360, 88 Stat. 395 (1974) (codified at 29 U.S.C. §§ 152, 158, 169, 183 (1982)).

unions give ten days' notice of a strike in a health-care facility;[67] it is another example of how current law tempers the pro-union policy introduced by the Wagner Act.

Professor Douglas Leslie has suggested that unions would often be better off with larger units because this would facilitate the mediation of conflicts among subgroups of employees.[68] If you have three local unions in a plant, however, their presidents should be able to negotiate some arrangement for mutual support; it is a negotiation among just three people, which the Coase Theorem suggests should be feasible, though there are possible "trilateral monopoly" problems and additional complications stemming from the fact that they will be negotiating in a representative capacity. But if the negotiation is within a unit, no faction has a representative who can negotiate on its behalf; the costs of negotiation will therefore be (I should think) higher; and if so the probability of unresolved conflict will also be higher. I am therefore led to predict that in periods when the NLRB is dominated by Democrats (whom most union leaders support), the Board will tend to certify smaller bargaining units than in periods when Republicans dominate. This would be a fruitful subject for empirical research.

If I am right in my contention that the National Labor Relations Act is best understood as a means of federal governmental support for the cartelization of the labor supply, this may also illuminate another feature of the Act: the vesting of primary responsibility for enforcing it in an administrative agency, the NLRB, rather than in the courts. Since the Act turned labor policy on its head, transforming a public policy of fostering competitive determination of wages and working conditions into one of fostering cartelization, it was quite sensible for Congress to be concerned that state and federal judges—who after all had largely fashioned the former policy—might resist its inversion. It would have made less sense if all the Act were doing was enhancing labor productivity—though Congress might have feared that the judges would misunderstand that this is what the Act was doing.

All that was years ago, and now there are very few judges, state or federal, who have any emotional or intellectual commitment to competitive labor markets. Although the word "cartelization" has negative overtones (more so, indeed, than in the 1930's, when the Depression was attributed in some quarters to excessive

---

[67] *See* National Labor Relations Act (as amended by Health Care Institutions Amendments Act) § 8(g), 29 U.S.C. § 158(g) (1982).

[68] Leslie, *supra* note 9, at 50.

competition), I am sure that most judges today would agree that if federal labor policy is one of facilitating the cartelization of labor, they should, and without much pain can, use this policy to guide them in reviewing the decisions of the NLRB. The only real difficulty is that with the Taft-Hartley amendments, the National Labor Relations Act no longer evinces a univocal policy of promoting cartelization. Even in its pristine Wagner Act form, the NLRA did not totally embrace such a policy. For example, the Act has since the early days been interpreted to allow employers to replace strikers, and has also been interpreted not to protect concerted activity that involves a danger of physical destruction (e.g., damaging the employer's machinery) or personal injury.[69] The rationale of this exception is not quite so obvious to an economist as it might appear to be. Strikes that destroy much more valuable intangible assets are protected. But there is a difference, and the exception for destruction of tangible assets does limit the power of unions. Destroying intangible assets (business goodwill, customers' time, etc.) usually requires a lengthy strike, which is costly to the workers as well as to the employer, his customers, and his suppliers; equally costly destruction of tangible assets might be accomplished in minutes.

A more ambiguous example of a limitation on the union-promoting policy of the Act (as it has been interpreted) is the requirement that the union get at least thirty percent of the workers in the bargaining unit to sign union authorization cards before a representation election will be ordered. It is not obvious that lowering the threshold would promote unionization. A weak union might get enough signatures to compel an election, then lose it resoundingly and by doing so make it harder for a stronger union to organize the plant subsequently.

But the Taft-Hartley Act did make a difference. Notably, by withholding the protection of federal law from supervisor unions (and as a result there are few such unions and most are powerless), the Act strengthened the hand of employers by enabling them to substitute for strikers other workers less likely than permanent replacements to be intimidated by returning strikers. It also outlawed the closed shop,[70] which is a device that minimizes free rid-

---

[69] See NLRB v. Fansteel Metallurgical Corp., 306 U.S. 240, 255 (1939) ("We are unable to conclude that Congress intended to . . . invest those who go on strike with an immunity from discharge for acts of trespass or violence against the employer's property . . . .").

[70] See National Labor Relations Act (as amended by Taft-Hartley Act) § 8(b)(2), 29 U.S.C. § 158(b)(2) (1982).

ing on union efforts by requiring the employer to hire from the ranks of those who already belong to the union, thus excluding those who join after the plant has been organized.

But the impact of the Taft-Hartley Act is easily exaggerated, as another example will show. Although the Act made no-strike clauses enforceable by damage suits against unions, it is very hard to see this provision as anti-union. A union doesn't have to agree to such a clause; and if it does, presumably it has been compensated for it. Expanding freedom of contract ought to benefit all parties to a potential transaction. It would be different if the Act allowed "yellow dog" contracts. Those are not contracts between unions and employers but between individual workers and employers and are a device by which employers can exploit the large-numbers problem that complicates unions' organizing efforts. Each worker knows that his signing an agreement with his employer not to strike while he is employed will have little effect on the success of any union organizing efforts in his plant because he is one of many; knowing this, he will sign such an agreement for only a modest consideration. If all or at least most workers think the same way (and why shouldn't they?), the employer will have succeeded in preventing union organizing at his plant for a total cost that may be much less than he would have to pay in higher wages if the plant were organized (provided there is not already in being a strong union that can pay the workers more than the company can pay to induce them not to sign "yellow dog" contracts). The banning of "yellow dog" contracts (accomplished in the Norris-La-Guardia Act a few years before the Wagner Act) not only is a rational component of a labor policy dedicated to facilitating labor cartels but is perfectly consistent with the provision in the Taft-Hartley Act allowing no-strike clauses to be enforced. Indeed, the federal labor laws as a whole appear to have a remarkable consistency and intelligibility when viewed as a legal regime for fostering (though not to the maximum possible extent) the cartelization of labor markets.

[9]

ESSAYS

THE EFFICIENCY AND THE EFFICACY OF TITLE VII

Richard A. Posner†

In a recent article in this journal,[1] John Donohue argues that Title VII of the Civil Rights Act of 1964,[2] which forbids employment discrimination on racial and other invidious grounds,[3] may well be an efficient intervention in labor markets, even if efficiency is narrowly defined as maximizing social wealth. His argument is of considerable interest. Social welfare legislation, notably including legislation designed to help minority groups, is usually thought to involve a trade-off between equity and efficiency, or between the just distribution of society's wealth and the aggregate amount of that wealth. If Donohue is right and equity and efficiency line up on the same side of the issue, these laws are considerably less problematic than they have seemed to some observers.

Donohue's argument builds on Gary Becker's theory of racial discrimination.[4] For Becker, discrimination by whites against blacks is the result of an aversion that whites have to associating with blacks.[5] This aversion makes it more costly for whites to transact with blacks than with other whites. Becker likens this additional transaction cost to transportation costs in international trade.[6] The higher those transportation costs are, the less international trade there will be. Countries such as Switzerland that are highly dependent on such trade because

---

† Judge, United Court of Appeals for the Seventh Circuit; Senior Lecturer, University of Chicago Law School. I thank John Donohue for his generous comments on a previous draft of this paper, and Lisa Heinzerling and Richard Porter for their comments.

[1] Donohue, *Is Title VII Efficient?*, 134 U. Pa. L. Rev. 1411 (1986).

[2] 42 U.S.C. §§ 2000e to 2000e-17 (1982).

[3] Donohue confines his attention to racial discrimination, as will I. Title VII also forbids discrimination on grounds of sex, religion, and national origin. *See* 42 U.S.C. § 2000e-2(a) (1982).

[4] *See generally* G. Becker, The Economics of Discrimination (2d ed. 1971). For a brief summary of Becker's theory, see R. Posner, Economic Analysis of Law § 27.1 (3d ed. 1986).

[5] *See* G. Becker, *supra* note 4, at 14, 153-54.

[6] *Id.* at 21 n.3.

(513)

their internal markets are small will suffer more than countries that, by virtue of the large size of their internal markets,[7] are more nearly self-sufficient. Similarly, blacks will be hurt more than whites by the whites' aversion to associations with them because the white community is more nearly self-sufficient than the black.[8]

Just as there are potential gains from measures that lower transportation costs, so there are potential gains from measures that lower the costs of association between whites and blacks. One of these measures is competition. White employers who are not averse to such associations will have lower labor costs and will therefore tend to gain a competitive advantage over their bigoted competitors. Hence competition should, over time, erode the effects of discrimination, not by changing preferences, to be sure, but by shifting productive resources to firms that are not handicapped by an aversion to associating with blacks.

Donohue's argument is simply that this process can be accelerated by a law against employment discrimination, such as Title VII.[9] By adding a legal penalty to the market penalty for discrimination, Title VII accelerates the movement toward the day when discrimination has been squeezed out of markets and the gains from trade have thereby been maximized.[10] In his analysis, Title VII is like an innovation that reduces the costs of transportation—to zero.[11]

The obvious objection to Donohue's argument is that he has failed to balance the costs of administering Title VII against the gains from lowering the costs of transacting between blacks and whites. In the year ending June 30, 1986, more than 9,000 suits charging employment discrimination, the vast majority under Title VII, were brought in federal court.[12] The aggregate costs of these cases, and of the many more matters that are settled without litigation, must be considerable. However, I want to emphasize two more subtle points. The first is that, to the extent it is effective, Title VII may generate substantial costs over and above the costs of administering the statute. The second point is that Title VII may not be effective, in which event its administrative costs are a dead weight loss.

---

[7] The size of the market should not be confused with the size of the country. The larger a country is, all other things being equal, the greater will be transportation costs in its national markets.

[8] *See* G. BECKER, *supra* note 4, at 22-24.

[9] *See* Donohue, *supra* note 1, at 1426.

[10] *See id.*

[11] *See id.* at 1426-27.

[12] *See* ANNUAL REPORT OF THE DIRECTOR OF THE ADMINISTRATIVE OFFICE OF THE UNITED STATES COURTS app. I, table C 2 (U.S. Government Printing Office pub. 1986).

A. *The Efficiency of Title VII*

An analogy in the international-trade sphere to Donohue's argument would be to advocate passage of a law requiring a nation's industries to increase their exports and imports. Such a law would increase the amount of the nation's international trade, but not by lowering the cost of transportation. It might bring the nation to a level of international trade that it would not otherwise have reached for another fifty years through falling costs of transportation, but there would be no gain in efficiency because those costs had not yet fallen.

In Becker's analysis, the costs to whites of associating with blacks are real costs, and a law requiring such associations does not, at least in any obvious way, reduce those costs.[13] Of course, it makes blacks better off, but presumably by less than it makes whites worse off; for if both whites and blacks were made better off, there would be net gains from association and the law would not be necessary.

Another analogy to international trade may help to clarify my disagreement with Donohue's argument. Consider a law that requires the international maritime industry to adopt a newly developed, more efficient technology; and suppose someone has just invented a type of hull design that enables a ship to sail faster on less fuel. If adopted, the design would lower the costs of international transportation. Donohue's argument implies that a law requiring the adoption of the new technology as soon as possible would increase economic welfare by accelerating attainment of the new, more efficient equilibrium made possible by the invention. The difficulty is that such a law is likely to distort the optimal path to the new equilibrium. It is rarely efficient to scrap an existing technology the minute a superior one is developed. We usually leave it to competition to determine the rate at which the new displaces the old.

The basic difficulty with Donohue's analysis should now be plain. He argues for the efficiency of government intervention in a market not marked by externalities, monopoly or monopsony, high costs of information, or any other condition that might justify such intervention on economic grounds.[14] It might of course be the case that the labor mar-

---

[13] *See* G. BECKER, *supra* note 4, at 153-54. Indeed, Becker argues that forced association between whites and blacks may increase the whites' aversion to blacks and thereby increase the amount of discrimination, but nothing in my analysis depends on the correctness of this argument.

[14] For discussions of how monopsony might affect the economic analysis of discrimination in labor markets, see Culp, *Federal Courts and the Enforcement of Title VII*, 78 AM. ECON. REV. 355 (1986) (Papers & Proceedings); Fischel & Lazear, *Comparable Worth and Discrimination in Labor Markets*, 53 U. CHI. L. REV. 891

kets likely to be affected by Title VII had one or more of these conditions but that is not his argument.[15] It might equally be the case that the costs to whites of being forced to associate with blacks are morally unworthy of consideration in the formulation of public policy. Stated differently, it might be that a tax on those whites for the benefit of blacks would be justifiable on grounds of social equity. But that would not be an *efficiency* justification in the wealth-maximization sense that Donohue employs.

Moreover, it is not altogether plain that a reluctance by white employers to employ blacks *at the same wage as whites* (an essential qualification, as we shall see) must reflect nothing more than an inexplicable aversion, whether by the employer itself or by its white employees, to associating with blacks. Suppose that, because of past exclusion of blacks from equal educational opportunities or for other reasons, the average black worker is less productive than the average white, and suppose further that it is costly for an employer to determine whether an individual worker deviates from the average for the worker's group. Then an unprejudiced employer might nonetheless decide to pay blacks less than whites. This would be unfair to blacks who were in fact above average, yet might still be an efficient method (in the presence of high information costs) of compensating black workers.[16] If Title VII comes along and forbids this method of classifying workers, as it assuredly does, then the employer will either incur additional information costs or, by lumping all workers together regardless of productivity, depart even further from the optimum wage, which is the wage equal to a worker's marginal product. Either way, efficiency will be reduced. Again, gains in social equity may trump losses in efficiency. But Donohue is not concerned, at least in the article under discussion, with equity.

B.   *The Efficacy of Title VII*

I have assumed thus far, as does Donohue, that Title VII is effective—that it improves the employment prospects of black people. If it

---

(1986); Holzhauer, *The Economic Possibilities of Comparable Worth*, 53 U. CHI. L. REV. 919 (1986).

   [15] *See* Donohue, *supra* note 1, at 1414 & n.10.

   [16] *See generally* Phelps, *The Statistical Theory of Racism and Sexism*, 62 AM. ECON. REV. 659, 659 (1972) ("A prior discrimination against minorities may be based on statistical expectations which seem to the employer more cost effective than making individual determination."). Such discrimination may be socially (as well as privately) efficient—or may not be, as argued in Lundberg & Startz, *Private Discrimination and Social Intervention in Competitive Labor Markets*, 73 AM. ECON. REV. 340 (1983); Schwab, *Is Statistical Discrimination Efficient?*, 76 AM. ECON. REV. 228 (1986).

does not, then its administrative costs yield no gains, either in efficiency or in equity. One's intuition is that a law, which imposes sanctions on employers who discriminate and which is enforceable not only by a federal agency (the Equal Employment Opportunity Commission) but by the victims of discrimination in private suits, *must* improve the employment opportunities of members of a group that, at the time the law was passed, was a frequent target of employment discrimination. But this may be incorrect, as Professor Landes showed many years ago in a study of state fair employment practices laws, the precursors of Title VII.[17] Suppose that, for whatever reason, the market wage rate of blacks is lower than that of whites. Title VII forbids the use of race as a ground for pay differentials. Because this part of the law is difficult to evade, and because (as I mentioned earlier) employers find it difficult to measure the marginal product of the individual worker, we can assume that blacks and whites will be paid the same wage by the same employer for the same job. This means, however, that the employer will be paying some or many of its black workers more than their marginal product.[18] The employer will therefore have an economic incentive to employ fewer blacks. The law also forbids making hiring or firing decisions on the basis of race, but this part of the law is very difficult to enforce. To see this, however, it is necessary to get more deeply into the structure of the law than Donohue attempts to do in his article.

There are two basic approaches that plaintiffs can use to make out a case under Title VII.[19] The first, the "disparate treatment" approach, requires proving intentional discrimination.[20] This turns out to be exceptionally difficult in practice. No employer of even moderate sophistication will admit or leave a paper record showing that it has refused to

---

[17] *See* Landes, *The Economics of Fair Employment Laws,* 76 J. POL. ECON. 507, 544-45 & n.32 (1968) (observing that gains in black wages were partially offset by increased unemployment among blacks).

[18] The employer cannot simply reduce the white workers' wages to the level of the black workers because then the white workers would receive less than their market wage and therefore would go elsewhere. Of course, if all or most employers are affected by the law, the white workers' market wage may fall. But it would not fall all the way to the level of the black workers.

[19] For a brief summary of the elaborate body of legal doctrines that has evolved in the interpretation and application of Title VII, see PLAYER, FEDERAL LAW OF EMPLOYMENT DISCRIMINATION, IN A NUTSHELL, pt. 5 (2d ed. 1981). For fuller treatments, see S. AGID, FAIR EMPLOYMENT LITIGATION: PROVING AND DEFENDING A TITLE VII CASE (2d ed. 1979); C. SULLIVAN, M. ZIMMER & R. RICHARDS, FEDERAL STATUTORY LAW OF EMPLOYMENT DISCRIMINATION (1982).

[20] *See* Texas Dep't of Community Affairs v. Burdine, 450 U.S. 248 (1981) (addressing the issue of an employer's intent when an individual claims disparate treatment); McDonnell Douglas Corp. v. Green, 411 U.S. 792 (1973) (same).

hire, or has fired, a worker because of the worker's race. In the absence
of such evidence, the worker may try to eliminate alternative explanations, but this usually is impossible. There are, it is true, some workers
who are so superior that no cause other than racial animus could explain a refusal to hire them or a decision to fire them. But even a
bigoted employer is unlikely to take out his racial animus against a
perfect worker. Most workers are not perfect. As to them, it is usually
easy to supply a plausible reason why they were not hired or why they
were let go. The plaintiff may try to rebut the reason by showing an
overall pattern of racial hiring or firing, but this type of proof is expensive and will rarely be cost-justified when all the plaintiff is seeking is
reinstatement or back pay, the most common remedies (along with attorney's fees) under Title VII.[21] Common law damages (including punitive damages) are not available in Title VII cases, and there is no
right to trial by jury.[22]

Occasionally, a group of workers will band together in a class action,[23] or the EEOC will bring suit against a company or even an industry on behalf of a large group of workers who have been discriminated against. But there are few such cases relative to the vast labor
market in the United States,[24] and the threat of such a suit may not
have much deterrent effect because the available sanctions are so mild.

The second basic approach under Title VII is the "disparate impact" approach. If a firm uses a screening device such as an aptitude
test or requiring a high-school degree that has the effect of excluding a
disproportionate number of blacks, the device is unlawful unless the
firm can show a strong business justification for it, even if the device is
not intended to keep out blacks.[25] The crux of the problem is identifying disproportionate exclusion. The usual solution is to compare the

---

[21] *See* 42 U.S.C. § 2000e-5(g) (1982) (Title VII's remedial provision); *see also* C.
SULLIVAN, M. ZIMMER, & R. RICHARDS, *supra* note 19, at 69-80 (discussing complexities of statistical proof under Title VII).
[22] The Supreme Court has observed that remedies under 42 U.S.C. § 2000e-5(g)
are equitable in nature. *See* Albemarle Paper Co. v. Moody, 422 U.S. 405 (1975). The
courts of appeals have held, therefore, that there is no right to a jury trial of claims
brought under Title VII alone. *See, e.g.,* Williamson v. Handy Button Mach. Co., 817
F.2d 1290 (7th Cir. 1987). The logic of *Albemarle* has also persuaded courts of appeals
that punitive damages are unavailable under Title VII, as well as common law com-
pensatory damages (as distinct from backpay). *See, e.g.,* Protos v. Volkswagen of
America, 797 F.2d 129, 138 (3d Cir. 1986); Richerson v. Jones, 551 F.2d 918 (3d Cir.
1977).
[23] *See* Frans v. Bowman Transp. Co., 424 U.S. 747 (1976); *Albemarle Paper Co.,*
422 U.S. 405.
[24] Eighty-two class action suits involving employment discrimination were filed in
1985. Telephone interview with David Cook, Chief of the Statistics Division of the
Administrative Office of the United States Courts (Oct. 13, 1987).
[25] *See* Griggs v. Duke Power Co., 401 U.S. 424 (1971).

percentage of blacks employed by the firm with the percentage in the labor pool from which the firm draws. This method of proof makes it more costly for a firm to operate in an area where the labor pool contains a high percentage of blacks, by enlarging the firm's legal exposure.[26] Therefore, when deciding where to locate a new plant or where to expand an existing one, a firm will be attracted (other things being equal) to areas that have only small percentages of blacks in their labor pools.[27]

This incentive exists even if the firm is not worried about disparate-impact suits. Title VII makes it more costly to employ black workers; it also makes it more costly to fire them because the firm may have to incur the expense of defending a Title VII disparate-treatment suit when a black employee is discharged. These costs operate as a tax on employing black workers and give firms an incentive to locate in areas with few blacks.

Thus Title VII can be expected to have several effects: to increase the wages of those blacks who are employed by wiping out racial pay differentials; to eliminate some discrimination in hiring and firing; but, in the case of some employers, to reduce the number of blacks who are employed.[28] When the wages of black workers are averaged over all blacks, both those who are employed and those who are not, the average black wage may not have increased (or increased much) as a result of Title VII, and may even have decreased. Any net loss of wealth might be offset by a gain in self-esteem from being freed from direct (though not, if the foregoing analysis is correct, indirect) racial discrimination, but that gain would be outside the scope of the analyses that Donohue and I are making.

Professor Landes, in his study of state fair employment laws, found that the employment and wage effects partially offset each other.[29] Unfortunately, it is difficult to make a parallel study of Title VII. Since Title VII is applicable nationwide, cross-sectional studies are not possible. Time studies are confounded by the number of other

---

[26] *See* C. SULLIVAN, M. ZIMMER, & R. RICHARDS, *supra* note 19, at 46-51.

[27] In a recent case, evidence was presented that the defendant "desire[d to] . . . build its plant in a city with a minority population no greater than 35% of the total population, allegedly because it had previously experienced difficulty meeting affirmative action goals in communities with proportionately larger minority populations." Terry Properties, Inc. v. Standard Oil Co., 799 F.2d 1523, 1527 (11th Cir. 1986). I am indebted to Professor Donohue for bringing this case to my attention.

[28] *See supra* notes 17-18 and accompanying text.

[29] *See* Landes, *supra* note 17, at 544-45 (finding, in fair employment states between 1939 and 1959, that "the increase in the ratio of non-white to white male wages was partly at the expense of greater unemployment differentials between non-whites and whites.").

developments affecting the wages and employment of blacks since Title
VII was enacted in 1964, including changes in welfare benefits (which
may affect the incentive to seek employment), changes in the taste for
discrimination (besides any such change attributable to Title VII itself),
expanded educational opportunities for blacks, the disintegration of the
lower-class black family, the shift in jobs from the industrial to the
service (including governmental) sector, the increased political clout of
blacks, the decline of unions, and a variety of other changes. Disentangling the effects of Title VII from all the other things that have been
going on since 1964 and that bear on the wages and employment of
blacks seems well-nigh impossible. Even disentangling the effects of all
governmental programs to combat racial discrimination from the effects
of other developments is extraordinarily difficult and thus far inconclusive, as shown in a recent and very scrupulous review essay by James
Heckman.[30] Although some studies find that Title VII has increased
both the wages and employment of blacks, and others that the wage
and employment effects have cancelled each other out,[31] the most responsible conclusion for the nonspecialist appears to be that the effects
of Title VII are unknown.

Of course, Title VII could have indirect effects as well as the direct effects that I have been emphasizing. By putting the government's
moral authority behind efforts to eradicate racial discrimination, Title
VII may have reduced the aversion of whites to associating with blacks
and may have helped blacks overcome the psychological legacy of slavery. As Heckman shows, however, when such indicia of black progress
as relative incomes of black and white workers and black and white
families, and the rate at which black versus white workers drop out of
the labor force before they reach retirement age, are taken into account,
one observes not only that black progress has been distinctly uneven,
but also that it is not well correlated with Title VII or any other government initiative. Moreover, both the decrease in overt expressions of
hostility toward blacks, and the existence of anti-discrimination laws
themselves, may reflect the growing political influence and assertiveness

---

[30] *See* J. Heckman, The Impact of Government on the Economic Status of Black
Americans (rev. May 1987) (unpublished manuscript) (on file with the *University of
Pennsylvania Law Review*).

[31] *Compare* Leonard, *Antidiscrimination or Reverse Discrimination: The Impact
of Changing Demographics, Title VII, and Affirmative Action on Productivity,* 19 J.
HUMAN RES. 145 (1984) (arguing that Title VII has played a significant role in increasing black employment) *with* Beller, *The Economics of Enforcement of an Antidiscrimination Law: Title VII of the Civil Rights Act of 1964,* 21 J. LAW & ECON. 359
(1978) (arguing that Title VII has not served as an efficient means of increasing the
overall wealth of blacks).

of black people and the growing racial tolerance of white people, rather than show that the laws have caused greater tolerance.

To conclude, I am not persuaded by Donohue's argument that Title VII can be defended on strictly economic grounds, as overcoming the transaction-cost barrier to market interactions between white and black people that Gary Becker identified in his economic study of racial discrimination. Title VII, to the extent effective, ignores, rather than reduces, the costs of undesired associations between whites and blacks. It may be correct on moral grounds to do so, but that is not Donohue's argument. Furthermore, it is an open question whether Title VII has improved the net welfare of black people, directly or indirectly. If it has not, then the costs of administering the law are a dead weight social loss that cannot be justified on grounds of social equity.

[10]

HEGEL AND EMPLOYMENT AT WILL:
A COMMENT

Richard A. Posner *

I applaud Professor Cornell's attempt to bring the thought of Hegel to bear on the contemporary issue of employment at will.[1] Hegel is an important figure in jurisprudence, and one too little known to legal scholars in the Anglo-American orbit; and Drucilla Cornell is a true student of Hegel. But precisely because Hegel is so little known to these scholars—for the easily understood reason that his writings, even when translated into English, are opaque, and alien to the Anglo-American sensibility[2]—anyone who wants to "sell" Hegelianism to Anglo-American jurisprudes would be well advised to wrap it in simpler packaging than Professor Cornell has employed in her interesting but difficult paper. The quotations from Hegel that punctuate the paper are, perhaps unavoidably, not lucid, and some of her own paraphrases of Hegel are Hegelian in style and therefore fully intelligible only to initiates (among whom I do not count myself). We know from the works of Charles Taylor and others—including Cornell herself in a previous article—that it is possible to explain Hegel's thought to an unschooled Anglo-American audience, and I wish Professor Cornell had made a greater effort along those lines.[3]

Her article is far-ranging, and will I am sure be of great interest to students of Hegel's legal thought whether they have any interest in employment at will—that is, employment terminable by either party, employer or employee, without notice or grounds. However, I shall confine my comments to those parts of her article that bear directly

---

* Judge, United States Court of Appeals for the Seventh Circuit; Senior Lecturer, University of Chicago Law School. This is the revised text of remarks delivered at the Conference on Hegel and Legal Theory held at Cardozo Law School on March 27-29, 1988. I thank Drucilla Cornell, Frank Easterbrook, Richard Epstein, William Landes, Edward Lazear, Eva Saks, Cass Sunstein, and participants at the Conference for many stimulating comments and suggestions, and Catherine Van Horn for her helpful research assistance.

[1] Cornell, Dialogic Reciprocity and the Critique of Employment at Will, 10 Cardozo L. Rev. 1575 (1989).

[2] This is not to deny that Hegel has influenced Anglo-American thinkers, not only indirectly through Marx, but directly—John Dewey being a notable example.

[3] See Cornell, Institutionalization of Meaning, Recollective Imagination and the Potential for Transformative Legal Interpretation, 136 U. Pa. L. Rev. 1135, 1178-93 (1988); S. Avineri, Hegel's Theory of the Modern State (1972); R. Plant, Hegel: An Introduction (2d ed. 1983); A. Ryan, Hegel and Mastering the World, in Property and Political Theory 118 (1984); C. Taylor, Hegel and Modern Society (1979); Rosenfeld, Hegel and the Dialectics of Contract, 10 Cardozo L. Rev. 1199 (1989).

1625

on the controversy over that doctrine. The article uses several strands in Hegel's thought to argue, primarily against Richard Epstein,[4] that employment at will should be outlawed. The natural inference from abolishing employment at will would be to entitle every employee in the United States to retain his or her job—for life—unless an arbitrator or some other neutral adjudicator determined that the employer had good cause to discharge the employee. Every employee would have the type of job rights enjoyed at present by tenured college teachers, civil servants (including public school teachers), and workers covered by collective bargaining agreements. But Cornell's actual proposal is slightly different. It is that statutes be enacted that would specify forbidden grounds for discharging an employee. The list of forbidden grounds, on which Cornell is surprisingly casual, must be specified precisely before one can be sure whether her proposal would curtail the freedom of action of employers substantially. Assuming it would, I disagree with it. I consider it inefficient and regressive. And I doubt whether Hegel can be squeezed hard enough to yield persuasive reasons for it.

I do however grant the force of Hegel's argument, which Cornell emphasizes, that individualism, upon which Epstein founded the ethical part of his argument for employment at will,[5] is socially constructed rather than presocial. Like Hegel, I do not believe that individuals have "natural" rights, whether to make contracts or to do anything else. The natural state of human beings is one not of equality but of dependence on more powerful human beings. Economic freedom in the classical liberal sense is one of the luxuries enabled by social organization. The long life, wide liberties, and extensive property of the average modern American are the creation not of that American alone but of society, that is, of a vast aggregation of individuals, living and dead; and of luck (in geography, climate, natural resources). As between two equally able and hard-working people, one living in a wealthy society and the other in a poor one, the former will have a higher standard of living; and the difference will be due to the efforts of other members, living and dead, of the wealthier society. The individual's "right" to property in such a society is not "natural," because his possessions are a product of social interactions rather than of his skills and efforts alone (and those skills may be, in part or

---

[4] See Epstein, In Defense of the Contract at Will, 51 U. Chi. L. Rev. 947 (1984).

[5] See id. at 951-55. I use the past tense because Epstein has since moved away from an effort to ground his jurisprudential views on natural-rights philosophy, and has begun to emphasize utilitarian justifications (more broadly, the kind of pragmatic justifications that I use in this Paper) instead. See Epstein, A Last Word on Eminent Domain, 41 U. Miami L. Rev. 253, 256-58 (1986).

whole, a social product too). I thus stand with Hegel and Cornell, and against Hobbes and (1984 vintage) Epstein, in believing that freedom of contract—the principle that undergirds the institution of employment at will—cannot be defended persuasively by reference to natural liberty.

But this concession will not carry the day for opponents of employment at will. To strip away one of the doctrine's philosophical struts is not to show that the doctrine should be abandoned. It would be odd to conclude that because individual well-being is, in an important sense, a social product, the state has a right to take away the difference between my income and that of the average resident of Bangladesh. Employment at will is a corollary of freedom of contract, and freedom of contract is a social policy with a host of economic and social justifications, even though nature is not of them. Employment at will happens to be the logical terminus on the road that begins with slavery and makes intermediate stops at serfdom, indentured servitude, forced servitude, and guild restrictions. That should be a point in its favor. Hegel himself, as Cornell notes, would have thought employment at will a fine thing. Just the pragmatic success of free markets in "delivering the goods"[6] warrants a presumption in their favor and places on Cornell some burden of making a case for public intervention. She cannot rest on Hegel's demonstration that rights are social rather than natural.

She knows she cannot and is therefore led to place great emphasis on Hegel's belief that the possession of property is essential to a person's sense of himself as a person.[7] Taken literally (but Cornell does not take it literally), this is an odd and not especially plausible idea. Do monks or nuns, or for that matter slaves, actually lack a sense of themselves as persons because they lack property rights? Hegel himself did not think so. Conversely, do the compulsive consumers of modern affluent society—the middle-class Americans for whom shopping is the preferred leisure activity—have as a consequence of their affluence, their property, a deep sense of self?

At the root of Hegel's belief that property is important to personality is the plausible idea that we are scarcely persons unless we are able to intervene in the external world in some way. One who cannot have any effect on his environment may not be aware of himself as a person, that is, aware of himself as being distinct from his environ-

---

[6] On which, see, e.g., S. Brittan, How British is the British Sickness?, in The Role and Limits of Government: Essays in Political Economy 219 (1983); A. Ryan, Why Are There So Few Socialists?, in Property and Political Theory, supra note 3, at 194.

[7] Hegel's theory of property is well described in A. Ryan, supra note 3.

ment in a way that a tree is not distinct from its environment. These interventions are constitutive of personality in an additional sense: our sense of ourselves as persons is a function in part of our recollections of past experience, and those recollections are kept fresh by the objects and activities associated with them. That is why it can be a terrible wrench (over and above the inconvenience) to lose one's house and personal possessions in a fire even if they are fully insured.

It may therefore be the case empirically that a person who has no property has a fainter awareness of himself as a separate person than one who does have property. Is it not a purpose of the monastic life to make its adherents feel themselves a part of a larger organism? To Margaret Jane Radin, Hegel's analysis of property implies that heirlooms should receive greater legal protection than cash or other fungible property.[8] This may seem a curious suggestion but bankruptcy law does place at least some of the bankrupt's personal property beyond the reach of his creditors,[9] and maybe the explanation is Hegelian.[10] But Cornell's version of Hegel's theory of property rights is less literal than this, and either version seems remote from employment at will. The employee at will can leave his job whenever he wants and go work for someone else. Far from being a slave of his employer he is not even tied to him by a contract for a fixed term. Employment at will lies, as I have said, at the opposite end of the spectrum from slavery, with contracts for a fixed term in the middle (not in the exact middle, to be sure). It is true that the employee at will can be fired at will, but the consequences of being fired, in our society at any rate, do not include becoming someone's slave; given unemployment insurance and welfare, they do not even include becoming a poor person, in the sense of someone utterly destitute and without property. Most poor people in the United States are wealthy by international standards—at least wealthy enough to retain a lively sense of themselves as persons.

But by pushing a little harder the idea that our sense of personal-

[8] See Radin, Property and Personhood, 34 Stan. L. Rev. 957 (1982) [hereinafter Radin, Property and Personhood]; see also Radin, Time, Possession and Alienation, 64 Wash. U.L.Q. 739, 741 (1986) ("the claim to an owned object grows stronger as, over time, the holder becomes bound up with the object").

[9] See 11 U.S.C. §§ 522(d)(3)-(4), (f)(2)(A) (1982 & Supp. IV 1986).

[10] Radin also suggests using Hegel's theory of property to give tenants a right to renew their leases indefinitely, provided they behave themselves. See Radin, Property and Personhood, supra note 8, at 991-96. This suggestion is much more troublesome. Carried to its logical extreme it would destroy the institution of tenancy by giving the tenant a right almost as extensive as fee simple. It is hard to see how the interests of people who cannot afford to own their homes would be helped by the destruction of tenancy. Existing tenants would benefit, but what of persons who will be seeking rental housing in the future?

ity is embodied in our accustomed possessions and activities we can begin to see a loosely Hegelian argument for job tenure, as for tenant rights. The person who has had the same job for a long time, like the tenant who has lived in the same place for a long time (but under a succession of one-year leases), may develop an attachment such that termination is wrenching. But we are now a long way from the idea that people who lack any property (the monk, the conscript soldier, the slave, the pauper) may in consequence have a precarious sense of self. We are now saying merely that everyone dislikes losing what he had grown accustomed to having. We have turned Hegel into a utilitarian, and a superficial utilitarian, who does not consider the long-range consequences of his happiness-maximizing proposals.

The fact that employment at will is a voluntary relationship on the part of the employee as well as the employer is an embarrassment for the Hegelian analyst. The right of property implies the right of alienation. If I own my labor I should be entitled to rent it on whatever terms I see fit. For reasons that will become clearer later in this paper, the employee at will is likely to have a higher wage than he would if he had an employment contract or other job tenure (including Professor Cornell's proposed "rational grounds" protection). With the higher wage he can acquire additional property. To force him to forgo his preferred wage-tenure package and to accept a lower wage in exchange for greater job security is, one might think, a denial of his personhood. Granted, this analysis would fail if employees did not know that they were employees at will unless they had an employment contract. But surely few employees at will think they have job tenure; losing one's job is not such a low-probability event that people have trouble thinking rationally about it. If, contrary to my belief, ignorance on this score really is a problem, it is one readily curable by the imposition of heavy sanctions on employers who mislead their employees into thinking that they have job protection when they do not.

Of course, any suggestion that one's property right in one's own labor should be freely alienable runs into the fact that one is not allowed in this society to sell oneself into slavery. But it is not clear that the ban against self-enslavement has much to do with notions of essential personhood. It may just be that we cannot think of any reason why a sane person in our society would make a contract to become a slave. However generous the price was for surrendering his freedom, as a slave the person would derive no benefit from the price unless he were intensely altruistic toward his family or others *and* they did not reciprocate his concern—for if they did they would suffer from seeing him a slave, and his altruistic gesture would fail.[11] And if they are so indifferent to his own welfare as to be untroubled by seeing him a slave, he is unlikely to be so altruistic toward them as to be willing to make such a sacrifice for them.

Our reaction to slavery is both culture-bound and semantically influenced. We are unlikely to say that if in ancient times a captive chose slavery over death he thereby surrendered his personhood. And today when a person does outwardly rather similar things to self-enslavement, but for a good reason—join the army, become a Catholic priest or nun, or even, having robbed a bank, become a "slave" of the state, maybe for life—we do not say that the person has surrendered his or her essential personhood. Slavery has become the name of the forms of involuntary servitude that we abhor; it does not signify the abhorrence of all forms of involuntary servitude. In any event, none of this has anything to do with employment at will, which as I have said is at the other end of the spectrum of "labor contracts" from slavery.

Professor Cornell lays great stress on what she calls "reciprocal symmetry" in personal relations: "The image is of two people looking one another in the eye, knowing the other is looking back. No one is on top."[12] This would appear to be an apt description of a regime of freedom of contract. The employer and employee meet as free individuals, and can strike any deal they want; presumably it will be mutually advantageous. It may or may not involve job tenure, as the parties prefer. If, perhaps by virtue of a statute, the employee could dictate the terms, he would be on top, and this would violate reciprocal symmetry. Cornell infers from reciprocal symmetry a quite different principle, not obviously related to it at all: that each of us is entitled to demand that someone who proposes to harm us, as by firing us, have and give us a compelling reason for doing so. Yet each of us is harmed every day by the actions of unknown others and harms unknown others by our own actions, if only through the action of competition in economic and other marketplaces. It would be absurd to require that all the harmed (The jilted boyfriend? The writer whose book is reviewed unfavorably? The consumer faced with an increase in the price of anchovies? The loser in a tennis match?) be given notice and a hearing. Granted, losing one's job may be a greater

---

[11] Notice the curious implication of this point: sacrifice is likely to be more rational, the less grateful the person on whose behalf the sacrifice is made to the person making the sacrifice; in other words, the existence of a reciprocal relationship may actually make sacrifice less rather than more likely. There is some merit to this odd, counterintuitive suggestion: parents are more likely to make sacrifices on behalf of their children than vice versa.

[12] Cornell, supra note 1, at 1587.

blow; but it is a known risk; and one who desires—and is willing to pay for—protection against it can negotiate for an employment contract, or enter the sector of the work force where such protection comes with the job.

Let us pause for a moment and consider conditions in that sector. For the truth is that many millions of American workers have job tenure. Does their experience suggest that universalizing the practice would improve human relations? Does the union worker have a greater sense of personality than the nonunion worker? Does the civil servant have a greater sense of personality than his counterpart who works without tenure in a private-sector job? Do public school teachers have a greater sense of personality than private-school teachers? Even if there is something, perhaps much, to the Hegelian notion that property is a part of personality, or to the notion that people should interact on terms of reciprocal symmetry, it is far from clear that Professor Cornell's proposal would if adopted cause these notions to be more fully actualized than they already are. It would, however, curtail the freedom of contract.

Another objection to entitling a person to demand a reason for being fired is that it logically entails a right (of the employer) to demand a reason for quitting—and if this seems to be pushing logic too hard, consider that in the Netherlands neither party to an employment relationship can terminate the relationship without cause, and workers can be sent to jail for trying to do so.[13] The relationship of the just-cause principle to slavery is nowhere clearer than in this example; the employee who could not show just cause for leaving his employment might be forced to spend his whole life in a job he hated.[14] Nevertheless, what is sauce for the goose should be sauce for the gander. Professor Cornell does not deny that an employee can sometimes hurt his employer, and hurt him badly, by quitting without notice or just cause. She thinks a discharge will on average hurt the employee more than a quit will hurt the employer, but this is not clear; the employee may be compensated ex ante for this risk (for example, by being paid a higher wage). Even if she is right, it would not provide a powerful justification for denying the employer a remedy in those cases where the quit really does hurt him.

She makes a good argument against employment at will (or at least against an argument made in favor of employment at will), and it

---

[13] Martin, The Economics of Employment Termination Rights, 20 J.L. & Econ. 187, 188-89 (1977).

[14] This is unlikely, of course; the costs of monitoring the effort of an unhappy worker would be too high. This is one reason why slavery has gone out of fashion.

is hardly important that the point owes nothing to Hegel. One argument used to defend employment at will is that the employment relationship is typically one of bilateral monopoly.[15] (I already hinted at this in my reference to the key employee, whose quitting hurts the employer.) The employee develops skills that are specialized to the particular job he is doing for the particular employer for whom he is doing it. As a result he would be less productive working for another employer; and knowing this, his current employer may be able to threaten him, explicitly or implicitly, with discharge if he demands a wage equal to his marginal product for this employer. But precisely because this employee is more productive than a new replacement would be, he can threaten the employer with quitting if the employer does not pay him his full marginal product. It is a game of chicken, likely to end in a stand-off, in which case both parties are protected against overreaching by the other.

The conclusion that the employee's specialized skills protect him from overreaching by the employer at the same time that they create the temptation for overreaching can be reached by an alternate route. Suppose a worker would be more valuable if he developed skills specialized to this employer. If the employer incurs the full costs of developing these skills in the worker, the worker can hardly complain if the employer refuses to pay him the higher marginal product made possible by the employer's own investment in the worker's skills; and to the extent that the worker (by threatening to quit) can extract any part of that higher marginal product in the form of a higher wage, the employer had been "had." Conversely, if the worker pays for the acquisition of these skills himself (maybe by accepting a lower wage initially), he will be at the mercy of the employer, who can expropriate the worker's investment by refusing to pay him his full marginal product; if the worker quits, he will have lost his entire investment, since by definition the skills are worth nothing in another employment.

Consideration of these alternatives leads to a prediction that the costs of developing specific human capital (as skills specialized to a particular employer are called) will be shared between worker and employer.[16] That way, neither party has as much to gain or lose from a termination of the employment relationship, and hence there is less incentive to engage in bluffing and other gaming, and less turnover.

But in either case the assumption is that the worker develops specialized skills; and, as Professor Cornell rightly points out, not

---

[15] See Epstein, supra note 4, at 973-76.

[16] See G. Becker, Human Capital: A Theoretical and Empirical Analysis, with Special Reference to Education 29-31 (2d ed. 1975).

every employee is so fortunate. This is a good point, but incomplete. If the employee lacks specialized skills, he loses a club over his employer's head, it is true, but by the same token the employer loses a club over the employee's head. The employee's wage will be as high in another job as it is in this one, since his skills, such as they are, are by hypothesis mobile. Of course, if there were a vast labor surplus, the wages of unskilled labor would be very low, but this situation would not be alleviated by job tenure.

There are other reasons to doubt whether employment at will is exploitive. The employer who encourages employees to develop a specialized skill and then takes advantage of their resultant immobility by refusing to compensate them adequately will find that he has to pay higher wages to induce people to work for him in the future. (A similar concern with reputation may restrain key employees from taking advantage of their employer's vulnerability bv walking off the job without notice, or by demanding a raise not to do so.) The employer will also find that his employees are highly susceptible to the enticements of labor unions. One of the curious byproducts of the universal "rational cause" rule that Cornell proposes is that it would weaken labor unions by giving every worker the kind of protection that he can get from a union only at the cost of having to pay union dues. Yet I had thought that Cornell (a former union organizer) was a supporter of unions for reasons that went beyond the tenure provisions in collective bargaining contracts.

The case for the just-cause or rational-cause principle[17] is a weak one, it seems to me; in addition there is a case against it that Cornell largely ignores. First, it is a costly principle. While not every employer in the United States is an effective profit-maximizer (and hence cost-minimizer), a free-market institution as persistent and widespread as employment at will is presumptively more efficient than an alternative imposed by government. The reason it might be more efficient is not hard to find. Litigation, even when conducted before arbitrators rather than before judges and juries, is costly. Apart from these direct costs of legally enforceable universal tenure rights there are the indirect costs, potentially enormous, from the weakening of discipline in the workplace when workers can be fired only after a costly and uncertain proceeding. The sum of these costs should not be underestimated. If they did not outweigh the benefits to workers, why would employers not offer just-cause protection voluntarily, the

---

[17] I realize that Professor Cornell distinguishes between these two methods of abrogating employment at will. But the differences do not appear to bear on my criticisms of her proposal.

way they offer other fringe benefits? Are the employers that do offer such protection—government agencies, unionized firms, and universities—the most efficient producers in the marketplace?[18]

We should consider the likely incidence of the costs of the just-cause or rational-cause principle. Consumers would be hurt, because these costs would be passed on (in part) to consumers in the form of higher product prices. Less obviously, workers would be hurt too. In figuring what he can afford to pay, an employer considers not only the direct costs of labor but indirect costs as well (such as the employer's social security tax, unemployment insurance premiums, and workers' compensation insurance premiums), of which the costs of the just-cause or rational-cause principle would be one. The higher the indirect costs, the less the employer will be willing to pay the employee in the form of wages and fringe benefits. Now in a sense just-cause protection is a fringe benefit, so the worker does not lose out completely, but it is by definition a benefit he did not want as much as he wanted a higher wage, or else the employer would have offered it to him, provided only that the employer is a rational maximizer of his own self-interest.

Just-cause protection would increase unemployment.[19] Employers would search longer before hiring a worker, because the cost of firing the worker if he did not pan out would be higher.[20] Therefore it would take longer to find a new job, which would increase the unemployment rate because most unemployed people are people searching for a new job to replace the one they have just lost. Second, and more serious, would be the effect on new hires. Just-cause (or rational-cause) protection raises the cost of labor to employers, and therefore reduces their demand for it; they hire less, automate more, relocate plants to foreign countries that do not have such protection. The

---

[18] One is amused to be told by another advocate of abolishing employment at will that we need not fear that abolition would be inefficient, because "[u]nder the British system, for example, industrial tribunals determine whether an employee has been improperly discharged." Leonard, A New Common Law of Employment Termination, 66 N.C.L. Rev. 631, 677 (1988).

[19] For empirical evidence, see Martin, supra note 13, at 199-201. The unemployment effects of European job-security laws are discussed in E. Lazear, Job Security and Unemployment (Hoover Institution Working Paper in Economics No. E-87-47, Oct. 1987) (available at Cardozo Law Review).

[20] This effect should be mitigated some, however, by the fact that just-cause protection usually does not start until some probationary period is completed. Cornell's proposal would allow for such periods.

Of course, if irrational firing of workers is widespread, a just-cause statute could lower the unemployment rate by dramatically reducing job turnover. But this seems highly unlikely, see DeFranco, Modification of the Employee at Will Doctrine—Balancing Judicial Development of the Common Law with the Legislative Prerogative to Declare Public Policy, 30 St. Louis U.L.J. 65, 70-72 (1985), and is not argued by Cornell.

brunt of the disemployment effect of job protection is invariably borne by newcomers to the work force and other marginal workers; and most of these will be women, non whites, or handicapped—the very workers that Cornell would most like to protect, in the interest of reciprocal symmetry or "horizontality." Employers in a regime of just-cause or rational-cause protection will be less willing to take chances on problem workers or workers who lack an impressive job history, since it will be harder to correct mistakes in hiring than under a system of employment at will.[21]

Professor Cornell does not see these problems, I conjecture, because she has committed that arch-sin that we "liberals" (in the sense of classic, not welfare-state, liberalism) are always being accused of: the sin of "reification." She has reified the employer, instead of treating the employer as a nexus of relationships with suppliers, workers, shareholders, managers, and consumers.

Another objection to the just-cause or rational-cause principle is that it would make discharges more painful and humiliating than they need be. When a worker is fired with no reasons given, at least he is not stigmatized by a determination that he is a bad worker. Under Cornell's proposal, fewer workers would be fired (and fewer hired either—my previous point) but those that were fired would be branded as bad workers and might have difficulty finding replacement jobs. This might be all to the good from the standpoint of efficiency but I would not expect Cornell to take quite so cold-blooded a view of the matter!

If experience in the unionized sector is a guide, we can expect arbitrators to react to the possibility of stigma by refusing to let employers fire employees for anything short of egregious misconduct. If they do this it will weaken the objection just made but strengthen the objection based on impairment of workplace discipline.

Cornell's proposal is underinclusive, not only because there is no justification for confining it to discharges and excluding quits, but also because business decisions other than to discharge workers may have greater consequences for employment than discharge decisions. An example is lay-off decisions, which are excluded from Cornell's proposal[22] even though lay-offs have a far greater aggregate impact on workers than discharges. But it is also overinclusive, because many

---

[21] Still another wrinkle is that if temporary and part-time workers are exempted from the just-cause law, as has been the pattern with European job-protection laws, see E. Lazear, *supra* note 19, at 7-9, employers will tend to substitute such workers for full-time workers.

[22] She does, however, propose that employers be required to give advance notice of layoffs. See Cornell, *supra* note 1, at 1622.

workers do not need the protection of just-cause or rational-cause protection. Henry Ford fired Lee Iaccoca without a statement of reasons or an effort to establish just cause; should the law have given Iaccoça job protection that he could have negotiated for had he been willing to accept a lower salary?

[11]

EXCHANGE

An Economic Analysis of Sex Discrimination Laws

Richard A. Posner†

There is now a substantial economic literature on discrimination. The literature focuses on racial discrimination but has implications for other forms of discrimination as well, including sex discrimination.[1] There is also a substantial economic literature on the extent and causes of disparities between men and women in wages, employment level, and other measures of professional attainment.[2] At the intersection of the two literatures one finds a number of studies of the economics of sex discrimination in employment.[3] There is also—it goes without saying—an enormous legal literature on sex discrimination law, again focused on employment. But there is relatively little writing on sex discrimination *law* from an eco-

† Judge, United States Court of Appeals for the Seventh Circuit; Senior Lecturer, The University of Chicago Law School. The comments of Mary Becker, Dennis Black, John Donohue, Lewis Kaplow, Cass Sunstein, and participants in the law and economics workshop at Harvard Law School, and the research assistance of Seung C. Kim, are gratefully acknowledged.

[1] See my book, Richard A. Posner, *Economic Analysis of Law* ch 27 (Little, Brown, 3d ed 1986), for an introduction to the economics of discrimination with references to some of the leading studies.

[2] See, for example, Gary S. Becker, *Human Capital, Effort, and the Sexual Division of Labor*, 3 J Labor Econ S33 (1985); Victor R. Fuchs, *Women's Quest for Economic Equality* (Harvard, 1988); Morley Gunderson, *Male-Female Wage Differentials and Policy Responses*, 27 J Econ Lit 46 (1989) (a thorough review of the literature); and a particularly accessible, as well as up-to-date, introduction to the literature, *Symposium: Women in the Labor Market*, 3 J Econ Perspectives 3 (1989).

[3] For a recent review of this literature, see Janice Fanning Madden, *The Persistence of Pay Differentials: The Economics of Sex Discrimination*, in Laurie Larwood, Ann H. Stromberg, and Barbara A. Gutek, eds, 1 *Women and Work: An Annual Review* 76 (Sage, 1985); and for an illustrative study see William T. Bielby and James N. Baron, *Sex Segregation Within Occupations*, 76 Am Econ Rev Papers & Proc 43 (May 1986).

nomic standpoint.[4] My objective in this paper is to examine the economic properties of the laws and doctrines relating to sex discrimination in employment. Although I am unable on the basis of existing information and analysis to estimate either the efficiency or the distributive effects of these laws and doctrines, I believe it is a plausible hypothesis—no stronger statement is possible—that sex discrimination law has not increased, and it may even have reduced, the aggregate welfare of women. Underlying this conclusion are four general arguments supported by smatterings of empirical evidence: (1) the sheer variety of practices that cluster together under the law's label "sex discrimination"; (2) the distributive complexities arising from interdependent positive utilities and joint consumption between men and women; (3) the pervasive conflicts of interest between different groups of women (for example, nonworking housewives and unmarried working women); and (4) the probably substantial, and growing, costs of administering sex discrimination laws. Arguments (2) and (3) are related[5] and together help explain why women, despite being a majority of voters, may not have succeeded in obtaining *effective* antidiscrimination legislation.

---

[4] What there is focuses mainly but not exclusively on (1) comparable worth, (2) eliminating sex distinctions in longevity tables used for computing annuities and life insurance premiums, and (3) the use of econometric evidence in sex discrimination litigation. The following list, although by no means complete, is an extensive sample of the literature: Arthur P. Dempster, *Employment Discrimination and Statistical Science*, 3 Stat Sci 149 (1988) (and comments following by other scholars); Robert L. Moore, *Are Male/Female Earnings Differentials Related to Life-Expectancy-Caused Pension Cost Differences?*, 25 Econ Inquiry 389 (1987); Samuel A. Rea, Jr., *The Market Response to the Elimination of Sex-Based Annuities*, 54 S Econ J 55 (1987); Daniel R. Fischel and Edward P. Lazear, *Comparable Worth and Discrimination in Labor Markets*, 53 U Chi L Rev 891 (1986); George E. Johnson and Gary R. Solon, *The Attainment of Pay Equity Between the Sexes by Legal Means: An Economic Analysis*, 20 U Mich J L Ref 183 (1986); Jonathan S. Leonard, *The Impact of Affirmative Action on Employment*, 2 J Labor Econ 439 (1984); Andrea H. Beller, *Occupational Segregation by Sex: Determinants and Changes*, 17 J Human Resources 371 (1982); George J. Benston, *The Economics of Gender Discrimination in Employee Fringe Benefits:* Manhart Revisited, 49 U Chi L Rev 489 (1982); Cotton M. Lindsay and Charles A. Shanor, County of Washington v. Gunther: *Economic and Legal Considerations for Resolving Sex-Based Wage Discrimination Cases*, 1 S Ct Econ Rev 185 (1982); Janet C. Hunt and Paul H. Rubin, *The Economics of the Women's Movement*, 35 Pub Choice 287 (1980); Butler D. Shaffer, *Some Economic Considerations in Sex Discrimination Cases*, 26 Labor L J 290 (1975); and Gunderson, 27 J Econ Lit at 53-68 (cited in note 2), and studies cited therein.

[5] This is noted briefly in Hunt and Rubin, 35 Pub Choice at 292-94 (cited in note 4), who find that sex discrimination legislation is more likely to be enacted the lower the marriage rate, since single women tend to gain more from such legislation than married ones.

I. The Legal Background[6]

A complex set of laws regulates sex discrimination in employment; its complexity may be an important reason why more economists have not studied sex discrimination law, as distinct from the phenomenon of sex discrimination. I begin with the federal statutes and judicial interpretation of them. The Equal Pay Act of 1963[7] requires employers to pay their employees the same wages for "equal work" regardless of sex. Equal work is narrowly defined, and unequal pay for equal work is permitted if the employer can show that the inequality is due to something other than the sex of the employees. Title VII of the Civil Rights Act of 1964[8] forbids sex discrimination in employment—in hiring, firing, promotion, and working conditions. Discrimination in pay is also included, so Title VII overlaps with the Equal Pay Act. "Discrimination" as used in Title VII essentially means disadvantage, but the employer can defend against a charge of sex discrimination by showing that the discrimination is necessary to its business. This is the "BFOQ" (bona fide occupational qualification) defense.[9] A standard example is refusing to consider male actors for female acting parts. Finally, Executive Order No 11246, as amended in 1967,[10] forbids discrimination on the basis of sex by federal contractors, under pain of loss of their contracts.

Title VII was amended in 1972 to extend its coverage to public employers and small private employers and to enlarge the powers of the Equal Employment Opportunity Commission (EEOC). In the Pregnancy Discrimination Act of 1978,[11] Congress, repudiating the Supreme Court's decision in *General Electric Co. v Gilbert*,[12] further amended Title VII to forbid discrimination based on pregnancy, with the result that an employer's refusal to classify pregnancy as a disability or to include the medical costs of pregnancy in a health benefits plan for employees is now unlawful discrimination. And the courts have interpreted Title VII discrimination to

---

[6] See generally Charles A. Sullivan, Michael J. Zimmer and Richard F. Richards, 1 *Employment Discrimination* ch 8 (Little, Brown, 2d ed 1988); see also index references to "sex discrimination" in volume 3 of this up-to-date, comprehensive, but one-sided treatise.

[7] 29 USC § 206(d) (1982).

[8] 42 USC § 2000e (1982).

[9] 42 USC § 2000e-2(e) (1982).

[10] Executive Order 11246, 3 CFR 1964-65 Comp 339 (1965), as amended 3 CFR 1966-70 Comp 684 (1967).

[11] 42 USC § 2000e(k) (1982).

[12] 429 US 125 (1976).

include sexual harassment.[13] Although Title VII has been held not to require employers to adopt "comparable worth,"[14] several states have required it of their public employers.[15] California has in addition required its private as well as its public employers to give female workers maternity leave; recently the Supreme Court held that such a requirement does not violate the Pregnancy Discrimination Act.[16]

The Equal Protection and Due Process Clauses have been held to forbid various forms of governmental sex discrimination, both state and federal. For example, the Equal Protection Clause has been interpreted to require the "degendering" of pension plans for public employees and to forbid differentiating spousal pension and fringe benefits on the basis of the employee's sex.[17] It can be taken for granted that laws excluding women from particular occupations, with narrow exceptions such as jobs involving military combat, are unconstitutional, and almost all such laws have in fact been repealed. On the other hand, in the Feeney decision the Supreme Court rejected a complaint by women that a state's policy of giving veterans a preference in public employment denied women equal protection because only a minuscule number of women are veterans.[18]

This hasty and oversimplified summary of a complicated legal pattern will make specialists in employment discrimination law wince, but it is sufficient for my economic analysis. Later, however, I shall have to consider a few of the details of the evidentiary and remedial scheme created by Title VII.

II.   Some Economics of Sex Discrimination

Before the economic effects of sex discrimination law can be evaluated, one must get a grip on the economics of sex discrimination. This section lists the basic assumptions of the analysis, then examines the causes of sex discrimination, and finally makes a stab at estimating what our labor markets would be like today without any sex discrimination laws.

---

[13] See Meritor Savings Bank v Vinson, 477 US 57 (1986).

[14] See, for example, AFSCME v Washington, 770 F2d 1401 (9th Cir 1985); American Nurses Ass'n v Illinois, 783 F2d 716 (7th Cir 1986).

[15] See, for example, Iowa Code § 602.1401 (1987); and Minn Stat § 471.991-.999 (1984).

[16] See California Federal Savings & Loan Ass'n v Guerra, 479 US 272 (1987).

[17] See, for example, Los Angeles Dept. of Water and Power v Manhart, 435 US 702 (1978).

[18] See Personnel Administrator v Feeney, 442 US 256 (1979).

A. Assumptions

I assume that all people—men and women alike—are rational in the usual economic sense. That is, they consistently act to maximize the excess of their private benefits over their private costs. It is consistent with this model, as we shall see, that some—or, for that matter, many or even most—men are misogynistic, exploitative, or ill-informed. I further assume that even if there is no discrimination against women, women will, on average, invest less than men in human capital, both general and job-specific. The qualification that it is only *on average* that women will invest less is important. The characteristics that are related to productive employment are unevenly distributed within each sex, so that even if the means of the distributions differ, the distributions themselves overlap, with the result that many women invest more in their human capital than many men invest in their own human capital. Nevertheless, the *average* woman expects to take more time out of the work force than the average man to raise children,[19] which makes the expected lifetime earnings of the average woman, and hence return to human capital, lower than those of the average man. The average woman will therefore invest less in her human capital, causing her wage to be lower than the average man's, since a part of every wage is repayment of the worker's investment in human capital.

It is possible that the greater propensity of women than men to take time out of the labor force is itself a product of sex discrimination, but I am skeptical of that proposition—I think child-rearing is an area where nature dominates culture—and I do not accept it for purposes of my analysis. However, I will not try to defend this assumption. It is also possible that the propensity will in time disappear, but again I am skeptical, and for the same reason. Even if it does eventually disappear, there can be little doubt that women's *current* wages are depressed because today's working women did not invest heavily in their human capital when they

---

[19] It is illustrative that in 1984, women who interrupted their work for more than six months gave "family reasons" as the cause of interruption in 40.7 percent of the cases; men mentioned family reasons in only 0.3 percent of the cases. Sara E. Rix, ed, *The American Woman 1988-89: A Status Report* 379 table 16 (Norton, 1988). In 1986, of all women with children up to the age of six, only a third were employed full time. Id at 375 fig 11. The Bureau of Labor Statistics estimated that in 1985 white males had a "worklife expectancy" at birth of 39.8 years, compared to 29.7 years for white females. U.S. Department of Commerce, Bureau of the Census, *Statistical Abstract of the United States* 364 table 606 (GPO, 108th ed 1988). In 1987, of married persons aged 20-24, 95.7 percent of the men were working outside the home but only 67.4 percent of the women. Id at 373 table 622.

were young. Table 7-3 in the 1987 *Economic Report of the President*[20] shows, for example, that while in 1968 only 27.5 percent of young white women expected to be working when they were 35 years old, in 1985 more than 70 percent of these women *were* working. The table also shows that, by 1979, young women had changed their expectations: almost exactly the same percentage of young women expected to be working at age 35 as were in fact working at that age in 1985. Since women now have more realistic expectations concerning their labor force participation, we can expect them to invest more heavily in their human capital and therefore earn higher wages in the future. Thus, although the fact that the average woman earns substantially less than the average man is often taken to be prima facie evidence of sex discrimination, it is not, and in any case the differential is likely to decline for reasons unrelated to sex discrimination law.

Finally, I assume that men's and women's utility functions are interdependent, and specifically that women derive a benefit from an increase in the income of a husband or other male relative (son, father, brother, etc.), even if no part of the increased income is consumed by the woman. This qualification is necessary because of the importance of joint consumption in the household. Normally if one spouse's income rises, the other spouse will benefit because so much of the consumption in a household is joint. We thus have separate interdependencies: the "pure" interdependency that results from altruism (the satisfaction that most people experience from an increase in the happiness of a close relative), and the interdependency resulting from joint consumption within the household. For simplicity's sake I shall confine my attention to the interdependencies between wife and husband and ignore other relatives.

It is important to note that the interdependencies between spouses often persist after divorce or the death of a spouse. If a widow's or divorcée's standard of living is a function of her husband's income, increases in that income will increase the wife's welfare. This increase will persist even after a woman is widowed, since her standard of living remains tied to her husband's former income; similarly, a divorced woman's standard of living often remains tied to her former husband's current income. Thus the large percentage of women who are unmarried exaggerates the economic independence of women from men. The vast majority of women marry at some time during their lives, and this is all that is neces-

---

[20] Council of Economic Advisors, *Economic Report of the President* 215 table 7-3 (GPO, 1987).

sary to establish a pervasive economic interdependence between the sexes.[21]

The relationship between majority and minority groups is not characterized by interdependence of either the joint-consumption or altruistic varieties, if only because racial intermarriage remains rare.[22] Interdependence gives the economics of sex discrimination a distinctive cast. To take the extreme case, suppose that all workers were married and that all consumption within the household were joint. Then discrimination against women in the labor force would be compensated for completely in the home, for while wives' wages would be lower than in a nondiscriminatory regime, wives would benefit dollar for dollar from the correspondingly higher wages of their husbands. Of course these assumptions are too strong, and they ignore the fact a woman's earning power may affect her influence over household expenditure decisions,[23] but they point to an important difference between sex discrimination and the other forms of discrimination with which sex discrimination is often, but perhaps facilely, linked.

B.   The Meaning and the Causes of Sex Discrimination

To avoid building a normative assessment into the word "discrimination," I shall follow the lead of Title VII and define sex discrimination as treating a woman differently from a man because she is a woman, without worrying at the definitional stage about whether the discrimination is invidious on the one hand, or justified or even beneficent on the other.[24] This definition is more prob-

---

[21] In 1986, of all white women 15 years and older, 20.9 percent had never been married, 56.4 percent were married and living with their husband, 2.7 percent were married but not living with their husband, 11.8 percent were widowed, and 8.2 percent were divorced. Rix, *The American Woman* at 354-55 fig 2 (cited in note 19). For black women, the figures are 36.4 percent, 32.4 percent, 8.9 percent, 11.6 percent, and 10.8 percent, respectively. Id. In 1986, among all women 55-64 years old, only 3.9 percent had never been married. *Statistical Abstract of the United States* at 40 table 49 (cited in note 19). Of course, this figure may decline since fewer women are marrying nowadays. On the changing demographics of American women, see Heidi I. Hartmann, *Changes in Women's Economic and Family Roles in Post-World War II United States*, in Lourdes Benería and Catharine R. Stimpson, eds, *Women, Households, and the Economy* 33 (Rutgers, 1987).

[22] In 1986, out of 51,704,000 married couples in the U.S., only 181,000 (0.35 percent) consisted of a white and a black. *Statistical Abstract of the United States* at 40 table 50 (cited in note 19).

[23] This depends in part, however, on the structure of family and divorce law, which determines the wife's entitlements in her husband's income.

[24] Although there is discrimination against men, I shall ignore it. A more important phenomenon that I do discuss is policy that is designed to combat discrimination against women and has the incidental effect of harming men.

lematic than it may appear to be, because it leaves unresolved the question whether it is discriminatory (in a sense pertinent to public policy) to treat a woman differently because of a characteristic that no men but only some women have, such as the capacity to bear children. The Supreme Court in *Gilbert* held that such differentiation was not discriminatory,[25] but the Court was overruled by Congress. I shall follow Congress's approach and assume that discrimination based on pregnancy is a form of sex discrimination—which is not to say, of course, that it necessarily is inefficient.

When discrimination is defined as broadly as I am defining it, the causes are multifarious. Here are the main ones, in (roughly) descending order of invidiousness. The discussion is confined to employment discrimination, the focus of this paper.

Misogyny. By this I mean an elemental distaste on the part of men for associating with women at work, not founded on any notions of productivity or efficiency. The misogynist, as I am using the word, is not someone misinformed about either the average or individual quality of female employees—he just doesn't like them in the workplace, maybe because he has traditional views of "the woman's place." Misogyny may appear to be a taste like any other, and therefore ethically neutral from an economic standpoint—a given. But this is not so clear. Insofar as it is expressed in hostile behavior, it may be more akin to a taste for assault than to a taste for chocolate ice cream. Perhaps misogyny is in between a harmless taste and an actual externality like rape or theft. But the precise status in economics of misogyny is not important to my analysis. To further complicate the picture I note that a disinclination to associate with women in the workplace need not reflect a dislike of women and could in fact reflect something nearly opposite to dislike—a desire, not necessarily insincere, to protect women from the hardships of the workplace.

Physical or Psychological Aggression. A straightforward case of exploitation, more clearly akin to theft or rape than to misogynistic refusal to accept women workers, is sexual harassment—conduct designed to elicit sexual favors from women against their will. This phenomenon is related to the "conduit" type of discrimination discussed below, because ordinarily it is not the employer himself (more often, itself) who harasses women, but male employees. The employer merely doesn't want to go to the

---

[25] 429 US at 133-46.

expense of preventing harassment by its employees. More precisely, the required expense would exceed the potential benefit to the employer from not having to compensate female employees for the disutility of being sexually harassed.

Ignorance About the Average Working Woman. A man who is not a misogynist may nevertheless labor under serious misconceptions concerning the abilities of working women. This is especially likely if there are few women in the workplaces with which the man is familiar. This ignorance may be rational, but that is not to say that it is admirable. Indeed, it may be rational for the entire market to be misinformed, because of the well-known externality problems with information. Whom would it pay to develop information about the working qualities of women in general? How would the social benefits of such information be translated into private benefits for the producer of the information? The pioneer in hiring women in a particular segment of the work force may simply be paving the way for his competitors to learn from his mistakes. Notice that in an era of minimum wage (and equal pay) laws, a woman cannot compensate her employer for taking a chance with an unknown quantity by accepting a lower wage. However, the minimum wage is not an important factor in professional and other well-paid employment or in periods such as the present when the minimum wage is far below the average wage.

Monopsony. Married women have high relocation costs when the husband earns more than the wife, as is usually the case. In areas where competition for labor among local employers is weak, these employers may be able to set a monopsonistic wage for female employees, so long as such women represent a large fraction of the female labor force or the employer is able to discriminate among women, paying less to those he believes would have difficulty relocating. Monopsony wage-setting is exploitation of female labor in a straightforward economic sense, although it is less invidious than certain other forms of discrimination because it does not rest on any premise that women are inferior workers to men.

Conduit of Discrimination. In many cases of discrimination the discriminator is merely reflecting the tastes of customers, employees, government agencies, or others with whom the discriminator has a commercial or regulatory relationship. If male employees don't like working with women, or if customers don't like female workers, the employer will perceive these aversions as additional costs of hiring women and will hire fewer of them, or will pay the women a lower wage to compensate the employer for their greater cost.

Statistical Discrimination. Even if employers and their male employees and customers have no discriminatory feelings *and* are perfectly well informed concerning the average characteristics of women in the various types of job, it may be rational for employers to discriminate against women because of the information costs of distinguishing a particular female employee from the average female employee. For example, the average woman may be physically or emotionally less suited for combat than the average man, even though the two distributions overlap. If it is too costly for the Department of Defense to identify women who are as well suited for combat as the minimally qualified male recruit, the Department may rationally, noninvidiously, decide to exclude *all* women from combat jobs.

Differentiation Infinitely Costly. Discussions of statistical discrimination normally assume that, while it would not be efficient to ascertain individual qualifications, it would be *possible* to do so—that is, the cost would not be infinite. But in the case of women, the cost sometimes *would* be infinite, because the uncertainty is inherent and ineradicable. For example, when an employer hires two 21-year-old workers, one male and one female, he knows that the former, being male, has a shorter life expectancy than the latter, but he doesn't know and ordinarily couldn't discover whether *this* female will outlive *this* male. Similarly, he knows that the man is likely to take less sick leave than the woman,[26] but this is just betting on the averages—he doesn't know whether these two workers will track the *average* experience of male and female workers. If differentiations are to be made, they must be made on a statistical basis.

Three things should be noted about my list of the causes of sex discrimination. The first is that it describes a world without sex discrimination laws; for example, we shall see that the problem of "rational ignorance" would be less serious if there were no Equal Pay Act. The second thing to note is the importance of information costs. Half the causes I have identified are based on such costs: ignorance of the average qualities of women workers, statistical discrimination, and inherent uncertainty. Third, only half the causes reflect market failure in a clear economic sense: monopsonistic exploitation of higher relocation costs, aggression against women, and ignorance of the average qualities of women due to

---

[26] In 1985, the average female worker lost six days of work because of illness or injury; the average male, 4.8 days. *Statistical Abstract of the United States* at 105 table 166 (cited in note 19).

information externalities. The other forms of discrimination are, or at least may be, efficient—which does not necessarily make them good from an ethical standpoint. Misogyny, for example, is a morally unattractive trait, but from an economic standpoint it *may* be no different in character from having an aversion to cabbage or rutabaga, though then again it may.

Of the three causes of sex discrimination in employment that clearly reflect a market failure, one has little or no contemporary importance: ignorance of the average qualities of women workers. So many women are employed in so many and diverse fields that few employers can be ignorant any longer concerning women's abilities as workers. The time when the law might have done something to eliminate this information externality is long gone. Another cause, high relocation costs conferring monopsony power on employers, has probably never been very important; I do not recall having seen it mentioned in the literature on female employment. The third cause, sexual harassment in the workplace, probably is largely self-correcting. As more and more women are employed, the employer's self-interest in curbing intrigue and harassment, which lower productivity, grows apace.

I conclude that there is no strong theoretical reason to believe that sex discrimination, even if not prohibited by law, would be a substantial source of inefficiency in American labor markets today. If I am correct, then the costs of administering that law will be largely a deadweight loss, from an economic standpoint. That does not make the law immoral or unjust, but any deadweight losses from law enforcement must be considered in deciding whether a particular law or set of laws furthers the public interest.

C. Discrimination Trends, Ex Law

How much sex discrimination of any sort could we expect today if there were no sex discrimination laws or other pertinent governmental interventions (for example, subsidies for day care)? Some, surely; for we have just seen that some, perhaps most, forms of differential treatment are efficient. But sex discrimination would probably be declining, perhaps steeply, even in the absence of any laws against sex discrimination.

The engine of decline is the increasing participation of women in the work force. No one thinks that discrimination would keep all women from working, any more than racial discrimination keeps blacks from working. The main effect would be to depress the wages women were paid, lower their fringe benefits, and alter the distribution of women among jobs. There would, however, be some effect on the total number of women employed—more so, indeed, than on the number (as distinct from wages and working conditions) of blacks employed. This is because the elasticity of the supply of labor is higher for women than for men, a phenomenon especially pronounced when a higher percentage of women were married and raising children than is the case today. A married woman, especially with children at home, is in an economic sense "employed" in the home, and her household income will be less if she works in the market. Therefore a small reduction in market wages may keep many women out of the labor market, and conversely a small increase in those wages may draw many women into the labor market.

Women began working in large numbers long before sex discrimination in the workplace was widely criticized, let alone prohibited, and certainly long before sex discrimination ceased to be rampant (some believe it is still rampant). The percentage of the labor force that is female has grown steadily since 1947,[27] and the primary causes of this growth could not be anti-discrimination laws. The other causes of the increased female participation in the work force are by now well-known. With the decline in infant and child mortality, with improved techniques of contraception, and with the advent of inexpensive household labor-saving devices, women spent less time pregnant and raising children and doing household chores, so their opportunity costs of working in the market fell. At the same time, work was becoming less strenuous, in part because the entrance of large numbers of women into the work force increased the demand for services, hence for service workers, who do lighter work than industrial workers. So the demand for female workers rose, and hence their wages rose. As their wages rose, the opportunity costs of pregnancy and child raising rose too, reinforcing the trend toward fewer pregnancies. This in turn reduced the benefits of marriage to both men and women. The improvement in female job opportunities also reduced women's dependence on men. For both reasons, marriage rates fell and divorce rates soared: the former trend increased women's incentive to invest in their human capital, because they were working more; the latter increased the pressure on women to work, both as insurance against divorce and to maintain their standard of living after divorce.[28]

---

[27] See Fuchs, *Women's Quest for Economic Equality* at 12 fig 2.1 (cited in note 2); Rix, *The American Woman* at 366 table 9 (cited in note 19).

[28] See references in note 2; see also Fredricka Pickford Santos, *The Economics of Mari-*

Assuming that the increased female participation in the labor force is largely independent of the laws forbidding sex discrimination, one may ask what effect the increase is likely to have had on the incidence of sex discrimination (still *ex* law). It should reduce that incidence. First, as more women enter the work force, misconceptions concerning the average qualities of female workers should become less common. Of course, if the misconception consisted of exaggerated those qualities, women would be worse off by the elimination of the misconception. But the likelier misconception about a class of people not commonly encountered in the work force is that they are not as good as the existing workers, and this misconception would tend to dissipate with the entry of large numbers of that class into all kinds of jobs.

Second, as more wives and daughters enter the work force, we can expect misogyny to decline. Men who love their wives and daughters and empathize with their wives' and daughters' efforts to find work and to cope with misogynistic coworkers or supervisors are less likely to be misogynists in the workplace than if they lacked this family experience. Third, as more women enter the work force misogynistic employers are placed at a competitive disadvantage: their labor costs are higher than nonmisogynists' because their employment decisions are constrained by misogyny. Fourth, with more and more women workers, sexual harassment becomes more costly. Apart from the impact on productivity noted earlier, a larger fraction of the work force is offended by it, so the total compensating differential that the employer must pay its female employees rises.

As discrimination falls, we can also expect the wage gap between men and women to fall. Another factor working in this direction is the growing value of women's work relative to men's as physical strength becomes a less important labor asset. The declining wage gap among current workers may be masked, however, by an influx of new women workers, since less experienced workers are paid less than more experienced ones.[29] Thus a reduction in discrimination can actually *lower* average female wages, rather than, as one would expect, raise them.

Because economic analysis predicts that sex discrimination

---

tal Status, in Cynthia B. Lloyd, ed, *Sex, Discrimination, and the Division of Labor* 244 (Columbia, 1975).

[29] See James P. Smith and Michael Ward, *Women in the Labor Force and in the Family*, 3 J Econ Perspectives 9 (1989); June O'Neill, *The Trend in the Male-Female Wage Gap in the United States*, 3 J Labor Econ S91 (1985).

would have declined and the wage gap between men and women narrowed since 1963, when the first federal sex discrimination law—the Equal Pay Act—was passed, these trends cannot automatically be attributed, even in part, to law. Law may have had little or even nothing to do with improvements in women's status in the labor force. This suggestion may seem paradoxical: if the law penalizes certain conduct, the economist's "Law of Demand" implies that the conduct will become less frequent. This assumes, however, that the law is effective, and it may not be, for reasons to be examined in the next section.

The effect of sex discrimination laws on discrimination is ultimately an empirical question—and a difficult one. As argued above, discrimination would have declined without those laws—indeed *was* declining, before those laws were enacted—and it is difficult to isolate the effect of one variable from the others pushing in this direction. Victor Fuchs remarks:

> It is easy enough to find particular instances where these laws opened up jobs that were previously closed to women or resulted in a realignment of women's pay scales, but it is difficult to see any major effects on broad trends in women's wages or employment. The Equal Pay laws were passed in 1963 and 1964 [Fuchs is referring to the Equal Pay Act of 1963 and to Title VII], but fifteen years later the women/men wage ratio was unchanged at about 60 percent. It was only in the 1980s that the ratio started to climb, but these were the 'Reagan years'—a period not noted for vigorous enforcement of antidiscrimination and affirmative action legislation. With regard to women's employment, the rate of increase prior to the legislation was as rapid as after the laws were passed.[30]

This is painting with a pretty broad brush; other scholars have found that sex discrimination law *has* helped to break down barriers to the employment of women in traditionally male occupations.[31] Here is Morley Gunderson's cautious summary: "Clearly, the evidence does *not* unambiguously indicate that the EEO [Equal Employment Opportunity] initiatives of Title VII were a resounding success, although there is some evidence of a positive

---

[30] Fuchs, *Women's Quest for Economic Equality* at 27 (cited in note 2).

[31] See, for example, Beller, 17 J Human Resources at 388-90 (cited in note 4); Leonard, 2 J Labor Econ at 459 (cited in note 4); James V. Koch and John F. Chizmar, Jr., *Sex Discrimination and Affirmative Action in Faculty Salaries*, 14 Econ Inquiry 16 (1976). There is, however, contrary evidence besides Fuchs's. See, for example, Smith and Ward, 3 J Econ Perspectives at 15-16 (cited in note 29).

effect on the earnings and occupational position of women. There is also some evidence that the legislation is more effective when it is strictly enforced and when the economy is expanding."[32] There is no evidence of *large* effects[33]—and we shall see that sex discrimination law may not have improved the net *welfare* of women even if it has somewhat reduced the amount of sex discrimination.

Moreover, the costs of administering the sex discrimination laws must be factored into any attempt at an overall evaluation of those laws. No laws are costless to enforce, not even ineffectual ones. The burdens that sex discrimination laws place on the courts are substantial, and are growing even as discrimination is declining. John Donohue and Peter Siegelman have shown in a recent paper that declining discrimination may be associated with a rise rather than (as one might expect) a fall in the number of cases brought, because as more women are employed in better-paying jobs the gains from suit rise, and because women working side by side with men have a benchmark for proving unequal treatment.[34]

III. An Economic Examination of Specific Laws and Doctrines

Having sketched the basic sex discrimination laws and the basic economics of sex discrimination, I am prepared to analyze those laws from an economic standpoint. The highly tentative character of the analysis should be self-evident.

A. Equal Pay Act

At first glance this is the least problematic of the sex discrimination laws. If work is really equal (and the Act has, as I have

---

[32] Gunderson, 27 J Econ Lit at 61 (cited in note 2) (emphasis in original). For a similar appraisal of Executive Order 11246, see id at 63-64. Notice in regard to the last sentence in the quoted passage that the more the government impedes the efficiency of labor markets the less likely the economy is to be expanding.

[33] See also Cynthia B. Lloyd and Beth T. Niemi, *The Economics of Sex Differentials* 304-07 (Columbia, 1979). But there is an exception: Leonard, 2 J Labor Econ at 459 (cited in note 4), found that the executive order had increased the demand for white women by employers subject to the order by 3.5 percent relative to the demand for white men, but the demand for black women by 11 percent relative to the demand for white women. The reason may be that hiring a black woman enables the employer to make progress toward two affirmative action goals at once.

[34] See John J. Donohue and Peter Siegelman, *The Changing Nature of Employment Discrimination Litigation* (Am Bar Found, unpublished April 1989). Their discussion covers racial as well as sexual discrimination, and reaches the same conclusion: as blacks move into higher-paid positions and work in integrated jobs, the net expected gains from filing employment discrimination suits rise.

noted, been narrowly construed in this regard), then it would seem that unequal pay could not be efficient—it must reflect price discrimination. But it is more correct to say that it *may* reflect price discrimination. If the employer is able to pay its female employees a monopsonistic wage because of their high relocation costs, then it is discriminating in the economic (price discrimination) sense. Another possibility, however, is that while the work is nominally equal, the men do it better—are more productive—on average than the women, yet the employer is unable to prove this "factor other than sex" (which, as mentioned above, is a defense under the Act).

A third possibility is that the employer pays its female employees less because the employer's male owners, male managers, or male employees have an aversion to women in the workplace. Then the Act will operate as a tax on misogyny. Such a tax is not objectionable in itself, but we must consider the employer's likely reaction. He (the male pronoun being particularly appropriate in this context) will try to reduce the tax, by hiring fewer female employees, creating working conditions that are not attractive to them, or—the simplest strategy—placing women in jobs where they are doing work that is not equal to men's work. These would not be feasible strategies if Title VII were totally effective, for virtually all the measures that an employer might take to avoid the mandate of the Equal Pay Act would be a form of sex discrimination forbidden in principle by Title VII. Even substituting computers for secretaries might violate Title VII if the employer's motive were to reduce the number of *female* employees. But if we assume, realistically, that the Equal Pay Act is easier to enforce than Title VII, then the Act will result in fewer women being employed even if the average wage of those women who are employed is higher.[35] And the average wage may not be higher if the employer responds to the Act by shifting women to jobs where their

---

[35] For some evidence that the Act (and its foreign counterparts) has had this effect, see Isabel V. Sawhill, *The Economics of Discrimination Against Women: Some New Findings*, 8 J Human Resources 383, 393-94 (1973); Shaffer, 26 Labor L J at 294 n 10 (cited in note 4); Jacob Mincer, *Intercountry Comparisons of Labor Force Trends and of Related Developments: An Overview*, 3 J Labor Econ S1, S30 (1985); Maureen Pike, *The Employment Response to Equal Pay Legislation*, 37 Oxford Econ Papers 304, 316 (1985). It has even been argued that the covert purpose of the Equal Pay Act was to help men compete with lower-paid women. See Nancy S. Barrett, *Women in the Job Market: Occupations, Earnings, and Career Opportunities*, in Ralph E. Smith, ed, *The Subtle Revolution* 31, 55 (Urban Institute, 1979), citing Jo Freeman, *The Legal Basis of the Sexual Caste System*, 5 Valp U L Rev 213, 226-27 (1971). A comparable effect on blacks was found in a study of state fair-employment laws. See William M. Landes, *The Economics of Fair Employment Laws*, 76 J Pol Econ 507, 544-45 (1968).

work is not equal to men's. In addition, the Act will prevent women from attempting to overcome any information barriers to hiring them that may exist by offering to work for a lower wage than men.

Even if the employer does not try to avoid or evade the Equal Pay Act there may be a disemployment effect. The Act operates as a payroll tax, and the tax is higher the more workers employed. The employer may raise price in an effort to offset the tax, but unless he faces a totally inelastic demand curve—which no seller does—the increase in his price will reduce the demand for his goods, leading him to curtail his output and hence inputs, including labor inputs. He will employ fewer women as well as fewer men.

Another point is that the employer may avoid the Act *unconsciously*. He may simply observe that a department which happens to employ many women now has higher costs and lower profits than it used to, and may decide to reduce the size of the department without knowing or caring *why* its profit margin has fallen. All he needs to know is that his capital will command a higher return in an alternative use.

To the extent that unequal pay reflects differences in productivity that the equal work standard of the Act is insufficiently sensitive to pick up, the Act's distributive consequences are complicated by the interdependencies between men and women noted earlier in this article. If employers must pay a single wage to workers of different average productivity (i.e., men and women), that wage will be lower than that which the more productive workers would command but for the prohibition of "discrimination." So both men (by hypothesis, the more productive group) and their wives will be worse off. By the same token, the husbands of married women whose pay rises as a result of the Equal Pay Act will be better off. But if women are more altruistic on average than men,[36] the increase in men's welfare resulting from an increase in their wives' income will be less than the decrease in women's welfare resulting from a decline in their husbands' income, even if the increase and decrease are identical in dollar terms. In addition, since more married men than married women work, the transfer of welfare to married women will be larger. When this consideration is added to the Equal Pay Act's potential disemployment effect on women, it becomes a plausible speculation (again, no stronger con-

---

[36] See generally, Carol Gilligan, *In a Different Voice: Psychological Theory and Women's Development* (Harvard, 1982).

clusion is possible) that the Act makes women as a group worse off.

B. Title VII

Two different types of Title VII sex discrimination cases should be distinguished. In a *disparate impact* case, the employee challenges a practice (for example, a height requirement, or a prohibition, as part of an "anti-nepotism" rule, on hiring employees' spouses) that has a disproportionate exclusionary effect on women, though it was not intended to exclude them. Traditionally, such a practice was unlawful unless the employer could show that it was a business necessity; in practice such a showing was difficult to make. Disparate impact litigation has been important in eliminating personnel practices that tended to exclude blacks (i.e., requiring a high-school diploma), but has not been very important in the area of sex discrimination. Most practices challenged under disparate impact theories involve tests and credentials, and these are rarely sex-biased. Recently, the Supreme Court watered down the "business justification" defense and shifted the burden of proof to the plaintiff, so we can expect disparate impact cases to decline.[37]

The other, and more common, type of sex discrimination case is the *disparate treatment* case. This requires proof that the employer intentionally treated the female employee (or applicant) less favorably than it would have treated a similarly situated male employee. The practical difficulties in such litigation are great. First, it is difficult to prove a complex counterfactual (for example, what would have happened if the employee had been male rather than female). Second, it often does not pay the plaintiff to invest in the necessary proof—which involves looking at similarly situated males to show that the plaintiff's inadequacies were not responsible for her being fired or otherwise mistreated.[38] The stakes are small. They consist of backpay minus whatever the plaintiff has earned in a substitute job (for the employee has a duty to mitigate her damages) plus reinstatement. But reinstatement will rarely be sought, since usually the plaintiff will have gotten another job while the litigation was pending and will be reluctant to go back to work for an employer who mistreated her and whom she sued. Finally, bringing an employment suit impairs the plaintiff's earning capac-

---

[37] *Wards Cove Packing Co., Inc. v Atonio*, 109 S Ct 2115 (1989).

[38] Rarely will an employer fire, or otherwise treat badly, a perfect worker, of whatever race or sex. Discrimination is more apt to be directed against workers who are not, or not much, better than average, and whose complaint is that the employer took a dimmer view of their failings than he would have of a white male's failings.

ity: employers are reluctant to hire people who sue employers![39]

Although the plaintiff's costs in bringing successful sex discrimination litigation under Title VII may well outweigh her gains, there is an important qualification. If class action treatment is possible, as where a large employer is alleged to be discriminating against all or most of its female employees, then plaintiffs will find safety in numbers and it will be feasible for them to develop statistical evidence of discrimination. Yet such evidence often is inconclusive. It usually comes down to an unexplained difference in the wages or number of men and women employed, and it is always possible for the employer to argue that the statistical methodology is insufficiently sensitive to identify all noninvidious explanatory variables.

To the extent that disparate treatment suits do succeed, it is uncertain whether they increase the net welfare of women. Since some forms of unlawful sex discrimination are efficient, Title VII litigation will reduce the efficiency with which employers use labor, and this will result in lower average wages and higher product prices. The direct costs of Title VII litigation—lawyers' fees, executive time, and so forth—will work in the same direction. Full-time housewives will bear a disproportionate share of these costs, since their husbands' wages will fall and the prices they and their husbands pay for goods and services will rise.[40] Conversely, single working women will tend to benefit, except to the extent that employers are reluctant to hire women in the first place out of fear that Title VII will restrict their ability to fire an unsatisfactory female employee without inviting a lawsuit.

C. Comparable Worth

Failure to achieve "comparable worth" has sometimes been challenged under the disparate impact theory of Title VII, but without success. Jobs traditionally dominated by women (the stereotypical examples are nursing and secretarial work) are on average less well paid than jobs traditionally dominated by men, such as truck driving. Proponents of "comparable worth" argue that the disparity reflects sex discrimination and can be eliminated by re-

---

[39] On the reluctance of women for this reason to bring sex-discrimination suits see Kristin Bumiller, *The Civil Rights Society: The Social Construction of Victims* 26 (Johns Hopkins, 1988).

[40] There are fewer full-time housewives today than there used to be, but there are still plenty. In 1985, 23.5 percent of all families had a full-time housewife. Rix, *The American Woman* at 374 table 14 (cited in note 19).

quiring employers to pay wages "objectively" commensurate with the skill, responsibility, and other attributes of each job. The short economic answer is that a competitive labor market will achieve comparable worth; for that is the equilibrium condition of such a market. If a particular job classification happens to be overpaid relative to skill, responsibility, and other considerations that determine the value and cost of a worker's time, workers will flow into the classification, reducing the wage until the excess demand is eliminated. And if the job classification happens to be underpaid, workers will leave for better jobs, causing the wage to rise.

There are, however, three important qualifications to this economic answer; the first two are closely related. First, the equilibrium that results will reflect any systematic wage differences that are due to efficient sex discrimination; and some, maybe most, discrimination is efficient. Second, to the extent that employers "steer" women into traditional women's jobs and men into traditional men's jobs, and this discrimination is not detected and prevented through enforcement of Title VII, competition will not eliminate discrimination based on sex. Finally, public employer labor markets may not be competitive; hiring and firing may be determined by political rather than economic considerations. Thus, requiring public employers to achieve comparable worth is less likely to produce market distortions than requiring private employers to do so.[41]

A deeper objection to making comparable worth mandatory in private markets is that comparable worth neglects important factors that bear on the determination of a competitive wage, such as investment in human capital. Women who because of voluntarily assumed family responsibilities expect to participate only intermittently in the labor market will be attracted to jobs that do not involve as great an investment in human capital, and such jobs will not (and from an economic standpoint) should not pay as well. Also, comparable worth does not take into account the desirability of allowing wages to fluctuate in order to correct temporary imbalances between supply and demand, when a particular labor market is not in equilibrium. Finally, if wages are set on the basis of what is deemed to be comparable worth and, as is likely, the resulting

---

[41] For evidence in support of these three points see Richard F. Kamalich and Solomon W. Polacheck, *Discrimination: Fact or Fiction? An Examination Using an Alternative Approach*, 49 S Econ J 450 (1982); Bielby and Baron, 76 Am Econ Rev Papers & Proc 43 (cited in note 3); and Elaine Sorensen, *Implementing Comparable Worth: A Survey of Recent Job Evaluation Studies*, 76 Am Econ Rev Papers & Proc 364 (May 1986), respectively.

pattern is not the equilibrium pattern for the labor market in question, entry or exit will occur until the old "discriminatory" pattern is restored. In other words, if women (for whatever reason) prefer "traditionally female" jobs, once the wages in those jobs rise women will enter these occupations in great numbers, driving the wage back down. Hence a commitment to comparable worth implies not merely one-time, but continuous, intervention in competitive wage-setting.

Even if comparable worth were fully achieved, women as a whole might not be better off. Women in the traditional women's jobs would have higher wages, but fewer of them would be employed, because employers would have an increased incentive to substitute capital for these jobs and, to the extent substitution was infeasible, to reduce the scale of the activity in which these women were employed. In general, then, comparable worth can be expected to reduce the employment of women[42] as well as to transfer wealth from childless women to mothers, since the latter are more likely to be attracted to traditional women's jobs, those being the jobs for women who want to balance family and career. In addition, the social costs resulting from so massive a public interference with labor markets would be great and would be borne in significant part by women, as we have seen.

D. Sexual Harassment

When efforts were first made to attack sexual harassment under Title VII they seemed an exotic extension of the statute, in part because of the strange implication that a bisexual harasser couldn't be liable under the Act, since his conduct was sex neutral. However, the case for prohibiting sexual harassment may actually be stronger from an economic standpoint than the case for prohibiting conventional sex discrimination. Sexual harassment, properly defined to exclude mere flirtations and solicitations, is a coercive practice related to such plainly inefficient practices as rape and extortion.[43] Sexual harassment is unlikely, save for the costs of prevention, to be in the employer's interest. While, in principle, grant-

---

[42] For evidence see June O'Neill, Michael Brien, and James Cunningham, *Effects of Comparable Worth Policy: Evidence From Washington State*, 79 Am Econ Rev Papers & Proc 305, 308 (May 1989); Mincer, 3 J Labor Econ at S29-S30 (cited in note 35); see also Johnson and Solon, 20 U Mich J L Ref at 202-03 (cited in note 4); Mark R. Killingsworth, *The Economics of Comparable Worth: Analytical, Empirical, and Policy Questions*, in Heidi I. Hartmann, ed, *Comparable Worth: New Directions for Research* 86 (National Academy, 1985).

[43] See Posner, *Economic Analysis of Law* at 201 (cited in note 1).

ing a "license" to male supervisory employees to harass female employees would enable the employer to pay a lower wage to those male employees, the reduced cost of hiring supervisors is unlikely to offset: (1) the higher wage the employer will have to pay its female employees to compensate them for being exposed to sexual harassment; (2) time lost by employees in harassing or warding off harassment; (3) distortion in promotions; and (4) adverse selection of employees (the employer would be a magnet for male employees wanting to harass females and for female employees desiring to use their wiles to gain advancement). The problem is that, like other antisocial behavior in the workplace (embezzlement, for example), the costs of prevention are high; and this is an argument for public enforcement—depending of course on *its* costs.

The novelty in the legal concept of sexual harassment is that the usual defendant in a Title VII sexual harassment case is not the harassing male employee, but the employer. It is as if banks were the defendants in cases involving embezzlement by bank employees. The proper analogy, however, is to the tort doctrine of respondeat superior. The most efficient method of discouraging sexual harassment may be by creating incentives for the employer to police the conduct of its supervisory employees, and this is done by making the employer liable. Because "employer" is broadly defined in Title VII, the supervisory employee himself can be and sometimes is made a defendant in a Title VII sexual harassment case; so again the analogy to respondeat superior (which is an additional ground of liability, not a defense for the primary tortfeasor) is a close one.

E. Pregnancy Discrimination Act

The requirement that the employer not differentiate among its employees on the basis of pregnancy is analytically the same as a requirement that the employer pay the same retirement benefits to male and female employees despite women's superior longevity, or a requirement that the employer grant maternity leave (in other words, agree to reinstate female employees who take time off to have or take care of their babies). In all three cases, the law compels the employer to ignore a real difference in the average cost of male and female employees. The result is inefficient, but a more interesting point is that it may not benefit women as a whole.[44]

---

[44] Moreover, unisex longevity tables penalize women buying life insurance, unisex liability insurance premium-setting penalizes women because they are safer drivers than men,

The employer is required in effect to pay them greater fringe benefits than men (since health care for pregnancy is a benefit men do not require). The employer cannot recoup by reducing women's wages—that would violate the Equal Pay Act—but he can minimize his costs by employing fewer women (as by automating secretarial work faster and more completely). To the extent that this succeeds, women will be hurt. To the extent it does not succeed, the employer will experience a rise in his average cost of labor, causing him to reduce the average wage he pays.

Women will lose not only directly, but also indirectly, in their role as the wives of men who will now be paid less. The clearest loser will be a married but childless working woman.[46] Her wage and that of her husband will fall, and she will not recoup the loss in higher fringe benefits, because the additional benefits are of value only to women with children. And even if the aggregate income of the household is higher, women may have less power within the household if their paychecks are smaller. This, however, is pure speculation—it is far from clear that women's consumption within the household depends on the relative size of the woman's paycheck, as distinct from her relative contribution to the full (nonpecuniary as well as pecuniary) income of the household. Housewives will also suffer from the Pregnancy Discrimination Act because their husbands' wages will fall. The point can be generalized: housewives, being economically identified with their husbands, are hurt by efforts to reduce sex discrimination. The clearest beneficiaries of sex-neutral fringe benefits are unmarried working women with many children—a small group.

This analysis, by illustrating the possibility of deep conflicts of interest among women, may help explain why many women are not feminists. Depending on age, marital status, number and age of children, and other factors, women may gain or lose from measures ostensibly designed to eliminate discrimination "against women." Indeed, women are so heterogeneous a group that it is hard to imagine what public policies would benefit them as a group—except

---

and preventing insurers from differentiating among risk groups on the most efficient basis increases the social costs of insurance. These effects illustrate the tendency of sex discrimination law to bring about offsetting redistributions of wealth. Such redistributions are not costless. The only argument for them is that they will contribute to breaking down stereotypes. This is implausible. It is not a stereotype, but a fact, that women live longer than men, have fewer accidents, incur greater medical expenses, and so forth.

[46] There are many women in this category. In 1985, 17.1 percent of all families were childless married couples in which both spouses were working. Rix, *The American Woman* at 374 table 14 (cited in note 19).

policies designed to maximize social wealth by maintaining and strengthening free markets.

F. Equal Protection

The interpretation of the Equal Protection Clause as prohibiting sex discrimination in employment unless the discrimination is justified by an important governmental interest has thus far had little effect. Much of the prohibition overlaps Title VII. Many cases have been brought by men rather than women, although women's groups generally support these cases on the ground that they combat stereotypes harmful to women's aspirations for job equality.[46] Many cases have the usual ambiguous effects. Consider the requirement that spousal benefits under social security programs be equalized regardless of the sex of the spouse, so that a widower is entitled to the same social security death benefit as a widow. If the total benefits payable under social security are assumed to be fixed, the result of this entitlement will be to benefit the better off at the expense of the worse off, since widowers are on average wealthier than widows. The *Feeney* decision,[47] upholding Massachusetts' policy of giving veterans a preference in public employment, illustrates the possibility that the optimal ideology for the women's movement may well be a libertarian one. Veterans' benefits programs, which of course systematically benefit men over women, are redistributive measures that are contrary to the principles of efficiency and limited government.

CONCLUSION

What has been the net effect of the cascade of laws and lawsuits aimed at eliminating sex discrimination in employment? This is maddeningly difficult to say, but it is possible that women as a whole have not benefited and have in fact suffered. Because of the heterogeneity of women as an economic class and their interdependence with men, laws aimed at combating sex discrimination are more likely to benefit particular groups of women at the expense of other groups rather than women as a whole. And to the extent that the overall effect of the law is to reduce aggregate social welfare because of the allocative and administrative costs of the law,

---

[46] The fact that laws ostensibly discriminating in favor of women may actually harm them suggests that laws ostensibly forbidding discrimination against women may also harm women.

[47] *Personnel Administrator v Feeney*, 442 US 256 (1979).

women as a group are hurt along with men. Sex discrimination has long been on the decline, for reasons unrelated to law, and this makes it all the more likely that the principal effect of public intervention may have been to make women as a group worse off by reducing the efficiency of the economy. The case for ambitious extensions of sex discrimination law—for example in the direction of comparable worth—is therefore weak.

These suggestions should not be surprising, in light of the extensive, and largely negative, economic literature on regulation. There is a tendency to suppose that laws forbidding discrimination are somehow exempt from the critique of regulation. This position is difficult to sustain.

It is possible that the economic costs of sex discrimination law are offset by gains not measured in an economic analysis—gains in self-esteem, for example. But it is not clear that, if the canvass is broadened in this fashion, the picture brightens. For example, if by reducing the wages of men sex discrimination law propels more wives into the job market, with the result that (since they still bear the principal burden of household production) they work harder, have fewer children, and have less stable marriages, it is not clear that they are better off on balance than they were when their husbands had higher wages and they stayed home. The social, like the economic, consequences of sex discrimination law are murky, and not necessarily positive. In any event it is important to know what the sex discrimination laws cost; the price tag for an increase in women's self-esteem, if known, might be thought too high by society.

[12]

COMMENT ON DONOHUE

RICHARD A. POSNER

Professor Donohue has written a serviceable defense of the economic approach to law, emphasizing the utility of the Coase Theorem and the political neutrality of economics. I would not use quite the terms Donohue does to describe myself, but I cannot believe that the readers of this journal would be interested in what I have to say on that subject, so I shall hold my peace.

I would not emphasize the Coase Theorem as much as Donohue does. The essential relevance of economics to law lies not in a particular theorem but in the fact that economics is the most advanced of the social sciences. Law is an important social institution. It is for the most part a nonmarket institution, but there is a thriving economics of nonmarket behavior, and it is no wonder that it should have many fruitful applications to law. The wonder is that legal scholars continue to resist as vigorously as they do the use of economic models and methods in law. The law and society movement is a conspicuous focus of resistance.

The resistance is based, in part at least, on a misunderstanding, or rather a series of misunderstandings, about economics. The one emphasized by Professor Donohue is that economics embodies a conservative ideology. It does not. The essential assumption that powers economic analysis is that people are rational, in the sense of adapting means to ends as effectively as possible given relevant constraints such as lack of information. Almost everything in economic theory follows from this assumption. The assumption can hardly be thought liberal or conservative. Whether specific results of economic analysis are liberal or conservative depends on the various auxiliary assumptions, priors, empirical findings, and what have you that particular economists bring to their work. For every Posner, there are at least two Donohues.

A second misunderstanding is that the attempts of economists to achieve greater rigor than has been customary in social science, by heavy use of mathematics and statistics, disables the economist from capturing the rich human complexity of so verbally and culturally dense an institution as law. The economist, in that dreaded term of academic opprobrium, is "reductionist." There is a confusion of terms here. All science involves abstraction. Newton's law of falling bodies abstracts from many of the particulars of bodies (for example, was the apple red?) in an effort to discover a law of nature—a law that describes the behavior of a wide variety of bod-

LAW & SOCIETY REVIEW, Volume 22, Number 5 (1988)

ies (from apples to tides to stars) that differ in many of their particulars. We do not describe this as reductionism. We reserve that word for what we sense are unsuccessful efforts to explain one thing in terms of another—for example, ideas in terms of molecular changes in the brain. The economic analysis of law attempts to formulate general laws about behavior in and of legal systems. The Coase Theorem can be viewed in this light. Donohue gives another example, the Priest-Klein hypothesis that plaintiffs win fifty percent of litigated cases. The hypothesis has a solid basis in economic theory, and some empirical support. It may someday be falsified (Newton's law of falling bodies was falsified), it will no doubt be refined, but it is not reductionist.

Economics is a cornucopia of interesting hypotheses on law. Here are some others: abrogating the laws against selling babies for adoption would reduce, not increase, the price that adoptive parents must pay to acquire a child; making the losing party pay the winning party's attorney's fees would reduce, not increase, the settlement rate; the Supreme Court's "anti-religion" cases of recent years have helped the fundamentalist movement at the expense of the main-line religious faiths; the switch from contributory to comparative negligence has raised insurance rates without affecting the accident rate (except insofar as the rate changes may have done so indirectly); no-fault accident insurance plans increase the number of highway fatalities compared to a pure fault system; reducing court delay increases caseloads. I should think that anyone seriously interested in the sociology of law—which I take to be the focal interest of the law and society movement—would, regardless of his or her ideological commitments or political persuasion, be fascinated by a body of thought that has generated such intriguing hypotheses.

Professor Donohue expresses concern that economics, as it becomes more mathematical, may lose touch with law. There is no danger of that. First, the whole society is, at long last, becoming more mathematical, more "numerate." And high time. The quality and quantity of mathematical education in this country are both disgraceful. Second, and more important, there is no reason economic analysts of law should feel duty-bound to use the most advanced mathematical techniques. They should use the techniques appropriate to their subject matter and to their audience. Economic analysis of law is an applied field of economics; it is not obliged to aspire to the headiest heights of theory.

Despite resistance from legal scholars—not only conventional legal scholars but practitioners of rival interdisciplinary schools such as the law and society endeavor—economics has made great strides in law in just the last twenty years. Today it is an established and significant part of the curriculum of most major and most minor law schools. It contributes a substantial part of the first-rate legal scholarship produced in this country and, increasingly, abroad. It has its own journals. It has a growing foothold in legal practice, and in the judiciary. It fascinates even those whom it repels. The law and society movement has much to learn from its successes, and among the things it has to learn is the importance of theory and the value of political diversity.

RICHARD A. POSNER is a judge of the United States Court of Appeals for the Seventh Circuit and a senior lecturer at the University of Chicago Law School. He has written extensively on issues related to law and economics.

PART IV

REGULATION AND ANTITRUST

[13]

Theories of economic regulation

Richard A. Posner

Professor of Law
University of Chicago
and Senior Research Associate
National Bureau of Economic Research

Several theories have been advanced to explain the observed pattern of government regulation of the economy. These include the "public interest" theory and several versions, proposed either by political scientists or by economists, of the "interest group" or "capture" theory. This article analyzes those theories. It argues that the public interest theory and the political scientists' versions of the interest group theory are unacceptable in their present form. The economists' version of the interest group theory is discussed at greatest length; its theoretical and empirical foundations are reviewed, and the conclusion is reached that, while promising, the theory requires both more analytical development and new sorts of empirical investigation before it can be accepted as an adequate positive theory of regulation.

1. Introduction

■ A major challenge to social theory is to explain the pattern of government intervention in the market—what we may call "economic regulation." Properly defined, the term refers to taxes and subsidies of all sorts as well as to explicit legislative and administrative controls over rates, entry, and other facets of economic activity. Two main theories of economic regulation have been proposed. One is the "public interest" theory, bequeathed by a previous generation of economists to the present generation of lawyers.[1] This theory holds that regulation is supplied in response to the demand of the public for the correction of inefficient or inequitable market practices. It has a number of deficiencies that we shall discuss. The second theory is the "capture" theory—a poor term but one that will do for now. Espoused by an odd mixture of welfare state liberals, muckrakers, Marxists, and free-market economists, this theory holds that regulation is supplied in response

Richard A. Posner received the A.B. from Yale University in 1959 and the LL.B. from Harvard University in 1962. His current research centers on the use of economic analysis to explain the behavior of the legal system.

The author wishes to thank Gary S. Becker, Ronald H. Coase, Paul W. MacAvoy, B. Peter Pashigian, and George J. Stigler for their helpful comments on an earlier draft.

This paper was originally given at a conference on regulation sponsored by the National Bureau of Economic Research, and is part of a series of studies in the area of law and economics being carried out by the Bureau under a grant from the National Science Foundation. It is not an official Bureau publication, since it has not yet undergone the full critical review accorded National Bureau publications, including approval by the Bureau's board of directors.

For an appendix to this article, see George Stigler's "Free Riders and Collective Action," pp. 359–365 in this issue.

[1] The theory is more often assumed than articulated. Some representative works embodying it are Bonbright [4], Davis [9], and Friendly [13].

to the demands of interest groups struggling among themselves to maximize the incomes of their members. There are crucial differences among the capture theorists. I shall argue that the economists' version is the most promising, but shall also point out the significant weaknesses in both the theory and the empirical research that is alleged to support the theory.

2. The public interest theory of regulation

■ **The original theory.** Two assumptions seem to have typified thought about economic policy (not all of it by economists) in the period roughly from the enactment of the first Interstate Commerce Act in 1887 to the founding of the *Journal of Law and Economics* in 1958. One assumption was that economic markets are extremely fragile and apt to operate very inefficiently (or inequitably) if left alone; the other was that government regulation is virtually costless. With these assumptions, it was very easy to argue that the principal government interventions in the economy—trade union protection, public utility and common carrier regulation, public power and reclamation programs, farm subsidies, occupational licensure, the minimum wage, even tariffs—were simply responses of government to public demands for the rectification of palpable and remediable inefficiencies and inequities in the operation of the free market. Behind each scheme of regulation could be discerned a market imperfection, the existence of which supplied a complete justification for some regulation assumed to operate effectively and without cost.

Were this theory of regulation correct, we would find regulation imposed mainly in highly concentrated industries (where the danger of monopoly is greatest) and in industries that generate substantial external costs or benefits. We do not. Some fifteen years of theoretical and empirical research, conducted mainly by economists, have demonstrated that regulation is not positively correlated with the presence of external economies or diseconomies or with monopolistic market structure. Few, if any, responsible students of the airline industry, for example, believe that there is some intrinsic peculiarity about the market for air transportation that requires prices and entry to be fixed by the government. The same may be said for trucking, taxi service, stock brokerage, ocean shipping, and many other heavily regulated industries. Even the danger of "market failure" in such traditionally unquestioned areas of regulation as health care, the legal profession, and the safety of drugs and other products is increasingly discounted. The conception of government as a costless and dependably effective instrument for altering market behavior has also gone by the boards.[2] Theoretical revision has both stimulated and been reinforced by a growing body of case studies demonstrating that particular schemes of government regulation—whether of taxicabs, or producers of natural gas, or truckers, or airlines, or stock brokers, or new drugs, or electricity rates, or broadcasting—cannot be explained on the

---

[2] Some examples of the emerging theory of "government failure" are Hirshleifer, DeHaven, and Milliman [16], pp. 74–82, and Posner [39] and [35].

ground that they increase the wealth or, by any widely accepted standard of equity or fairness, the justice of the society.[3]

☐ **A reformulation.** The empirical evidence is sometimes challenged on the ground that the disappointing performance of the regulatory process is the result not of any unsoundness in the basic goals or nature of the process but of particular weaknesses in personnel or procedures that can and will be remedied (at low cost) as the society gains experience in the mechanics of public administration.[4] Thus reformulated, the public interest theory of regulation holds that regulatory agencies are created for bona fide public purposes, but are then mismanaged, with the result that those purposes are not always achieved.

This reformulation is unsatisfactory on two grounds. First, it fails to account for a good deal of evidence that the socially undesirable results of regulation are frequently desired by groups influential in the enactment of the legislation setting up the regulatory scheme. The railroads supported the enactment of the first Interstate Commerce Act, which was designed to prevent railroads from practicing price discrimination, because discrimination was undermining the railroads' cartels. American Telephone and Telegraph pressed for state regulation of telephone service because it wanted to end competition among telephone companies. Truckers and airlines supported the extension of common carrier regulation to their industries because they considered unregulated competition "excessive." Sometimes the regulatory statute itself reveals an unmistakable purpose of altering the operation of markets in directions inexplicable on public interest grounds, as in the reference in the ICC's statutory mandate to the desirability of maintaining "balance" among competing modes of transportation.[5] None of this evidence is decisive against the public interest theory—in each case other groups besides the industry directly regulated supported the legislation. Whether the other groups were also interest groups is discussed later on.

Second, the evidence that has been offered to show mismanagement by the regulatory agency is surprisingly weak. Much of it is consistent with the rival theory (which is considered more closely in Section 3) that the typical regulatory agency operates with reasonable efficiency to attain deliberately inefficient or inequitable goals set by the legislature that created it. The proclivity of some agencies for concentrating their resources heavily on cases of small indi-

---

[3] See, for example, Baxter [1], Cabinet Task Force on Oil Import Control [6], Coase [7], Hilton [15], Jordan [19], Kitch, Isaacson, and Kasper [21], MacAvoy [25], Peltzman [30, 31], and, for a general summary of the literature, Jordan [20].

[4] An interesting example of this point of view is provided by Herring in [14], which argues that the challenge to public administration is to develop techniques of overcoming the interest group pressures that threaten to deflect legislative programs from serving the public interest. He may underestimate the difficulties of doing this because of a certain economic naivete that leads him to suggest that opposing group interests can often be harmonized in a way that vindicates the public interest. Ordinarily harmony is achieved at the expense of the public interest. See text at notes 38–41, *infra*.

[5] National Transportation Policy, 49 U.S.C. preceding § 1.

vidual consequence—a proclivity often thought to be convincing evidence of mismanagement—is in fact consistent with an efficient allocation of resources within the agency.[6] The frequent criticisms of agencies for relying on case-by-case adjudication to make policy, rather than engaging in elaborate planning exercises, are extremely superficial since they ignore, first, the intrinsic difficulty of forecasting the future and, second, the disastrous consequences for agencies, notably the Federal Communications Commission, that have engaged in such planning.[7] The common argument that the employees of regulatory agencies must be less able than their counterparts in the private sector, since they are paid lower salaries,[8] ignores the fact that service with an agency frequently increases the later earning capacity of the employee in the private sector. The agency makes a contribution to the employee's human capital. This contribution, when added to his salary, may equal the value of the salary (plus contributions of human capital) that he would have received in the private sector.[9] In sum, one is left puzzled as to why such failures of regulation in the public interest as one observes should be ascribed so confidently to bureaucratic ineptitude.

Third, no persuasive theory has yet been proposed as to why agencies should be expected to be less efficient than other organizations. The motivation of the agency employee to work diligently and honestly is similar to that of the employee of a business firm. Both want to obtain advancement (not necessarily within the employing firm or agency) and to avoid being fired, demoted, or humiliated. To some extent, these motivations are independent of the incentive of the agency's head to enforce standards of diligence and honesty against the employees. Many employees will want to demonstrate the possession of excellent qualities in order to improve their prospects for superior private employment anyway. In any event, the agency head's incentive is clear. He derives few benefits from the slackness of his staff—not even the famous "quiet life." His life would not be so quiet, for many employees would be restless and dissatisfied, knowing that their opportunities for private employment were being impaired by the agency's reputation for laxity and sloth.

Furthermore, the agency's head is answerable both to the legislative and (if he desires promotion or reappointment) to the executive branches. Legislative oversight of agencies is too little emphasized. Unlike business firms, government agencies must go to *their* capital markets—the legislative appropriations committees —every year. There is competition among agencies for the largest possible slice of the appropriations pie, and the agency that has a reputation for economy and hard work enjoys an advantage in the competition, for only in the exceptional case will it be to the legislators' advantage that the agency's personnel be lining *their*

---

[6] Posner [33].

[7] See, for example, Posner [32] and Comanor and Mitchell [8].

[8] The question is never asked whether their jobs might be less risky or require less skill than the private-sector jobs with which they are compared.

[9] See Posner [34] and Eckert [11].

pockets (whether with pecuniary income or with nonpecuniary income such as leisure).[10]

One objection to the foregoing argument is that the agency differs from the private firm in not competing in any product market. But that is to say only that the agency is like a private monopolist, and there is no convincing theoretical or empirical support for the proposition that the internal management of monopolistic firms is any laxer than that of competitive firms. Another objection is that the agency has little incentive to minimize costs because, unlike a business firm, it cannot keep the profits generated by its cost savings. Yet most employees of business firms do not share in the profits of the enterprise, and they are somehow motivated to work efficiently. Moreover, I have suggested several ways in which agency employees, from the head of the agency down, do "profit" from efficient management, and lose if the agency is managed inefficiently.

□ **A further reformulation of the public interest theory.** The idea that regulation is an honest but frequently an unsuccessful attempt to promote the public interest becomes somewhat more plausible if we introduce two factors often ignored. The first is the intractable character of many of the tasks that have been assigned to the regulatory agencies. The clearest example is the regulation of price levels under public utility and common carrier statutes. These statutes require the agencies to determine the costs of the regulated firms and to hold their prices to those costs, and there are good grounds for believing that the necessary instruments of measurement and control simply do not exist.[11] The agencies are asked to do the impossible and it is not surprising that they fail, and in attempting to succeed distort the efficient functioning of the regulated markets. But this does not explain why legislatures assign such tasks to agencies.

The second factor is the cost of effective legislative supervision of the agencies' performance. In a recent article on legal rulemaking, Isaac Ehrlich and I point out that legislative bodies are a type of firm in which the costs of production are extremely high and, moreover, rise very sharply with increases in output.[12] The reason is that legislative "production" is a process of negotiation among a large group, the legislators, and the analysis of transaction costs in other contexts suggests that bargaining among a number of individuals is a costly process (and explains why legislatures require only a majority and not a unanimous vote in the conduct of their business). Because costs of bargaining rise rapidly with the number of bargainers, a legislature cannot respond efficiently to a growth in workload by increasing the number of its members. Hence, as

---

[10] One could argue that the legislator may not have much incentive to ride herd on the agency: he will not get paid more and his popularity with the voters will be increased only marginally. But this ignores the fact that the actual audit will be conducted by an employee of the legislative body, who will have the same incentive to conduct a searching audit as any privately employed auditor.

[11] See, for example, Posner [35].

[12] Ehrlich and Posner [12].

the business of a legislature rises, it can be expected to delegate more and more of its work to agencies, and to exercise progressively less control over those agencies. This theory has various testable implications. It suggests, for example, a "life cycle" theory of administrative regulation. The agency is created at a time when the legislature has a strong interest in the problem to be dealt with by the agency. But as time passes, and other problems come before the legislature, the legislature finds itself unable at reasonable cost to continue to devote time to properly monitoring the agencies created previously. The theory also implies that administrative failure will become, on average, a more serious problem over time, with the growth of the size and complexity of the economy. As we shall see shortly, however, the inquiries suggested by these hypotheses might not discriminate adequately between the version of the public interest theory suggested here and some versions of the capture theory of regulation.

☐ **Behavioral assumptions of the public interest theory.** A serious problem with any version of the public interest theory is that the theory contains no linkage or mechanism by which a perception of the public interest is translated into legislative action. In the theory of markets, it is explained how the efforts of individuals to promote their self-interest through transacting bring about an efficient allocation of resources. There is no comparable articulation of how a public perception as to what legislative policies or arrangements would maximize public welfare is translated into legislative action. It is not enough to say that a voter will vote for the candidate who promises to carry out the policies that the voter perceives to be in the public interest; other policies might benefit the particular voter more. Policies that benefitted 51 percent of the voters might impose much greater costs on the other 49 percent, in which event the majority would be confronted with a conflict between principle and interest—and no body of theory or of evidence suggests that they would be likely to vote the former.

There are two possible ways around this problem. One, suggested by Ronald Coase, emphasizes the moral differences between private and political action. The assumption that market behavior is normally motivated by fairly narrow considerations of self-interest is plausible, because most market decisions are social goods rather than bads. To be sure, a decision to sell a new product may harm a competitor or a locality or a group of workers or of customers, but the decision makers can be reasonably confident that these harms are more than offset by the gains to others. Where, however, an individual votes for policies designed to exploit his fellows, he can hardly avoid confronting the moral implications of his action and the moral code may constrain him from voting in that manner.

A second approach is to observe the potentiality for collusion among politicians. There are only two important political parties in this country, and there are barriers not only to the formation of additional parties but to the takeover of either of the major parties by disgruntled members or outsiders. Thus, there would appear to be opportunities for the politicians who dominate the parties to agree to impose some of their own policy preferences on the electorate. They could also use their monopoly power to obtain pecuniary income—and doubtless do—but I am assuming that they take at least some of their monopoly profits in the form of satisfaction from imposing on the public their conception of the public interest (which might differ from the conception held by the electorate and from the desires of any particular interest group). If this analysis is accepted, it becomes plausible to suppose that some policies are adopted because they conform to the public interest—as conceived by the politicians.

■ **The Marxists and the muckrakers.** The theory that economic regulation is not about the public interest at all, but is a process by which interest groups seek to promote their (private) interests, takes several distinct forms. One, which is put forward by Marxists and by Ralph Nader-type muckrakers, can be crudely summarized in the following syllogism. Big business—the capitalists—control the institutions of our society. Among those institutions is regulation. The capitalists must therefore control regulation. The syllogism is false. A great deal of economic regulation serves the interests of small-business—or nonbusiness—groups, including dairy farmers, pharmacists, barbers, truckers, and, in particular, union labor. Such forms of regulation are totally unexplained (and usually either ignored or applauded) in this version of the interest-group or "capture" theory.

□ **The political scientists' formulations.** A more interesting version of the "capture" theory derives from political science, and in particular from Bentley and Truman and their followers, who emphasize the importance of interest groups in the formation of public policy.[13] The political scientists have developed some evidence of the importance of interest groups in legislative and administrative processes, but unfortunately their work is almost entirely devoid of theory. They do not tell us why some interests are effectively represented in the political process and others not, or under what conditions interest groups succeed or fail in obtaining favorable legislation.[14]

A few political scientists have proposed the rudiments, at least, of a usable theory. This theory—which the term "capture" describes particularly well—is that over time regulatory agencies come to be dominated by the industries regulated.[15] This formulation is more specific than the general interest group theory. It singles out

3. Some versions of the capture theory

---

[13] See Bentley [2] and Truman [44]. For a specific application of the approach to regulatory agencies, see Truman [44], pp. 416–421. For the position of Herring on the role of interest groups in regulation see note 4, *supra*. It is interesting to note that "interest group" is not a pejorative term for most of the political scientists, since they are either indifferent to or unaware of the fact that the economic costs of regulation procured by an interest group normally exceed the economic benefits.

[14] The vagueness of the theorizing in Truman's book [44], especially pp. 506–507 and 515, is typical.

[15] See Bernstein [3], Huntington [17], Leiserson [23], and Ziegler [46].

a particular interest group—the regulated firms—as prevailing in the struggle to influence legislation, and it predicts a regular sequence, in which the original purposes of a regulatory program are later thwarted through the efforts of the interest group.

Unfortunately, the theory is still unsatisfactory. First, it is confusingly similar to, and in practice probably indistinguishable from, some versions of the public interest theory discussed in Section 2. Second, while I have generously called it a "theory," it is actually a hypothesis that lacks any theoretical foundation. No reason is suggested for characterizing the interaction between the regulatory agency and the regulated firm by a metaphor of conquest, and surely the regulatory process is better viewed as the outcome of implicit (sometimes explicit) bargaining between the agency and the regulated firms. No reason is suggested as to why the regulated industry should be the only interest group able to influence an agency. Customers of the regulated firm have an obvious interest in the outcome of the regulatory process—why may they not be able to "capture" the agency as effectively as the regulated firms, or more so? No reason is suggested as to why industries are able to capture only existing agencies—never to procure the creation of an agency that will promote their interests—or why an industry strong enough to capture an agency set up to tame it could not prevent the creation of the agency in the first place.

The "theory" answers none of these questions. In addition, it is contradicted by three important bodies of evidence. First, not every agency is characterized by a pristine virtue; often there is no occasion for conquest. As mentioned earlier, there is now considerable evidence that a major purpose (in fact) of the original Interstate Commerce Act was to shore up the railroads' cartels.[16] Later amendments, typically passed at the behest of the Commission itself, seem to have been less rather than more favorable to railroads (an example is the Hepburn Act which gave the ICC the power to fix maximum rates). The sequence is opposite to what the capture hypothesis predicts.

Second, the theory has no predictive or explanatory power at all when a single agency regulates separate industries having conflicting interests. The ICC is again a conspicuous example. It regulates competing modes of transportation—truckers, railroads, and barge lines—and the theory does not tell us which one the ICC can be expected to favor. This difficulty is not limited to the agency with a multiindustry "clientele." There are always competing groups within an industry. The interests of the trunk airlines are not identical to those of the regional or of the local service lines: which will the CAB decide to promote? The interests of the telephone companies, primarily AT&T, are in conflict with those of Western Union and other "record" carriers: which competing group will the Federal Communications Commission promote?

Third, the capture theory ignores a good deal of evidence that the interests promoted by regulatory agencies are frequently those of customer groups rather than those of the regulated firms themselves. Indeed, not only many examples of specific regulatory

---

[16] See Hilton [15], Kolko [22], and MacAvoy [24].

policies, but some of the structural characteristics of the regulatory process, seem best explained by reference to the influence on the regulatory process of interest groups consisting of customers of the regulated industry.[17]

☐ **The economic theory of regulation.** What I shall call "the economic theory of regulation" was proposed by George Stigler in a pathbreaking article.[18] The theory seems at first glance merely a refined version of the capture theory just discussed. It discards the unexplained, and frequently untrue, assumption of pristine legislative purpose; it admits the possibility of "capture" by interest groups other than the regulated firms; and it replaces the "capture" metaphor, with its inappropriately militaristic flavor, by the more neutral terminology of supply and demand. But it insists with the political scientists that economic regulation serves the private interests of politically effective groups.

More is involved, however, than merely a recasting of the work of the political scientists. The economic theory is more precise and hard-edged—easier to confront and test with a body of data—than the political theory (which, as I pointed out, is not really a theory at all). Moreover, the economic theory is committed to the strong assumptions of economic theory generally, notably that people seek to advance their self-interest and do so rationally. A political scientist can argue that regulation is more likely to be imposed in a declining industry because adversity is a greater spur to effort than opportunity[19] (an example that assumes that regulation is normally obtained for the benefit of the regulated firms). The economist is reluctant to accept such an explanation. He does not distinguish between a profit foregone and a loss incurred—the former is a cost too, indeed the same kind of cost.[20] (I note parenthetically that the hypothesis is contradicted by a good deal of evidence.[21])

It is, of course, a weakness rather than a strength in a theory that it is so elastic as to fit any body of data with which it is likely to be confronted. The political science theory of regulation is such a theory. Exceptions to the general rule that regulatory agencies are captured by the regulated firms are explained away by facile references to the personality of the legislators, public opinion, ignorance,

---

[17] See Posner [40].

[18] Stigler [42]. For an attempt to marshal empirical support for the theory see Jordan [20]. Stigler, it should be noted, builds on earlier work by economists on the political system. See Buchanan and Tullock [5], Downs [10], and Olson [28].

[19] Wilson [45].

[20] Coase, however, suggests the interesting possibility that when a business is in decline, managers may find it profitable to shift their attention from improving their business operations to improving the political environment, another potential source of profits. There is a further point: the costs of becoming informed about opportunities for enhanced profits through government regulation may be greater than the costs of perceiving losses that regulation might reduce.

[21] For example, the airline industry was not declining in 1938 when the Civil Aeronautics Act was passed, nor the railroad industry in 1887 when the first Interstate Commerce Act was passed. One tends to associate regulation with declining industries primarily because so many regulatory programs were instituted during the depression of the 1930s.

folk wisdom,[22] etc. The economic theory insists that regulation be explained as the outcome of the forces of demand and supply. Outcomes that cannot be so explained count as evidence against the theory.

4. A closer look at the economic theory of regulation

■ **The theory.** I shall now try to describe the economic theory more precisely and to state what I believe to be its strengths and weaknesses. The theory is based on two simple but important insights. The first is that since the coercive power of government can be used to give valuable benefits to particular individuals or groups, economic regulation—the expression of that power in the economic sphere—can be viewed as a product whose allocation is governed by laws of supply and demand. The second insight is that the theory of cartels may help us locate the demand and supply curves.

Viewing regulation as a product allocated in accordance with basic principles of supply and demand directs attention to factors bearing on the value of regulation to particular individuals or groups, since, other things being equal, we can expect a product to be supplied to those who value it the most. It also directs our attention to the factors bearing on the cost of obtaining regulation. The theory of cartels illuminates both the benefit and the cost side. The theory teaches that the value of cartelization is greater, the less elastic the demand for the industry's product and the more costly, or the slower, new entry into the industry (or cartelized markets within the industry) is. The theory identifies two major costs of cartelization (besides punishment costs, which are relevant only where cartelization is forbidden by law). The first is the cost to the sellers of arriving at an agreement on the price to be charged by and the output of each seller. This agreement determines the profits of each cartel member. The second cost is the cost of enforcing the cartel agreement against nonparticipants or defectors. Cartels are plagued by "free rider" problems. After the sellers agree to charge the price that maximizes their joint profits, each seller has an incentive to sell at a slightly lower price, because his profits are likely to be higher at the much greater sales volume that a slightly lower price will enable him to obtain. If enough sellers submit to the temptation, the cartel will collapse. A cartel is particularly fragile if members are able to conceal price cuts from one another; then each has the hope of being able to obtain substantial short-term profits before the other members realize that he is cutting price and match him.[23]

Since the effect of typical regulatory devices (entry control, minimum rates, exemption from the antitrust laws) is the same as that of cartelization—to raise prices above competitive levels— the benefit side of cartel theory is clearly relevant. The cost side also seems relevant. The members of the industry must agree on the form of regulation. And just as the individual seller's profits are maximized if he remains outside of the cartel (as long as his competitors remain inside), so any individual or firm that would be benefitted by a type of regulation will have some incentive to avoid

---

[22] See Truman [44], p. 512.

[23] For a summary of the theory of cartels, see Posner [36].

joining in the efforts of his group to obtain the regulation. If the regulation is forthcoming, he will benefit from it—he cannot be excluded from the protection of a general regulation, just as a seller cannot be excluded from the benefits of his competitors' charging a monopoly price—but, unlike the active participants in the coalition, he will benefit at no cost.

The theory of cartels teaches that the reluctance to cooperate in maintaining a monopoly price is most likely to be overcome if the number of sellers whose actions must be coordinated is small, which tends to reduce the costs of coordination and of policing, and if the interests of the sellers are identical or nearly so, which should reduce the cost of securing agreement.[24] Likewise in the regulatory sphere, the fewer the prospective beneficiaries of a regulation, the easier it will be for them to coordinate their efforts to obtain the regulation. Also, it will be more difficult for one of them to refuse to participate in the cooperative effort without causing the effort to collapse. Thus, all will tend to participate, knowing that any defection is likely to be followed promptly by the defection of the remaining members of the group, leaving the original defector worse off than if he had not cooperated. The homogeneity of the interests of the members is also significant. The more homogeneous their interest in the regulation in question, the easier (cheaper) will it be for them to arrive at a common position and the more likely will it be that the common position does not so disadvantage one or more members as to cause them to defect from the group.[25]

The analysis of cartels is plainly relevant to the development of an economic theory of regulation, but it is not that theory. If it were, we would observe the same industries obtaining regulatory protection as form durable cartels. We do not. Many industries, such as agriculture, certain occupations, many branches of retail trade, and some manufacturing industries such as textiles, which have obtained favorable regulation, lack the characteristics that predispose a market to cartelization, in particular fewness of sellers. Casual observation suggests that highly concentrated industries are actually *less* likely to obtain favorable regulation than less concentrated industries,[26] reversing the usual expectation with regard to the incidence of cartelization.

There are two reasons why the pattern of regulation and the pattern of private cartelization are different. First, the demand for regulation (derived from its value in enhancing the profits of the regulated firms) is greater among industries for which private cartelization is an unfeasible or very costly alternative—industries that lack high concentration and other characteristics favorable to cartelizing. They lack good substitutes for regulation. (This point

---

[24] The characteristics that predispose a market to cartelization are discussed in Posner [34], pp. 116–117.

[25] On the other hand, the more successful and profitable the cartel, the greater the costs to consumers, and so the greater the incentive of consumers to organize against the cartel. Stigler has suggested that the role of the "outsider" (e.g., the consumer) is greater in the public regulation than in the private cartelization context (see [42], p. 16), but it is not clear why a cohesive group of customers would not be equally effective in exacting concessions from a private cartel.

[26] For some evidence in support of this hunch, see MacPherson [26].

suggests, incidentally, a testable—in principle anyway—hypothesis of the economic theory of regulation: among randomly selected unconcentrated industries the presence of cartel-like regulation will be negatively related to the price elasticity of demand for the industry's product *at the competitive price.* The qualification, which is critical, makes the test difficult to carry out in practice.)

Second, whereas cartelization is the product purely of the cooperative action of the firms, favorable regulation requires, in addition, the intervention of the political process. Some industries may be able to influence that process at lower cost than others and these may not be the same industries that are able to cartelize at low cost. In particular, the political dimension of regulation requires two modifications of the theory of cartels as applied to regulation. First, as Stigler proposes in his paper on the free-rider problem, which appears as an appendix to this article, each member of an industry will have an interest in participating in the coalition seeking protective regulation when there is significant asymmetry among the positions of industry members. Protective regulation can take a variety (greater than in the case of private cartelization) of forms—limitation of entry, cash subsidy, tariff, etc.—and the choice of the form may, assuming asymmetry among the positions of the industry's members, affect differentially the welfare of those members. If so, each will want to participate in the industry campaign for regulation so that the choice of the form of regulation to seek will reflect his views. The free-rider problem will still be easiest to overcome where the number of firms in an industry is small, but if the asymmetry condition is fulfilled, even the presence of many firms may not erect an insurmountable obstacle to the formation of an effective coalition. This suggests that it may be cheaper for large-number industries to obtain public regulation than to cartelize privately.

Second, the determinants of political influence must be worked into the supply side of the market in regulation. But before this can be done it is necessary to specify the character of the political system under discussion: the political system of the Soviet Union—or of the City of Chicago—is not identical to that of the United States.

One can distinguish three distinct forms of political system, all of which play some role in the actual political systems of democratic countries such as the United States. One system I shall call "entrepreneurial:" favorable legislation is sold[27] to the industries that value it most. For the reason just mentioned, these would not be the same industries that form private cartels. The costs of cooperative action are irrelevant under this system: the government can use its taxing or other powers of coercion to enable the industry to overcome any free-rider problem it might have, in order that the industry can raise the maximum purchase price for the legislation.

The next system to be considered is the "coercive:" legislation

---

[27] At what price? The government has a monopoly of the sale of regulation so presumably it will be able to charge a positive price even if the cost of supplying regulation is zero. In fact the cost is greater than zero, both because the production of legislation is costly (see text at note 12, *supra*) and because regulation that favors one group imposes costs on others.

is awarded to groups that are able to make credible threats to retaliate with violence (or disorder, or work stoppages, or grumbling) if society does not give them favorable treatment. We lack good theories of threats or violence but as a first approximation it would seem that the number of people in the group would be an important determinant of its ability to make credible threats of *serious* disorder or violence (as opposed to threats of minor sabotage, annoying and costly but not deeply threatening).

The third system is the "democratic:" legislation is awarded by the vote of elected representatives of the people. This system, like the coercive, emphasizes the importance of numbers: not of threateners but of voters. The groups are not identical, but there is great overlap, so we are led to predict that the economic legislation of dictatorial regimes will broadly resemble that of democratic ones— as seems on casual observation to be the case. Willingness to pay is also important in the democratic as in the enterpreneurial political system, since legislators are elected in campaigns in which the amount of money expended on behalf of a candidate exerts great influence on the outcome. However, unlike the case of an entrepreneurial system, in a democratic system the free-rider problem remains a serious one: it may limit the ability of an industry or other interest group to make substantial campaign contributions.

The foregoing analysis suggests that while the characteristics that predispose an industry to successful cartelization may also help it to obtain favorable government regulation, one characteristic that discourages cartelization—a large number of parties whose co-operation is necessary to create and maintain the cartel—encourages regulation. Large numbers have voting (and, potentially, coercive) power and also increase the likelihood of an asymmetry of interests that will encourage broad participation in the coalition seeking regulation. In addition, large numbers, and other factors that discourage private cartelization, increase the demand for protective legislation.

The economic theory can thus be used to explain why we so often observe protective legislation in areas like agriculture, labor, and the professions, where private cartelization would hardly be feasible. This is an important advance over the other theories that we have examined. However, the economic theory has not been refined to the point where it enables us to predict specific industries in which regulation will be found. That is because the theory does not tell us what (under various conditions) is the number of members of a coalition that maximizes the likelihood of regulation. Formally, this is the number beyond which the loss of group cohesiveness caused by adding another member would outweigh the increase in the feasibility and attractiveness of becoming regulated produced by greater voting power and by greater demand for regulation due to greater difficulty of cartelizing privately.

I used to think that there was one case in which the theory yielded an unequivocal and testable prediction. That is where the number of *firms* in the industry is small, thereby facilitating the organization of the industry for effective political action,[28] but

---

[28] I assume that the free-rider problem is least serious when the number

the number of *employees* in the industry is great.[29] Since the profits from protective regulation can be divided between the employees and the firms through collective bargaining, it should be possible for the firms to induce the employees to "lend" their voting power to obtaining such regulation. The industry does not quite have the best of both worlds, because the firms' profits from favorable legislation, and hence their incentive to seek it, will be diminished by the amount of the payoff to the employees. This may be considerable. Legislation favorable to the industry, by raising prices, will reduce output and hence the industry's demand for inputs, including labor. The reduction in demand will harm not only the employees who are laid off but the remaining employees as well, since the diminution in the number of employees will reduce their voting power, which they might want to exercise in other areas. These costs will presumably be considered by the union when it negotiates for its share of the profits conferred by the regulation being sought by the firms.

The major problem with this hypothesis is that the small number of firms is a factor that, by reducing the costs of private collusion, reduces the industry's demand for favorable legislation. So the economic theory is not refuted by observing that the most conspicuous example of such an industry—the automobile industry—seems to have been unsuccessful either in obtaining favorable regulation or in warding off unfavorable regulation (such as safety and emission controls). Anyway, the automobile example—like so many in this field—is ambiguous.[30]

As this example suggests, the economic theory is still so spongy that virtually any observations can be reconciled with it. Consider, as a further example, the apparent paradox that so many regulated industries appear to be either extremely atomistic (like agriculture) or extremely concentrated (like local telephone or electrical service). The former would appear to encounter substantial free-rider problems in organizing a politically effective group; the latter would appear to have little demand for regulation. The moderately con-

---

of parties is very few, albeit larger coalitions might also be able to overcome the problem.

[29] The fundamental distinction between number of firms and number of voters undermines Stigler's hypothesis ([42], p. 7) that small firms will enjoy disproportionate political influence. If the number of employees is proportional to sales, it is not obvious why small firms should be any more important in obtaining favorable regulation than in the formation of a private cartel.

[30] Conceivably safety and emission controls hurt foreign manufacturers more than domestic ones. Without evidence, I find this suggestion somewhat implausible, however. For example, the emission controls reduce engine performance—always a big selling point for American cars—which would seem to hurt the domestic manufacturer more. Also, the argument ignores the fact that many imported cars are manufactured by foreign subsidiaries of domestic manufacturers. The foreign entanglements of the domestic companies may explain, however, why the industry does not enjoy tariff protection. Also to be considered is the fact that while the gasoline tax would seem to reduce the demand for automobiles, the proceeds of the tax are largely earmarked for highway construction—and highways are complementary to automobiles—so the tax may have little adverse effect on the industry after all. The need for further research in this area is dramatically apparent.

centrated industry would seem to have the optimal structure in terms of the costs of obtaining legislation and the benefits to be derived from it. But theory can worm its way out of this hole, too. For the small-number case, we can point out: (1) even a naturally monopolistic industry would gain from legislation that increased the demand for its product (e.g., by suppressing substitutes) or prevented entry;[31] (2) even if the members of the regulated industry do not gain from regulation, other groups, for example groups of customers, may;[32] and (3) concentration or monopoly may itself be the result of regulation. In the large-number case, we can point out that the reluctance of each member of a coalition to participate substantially in it may be dominated by the number of members who participate, albeit very modestly. Is industry X, having 10 members, likely to spend more money on trade association activities than industry Y, which differs only in that it has 10,000 members? Free-rider problems are presumably not serious in the case of industry X. Let us assume that each member of that industry contributes $1,000 for a total of $10,000 and that this approximates the optimal expenditure for the industry. Free-rider problems may be serious in industry Y, so serious that it would be impossible for the industry to raise $1,000 from each member were that necessary to reach an optimal level of expenditures. But the industry does not have to raise that amount from each member in order to match industry X—to do that it need only raise $1 from each member.

As part of the search for a harder-edged theory of regulation, it has been suggested that the geographic concentration of the people who would benefit from favorable regulation is an important element since a legislator will exert greater efforts on behalf of a voter bloc large enough to influence the outcome of an election materially. But it has not been demonstrated that this is a generally valid proposition. If the same number of voters are more widely dispersed, no legislator will pay as much attention to their demands, but more legislators will pay some attention, and the net effectiveness of the interest group in the legislature *may* (it is an empirical question whether it *will*) be greater. The proposition also ignores the importance of the President in the legislative process. A Presidential candidate has little reason to respond to the desires of voter blocs concentrated in states in which the vote is not expected to be close. Thus we are at a loss to say whether observing a geographically concentrated—or dispersed—group obtaining—or failing to obtain—regulation confirms or refutes the economic theory of regulation. And this illustrates the essential deficiency of the economic theory of regulation in its present form. At best it is a list of criteria relevant to predicting whether an industry will obtain favorable legislation. It is not a coherent theory yielding unambiguous and therefore testable hypotheses.

Another sort of weakness is that the theory, pushed to its logical extreme, becomes rather incredible, because it excludes the

---

[31] Even under conditions of natural monopoly, the profit-maximizing monopoly price will induce entry, albeit of firms having higher costs than the monopolist.

[32] See Posner [40].

possibility that a society concerned with the ability of interest groups to manipulate the political process in their favor might establish institutions that enabled genuine public interest considerations to influence the formation of policy. One can certainly argue that the U.S. Constitution, in establishing an independent judiciary, did just this (and this point is discussed further below). The constitutional requirement of payment of compensation in eminent domain cases is a similar example.[33] More generally, the many features of law and public policy designed to maintain a market system are more plausibly explained by reference to a broad social interest in efficiency than by reference to the designs of narrow interest groups.[34] One can of course say that on some issues the relevant interest group consists of everyone, or almost everyone, in the society. But this usage robs the interest group concept of its utility by collapsing it into the public interest theory.

☐ **The evidence.** Let us turn now to the empirical evidence bearing on the economic theory of regulation. There are a fair number of case studies—of trucking, airlines, railroads, and many other industries—that support the view that economic regulation is better explained as a product supplied to interest groups than as an expression of the social interest in efficiency or justice.[35] I shall discuss in a moment the question just how much support for the economic theory of regulation do these studies really provide. But first I want to discuss another type of empirical evidence, so far largely neglected, that provides additional support for the economic interest group approach. This is evidence concerning the procedures employed in the regulatory process.

A corollary of the economic theory of regulation is that the regulatory process can be expected to operate with reasonable efficiency to achieve its ends. The ends are the product of the struggle between interest groups, but, as suggested earlier, it would be contrary to the usual assumptions of economics to argue that wasteful or inappropriate means would be chosen to achieve those ends. We saw that the evidence traditionally adduced to show that regulatory agencies are inefficient is highly ambiguous. I want to go beyond that evidence and note some general features of the regulatory process that suggest it is well designed to achieve the ends posited by the economic theory of regulation.

One is the delegation of regulatory authority by legislatures to administrative agencies. As mentioned earlier, legislatures cannot continuously regulate a complex area; they must delegate much of the regulatory function either to the courts or to administrative agencies. In the area of economic regulation the legislative choice has generally been the administrative agency rather than the court. Lawyers defend this choice on the ground that the public interest purposes assumed to lie behind the legislation can be achieved more efficiently due to (1) the agency's specialization and (2) its independence from political control. The first reason seems specious.

---

[33] See Posner [34], p. 22, note 2.
[34] The role of legal institutions in supporting the market system is a major theme in Posner [34].
[35] See references in note 3, *supra*.

Courts have long handled highly complex economic questions, such as those which arise in antitrust cases, no less efficiently (or more inefficiently) than the agencies. Is a merger case tried before a federal district court likelier to be mishandled than one tried before the FTC, or the ICC?[36] The second reason is illogical. The choice is not between agency and direct legislative regulation—the latter is assumed to be impracticable. The choice is between agency and court, and the court is more insulated from political control than the agency. The terminal character of many judicial appointments, the general jurisdiction of most courts, the procedural characteristics of the judicial process, and the freedom of judges from close annual supervision by appropriations committees, all operate to make the courts freer from the interest group pressures operating through the legislative process, and more disposed to decide issues of policy on grounds of efficiency, than any other institution of government—specifically the administrative agency, where these features are absent or attenuated.[37] If I am correct in suggesting that the judicial process is designed to resist interest group pressures, it would seem to follow that the delegation phenomenon should count as evidence in support of the interest group theory of regulation.

My article, "Taxation by Regulation,"[38] presented some additional evidence of the influence of interest group pressures on the structure and procedures (as distinct from the substantive outcomes) of the regulatory process. The article suggests that a number of standard features of public utility and common carrier regulation, including controls over construction of new plant and over abandonment of service, the duty of the common carrier to serve all comers, and the tendency to impose public utility and common carrier controls on industries that sell services rather than goods, are best explained on the theory that regulation is designed in significant part to confer benefits on politically effective customer groups. Much regulation, I argued, may be the product of coalitions between the regulated industry and customer groups, the former obtaining some monopoly profits from regulation, the latter obtaining lower prices (or better service) than they would in an unregulated market—all at the expense of unorganized, mostly consumer, groups.[39]

Since that article was written, an example has occurred to me where regulation may be the product of an alliance between the

---

[36] For some evidence that it is not, see Posner [39].

[37] See Posner [34], chapters 23, 27. An interesting point here is the traditional reluctance of the courts to permit groups to litigate, which is manifested in requirements of "standing" to sue and in prohibitions against "lay intermediaries" between client and lawyer. A trade association cannot bring a lawsuit seeking a legal rule favorable to its members. The member must sue on his own behalf. This reduces the influence of interest groups in the litigation process. But see *NAACP* v. *Button*, 371 U.S. 415 (1963).

[38] [40].

[39] This extension of the economic theory of regulation helps explain, for example, why the original Interstate Commerce Act was supported by (some) shippers as well as the railroads themselves: the railroads' discriminatory pricing—the target of the Act—both undermined the railroads' cartels and harmed shippers competing with favored purchasers.

industry and a supplier group. A perplexing feature of airline regulation is that although the CAB has evidently been effective in facilitating cartel pricing by the airlines, it has (until very recently[40]) exercised no control whatever over nonprice competition. The effect of unrestricted nonprice competition when price competition is constrained is to increase the costs of the competing firms and thereby reduce their profits, but, under plausible as-assumptions, by less than if they competed in price.[41] It seems that the airline industry has incurred additional costs largely from equipment purchases. The airlines compete with one another by purchasing newer and more comfortable aircraft and by offering more flights and therefore greater convenience to travelers. The airlines may have purchased *more* equipment than they would if they were competing in price as well as in service (although a possibly offsetting fact is that the demand for air travel is less than it would be if the industry's prices were lower). If so, this would suggest that an apparently inexplicable omission in the regulatory scheme may actually be the calculated result of a coalition of interest groups.

The body of empirical evidence supporting the economic theory of regulation has, however, several shortcomings.

(1) Most of the evidence is consistent with *any version* of the interest group theory. The evidence relating to the internal efficiency of regulatory agencies does not enable one to discriminate among any specific such theories (such as the economic theory), because none asserts that regulatory agencies are inept.[42] Only the public interest theory is damaged by such evidence. The case studies on the substance of regulatory policy suffer from the same inadequacy. To show that the Interstate Commerce Act was enacted to benefit the railroads, or the Civil Aeronautics Act the airlines, or that the licensure of physicians benefits them rather than their patients, or that much regulation seems subservient to special-interest customer groups, is to show only that interest groups influence public policy. For these case studies to support the economic theory of regulation they would have to demonstrate that the characteristics and circumstances of the interest groups were such that the economic theory would have predicted that they, and not some other groups, would obtain the regulation that we observe them enjoying. Otherwise *any* legislation that benefitted some group at the expense of the general public would count as support for the economic theory of regulation.

I am aware of only three studies that have tried to test the economic theory of regulation, as distinct from the general interest group theory: two by Stigler (of highway weight limitations for

---

[40] When it approved capacity-limitation agreements among airlines in certain markets.

[41] See Stigler [41].

[42] The theory, discussed in Section 3, that regulatory agencies eventually knuckle under to the regulated firms comes close to implying that regulatory agencies are ineptly managed (otherwise they would not be so easily conquered). This is an example of the confusing overlap, noted earlier, between this version of the capture theory and the public interest theory.

trucks and of occupational licensure)[43] and one by McPherson (of tariffs).[44] Only the results of one of the studies (trucks) clearly support the theory.[45]

(2) The empirical research has not been systematic. The researcher does not draw a random sample of, say, the economic legislation passed in the last ten years and ask how much of that legislation can be explained by the economic theory of regulation. Instead, he picks the cases that seem from a distance to support the theory[46] and seeks to determine whether that initial impression was correct. I am not criticizing these studies. Had they shown that trucking, and airline, and railroad regulation could *not* be explained by reference to the operation of interest groups, the significance for scholarship would have been immense. But even a lengthy series of case studies cannot provide much support for the economic theory of regulation, given that the industries studied do not appear to be—and were not selected as—typical and that apparent counterexamples abound. The "consumerist" measures of the last few years—truth in lending and in packaging, automobile safety and emission controls, other pollution and safety regulations, the aggressiveness recently displayed by the previously lethargic Federal Trade Commission—are not an obvious product of interest group pressures,[47] and the proponents of the economic theory of regulation have thus far largely ignored such measures. Nor have there been case studies of industries that fail (or never try) to obtain favorable regulation. Furthermore, there is a serious question whether it is proper to define the subject of study as "economic" regulation. Criminal laws, civil rights legislation, legislative reapportionment, and other "noneconomic" regulations affect economic welfare no less than the conventional forms of economic regulation, and it seems arbitrary to exclude them from the analysis: presumably they obey the same laws of social behavior that we think explain economic regulation.

(3) Some of the case studies of regulation have produced evidence difficult to reconcile with the economic theory. I refer in particular to studies which indicate that maximum-price regulation has little or no effect on the price levels of public utilities[48] and that some forms of regulation generate costs in resource misallocation that seem large in relation to the benefits to the favored interest group.[49] Both sorts of evidence may seem to confirm the influence of interest groups in the regulatory process but it is only the crudest form of interest group analysis that they support. There is no basis

---

[43] In [41, 42].

[44] In [26].

[45] Stigler's tests of occupational licensure produced mixed results. A partial test of the theory is also attempted in Pashigian [29], again without successful results.

[46] However, this does not appear to be true of Stigler's study of state limitations on truck weights.

[47] See Peltzman's recent study of the regulation of new drugs by the Food and Drug Administration in [31]; cf. Posner [37].

[48] See Moore [27], Jackson [18], and Stigler and Friedland [43].

[49] The oil import quota program is a notable example. See Cabinet Task Force on Oil Import Control [6], pp. 28–30.

in the economic theory of regulation for ineffectual regulation—for trying and failing to limit the prices of the regulated firms. The obvious explanation is that maximum price controls are a fig leaf which the regulatory agency dons to conceal from the public its domination by an interest group. But the economic theory of regulation—as thus far developed—does not predict that regulatory agencies will practice fraud on the general public.[50]

Nor does the theory predict that legislatures will choose unnecessarily expensive methods of conferring benefits upon effective political groups. Perhaps they do not. It has been estimated that hundreds of millions of dollars a year could have been saved had oil companies received outright grants from the Treasury rather than oil import quotas which, in the process of enriching the companies and the owners of domestic oil-producing property, induce consumers to make inefficient substitutions for oil.[51] But the underlying assumption—that there is a large avoidable deadweight loss—may well be incorrect. An increase in income tax rates to finance an outright grant to the oil companies could have costly substitution effects (e.g., leisure for work) of its own. If the assumption *is* correct, the implications for the economic theory of regulation are disturbing. It is in everyone's interest to use a more rather than a less efficient way of transferring money to the oil companies. Stigler, in his search for a rational explanation of the quotas, has argued that it would be impracticable to give money to the oil companies directly, because then firms would have an incentive to create oil-company affiliates in order to be entitled to the subsidy.[52] However, that danger could be averted by limiting the subsidy to oil companies in existence as of the date of the grant. The CAB gave cash subsidies to the airlines for many years: its control over entry prevented the subsidies from attracting new entrants. Nor are entry controls strictly necessary: the cash grant can be limited to the firms in the industry at the date of the grant (or some earlier date to prevent entry in anticipation of the grant).

(4) The empirical evidence depends heavily on a confident rejection of the public interest rationales in which all legislation is —for reasons not yet illuminated by the economic theory of regulation—cloaked. Sometimes these rationales have just enough plausibility to make such rejection questionable. The oil import quota case is again an interesting one. The recent Arab oil embargo suggests that it is not palpably absurd to adopt governmental policies designed to reduce U.S. dependence on the oil produced by the Arabs. Stigler has argued that if this were the actual purpose behind the oil import quota system, it would have been carried out not by a quota system but by a tariff, since the revenues generated by a tariff would go to the taxpayers rather than to the oil com-

---

[50] Such a prediction would be a logical extension of Stigler's remarks on the relevance of information costs in the analysis of the political process (in [42], pp. 11–12), but the extension has not been made. On the economics of fraud, see Posner [38], pt. 1, and references cited therein. The possible application of the economic theory of fraud to the theory of regulation is discussed in the text below.

[51] See [6].

[52] See Stigler [42], pp. 4–5.

panies' stockholders.[53] (Another alternative would be stockpiling imported oil.) But the argument proves only that the purpose behind the system may have been a mixture of public interest considerations and interest group pressures.[54]

(5) The effects of economic regulation are difficult to trace. A tax on gasoline might help the railroad industry. The cartelization of the airline industry under the CAB's aegis benefits surface transportation (the demand for which is increased by anything that increases the price of a substitute service). These complications make it difficult to identify the industries that benefit from and those that are injured by regulation. It is superficial to point to an industry as an example of an effective political group because it enjoys a high tariff without considering the impact on it of other governmental policies, including many ostensibly imposed on different industries. We do not know whether to regard automobile emission controls as a sign of the industry's inability to ward off adverse regulation or as a token of how limited, and late, government regulation of the automobile industry has been.

(6) An important, but as yet unexplained, datum is the characteristic public interest rhetoric in which discussions of public policy are conducted and the policies themselves framed. The use of language that, if the economic theory of regulation is correct, is utterly uninformative and indeed misleading is not costless; presumably it is employed only because there are offsetting benefits. These benefits must have to do with increasing the costs to members of the public of obtaining accurate information about the effect of the actions of their legislative representatives on their welfare.

Recent developments in the economic theory of fraud may prove helpful in explaining the prevalence of misleading rhetoric in discussions of public policy. The propensity to engage in fraud seems to be related to such factors as the difficulty (cost) of the buyer's determining the performance characteristics of the product (by inspection, use, or whatever) and the value of the buyer's time. The greater the cost of determining the product's performance characteristics, or of the time spent by the buyer in trying to ascertain those characteristics, the more fraud we can expect to find. Where the product is legislation, the cost of determining its quality is often extremely high. With respect to the value of the buyer's time, it is important to note that a legislative proposal must be "sold" to two groups: the legislators and the electorate. Our earlier discussion of the costs of legislation implied that the cost of a legislator's time is very high, which in turn implies that the amount of time he can efficiently devote to appraising the merits of proposed legislation is small.

The introduction of considerations based on the economic analysis of fraud, or more broadly of the costs of information, suggests that it may be possible to revive the public-interest-miscarried

---

[53] *Id.* p. 4.

[54] Another consideration is that the oil import quota program could be and was established by Executive Order rather than by statute, whereas imposition of a tariff would have required congressional action.

theory of regulation in a form that it can be made rigorous and empirically testable.

5. Conclusion

■ This article has offered a number of criticisms of both the traditional public interest theory of regulation and the newer economic theory which conceives regulation as a service supplied to effective political interest groups. Neither theory can be said to have, as yet, substantial empirical support. Indeed, neither theory has been refined to the point where it can generate hypotheses sufficiently precise to be verified empirically. However, the success of economic theory in illuminating other areas of nonmarket behavior leads one to be somewhat optimistic that the economic theory will eventually jell: the general assumption of economics that human behavior can best be understood as the response of rational self-interested beings to their environment must have extensive application to the political process.

References

1. BAXTER, W. F. "NYSE Fixed Commission Rates: A Private Cartel Goes Public." *Stanford Law Review.* Vol. 22 (April 1970), pp. 675–712.

2. BENTLEY, A. F. *The Process of Government.* Chicago: University of Chicago Press, 1908.

3. BERNSTEIN, M. *Regulating Business by Independent Commission.* Princeton: Princeton Univ. Press, 1955.

4. BONBRIGHT, J. C. *Principles of Public Utility Rates.* New York: Columbia Univ. Press, 1961.

5. BUCHANAN, J. AND TULLOCK, G. *The Calculus of Consent.* Ann Arbor: University of Michigan Press, 1962.

6. CABINET TASK FORCE ON OIL IMPORT CONTROL. *The Oil Import Question.* Washington, D.C.: U.S. Government Printing Office, 1970.

7. COASE, R. H. "The Federal Communications Commission." *Journal of Law and Economics,* Vol. 2, No. 2 (October 1959), pp. 1–40.

8. COMANOR, W. S. AND MITCHELL, B. "The Costs of Planning: The FCC and Cable Television." *Journal of Law and Economics,* Vol. 15, No. 1 (April 1972), pp. 177–231.

9. DAVIS, K. C. *Administrative Law Treatise.* St. Paul: West, 1958 and 1970 supplement.

10. DOWNS, A. *An Economic Theory of Democracy.* New York: Harper, 1957.

11. ECKERT, R. D. "What Do Regulatory Commissions Maximize?" Unpublished manuscript, University of Southern California, 1972.

12. EHRLICH, I. AND POSNER, R. A. "An Economic Analysis of Legal Rulemaking." *Journal of Legal Studies.* Vol. 3, No. 1 (January 1974), pp. 257–286.

13. FRIENDLY, H. J. *The Federal Administrative Agencies: The Need for Better Definition of Standards.* Cambridge: Harvard Univ. Press, 1962.

14. HERRING, E. P. *Public Administration and the Public Interest.* New York: McGraw-Hill, 1936.

15. HILTON, G. W. "The Consistency of the Interstate Commerce Act." *Journal of Law and Economics,* Vol. 9, No. 2 (October 1966), pp. 87–113.

16. HIRSHLEIFER, J., DeHAVEN, J. C., AND MILLIMAN, J. W. *Water Supply: Economics, Technology, and Policy.* Chicago: University of Chicago Press, 1960.

17. HUNTINGTON, S. P. "The Marasmus of the ICC: The Commission, the Railroads, and the Public Interest" in P. Woll, ed., *Public Administration and Policy: Selected Essays*, New York: Harper & Row, 1966.

18. JACKSON, R. "Regulation and Electric Utility Rate Levels." *Land Economics*, Vol. 45, No. 3 (August 1969), pp. 372–376.

19. JORDON, W. A. *Airline Regulation in America: Effects and Imperfections.* Baltimore: Johns Hopkins Press, 1970.

20. ———. "Producer Protection, Prior Market Structure and the Effects of Government Regulation." *Journal of Law and Economics*, Vol. 15, No. 1 (April 1972), pp. 151–176.

21. KITCH, E. W., ISAACSON, M., AND KASPER, D. "The Regulation of Taxicabs in Chicago." *Journal of Law and Economics*, Vol. 14, No. 2 (October 1971), pp. 285–350.

22. KOLKO, G. *Railroads and Regulation, 1877–1916.* Princeton: Princeton Univ. Press, 1965.

23. LEISERSON, A. "Interest Groups in Administration" in F. Morstein Marx, ed., *Elements of Public Administration*, New York: Prentice-Hall, 1946.

24. MACAVOY, P. W. *The Economic Effects of Regulation: The Trunk-Line Railroad Cartels and the Interstate Commerce Commission before 1900.* Cambridge: M.I.T. Press, 1965.

25. ———. "The Regulation-Induced Shortage of Natural Gas." *Journal of Law and Economics*, Vol. 14, No. 1 (April 1971), pp. 167–199.

26. MACPHERSON, C. B. "Tariff Structures and Political Exchange." Unpublished Ph.D. dissertation, University of Chicago, 1972.

27. MOORE, T. G. "The Effectiveness of Regulation of Electric Utility Prices." *Southern Economic Journal*, Vol. 36, No. 4 (April 1970), pp. 365–375.

28. OLSON, M., JR. *The Logic of Collective Action.* Cambridge: Harvard Univ. Press, 1965.

29. PASHIGIAN, B. P. "Public vs. Private Ownership: Consequences and Determinants of Local Transit Systems." Unpublished manuscript, University of Chicago Graduate School of Business, October 1973.

30. PELTZMAN, S. "Entry in Commercial Banking." *Journal of Law and Economics*, Vol. 8, No. 2 (October 1966), pp. 11–50.

31. ———. "An Evaluation of Consumer Protection Legislation: The 1962 Drug Amendments." *Journal of Political Economy*, Vol. 81, No. 5 (September–October 1973), pp. 1049–1091.

32. POSNER, R. A. "The Appropriate Scope of Regulation in the Cable Television Industry." *The Bell Journal of Economics and Management Science*, Vol. 3, No. 1 (Spring 1972), pp. 98–129.

33. ———. "The Behavior of Administrative Agencies." *Journal of Legal Studies*, Vol. 1, No. 2 (June 1972), pp. 305–323.

34. ———. *Economic Analysis of Law.* New York: Little, Brown and Co., 1973.

35. ———. "Natural Monopoly and Its Regulation." *Stanford Law Review*, Vol. 21 (February 1969), pp. 548–643.

36. ———. "Oligopoly and the Antitrust Laws: A Suggested Approach." *Stanford Law Review*, Vol. 21 (June 1969), pp. 1562–1575.

37. ———. "Reflections on Consumerism." *University of Chicago Law School Records*, Vol. 20, No. 3 (Spring 1973), pp. 19–25.

38. ———. *Regulation of Advertising by the FTC.* American Enterprise Institute, November 1973.

39. ———. "A Statistical Study of Antitrust Enforcement." *Journal of Law and Economics*, Vol. 13, No. 2 (October 1970), pp. 365–419.

40. ———. "Taxation by Regulation." *The Bell Journal of Economics and Management Science*, Vol. 2, No. 1 (Spring 1971), pp. 22–50.

41. STIGLER, G. J. "Price and Nonprice Competition" in G. J. Stigler, ed., *Organization of Industry*, Homewood, Ill.: Richard D. Irwin, 1968.

42. ———. "The Theory of Economic Regulation." *The Bell Journal of Economics and Management Science*, Vol. 2, No. 1 (Spring 1971), pp. 3–21.

43. ———— AND FRIEDLAND, C. "What Can Regulators Regulate? The Case of Electricity." *Journal of Law and Economics*, Vol. 5, No. 2 (October 1962), pp. 1–16.

44. TRUMAN, D. B. *The Government Process: Political Interests and Public Opinion.* New York: Knopf, 1951.

45. WILSON, J. *The Politics of Regulation.* Washington, D.C.: The Brookings Institution, forthcoming.

46. ZIEGLER, H. *Interest Groups in American Society.* Englewood Cliffs, N.J.: Prentice-Hall, 1964.

[14]

Taxation by regulation

Richard A. Posner

Professor of Law
The University of Chicago

Students of the regulated industries often assume that regulation is designed either to approximate the results of competition or to protect the regulated firms from competition. But neither view explains adequately a number of important phenomena of regulation and regulated industries. Foremost among them is the prevalence of "internal subsidies," whereby unremunerative services are provided, sometimes indefinitely, out of the profits from other services. To understand this and other phenomena, we must assign another important purpose to regulation: we can call it "taxation by regulation." The purpose of this paper is to explore this dimension of the regulatory process, to demonstrate that it explains some otherwise perplexing features of the process and the industries subject to it, and to compare it with other methods of public finance.

■ Two views of the purpose in fact of public utility and common carrier regulation[1] vie in current scholarly debate. One, the more familiar, holds that regulation is a device for protecting the public against the adverse effects of monopoly[2]; the other holds that regulation is procured by politically effective groups, assumed to be composed of the members of the regulated industry itself, for their own protection.[3] In my opinion neither view, at least as thus far formulated, explains an important phenomenon of regulated industries: the deliberate and continued provision of many services at lower rates and in larger quantities than would be offered in an unregulated competitive market or, *a fortiori*, an unregulated monopolistic one.

Richard A. Posner, who received the A.B. degree from Yale University and the LL.B. from Harvard, is Professor of Law at the University of Chicago Law School. Among his major interests is the application of economic theory to law, and he also is the editor of a new journal to be published under the auspices of the University of Chicago. It is entitled *The Journal of Legal Studies*, and its first appearance will be in January 1972. The author would like to thank Edmund W. Kitch and George J. Stigler for their helpful comments on an earlier draft.

[1] By the awkward term "purpose in fact" I mean to distinguish sharply between the reasons ascribed to regulatory laws and decisions by the legislators and regulators themselves and the reasons, whether or not anywhere avowed, that provide a consistent explanation of the actual course and consequences of regulation. It is with the latter that I am concerned here.

Although the emphasis throughout this paper is on the full panoply of rate and entry controls characteristic of public utility and common carrier statutes, where the analysis can be extended to markets having somewhat different regulatory arrangements I have not hesitated to do so.

[2] For example, see Bonbright [3], p. 23.

[3] A rigorous statement of this theory appears in the article by G. J. Stigler in this issue of *The Bell Journal* [59]. The "capture" of regulation by the regulatees is, of course, an old theme in the literature of regulation. Professor Stigler's theory allows for capture by effective political groups other than the regulated firms themselves, and there is accordingly no necessary inconsistency between it and the analysis in this paper.

22 / RICHARD A. POSNER

This phenomenon can be explained, I believe, only if we modify existing views by admitting that one of the functions of regulation is to perform distributive and allocative chores usually associated with the taxing or financial branch of government. And we shall see that an analysis of taxation by regulation explains other perplexing phenomena. But it would be error to think that the analysis compels rejection, as distinct from modification, of the existing views of regulation. I hope to show that any theory that conceives the function of regulation to be to approximate the results of competition, or to enrich the regulated firms, or to do sometimes the one and sometimes the other, is incomplete. But it does not follow that a broadened public-interest approach (one that accommodated certain subsidy elements) or a broadened effective-political-group approach (one that viewed certain customer classes as effective political groups) might not be tenable.

■ The best known example of a regulated service that an unregulated competitive market would not provide on the same scale is railroad passenger service,[4] but it is far from being an isolated example.[5] Like railroad passenger service, domestic telegraph service would be declining even more rapidly than it is, were it not for the Federal Communications Commission's stubborn rearguard action against further rate increases and service degradation by Western Union.[6] Local airline service provides another example,[7] complicated though by the presence of direct as well as internal subsidies.

The phenomenon is by no means limited to declining industries. The American Telephone and Telegraph Company may soon be required to provide electronic interconnection free of charge (or nearly so) to the National Educational Television network.[8] Broadcasters are required to provide at least some nonremunerative news and public-affairs programming.[9] Liability insurance for high-risk automobile drivers in many states is written at a loss.[10] Producers of natural gas are constrained to sell at a price that does not include scarcity rents, thereby benefiting present consumers of natural gas at the expense of future consumers, who may encounter shortages.[11] Uniform rates, based on averaging together the costs of services whose cost characteristics are in fact very different, are a conspicuous feature of regulated rate structures. Examples are statewide telephone rates, the uniform long-distance rate for telephone calls of the same distance and duration regardless of route, the pegging of airline and rail passenger rates to distance with little or no consideration for cost differences over different routes, and the flat rates characteristic of

1. Internal subsidies

---

[4] See Conant [10], p. 132, Hilton [23], p. 136, and Nelson [40], pp. 286–301.

[5] In at least one respect, we shall see, it is atypical of the general class. See p. 43 and fn 69 *infra*.

[6] See President's Task Force on Communications Policy [50], and U. S. Federal Communications Commission [75].

[7] See Eads [14], pp. 1, 13–14.

[8] See The Communications Act of 1934 [78], sec. 396(h), Interconnection Service [73].

[9] See Public Service Responsibility of Broadcast Licensees [74].

[10] See Keeton and O'Connell [30], pp. 93–94; cf [67], Price Variability in the Automobile Insurance Market.

[11] See MacAvoy [35], p. 271.

urban transit systems.[12] Electrical companies grant discounts, unrelated to any cost savings, to hospitals and other worthy groups,[13]
while water companies are often required to furnish water for household use at rates below marginal cost—and to fire departments and
schools for nothing.[14]

These practices are very old. In 1827, the State of Illinois required
by statute that every keeper of a ferry, toll bridge, or turnpike road
"give passage to all public messengers and expresses; to all grand
and petit jurors, when going to and returning from court, without
any fee or reward whatever" [26].

In all of these examples, as in many others one could cite (including some to be discussed later), a service is provided that does not
pay its way in the market. Someone must pay its way, however.
Normally it is other customers of the firm rendering the service, who
pay a price higher than the cost of serving them. Sometimes it is
future generations of consumers (as in the gas example) or the stockholders or creditors of the firm (as, perhaps, in the railroad and telegraph examples). Examples of internal or cross-subsidization, as we
may call the practice, lie everywhere at hand in the regulated industries.[15] They are also commonly found among public enterprises here
and abroad,[16] the structure of postal rates providing a conspicuous
example.[17] They seem much less common in unregulated private
markets. The contrast is instructive: it suggests that the provision of
internal subsidies is associated with distinctively governmental purposes and functions. We shall return to this point.

Before proceeding, I should caution the reader that identification
of our phenomenon—internal subsidization—is often difficult.[18] In
practice an internal subsidy is not always easy to distinguish from
certain familiar profit-maximizing practices. A monopolist may be
able to maximize profit by setting different markups on different
sales, depending on the elasticities of demand of particular customers
or groups of customers. Like the internal subsidy, this practice involves a departure from cost-based pricing. But it does not involve
any unremunerative services. Were the lower-priced services unprofitable, the monopolist could increase his profits still further by
terminating them. To take another example, a firm that has a
monopoly in some markets can, under certain restricted conditions,
increase its profits by selling below cost in other markets where it
still faces competition. Unlike internal subsidization, however, such
"predatory price discrimination" is strictly a temporary tactic to

---

[12] See Caves [5], p. 369; Davidson [12], p. 217; Johnson [27]; Garfield and
Lovejoy [18], pp. 200–203, 243; Meyer, Kain and Wohl [37], pp. 354, 357; Meyer
Peck, Stenason and Zwick [38], pp. 166–67; Watkins [82], p. 623.

[13] See Bonbright [3] p. 111.

[14] Hirshleifer, DeHaven & Milliman [24], pp. 109–11; Garfield and Lovejoy
[18], p. 225; cf. Keig, Fristoe and Goddard [31].

[15] For additional examples see Bonbright [3], pp. 111–12; Friedlaender [15],
pp. 66–68; Meyer, Peck, Stenason and Zwick [38], pp. 194–95; Nelson [40], p.
331; Hearings on Transportation Acts Amendments [66].

[16] See, for example, Coase [8], pp. 1, 13–14; Crew [11], p. 258; Peltzman [44];
Sargent [51], p. 248; Sharp [52], p. 53; Shepherd [53], p. 132. Sargent and Shepherd
analyze internal subsidization in the context of public enterprises in terms somewhat parallel to mine in this paper.

[17] See Baratz [2], p. 305; Coase [9], p. 25; Kennedy [29], pp. 93–94.

[18] As emphasized by Nove [42], p. 847.

drive out competitors; prolonging it indefinitely would make no business sense.

Peak-load pricing also involves different prices for the same service, and is also different. One observes resort hotels charging, for identical accommodations, higher prices in peak seasons than in off-seasons. But the reason for the off-season discount is that it attracts customers who would otherwise not buy the service. So long as the price they pay covers the marginal or additional cost of serving them, the discount is profitable. It is therefore not a case of internal subsidization as I use the term.

Temporary below-cost selling might of course stem from errors of various kinds. And even persistent departures from a proper matching of price and cost could reflect simply the difficulty and expense of determining which costs were incurred in making which sales; some averaging of costs over different services is certainly explicable on this ground. Other cases of apparent below-cost selling evaporate on examination. Professor Bonbright gives as an instance of internal subsidization (he calls it "social principles of rate making," but it is the same concept) the granting of special rail fares to clergymen[19]; but one suspects that such a discount is simply a public-relations gesture. In view of the low income of clergymen, which may make their demand for some services relatively elastic, the discount might even be an example of price discrimination.

Finally, some services may appear unremunerative only because an inappropriate conception of cost is employed. As the resort example shows, a price below average cost, but equal to or above marginal cost, may still be remunerative. On the other hand, a price above even long-term marginal cost may be unremunerative.

The last point requires some explanation. In the case of an industry in which average cost decreases with output, a firm that charged a uniform price equal to its marginal cost would not recover its total costs. It could recover them by setting a uniform price equal to average cost. This would force customers willing to pay a price equal to or slightly above marginal cost but not the higher price equal to average cost to turn to more costly substitutes. Neither result is optimal, and the proper solution to the dilemma is a matter of fair debate. One attractive possibility is to charge a price equal to marginal cost for marginal purchases and a sufficiently higher price for inframarginal purchases to cover total costs without losing those sales. Although the proper design of the rate structure is not easy, this approach seems preferable to either the uniform marginal-cost price, which necessitates a government subsidy to make up the deficit in covering total costs, or the uniform average-cost price, which excludes the marginal sale.[20]

It is implicit in this solution, however, that some customers may end up paying a higher price than under average-cost pricing. A simple arithmetical example will illustrate. Suppose the fixed costs of providing a service are $1000 and marginal cost is $1, and suppose further that when price is made equal to average cost 500 units are demanded and supplied at a price of $3 per unit. Therefore, Buyer

---

[19] See Bonbright [3], p. 61.
[20] See Coase [7]; Henderson [22], p. 223; Hirshleifer, DeHaven and Milliman [24], pp. 91–92.

X, who purchases 20 units, pays a total price of $60. Now suppose the industry adopts a two-part pricing system (one version of the preferred solution to the dilemma of proper pricing under conditions of decreasing average cost) under which anyone wishing to purchase service must pay (a) a share of the fixed costs (ideally, the shares should vary inversely with the elasticity of the buyers' demands) plus (b) the marginal cost of each unit he buys. And suppose that X's share of the fixed costs is set at $100. He must now pay $120 for the same 20 units.

To the extent that regulatory agencies are unwilling to visit such consequences upon particular customers of the firms they regulate, output is not carried to the efficient point. The subsidy is indirect but inescapable: the additional price that the rejected marginal customers must pay for substitute products is a cost imposed on them in order to enable inframarginal customers to buy at a cheaper price than if an efficient pricing system were employed. Profit-maximizing price discrimination would also result in the inframarginal customer paying a higher price. The pricing actually employed in decreasing-cost industries appears often to be neither efficient nor profitable.

"Value-of-service" pricing in the railroad industry provides good examples of this point. Before the development of truck transportation, the practice of proportioning rail rates to the price of the commodity transported may have been a roughly adequate method of concentrating the fixed costs of railroad service on those customers whose demands for rail transportation were least elastic. But once there was a good substitute service, the method ceased to have a rational basis, at least under the usual views of regulation, since the price of the commodity shipped bears no necessary relation to the adequacy of trucking as a substitute for transportation by rail. Wristwatches are more expensive per unit of weight than grain, but it does not follow that the demand of the wristwatch shipper for rail service is less elastic; it is probably more elastic, because trucking is a more feasible alternative for the shipper of wristwatches than for the shipper of grain.

Value-of-service pricing may have persisted because it is a convenient method of subsidizing some shippers regardless of the elasticity of demands for rail transportation. The favorable rates at which agricultural commodities continue to be transported seem a case in point.[21] Considering the broad range of subsidies that farmers have managed to obtain for themselves, it is perhaps not surprising that they have obtained internal subsidies as well. And they are not the only group, or railroading the only industry, where we find value-of-service pricing used as a method of internal subsidization.[22] Notice that keeping rates low to customers so favored is not only inefficient but can destroy a decreasing-cost industry.[23] These consequences only underscore the limitations of existing theories of regulation.

A final problem of characterization, one that also arises from the phenomenon of decreasing average costs in some regulated industries, requires brief mention. A pricing system for a decreasing-cost in-

---

[21] See Friedlaender [15], pp. 18–20; The Hoch-Smith Resolution [80], p. 801; cf Meyer, Peck, Stenason and Zwick [38] pp. 175, 187–88.

[22] See, for example, Johnson [27], pp. 42, 67; Wilson [83], p. 337.

[23] Stigler [60], pp. 213–14.

dustry, to be efficient, must satisfy three criteria: (1) it must enable the total costs of the enterprise to be recovered; (2) it must be so designed that no customer willing to pay at least the marginal cost of serving him is turned away; (3) there should be no sales below marginal cost. Now there are many different formulae for allocating overhead costs consistently with these criteria and the choice of one inescapably affects the distribution of wealth as between various customers. For example, suppose the fixed costs of an enterprise are $100; there are 10 customers who can be made to contribute to those costs; and each of them would pay $20 rather than do without service. The regulatory agency can insist on a pricing scheme under which each pays $10, or on one under which some pay $20 and some less (perhaps zero). Whichever choice is made makes some customers worse off and some better off than they would be under an alternative arrangement.

Because this type of "subsidization" does not involve the maintenance of any uneconomic service, and thereby avoids most of the problems with which this paper is concerned, I exclude it (perhaps arbitrarily) from the category of internal subsidies. That regulation unavoidably involves issues of wealth distribution as between customer classes does, however, emphasize the relevance of notions of taxation and public finance to the theory of public regulation—but on this, more shortly.

■ The existence of the internal subsidy is an embarrassment to proponents of the first view of regulation (at least as usually formulated) mentioned at the beginning of this paper—the view that regulation is imposed in order to bring about results approximating those of competition. As we have seen, the internal subsidy brings about results unthinkable in a competitive market, which is perhaps why a distinguished proponent of the first view, Professor Bonbright, who believes that "public utility services are designed to be sold at cost, or at cost plus a fair profit"[24], considers the internal subsidy aberrational.[25]

Nor is it explicable if regulation is conceived purely as a service demanded by and supplied to the regulated firms themselves, although here the demonstration is more complicated. While an unregulated firm, whether monopolist or competitive, would not profit from engaging in internal subsidization, regulation alters normal business incentives. Under certain conditions, a regulated firm can increase its profits by expanding the size of its plant even if some of the output of the enlarged plant must be sold at a loss.[26] In addition, a regulated firm might provide some unremunerative services as an unintended byproduct of a policy of deliberately not keeping detailed cost information. The purpose of such a policy would be to prevent the regulatory agency, which is normally dependent on the regulated firm for information about the firm and its markets, from acquiring sufficiently detailed knowledge of the firm's operations to enable more stringent regulation. Such a strategy is less risky than it may seem. A regulated monopolist can get by with less information about

2. Internal subsidization and the received views of regulation

---

[24] See Bonbright [3], p. 23.
[25] *Id.*, Ch. 8.
[26] Averch and Johnson [1], p. 1052.

the costs of particular sales than a nonregulated firm. It may be able to earn the overall profit permitted by the agency, even though many of its sales are unprofitable, by charging supracompetitive prices in markets where its monopoly is secure.

Furthermore, a firm that engages in internal subsidization can argue forcefully to the regulatory agency that the agency should not permit, or at least should strictly limit, the entry of competitors into those markets where the firm makes large profits, because those profits—which new entrants would erode—are necessary in order to cover the losses in the subsidized markets. Finally, regulated monopolists may believe that differential rates, even where cost justified, strike the public as discriminatory and may in consequence invite sterner regulation of the firm's profits.

These considerations do not explain, however, those instances, such as railroad passenger service and natural gas production, where the regulated industry does not appear to be benefiting, directly or indirectly, from internal subsidization. Nor do they explain very convincingly why the practice is ever instituted in the first place. If regulated firms dominate an agency, as the view under examination posits, they can use their position to increase profits directly by getting the agency to fix a high permitted level of profits and forbid the entry of new competitors. A program of internal subsidies seems a needlessly roundabout method for achieving these ends, and also a costly one: it entails smaller profits for the regulated firms since, as mentioned earlier, a profit-maximizing firm is always better off terminating a losing service. If firms do not yet dominate a regulatory agency but seek to do so, a program of internal subsidies is not likely to help them to reach their goal. A regulatory agency that is not a creature of the firms being regulated will not permit plant used for rendering unremunerative services to be figured in the rate base. It will not reason from the fact that the regulated firms are losing money in some markets to the conclusion that it should forbid the entry of new firms into others; rather, it will invite the firms to terminate the losing services. It will insist that the regulated firm adopt accounting procedures that reveal the true costs of serving various classes of customers. These regulatory checks may be far from entirely effective in practice, but it does seem unlikely that, if regulatory agencies had no independent reasons for encouraging internal subsidization, regulated firms could nonetheless engage in the practice on the scale they do.

In sum, existing views of regulation do not explain well the important phenomenon of internal subsidization. A new approach is needed and, in the next part, proposed.

3. Internal subsidization as a branch of public finance

■ Regulation and public finance are ordinarily considered unrelated activities. Occasionally the language of one laps over to the other, and we speak of a monopolist "taxing" his customers, redistributing wealth from them to him, by charging a price above cost. The internal subsidy, it seems to me, is an aspect of public finance in what is at once a more exact and a more natural sense. Taxation in common parlance refers to the use of the powers of the state to extract money from its subjects in order (1) to defray the cost of services that the politically dominant elements of the state wish to provide and that the market would not provide in the desired quantity and at the desired price, or (2) to transfer money from one group to another, or (3), often, to do both. By this test regulation is in part a system of taxation or public finance. The basic mechanism is the internal subsidy. A firm provides a service below its real cost, and the deficit is made up by (usually) other customers of the firm who pay higher prices than they would otherwise. Were it not for the power of the state, acting through the regulatory agency, to control entry, the system would not be viable. A firm would not institute a losing service. If by mistake it did, it would terminate the service rather than subsidize the losses from profits in other markets. If foolishly persisted, firms not burdened with the costs of losing services would enter the high-profit markets and their competition would drive down the price; deprived of the necessary supernormal profits, the firm would finally be compelled to terminate the unprofitable service.

Internal subsidization may thus be viewed as an exertion of state power whose purpose, like that of other taxes, is to compel members of the public to support a service that the market would provide at a reduced level, or not at all. It is in fact a form of excise tax, with the burden falling on purchasers of certain goods or services, and the proceeds earmarked for specific uses. As a form of excise tax, it invites comparison with other methods and objects of taxation.

■ It may be helpful at this point to illustrate the thesis that regulation is a method of public taxation and expenditure by some cases. I confine myself to two: the wall of protection thrown up around the international telegraph carriers by the Federal Communications Commission, and the methods of regulation used in the cable television industry. These case histories are no more than suggestive, but I believe a broader study of regulated markets would confirm the picture they present.

□ **International telegraph service.** Since this is one of the less well known regulated industries, it may be well to begin with some background.[27] U. S. companies providing international telegraph service (which includes telegrams, teletype, and transmission of computer data) are regulated by the FCC and known as "record carriers," because they transmit communications in the form of a written or otherwise stored record, as distinct from voice-only telephone transmission. There are three principal record carriers: ITT World Com, RCA Global Communications, and Western Union International. Until the 1950's they owned and operated submarine telegraph cables and high-frequency radio transmitting and receiving equipment. AT&T owned high-frequency radio equipment too, with which it supplied overseas telephone service (underwater cables lacked sufficient capacity for such service). AT&T did not offer record services. It seems to have been understood that the FCC would not permit the telephone company to enter the record market in competition with the record carriers.

A technological revolution in the provision of international telecommunication service occurred in the 1950's with the perfection of

4. Two case studies

---

[27] A more detailed description of the industry is given by the President's Task Force on Communications Policy in [49] and [50].

the voice-grade submarine cable, developed and installed by AT&T. These cables had sufficient capacity not only to enable telephone communication but also to permit the derivation of telegraph circuits at much lower cost than was possible to the record carriers using their existing, and now largely obsolete, equipment. Overseas telephone calls were cheaper and of much better quality than before, and since a telephone call is a substitute for a telegram or other record service, the new development placed a good deal of pressure on the record carriers. In addition, AT&T began to offer a new service, called "AVD" (alternative voice-data), under which the customer leased a circuit in the AT&T cable which he could use for voice or record service or both. Leased lines represented the most lucrative portion of the record carriers' services, and AT&T's new offering posed a serious threat to those carriers' continued profitability and even to their survival.[28]

They complained to the FCC. The Commission forbade AT&T to offer further AVD service (although AT&T was permitted to continue serving a few markets where the service had already been instituted) and granted the record carriers rights of co-ownership in AT&T's cable.[29]

The record carriers thus weathered this storm, but another was brewing. In 1962 the Communications Satellite Corporation was created to exploit the newly developed communications satellite. The enabling legislation[30] was ambiguous as to whether Comsat was free to deal directly with communications customers in addition to leasing circuits to the record carriers and AT&T. The issue came to a head when Comsat and the Department of Defense negotiated for the lease of thirty circuits in Comsat's Pacific satellite to the Department directly. Comsat offered a rate that was 32-to-40 percent of the rates offered by the record carriers.[31] The disparity was puzzling, since on leased circuits the record carriers do little more than arrange for obtaining a circuit either in one of AT&T's submarine cables, or, in the present case, in one of Comsat's satellites. After the record carriers agreed on a general rate reduction, although not to the level offered by Comsat, the Commission held that as a matter of policy (not law) it would forbid Comsat to deal directly with the communications user.[32]

Bare as this summary is, it indicates the salient fact of regulation in the international communications industry: the insulation of the record carriers from direct competition. AT&T could have competed directly with the record carriers before the invention of the modern submarine cable and especially afterward, as could Comsat, but the regulatory agency prevented such competition. The received views of regulation do not explain well this persistent, indeed dogged, policy of regulatory protection.

If regulation is imposed in order to prevent monopolistic distortions, one must find reasonable grounds for thinking that the entry of AT&T or Comsat into the record business would have reduced

---

[28] See FCC proceedings re the American Telephone and Telegraph Company [68], p. 1159 and [70], p. 433, n 9.

[29] Re The American Telephone & Telegraph Co. [68].

[30] Communications Satellite Act of 1962 [79].

[31] President's Task Force on Communications Policy [49], p. 19.

[32] *Authorized Entities and Authorized Users* [72].

rather than increased competition in that industry. Only if one attributes simplistic, although admittedly common, notions of competition to the FCC is it possible to construct a competitively based rationale for the denial of entry. The argument would be that AT&T controls the domestic leg of most international record traffic, and if permitted to offer international service as well would use its domestic position to monopolize the international service by routing all traffic to itself.

The fallacy in this reasoning lies in the assumption that a monopolist of one stage in the distribution of a good can increase his monopoly return by annexing successive stages as well. The assumption is in general false.[33] The successive stages of distribution are exactly analogous to the sale of complementary products, for example the head and shaft of a hammer. A monopolist of hammer heads could not increase his profits by getting control of the production and sale of the shafts as well. Any monopoly profits to be earned from controlling the manufacture of hammers could be captured by control of one essential component of hammers such as the heads. A monopolist's interests are ordinarily best served by minimizing the cost of complementary products, which will usually require the encouragement of competition in their provision. Thus, if AT&T indeed enjoys an effective monopoly of the domestic leg of international telegraph service, it should be able to extract all possible monopoly profits by means of appropriate charges for that leg. It would have an incentive to enter the international end of the business only if its costs in providing that service would be less than the rates charged by the existing carriers, in which event permitting it to enter would further the ends of competition.

Even if fear of AT&T's monopolizing the international business were plausible, it would not explain why the Commission also forbade Comsat to enter, or why the record carriers' rates at the time of Comsat's attempted entry were more than twice their costs.

The interest of the record carriers in repelling new entry is of course evident, but it seems unlikely that the protective measures taken by the Commission were merely in response to their demand. Although the determinants of political power are unfortunately not clearly understood, one is skeptical that the record carriers by themselves could have induced the Commission to subordinate to their protection the interests of AT&T and the Department of Defense, two of the nation's largest institutions, and of Comsat. The record carriers appear to lack the most important constituents of political influence. Their total revenues in 1968 were $173 million, in contrast to the Bell System's total earnings of $2.4 billion.[34] The record carriers have few employees[35] to go to bat on their behalf,

---

[33] See Bowman [4], p. 19. This statement and the analysis that follows in the text do not hold in a few special cases. Forward integration might facilitate price discrimination, enable the transfer of profits to an unregulated affiliate, forestall new entry, or simply complicate regulation of the primary market. None of these seem likely factors in the case under discussion.

[34] See Federal Communications Commission Annual Report [71].

[35] I am informed by the FCC that as of October 31, 1969, the international record carrier industry (the three major record carriers plus four smaller ones) had a total of 5623 employees in the United States and another 2432 abroad, of whom an undisclosed number are foreigners.

and the carriers' operations are confined to a handful of major cities—principally New York, San Francisco, and Washington[36]—in whose economies they play an insignificant role. One can challenge the comparison with Bell. Since two of the record carriers are parts of very large firms,[37] perhaps the proper comparison is between the parents' revenues (employees, etc.) and Bell's, or between the record carriers' revenues and those revenues of the Bell System that are earned in the international market alone. What this point ignores, however, is that virtually all of the Bell System's operations (even those regulated by state agencies) are directly or indirectly subject to control or influence by the FCC. The entire system, therefore, has a stake in decisions affecting a part. A decision limiting competition by AT&T in the international market could have precedential force in cases involving its right to compete in other markets. The common carrier interests of RCA and ITT, in contrast, are limited to the international telegraph industry.[38] The impact of regulatory decisions in that industry on the parent companies of the record carriers is consequently much smaller than the impact on the Bell System, so one would not expect them to devote comparable efforts to prevailing before the Commission.

A public finance view of regulation provides a clue to the curious success of the international telegraph industry in insulating itself from competition. The record carriers have long provided telegram service at a loss which they recoup by charging supracompetitive prices for other services, principally leased lines, where their costs, as mentioned, are small.[39] As a result, there is a class of customers who receive a service for which they would have to pay much higher prices were it provided in a free market; possibly the service would not be offered at all. These customers would be injured by any policies, such as free entry, which jeopardized the continued provision of international telegram service at the present attractive rates. They constitute allies of the record carriers in seeking the protection of the Commission against new entry and help to explain why such protection has been obtained in the face of strong opposition.

One would like to have a clearer idea of who the class of benefited customers is and how important cheap international telegraph service is to them. We can speculate that they are mostly small firms and individuals—travel agents, some importers, many tourists and their families—rather than large firms: a large user of international telecommunications service would lease circuits or at least subscribe to teletype service. But we know from other industries, notably the retail-drug industry, that small firms (when many in number) are frequently an effective political group in obtaining protective legislation for themselves. And even if the favored telegraph customers do not constitute an effective political group, perhaps they are viewed for one reason or another as particularly deserving, and on that ground favored. A careful empirical study might refute the suggestion that the interests of this customer class are a significant factor in the

---

[36] In re American Telephone & Telegraph Company [68], p. 1158.

[37] Western Union International is not affiliated with the domestic Western Union Company.

[38] ITT owns some South American telephone companies, but they are, of course, not regulated by the FCC.

[39] See *Authorized Entities and Authorized Users* [72], pp. 432–35.

actions of the Commission, but the important point is that such a study seems clearly indicated.

☐ **Cable television.** The cable television industry,[40] in both its economic and its regulatory characteristics, resembles the public utility industries of the late nineteenth century. The industry is in its promotional phase. The systems already installed may be only a small fraction of what we can expect when it is mature. As with the earlier public utility industries, it appears that the returns to scale are large, and it may be inefficient for more than one cable television system to serve any given local area. There is a growing momentum of regulation. All municipalities now require providers of cable television service to obtain a municipal franchise; the franchises are becoming more elaborate; and some states are beginning to regulate the rates charged by cable firms.

On the basis of the received views of regulation, one might hypothesize that regulation had been imposed because the service was thought to be a natural monopoly, or had been demanded by the cable companies themselves in order to create or entrench a monopoly position. But neither hypothesis, separately or in combination, explains the specific types of regulation that have been imposed. On the one hand, the rates charged by the cable companies to their subscribers are rarely regulated (although, as mentioned, there is some movement in that direction); the thrust of regulation thus far has not been to eliminate monopoly pricing. On the other hand, municipal authorities have required cable franchisees to pay substantial fees, in money and kind, to the municipal government. These commonly take the form of the franchisee's agreeing to pay a percentage, sometimes as high as six percent, of gross revenues, coupled with his assuming an obligation to provide several channels in the cable system, without charge, to various municipal bodies such as the schools and the fire department. These exactions both reduce the value of the franchise to the cable firm and raise the price to the subscriber above what it would be if the service were an unregulated monopoly.[41]

Thus neither the subscribers nor the cable companies are clear gainers from the current regulatory policies. But they do generate municipal revenues. A tax is imposed on cable subscribers for the benefit of whoever watches the dedicated channels or partakes (either in reduced other taxes or greater municipal services) of the revenues generated by the franchise. In the latter case, indeed, internal subsidization has become conventional taxation in all but name.[42]

Possibly these burdens have been placed on the cable television industry at the behest of competitors, such as theater owners or local television stations (a hypothesis more plausible in the case of the percentage-of-receipts fee than in the case of the dedicated

---

[40] The discussion that follows draws heavily on Posner [45].

[41] See *id.* at pp. 16–19.

[42] Another interesting example of the interplay of explicit taxation and internal subsidies is found in *Student Educational Group Fares* [62], a decision of the Civil Aeronautics Board dealing with a recent Hawaiian statute that granted a tax rebate to airlines establishing a special group rate for students.

channels). In that event, the analogy would be to a tariff—another exercise of the public finance power.

5. Some general characteristics of regulation and the regulated industries that a public finance approach illuminates

■ We have seen that viewing regulation as a method of taxation or public finance appears to account, better than alternative views, for a major phenomenon found in regulated industries—internal subsidization. But beyond that, the view provides a consistent explanation of many other features of regulation and regulated industries, some of which fit poorly the received views.

☐ **Regulatory control over entry.** Control of entry is an essential feature of regulation under the view advanced here because the adoption of a system of internal subsidies creates false pricing signals. Prices in certain markets must exceed costs if the losses sustained in providing the subsidized services are to be recouped. The price-cost spread in the subsidizing markets will naturally attract new entrants. But their costs may actually be higher than those of the existing firms, in which event their entry would produce a misallocation of resources. Entry would also impair or destroy the system of internal subsidies. With free entry, then, both efficiency and the subsidy scheme would be gravely endangered, so the regulatory agency must control entry.

To be sure, were regulation imposed for the sole benefit of the firms regulated, control over entry would also be necessary to prevent the dissipation through competition of the advantages secured to the incumbent firms by regulation. But not all important instances of entry control can be explained on this ground. The Post Office is not a profit-maximizing enterprise—it is in fact run at a deficit—but new entry into postal service is, and must be, barred, in order to preserve the uniform-rate structure and interclass subsidies that are a prominent feature of the Post Office's operation. Given the financial position of the railroads, it is doubtful that the control of entry in that industry is to be explained in terms of the interests of the regulated firms either.

The theory that regulation seeks to approximate the results of competition cannot explain the control of entry at all. If the regulated firm is constrained to sell at a price approximating cost, there will be no incentive for an inefficient firm to enter. If, despite regulation, the firm is charging a higher price, the matter is more complex. In general, however, assuming that differential pricing is feasible, as seems generally the case in decreasing-cost industries, a new entrant will not be attracted into such an industry by monopoly profits unless it is more efficient than the existing seller. The latter can repel entry by fixing a price near marginal cost to any customer solicited by the new entrant and will, because such a policy will not reduce his profits on any other sales (we have assumed he can maintain different prices) and the alternative is to lose a customer whom it is still profitable to serve even at the reduced price. Unless it is a more efficient firm, the new entrant will have higher costs and will not be able to meet the low price. Thus, in the case where public utility regulation is most plausibly explained in terms of an efficiency rationale—where the industry regulated is a decreasing-cost industry—the rationale still will not explain an important feature of that regulation, the control of entry, because there is no reason to anticipate inefficient or excessive entry in the absence of public control.

□ **Regulatory review of new construction.** Firms subject to public utility or common carrier regulation are commonly required to obtain the permission of the regulatory agency for any major new construction.[43] This control is to be distinguished from control over entry: it applies whether the purpose of the construction is to enable the firm to enter a new market or to serve an existing market. In arguing that regulation is for the exclusive benefit of the regulated firms, one could point out that such control enables an agency to prevent the firms from expanding production in a way that might undermine cartel pricing. Although the provisions of regulatory statutes giving the agencies authority to fix prices and levels of service, requiring the regulated firms to embody all offerings in published tariffs, and forbidding under severe penalty any deviation from the tariff filings, already give an agency broad authority to enforce cartel pricing,[44] control of new construction makes the agency an even more effective enforcer of the cartel.

A consumer-interest view of regulation also provides an explanation, although not a very satisfactory one, of the control of new construction. While there is little solid basis for fear that an unregulated firm, even if a monopolist, would adopt an extravagant construction program,[45] there are, as noted earlier, some reasons for concern that regulated firms would not minimize costs. But it is unlikely that recognition of the side effects of regulation provides a general explanation of the power over new construction. Many regulated firms subject to the power are not monopolists, and the earlier analysis would not apply. If simply a fear of poor management was in the minds of those who framed the various public utility and common carrier statutes, one wonders why such statutes do not give the regulators more direct authority over management.

I suspect that the framers may have been motivated by a somewhat different concern from those previously mentioned—one that arises from the public finance function of regulation. An illustration, again drawn from the international communications industry, will help explain. In 1967, AT&T, acting this time in concert with the record carriers (and several foreign carriers), applied to the FCC for permission to build a fifth voice-grade cable across the Atlantic Ocean ("TAT 5").[46] The cost of constructing the facility was estimated to be $70 million and the planned capacity was 720 voice circuits. Comsat opposed the application. It pointed out that by the time TAT 5 was installed, very large satellites (5000 circuits each) would be in service above the Atlantic and these satellites would provide sufficient capacity to meet all reasonably foreseeable increments of demand for transatlantic telecommunications service at

---

[43] See, for example, the Communications Act of 1934 [78], sec. 214(a); the Natural Gas Act [81]; and the Transportation Act of 1920 [65].

[44] MacAvoy [36] is a case study of the role of regulatory controls in effectuating cartel pricing.

[45] See Posner [47], pp. 573–77.

[46] The incident is discussed by the staff of the President's Task Force on Communications Policy in [49], pp. 35–49.

a cost per circuit that would be only a small fraction of TAT 5's. AT&T, in reply, noted that the satellites in question might not be in service in time to avoid a shortage. But in that event, judging from subsequent filings and analysis in the proceeding, the economical solution would be to permit queuing, or use peak-load pricing, or launch an additional satellite of an older model. The staff of President Johnson's Task Force on Communications Policy, which analyzed AT&T's application in some depth, concluded that TAT 5 was the least economical alternative.[47]

The cost questions were in fact quite complex and the correctness of the staff's analysis perhaps debatable. The opinions in the case suggest, however, that the FCC itself doubted whether TAT 5 was cost justified. The Commission expressly refused to compare the costs of the cable with those of alternative satellite facilities,[48] adhering to this position in the face of a strong dissenting opinion in which it was urged that the cable was indeed more costly.[49] The majority cannot have been optimistic as to what an analysis of costs would have shown.

In approving the application, the Commission appears to have been strongly influenced by considerations that cannot be understood save in terms of a public finance approach to regulation, such as AT&T's representation that if TAT 5 were approved, it would be able to reduce its transatlantic telephone rates by 27 percent. It is at first glance surprising that the FCC should have been impressed by this offer. If satellites were a cheaper means of meeting demand than the cable, then rates could be reduced by even more than 27 percent if AT&T, rather than building a new cable, leased circuits from Comsat: so why did the Commission refuse to compare cable and alternative satellite costs? The probable explanation lies in Comsat's rate structure. Comsat is wedded, largely it appears for reasons of foreign relations, to a system of uniform global pricing under which the price of a circuit in a Comsat Pacific satellite is roughly the same as the price of a circuit in one of its Atlantic satellites. Because the Atlantic routes are busier, the Atlantic satellites are more fully utilized and the cost per circuit accordingly lower than in the Pacific. But this cost difference is not reflected in the rates, which, as noted, are roughly the same in both markets. Consequently, when AT&T leases circuits from Comsat for transatlantic service, it is forced to pay a considerable premium above the actual cost of the circuits to Comsat, so much so that the price to AT&T (after correcting for certain quality differences) is not clearly lower than the cost to it of circuits in a new cable. It is thus understandable why AT&T should have pushed for approval of TAT 5. But while from its standpoint cable costs may not have been higher than satellite costs, from the broader social standpoint they were (assuming that the staff analysis referred to earlier was correct). It is to prevent unwarranted

---

[47] See *id.*, pp. 36–41a.

[48] Re American Telephone & Telegraph Company [70], pp. 242–43 and n. 4.

[49] Re American Telephone & Telegraph Company [69], pp. 962–63 and [70], pp. 261–62.

[50] The staff of the President's Task Force on Communications Policy estimated that if the price per circuit in an Atlantic satellite had been determined on the basis of the costs of that satellite (and its associated ground facilities), it would have been $22,400 per half circuit per year in 1970, rather than the actual price of $31,300 set by Comsat.

investments based on divergences between private and social cost calculations caused by internal subsidization that regulatory agencies must have authority over the construction programs of regulated firms even when entry into a new market is not contemplated.

In this case, to be sure, the agency's exercise of its duty was per-functory at best. Given the circumstances, however, that is not sur-prising. First of all, the program of internal subsidies that was jeopardized by the grant of the application—Comsat's policy of uniform global pricing of satellite circuits—is not one that the Com-mission has particularly encouraged. The motives behind it are rooted, as mentioned, in foreign-policy considerations that are the responsibility of other agencies. By granting the application the Commission was able to obtain immediate rate reductions for one of its constituencies, users of transatlantic telecommunications service, and the costs to the Commission cannot have seemed large.

Secondly, the Department of Defense made strong representa-tions to the Commission[61] that the construction of TAT 5 would promote national security—another example of internal subsidiza-tion at work. The Department could have requested an appropria-tion from Congress to contribute to the cost of building a cable not justified by purely civilian demands; prevailing upon the FCC to authorize such a facility was an alternative mode of financing this defense project. The method of obtaining the "appropriation" and the class of "taxpayers" were different, but the object was the same. The subsidization of defense needs appears to be a rather general feature of regulation.[62]

□ **The duty of the regulated firm to serve and regulatory power over the abandonment of service.** Two long-established and complementary features of the regulatory process are the duty of regulated firms to serve all who demand service and the prohibition against such firms' discontinuing a service without the authorization of the regulatory agency. Although the prohibition of arbitrary refusals of service lies close to the heart of the traditional common-law concept of a public utility or common carrier (as the very name, common carrier, sug-gests) and is a settled feature of regulatory law,[63] it is difficult to explain under existing views of the purpose in fact of regulation. It is not apparent why regulated firms would want to be placed under such a duty or how they might benefit from it; it is only a little less difficult to see why, from the standpoint of consumer interests, the imposition of such a duty would be thought an appropriate part of the regulatory system. To be sure, a monopolist, if he has his way, will establish a schedule of prices under which fewer customers are served than if a competitive price were set; but once the schedule is adopted there is no reason to expect him to refuse service, on any

---

[61] Alluded to in [69], p. 961, the dissenting opinion of Commissioner Johnson.

[62] See, for example, Bonbright [3], p. 113, and National Transportation Policy in [64].

[63] A typical statement of the duty appears in the Interstate Commerce Act [63]: "It shall be the duty of every common carrier subject to this part to provide and furnish transportation upon reasonable request therefor . . . ." Other examples are given in Jones [28], pp. 376–85. See also *id.* at pp. 26–27. The sub-ject is treated exhaustively by Wyman in [84].

but good business grounds, to any customer willing to pay the price.[54] Arbitrary refusals do not make good business sense. There is similarly no reason to expect a commercial enterprise to abandon a profitable service. Yet regulated firms are forbidden to abandon any route without obtaining the permission of the regulatory agency,[55] and bitterly contested abandonment proceedings are a commonplace occurrence, especially in the railroad industry.

Perhaps these controls are designed in many instances to reinforce regulatory control over the profits of the regulated firms: a firm might refuse or terminate service in order to coerce a higher rate from the customer, or as part of a scheme for enhancing its profits by reducing the level of service on which the rates it was permitted to charge had been based. Possibly they were intended to reinforce ordinary contractual remedies for nonperformance of services considered "essential." But these considerations do not provide a complete explanation. They do not explain why regulatory agencies are empowered to require the extension of utility services to new areas and to prevent the discontinuance of manifestly unremunerative services such as long-distance passenger transportation in the railroad industry. These cases can only be explained, I believe, in terms of a public finance view of regulation. Regulated firms, were they not subject to the duty to institute and not to terminate service, could not be relied upon to implement policies of internal subsidization. For reasons to be noted later, they might still offer some unremunerative services and they might still not always discontinue services when they ceased to be remunerative. But there would be no assurance of their cooperation.

☐ **Competitive market structures.** The public finance hypothesis also illuminates some of the important characteristics of the regulated industries themselves (as distinct from characteristics of the regulatory schemes). It suggests, for example, why so many regulated industries do not have a monopolistic structure. A program of internal subsidies does not depend on the regulated industry's being a monopoly. So long as the demand for the industry's product is not perfectly elastic, and so long as the obligation to provide internal subsidies is imposed on all the firms in the industry, such a program is feasible just as it is feasible to impose an excise tax on a competitive industry. It is therefore not surprising, under the view advanced here, that many regulated industries are not monopolistic in structure. To be sure, were regulation imposed solely at the behest of regulated firms, one would also expect many regulated industries to be competitive in structure. But one would not expect so many regulated markets (especially in the communications, power, and water-supply industries) to exhibit pronounced characteristics of natural monopoly. These are the least likely settings for firms to seek governmental protection from competition since the existence of a natural monopoly substantially reduces the danger of competition.

---

[54] See Posner [47], p. 584. I except refusals to serve based upon widespread racial prejudice in a community and refusals to serve business customers for monopolistic reasons. These are special cases, and the scope of the duty to serve is considerably broader.

[55] See Jones [28], pp. 385–95.

☐ **Regulated industries produce services.** It is a curiosity that public utility and common carrier industries invariably provide services (in the sense of a good that is difficult or impossible to store or transfer) rather than commodities. The public finance view supplies an answer. A subsidized good or service will not in fact be used by those for whom it is intended if they are free to resell it on the free market, which is why direct subsidies are commonly of services rather than commodities.[56]

☐ **Regulated industries provide "infrastructure" services.** The specific complex of controls over entry and over the level and structure of rates that is characteristic of public utility and common carrier regulation is confined, for the most part, to the transportation, telecommunication, and power (electricity and gas) industries. Neither of the received views of regulation explains adequately why these particular industries have been singled out. The consumer-interest view of regulation would suggest that these were industries in which monopolistic misallocations of resources were most likely to occur, yet, as mentioned, many of the industries are naturally competitive rather than monopolistic, while a number of important industries, such as computers, drugs, newspapers, and certain non-ferrous metals, which appear to have monopoly problems, sometimes quite serious ones, have escaped regulation. On the other hand, if we assume that regulation is imposed primarily for the benefit of the regulated firms, it must be shown why other industries have not obtained the same kind of regulation as public utilities and common carriers.

A partial explanation of the identity of the regulated industries may be that society frequently subjects to the public utility type of control services that it wants provided on the broadest possible basis (in a sense to be defined). The regulated industries are part of the "infrastructure" of economic growth. Adequate transportation, communications, and power (especially electrical) must be in place before the development of modern industry is possible, and most countries, including this one at various periods, have undertaken to subsidize these services or provide them directly in the hope thereby of attracting industrial developers.[57] One can deny the necessity or appropriateness of this state promotional role but hardly its prevalence. And internal subsidization is one method whereby the expansion of the infrastructure services can be promoted.

To be sure, it is not "expansion" in any simple or obvious sense that is involved. In the case of a naturally competitive industry, internal subsidies expand the provision of service to one class of customers, the beneficiaries of the program, but contract it to another: those who must pay a higher price to defray the subsidy and who consequently demand (and are supplied) a smaller quantity. The overall output of the industry is not necessarily larger, and may (as we saw in discussing value-of-service pricing) be smaller. If the industry is monopolistic in structure and it is not feasible to control its monopoly profits directly, a program of internal subsidies may well

---

[56] Shoup [55], p. 160; Stigler [58], p. 5.

[57] See, for example, Locklin [34], pp. 101–11, and Smead [56]. The theory of social overhead capital (as investment in infrastructure is often called by economists) is discussed by Hirschman [25], pp. 83–97.

bring about a larger output than otherwise. But in either case it would appear that the primary effect of such a program is not to increase the amount of transportation, communication, or power produced but rather to extend the service to classes of customers and geographical areas that might not be served in a free market.

Such a result is nonetheless consistent with the thinking that underlies the desire to force the creation of an adequate infrastructure rather than let the market take its course. The basic assumption, correct or incorrect, is that private enterprise, due to lack of foresight, or imperfections in the capital market, or external economies, will forgo many investments in infrastructure that would be socially profitable.[58] One can argue from this that it is the role of the state to encourage precisely those infrastructure services that are unremunerative.

This view may be reinforced in some cases by another: concern with geographical concentration of population and economic activity. A program of internal subsidies that denies the cost advantages of proximity and density, as is often the case, encourages greater geographic dispersion. Cost advantages based on location, it need hardly be said, are no less real than those based on other factors. But governments, including our own, have frequently followed policies aimed at denying those advantages. Utility regulation is perhaps one of them.

The industries in which we find internal subsidies are commonly also recipients of at least some direct subsidies.[59] This correlation supports the view of regulation as a method of public finance, especially where, as in the case of the electrical and telephone subsidies doled out by the Rural Electrification Administration, the recipients of direct subsidies are not members of the industry at all (in the REA case, they are consumer cooperatives). In such a case the established firms in the industry benefit only insofar as the existence of the direct subsidy reduces the pressure on them to provide an internal subsidy, and the subsidy scheme is more convincingly interpreted as a method of obtaining greater service than as a device for enriching corporate treasuries.

To suggest that regulation is a method of promoting the expansion of infrastructure services is not, of course, to explain why it is chosen in preference to alternative methods, such as direct subsidies, or why, with respect to some infrastructure services, such as education, the public utility approach plays a very subordinate role.[60] A framework for answering this question is sketched in part 6, where we look at some of the advantages and disadvantages of regulation in comparison with other methods of taxation, and a highly tentative answer is suggested.

The infrastructure explanation for the identity of the regulated industries is far from being completely satisfactory. It hardly seems applicable when an internal subsidy is used to retard the decline of an old industry, such as railroad passenger service or telegraph service. In addition, the economic case for subsidizing infrastructure

[58] See, for example, Hagen [19], pp. 126–29, and Kindleberger [32].

[59] Cf. Harriss [21], p. 270.

[60] Although not an entirely negligible one, as attested by free cable-television channels for schools, the public-affairs programming obligations of broadcast licensees, and the proposed free interconnection for educational television.

services is often dubious. And internal subsidization seems a somewhat curious way to encourage the expansion of an industry since,
as mentioned, the cost of the subsidy is borne by customers of the
industry. Indeed, the obligation to provide service to all at a uniform
price may retard the undertaking of new extensions of service.[61]

At the least, these considerations suggest that a thoroughgoing
justification of internal subsidies on efficiency grounds is impossible.
One can easily find examples where an internal subsidy works directly contrary to the dictates of efficient resource allocation. Thus,
the subsidization of commuter railroad service aggravates an existing
imbalance between private and social costs caused by the fact that
individuals who are employed in cities and utilize urban public
services can escape the costs of those services by living in a suburb
and commuting. It would appear, therefore, that internal subsidies
are frequently designed to redistribute wealth rather than to correct
imperfections in the market.

■ **Limitations of the device.** To summarize the discussion at this
point, there is persuasive evidence that an important purpose in fact
of public utility and common carrier regulation is to compel, by the
device of the internal subsidy, the provision of certain services in
quantities and at prices that a free market would not offer, much as
the conventional taxing-spending power is used to the same end.
Serious discussion of the public finance component of regulation has
been retarded, however, by a tendency to dismiss it out of hand as
an implausible and inappropriate alternative to more conventional
exertions of the taxing power. Two objections are usually advanced
as conclusive. The first is that internal subsidization distorts the
efficient allocation of resources; the second, that it tends to be arbitrary and inequitable. One sometimes hears it said, too, that taxation
is the proper business of the legislature and not of regulatory agencies.

1) *Delegation.* To take the last point first, it is difficult to understand why the delegation of a part of the taxing power to appointive
agencies, the regulatory commissions, should be thought to offend
the principles on which our government is organized. Congress,
acting from imperative reasons of practicality, has delegated much
of its lawmaking power to appointive agencies. The Federal courts
provide a conspicuous example, and the Internal Revenue Service
one that is directly in point.

2) *Efficiency.* It is true that internal subsidization, by forcing
prices in some markets above cost and prices in others below, distorts the allocation of resources. It creates a secondary inefficiency
as well: the entry of new competitors into the high-price markets
must be prevented by the regulatory agency lest the source of the
internal subsidy be wiped out.[62] Where the high-price market is

**6. Internal
subsidization
compared with
other methods of
public finance**

---

[61] Coase [6], p. 139. The effect of uniform price systems with which Professor
Coase was concerned—denial of service to high-cost customers willing to pay
the full cost of serving them—can be avoided by combining a uniform price system for most customers with a system of surcharges for those who would not be
served at the uniform price. This appears on casual observation to be the practice
of the telephone industry in this country.

[62] For a good example, see Caves [5], p. 314.

a natural monopoly, this is not an acute problem, but of course not all markets subject to regulation are naturally monopolistic.

The criticism of internal subsidization as inefficient points to a real characteristic of the device; but as a criticism it is superficial. It measures the device against an ideal standard, and of course finds it wanting. The proper comparison is to other exercises of the taxing power. All methods of taxation distort the "optimum" allocation of resources—optimum, that is, without regard to any need or demand to provide certain services publicly—and there are no *a priori* grounds for assuming that excise taxes, such as the internal-subsidy programs imposed by regulatory agencies, produce worse misallocations than income or other taxes.[63] To consider an important example, the exemption from income taxation of the real but not pecuniary income generated by housewives must cause a significant misallocation of resources by inducing many women to stay at home who would be more productive in other employments. The administrative costs of implementing a broader income concept would be so great, however, that this exemption is probably a permanent feature of income taxation. Because of pervasive and ineradicable distortions of this kind, it is not obvious that raising income tax rates would be a more efficient method of providing particular services at below-market prices than internal subsidization.[64] Indeed, insofar as the burden of internal subsidies tends to be borne by customers whose demands are highly inelastic, the allocative effects may be less adverse than those of alternative taxation methods.[65] And in those cases where the regulated firms are obtaining monopoly profits, the adverse allocative effects of the tax will be even fewer.[66]

Internal subsidies are also criticized on the ground that a subsidy in kind is inefficient compared to an unrestricted cash subsidy, because different people have different needs and wants. This is a valid and important point but it is not a criticism of internal subsidies as such, since it applies with equal force to most direct subsidies.

3) *Equity.* Because the determination of the incidence of particular taxes is immensely complex, it is very difficult to gauge the effect of internal subsidies on the distribution of income. At a rough guess, internal subsidization may sometimes benefit the poor[67] but has no general tendency to do so; and as our commuter example shows it may sometimes work in the opposite direction. But poverty is not the only possible justification for the redistribution of income. It is notable that internal subsidization is frequently employed to bolster declining services or sectors; perhaps in these cases it is felt that there are important reliance interests (for example, in location proximate to a railroad line) that deserve protection. And even if no consistent equity justification is possible, that is no special criticism

[63] See Friedman [16], pp. 56-67, and Little [33], p. 608.
[64] Cf. Harberger [20], p. 58.
[65] Cf. Musgrave [39], p. 157.
[66] Cf. Shilling [54], p. 224; Shoup [55], p. 276; Dirlam and Kahn [13], p. 494.
[67] Some rather dubious examples are given in Bonbright [3], pp. 111–12. Lower prices to the poor could in some cases be explained as profit-maximizing price discrimination, and his examples may well be of this type. A better example is provided by the low rail rates for agricultural commodities (see p. 26 and fn. 21 *supra*), but it is possible that the benefits are largely captured by farmers (who may or may not be poor) rather than by consumers. Staudinger [57], p. 259, argues for using public utility pricing to redistribute income to the poor.

of internal subsidies: the redistributive effects of tax-cum-direct-subsidy programs appear in a surprising range of cases to be perverse.[68] If one is to oppose internal subsidies on equity grounds, it must be as part of a broader objection to the redistributive policies of the state.

I turn now to some other, less frequently discussed attributes of regulation as a method of public finance.

4) *Enforcement.* An important characteristic of taxation by regulation is difficulty (and expense) of enforcement. A firm that finds the provision of an unremunerative service irksome may try to terminate it by drastically reducing the quality of the service and then citing the resulting fall in demand as evidence that the public no longer wants the service. This is not so transparent a gambit as it may seem. Since the public is not paying the full cost of the service, it has a natural tendency to demand a very high (and correspondingly costly) level of service. The specification of an appropriate level involves an essentially arbitrary judgment and accordingly gives the firm some room for maneuver. Evidently degradation of service has played an important role in the termination of railroad passenger operations.[69]

The tendency of regulated firms to cheat in providing unremunerative services is probably quite general since, unless regulation is more effective than anyone thinks, a penny saved in skimping on an unremunerative service will not result immediately in a full penny reduction in the rates paid by customers of the firm's lucrative services. The finding in a recent study that the rates set by publicly owned electric utilities[70] are more uniform than those set by privately owned electric utilities supports this suggestion. Uniform rates, we saw, are a common method of internal subsidization; and one would expect a privately owned company to resist providing unremunerative services more energetically than a publicly owned one.

The tendency to cheat is not entirely a bad thing. It may result in a smaller subsidy than if direct subsidization were used, and given the forceful objections to many subsidies, this may be distinctly to the good.

5) *Public scrutiny.* A troubling characteristic of the internal subsidy is its low visibility, which impedes responsible review. The amounts and recipients of direct subsidies are ordinarily specifically stated, but this is not the case with internal subsidies. Since information is not a free good, a subsidy program whose magnitude requires computation is less apt to be challenged than one whose magnitude is patent.

This is a general criticism of hidden subsidies, of which internal subsidies in the regulated industries are only one variety. And it is easily overstated: extravagant subsidy programs sail through Congress with monotonous regularity. Full disclosure is a far from dependable test of whether legislation in the public interest will be adopted, because the public does not vote on specific pieces of legislation, but on representatives, and it is demonstrable that in a repre-

---

[68] Stigler [58], p. 1.

[69] Doubtless encouraged by the ICC's recent holding that it has no authority over the quality of rail passenger service [76].

[70] Peltzman [44].

sentative system much legislation benefiting special interests at the expense of the larger public will be enacted.[71] This is a basic insight of the effective-political-group theory of regulation. Furthermore, given the size of the Federal budget, the disclosure in an appropriation hearing of the amount of a subsidy may not always be an effective method of assuring a responsible review of the proposal's merits. Suppose that buried in the Defense Department's appropriation request there had been a small item for a contribution to the cost of building a transatlantic cable: can one be confident that it would have received the careful scrutiny of Congress?

Despite the last point, the concern about adequacy of scrutiny has greatest force, I believe, precisely with regard to internal subsidies for national defense. The Defense Department's role in the TAT 5 matter affords a good illustration. Had the Department been forced to include the item in its budgetary request to Congress, it would have had to weigh its importance against that of other national-defense programs. The defense budget is not limitless. The inclusion of the cable item might have compelled the Department to modify some other request. In the context of a regulatory proceeding, however, the cable represented a free good to the Department. The Department had no incentive to evaluate the benefits of TAT 5 to the national defense objectively; indeed, it had an incentive to exaggerate those benefits. The FCC could not exercise a critical scrutiny because it has no competence to deal with military questions. The competent agencies—Congress and the Bureau of the Budget (which reviews all Federal budgetary proposals before submission to Congress)—were bypassed.

6) *Manageability of regulation.* Another problem with internal subsidization is that it complicates an already barely manageable regulatory process. Because there is no objective basis for balancing off distributive benefits against allocative costs,[72] an agency concerned with subsidizing worthy groups is deprived of a clear-cut standard for resolving controversies over pricing and entry. Clear and definite standards are necessary to tolerable regulation.[73] Without a definite standard at the agency level, moreover, judicial review, a potentially

---

[71] See Stigler [59].

[72] In his recent study of the Federal Power Commission [35], pp. 288–89, Paul MacAvoy makes a valiant but, I believe, unsuccessful effort to do so. His position on determining the dollar value of an income redistribution is "that the government should decide, and it indicates value by the amount that consumer X can keep after taxes . . . ." The difficulty with such an approach is that the scheme of Federal taxation does not reflect any consistent or intelligible policy toward the equity of income redistribution—unless we are to assume, for example, that because some dividend income is exempt from tax, stockholders are to be deemed a favored class for purposes of evaluating the redistributions brought about by a monopolist or a regulatory agency. See Pechman [43] for a lively recent discussion. And many of the apparently distributive features of Federal income taxation, including the progressive principle itself, have been justified on grounds (such as benefits received) that have nothing to do with the equity of redistributing income, while other features (such as the nontaxability of real income received in the form of reductions in the prices of consumer goods) reflect purely administrative considerations.

[73] Friendly [17]. For a somewhat different path to the same conclusion, see Posner [46], pp. 84–85.

important check on regulatory excesses,[74] is likely to be ineffectual; the agency can give a plausible justification for any result. Multiple and conflicting standards also breed corruption.[75]

7) *Private demand.* Taxation by regulation, to be feasible, requires that there be sufficient demand in the private market to justify the imposition of the burden of the subsidy on the regulated firms. Where there is not, as in the railroad industry, the results can be disastrous for the industry. One may hazard the guess that regulation has frequently been the principal means of subsidizing infrastructure services for which there is a strong private demand, while in areas like national defense and education, where the market demand is probably small in relation to the amount of service that the state wishes to provide, other methods of subsidization have predominated.

☐ **And some advantages.** The balance of advantages is not wholly against the choice of the internal subsidy as a method of public finance. We have indicated several respects in which it may be preferable to other methods, and there are others.

1) *Administrative expense.* Although enforcement of internal subsidization can, as mentioned, be quite costly (railroad abandonment proceedings are a case in point), there are certain offsetting factors. Since no cash transfers are involved in internal subsidization, it is possible to dispense with the frequently elaborate apparatus of a formal transfer program—application forms, disbursement machinery, and the like. Often, too, a program of internal subsidies is implemented simply by the regulated firms' averaging the costs of many customers in setting a rate, and where this is done the firms avoid the expenses that would be incurred in identifying the costs of finer groups of customers and adopting a more complex rate structure tailored to the different costs. This is not to suggest that expenses incurred in implementing the price system are normally wasted; but once it is decided not to allow the price system to control the allocation of resources, a choice implicit in the decision to subsidize, the elimination of some of those expenses may represent a real saving.

2) *Legislative capacity.* By shifting taxing power from Congress (or state legislative bodies) to administrative agencies, internal subsidization economizes on the legislature's time. This is an especially important consideration where the subsidy is of a kind that requires frequent adjustment or review. The ability of a legislature to transact business is obviously limited. Among the ways in which it can be conserved, perhaps the delegation of minor taxing functions to regulatory agencies is relatively efficient.

3) *Protection of expectations.* At least when imposed on a service from the outset, internal subsidies may be less disruptive of public and

---

[74] An expanded role for the courts in the review of regulatory action is urged in Turner [61], p. 386. His position can be defended on the ground that judges are more insulated from political-group pressures than regulatory agencies. Cf. Posner [46], p. 89.

[75] The classic instance is the corruption that beset the FCC, at the highest levels, in the 1950's. The problem revolved around the initial grant of broadcast licenses, where the Commission applied no standard but used a check-list of criteria, enabling any preconceived result to be rationalized. Jones [28], pp. 1081–84, lists 15 criteria.

commercial expectations than other new taxes. An example will illustrate. Suppose a community has pending before it several applications for a cable television franchise and would like to use a few channels in any cable television system that is constructed for municipal functions such as education. And suppose further that the feasible alternative methods of obtaining this service have been narrowed to two: a tax on the gross receipts of the barbers in the community, the proceeds to be used to purchase the channels from the cable franchisee, and a condition in the franchise requiring the franchisee to provide the channels to the school system at no charge. If the first alternative is chosen, the result will be a rise in the cost (and hence presumably price) of barbering, which will lead to a fall in the amount of barbering demanded and supplied. As a result, some of the resources used in barbering in the community will be idle during the period in which they are being redeployed. And there will be an outcry from the barbers. These economic and political costs, incurred by virtue of the change in the economic conditions of the business brought about by a new tax, can be avoided if the second alternative, an internal subsidy by the cable industry, is selected. Since the costs of the cable system are now higher, a smaller system will be built. But the efficient scale (consistent with the obligation to provide free channels to the franchising authority) will be known in advance; there will be no waste in achieving it, as in the barbering example. In fact one observes that public utility and common carrier regulation has typically been imposed upon new services, where it was possible by a system of internal subsidies to finance desired extensions of the service without disturbing settled activities. And perhaps these considerations explain why municipalities have latched onto cable television as an important new source of revenue.[76]

Nonetheless, the explanation is severely limited. The alternatives in our example were too narrow: the municipality could also have placed a gross-receipts or other tax on cable service and raised the money for the free channels that way. It did not have to use internal subsidization, although we have previously discussed some reasons why internal subsidization might sometimes be preferred to alternative forms of excise taxation.

4) *Justice.* There may be some appeal to the notion that it is more "just" for other customers of the same industry to bear the cost of a subsidy of the industry's service than to distribute that cost among the taxpaying public at large. The notion is a little peculiar, however. It is one thing to say that those who benefit from a service should bear its costs, and quite another to impute the cost of a subsidy to those customers who are quite prepared to pay the full cost of serving them.

A final reason for the choice of internal subsidization over alternative methods of public finance has nothing to do with its relative merits. The regulated firms may cast their weight on the side of the internal subsidy, viewing customers who enjoy subsidized rates as useful allies in the maintenance of regulatory barriers to entry. Subsidizing some customers may be the "price" that the franchised monopolist pays for his monopoly. Perhaps careful study would disclose that most regulation is demanded by and supplied to a coalition

[76] See, for example, the Mayor's Advisory Committee [41].

of regulated firms and those of their customers who receive services below cost as a consequence of regulation.

■ I trust that the foregoing remarks will not be construed as a "defense" of taxation (and subsidization) by regulation. They may, however, help explain the prevalence and tenacity of the practice, and they do suggest that, short of a thorough overhauling of government subsidy policy, it is less easy to condemn the practice out of hand as inefficient and inequitable than has usually been assumed. Perhaps few subsidies are in the public interest; there may still be cases where, given a decision to subsidize, regulation is the cheapest means of doing so.

But if we are stuck with taxation by regulation, perhaps we are not stuck with its worst features. I propose two modest reforms. The first is that agencies and reviewing courts insist, in proceedings where the maintenance of an internal subsidy is an issue, that the amount and cost of the subsidy, together with the identity of the recipients and of the payors, be calculated and placed in the public record. Perhaps this would eliminate some of the more captious instances of the phenomenon; at least it would bring an important issue of public policy into the open.

Second, more consideration should be given to the most efficient method of attaining the ends of internal subsidization. Accepting the decision to subsidize a specific service and to impose the cost of the subsidy on other customers of the firm providing the service, there may be better ways of achieving this end than control of prices, entry, abandonments, and the like by a regulatory agency. In particular, an explicit excise tax (such as the percentage-of-gross-receipts fee in many cable television franchises), with the proceeds earmarked for the service that the state wants to subsidize, may be preferable to the internal subsidy proper because it entails no limitation on entry into the high-price market; lump-sum fees may be preferable to either.[77] A likely reason why such alternatives are rarely considered is that the usual regulatory agency lacks authority to impose an explicit tax or other fee. In franchise regulation, as the case of cable television suggests, this option is open. Perhaps, therefore, a modest enlargement of the taxing power of regulatory agencies, to permit them to exact a uniform and limited fee from any firm desiring to enter a regulated market in lieu of other regulatory controls, would foster the more efficient use of what appears to be a settled device of public finance.

■ This paper merely scratches the surface of an interesting and important question of public policy. I have tried to show that certain views of the purpose in fact of public utility and common carrier regulation—that it is to approximate competitive results, or that it is to benefit the regulated firms—fail to account for a number of significant observed features of the regulatory process and the regulated industries. And I have argued that a consistent and comprehensive explanation of those features requires that we assign an important place to taxation and subsidization among the purposes that regula-

---

[77] See Posner [45] pp. 19–20.

tion in fact serves. I have attempted further to compare taxation by regulation with other methods of taxation and subsidization, in the hope of assisting evaluation of the pros and cons of alternative methods in particular cases. What I have not attempted to do is explain why some groups are subsidized and others not, or why the same group will receive some internal subsidies but not others (in the case of fire departments, for example, free water but not free telephone service). These fascinating and important questions, which require a better understanding of the magnitude and incidence of taxation by regulation than existing information permits, constitute the agenda for further research into a heretofore rather neglected aspect of public regulation.

References

1. AVERCH, H. and JOHNSON, L. L. "Behavior of the Firm Under Regulatory Constraint," *American Economic Review,* Vol. 52 (December 1962), pp. 1053–69.
2. BARATZ, M. "Cost Behavior and Pricing Policy in the Post Office," *Land Economics,* Vol. 38 (1962).
3. BONBRIGHT, J. C. *Principles of Public Utility Rates.* New York: Columbia University Press, 1961.
4. BOWMAN, W. "Tying Arrangements and the Leverage Problem," *Yale Law Journal,* Vol. 67 (1957).
5. CAVES, R. E. *Air Transport and its Regulators: An Industry Study.* Cambridge, Mass: Harvard University Press (Economic Studies Series, No. 120), 1962.
6. COASE, R. H. "The Economics of Uniform Pricing Systems," *Manchester School of Economic and Social Studies,* Vol. 15 (1947).
7. ———. "The Marginal Cost Controversy," *Economica,* Vol. 13 (1946), pp. 169–82.
8. ———. "The Nationalization of Electricity Supply in Great Britain," *Land Economics,* Vol. 26 (1950).
9. ———. "The Postal Monopoly in Great Britain: An Historical Survey," In *Economic Essays in Commemoration of the Dundee School of Economics, 1931–1955,* J. Eastham, editor, 1955.
10. CONANT, M. *Railroad Mergers and Abandonments.* Berkeley, California: University of California Press, 1965.
11. CREW, M. "Electricity Tariffs," In *Public Enterprise.* Edited by Ralph Turney. 1968.
12. DAVIDSON, R. *Price Discrimination in Selling Gas and Electricity.* 1954.
13. DIRLAM, J. and KAHN, A. "The Merits of Reserving the Cost Savings from Domestic Communications Satellites for the Support of Educational Television," *Yale Law Journal,* Vol. 77 (1968).
14. EADS, G. "The Effect of Regulation on the Cost Performance and Growth Strategies of the Local Service Airlines," unpublished manuscript, Princeton University Department of Economics, 1970.
15. FRIEDLAENDER, A. F. *Dilemma of Freight Transport Regulation.* Washington, D. C.: The Brookings Institution, 1969.
16. FRIEDMAN, M. *Price Theory: A Provisional Text.* Chicago, Ill.: Aldine Press, 1966 (rev. ed).
17. FRIENDLY, H. J. *Federal Administrative Agencies: The Need for Better Definition of Standards.* Cambridge, Mass.: Harvard University Press, 1962.
18. GARFIELD, P. and LOVEJOY, W. *Public Utility Economics.* Englewood Cliffs, New Jersey: Prentice-Hall, 1963.
19. HAGEN, E. E. *The Economics of Development.* Homewood, Ill.: Richard D. Irwin, 1968.
20. HARBERGER, A. C. "Taxation, Resource Allocation, and Welfare," in NATIONAL BUREAU OF ECONOMICS RESEARCH and THE BROOKINGS INSTITUTION, *The Role of Direct and Indirect Taxes in the Federal Revenue System: A Conference Report.* Princeton, N. J.: Princeton University Press, 1964.
21. HARRISS, L. "Subsidies in the United States," *Public Finance,* Vol. 16 (1961).

22. HENDERSON, A. "The Pricing of Public Utility Undertakings," *Manchester School of Economic and Social Studies*, Vol. 15 (1947).

23. HILTON, G. W. *The Transportation Act of 1958: A Decade of Experience.* Bloomington, Indiana: Indiana University Press, 1969.

24. HIRSHLEIFER, J., DE HAVEN, J. and MILLIMAN, J. *Water Supply: Economics, Technology, and Policy.* Chicago, Ill.: University of Chicago Press, 1960 (rev. ed, 1969).

25. HIRSCHMAN, A. O. *The Strategy of Economic Development.* New Haven, Conn.: Yale University Press, 1958.

26. ILLINOIS, STATE OF. "An Act to provide for the establishment of ferries, toll bridges, and turnpike roads," *Revised Code of Laws of Illinois*, Sec. 5 (1827).

27. JOHNSON, L. *Communications Satellites and Telephone Rates: Problems of Government Regulation.* Rand Memorandum RM-2845-NASA (October 1961).

28. JONES, W. K. *Cases and Materials on Regulated Industries.* 1967.

29. KENNEDY, J. "Structure and Policy in Postal Rates," *Journal of Political Economy*, Vol. 65 (1957).

30. KEETON, R. E. and O'CONNELL, J. *Basic Protection for the Traffic Victim: A Blueprint for Reforming Automobile Insurance.* Boston, Mass.: Little, Brown & Company, 1966.

31. KEIG, N. G., FRISTOE, C. W. and GODDARD, F. O. "A Critique of the Policy Objectives of Publicly Owned Water Utilities," Unpublished manuscript, University of Florida, 1970.

32. KINDLEBERGER, C. P. *Economic Development.* New York, N. Y.: McGraw Hill, 1958 (2nd ed. 1965).

33. LITTLE, I. M. D. "Direct Versus Indirect Taxes," *Economic Journal.* Vol. 61 (1951). Reprinted in AMERICAN ECONOMICS ASSOCIATION, *Readings in Welfare Economics*, 1969.

34. LOCKLIN, D. P. *Economics of Transportation.* Homewood, Ill.: Richard D. Irwin, 1966 (6th ed.).

35. MACAVOY, P. W. "The Effectiveness of the Federal Power Commission," *Bell Journal of Economics and Management Science*, Vol. 1, No. 2 (Autumn, 1970), pp. 271–303.

36. ———. *The Economic Effects of Regulation: The Trunk-Line Railroad Cartels and the Interstate Commerce Commission before 1900.* Cambridge, Mass.: MIT Press, 1965.

37. MEYER, J. R., KAIN, J. F. and WOHL, M. *The Urban Transportation Problem.* Cambridge, Mass.: Harvard University Press, 1965.

38. ———, PECK, M., STENASON, J. and ZWICK, C. *The Economics of Competition in the Transportation Industries.* Cambridge, Mass.: Harvard University Press, 1959.

39. MUSGRAVE, R. *The Theory of Public Finance: A Study in Public Economy.* New York: McGraw Hill, 1959.

40. NELSON, J. C. *Railroad Transportation and Public Policy.* Washington, D. C.: The Brookings Institution, 1959.

41. NEW YORK MAYOR'S ADVISORY COMMITTEE ON CATV AND TELECOMMUNICATIONS. *A Report on Cable Television and Cable Telecommunications in New York City.* New York, 1968.

42. NOVE, A. "Internal Economies," *Economic Journal*, Vol. 79 (1969).

43. PECHMAN, J. A. "The Rich, the Poor, and the Taxes They Pay," *The Public Interest*, No. 17 (Fall 1969), pp. 21–43.

44. PELTZMAN, S. "Pricing in Public and Private Enterprises: Electric Utilities in the United States," *Journal of Law and Economics*, forthcoming.

45. POSNER, R. A. *Cable Television: The Problem of Local Monopoly.* Rand Memorandum RM-6309-FF (May 1970).

46. ———. "The Federal Trade Commission," *University of Chicago Law Review*, Vol. 37 (1969).

47. ———. "Natural Monopoly and Its Regulation," *Stanford Law Review*, Vol. 21 (1969).

48. PRESIDENT'S TASK FORCE ON COMMUNICATIONS POLICY. *Final Report.* Washington, D. C.: Government Printing Office, 1968.

49. ———. *Organization of the United States International Communications Industry.* U. S. Department of Commerce, Clearinghouse for Federal Scientific and Technical Information, PB 184 424 (June 1969). Staff Paper 2.

50. ———. *The Western Union Telegraph Company*. U. S. Department of Commerce, Clearinghouse for Federal Scientific and Technical Information, PB 184 418 (June 1969). Staff Paper 5.
51. SARGENT, J. R. "Nationalized Industries and Public Policy," in *The Lessons of Public Enterprise*, edited by Michael Shanks (1963).
52. SHARP, C. *Problems of Urban Passenger Transport with Special Reference to Leicester*. 1967.
53. SHEPHERD, W. G. "Cross-Subsidizing and Allocation in Public Firms," *Oxford Economic Papers*, Vol. 16 (N.S., 1964).
54. SHILLING, N. *Excise Taxation of Monopoly*. New York: Columbia University Press, 1969.
55. SHOUP, C. S. *Public Finance*. Chicago, Ill.: Aldine Press, 1969.
56. SMEAD, E. E. *Governmental Promotion and Regulation of Business*. New York: Appleton-Century Crofts, 1969.
57. STAUDINGER, H. "Social Rates in Electricity," *Social Research*, Vol. 3 (1936).
58. STIGLER, G. J. "Director's Law of Public Income Redistribution, " *Journal of Law and Economics*, Vol. 13 (1970).
59. ———. "Theory of Economic Regulation," *Bell Journal of Economics and Management Science*, Vol. 2, No. 1 (Spring 1971).
60. ———. *The Theory of Price*. New York: The Macmillan Company, 1966 (3rd ed).
61. TURNER, D. "The Scope of Antitrust and Other Economic Regulatory Policies," *Harvard Law Review*, Vol. 82 (1969).
62. U. S., CIVIL AERONAUTICS BOARD. *Student Educational Group Fares*. Docket No. 22402, order of investigation and suspension, July 29, 1970.
63. *U. S. Code*. "Interstate Commerce Act," Vol. 49, Sec. 1(4).
64. ———. "National Transportation Policy," Preceding Vol. 49, Sec. 1.
65. ———. "Transportation Act of 1920," Vol. 49, Secs. 1(18), 1(20), and 1(22).
66. U. S., CONGRESS, HOUSE, COMMITTEE ON INTERSTATE AND FOREIGN COMMERCE. *Transportation Acts Amendments, 1962, Hearings on*. 87th Cong., 2nd Session.
67. U. S. DEPARTMENT OF TRANSPORTATION. *Price Variability in the Automobile Insurance Market*. Automobile and Compensation Study, August 1970.
68. U. S., FEDERAL COMMUNICATIONS COMMISSION. *Re American Telephone and Telegraph Company*, 37 F.C.C. 1151 (1964).
69. ———. *Re American Telephone and Telegraph Company*, 11 F.C.C. 2d 957 (1968).
70. ———. *Re American Telephone and Telegraph Company*, 13 F.C.C. 2d 235 (1968).
71. ———. *Annual Report, 1969*. Washington, D. C.: U. S. Government Printing Office, 1970.
72. ———. *Authorized Entities and Authorized Users Under the Communications Satellite Act of 1962*, 4 F.C.C. 2d 421 (1966).
73. ———. *Interconnection Service*, 14 F.C.C. 2d 599 (1968).
74. ———. *Public Service Responsibility of Broadcast Licensees* (1946).
75. ———. *Re Western Union Telegraph Company*, 12 F.C.C. 2d 980 (1968).
76. U. S, INTERSTATE COMMERCE COMMISSION. *Adequacy—Passenger Service— Southern Pac. Co. Between California and Louisiana*, 335 I.C.C. 415 (1969).
77. ———. *Increased Freight Rates, E.W. & S. Territories, 1956*, 299 I.C.C. 429, 441, 451–59 (1956).
78. *U. S. Statutes at Large*. Communications Act of 1934, as amended by the Public Broadcasting Act of 1967 (U. S. Statutes at Large, vol. 81, p. 365), U. S. Code Vol. 47, Secs. 1 *et seq*.
79. ———. Communications Satellite Act of 1962, Vol. 76; U. S. Code, Vol. 47, Secs. 701 *et seq*.
80. ———. Hoch-Smith Resolution, Vol. 43 (1925).
81. ———. Natural Gas Act, sec. 7(c), as amended. U. S. Code, Vol. 15, sec 717 ff.
82. WATKINS, G. P. "Street-Railway Rates, with Especial Reference to Differentiation," *Quarterly Journal of Economics*, Vol. 25 (1911).
83. WILSON, G. "Effects of Value-of-Service Pricing Upon Motor Common Carriers," *Journal of Political Economy*. Vol. 63 (1965).
84. WYMAN, B. *Public Service Corporations*. Vol. 1 (1911), Parts II–IV.

[15]

The Social Costs of Monopoly and Regulation

Richard A. Posner

University of Chicago Law School and National Bureau of Economic Research

This paper presents a model and some highly tentative empirical estimates of the social costs of monopoly and monopoly-inducing regulation in the United States. Unlike the previous studies, it assumes that competition to obtain a monopoly results in the transformation of expected monopoly profits into social costs. A major conclusion is that public regulation is probably a larger source of social costs than private monopoly. The implications of the analysis for several public policy issues, such as appropriate policy toward mergers and price discrimination, are also discussed.

When market price rises above the competitive level, consumers who continue to purchase the sellers' product at the new, higher price suffer a loss (L in fig. 1) exactly offset by the additional revenue that the sellers obtain at the higher price. Those who stop buying the product suffer a loss (D) not offset by any gain to the sellers. This is the "deadweight loss" from supracompetitive pricing and in traditional analysis its only social cost, L being regarded merely as a transfer from consumers to producers. Loss D, however, underestimates the social costs of monopoly. The existence of an opportunity to obtain monopoly profits will attract resources into efforts to obtain monopolies, and the opportunity costs of those resources are social costs of monopoly too (Tullock 1967). Theft provides an instructive analogy. The transfer of wealth from victim to

Research on this paper was supported by a grant from the National Science Foundation to the National Bureau of Economic Research for research in law and economics. The paper is not an official National Bureau publication, since it has not yet undergone the full critical review accorded Bureau publications, including approval by the Bureau's Board of Directors. I am grateful to William F. Baxter, Gary S. Becker, Harold Demsetz, Victor R. Fuchs, William M. Landes, Sam Peltzman, and George J. Stigler for helpful comments on previous drafts of the paper.

[*Journal of Political Economy*, 1975, vol. 83, no. 4]

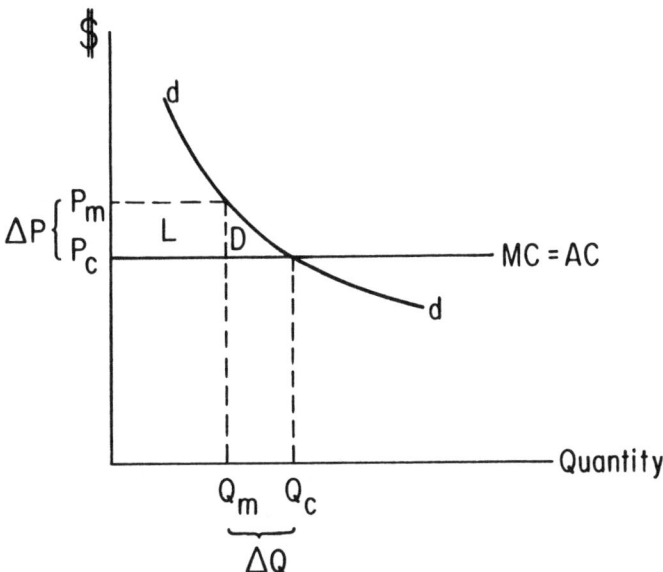

FIG. 1.—Social costs of supracompetitive pricing

thief involves no artificial limitation of output,[1] but it does not follow that the social cost of theft is zero. The opportunity for such transfers draws resources into thieving and in turn into protection against theft, and the opportunity costs of the resources consumed are social costs of theft (Tullock 1967; Becker 1968, p. 171, n. 3).

This sort of analysis has long been familiar in a few special contexts. Plant's criticism of the patent system, made more than a generation ago, was based on the effect of the patent monopoly in drawing greater resources into invention than into activities that yield only competitive returns (Plant 1934). Telser's theory of resale price maintenance is in the same vein (Telser 1960), as is the literature on nonprice competition among members of a cartel (Stigler 1968, pp. 23–28; Douglas and Miller 1974). But, while the tendency of monopoly rents to be transformed into costs is no longer a novel insight, its implications both for the measurement of the aggregate social costs of monopoly and for a variety of other important issues relating to monopoly and public regulation (including tax policy) continue for the most part to be ignored. The present paper is an effort to rectify this neglect.[2]

---

[1] If a thief took three radios from a home and on the way out dropped one, which broke, the resulting loss would correspond to the deadweight loss of monopoly.

[2] See Krueger (1974) for a parallel approach to the measurement of the social costs of import licenses in India and Turkey.

Part I presents a simple model of the social costs of monopoly, conceived as the sum of the deadweight loss and the additional loss resulting from the competition to become a monopolist. Part II uses the model to estimate the social costs of monopoly in the United States and the social benefits of antitrust enforcement. The estimates are crude; their primary value may simply be to induce skepticism about the existing empirical literature on the social costs of monopoly. Part III considers the implications of the analysis for several qualitative issues relating to monopoly and public regulation.

I. A Model of the Social Costs of Monopoly

A. Assumptions

The critical assumptions underlying the model are the following:

1. Obtaining a monopoly is itself a competitive activity, so that, at the margin, the cost of obtaining a monopoly is exactly equal to the expected profit of being a monopolist. An important corollary of this assumption is that there are no intramarginal monopolies—no cases, that is, where the expected profits of monopoly exceed the total supply price of the inputs used to obtain the monopoly. If there were such an excess, competition in the activity of obtaining the monopoly would induce the competing firms (or new entrants) to hire additional inputs in an effort to engross the additional monopoly profits.

2. The long-run supply of all inputs used in obtaining monopolies is perfectly elastic. Hence, the total supply price of these inputs includes no rents.

3. The costs incurred in obtaining a monopoly have no socially valuable by-products.

The first two assumptions assure that all expected monopoly rents are transformed into social costs, and the third that these costs do not generate any social benefits.[3] But how reasonable are such assumptions?

1. The first is a standard assumption of economics and, pending better evidence than we have, seems a reasonable one in the present context. Anyone can try to obtain a patent, a certificate of public convenience and necessity, a television license, a tariff, an import quota, or a minimum-wage law; and anyone can try to form a cartel with his competitors or, if he is a member of a cartelized industry, try to engross a greater share of the monopoly profits of the industry.[4] Nonprice competition in the airline

---

[3] Another assumption, but one that does not affect the analysis, is that the monopoly is enjoyed for one period only; otherwise the optimum expenditures on obtaining a monopoly could not be compared directly with L in fig. 1.

[4] Other than by reducing price, a method of obtaining a larger share of the cartel's profits that would not involve a socially wasteful use of resources.

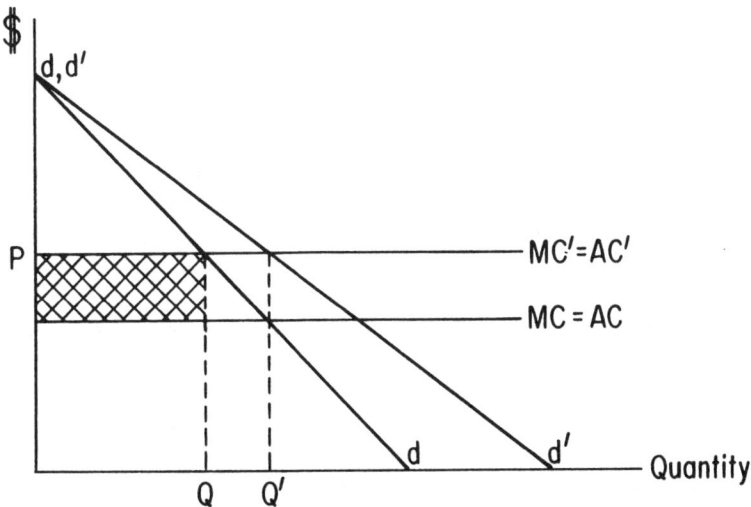

Fig. 2.—Nonprice competition when market price exceeds competitive level

industry illustrates the last point. If the Civil Aeronautics Board places a floor under airline prices that exceeds the marginal cost of providing air transportation under competitive conditions, the situation initially is as depicted in figure 2 and is unstable. Since nonprice competition is not constrained, the airlines will expend resources on such competition (better service, etc.) until the marginal costs of air transportation rise to the level (P in fig. 2) where the industry is earning only a normal return (see Douglas and Miller 1974). The result will be the transformation of the monopoly profits initially generated by the regulatory price floor—the shaded rectangle—into higher costs for the industry. The demand curve shifts to the right because the increased expenditures on service improve the product from the standpoint of the consumer. But the additional consumer surplus is not great enough to offset the higher costs—otherwise the higher level of service would have been provided without the spur of monopoly pricing.

If nonprice competition were forbidden (say, at zero cost) or were somehow not feasible, it would not follow that our assumption that monopolizing is a competitive activity would be overthrown. It would mean simply that the expected profits of the airline business would be greater than if the airlines could expect those profits to be dissipated in nonprice competition. Hence, more resources would be devoted to obtaining a license from the CAB in the first place. The expected profits from monopoly pricing of air transportation would still be zero.

2. Although the assumption that obtaining monopolies involves constant costs seems plausible as a first approximation—there seems little

reason to think that it involves using resources whose long-run supply is inelastic—a more important point is that the assumption may not be a crucial one. Assume that suppliers of inputs into monopolizing do obtain rents. In the long run, the availability of such rents will attract additional resources into the production of those inputs, and these resources will be wasted from a social standpoint. Some possible exceptions are considered in part III(7). Clearly, however, the production function of monopolies requires greater attention than I give it in this paper. The assumption of a perfectly elastic long-run supply may fail for an input as foreign to conventional economic analysis as political power.

3. In the airline example, the expenditures on monopolizing had a socially valuable by-product (improved service), although the value was less than its cost. However, the possibility that expenditures on monopolizing will yield such by-products will be ignored in the development of the model, and its principal relevance, therefore, is to methods of monopolizing that have little or no social value. The formation of a cartel, the procuring of a tariff or other protective legislation, and the merging of competing firms in a market to produce a monopoly (where the merger does not enable economies of scale or other efficiencies to be realized) are examples of such methods. (Even in these cases, there will be some socially valuable by-products [e.g., information] if, for example, the cartel agreement fails to limit nonprice competition.) At the opposite extreme, obtaining a monopoly by cutting costs or prices or by innovation will normally yield social benefits greater than the expenditures on monopolizing.

Several more preliminary points should be noted briefly.

1. Legal and illegal monopolies must be distinguished. The threat of punishment can be used to increase the expected costs of monopolizing and thereby reduce the amount of resources invested in the activity. To the extent that enforcers' resources are merely substituted for monopolizers', there will be no social savings (see Becker 1971, p. 101); but the literature on punishment (e.g., Becker 1968) suggests that activities such as monopolizing can be deterred at low social cost by combining heavy monetary penalties (i.e., transfer payments) with modest resources devoted to apprehending and convicting offenders.[5] Hence, under an optimum system of penalties, the social costs of *illegal* monopolies might be quite low.

2. As an extension of the last point, note that the observed monopoly profits in an industry may actually underestimate the social costs of monopoly in that industry. Considerable resources may have been

---

[5] This could, to be sure, merely shift the problem to a new level: the opportunity to obtain substantial rents from apprehending and convicting monopolists will induce enforcers to pour resources into enforcement activities. This problem is analyzed in Landes and Posner (1975).

expended by consumers or enforcers to reduce those profits. Monopoly profits in an industry could be zero, yet the social costs of monopoly in that industry very high, if enforcement of antimonopoly measures were both expensive and effective.

3. Given uncertainty, the expected monopoly profits of any firm seeking a monopoly may be much smaller than the actual monopoly profits, and so will its expenditures. If 10 firms are vying for a monopoly having a present value of $1 million, and each of them has an equal chance of obtaining it and is risk neutral, each will spend $100,000 (assuming constant costs) on trying to obtain the monopoly. Only one will succeed, and *his* costs will be much smaller than the monopoly profits, but the total costs of obtaining the monopoly—counting losers' expenditures as well as winners'—will be the same as under certainty. If the market for monopoly is in fact characterized by a high degree of uncertainty, this would explain why the costs of obtaining monopoly have largely eluded detection. Most of the costs are incurred in unsuccessful efforts to obtain a monopoly—the lobbying campaign that fails, the unsuccessful attempt to obtain a bank charter or form a cartel.

4. It might seem that where monopoly is obtained by bribery of government officials, the additional loss of monopoly with which this paper is concerned would be eliminated, since a bribe is a pure transfer. In fact, however, bribery merely shifts the monopoly profits from the monopolist to the officials receiving the bribe and draws real resources into the activity of becoming an official who is in a position to receive these bribes (Krueger 1974, pp. 292–93).

B. The Model

Given the assumptions explained above, the total social costs of monopoly prices in figure 1 are simply $D + L$, and since $D \simeq \frac{1}{2}\Delta P\Delta Q$ and $L = \Delta P(Q_c - \Delta Q)$, the relative sizes of D and L are given by

$$\frac{D}{L} \simeq \frac{\Delta Q}{2(Q_c - \Delta Q)} . \tag{1}$$

This ratio can also be expressed in terms of the elasticity of demand for the product in question at the competitive price and the percentage increase in price brought about by monopolization (p):

$$\frac{D}{L} \simeq \frac{p}{2(1/\varepsilon - p)} . \tag{2}$$

The partial derivatives are

$$\frac{\partial(D/L)}{\partial \varepsilon} \simeq \frac{2p}{(2 - 2p\varepsilon)^2} > 0;$$

$$\frac{\partial(D/L)}{\partial p} \simeq \frac{2\varepsilon}{(2 - 2p\varepsilon)^2} > 0. \tag{3}$$

In words, the ratio of D to L is smaller, the less elastic the demand for the industry's product at the competitive price and the smaller the percentage price increase over the competitive level. At moderate elasticities and percentage price increases, D is only a small fraction of L (and hence of the total costs of monopoly). For example, at an elasticity of one[6] and a price increase over the competitive level of 10 percent, D is only 5.6 percent of L.

Observe that the model does *not* assume that the actual supracompetitive price being charged (P_m in fig. 1) is the optimum monopoly price for the industry (otherwise the supracompetitive price increase would not be determined independently of the elasticity of demand, as in [2]). The rationale of this procedure is that perfect monopoly is presumably rare; it will, however, be considered as a special case later.

Using R_c to denote total sales revenues at the competitive price, C, the total social costs of monopoly, is approximated by

$$D + L = pR_c - \tfrac{1}{2}\Delta P\Delta Q \tag{4a}$$

$$= R_c(p - \tfrac{1}{2}\varepsilon p^2). \tag{4b}$$

The partial derivatives of C are (approximately)

$$\frac{\partial C}{\partial R_c} = p - \tfrac{1}{2}\varepsilon p^2 > 0 \text{ iff } \varepsilon p < 2;$$

$$\frac{\partial C}{\partial p} = R_c(1 - \varepsilon p) > 0 \text{ iff } \varepsilon p < 1; \tag{5}$$

$$\frac{\partial C}{\partial \varepsilon} = -\tfrac{1}{2}p^2R_c < 0.$$

In words, the social costs of monopoly will usually—not always—be higher, the larger the industry's sales revenues at the competitive price and output and the greater the percentage price increase over the competitive level. And they will always be higher, the less elastic the demand for the product at the competitive price—the costs of monopoly being greatest when demand is totally inelastic at the competitive price.

Formulas (2) and (4b) are accurate only for small changes in the price level. Yet monopolization might result in large price increases. Hence (1) and (4a) remain useful. For purposes of empirical estimation, it is helpful to derive two additional formulas: one for the case where data on the deadweight loss, the elasticity of demand, and the monopoly price increase are available and the elasticity of demand is assumed to be constant, and the other for the case where data on the monopoly price increase, the monopoly output, and the elasticity of demand at the

---

[6] Throughout this paper, ΔQ is treated as a positive number. Therefore, $\varepsilon \, [= (\Delta Q/\Delta P)/(Q/P)]$ is also positive.

monopoly price are available and the demand curve is assumed to be linear.

1. For the case of constant elasticity, let $k \equiv P_c/P_m$ and $R_m \equiv$ total sales revenue at the monopoly price and output. Then, since $Q_c = \alpha P_c^{-\varepsilon}$ and $Q_m = \alpha P_m^{-\varepsilon}$, and therefore $\Delta Q = \alpha(P_c^{-\varepsilon} - P_m^{-\varepsilon})$, D/L and C are approximately

$$\frac{D}{L} = \frac{(kP_m)^{-\varepsilon} - P_m^{-\varepsilon}}{2P_m^{-\varepsilon}} = \frac{k^{-\varepsilon} - 1}{2}; \tag{6}$$

$$C = D + L = D\left(1 + \frac{2}{k^{-\varepsilon} - 1}\right) = R_m(1 - k)\left(\frac{k^{-\varepsilon} + 1}{2}\right). \tag{7}$$

The partial derivatives of D/L are (approximately)

$$\frac{\partial(D/L)}{\partial k} = \frac{-\varepsilon}{2k^{\varepsilon+1}} < 0;$$

$$\frac{\partial(D/L)}{\partial \varepsilon} = \frac{-k^{-\varepsilon} \ln k}{2} > 0. \tag{8}$$

[7] For the special case where the firm is able to charge the optimum monopoly price for the industry, so that $P_c = MC = P_m(1 - 1/\varepsilon)$, equation (6) becomes

$$\frac{D}{L} = \frac{(1 - 1/\varepsilon)^{-\varepsilon} - 1}{2} \tag{6'}$$

and equation (7) becomes

$$C = \frac{R_m[(1 - 1/\varepsilon)^{-\varepsilon} + 1]}{2\varepsilon}. \tag{7'}$$

Since a demand curve of constant elasticity is nonlinear, the question arises whether the linear approximation of the deadweight loss used in equations (6) and (7) (and [6'] and [7']) introduces a source of serious inaccuracy. It appears not to, at least in the simple case where $\varepsilon = 1$ and therefore

$$\frac{D}{L} = \frac{\int_{Q_m}^{Q_c} P \, dQ - P_c \, \Delta Q}{(P_m - P_c)Q_m} = \frac{\ln(1/k) - 1 + k}{1 - k}. \tag{6''}$$

Table 1, which compares D/L as calculated from equation (6) (with $\varepsilon = 1$) and from equation (6''), shows that the linear approximation overestimates the deadweight loss, but not seriously.

TABLE 1

P*	D/L†	
(%)	Eq. (6)	Eq. (6'')
5	.025	.025
10	.050	.049
15	.075	.072
20	.100	.094
50	.250	.216

* Monopoly price increase.
† Ratio of deadweight to additional loss.

In words, the ratio of the deadweight loss of monopoly to the additional loss is smaller, the smaller the monopoly price increase (k, the ratio of the competitive to the monopoly price, is larger, the smaller the relative price increase) and greater, the more elastic the demand.

2. For the case where the elasticity of demand at the monopoly price (as well as the monopoly price increase and the quantity sold at the monopoly price) is known or can be computed, and the demand curve can be approximated by a straight line, we begin by determining the slope of the demand curve at the monopoly price:

$$\frac{\Delta Q}{\Delta P} = \frac{\varepsilon Q_m}{P_m}. \tag{9}$$

Since the slope of a linear demand curve is constant, this equation can be used to find ΔQ and hence C and D/L:

$$C = R_m(1 - k)[1 + \tfrac{1}{2}\varepsilon(1 - k)]; \tag{10}$$

$$\frac{D}{L} = \frac{\varepsilon(1 - k)}{2}.^8 \tag{11}$$

The estimates produced by our two formulas for the ratio of the deadweight to the additional loss from monopoly—equations (6) and (11)—turn out not to be very different for price increases of less than 25 percent, and even for much larger price increases if the elasticity of demand is no greater than one (see fig. 3).

II. Empirical Estimates

The formulas developed in the preceding part can be used to derive, from the estimates of the deadweight loss of monopoly made by Arnold Harberger and others, an estimate of the total social cost of monopoly. Harberger (1954), estimating an average monopoly price increase of about 6 percent and assuming that the elasticity of demand was constant and equal to unity, found the deadweight loss from monopoly in the manufacturing sector to be equal to (at most) 0.1 percent of GNP. Harberger's (implicit) k is 0.9434, and from equation (6) the ratio of D to L in Harberger's analysis is, therefore, 0.03. Hence, if D is 0.1

---

[8] In the special case where the firm is able to charge the optimum monopoly price,

$$C = \frac{R_m}{2\varepsilon}; \tag{10'}$$

$$\frac{D}{L} = \frac{1}{2}. \tag{11'}$$

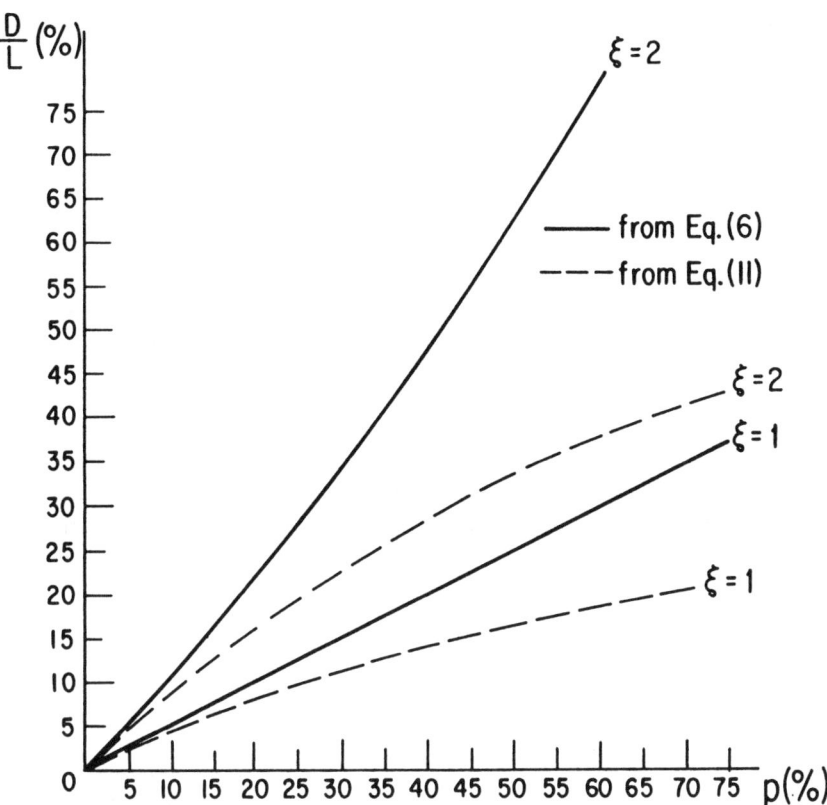

Fig. 3.—Ratio of deadweight to additional loss of monopoly, for different price increases and demand elasticities.

percent of GNP, L is about 3.3 percent and C about 3.4 percent of GNP. Schwartzman (1960) used similar methods and found D equal to about 0.1 percent of GNP too. But he assumed a price increase of 8.3 percent and an elasticity of demand of 1.5. Plugging these values into equation (6) yields $D/L = 0.06$. Hence, if $D = 0.1$ percent of GNP, $L = 1.7$ percent and $C = 1.8$ percent.

Neither estimate can be given much credence, however, because of the method that both Harberger and Schwartzman employed to determine the monopoly price increase. Persistently above average rates of return were used both (1) to identify the monopolized industries and (2) to calculate the monopoly price increase. If the approach of this paper is correct, such a procedure is improper, especially the second step. Because of uncertainty, many monopolists may enjoy supernormal rates of return ex post, but those rates will understate the percentage of the monopolist's

revenues that is attributable to monopoly pricing, unless no cost whatever
was incurred in obtaining (or maintaining) the monopoly.[9]

A better method of calculating the social costs of monopoly (deadweight
plus additional loss) is to obtain from industry studies estimates of the
monopoly price increase and of the elasticity of demand at the relevant
points along the demand curve. An independent estimate of the elasticity
of demand would be unnecessary if we could assume that, after the price
increase, the price charged was the optimum monopoly price; and where
an independent estimate of ε is available, it can serve as a check on that
assumption. To illustrate, there have been a number of estimates of the
percentage by which CAB regulation has increased the price of airline
travel. The simple average of these estimates is .66 (computed from
Caves 1962, p. 372; Jordan 1970, pp. 110–11, 124–25; and Yale Law
Journal 1965, pp. 1435–36). If a 66 percent price increase over competitive
levels is assumed to raise the price of air travel to the optimum monopoly
level, then the elasticity of demand at the monopoly price can be calculated, from the formula which equates marginal cost to marginal
revenue,[10] to be 2.5 at the monopoly price. An independent estimate of
the long-run elasticity of demand for air travel made by Houthakker and
Taylor (1966, p. 124) is 2.36,[11] which is virtually identical to my
calculation.

If we assume a constant elasticity of 2.5 and solve for D/L using equation
(6'), $D = 1.29L$, and (from equation [7']) it is readily calculable that
the total social cost of the airline monopoly is equal to 92 percent of the
total revenue of the industry at the monopoly price. However, the
assumption of a linear demand curve seems more plausible than
the assumption of constant elasticity, especially for large relative price
increases, which one expects to find associated with a rising elasticity of
demand as substitutes become increasingly attractive. If, therefore,
equations (10') and (11') are used instead of (6') and (7'), $D = 0.5L$ and
$C = 0.2R_m$—still a very large social loss from the regulation-induced
airline monopoly. (These estimates ignore, however, the partially offsetting benefits of excessive nonprice competition in the airline industry.)

---

[9] This point is distinct from the (also valid) objections to Harberger's procedure
raised by Stigler (1956)—that monopoly profits are often capitalized into the valuation of
a firm's assets and that some of the profits may be received as rents by suppliers of the
firm's inputs.

[10] This was essentially the procedure used by Kamerschen (1966) to estimate the
deadweight loss from monopoly in manufacturing. He has been criticized, rightly, for
assuming that firms in concentrated industries subject to the Sherman Act's prohibition
of collusive pricing are typically able to charge the profit-maximizing monopoly price.
The assumption is more plausible with regard to a regulated industry in which entry and
price competition are limited by the regulatory agency and the Sherman Act is inapplicable.

[11] This is presumably the elasticity of demand at the regulated price, since only a small
part of the airline industry is exempt from CAB regulation.

TABLE 2

SOCIAL COSTS OF REGULATION

INDUSTRY	REGULATORY PRICE INCREASE (%)	ELASTICITY		COSTS (AS % OF INDUSTRY'S SALES)	
		ε_1	ε_2	C_1*	C_2*
Physicians' services	.40†	3.500	0.575‡	.14	.31
Eyeglasses........	.34§	0.394	0.450‖	.13	.24
Milk	.11#	10.000	0.339**	.05	.10
Motor carriers ...	.62††	2.630	1.140‡‡	.19	.30
Oil	.65§§	2.500	0.900§§	.20	.32
Airlines	.66	2.500	2.360	.20	.19

* C_1 based on ε_1; C_2 based on ε_2.
† Kessel 1972, p. 119.
‡ Houthakker and Taylor 1966, p. 99 (short run).
§ Benham 1973, p. 19.
‖ Benham 1973, p. 30 (simple average).
Kessel 1967, p. 73.
** Houthakker 1965, p. 286. This estimate is for all food; an estimate limited to dairy products in the Netherlands was not significantly different (Ayaynian 1969).
†† Average estimates in Department of Agriculture studies cited in Moore (1972) and Farmer (1964).
‡‡ Simple averages of various estimates for transportation in Scandinavia (see Frisch 1959 and Parks 1969, p. 649).
§§ Cabinet Task Force on Oil Import Control 1970.

All of the previous studies of the cost of monopoly to the economy have been based on supposed monopoly pricing in manufacturing alone. Yet the ability of firms to maintain supracompetitive prices must be greater in industries in which a regulatory agency limits entry and price competition than in the manufacturing sector, where express collusion is forbidden by the Sherman Act. Table 2 collects estimates of the regulation-induced price increase and the elasticity of demand at the current price for several industries for which these data are available. Two estimates of elasticity are given: one (ε_1) is derived from the price-increase data, on the assumption that the industry is charging the optimum monopoly price; the other (ε_2) is an independent estimate of elasticity. The estimates of the total social costs of the regulation in question $(C_1$, where ε_1 is the estimate of elasticity used, and C_2, where ε_2 is used) are based on the assumption that the industry's demand curve is linear in the relevant region and are expressed as a percentage of the total revenues of the industry.

These estimates are, of course, very crude, but they do suggest that the total costs of regulation may be extremely high, given that about 17 percent of GNP originates in industries—such as agriculture, transportation, communications, power, banking, insurance, and medical services—that contain the sorts of controls over competition that might be expected to lead to supracompetitive prices.[12] Indeed, the costs of

[12] Of course, not all of the markets in the regulated industries are in fact subject to the relevant regulatory controls (almost half of the trucking industry, for example, is exempt from regulation by the Interstate Commerce Commission). On the other hand, tariffs and similar restrictions (e.g., the oil import quota) are excluded from the estimate of the percentage of GNP affected by regulation.

regulation probably exceed the costs of private monopoly. To be sure, a higher percentage of GNP—30 percent—originates in manufacturing and mining, a highly concentrated sector of the economy, and the conventional wisdom associates high concentration with supracompetitive pricing. But only about one-fifth of the output of this sector comes from industries in which four firms account for 60 percent or more of sales, and there is little theoretical basis for believing that the sellers in less concentrated industries could collude effectively without engaging in behavior prohibited by the Sherman Act.[13] Not all violations of the Sherman Act are detected and punished, but the secret conspiracies that escape detection are probably not very effective—even the great electrical conspiracy, an elaborate and relatively durable conspiracy among a very small group of firms, apparently succeeded in raising prices by less than 10 percent on average (see U.S. Congress 1965, p. 39). It would be surprising if the price level of the manufacturing and mining sector as a whole were more than about 2 percent above the competitive level.[14] Assume that it is 2 percent, and that the average elasticity of demand for the products of this sector, at current prices, is 1.1607.[15] Then the total social costs of monopoly in this sector are 1.9 percent of the total revenues generated in the sector (from equation [10]). This amounts to a total dollar loss substantially smaller than that generated in the regulated sector.[16] And this is true even if we assume that prices in the manufacturing and mining sector are, on average, 4 percent above the competitive level, rather than 2 percent.[17]

This comparison excludes, of course, both the relative costs of regulation

[13] Thus, Kessel's study of underwriting costs (1971, p. 723) shows that an increase beyond eight in the number of bids does not reduce those costs substantially—and an industry where the four largest firms have less than 60 percent of the market is apt to contain at least eight significant competitors.

[14] If we assume that only in industries where the four-firm concentration ratio exceeds 60 percent is effective, undetected collusion likely, and that collusion allows these industries to maintain prices, on average, 5 percent above the competitive level while in the rest of the manufacturing and mining sector the average price level is only 1 percent above the competitive level, then average prices for the entire sector would be only 1.83 percent above the competitive price level. (Statistics on the distribution of output among industries in different four-firm concentration ratio groups are from the 1963 Census of Manufactures.)

[15] This figure is a simple average of the long-run price elasticities for nine product groups within the manufacturing and mining sector estimated in Houthakker and Taylor (1966, pp. 72, 74, 83, 112–14, 116, 128–31).

[16] The simple average of the social-cost estimates presented in table 2 is 19.8 percent of the total revenues of the regulated industry. Assuming that 50 percent of the output of that sector is produced in markets that are regulated in a manner similar to the industries in table 2 and that the average social cost of regulation in each such market is 19.8 percent of total revenue, the social costs of regulation would be equal to 1.7 percent of GNP, while the social costs of monopoly in manufacturing and mining would be equal to 0.6 percent of GNP.

[17] In which event the social costs of monopoly in that sector would be about 1.2 percent of GNP.

TABLE 3

SOCIAL COSTS OF CARTELIZATION

INDUSTRY	CARTEL PRICE INCREASE (%)	ELASTICITY		COSTS (AS % OF INDUSTRY'S SALES)	
		ε_1	ε_2	C_1	C_2
Nitrogen	0.75*	2.3256	1.4493†	.21	.30
Sugar	0.30‡	4.3276	0.3390§	.12	.22
Aluminum	1.00‖	2.0000	...	.25	...
Aluminum	0.38#	3.6311	...	.14	...
Rubber	1.00**	2.0000	...	.25	...
Electric bulbs	0.37††	3.7023	...	.14	...
Copper	0.31‡‡	4.2499	...	.12	...
Cast-iron pipe	0.39§§	3.5641	...	.14	...

* Stocking and Watkins 1946, p. 163.
† Stocking and Watkins 1946, p. 166.
‡ Stocking and Watkins 1946, p. 46.
§ Houthakker 1965, p. 286; obviously a much too low estimate for one food product sold at a cartel price!
‖ Stocking and Watkins 1946, p. 228.
Stocking and Watkins 1946, p. 251.
** Stocking and Watkins 1946, pp. 64–65.
†† Stocking and Watkins 1946, p. 343.
‡‡ Stocking and Watkins 1948, p. 127.
§§ United States v. Addyston Pipe & Steel Co., 85 F. 271 (6th Cir. 1898).

and of antitrust enforcement and the relative benefits of monopoly in the two sectors.[18] Were these additional factors included, however, it is doubtful that the comparison would become more favorable to the regulated sector. In particular, while there are theoretical reasons for believing that concentration in unregulated markets is associated with economies of scale and other efficiencies (Demsetz 1973), there is no accepted theory or body of evidence that ascribes social benefits to regulation limiting entry and price competition.

The analysis developed here can also be used to estimate the social benefits of the antitrust laws. Table 3, which is constructed on the same basis as table 2, presents estimates of the social costs of several well-organized (mainly international) private cartels.[19]

Presumably, collusive price increases of this magnitude and the attendant very substantial social costs are deterred by current enforcement of the American antitrust laws. A complete cost-benefit analysis of the antitrust laws would, however, also require estimation of (1) the costs of administering those laws[20] and (2) the large social costs imposed by the

[18] To recur to an earlier point, the assumed monopoly price increase in the manufacturing and mining sector may underestimate the social costs of monopoly in that sector. Those costs may be reflected in expenditures by consumers and enforcers in preventing monopoly pricing.

[19] As distinct from the sorts of covert conspiracies that might escape detection under present enforcement of the Sherman Act (see Stigler 1968, pp. 268–70).

[20] A point to be kept in mind is that, while these costs are incurred annually, private—unlike governmentally protected—cartels eventually collapse (although they often re-form later). Hence, table 3 gives an exaggerated picture of the *average* annual costs of cartelization as it would exist in the absence of the Sherman Act.

many perverse applications of antitrust laws that are, perhaps, an inevitable by-product of having such laws.

A very large disclaimer concerning the accuracy of the estimates presented in this part of the paper needs to be entered at this point. Quite apart from any reservations about the realism of the assumptions on which the model used to generate these estimates is based, the crudeness of the data on price increases and elasticities of demand precludes treating the estimates of the costs of the monopoly and regulation as anything more than suggestive. The suggestions are, however, interesting ones: (1) previous studies of the costs of monopoly may have grossly underestimated those costs; and (2) the costs of monopoly are quite probably much greater in the regulated than in the unregulated sector of the economy, despite the greater size of the latter sector.

III. Other Applications

1. In a recent paper Comanor and Smiley (in press) attempt to show that a large part of the inequality in the distribution of wealth in contemporary America is attributable to monopoly. They use studies such as Harberger's (1954) to determine the aggregate wealth transfer from consumers to the owners of monopoly firms and, by a series of additional assumptions concerning the incomes of consumers and shareholders, family size, the savings rate, etc., derive an estimate of the distributive impact of monopoly. Many of the assumptions are questionable, but even if their correctness were conceded the conclusion would be highly doubtful. There is no reason to think that monopoly has a significant distributive effect. Consumers' wealth is not transferred to the shareholders of monopoly firms; it is dissipated in the purchase of inputs into the activity of becoming a monopolist.

2. Oliver Williamson (1968) has argued that the refusal of the courts to recognize a defense of economies of scale in merger cases under the Clayton Act is questionable because, under plausible assumptions concerning the elasticity of demand, only a small reduction in the merging firms' costs is necessary to offset any deadweight loss created by the price increase that the merger enables the firms to make (see fig. 4).

This analysis is incomplete, however. The expected profits of the merger (*ABEF*) will generate an equivalent amount of costs as the firms vie to make such mergers or, after they are made, to engross the profits generated by the higher postmerger price through service competition or whatever. As a first approximation, the total social cost of the merger is *ABEF* + *BCD* and exceeds the cost savings (*GDEF*) made possible by it. The curves could, of course, be drawn in such a way that the merger would generate net cost savings; the point is only that there is no presumption that anticompetitive mergers generate net savings. This consideration, together with the high cost of litigating issues of cost

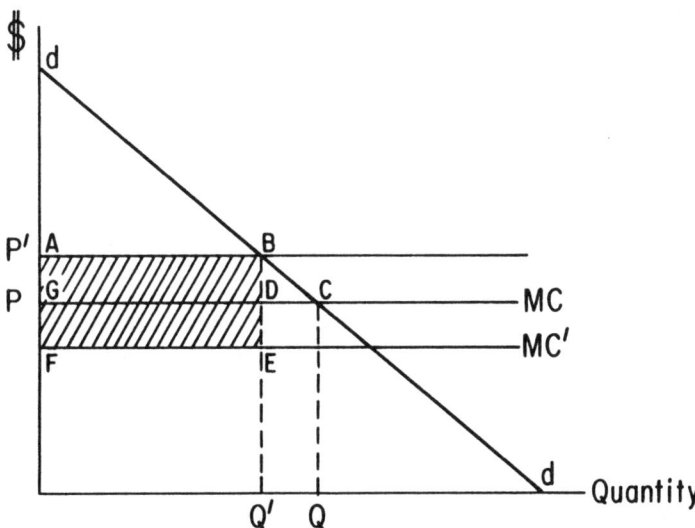

FIG. 4.—The costs of mergers

savings, may provide a justification for refusing to recognize a defense of efficiencies in merger cases where the merger is likely to produce a substantial increase in monopoly power.

3. It has been argued (e.g., Bowman 1973) that the antitrust laws should not concern themselves with practices that are merely methods of price discrimination, since there is no basis for thinking that discrimination increases the deadweight loss of monopoly, and it may reduce it (it will reduce it to zero if discrimination is perfect). The conclusion may be justifiable by reference to the costs of administering antidiscrimination rules, but the basis on which it has been defended by its proponents is incorrect. Even when price discrimination is perfect, so that the dead-weight loss of monopoly is zero, the total social costs of a discriminating monopoly are greater than those of a single-price monopoly.[21] Under perfect price discrimination, C is the entire area between the demand curve and the marginal ($=$ average) cost curve, and it is greater than $D + L$ at any single price (see fig. 1).

4. It is occasionally suggested that the case for antitrust enforcement has been gravely weakened by the theory of the second best. Since the elimination of one monopoly in an economy containing other monopolies (or other sources of divergence between price and marginal cost, such as

[21] I abstract from the costs of administering the price-discrimination scheme; these increase the costs of discriminating monopoly relative to those of nondiscriminating monopoly.

taxation) may reduce the efficiency of resource allocation, antitrust enforcement may increase, rather than reduce, D. The true economic basis for antitrust enforcement, however, is not D but $D + L$, and we have seen that, under plausible assumptions as to the elasticity of demand, D is only a small fraction of $D + L$, at least for moderate increases in price above the competitive level. The social costs measured by L, like the social costs of theft (i.e., the opportunity costs of thieves' and police-men's time and of the labor and capital inputs into locks, burglar tools, etc.), are unaffected by the existence of second-best problems (cf. Markovits 1972).

5. The analysis in this paper suggests a possible explanation for the positive correlation that has been found between concentration and advertising.[22] It may be easier to collude on price than on the amount of advertising. Although there is no great trick to establishing an agreed-upon level of advertising and detecting departures from it, the incentives to violate any such agreement are strong, because the gains from a successful advertising campaign may be difficult to offset immediately and hence offer promise of a more durable advantage than a price cut would. In that event the situation is similar to nonprice competition in the airline industry. If price is fixed by the cartel but the level of advertising is not, or at least not effectively, the monopoly profits generated by the cartel price will be transformed into additional expenditures on advertising. Cartelization is presumably more common in concentrated industries.

This analysis suggests, incidentally, a possible difficulty in distinguishing empirically between Telser's theory of resale price maintenance (1960) and an alternative explanation which stresses cartelization by dealers. In Telser's theory, manufacturers impose resale price maintenance in order to induce dealers to provide services in connection with the resale of the manufacturer's brand. If Telser's theory is correct, we would expect to find resale price maintenance imposed where the efficient merchandising of a product involved the provision of extensive point-of-sale services. However, a dealer's cartel might also result in the dealers' competing away the cartel profits through service competition.

6. Discussions of the "social responsibility" of large corporations generally assume that a firm (or group of firms) having some monopoly power could, without courting bankruptcy, decide to incur somewhat higher costs in order to discharge its social responsibilities. Thus, in figure 1, even if MC rose to P_m the firm would still be covering its costs. However, if the analysis in this paper is correct and the expected profits of monopolizing are zero, it follows that the entire area L in figure 1 will represent fixed costs to the firm unless the monopoly was obtained under conditions

---

[22] The finding has been questioned, however (e.g., Ekelund and Gramm 1970).

of uncertainty. In the latter case the fixed costs will be somewhat lower, but in the former *any* increase in MC will jeopardize the firm's solvency.

7. Assuming that the decision to create or tolerate a monopoly has been made, it may still be possible to prevent the expected monopoly profits from being completely transformed into social costs. The basic technique is to reduce the elasticity of supply of the inputs into monopolizing. (Thus, the present discussion modifies my original assumption of perfect supply elasticity.) Consider, for example, a market that is a natural monopoly. If the monopolist is permitted to charge a monopoly price—and suppose that he is—he may set a price that exceeds the average costs of new entrants, albeit those costs are higher than his; and new entry will presumably occur. The resulting increase in the average costs of serving the market is an example of the social costs of monopoly (independent of the welfare triangle). These costs can be reduced, however, by a rule limiting entry. Such a rule will reduce the responsiveness of a key input into monopolizing—capacity to produce the monopolized product—to increases in the expected value of the monopoly. But the rule is not very satisfactory. Prospective entrants will have an incentive to expend resources on persuading the agency to change or waive the rule—and the monopolist to expend them on dissuasion. Moreover, the more efficient the rule is at keeping out new entrants at low cost to the monopolist, the greater will be the expected value of having a natural monopoly—and, hence, the greater will be the resources that firms expend on trying to become the first to occupy a natural-monopoly market.[23]

As another example, consider the recurrent proposal to replace the present method of assigning television licenses (now awarded to the applicant who convinces the Federal Communications Commission in a formal hearing of his superior ability to serve the public interest) by an auction system. This proposal is frequently supported on distributive grounds—why should the licensee, rather than the public, receive the rents generated by the limited allocation of electromagnetic spectrum for broadcasting? But there is also an efficiency justification for the proposal. The auction would substitute a transfer payment for a real cost, the expenditures on the hearing process by competing applicants. To be sure, these expenditures might simply be redirected into rigging the bidding. But this could be discouraged, possibly at low cost, by appropriate legal penalties. The objective would be to increase the expected costs of obtaining the license (other than by an honest bid), which include any expected punishment costs, to the point where the applicants are induced to make the costless transfer rather than to expend real resources on trying to obtain the license outside the auction

---

[23] This is the obverse of the situation discussed in Demsetz (1968), where competition to become a monopolist results in a competitive price level.

process. As mentioned earlier, in an optimum system of penalties the resources expended on enforcement would be slight.

The patent laws embody a somewhat similar economizing technique. In their absence inventors would expend substantial resources on preserving the secrecy of their inventions. Their efforts in this direction would generate indirect as well as direct social costs, by retarding the spread of knowledge. By providing a legal remedy against "stealing" inventions, the patent laws reduce the level of such expenditures in much the same way as the existence of legal penalties for theft reduces the level of resources that people devote to protecting their property from thieves.

An interesting method of reducing the social costs of monopoly is used by labor unions. The existence of a monopoly wage might be expected to induce the expenditure of more and more resources by workers seeking entry into the union, until the expected benefits of union membership were reduced to zero. However, unions traditionally have rationed membership in a way that greatly reduces the marginal benefits of expenditures on obtaining membership, and hence the resources expended in that pursuit, by conditioning membership on a status that is difficult or impossible for the job seeker to buy at any price—such as being white or the son of a union member.[24] In the limit, this method of rationing would reduce the elasticity of the supply of inputs into obtaining union membership, and hence the social costs of labor monopolies (excluding the welfare triangle), to zero, disregarding the costs resulting from the exclusion of possibly better qualified workers who do not meet the membership criterion. Yet even this method may not be ultimately effective in preventing the transformation of monopoly rents into social costs. The more profitable union membership is, the greater are the resources that workers will be willing to invest (e.g., in forgone earnings due to being on strike) in union-organizing activities.

8. One reason why most students of tax policy prefer income to excise taxes is that the misallocative effect of an income tax is believed to be less than that of an excise tax: the cross-elasticity of demand between work and leisure is assumed to be lower than that between a commodity and its substitutes. Even if correct, this does not mean that the total social costs of collecting a given amount of revenue by means of an income tax are lower than those of an excise tax. The amount of the tax transfer represents potential gain to the taxpayer, and he will expend real resources on trying to avoid the tax until, at the margin, cost and gain are equated. A critical question in comparing the costs of income and excise taxation is therefore the shape and location of the supply curves for avoiding income tax liability and excise tax liability, respectively. In the case of a highly progressive income tax system in which

[24] The use of these methods by unions is being increasingly limited by government regulations designed to eliminate racial discrimination.

expenses for the production of income are deductible, the comparison is likely to be unfavorable to income taxation. Were the marginal income tax rate in the highest bracket 90 percent (as it once was in this country), the taxpayer would continue expending resources on tax avoidance until the expected value of a dollar so expended fell below 10 cents. Thus, he might spend as much as 10 times his marginal tax liability in order to reduce that liability to zero. (How much he would actually spend would depend on the location and shape of the supply curve for avoidance and on his resources and attitude toward risk.) This analysis is not conclusive against the income tax. It might be possible to increase the private marginal costs of avoidance by punishment or by disallowing the deduction of expenses on avoidance. The main problem would be to distinguish legitimate from illegitimate avoidance efforts.[25] Still, no general presumption that excise taxation is less costly than income taxation can be derived from an analysis limited to the allocative costs of taxation, corresponding to the deadweight loss of monopoly.

References

Ayaynian, Robert. "A Comparison of Barten's Estimated Demand Elasticities with Those Obtained Using Frisch's Method." *Econometrica* 37 (January 1969): 79–94.

Becker, Gary S. "Crime and Punishment: An Economic Approach." *J.P.E.* 76, no. 2 (March/April 1968): 169–217.

———. *Economic Theory*. New York: Knopf, 1971.

Benham, Lee. "Price Structure and Professional Control of Information." Mimeographed. Univ. Chicago Graduate School Bus. (March 1973).

Bowman, Ward S., Jr. *Patent and Antitrust Law: A Legal and Economic Appraisal.* Chicago: Univ. Chicago Press, 1973.

Cabinet Task Force on Oil Import Control. *The Oil Import Question.* Washington: Government Printing Office, 1970.

Caves, Richard E. *Air Transport and Its Regulators.* Cambridge, Mass.: Harvard Univ. Press, 1962.

Comanor, William S., and Smiley, Robert H. "Monopoly and the Distribution of Wealth." *Q.J.E.* (in press).

Demsetz, Harold. "Why Regulate Utilities?" *J. Law and Econ.* 11 (April 1968): 55–65.

———. "Industry Structure, Market Rivalry, and Public Policy." *J. Law and Econ.* 16 (April 1973): 1–9.

Douglas, George W., and Miller, James C., III. "The CAB's Domestic Passenger Fare Investigation." *Bell J. Econ. and Management Sci.* 5 (Spring 1974): 204–22.

Ekelund, Robert B., Jr., and Gramm, William P. "Advertising and Concentration: Some New Evidence." *Antitrust Bull.* 15 (Summer 1970): 243–49.

Farmer, Richard N. "The Case for Unregulated Truck Transportation." *J. Farm Econ.* 46 (May 1964): 398–409.

---

[25] It would make no sense to punish everyone who believed that some provision of the Internal Revenue Code was not intended to apply to his activity.

Frisch, Ragnar. "A Complete Scheme for Computing All Direct Costs and Cross Demand Elasticities in a Market with Many Sectors." *Econometrica* 27 (April 1959): 177–96.

Harberger, Arnold C. "Monopoly and Resource Allocation." *A.E.R.* 44 (May 1954): 77–87.

Houthakker, H. S. "New Evidence on Demand Elasticities." *Econometrica* 33 (April 1965): 277–88.

Houthakker, H. S., and Taylor, Lester D. *Consumer Demand in the United States, 1929–1970.* Cambridge, Mass.: Harvard Univ. Press, 1966.

Jordan, William A. *Airline Regulation in America.* Baltimore: Johns Hopkins Univ. Press, 1970.

Kamerschen, David. "Estimation of the Welfare Losses from Monopoly in the American Economy." *Western Econ. J.* 4 (Summer 1966): 221–36.

Kessel, Reuben A. "Economic Effects of Federal Regulation of Milk Markets." *J. Law and Econ.* 10 (October 1967): 51–78.

———. "A Study of the Effects of Competition in the Tax-exempt Bond Market." *J.P.E.* 79, no. 4 (July/August 1971): 706–38.

———. "Higher Education and the Nation's Health: A Review of the Carnegie Commission Report on Medical Education." *J. Law and Econ.* 15 (April 1972): 115–27.

Krueger, Anne O. "The Political Economy of the Rent-seeking Society." *A.E.R.* 64 (June 1974): 291–303.

Landes, William M., and Posner, Richard A. "The Private Enforcement of Law." *J. Legal Studies* 5 (January 1975): 1–46.

Markovits, Richard S. "Fixed Input (Investment) Competition and the Variability of Fixed Inputs (Investment): Their Nature, Determinants, and Significance." *Stanford Law Rev.* 24 (February 1972): 507–30.

Moore, Thomas Gale. *Freight Transportation Regulation.* Washington: American Enterprise Inst., 1972.

Parks, Richard W. "Systems of Demand Equations: An Empirical Comparison of Alternative Functional Forms." *Econometrica* 37 (October 1969): 629–50.

Plant, Arnold. "The Economic Theory Concerning Patents." *Economica* 1 (n.s.) (February 1934): 30–51.

Schwartzman, David. "The Burden of Monopoly." *J.P.E.* 68, no. 6 (November/December 1960): 627–30.

Stigler, George J. "The Statistics of Monopoly and Mergers." *J.P.E.* 64, no. 1 (January/February 1956): 33–40.

———. *The Organization of Industry.* Homewood, Ill.: Irwin, 1968.

Stocking, George W., and Watkins, Myron W. *Cartels in Action.* New York: Twentieth Century Fund, 1946.

———. *Cartels or Competition?* New York: Twentieth Century Fund, 1948.

Telser, Lester. "Why Should Manufacturers Want Fair Trade?" *J. Law and Econ.* 3 (October 1960): 86–105.

Tullock, Gordon. "The Welfare Costs of Tariffs, Monopolies, and Theft." *Western Econ. J.* 5 (June 1967): 224–32.

U.S. Congress, Joint Committee on Internal Revenue Taxation. *Staff Study of Income Tax Treatment of Treble Damage Payments under the Antitrust Laws.* Washington: Government Printing Office, 1965.

Williamson, Oliver E. "Economics as an Antitrust Defense: The Welfare Tradeoffs." *A.E.R.* 58 (March 1968): 18–36.

Yale Law Journal. "Is Regulation Necessary? California Air Transportation and National Regulatory Policy." *Yale Law J.* 74 (July 1965): 1416–47.

[16]

A STATISTICAL STUDY OF
ANTITRUST ENFORCEMENT*

RICHARD A. POSNER
University of Chicago Law School

T HIS paper reports the results of a statistical study of antitrust enforcement by the Department of Justice, the Federal Trade Commission, state agencies, and private plaintiffs since the enactment of the Sherman Act in 1890.[1] The purpose of the study was threefold:

1. To show by example that the collection and analysis of statistical data on the operation of legal institutions is a fruitful and practicable undertaking for students of those institutions.

2. To set forth compactly such statistics on antitrust enforcement as could be obtained without elaborate and costly field research or computer operations, and to explore their implications for issues of antitrust policy.

3. To identify gaps and deficiencies in the existing statistical sources and to suggest methods for improving antitrust statistics.

In the following pages we shall be looking at the number of cases filed by the various enforcement institutions, the length of proceedings, the record of success of antitrust claimants, the use of various civil and criminal remedies, the pattern of violations alleged, the industries involved, the possible explanative role of politics, and some steps whereby antitrust statistics could be improved. We shall close with a discussion of the importance of statistical analyses of antitrust enforcement to effective policy planning in the antitrust field.

I. The Number of Cases Filed

Table 1 records the number of cases instituted by the Department of Justice by year (and also by five-year periods) since 1890. The source of

* I should like to express my gratitude to Jewel Klein, who helped prepare the tables on the FTC cases; to David F. Grosse, Richard I. Janvey, and Tefft W. Smith, who helped prepare the tables on the private and state cases; to the Law and Economics Program of the University of Chicago Law School, which provided financial assistance; and to Aaron Director and George J. Stigler, who first suggested the study and have made many helpful suggestions as to its conduct. An earlier uncompleted study covering much of the same ground, by Michael Marks, contributed valuable leads for my own study.

[1] Sherman Antitrust Act, 15 U.S.C. sec's 1-7 (1964).

365

TABLE 1
ANTITRUST CASES INSTITUTED BY THE DEPARTMENT OF JUSTICE

1890	1		1918	10		1945	20
1891	0		1919	3		1946	37
1892	5		1915-1919		43	1947	25
1893	1		1920	8		1948	44
1894	2		1921	20		1949	31
1890-1894		9	1922	17		1945-1949		157
1895	1		1923	8		1950	48
1896	3		1924	13		1951	42
1897	2		1920-1924		66	1952	27
1898	0		1925	12		1953	18
1899	1		1926	9		1954	24
1895-1899		7	1927	13		1950-1954		159
1900	0		1928	17		1955	34
1901	0		1929	8		1956	30
1902	3		1925-1929		59	1957	38
1903	2		1930	7		1958	47
1904	1		1931	3		1959	46
1900-1904		6	1932	5		1955-1959		195
1905	5		1933	9		1960	35
1906	14		1934	6		1961	47
1907	10		1930-1934		30	1962	56
1908	7		1935	4		1963	26
1909	3		1936	5		1964	51
1905-1909		39	1937	7		1960-1964		215
1910	15		1938	10		1965	35
1911	23		1939	31		1966	36
1912	20		1935-1939		57	1967	34
1913	22		1940	65		1968	47
1914	11		1941	71		1969	43
1910-1914		91	1942	46		1965-1969		195
1915	7		1943	22			
1916	2		1944	19		Total		1551
1917	21		1940-1944		223		

Source: Computed from CCH The Federal Antitrust Laws With Summary of Cases Instituted by the United States 1890-1951 (1952); 1952-1956 Supp. (1957). Trade Reg. Rep., 10th ed., Transfer Binder, New U.S. Antitrust Cases—Complaints, Indictments, Developments 1957-1961; 5 Trade Reg. Rep. ¶ 45003-45064 (current). Hereinafter cited Bluebook. I have also included, in this and subsequent tables, one case that was inadvertently omitted from the Bluebook. See Hans Berger Thorelli, The Federal Antitrust Policy—Origination of an American Tradition 429 (1955).

these data, as of most of the data presented in this study, is a series of volumes published by Commerce Clearing House and known popularly as the "Bluebook."[2] The Bluebook contains brief summaries of all Department of Justice antitrust cases in the order of their filing. Although the Bluebook number of the last case filed by the Department in 1969 is 2081, the reader

2 CCH, The Federal Antitrust Laws, With Summary of Cases Instituted by the United States 1890-1951 (1952); 1952-1956 Supp. (1957); Trade Reg. Rep., 10th ed., Transfer Binder, New U.S. Antitrust Cases—Complaints, Indictments, Developments 1957-1961; and 5 Trade Reg. Rep. ¶ 45003-45069 (current). Hereinafter cited as Bluebook.

will note in Table 1 that the sum of cases through 1969 was only 1551. The reason for this discrepancy is that, with trivial exceptions, every antitrust complaint, indictment, and information is assigned a separate Bluebook number when it is filed, with the result that frequently what I consider a single proceeding is counted two or more times.[8]

What explains the variations in the antitrust activity, measured by number of cases brought, of the Department of Justice? A plausible hypothesis is that it is changes in the level of overall economic activity. Both the incidence of antitrust violations and the resources available to combat them could be expected to increase as the economy expanded, and decrease as the economy contracted. This hypothesis is explored in Figure I. It reveals a fair correlation between changes in antitrust and in overall economic activity until about 1940. Since that time, however, the number of cases brought by the Department has not increased significantly, despite the tremendous growth of the economy. There are a number of possible explanations for this discrepancy. Cases are not fungible; perhaps the Department is bringing fewer, but bigger, cases today. This is unlikely: if the Department were bringing bigger cases one would expect the average duration of its cases to be increasing, but it is not.[4] Another possibility is that the price of resources employed in antitrust enforcement has been rising faster than prices in general, so that the same percentage of Gross National Product devoted to antitrust enforcement buys less of it than formerly. There is some evidence to support this hypothesis. Between 1956 and 1967, the Antitrust Division's appropriations rose from $3.4 million to $7.5 million, an increase of 121 per cent. Yet the personnel of the Antitrust Division rose by only 30 per cent.[5] What these figures do not explain, of course, is why the 30 per cent increase in the Division's personnel led to no significant increase in the number of cases brought.

Table 1 and Figure I can be used to test two other plausible hypotheses concerning changes in the volume of antitrust activity over time. One is that such activity increases in periods of economic contraction—either because contractions are thought to be aggravated by monopoly, or because the pub-

---

[8] Sometimes, an indictment merely supersedes an earlier one that was dismissed because it was technically defective. Often, several indictments are returned that relate to the same transactions and are disposed of in the same proceeding, the only reason for the plural indictments being a slight difference in the product or in the identity of some of the defendants. Often, too, a civil complaint will be filed solely in order to obtain an injunction against defendants in a pending or recently completed criminal proceeding arising from the same transaction. Occasionally a case is brought for contempt of a previous order; I prefer to classify the contempt proceeding as a reopening or continuation of the earlier action rather than as a separate new suit. In all of these cases, I have counted one proceeding where the Bluebook counts several.

[4] See Table 7, *infra*.

[5] Computed from 1964 Att'y Gen. Ann. Rep. 116; 1967 Att'y Gen. Ann. Rep. 105.

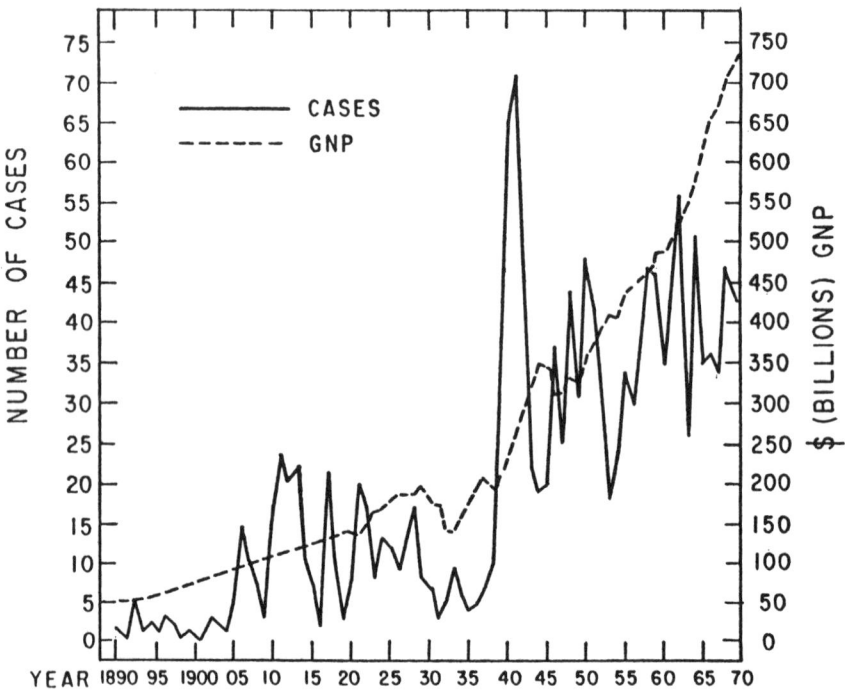

FIGURE I
DEPARTMENT OF JUSTICE ANTITRUST CASES AND THE GROSS
NATIONAL PRODUCT IN CONSTANT—1958—DOLLARS

Sources: Table 1; U.S. Bureau of the Census, Dep't of Commerce, Historical Statistics of the United States, Colonial Times to 1957; U.S. Bureau of the Census, Dep't of Commerce, Statistical Abstract[s] of the United States, 1958-1969.

lic wants a scapegoat. The other is that antitrust activity decreases in periods of war—because economic controls are substituted for the market, or because of the philosophy that underlies wartime economic controls (a distrust of economic freedom in times of national crisis), or because antitrust prosecutions are felt to be divisive or distracting at such times. The statistics support neither hypothesis.

For cases brought by the Federal Trade Commission, there is no exact counterpart to the Bluebook. Commerce Clearing House does publish an "FTC Docket of Complaints,"[6] which, like the Bluebook, contains brief summaries of each case in the order brought. But the summaries contain the barest possible description of the violation alleged. And restraint-of-trade

---

[6] 3 Trade Reg. Rep. 24051, hereinafter cited as FTC Docket of Complaints. In addition, all FTC complaints are eventually published in Federal Trade Commission Decisions, the official report of the Commission's adjudicative actions.

cases are not separated from the false-advertising and mislabeling cases that constitute the major part of the Commission's docket. It is possible, however, to make the separation; and Table 2 lists by year and by five-year

TABLE 2
FTC RESTRAINT-OF-TRADE CASES*

Year Initiated	Number	Year Initiated	Number	Year Initiated	Number
1915	0	1935	30	1955	29
1916	1	1936	33	1956	22
1917	20	1937	18	1957	16
1918	64	1938	28	1958	13
1919	121	1939	31	1959	12
1915-1919	206	1935-1939	140	1955-1959	92
1920	18	1940	33	1960	26
1921	26	1941	32	1961	7
1922	32	1942	16	1962	15
1923	50	1943	14	1963	9
1924	51	1944	8	1964	12
1920-1924	177	1940-1944	103	1960-1964	69
1925	21	1945	6	1965	18
1926	4	1946	9	1966	19
1927	8	1947	11	1967	9
1928	10	1948	11	1968	15
1929	17	1949	10	1969	15
1925-1929	60	1945-1949	47	1965-1969	76
1930	12	1950	5		
1931	4	1951	18	Total	1,061
1932	3	1952	16		
1933	4	1953	7		
1934	14	1954	11		
1930-1934	37	1950-1954	57		

Source: Computed from FTC Docket of Complaints and F.T.C. Decisions. [See text].
* Excluding Robinson-Patman cases that do not allege predatory pricing.

periods the restraint-of-trade cases brought by the Commission since its establishment in 1915. I have excluded not only deceptive-practice cases, but also those cases involving in essence a private business tort (such as commercial bribery), and all Robinson-Patman Act[7] cases other than those charging predatory (or in the jargon of antitrust lawyers, "primary line") price discrimination. This last, and perhaps most questionable, exclusion is based on the view that other practices forbidden by the Robinson-Patman Act lack an arguable tendency to impair competition—the Act being in reality a price-control rather than an antitrust statute—and on a desire to facilitate comparison with the Department of Justice. The Department has brought virtually no cases under the Robinson-Patman Act, although it

[7] Robinson-Patman Act, amending 15 U.S.C. sec. 13 (1964). Hereinafter cited as Robinson-Patman Act.

has occasionally charged predatory price discrimination under the Sherman Act.

One result of this procedure is to undermine the recent assertion "that available measurements of all FTC activities, formal and informal, show a consistent and serious decline between 1961-1963 and 1969 (except in textiles and furs)."[8] Had the study separated the Commission's restraint-of-trade from its Robinson-Patman Act cases, it would have found an increase rather than a decrease in restraint-of-trade cases filed (see Table 2).

The most striking result in Table 2 is that the number of restraint-of-trade cases (as I have defined them) brought by the FTC in each period has shown no tendency to increase over time. Indeed, it brought more cases between 1916 and 1939 than it has in the 31 years since. Three reasons may be conjectured. The first is that the enactment of the Robinson-Patman Act in 1936, coupled with the Department's lack of interest in enforcing it, deflected the Commission's attention from the restraint-of-trade field.[9] The second is that the Commission has shifted resources from adjudication to nonadjudicative enforcement methods such as Trade Practice Conferences and advisory opinions. The third, and probably most important, is that the screening of complaints was extremely casual in the early periods, as indicated by the very high percentage of dismissals,[10] and that the Commission's adjudicative procedures in general were much more casual and summary than in later periods.[11] In these circumstances, it was possible to produce many more cases with the same expenditure of resources. Withal, there is plainly no reason for supposing that the Commission's level of antimonopoly activity has increased over the years; and this further undermines the hypothesis that antitrust activity is determined by overall economic activity.

Table 3 records the number of private antitrust cases brought since the enactment of the Sherman Act. The available data with respect to the private cases are very poor. There is no record of the private cases filed before

[8] ABA Comm'n to Study the Federal Trade Comm'n, Report 26 (1969). See also *id.* at 1.

[9] The number of Robinson-Patman cases, not included in Table 2, brought by the Commission since the enactment of the Act in 1936 is as follows:

1936-1939	75
1940-1944	106
1945-1949	94
1950-1954	66
1955-1959	227
1960-1964	545
1965-1969	102
Total	1,215

Source: Computed from FTC Docket of Complaints.

[10] See Table 12, *infra.*

[11] The Commission's early procedures are described in Gerard C. Henderson, The Federal Trade Commission, 49-104 (1924).

TABLE 3
PRIVATE ANTITRUST CASES

Period	Reported	Initiated (Excluding Electrical-Equipment Cases)	Electrical-Equipment Cases Initiated	Total Initiated
1890-1894	2	5[a]		5[a]
1895-1899	4	11[a]		11[a]
1900-1904	8	21[a]		21[a]
1905-1909	20	53[a]		53[a]
1910-1914	23	64[a]		64[a]
1915-1919	17	45[a]		45[a]
1920-1924	17	45[a]		45[a]
1925-1929	13	35[a]		35[a]
1930-1934	20	53[a]		53[a]
1935-1939	34	91[a]		91[a]
1940-1944	68	270[b]		270[b]
1945-1949	82	399		399
1950-1954	183	1,002		1,002
1955-1959	286	1,144		1,144
1960-1964	1,133	1,435	1,919	3,354
1965-1969	638	2,822	314	3,136
Total	2,548	7,495	2,233	9,728

Source: Hearings on S. 2512, Nolo Contendere and Private Antitrust Enforcement, Before the Subcomm. on Antitrust & Monopoly of the Senate Comm. on the Judiciary, 89th Cong., 2d Sess., at 180-324 (1966); United States Courts, Administrative Office, Ann. Rep.

[a] Estimated; see text.

[b] Excluding 1940, for which I have been unable to obtain information.

1938, except for those in which there is a reported decision, and to compile one would require visits to every district court in the country, none of which, to my knowledge, maintains any subject-matter index of its past cases. Since 1938, the Administrative Office of the United States Courts, in its annual reports, has recorded the number of private antitrust cases filed each year. But that is all the information it has reported about them, except that it did break out the electrical-equipment cases of the early 1960's and report their number separately. Since at least 1964 the Administrative Office has collected more information about the private antitrust cases than it publishes, but the additional information, although doubtless useful for the purposes of judicial administration for which it is collected, is of only limited interest to the student of antitrust policy.[12]

An anonymous public benefactor, however, has catalogued all *reported* private antitrust cases,[13] and by computing the ratio of reported to initiated cases during those years in which the catalog and the records of the Adminis-

[12] But see Table 13, *infra.*

[13] Nolo Contendere and Private Antitrust Enforcement, Hearings on S.2512, Before the Subcomm. on Antitrust & Monopoly of the Senate Comm. on the Judiciary, 89th Cong., 2d Sess., app. I, 180-324 (1966).

trative Office overlap, and applying it to the number of reported cases in the years prior to 1938, one can derive a very crude estimate of the number of cases brought in the earlier years. This is the estimate used in Table 3. In no event would it be proper to add the number of private cases to the number of Department of Justice and Federal Trade Commission cases in an attempt to estimate overall levels of antitrust activity. In the first place, as shown in Table 4, many private suits follow a government judg-

TABLE 4

REPORTED PRIVATE ANTITRUST CASES PRECEDED BY A
DEPARTMENT OF JUSTICE JUDGMENT

Period	Total Cases	Cases Preceded by Justice Department Judgment			
		Nolo	Consent	Other	Total
1890–1900	10			2	2
1901–1905	5				
1906–1910	23			6	6
1911–1915	22		1	5	6
1916–1920	15		2	4	6
1921–1925	15		2	4	6
1926–1930	17			1	1
1931–1935	19		1	2	3
1936–1940	43	1	7	4	12
1941–1945	71	3	1	23	27
1946–1950	99	3	8	34	45
1951–1955	199	1	20	60	81
1956–1960	278	1	19	81	101
1961–1963	880		11	748	759

Source: Computed from Hearings on S. 2512, Nolo Contendere and Private Antitrust Enforcement, Before the Subcomm. on Antitrust & Monopoly of the Senate Comm. on the Judiciary, 89th Cong., 2d Sess., at 180–324 (1966).

ment, and thus arise from the same transaction. Table 4 probably under-states this phenomenon (although one does not know by how much), since it deals only with reported cases: one would expect more controversy, and hence a higher ratio of judicial opinions, among those cases not preceded by a government action, in which action many of the important issues would have been determined. In the second place, a single antitrust violation may give rise to many private suits, for there is usually more than one victim of a monopolistic practice. The 2,233 electrical equipment cases noted in Table 3 arose from a few indictments. One does not know how many separate vio-lations have been attacked by private suits; it may be only a small fraction of the total number of private antitrust cases.[14]

Figure II shows that until the 1945-1949 period fluctuations in the num-ber of private cases paralleled those in Department of Justice cases. This

[14] Furthermore, the catalog included Robinson-Patman cases. See Table 32, *infra*.

FIGURE II
DEPARTMENT OF JUSTICE AND PRIVATE ANTITRUST CASES

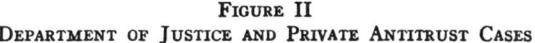

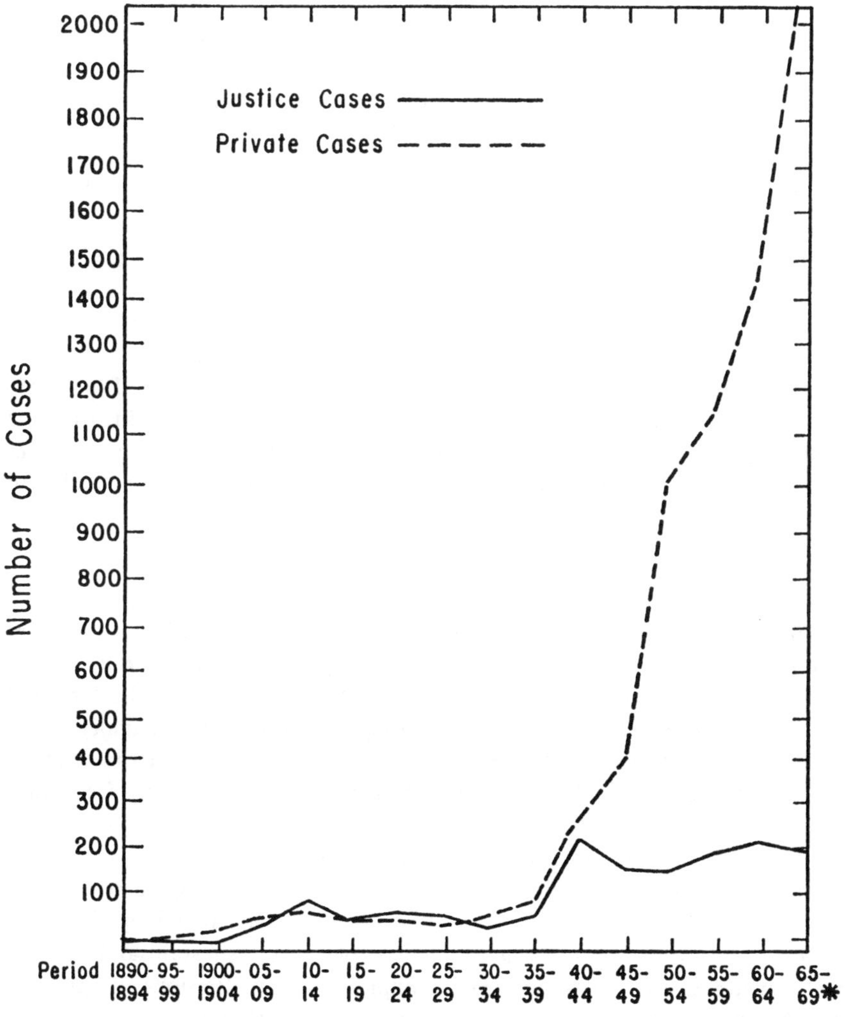

Sources: Tables 1 and 3.
* The total for 1965-1969 is 2822, which is off the graph.

is not surprising in light of the tendency of private plaintiffs to move in the wake of government action. What is surprising is that beginning with that period the patterns diverge: the number of private suits rises in each period and the increase is proportionately greater than in the Department's activity. The reasons are not wholly clear, but it is noteworthy that the divergence coincides roughly with the decision in the *Bigelow* case,[15] which greatly simplified the proof of damages in private antitrust cases. The veritable explosion of private cases in the most recent period may similarly reflect a recent rash of procedural rulings highly favorable to antitrust plaintiffs.[16]

The data with respect to cases brought under state antitrust laws are no better, and in fact worse, than the data regarding private cases under federal antitrust law, although better data with respect to state government cases could perhaps be obtained by inquiry of each state government. The only public source of information is *CCH Trade Cases,* which reports those state cases in which an opinion was issued by the court. A partial search of *Trade Cases* indicates that the pace of state antitrust activity has quickened in recent years, and tells something of the pattern of violations alleged (see Table 33, *infra*). Between 1935 and 1944, only 18 state cases were reported, six of them brought by state agencies; for the shorter period 1965-1969, these numbers are 91 and 25 respectively. The number of cases instituted is doubtless larger, but since we have no information as to the actual number of cases instituted under state law in any year or period, it is impossible to estimate how much larger.

II. The Length of Antitrust Proceedings

The antitrust field is notorious for protracted proceedings, but a recital of examples tells little about the central tendency of the field. A difficulty in measuring the length of the average antitrust case arises from the fact that most antitrust cases are terminated either by a consent judgment (see Table 5), in civil cases, or by a *nolo contendere* (no-contest) plea in criminal cases (see Table 18). Since consent and no-contest cases are frequently concluded without any litigation, the inclusion of all such cases in calculating the length of the average case would significantly understate the length of contested proceedings. But it would be equally misleading to exclude all consent and no-contest cases, since often a case is terminated by the entry of a consent judgment or *nolo contendere* plea after substantial litigation, and sometimes after one—or several—Supreme Court decisions in the case. The Bluebook, however, while it frequently indicates that a case has involved some litigation, almost never indicates when a case in which a consent judgment or no-contest plea was entered involved no litigation.

Table 7 adopts the following compromise. All cases settled within six

---

[15] Bigelow v. RKO Radio Pictures, Inc., 327 U.S. 251 (1946).

[16] See, for example, Perma Life Mufflers, Inc. v. International Parts Corp., 392 U.S. 135 (1968); Hanover Shoe, Inc. v. United Shoe Machinery Corp., 392 U.S. 481 (1968); Leh v. General Petroleum Corp., 382 U.S. 54 (1965).

TABLE 5
CONSENT JUDGMENTS IN CIVIL ANTITRUST CASES BROUGHT BY
THE DEPARTMENT OF JUSTICE

Period in Which Case Was Instituted	All Civil Antitrust Judgments in Favor of Government	Consent Judgments	Percentage of Consent Judgments
1890-1894	4	0	0
1895-1899	4	0	0
1900-1904	4	0	0
1905-1909	10	3	30
1910-1914	40	19	50
1915-1919	17	15	88
1920-1924	27	20	74
1925-1929	39	33	85
1930-1934	15	12	80
1935-1939	26	17	65
1940-1944	50	36	72
1945-1949	81	67	83
1950-1954	70	58	83
1955-1959	90	71	79
1960-1964	115	93	81
1965-1969	48	43	90
Total	640	486	76

Source: Computed from the Bluebook.

months (see Table 6) are excluded from the computation of average lengths unless it appears that there was litigation; otherwise, such cases are assumed, by reason of their short length, to have involved no litigation. All other cases are included in figuring the average. As a result some cases are included that involved no litigation but simply took a long time to settle out of court. But that is not too troublesome. The interval between the filing and conclusion of an antitrust case is itself an important datum. And I have computed averages for two classes of cases actually litigated: cases (including consent and no-contest proceedings) in which it appears from the Bluebook that there was definitely some litigation (see Table 6) and cases decided by the Supreme Court on the merits (thus excluding denials of certiorari and *per curiam* dismissals of appeals).

One implication of Table 7 is that criminal cases are in general disposed of more rapidly than civil; probably the reason is that the government tends to avoid proceeding criminally when substantial legal questions are involved. Those cases in which the Bluebook indicates that there has been actual litigation take longer to dispose of than the larger class consisting of all cases not settled within six months, and litigated *civil* cases, consistent with the previous finding, take longer on average to dispose of than all litigated cases as a group. Not surprisingly, cases decided by the Supreme Court take still longer.

TABLE 6
DEPARTMENT OF JUSTICE CASES
(a) SETTLED WITHIN SIX MONTHS, (b) LITIGATED

Period in Which Case Was Instituted	Total Cases	Number of Cases Settled Within 6 Months	Percentage of Cases Settled Within 6 Months	Number of Litigated Cases	Percentage of Litigated Cases
1890-1894	9	0	0	9	100
1895-1899	7	0	0	7	100
1900-1904	6	0	0	3	50
1905-1909	39	13	13	17	44
1910-1914	91	18	18	52	57
1915-1919	43	35	35	22	51
1920-1924	66	23	23	31	47
1925-1929	59	44	44	15	25
1930-1934	30	20	20	10	33
1935-1939	57	21	21	27	47
1940-1944	223	22	22	101	45
1945-1949	157	12	12	54	34
1950-1954	159	11	11	60	38
1955-1959	195	26	26	76	39
1960-1964	215	16	16	94	44
1965-1967	105	23	23	27	26

Source: Computed from the Bluebook.

What is interesting to note is that there has been no tendency over the years for the length of the average antitrust case to increase. If there is a general problem of mounting delays in the federal courts, it has not yet infected the Department of Justice antitrust cases. Furthermore, despite the fearsome reputation of antitrust for unwieldy and protracted litigation, highly protracted proceedings—which I define arbitrarily as those that require more than 6 years to complete—are, as shown in Table 8, decidedly the exception, even in the class—litigated civil cases—where they occur most frequently. Highly protracted proceedings are a modest fraction of all litigated civil antitrust cases and a small fraction of all civil antitrust cases. Nonetheless, it is certainly true that antitrust cases on average take substantially longer to dispose of than the average case brought by the government. As of June 30, 1968, of 566 cases brought by the United States in a federal court that had been pending for more than three years, 25, or 4.4 per cent, were antitrust cases,[17] even though less than one-half of one per cent of all U.S. government cases instituted each year are antitrust cases.[18]

Although Table 7 provides, I believe, a tolerably accurate picture of the length of the average antitrust *proceeding*, it understates the length of time between the filing of the complaint or indictment and actual application of

[17] 1968 Administrative Office of the United States Courts Ann. Rep. 116.

[18] See, *id.* at tab. C2, 194-95; 1965 *id.* at tab. C2, 178-79; 1964 *id.* at tab. C2, 218; 1962 *id.* at tab. C2, 196.

TABLE 7
LENGTH OF DEPARTMENT OF JUSTICE ANTITRUST CASES (in Months)[a]

Period in Which Cases Were Initiated	Criminal	Civil	All Cases	Litigated Civil Cases	All Litigated Cases	Supreme Court Cases
1890-1894	24	36	29	36	46	50
1895-1899	27	29	29	30	39	31
1900-1904	—	31	31	29	29	29
1905-1909	31	66	42	81	53	85
1910-1914	23	58	44	60	45	62
1915-1919	37	52	40	59	43	80
1920-1924	30	42	36	50	44	63
1925-1929	32	31	32	39	37	45
1930-1934	51	40	45	42	54	42
1935-1939	26	62	43	83	56	71
1940-1944	32	57	38	65	42	49
1945-1949	34	46	42	56	53	62
1950-1954	26	50	40	65	53	67
1955-1959	23	44	33	59	45	70
1960-1964[b]	31	41	38	47	42	57

Source: Computed from the Bluebook.
[a] Excluding cases settled within six months after being filed.
[b] The figures in this row contain a downward bias, since many cases brought in that period have not been terminated.

the penalty or effectuation of the civil relief. I measure the duration of a proceeding by the interval between the filing of the complaint and the entry of the last judicial order (later orders reopening the case for modification of the decree are not treated as extending the length of the case), except in a few cases where the Bluebook indicates when the relief decreed was actually carried out. The distinction will become important when we discuss divestiture decrees.

The duration of FTC restraint-of-trade proceedings is summarized in Tables 9 and 10.[19] In general, the results are similar to those obtained for Department of Justice antitrust cases and summarized in Tables 7 and 8. The use of administrative procedures to enforce the antitrust laws has not contributed to expedition—rather the contrary. Between 1930 and 1964, highly protracted cases (more than 72 months) comprised 11 per cent of the Commission's total restraint-of-trade cases, but only 10 per cent of the Department's civil cases (the figure would be even lower if criminal cases were involved), although the FTC brought many fewer monopolization cases than the Department.[20] For the period of 1940-1964, the figures are 14 and 9 per cent respectively. The average length of FTC cases in which

[19] Gerard C. Henderson, *supra* note 11, at 89, contains a rather similar table covering the Commission's earliest period. His differs from mine chiefly in that he includes non-binding stipulations of compliance and I do not.

[20] Compare Tables 28 and 31, *infra*.

TABLE 8

FREQUENCY DISTRIBUTION OF LENGTHS OF DEPARTMENT OF JUSTICE LITIGATED CIVIL ANTITRUST CASES

Period in Which Case Was Instituted	12 Months or less	13-24 Months	25-36 Months	37-48 Months	49-60 Months	61-72 Months	73-84 Months	85-96 Months	97-124 Months	125 Months or More
1890-1894	1		1			1				
1895-1899		2	2	2						
1900-1904		1	1							
1905-1909		1	5	2						2
1910-1914	3	1	1		2	1	1	1	4	
1915-1919					3	3	7			
1920-1924	2	5	4	3		1	1			
1924-1929		1	3	4		1	1		1	1
1930-1934					1	1				
1934-1939	2	3	2	1	1	1		2	1	4
1940-1944		3	4	3	4	5	4	1	4	3
1945-1949		4	5	11	5	2	3	1	2	2
1950-1954		4	4	9	8	3	3	2	5	3
1955-1959	1	5	6	4			5	2	6	1
1960-1964	7	7	10	4	10	4		7	2	
Total	16	37	48	43	34	23	28	16	25	16

Grand Total: 286

Highly protracted cases (73 months or more): 85

Percentage of all litigated civil cases: 34%

Percentage of all civil cases (computed from Table 15): 10%

Source: Computed from the Bluebook.

TABLE 9

DURATION OF FTC RESTRAINT-OF-TRADE CASES

Period in Which Case Was Instituted	Number Settled Within Six Months	Other Consent or No Contest	Contested	Judicially Reviewed	Reviewed by Supreme Court	Average Duration, All Cases Not Settled Within Six Months	Average Duration, All Contested Cases	Average Duration, All Judicially Reviewed Cases	Average Duration, All Cases Reviewed by Supreme Court
1915-1919	9	8	184	23	10	34	34	42	53
1920-1924	0	4	177	26	5	28	28	52	60
1925-1929	2	3	50	5	1	25	26	62	72
1930-1934	5	2	32	3	1	21	21	44	73
1935-1939	26	29	87	22	4	32	36	63	82
1940-1944	7	28	73	21	4	49	60	85	137
1945-1949	4	8	36	10	1	48	55	77	72
1950-1954	15	18	26	7	0	44	50	72	—
1955-1959	7	32	62	30	8	49	64	82	94
1960-1964	14	17	38	9	0	38	43	61	—

Sources: Computed from FTC Docket of Complaints; F.T.C. Decisions.

TABLE 10

FREQUENCY DISTRIBUTION OF DURATIONS OF CONTESTED FTC RESTRAINT-OF-TRADE PROCEEDINGS (SINCE 1930)

Period in Which Case Was Instituted	Number of Cases—Duration in Months									
	12 Months or Less	13-24 Months	25-36 Months	37-48 Months	49-60 Months	61-72 Months	73-84 Months	85-96 Months	97-124 Months	125 Months or More
1930-1934	12	11	5	2	1	1				
1935-1939	22	23	15	6	9	1	3	1	3	3
1940-1944	4	12	14	5	5	6	7	5	4	7
1945-1949	2	5	1	6	9	3	2	3	1	
1950-1954	2	4	5	4	4	4	1			2
1955-1959	1	6	7	6	6	7	7	2	3	1
1960-1964	4	3	8	5	10	4	6	1		
TOTAL	47	64	55	34	44	26	26	12	11	13

Grand Total: 332
Highly protracted cases (73 months or more): 62
Percentage of total of highly protracted cases: 19%
Percentage of all cases in period (computed from Table 2): 11%

Sources: Computed from FTC Docket of Complaints; FTC Decisions.

the respondent exercised his right to judicial review is far greater than the average length of litigated Department of Justice cases; and the length of FTC cases reviewed by the Supreme Court is greater than that of Department of Justice cases reviewed by the Court.

Comparable data with respect to private antitrust cases are not available. However, from information furnished the writer by the Administrative Office of the U. S. Courts, it was possible to determine the duration of those private antitrust cases disposed of since 1964. The average duration of cases terminated in 1964 was 21.5 months, and of those terminated in 1969, 25.8. These figures are misleading, however, in that only a small percentage of private antitrust cases go to judgment (see Table 13); of those that did, the average duration was 37.4 for cases disposed of in 1964 and 46.7 for those disposed of in 1969. The incidence of highly protracted cases is smaller in private than in governmental antitrust cases: only 1.4 per cent for private cases terminated in 1964, and 6.5 per cent for those terminated in 1969.

III. THE RECORD OF SUCCESS OF THE ANTITRUST CLAIMANT

Table 11 gives the won-lost record of the Department of Justice, both generally and in the Supreme Court. Consent judgments and *nolo contendere* pleas are included. The Department's high degree of success in the cases it undertakes is not of recent origin. Since 1910, there has been no five-year

TABLE 11
THE DEPARTMENT'S WON-LOST RECORD[a]

Period in Which Case Was Instituted	Number Won	Number Lost	Percentage Won	Number Won in Supreme Court	Number Lost in Supreme Court	Percentage Won in Supreme Court
1890-1894	3	5	38	1	1	50
1895-1899	4	3	57	2	2	50
1900-1904	5	1	83	2	0	100
1905-1909	21	17	55	6	1	86
1910-1914	61	30	67	8	8	50
1915-1919	31	12	72	2	2	50
1920-1924	42	24	64	6	6	50
1925-1929	53	4	93	6	0	100
1930-1934	23	6	79	2	1	67
1935-1939	45	12	79	12	6	67
1940-1944	173	50	78	12	9	57
1945-1949	131	28	82	20	6	77
1950-1954	135	22	86	12	4	75
1955-1959	176	18	91	19	5	79
1960-1964	180	31	85	32	3	91
1965-1967	78	3	96	6	0	100

Source: Computed from the Bluebook.
[a] See note to table 14, *infra*.

period in which the Department did not prevail in at least 64 per cent of the cases initiated in the period. And its record has been even better since 1925. Although some additional improvement seems evident since 1950, it is as yet too early to tell whether the most recent period will match the previous high water mark, 1925-1929. (The 1965-1967 results are biased in favor of the government since most of the cases instituted in this period that defendants have decided to contest have not yet been decided.)

The FTC has not attained the same high percentage of success as the Department; even in quite recent periods, the ratio of dismissals to total cases has been higher (Table 12). But it would be a mistake to infer from

TABLE 12
THE FTC's RECORD OF SUCCESS IN RESTRAINT-OF-TRADE CASES

Period in Which Case Was Instituted	Order Entered	Case Dismissed	Total	Judicial Review— FTC Won	Judicial Review— FTC Lost	Total Cases Judicially Reviewed
1915-1919	55	151	206	6	18	24
1920-1924	40	136	176	15	10	25
1925-1929	20	31	51	2	3	5
1930-1934	18	18	36	1	0	1
1935-1939	102	37	139	20	1	21
1940-1944	80	25	105	19	2	21
1945-1949	31	16	47	7	4	11
1950-1954	43	12	55	4	2	6
1955-1959	66	27	93	16	5	21
1960-1964	54	15	69	8	1	9

Sources: Computed from F.T.C. Docket of Complaints; F.T.C. Decisions.

this that the Commission should be criticized and the Department commended. Conceivably, the Department's high percentage of wins may reflect an excessively cautious enforcement policy, although that is not my impression.

As for the private cases, the requisite data, once again, are lacking. Previous writers on the subject concluded that private antitrust plaintiffs were rarely successful.[21] But they were looking only at cases that went to judgment or, worse, only at cases that were reported. As shown in Table 13, even in the most recent period most cases that went to judgment were decided in favor of the defendant. But what is at least as significant is that the vast majority of the cases were dismissed by action of the parties. Presumably, the plaintiff would not consent to dismissal unless the defendant had offered

[21] For example, Robert A. Bicks, The Department of Justice and Private Treble Damage Actions, 4 Antitrust Bull. 5 (1959); Comment, Antitrust Enforcement by Private Parties: Analysis of Developments in the Treble Damage Suit, 61 Yale L.J. 1010 (1952).

TABLE 13
DISPOSITION OF PRIVATE ANTITRUST CASES: 1964-1969[a]

	Number of Cases Terminated in:					
Disposition	1964	1965	1966	1967	1968	1969[b]
No Entry				10	26	23
Default Judgment				1	1	
Consent Judgment	9	3	4	4	5	3
Dismissed, Want of Prosecution	15	21	11	10	14	9
Dismissed, Action of Parties	556	911	1019	340	304	156
Remanded to State Court	4	5	8	1	1	1
Judgment for Plaintiff	8	16	17	13	11	8
Judgment for Defendant	161	74	90	68	67	21
Judgment for Both or Other	1				1	

Source: Correspondence with Administrative Office of the United States Courts.
[a] Fiscal Years.
[b] Information for 1969 is incomplete.

him something in settlement of his claim. Unfortunately, whether these settlements are small or large in relation to the damage suffered we do not know.

Table 11 lends some support to the widespread view that the Supreme Court is increasingly well disposed toward the vigorous enforcement of the antitrust laws. But Table 14, in which the Supreme Court cases are ordered by the date decided and FTC restraint-of-trade and private antitrust cases (including cases where an antitrust claim is asserted by way of defense in a patent-infringement or contract suit) are included, suggests a more cautious appraisal. Judging by that table, the period 1890-1914 was almost as bright a one for antitrust claimants as the period since 1945. The Department of Justice has done consistently very well since 1945, and the FTC has not lost a case since the 1950-1955 period.[22] But a high order of success is not more recent than those dates, while no consistent tendency is discernible with respect to the success of private claimants.

The interpretation of such statistics is again ambiguous. The high ratio of wins to losses in government antitrust cases may reflect not a favorable disposition on the part of the Court but merely careful screening by the Solicitor General; the spottier success of private antitrust claimants supports this view. The low win-loss ratio of private claimants in some periods could mean nothing more than that there were many cases whose merits were negligible even under a most generous view of the scope of the antitrust laws.

[22] The virtually identical won-lost records of the Department of Justice and the FTC (74% and 75%, respectively; Table 14) is consistent with a suggestion I have made elsewhere that the courts have not felt bound to accord special weight to the FTC's judgment in antitrust cases. Richard A. Posner, The Federal Trade Commission, 37 U. Chi. L. Rev. 47, 52 (1969). But this conclusion is subject to the qualification noted in the next paragraph of text.

TABLE 14

THE RECORD OF ANTITRUST CLAIMANTS IN THE SUPREME COURT[a]

	1890 to 1894	1895 to 1899	1900 to 1904	1905 to 1909	1910 to 1914	1915 to 1919	1920 to 1924	1925 to 1929	1930 to 1934	1935 to 1939	1940 to 1944	1945 to 1949	1950 to 1954	1955 to 1959	1960 to 1964	1965 to 1969	Total
Period in Which Supreme Court Decided Case																	
Justice Department Won	3	4	1	5	11	1	8	7	5	6	10	20	13	11	26	17	144
Justice Department Lost	4	7			1	6	6	4	4	1	7	4	5	2	2	4	50
Total	7	11	1	5	12	7	14	11	9	7	17	24	18	13	28	21	194
Percentage Won	43		100	100	92	14	57	64	56	86	59	83	72	85	93	81	74
FTC—Won							5	6	3	1	2	6	5	4	3	4	39
FTC—Lost							4	3	3	1	1	3	2	1	1	1	13
Total							9	7	6	3	6	9	7	7	16	12	52
Percentage Won							57	57	50	100	67	100	57	100	100	100	75
Private Claimant Won	3	4	3	4	2	5	5	5	3	1	8	4	4	6	9	11	75
Private Claimant Lost	1	1	3	3	5	4	11	1	6	3	2	3	1	7	1	1	80
Total	4	4	7	5	9	17	35	18	20	8	30	19	11	13	9	16	48
Percentage Won	75	100	75	57	40	55	35	83	50	20	80	67	57	86	56	92	63
Grand Total—Won	3	7	4	9	13	6	18	16	11	8	20	30	19	21	41	37	263
Grand Total—Lost	1	4	1	3	4	10	20	8	10	5	10	7	11	13	9	5	111
Total	4	11	5	12	17	16	38	24	21	13	30	37	30	24	50	42	374
Percentage Won	75	64	80	75	76	38	47	67	52	62	67	81	63	88	82	88	70

Source: Computed from Michael A. Duggan, Antitrust and the U.S. Supreme Court, 1829–1967 (1968).

a The sum of Supreme Court decisions in Justice Department cases is smaller in table 14 than in table 11. The reason is that the Duggan abstracts from which table 14 was computed exclude summary decisions even if on the merits, whereas table 11 includes such decisions.

IV. THE CHOICE OF REMEDIES

A. *Federal Equitable Remedies*

Table 15 shows the breakdown between civil and criminal antitrust cases filed by the Department of Justice in the various periods since 1890. The

TABLE 15

BREAKDOWN BETWEEN CRIMINAL AND CIVIL CASES BROUGHT BY
THE DEPARTMENT OF JUSTICE

Period in Which Case Was Instituted	Total Number of Cases	Criminal	Civil	Percentage Criminal	Percentage Civil
1890-1894	9	4	5	44	56
1895-1899	7	1	6	14	86
1900-1904	6	1	5	17	83
1905-1909	39	26	13	67	33
1910-1914	91	37	54	41	59
1915-1919	43	25	18	58	42
1920-1924	66	25	41	38	62
1925-1929	59	16	43	27	73
1930-1934	30	11	19	37	63
1935-1939	57	27	30	47	53
1940-1944	223	163	60	73	27
1945-1949	157	58	99	37	63
1950-1954	159	73	86	46	54
1955-1959	195	97	98	50	50
1960-1964	215	78	137	36	64
1965-1969	195	52	143	27	73
TOTAL	1551	694	857		

Source: Computed from the Bluebook.

proportion of civil cases has varied from 50 to 73 per cent in recent years. These figures understate the government's reliance on civil remedies since they exclude cases where civil relief is sought ancillary to a criminal proceeding. It is interesting to note that the periods of greatest increase over the previous period in the total number of cases filed (1905-1909 and 1940-1944) were periods in which the proportion of criminal to civil cases was unusually high.

The Department's civil antitrust decrees can be classified under three heads, which I shall call the "statutory language" decree, the "once-for-all" decree, and the "regulatory" decree. It is extremely common for the Department in price-fixing cases to obtain a decree that, stripped of the redundancies that are dear to lawyers, merely forbids further price fixing. Since the illegality of price fixing under the Sherman Act is well established, and directly punishable as a crime, the purpose of such an injunction is not obvious, especially in the many cases in which it is entered simultaneously with or shortly after the imposition of criminal punishment. (In other cases, where the rule of law is not well established, a civil proceeding makes obvious good sense.) One possible explanation for the practice is that it is an attempt to increase the deterrent effect of the rule against price fixing by adding to the penalties provided by section 1 of the Sherman Act the much heavier penalties that, in principle at least, can be imposed on a corporation that is found guilty of criminal contempt. Table 16, which records the criminal-contempt proceedings brought for violation of Department of Justice antitrust decrees, indicates, however, that few such proceedings have been brought, that the government's record of success in such proceedings has been poor by its usual standards, and (in conjunction with Table 20) that the penalties imposed in such proceedings are not generally higher than those imposed in original criminal antitrust actions. I am led to question whether the "statutory language" decree serves much purpose, except in cases where the rule of law is in doubt.

The "once-for-all" decree is one that eliminates the violation by a change in the defendant's business that, once effected, permits the Department and the court very largely to wash their hands of the case. An example would be a decree requiring the defendant to divest a firm unlawfully acquired or to dedicate its patents to the public, or enjoining an acquisition. Such a decree may, of course, take some time to carry out, but once it is carried out nothing more remains to be done. Despite this attractive feature, we shall see later that divestiture, at least in monopolization cases, involves major problems of delay.

The "regulatory" decree is one whose terms are such as to establish a continuing supervisory relationship between the court in which the decree was entered and the defendant; more realistically, perhaps, between the Judgments Section of the Antitrust Division and the defendant. A good example is the old *Terminal Railroad Association* decree, which ordered the defendant association to furnish its terminal services to all seekers on reasonable and nondiscriminatory terms.[23] In effect, the decree created a little Interstate Commerce Act for the terminal association, with the court cast in the role of the ICC. The example has been followed in a large number of decrees that require defendants to grant patent licenses on nondiscriminatory and reasonable-royalty terms. Of related character are decrees that forbid the defendant to make any further acquisitions, or to enter specified businesses, or to exceed a certain share of the market. The last two are manifestly anticompetitive, and all three seem highly questionable in that they implicitly grant the courts and the Department broad and lasting discretion over business decisions that may be only remotely related to the original purposes of the antitrust suit. The *Swift* decree provides a notorious example.[24]

[23] United States v. Terminal Railroad Ass'n of St. Louis, 224 U.S. 383, 411 (1912).

[24] The most recent episode is United States v. Swift & Co., 1969 Trade Cas. ¶ 72701

TABLE 16

CRIMINAL CONTEMPT PROCEEDINGS FOR VIOLATION OF DEPARTMENT OF JUSTICE ANTITRUST DECREES

	1890 to 1894	1895 to 1899	1900 to 1904	1905 to 1909	1910 to 1914	1915 to 1919	1920 to 1924	1925 to 1929	1930 to 1934	1935 to 1939	1940 to 1944	1945 to 1949	1950 to 1954	1955 to 1959	1960 to 1964	1965 to 1969	TOTAL
Year in Which Original Action Was Brought																	
Number of Criminal Contempt Proceedings Arising Out of Orders Entered in Those Actions	1			1	3			2	2	1	3	3	3	1	2		22
Number on Which Some Penalty Was Imposed	1				3			1	1		1	3	1[a]	1			12
Total Penalties [b]					$32,500			10,000	4,000		102,500	243,700	35,000	75,003			502,703
Average Penalty [b]					$10,833			10,000	4,000		102,500	81,233	35,000	75,003			45,700
Year in Which Contempt Proceedings Was Brought																	
Total Penalties [b]					$ 5,500			2,000		14,000	25,000		153,200		268,003	35,000	502,703
Average Penalty [b]					$ 5,500			2,000		7,000	25,000		76,250		89,334	35,000	45,700

Source: Computed from the Bluebook.

[a] One other case is pending.

[b] 3–6 months imprisonment.

Table 17 uses two methods to estimate the number of regulatory decrees that have been entered in Department of Justice antitrust cases. Column 1 reports the cases in which proceedings (other than for contempt of the original order) occurred after the termination of the original action: proceedings to reopen the case in order to modify the decree or determine its application. Since a regulatory decree, as I define it, is one that requires continuing attention after its entry, column 1 gives a partial glimpse of the importance of such decrees; it is partial because many regulatory decrees doubtless are administered without additional formal proceedings and hence do not show up in column 1. Column 2 indicates, again and for the same reason inadequately, the long span of time that often separates the original from the reopened proceeding. Columns 3 through 5 attempt a direct count of the regulatory decrees based on the Bluebook summaries. Because the summaries typically contain very scanty descriptions of the relief granted,[25] the actual number of regulatory decrees is understated, probably seriously so.

It would seem, at all events, that a significant fraction of civil antitrust decrees are regulatory in character. This finding is disturbing. First, as mentioned, such decrees are sometimes anticompetitive and often inappropriately far-reaching in their effect on future business behavior. Second, the entry of such a decree is tantamount to a confession that the antitrust action has not succeeded in restoring competitive conditions. And third, in view of persistent and serious questions that have been raised concerning the wisdom and efficacy of formal systems of regulation in the transportation, public utility, and other industries, the creation of new schemes of regulation on an *ad hoc* basis is a questionable expedient, especially when their administration must be left in the hands of scattered federal district courts and an obscure section in the Department of Justice.

B. Criminal Remedies[26]

Table 15 showed the breakdown between criminal and civil antitrust cases brought by the Department of Justice. Table 18 indicates the importance of the *nolo contendere* plea in the disposition of such cases since 1935-1939,

---

(N.D. Ill. 1969). For a critical discussion of experience with the administration of a group of regulatory decrees, see Comment, An Experiment In Preventive Anti-Trust; Judicial Regulation of the Motion Picture Exhibition Market Under the *Paramount* Decrees, 74 Yale L.J. 1040 (1965).

[25] Good summaries of most of the decrees may be found in American Enterprise Institute, Antitrust Consent Decrees 1906-1966—Compendium of Abstracts (1968), plus 1967-1968 Supp.

[26] For a study of criminal antitrust cases that partially overlaps my own, see James M. Clabault and John F. Burton, Sherman Act Indictments 1955-1965—A Legal and Economic Analysis (1966), and the 1968 Cumulative Statistical Supp.

TABLE 17
"REGULATORY" DECREES IN DEPARTMENT OF JUSTICE ANTITRUST CASES[a]

Period in Which Case Was Instituted	Decrees Later Reopened or Modified (1)	Average Number of Years from Original Complaint to Latest Reopening Proceedings (2)	Reasonable-Royalty Decrees (3)	Other "Regulatory" Decrees (4)	Total of Columns 3 and 4 (5)
1890-1894					
1895-1899					
1900-1904					
1905-1909	3	17		1	1
1910-1914	15	22			
1915-1919	5	9			
1920-1924	7	16		1	1
1925-1929	5	13			
1930-1934	7	11			
1935-1939	7	20	1	1	2
1940-1944	19	9	14	2	16
1945-1949	6	15	24	17	41
1950-1954	14	9	12	12	24
1955-1959	2	5	8	11	19
1960-1964	3	3	1	4	5
1965-1969					
TOTAL	93	13	60	49	109

Source: Computed from the Bluebook.

[a] There is some double counting in this table. Some regulatory decrees have been entered in cases ancillary to criminal proceedings and not counted as separate proceedings in other tables. And a few decrees containing both reasonable-royalty and other regulatory provisions have been counted twice.

and also (in conjunction with Table 11) that the Department's record of success in criminal cases is not significantly different from its overall record. Tables 19 through 21 and Figure III record the nature and severity of the sanctions imposed in criminal antitrust cases. As Table 19 indicates, imprisonment is a rarely used sanction; it has been imposed in fewer than 4 per cent of the Department's criminal cases, and then mostly in cases involving either acts of violence or union misconduct. The first prison sentence for "pure" price fixing was imposed in the 1955-1959 period. The next such was in the electrical-equipment case of 1960, where seven company officials were given 30-day terms. Prison sentences have been imposed in two cases since then, but it is too early to tell whether the reluctance of judges to impose prison sentences in antitrust cases is diminishing significantly.

Table 20 and Figure III indicate that the total antitrust fines imposed in cases brought in the various periods since the enactment of the Sherman Act kept at least rough pace with the growth of the economy and the decline in the purchasing power of the dollar—until the most recent period.

TABLE 18
CRIMINAL CONVICTIONS

Period in Which Case Was Instituted	Disposed of on Nolo Contendere Plea	Other Convictions	Total Convictions	Acquittals and Dismissals	Percentage of Convictions
1890-1894	0	0	0	4	0
1895-1899	0	0	0	1	0
1900-1904	0	1	1	0	100
1905-1909	0	11	11	14	44
1910-1914	9	12	21	16	57
1915-1919	5	8	13	10	57
1920-1924	1	14	15	10	60
1925-1929	4	10	14	2	88
1930-1934	2	6	8	3	73
1935-1939	13	6	19	8	70
1940-1944	110	13	123	40	75
1945-1949	41	9	50	8	86
1950-1954	55	10	65	8	89
1955-1959	65	21	86	11	89
1960-1964	47	17	64	14	82
1965-1969	40	6	46	1	98
TOTAL	395	143	538	150	

Source: Computed from the Bluebook.

And it is not yet clear how exceptional that period was since fines have not been assessed in all of the cases filed in the period.

Table 20 indicates that the amendment to the Sherman Act in 1955 raising the maximum penalty from $5,000 to $50,000[27] has had some impact on the aggregate, and even more on the average, antitrust fines imposed. But the impact was neither immediate—the average fine in the 1955-1959 period, while considerably higher than the average fine in the immediately preceding period, was lower than the average fine in several earlier periods —nor anything like tenfold in magnitude. The average fine for the period 1890-1954 was $38,479; the average fine for the period 1960-1969 was $122,326, less than a fourfold increase. The explanation for the lagged effect of the penalty increase is obvious. The new penalties could be imposed, consistently with constitutional requirements, only on conspiracies begun or continued after 1955, when the amendment became effective. The explanation why the amendment has thus far effected less than a fourfold increase in the average fine imposed should be obvious too: the amendment simply raised the maximum fine, and a judge is not required to impose the maximum. Judges apparently took the congressional action as a signal for increasing fines somewhat, but not by a factor of ten.

In view of the recent proposal of the Department of Justice to increase

[27] Act of July 7, 1955, ch. 281, 69 Stat. 282, amending 15 U.S.C. sec's 1-3 (1952).

TABLE 19
CRIMINAL SANCTIONS—IMPRISONMENT

Period in Which Case Was Instituted	Total Number of Criminal Cases	Total Number of Convictions	Prison Sentence Imposed[a]	Length of Sentence	Characteristics of Case
1890-1894	4	0	0		
1895-1899	1	0	0		
1900-1904	1	1	0		
1905-1909	26	11	0		
1910-1914	37	21	1	4 hours	labor
1915-1919	25	13	3	4 hours	labor
				1 year	labor-sabotage
				1 year	labor
1920-1924	25	15	5	N.A.	price fixing-labor
				10 days	labor
				10 months	labor
				8 months	labor
				1 year	labor
1925-1929	16	14	3	6 months	labor
				N.A.	price fixing-labor
				10 days	price fixing-violence
1930-1934	11	8	6	3 months	monopolization-violence
				6 months	
				6 months-2 years	price fixing-violence
				2 years	price fixing-violence
				2-5 months	price fixing-labor violence
				3-6 months	labor-violence
1935-1939	27	19	1	1 year	labor-violence
1940-1944	163	123	0		
1945-1949	58	50	0		
1950-1954	73	65	2	6 months	price fixing-labor
				9 months	price fixing-labor
1955-1959	97	86	2	90 days	price fixing-labor
				1 year	
1960-1964	78	64	2	30 days	price fixing
				N.A.	price fixing
1965-1969	51	46	1	24 hours-60 days	price fixing
TOTAL	693	536	26		

Source: Computed from the Bluebook.
[a] Suspended and remitted prison sentences and probation are excluded.

the maximum fine in the Sherman Act from $50,000 to $500,000,[28] it bears emphasizing that a change in maximum penalties is an indirect, and in magnitude uncertain, method of changing the actual penalties. Another tenfold

[28] See 429 BNA Antitrust & Trade Reg. Rep. (Sept. 30, 1969); S.3036, 91st Cong., 1st Sess. (1969); H.R. 14116, 91st Cong. 1st Sess. (1969).

TABLE 20
CRIMINAL SANCTIONS—FINES

Period in Which Case Was Instituted (1)	Total Criminal Convictions (2)	Number of Cases in Which Fine Was Imposed (3)	Aggregate Amount of Fines Imposed in Period (4)	Average Fine per Case (Col. 4 ÷ Col. 3)
1890-1894	0	0		
1895-1899	0	0		
1900-1904	1	1	1,000	1,000
1905-1909	11	10	218,875	21,876
1910-1914	21	19	400,090	21,057
1915-1919	13	13	145,857	11,220
1920-1924	15	13	764,850	58,835
1925-1929	14	12	796,510	66,376
1930-1934	8	7	142,444	20,349
1935-1939	19	17	882,914	51,936
1940-1944	123	123	6,319,506	51,378
1945-1949	50	50	1,790,123	35,802
1950-1954	65	64	1,197,537	18,711
1955-1959	86	86	4,306,375	50,074
1960-1964	64	62	7,846,552	126,557
1965-1969	46	46	5,364,633	116,622

Source: Computed from the Bluebook.

increase in the maximum today might have even a smaller effect than the last. In 1955, the maximum penalty under the Sherman Act had remained unchanged since its enactment in 1890, a period that had seen a tremendous growth in economic activity and a large decline in the purchasing power of the dollar. Judges would be less likely to consider the 1955 penalty structure so soon obsolete.

One would most like to know whether the antitrust criminal remedies, as they are actually applied, effectively deter price fixing and other concealable antitrust violations, where the need for punitive rather than merely remedial sanctions is evident.[29] The question cannot be answered directly. Not only is the incidence of undetected antitrust violations unknown, but there is another punitive sanction besides the criminal—the penalty component of the treble-damage awards in private antitrust cases—and it would be difficult to disentangle the deterrent effects of each. As a first step, it would be worthwhile to determine the frequency of successful private suits following government price-fixing actions and the magnitude of the awards decreed (or negotiated) in such suits. I have been unable to make this determination because of the statistical deficiencies in the recording of private antitrust actions noted earlier.

[29] See Gary S. Becker, Crime and Punishment: An Economic Approach, 76 J. Pol. Econ. 169, 199 n.55 (1968); Richard A. Posner, Oligopoly and the Antitrust Laws: A Suggested Approach, 21 Stan. L. Rev. 1562, 1588 (1969).

TABLE 21

FREQUENCY DISTRIBUTION OF ANTITRUST FINES

Period in Which Case Was Instituted	Percentage of Fines in Various Size Classes									
	$0-10,000	$10,001-25,000	$25,001-50,000	$50,001-75,000	$75,001-125,000	$125,001-200,000	$200,001-300,000	$300,001-500,000	$500,001-1,000,000	$1,000,001-2,000,000
1890-1894										
1895-1899										
1900-1904	100									
1905-1909	50	10	20	20						
1910-1914	63	21		5	5	5				
1915-1919	54	38	8							
1920-1924	23	15	23	15	8	8	8			
1925-1929	25	17	25	8	8	8		8		
1930-1934	57	29	14							
1935-1939	41	18	24	6	6				6	
1940-1944	19	20	27	10	14	7	2	1		
1945-1949	18	30	34	6	10	2				
1950-1954	45	38	18	2	2	2				
1955-1959	31	28	20	3	6	7	1	5		
1960-1964	11	6	27	11	17	11	11	2		
1965-1969	19	24	13	2	13	9	15		7	3

Source: Computed from the Bluebook.

FIGURE III
AGGREGATE ANTITRUST FINES AND THE GROSS NATIONAL PRODUCT
(CURRENT DOLLARS)

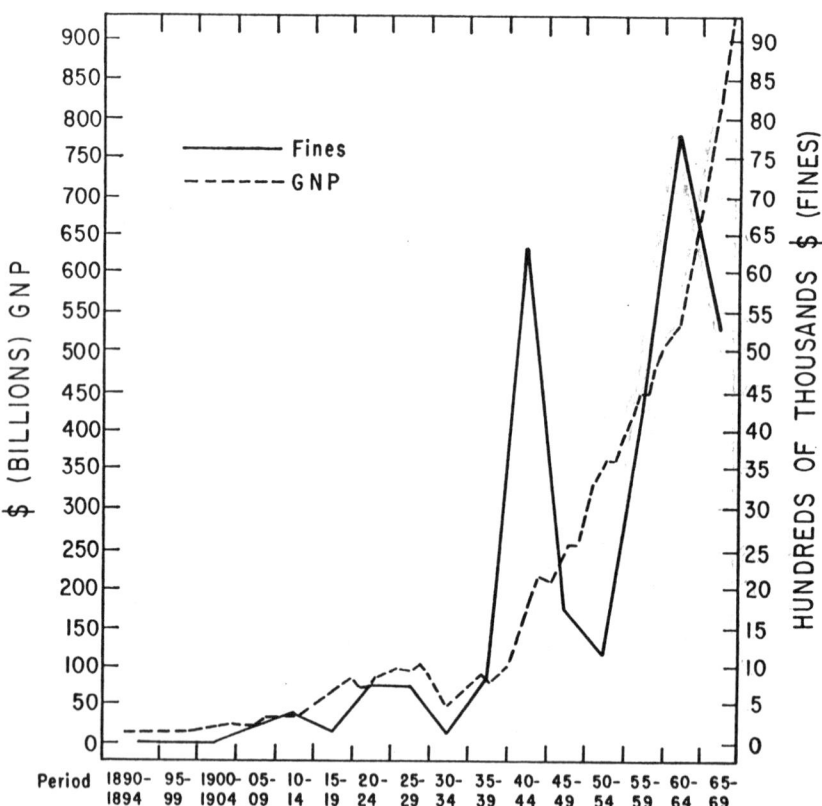

Sources: Table 20; U.S. Bureau of the Census, Dep't of Commerce, Historical Statistices of the United States, Colonial Times to 1957; U.S. Bureau of the Census, Dep't of Commerce, Statistical Abstract[s] of the United States, 1958-1969.

Another possibly fruitful and somewhat easier line of attack is to consider the incidence of repeated violations of antitrust law and the punishments meted out to the recidivist. Two obstacles are that the Bluebook, in cases brought before 1952, frequently fails to identify all of the defendants and that it rarely indicates when one defendant, due to a change of name or merger, is the same corporation as, or a predecessor (or successor) to, a defendant in another case. It is possible to ascertain from the Bluebook that 46 of the 320 corporations that were convicted of a criminal violation of the antitrust laws in cases brought between 1964 and 1968 had previously been convicted, in either a civil or criminal case (or several cases), of the same offense (usually price fixing); and in view of the deficiencies just mentioned, the true percentage of recidivists is undoubtedly higher. Ten of the 46 firms had three or more prior convictions.

The courts appear to take a rather lenient attitude toward the antitrust recidivist. The 46 recidivists were not punished more severely than other defendants in the same case who had a clean record; nor were their officers, in cases where individuals as well as corporations were charged. These results cannot be explained by the limitations on the judge's sentencing discretion imposed by the statutory maximum, because in only 15 of the 46 cases was the maximum penalty imposed in the latest conviction, and in no case was an officer fined more than one-half the maximum. Even in the ten cases where the corporation had three prior convictions, the maximum penalty was not imposed on the corporation in three. Perhaps the explanation for the courts' lenience is that the concept of corporate, as opposed to individual, recidivism is felt to be unsatisfactory. A widely diversified corporation is quite likely to commit more antitrust violations than one that operates in a single market: Should the first be punished more severely on that account? Should a corporation be charged with the old antitrust violations of a recently acquired division, or with the violations of a previous generation of officers?

Considering the virtual nonuse of imprisonment as a sanction, the rather low average fine in price-fixing cases even in the period since the maximum fine was increased, the high incidence of repeat offenses, and the lenient attitude of the courts toward the repeat offender, I am inclined to question the adequacy of the criminal antitrust remedies, standing alone, as a deterrent to concealable violations, especially price fixing. The long average duration of those conspiracies that are detected, discussed below, adds to one's sense of uneasiness concerning the deterrent adequacy of the present system.

V. THE VIOLATIONS ALLEGED

A. *Department of Justice Cases*

Tables 22 through 30 present information relating to the violations alleged in Department of Justice antitrust cases. I emphasize that these are allegations. Since most of the Department's antitrust suits are terminated without a determination or acknowledgment of guilt, and since in any event the factual statements in antitrust opinions cannot be assumed, without a careful examination of the record of the case, to be accurate,[30] the infor-

---

[30] See for example, John S. McGee, Predatory Price Cutting: The Standard Oil (N.J.) Case, 1 J. Law & Econ. 137 (1958).

mation recorded in these tables is of interest chiefly for what it tells us about enforcement policy, although I believe we get occasional glimpses of the underlying business behavior.

Our first question is what headway an "abuses" theory of antitrust policy has made with the Department of Justice. By an abuse I mean a practice by which a single firm, without combining in any way with its competitors, can enlarge or better exploit its monopoly or market power. Predatory pricing is an example of an abuse, and so—when it is challenged as a violation of the antitrust laws—is vertical integration. Simple price-fixing and horizontal mergers—what we may call combinations—are not abuses. It has been argued that concern with abuses is largely misplaced,[31] so it is interesting to note that, despite much talk about abuses, cases in which an abuse is charged constitute only 27 per cent of the cases that the Department has brought. The share of abuses cases has remained quite stable since the 1930-34 period, although at a somewhat higher level than before.[32]

TABLE 22

THE SIGNIFICANCE OF ABUSES IN THE ANTITRUST ENFORCEMENT PROGRAM
OF THE DEPARTMENT OF JUSTICE[a]

Period in Which Case Was Instituted	Number of Cases Involving Horizontal Combinations or Conspiracies	Cases Involving Abuse	Percentage of Abuse Cases
1890-1894	5	2	29
1895-1899	7	0	0
1900-1904	6	0	0
1905-1909	32	4	11
1910-1914	78	23	23
1915-1919	32	6	16
1920-1924	55	5	8
1925-1929	46	11	19
1930-1934	23	11	32
1935-1939	41	19	32
1940-1944	192	75	28
1945-1949	127	79	38
1950-1954	137	58	30
1955-1959	157	65	29
1960-1964	172	66	28
1965-1969	146	50	26

Source: Computed from the Bluebook.
a Cases in which both an abuse and a combination are alleged are counted twice in the table.

Although Table 22 gives, I believe, a tolerably accurate picture of the relative importance of abuses cases, it conceals some difficult problems of

[31] See Aaron Director & Edward H. Levi, Law and the Future: Trade Regulation, 51 Nw. U.L. Rev. 281 (1956).

[32] Table 22, *infra.* Cases in which both an abuse and a combination are alleged are counted twice in the table.

classification, at least one of which merits discussion: the treatment of resale-price-maintenance cases. Resale price maintenance may be a device for collusion among dealers or distributors, in which case it should be classified as a form of horizontal conspiracy or combination, or it may be imposed on the dealers or distributors by a manufacturer for his own ends. The most persuasive explanation that has been offered as to why a manufacturer might want to fix minimum resale prices, other than as a part of a scheme of colluding with his competitors, which would clearly place the arrangement in the horizontal-conspiracy category, relates to products that are sold in conjunction with costly display or other services.[33] A dealer who sold the product alone, relying on other dealers in the product to provide the services, could undercut those dealers to the detriment of the manufacturer. An example would be an automobile dealer without a showroom (a "bootlegger") who offered to sell at a discount any automobile that the customer picked out from an authorized dealer's showroom. Resale price maintenance is a method of preventing such free loading. I have divided the resale-price-maintenance cases into two categories, those involving a product sold without ancillary services (a "simple" product) and those where such services are involved (a "complex" product). I have assigned the former (40 per cent of the total) to the horizontal-conspiracy category and the latter to the abuse category.[34] There is a good deal of doubt whether the second group of cases involves an "abuse" that the law should attempt to discourage, but that is another question.

Table 23 summarizes the pattern of violations alleged in the Department's cases. Some explanation of the categories in this table is necessary, especially since they are employed in subsequent tables as well. Column 1, horizontal conspiracy, includes all cases in which competitors agree or conspire to eliminate competition among themselves, usually although not always price competition. Conspiracies among retailers or other distributors are included in this column, and so are conspiracies among manufacturers to establish resale prices; the resale-price-maintenance column is reserved for cases where a single manufacturer is involved and the restraint is imposed, ostensibly at least, by him. Column 2, monopolization, includes all cases in which a firm or group of firms seeks to enlarge rather than merely enjoy monopoly power. Included are attempts by previously competing firms to obtain monopoly power through merger or consolidation, and attempts by large firms or cartels to repel entry or destroy remaining competition by below-cost selling, by improper use of patents, or by other abusive conduct. The distinction between a case in column 1 and one in column 2, to be sure, is sometimes

---

[33] See Lester G. Telser, Why Should Manufacturers Want Fair Trade?, 3 J. Law & Econ. 86 (1960).

[34] With the exception of a few cases in which, although a complex product was involved, there was a strong flavor of horizontal action.

TABLE 23

TOPICAL CLASSIFICATION OF DEPARTMENT OF JUSTICE ANTITRUST CHARGES[a]

	Period in Which Case Was Instituted																
	1890 to 1894	1895 to 1899	1900 to 1904	1905 to 1909	1910 to 1914	1915 to 1919	1920 to 1924	1925 to 1929	1930 to 1934	1935 to 1939	1940 to 1944	1945 to 1949	1950 to 1954	1955 to 1959	1960 to 1964	1965 to 1969	Total
Horizontal Conspiracy	3	7	5	28	62	29	50	36	19	34	179	114	122	122	104	75	989
Monopolizing	3	1	1	9	25	3	7	8	9	14	65	60	62	45	40	19	370
Acquisitions Short of Monopoly		1	2	2	1	1	1	5	1	3	2	5	3	26	61	80	194
Boycott			2	1	15	9	10	20	5	8	43	20	44	38	18	12	245
Resale Price Maintenance							2			1	1	5	4	4	8	2	27
Vertical Integration				2		4		1	2	7	6	11	6	6	7	1	53
Tying Arrangements					3	2	1	1		4	8	23	12	5	4	2	65
Exclusive Dealing	1				9	1	3	1	1	4	16	24	29	23	22	6	140
Territorial and Customer Limitations										1	8			28	24	13	74
Violence	4	1		2	2		8		10	7	7			4		2	47
Price Discrimination	1		3		6	2	4	2		5	29	20	16	15	14	6	123
Other Predatory or Unfair Conduct	1			3	2	3	1	2	1	5	27	17	7	4	11	4	88
Interlocking Directorates								2		1		5	4	2	2		16
Clayton Act, sec. 10																	3
Labor Cases	3			2	6		16	6	7	18	35	2	17	7	5	1	125
Patent and Copyright Cases					6	1	8	3	2	3	36	45	22	15	13	11	165
Total Cases in Period	9	6	39	91	43	66	69	30	57		223	157	159	195	215	195	1551

Source: Computed from the Bluebook.

[a] Table shows distribution of allegations not of cases.

hazy. In general, I exclude from column 2 cases in which members of a cartel merely seek to discipline refractory members or merely boycott suppliers of their competitors.

Table 23 contains a good deal of double counting. In particular, all cases in the patent and copyright column are also classified in one (or more) of the violation columns, and all cases in the boycott column and in the price-discrimination and other-unfair-conduct columns are also recorded elsewhere, usually in column 1 or column 2. Table 23, then, shows the distribution of allegations, not of cases.

Tables 24 and 25 tabulate some characteristics of the price-fixing conspiracies attacked by the Department. Of particular interest in Table 24 is the frequency with which more than a simple agreement to fix prices is involved (for example, a division of territories, a system of fines and audits, a patent agreement, or an agreement on resale prices), and in particular, the large proportion of cases involving trade associations. Either conspiracies to fix prices are difficult to effectuate without such ancillary arrangements, or the adoption of such arrangements increases the probability of detection.

Table 25 indicates, rather surprisingly, that the conspiracies attacked by the Department are of long average duration and involve quite large annual sales. These findings, however, should be taken with a grain of salt. It is rarely clear from the Bluebook summaries whether a conspiracy alleged to have begun many years previously in fact continued throughout the period or was intermittent, or how much of the sales of the product in question were actually subject to the price-fixing agreement. The inadequacy of the summaries on these points is symptomatic of a larger failing. It is that the agencies enforce the rule against price fixing substantially without reliance on economic evidence. What is attacked, judging from the summaries, is the act of agreement—the attempt to affect the market price. The actual effect on price is not considered systematically, which is why the summaries are so lacking in good information about the gravity of the restraint.

Another surprising result in Table 25, the large average number of conspirators, is a statistical illusion. As shown in Table 26, the vast majority of cases involve 20 or fewer conspirators[35] and almost two-thirds involve 10 or fewer; and where large numbers are involved, invariably a trade association, commodity exchange, patent pool or other organization is instrumental in effectuating the conspiracy. The prevalence of small-number express-collusion cases (twice only has the Department ever challenged

---

[35] *Not* defendants alone. When the Bluebook indicates the number of defendants, it usually indicates the number of coconspirators as well. When it does not, the case has not been counted in Table 26. In some cases, coconspirators are not mentioned but the Bluebook indicates that the defendants were the only conspirators, and where this is so, and the number of defendants is indicated, the case is counted.

TABLE 24

HORIZONTAL CONSPIRACIES (DEPARTMENT OF JUSTICE)—MEANS EMPLOYED

	Period in Which Case Was Instituted																Total
	1890 to 1894	1895 to 1899	1900 to 1904	1905 to 1909	1910 to 1914	1915 to 1919	1920 to 1924	1925 to 1929	1930 to 1934	1935 to 1939	1940 to 1944	1945 to 1949	1950 to 1954	1955 to 1959	1960 to 1964	1965 to 1969	
Number of Cases	3	7	5	28	62	29	50	36	19	34	179	114	122	122	104	75	989
Exclusive Sales Agency or Pool		1	1		5	2	3	4	1	4	6	4	7	8	5	4	55
Production or Sales Quota											11	1	1		2	1	16
Trade Association or Equivalent	2	6		3	19	13	22	18	12	17	96	41	62	60	28	32	431
Policing, Fines, Audits, etc.								1	1	3	7	5	8	10	5	3	43
Division of Product Markets											3	5	7			3	18
Division of Territories				1	2	1		1	2		32	31	30	24	15	5	144
Allocation of Customers				1	1		2	3		4	11	8	15	14	7	11	77
Collusion on Terms Besides Basic Price							7	4	7	3	32	25	18	23	7	13	139
Exchange of Information						2	18	2	3	2	14	5	9		5	1	61
Delivered Pricing						1	1		1		5	4	4	1	5		22
Resale Prices or Other Restricted Distribution			1		2	1	1	3	1	1	26	6	9	8	9	3	71
Patents or Copyrights				1	1		6	2			28	27	13	7	5	6	96

Source: Computed from the Bluebook.

TABLE 25
HORIZONTAL CONSPIRACIES (DEPARTMENT OF JUSTICE)—OTHER CHARACTERISTICS

	1890 to 1894	1895 to 1899	1900 to 1904	1905 to 1909	1910 to 1914	1915 to 1919	1920 to 1924	1925 to 1929	1930 to 1934	1935 to 1939	1940 to 1944	1945 to 1949	1950 to 1954	1955 to 1959	1960 to 1964	1965 to 1969	Total
Number of Cases	3	7	5	28	62	29	50	36	19	34	179	114	122	122	104	75	989
Sales to Government Involving Bidding										1	6	5	5	14	29	13	73
Other Bidding Cases		1					1			9	18	11	8	4	10	4	66
Buying Conspiracy			1		3	4		2	1		23	6	8	8	5	3	64
Average Number of Conspirators		14	24	35	28	14	53	95	56	14	19	13	21	15	21	15	
Average Duration of Conspiracy (Years)													11	7	6	6	
Average Annual Sales Affected ($ Mill.)													55.3	27.0	161.5	166.7	
Nationwide Conspiracy			1	3	13	9	28	10	8	10	86	59	45	41	38	21	372
Local or Regional		7	3	14	24	11	11	16	3	19	74	38	71	73	57	45	469
Foreign Trade Involved	3				6					3	24	28	13	10	2		86

Source: Computed from the Bluebook.

TABLE 26
FREQUENCY DISTRIBUTION OF NUMBER OF CONSPIRATORS IN HORIZONTAL
CONSPIRACY CASES, DEPARTMENT OF JUSTICE

Period in Which Case Was Instituted	0-5	6-10	11-20	21-50	51-100	over 100	Number of Observations
1890-1894							
1895-1899			1				1
1900-1904				1			1
1905-1909		1			1		2
1910-1914				4			4
1915-1919		1	1				2
1920-1924		1		1		1	3
1925-1929			1		1	2	4
1930-1934			2	1		1	4
1935-1939	1	5	2	2			10
1940-1944	20	9	10	3	4	1	47
1945-1949	19	10	10	4	4	1	48
1950-1954	21	18	13	2	2	2	58
1955-1959	29	18	19	5	1	1	73
1960-1964	28	23	10		1	3	65
1965-1969	12	16	7	6	1	1	43
Total	130	102	76	29	15	13	365

Source: Computed from the Bluebook.

"conscious parallelism," or tacit collusion, as such) casts some doubt on the practical importance of tacit collusion. And small-numbers cases may be underrepresented in a sample that consists of Department of Justice proceedings. The Department's price-fixing cases, I am informed by Department sources, are frequently based on tips and testimony of defecting conspirators or disgruntled employees, and the larger the number of conspirators the greater the likelihood of evidence of this sort turning up and leading to prosecution. On the other hand, buyers are an important source of information too, so that number of conspirators is plainly not the only variable in detectability. Moreover, a test of the hypothesis that large-number conspiracies are more fragile than small, made by comparing the number of conspirators with the length of time between the inception of the conspiracy and the filing of the complaint (in those cases where the Bluebook disclosed the necessary information), yielded a negative result: of 79 conspiracies involving 10 or fewer conspirators, 41, or 52 per cent, persisted for six years or more. Of 28 conspiracies involving more than 10 conspirators, 18, or 64 per cent, persisted that long. Of the first group, 19, or 24 per cent, lasted more than 10 years, while of the second group 9, or 32 per cent, lasted more than 10 years.

Two other results in Table 25 are of note. The first is the large number of regional or local conspiracies; indeed, they are in the majority (the foreign-trade category largely overlaps the nationwide-conspiracy one). One implication of this finding relates to the point made earlier about economic evidence. A practical method of introducing such evidence into the administration of the antitrust laws would be by comparison of the price in a region where a conspiracy is suspected with the price of the same product in other areas. Of course, area differences may reflect factors other than a price-fixing conspiracy, but it should be possible to allow for the other factors. If most conspiracies are less than nationwide, such price evidence could be extremely important.

A second interesting result in Table 25 is the small number of conspiracies by purchasers. Monopsony is treated symmetrically with monopoly in most textbooks, but its practical incidence appears to be far less, and this is so even if we add the boycott-by-buyers cases in Table 27. Moreover, buying

TABLE 27
DEPARTMENT OF JUSTICE BOYCOTT CASES

Period in Which Case Was Instituted	Number of Cases	Buyers' Boycotts	Sellers' Boycotts	Membership and Refusal to Cooperate with Competitor Cases	Private Law-making[a]
1890-1894					
1895-1899	1	1		2	
1900-1904					
1905-1909	2	1	1	1	
1910-1914	15	9	4	2	
1915-1919	9	5	2	4	
1920-1924	10	7	2		
1925-1929	20	13	2	1	1
1930-1934	5		2	1	
1935-1939	8	1	4	2	
1940-1944	43	15	17	11	1
1945-1949	20	9	10	4	
1950-1954	44	14	15	16	3
1955-1959	38	15	21	8	1
1960-1964	18	6	10	5	1
1965-1969	12	2	4	6	1
Total	245	98	94	63	8

Source: Computed from the Bluebook.
[a] As in Paramount Famous Lasky Corp. v. United States, 282 U.S. 30 (1930).

conspiracies are more likely to be reported to the Department than selling ones, since in the former case the victims are almost always businessmen rather than consumers, so buying conspiracies are probably overrepresented in Table 25. A possible explanation of the infrequency of the buying conspiracy is that it is an effective tactic only if the supplying industry employs resources that are specialized to that industry. Otherwise, a concerted reduction of the price will simply cause the suppliers to switch to another market. And even if there are specialized or immobile resources, additional capital for replacement or expansion will not flow into the supplying industry without assurance of a normal return.

Monopolization cases are analyzed in Tables 28 and 29. Table 28 indicates that a very high proportion—80 per cent—of the cases involve aggressive cartels rather than single-firm monopolists. It appears also that the incidence of dissolution or substantial divestiture, the traditional monopolization remedies, is very small. Table 29 indicates, confirming an impression I have recorded elsewhere,[36] that the average dissolution or divestiture proceeding[37] is substantially more protracted than the average civil antitrust case. If we exclude local and small regional monopoly cases (local newspaper monopolies being the most common), dissolution or significant divestiture in a monopolization case has taken an average of almost eight years. And, to return to an earlier point, that is only the interval between the filing of the complaint and the last judicial order. The interval between the formation of the monopoly and the actual carrying out of divestiture is greater.

The last table in this section, Table 30, reveals the continued predominance of the horizontal merger in the Department's enforcement of section 7 of the Clayton Act.[38] It also reveals the dramatic impact of the amendment of section 7 in 1950[39] to cover mergers as well as stock acquisitions; the fact that the Department's interest in stock acquisitions also increased after the amendment even though such acquisitions were fully subject to the Clayton Act before; and, perhaps most interesting, the relative paucity of divestitures (due partly, however, to the fact that a number of cases are still pending) and the fact that challenged acquisitions are enjoined or abandoned as often as they are divested.

B. *FTC, Private, and State Antitrust Cases*

Table 31 summarizes the violations alleged in FTC restraint-of-trade cases. With the exception of the earliest periods, when as mentioned so many cases were dismissed, the resulting pattern is much like that of the Department of Justice cases. Like the Department, the Commission has devoted the bulk of its attention in the restraint-of-trade area, as measured by number of cases, to horizontal price fixing. The major difference is that the Commission has given proportionately much less attention to monopolization. The Com-

---

[36] Richard A. Posner, *supra* note 29, at 1597.

[37] I am speaking here of monopolization cases. The divestiture of recent acquisitions challenged under the antimerger law, Clayton Act, sec. 7, 15 U.S.C. sec. 18 (1964), hereinafter cited as Clayton Act, poses fewer difficulties.

[38] *Id.*

[39] Act of Dec. 29, 1950, ch. 1184, 64 Stat. 1125, amending 15 U.S.C. sec. 18 (1946).

TABLE 28

MONOPOLIZATION CASES—DEPARTMENT OF JUSTICE

| | Period in Which Case Was Instituted | | | | | | | | | | | | | | | | |
	1890 to 1894	1895 to 1899	1900 to 1904	1905 to 1909	1910 to 1914	1915 to 1919	1920 to 1924	1925 to 1929	1930 to 1934	1935 to 1939	1940 to 1944	1945 to 1949	1950 to 1954	1955 to 1959	1960 to 1964	1965 to 1969	Total
Number of cases	3	1	1	9	25	3	7	8	9	14	65	60	62	45	40	19	370
Consolidation	1	1	1	2	5							2	1		2	1	16
Consolidation Plus Abuses	1		2		12	1	1	2	1		2	8	3	4	5	1	43
Single-Firm Abuses	1			1	3		2	2	3	5	7	8	10	9	6	7	64
Single Firms—Patents							1					6	2	2	3	1	14
Plural Firms—Acquisitions					1		1		2		2	9	10	3		1	28
Plural Firms—Patents									2	1	17	26	13	8	5		72
Plural Firms—Other				2	4	2	3	4		8	43	21	36	26	20	8	180
Dissolution or Significant Divestiture			3		5	2	2	1		4	1	7	5		2		32

Source: Computed from the Bluebook.

TABLE 29
THE USE OF DISSOLUTION OR DIVESTITURE DECREES
IN DEPARTMENT OF JUSTICE MONOPOLIZATION CASES

Period in Which Case Was Instituted	Number of Cases in Which Significant Divestiture or Dissolution Was Carried Out	National or Large Regional Monopolist	Local or Small Regional Monopolist	Average Length of Proceeding (Months)[a]	Average Length— National or Large Regional (Months)	Average Length— Local or Small Regional (Months)
1890-1894						
1895-1899						
1900-1904						
1905-1909	3	3		59	59	
1910-1914	5	5		84	84	
1915-1919						
1920-1924	2	2		145	145	
1925-1929	1		1	16		16
1930-1934	2		2	10		10
1935-1939	4	2	2	124	136	107
1940-1944	1	1		82	82	
1945-1949	7	6	1	65	71	32
1950-1954	5	3	2	· 89	110	56
1955-1959						
1960-1964	2	2		76	76	
1965-1969						
Total	32	24	8	84	93	55

Source: Computed from the Bluebook.
[a] Excluding three settled within 6 months.

mission's emphasis on price fixing is at least curious in light of its inability to impose punitive sanctions, a point on which I have commented elsewhere.[40]

The only source from which it is possible to determine the violations alleged in private or state antitrust cases is the published opinions. Such a sample is likely to be biased toward cases involving novel legal questions, and hence to distort the actual emphasis of enforcement. Thus, the preponderance of abuses cases among the reported private cases (see Table 32) may indicate nothing more than that horizontal conspiracies are unlikely to generate as much opinion writing as abuses, the law as to horizontal conspiracies being better settled. What is more, the opinions frequently contain inadequate statements of the violations alleged. Still, one can infer that abuses cases probably comprise a larger fraction of private than of governmental cases, and not merely on *a priori* grounds (an abuses case is more likely to involve a victim having an incentive to sue). Table 33 compares the violations alleged in reported public and private antitrust cases brought

[40] Richard A. Posner, *supra* note 22, at 58-59.

TABLE 30

ACQUISITIONS (SHORT OF MONOPOLY) CASES—DEPARTMENT OF JUSTICE

	Period in Which Case Was Instituted																
	1890 to 1894	1895 to 1899	1900 to 1904	1905 to 1909	1910 to 1914	1915 to 1919	1920 to 1924	1925 to 1929	1930 to 1934	1935 to 1939	1940 to 1944	1945 to 1949	1950 to 1954	1955 to 1959	1960 to 1964	1965 to 1969	Total
Number of Cases	1		1	2	3	1	1	5	1	3	2	5	3	26	61	80	194
Stock Acquisition	1		1	2	3	1	1	5	1	3	2	3	1	2	13	10	48
Merger or Consolidation												2	2	21	48	69	142
Other Asset Acquisitions														3	1	1	5
Horizontal	1		1	2	3	1	1	5	1	3	2	3	1	24	46	50	143
Vertical								1				3		4	17	8	33
Potential Competition														3	3	17	23
Reciprocity															1	9	10
Other Conglomerate Allegations																4	4
Joint Venture													2		4	1	7
Divestiture	1		1	2	1	1		4	1	2	2	2		12	17	16	64
Enjoined or Abandoned														2	14	19	35

Source: Computed from the Bluebook.

TABLE 31

VIOLATIONS ALLEGED IN FTC CASES

Violation	1915 to 1919	1920 to 1924	1925 to 1929	1930 to 1934	1935 to 1939	1940 to 1944	1945 to 1949	1950 to 1954	1955 to 1959	1960 to 1964	1960 to 1965	Grand Total	1930 to 1969 Total
					Year in Which Case Was Brought								
Horizontal Price Fixing	11	35	9	14	74	64	26	25	22	7	4	291	236
Monopolization	3	11	3	2	10	8	1	3	1	12	6	60	43
Acquisition Short of Monopoly	17	18	18	3	18	2	1	6	22	31	51	187	134
Boycott	8	20	5	5	23	28	6	14	9	5	2	125	92
Resale Price Maintenance	62	70	21	6	14	0	2	1	9	6	6	197	44
Tying	25	17	1	2	10	15	7	7	3	2	0	89	46
Exclusive Dealing	47	24	2	4	11	5	11	11	29	7	1	152	79
Price Discrimination[a]	72	28	3	5	11	10	1	1	5	6	2	144	41
Violence	4	3	4	0	3	0	0	0	2	2	0	18	3
Labor	0	0	0	0	5	4	0	0	2	0	0	11	11
Patents	0	0	0	0	2	2	3	0	0	0	0	7	7
Other or N.A.	4	4	1	4	2	1	0	1	3	2	2	24	15
TOTAL	253	230	67	45	183	139	58	69	107	80	74	1305	751

Source: Computed from F.T.C. Docket of Complaints; F.T.C. Decisions.

[a] Excluding Robinson-Patman Act cases, save those charging predatory price discrimination.

TABLE 32
PRIVATE CASES BROUGHT UNDER THE FEDERAL ANTITRUST LAWS—
VIOLATIONS ALLEGED IN REPORTED CASES

| | Period Reported | |
Violation	1935-1944	1965-1969
Monopolization	17	52
Price Fixing	25	138
Exclusive Dealing	6	36
Tying	3	28
Price Discrimination	13	92
Other Vertical Restraints	5	33
Acquisitions	2	27
Boycotts	15	74
Other Refusals to Deal	0	48
Interlocking Directorates	2	2
Covenants Not to Compete	0	4
Violence	3	0
Other Practices	1	9
Patents	7	3
Labor	9	12

Source: Computed from CCH Trade Cas. (1944-1969).

under state antitrust laws in the most recent period. A striking disparity in emphasis is evident. The public cases are overwhelmingly price-fixing cases, the private cases overwhelmingly abuses cases.

VI. INDUSTRIES INVOLVED

An attempt was made to classify the antitrust cases brought both by the Department of Justice and by the FTC in each five-year period according to industry group and, in some groups, the three-digit SIC industry, involved

TABLE 33
VIOLATIONS ALLEGED IN REPORTED STATE ANTITRUST CASES, 1965-1969

Violation	Cases Brought by State	Private Cases	Total
Price Fixing	17	9	26
Boycott	7	4	11
Monopolization	3	7	10
Acquisition	1	1	2
Price Discrimination	2	4	6
Tying	1	4	5
Restriction in distribution	0	13	13
Covenant not to compete	0	19	19
Labor dispute	0	1	1
Other or N.A.	2	5	7
Total	33	67	100

Source: Computed from CCH Trade Cas. (1944-1969).

in the case.[41] The resulting tables are too voluminous for inclusion in this article,[42] nor have I yet attempted to analyze them fully.[43] The one observation to which I shall limit myself here is that a large proportion of the Department's cases—and an even larger proportion of the FTC's—are brought in industries not normally regarded as highly concentrated. Cases involving agricultural production, wholesale or retail trade, contract construction, services (excluding motion pictures), or the manufacture of food products, textile mill products, apparel, lumber products, or furniture or fixtures, account for approximately 45 per cent of all of the Department's antitrust cases, and for 55 per cent of the Commission's.[44] There are two possible explanations for this emphasis. One is that, regardless of the overall concentration of the industry, the actual markets involved in the cases, be they geographical or product submarkets, are highly concentrated. There is some support for this view in our earlier finding that the number of conspirators involved in a price-fixing case is typically quite small; and they are likely to comprise the important sellers in the market, else the conspiracy could not succeed. The other, and I think more plausible, explanation is that the methods used by the Department to detect and prove price fixing are such that marginal conspiracies in markets of low concentration are likely to be substantially overrepresented in the Department's "catch." Although the point is both too complex and too important to develop here, it would appear that both legal doctrine and the enforcement machinery are geared more to the apprehension of unsuccessful attempts to fix prices than to the apprehension of successful price fixing. In general, the fact of an agreement or conspiracy to fix prices is all that the government need prove in a price-fixing case and all that it attempts to prove. That fact is ordinarily most readily provable when one of the conspirators defects, or when a disgruntled employee turns government informer. Hence, conspiracies that have a large number of members or that fail to satisfy all of them are most likely to generate the crucial evidence of agreement, and hence are most vulnerable to government prosecution. But these are the very conspiracies that are least likely to succeed, and often because the market involved is not sufficiently concentrated to make price fixing a feasible strategy. Since the government rarely employs economic evidence to estab-

---

[41] James M. Clabault & John F. Burton, *supra* note 26, at Index of Cases By Industry, Index III, classify the criminal cases brought by the Department between 1955 and 1968 in four-digit SIC industries.

[42] I shall be happy to provide copies of the tables to any reader on request.

[43] Such analysis would include an attempt to account for shifts over time in the number of cases brought in each market and an attempt to relate the agencies' enforcement emphases to the degree of concentration in the various markets.

[44] Only cases brought since 1930 were included in computing the Commission's percentage.

lish price fixing, it is unfortunately quite likely that many conspiracies escape prosecution, and especially those that have marked effects on output and price. I do not consider this highly unsatisfactory state of affairs to be inevitable, but a discussion of solutions—which I have begun elsewhere—[45] would take us too far afield.

VII. Politics as an Explanative Factor

I have not attempted to account systematically for most of the variations in the various quantitative indicia of antitrust enforcement presented in this study, although I suggested earlier that changes in the level of overall economic activity could not explain changes in the overall level of antitrust activity. One factor of potentially great explanative power is politics, the identity of the party in the White House. The parties have, or at least avow, different economic philosophies and antitrust has always been—or seemed—politically controversial.[46] The possibility that the politics of the Administration affects either the quantity or quality of antitrust activity is explored, with negative results, in Tables 34 and 35 and Figure IV. If we exclude the period before 1905, when antitrust activity was quantitatively negligible, Democratic administrations have brought 979 antitrust cases and Republican administrations 550. During this period the Democrats have occupied the White House 58.2 per cent of the time. If their share of the cases were proportional to their occupancy of the White House, they would have brought 890 cases; and they have thus exceeded their quota. But this method of measurement is obviously unfair to the Republicans, whose Presidential terms are bunched in the early part of the period when the level of antitrust activity, regardless of the party in power, was much lower than later. Let us therefore split the period since the enactment of the Sherman Act into two parts, an earlier and a later period. A natural break between them comes at the end of Franklin D. Roosevelt's first term, in which 24 cases were filed; his next term the figure jumped to 115. In the earlier period, the Democrats occupied the White House 40.1 per cent of the time and if their share of cases were the same they would have brought 144; they brought only 110. In the later period the Democrats occupied the White House 72.8 per cent of the time and "should" have brought 868. They exceeded this quota very slightly, bringing 876.

---

[45] Richard A. Posner, *supra* note 29, at 1562 presents the case for using economic evidence to attack the problem of tacit collusion. But the argument can be extended to other price-fixing cases. Of general relevance is L. J. Zimmerman, The Propensity To Monopolize (1952).

[46] For an interesting discussion of the politics of antitrust see Richard Hofstadter, What Happened to the Antitrust Movement? in The Paranoid Style in American Politics and Other Essays 188 (1966).

TABLE 34

DEPARTMENT OF JUSTICE ANTITRUST CASES BY PRESIDENTIAL TERM

Term in Which Instituted	Party in White House	Number Instituted
1890-1893	R	6
1893-1897	D	7
1897-1901	R	3
1901-1905	R	6
1905-1909	R	36
1909-1913	R	74
1913-1917	D	31
1917-1921	D	48
1921-1925	R	51
1925-1929	R	54
1929-1933	R	19
1933-1937	D	24
1927-1941	D	115
1941-1945	D	157
1945-1949	D	126
1949-1953	D	148
1953-1957	R	106
1957-1961	R	171
1961-1965	D	176
1965-1969	D	154
1969	R	39

Source: Computed from the Bluebook.

A further refinement is to compare Republican and Democratic antitrust enforcement (for the period since 1936) eliminating those years in which the economy was in recession (GNP declined). The results are as before. The total number of cases brought in nonrecession years since 1936 is 1,008. Based on the number of nonrecession years in which they occupied the White House during this period, the Democrats "should" have brought 747; they in fact exceeded this quota very slightly, bringing 763. An additional test of the impact of politics on antitrust enforcement is whether the number of cases brought in Presidential election years is above or below average. If politics had no effect, we would expect that 25 per cent of all Department of Justice antitrust cases would have been initiated in such years; in fact 26.7 per cent have been initiated in such years. Finally, as shown in Figure IV, in which the solid bars indicate the number of cases brought in the first term after a change of parties, no systematic tendency of one party to increase or decrease antitrust activity upon taking office appears.

Table 35 takes a more qualitative approach to the problem. Landmark cases selected from a variety of sources have been grouped by Presidential term, and a composite figure representing the average of the three sources determined for each term. Since the enactment of the Sherman Act the Democrats have been in the White House 48.1 per cent of the time and their "quota" of landmark cases is therefore 22.8. They have modestly exceeded this, bringing a total of 24.2, in fact.

A STATISTICAL STUDY OF ANTITRUST ENFORCEMENT 413

FIGURE IV
DEPARTMENT OF JUSTICE CASES INITIATED BY PRESIDENTIAL TERM*

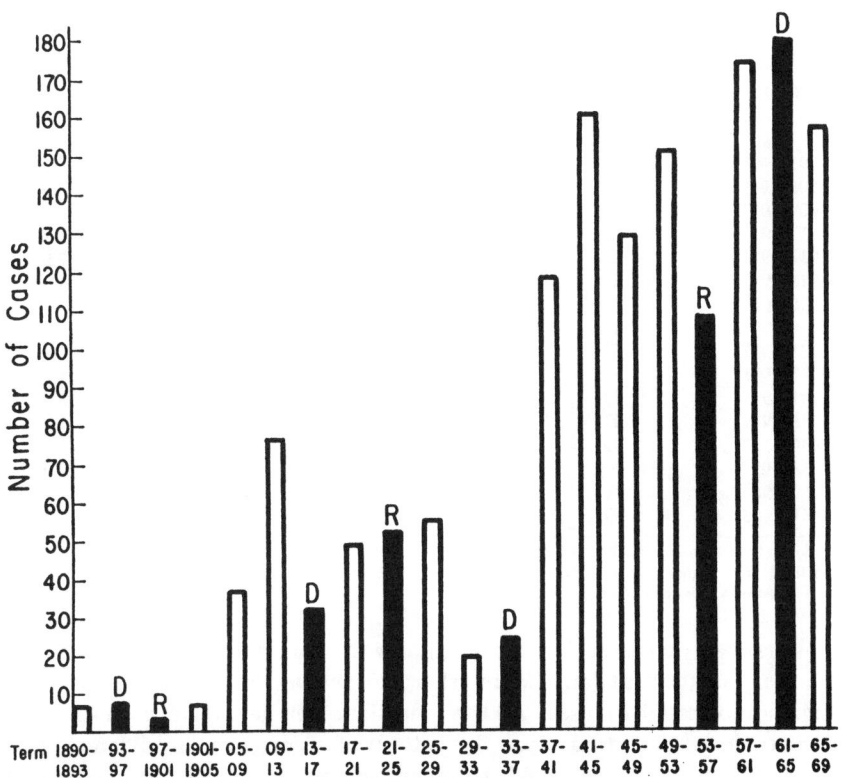

Source: Table 34.
* Terms in which party in White House changed are indicated by a solid bar.

On such evidence as I have been able to gather, it does not appear that the identity of the party in power has much influence on the quantity of quality of the Justice Department's antitrust activity.

VIII. CONCLUSION: THE IMPORTANCE OF GOOD STATISTICS TO SOUND POLICY PLANNING

The foregoing analysis of the statistics of antitrust enforcement does not purport to be exhaustive. It could be improved and extended in many ways. It could be improved by going back to the original records of cases kept by the Department of Justice, the FTC, and state agencies rather than relying on the summaries done by Commerce Clearing House. Sampling techniques could be utilized to learn more about the private cases. Interviews with

TABLE 35
"LANDMARK" CASES BY PRESIDENTIAL TERM

Term	Party	Blake and Pitofsky Casebook	U. Chi. Antitrust Materials	Most Frequently Cited[a]	Average
1890-1893	R	1	1		.7
1893-1897	D	1	2	1	.8
1897-1901	R	0	0		
1901-1905	R	1	1		.7
1905-1909	R	2	6	2	3.3
1909-1913	R	2	5	4	3.7
1913-1917	D	1	3	1	1.7
1917-1921	D	3	1	2	2.0
1921-1925	R	5	3	5	4.3
1925-1929	R	1	1		.7
1929-1933	R	3	3	3	3.0
1933-1937	D	2	2	2	2.0
1937-1941	D	3	3	5	3.7
1941-1945	D	4	1	4	3.0
1945-1949	D	6	5	7	6.0
1949-1953	D	4	2		2.0
1953-1957	R	2	2	2	2.0
1957-1961	R	7	4	3	4.7
1961-1965	D	6	3		3.0

Source: Harlan M. Black & Robert Pitofsky, Cases and Materials on Antitrust Law (1967); materials on the Law of Competition and Monopoly (U. Chi. Law School, mimeo.).

[a] Based on a survey of recent legal literature.

businessmen and their lawyers might reveal more about the deterrent impact of the antitrust laws. More refined techniques for measuring statistical significance could be used. And, as mentioned earlier, there is much more that could be done to analyze the pattern of enforcement in different markets. All these things could be done without changing the underlying methods by which antitrust statistics are now obtained and recorded, and are interesting projects in themselves. But those methods should be changed, and in the interest not merely of scholarship, but also of intelligent law enforcement.

Without the Bluebook, this study would have been much more difficult. But while the Bluebook is an invaluable source of information, it is limited to Department of Justice cases and contains much less information than could be desired and readily obtained.[47] The situation would be greatly improved for the future, and at little cost, by initiation of a program having the following essential features:

1. Every new case filed by the Department, the FTC, states, and private antitrust plaintiffs would be summarized and the summaries placed on computer cards

[47] As mentioned earlier, its counterpart for FTC cases, the FTC Docket of Complaints, is even skimpier.

or tape and revised (as the Bluebook summaries now are) whenever judicial or other new developments occurred. (Private cases could easily be monitored for this purpose by the United States Attorney in each district.)

2. Revisions would indicate not only later developments, the present Bluebook practice, but any new information developed in the proceeding with respect to number of conspirators, duration of conspiracy, sales involved, and other facts included in the summary (see 3 next).

3. Each summary would include the following information (I exclude information that is already routinely included in the Bluebook summaries), which would be added as it became known:

   a. The number of conspirators.

   b. The duration of the conspiracy (if it is a horizontal-conspiracy case), when it was first detected, and how.

   c. The assets and annual sales of each defendant and coconspirator.

   d. The amount of sales actually involved in the violation.

   e. Whether there has been any, or no, litigation.

   f. When the relief decreed was actually carried out.

   g. The terms of the decree.

   h. Whether, in the case of a government proceeding, there was a subsequent private suit and if so what its outcome was.

   i. The major factual findings of each court.

   j. The damages and attorney's fee, if known, in all private cases.

   k. Prior related violations of the antitrust laws by any defendant or coconspirator in the case.

   l. The 4-digit Standard Industrial Classification of the product or service involved.

4. Statistical summaries and analyses of the information thus obtained would be made and published on a regular basis.

A more costly but I think eminently worthwhile undertaking would be to prepare similar summaries of past cases. This should be possible for all but some private cases, and would permit studies such as the present one to be greatly improved.

Such a program as outlined above could be conducted by a government agency, perhaps a joint committee of the FTC and the Antitrust Division, or by a private group like Commerce Clearing House, or by a mixed public-private group. That is essentially a detail. Whoever conducts the program, the principal immediate beneficiary will be the enforcement agencies. They have the most direct and substantial interest in the statistics of antitrust. The interest is as yet unrecognized: the antitrust agencies collect few such statistics at present, even for internal use.[48]

---

[48] Some improvement in recent years is apparent. See, for example, 1967 Att'y Gen. Ann. Rep. 101-08. Inquiries of the Department have failed to elicit detailed information on the antitrust statistics currently being gathered.

To explain why the government has an important interest in antitrust statistics requires that we consider the perennial, and heretofore rather empty, subject of policy or program planning in the enforcement of regulatory policies. The need for better planning is widely conceded but no substantive measures to meet it have been taken, at least in the antitrust field. Although the FTC has a Program Review Officer and the Antitrust Division has had a succession of very able Directors of Policy Planning, in neither agency has much activity worthy of being called planning occurred. The absence of a statistical program is at least part of the problem.

A "planned" approach to antitrust enforcement, let us agree, would have the following main features:

1. Rational allocation of enforcement responsibilities among the different enforcement institutions;

2. Within each agency, evaluation of the agency's various programs, and movement of resources from those programs that the evaluation reveals to have a low payoff to those having a higher payoff;

3. Identification of areas in which the agency's existing resources or authority are inadequate.

The present approach lacks these features, and must continue to so long as the agencies manifest uninterest in antitrust statistics.

1. The power to initiate antitrust proceedings is shared by the private bar, the Department of Justice, the Federal Trade Commission, and state agencies. Although this dispersion of authority is of long standing, no reasoned principles for dividing the work of antitrust enforcement among the various enforcement institutions have yet evolved; the operative principle is catch-as-catch-can. The statistics of enforcement might be helpful in developing sensible principles. Consider the enormous recent increase in private antitrust actions and the fact that today a large fraction of private antitrust plaintiffs are at least partially successful. These findings, reported elsewhere in this paper, indicate that the private action is probably an effective remedy in cases where the size of the injury to the individual victim of the violation is sufficiently large to justify his bearing the costs of a lawsuit. If so, the continued proclivity of the Department (and the Federal Trade Commission) for bringing "abuses" cases, where there is ordinarily a businessman-victim who should be quite capable of suing on his own, seems contrary to the dictates of sound planning. For the government to proceed in such cases deflects resources from the violations (including most price-fixing conspiracies and anticompetitive mergers) in which a private suit providing complete relief is unlikely to be brought. In addition, as I have noted elsewhere in a slightly different context, there is a danger that a businessman who complains to the government about the conduct of a business rival is seeking to inhibit the competition of that rival by forcing

him to sustain litigation costs that the complainant, by getting the government to sue for him, escapes altogether.[49] On both counts, most abuses cases should, in the interest of efficient antitrust enforcement, be left to the private bar.

Another area where the statistics of enforcement point to a possible reallocation of antitrust responsibilities involves the division of cases between federal and state antitrust agencies. As we saw earlier, more than one-half of the conspiracy cases brought by the Department of Justice have involved regional or local rather than nationwide conspiracies (Table 25). Most of these conspiracies take place entirely within one state. It is far from certain that a federal agency should concern itself with a conspiracy, say, of the refuse collectors in a single city, especially now that many states have enacted antitrust statutes and established antitrust divisions. Perhaps the Department of Justice, rather than continuing to bring so many local cases, should be referring local complaints to state agencies for action, or endeavoring to strengthen local antitrust enforcement by advice or grants. We cannot be sure that a greater decentralization of antitrust enforcement would be an improvement over the present situation without knowing more about the efficient scale of antitrust enforcement and the costs of centralization. But it is enough to note that the question is an important and ignored one, and that, once again, a prerequisite to progress is the collection of systematic information, here, concerning the geographical scope of federal antitrust cases and the authority, activities, and resources of local antitrust agencies.

2. The Antitrust Division of the Department of Justice has an Evaluation Section under the Director of Policy Planning and the FTC has a Program Review Officer; but in neither agency is there any systematic review of programs, and there cannot be when neither agency collects adequate statistical data on what it is doing. Let me indicate some possible benefits from using such data as the basis of program evaluation. A careful review of the duration, decrees, and aftermaths of the Department's major monopolization cases—going beyond Table 29—might indicate that the payoff from cases seeking to restructure markets is smaller in relation to the resources expended than that from other cases brought by the Department.[50]

---

[49] Richard A. Posner, *supra* note 22, at 70.

[50] In this regard, it is interesting to note that a recent study found that a high level of concentration in an industry tends to dissipate by natural forces within an average period of 10 years. Yale Brozen, The Antitrust Task Force Recommendation for Deconcentration, 13 J. Law & Econ. 279 (1970). My table 29 discloses that the average length of a divestiture proceeding in a monopolization case involving a major regional or national market is 8 years, so assuming that a proceeding will not normally be brought immediately upon the attainment of monopoly, it seems unlikely that administrative methods of deconcentration will work significantly more rapidly than the market. Kenneth G. Elzinga, The Antimerger Law: Pyrrhic Victories?, 12 J. Law & Econ. 43, 74-75 (1969), makes a similar point with respect to divestiture in merger cases.

A similar review of experience in merger cases might indicate that the government should drop any merger case in which it fails to obtain a preliminary injunction barring consummation of the merger. A review of the Department's "regulatory" decrees might indicate that many or most of them should not continue to be enforced and, furthermore, that cases likely to terminate in such a decree should no longer be brought.[51] Similarly, the Department could determine how many of its cases involve violations in markets that, by virtue of low concentration or other factors, are not seriously prone to monopolization, with a view toward deciding whether too many resources are now being devoted to such markets. These are only a few examples of the fruitful program evaluations that could be conducted by antitrust agencies if they kept simple quantitative records of their activities.

3. I have thus far assumed that the resources and authority of the agency in question are taken as given. But they need not be, and an important planning function is to identify areas in which the marginal product of augmenting the agency's resources or authority would exceed the marginal political and other costs. This function, once again, cannot be performed without an adequate statistical base. The matter of criminal penalties will illustrate. As noted earlier, the Department of Justice has recently recommended that the maximum penalty under the Sherman Act be increased from $50,000 to $500,000. But, as we saw, the statistics of the actual penalties imposed in Sherman Act cases cast doubt on whether a marked increase in actual penalties would follow from the proposed change. Lacking systematic information concerning either the actual incidence of antitrust fines or the penalties imposed in private suits that follow government actions, the Department is simply in no position at present to make responsible legislative proposals in the penalty area.

I conclude that the antitrust agencies are ignoring the prerequisites—and particularly the statistical prerequisites—of serious planning and I should like in closing to venture a partial explanation of why this is so. The people who manage the antitrust agencies—who, not incidentally, are lawyers—do not view antitrust enforcement as a means, but as an end. They do not view it as a "business" whose "output" is reductions in monopoly power and whose "inputs" are the legal and related activities (private as well as public) employed in bringing about such reductions. If such a view of the matter

---

[51] As suggested by the Report of the President's Task Force on Productivity and Competition (the Stigler Report), reprinted in Hearings, Small Business and the Robinson-Patman Act, before the Special Subcomm. on Small Business and the Robinson-Patman Act of the House Select Comm. on Small Business, 91st Cong., 1st Sess., vol. 1, at 271, 281 (1969). See Kenneth G. Elzinga, *supra* note 50, at 66-72, for a critical analysis of the regulatory decree in cases under Section 7 of the Clayton Act.

were taken, it would become obvious that the various "factors of production" used in the "business," such as the Antitrust Division's personnel and the private antitrust bar, might be more productive in some combinations than in others; that small distortions in competitive behavior that require costly and protracted trials to rectify are not cost-justified and should therefore be ignored; that proceedings that do not terminate in effective remedies should be avoided; that the penalty system should be designed to make the cost of being detected violating the antitrust laws, discounted by the probability of escaping detection, greater than the benefit to the violator of his violation; and that careful records of antitrust activity should be kept and consulted. Because the lawyers who manage the antitrust agencies do not conceive of antitrust enforcement in the way I have suggested, they largely ignore the facts and implications that have been the subject of this study, and they conduct an enterprise that, if it made shoes instead of an intangible called competition, would rightly be considered mismanaged. So far as I am able to determine, the Department of Justice, to take the most distinguished component of the antitrust enforcement system, makes little effort to identify those markets in which serious problems of monopoly are likely to arise; except in the merger area, does not act save on complaint; makes no systematic effort to see whether its decrees are being complied with; keeps few worthwhile statistics on its own activities—and none on those of other components of the enforcement system; does not have adequate records of the criminal and civil penalties imposed on the defendants in its cases; makes no systematic effort to identify repeated violators of the antitrust laws; routinely prosecutes all reported *per se* violations, including agreements to fix prices that, considering the nature of the product and the conspirators' market share, are almost surely unsuccessful attempts; and is, in short, inappropriately run as a law firm, where the workload is determined by the wishes of the clients (in this case mostly unhappy competitors, aggrieved purchasers, and disgruntled employees), and where the social product of the legal services undertaken is not measured.

There is doubtless some element of overstatement in this indictment, but I believe it essentially correct. Antitrust enforcement is inefficient, and the first step toward improvement must be, I am convinced, a much greater interest in the dry subject of this paper, antitrust statistics.

[17]

The appropriate scope of regulation in the cable television industry

Richard A. Posner

Professor of Law
University of Chicago

The development of cable television has been subjected to a comprehensive and complex array of federal, state, and local regulations; and many new proposals for regulation are being discussed. This paper attempts a critique of the emerging pattern of regulation. The author analyzes the major policy choices and concludes that only limited regulation can be justified. He proposes a new federal statute that would carefully delimit the respective roles of federal, state, and municipal regulators of cable television.

1. Introduction

■ The government has not left development of cable television to the free market. Extensive regulation of rates, programs, ownership, and other facets of cable television service has been proposed and, in large measure, already implemented. A critique of the emerging pattern of regulation would seem to be timely.

I limit discussion here to the fundamental policy choices. To expound the details of particular regulations and proposals, most of which are in the nature of ephemeral and unprincipled comprises, would serve only to obscure the basic issues. Section 2 of this paper deals with a theme of growing importance in a number of substantive areas of cable television regulation: the use of regulation to compel the provision of services that do not pay their way in the market—what I call "taxation by regulation." Sections 3–5 analyze the substantive areas of regulation, divided into three broad groups: (1) regulation concerned with the content of programming on cable television; (2) regulation concerned with the level of the rates charged to the subscribers by cable television companies; and (3) regulation designed to reduce the impact on the television broadcasting industry of the competition of cable television. Section 6 considers the in-

Richard A. Posner received the A.B. from Yale University and the LL.B. from Harvard Law School. He is a Research Associate of the National Bureau of Economic Research and editor of *The Journal of Legal Studies*, a new journal published by the University of Chicago Law School. Professor Posner's interests include the application of economic theory to law, especially in the regulated industries, and the empirical study of the legal system.

This paper was commissioned by the Sloan Commission on Cable Communications. Section 4 is an abridgment of Posner, "Cable Television: The Problem of Local Monopoly" [23], and Sections 3 and 5 draw in part on research supported by The Rand Corporation under a grant from the Ford Foundation. In addition, ideas expressed in this paper were developed in part in the Workshop in Regulation of Economic Activity of the University of Chicago Law School, supported by The Brookings Institution. None of the views or conclusions expressed in this paper should be interpreted as reflecting the policies or opinions of the Sloan Commission, the Ford Foundation, The Rand Corporation, or The Brookings Institution.

stitutional problems created by the fact that three levels of government—municipal, state, and federal—are vying to regulate the industry, and summarizes the article's major recommendations.

■ Regulatory agencies often use their control over the rate structure of regulated firms to compel the provision of unremunerative services, in much the same way that the taxing and spending powers of legislatures are used to compel the provision of services that the market would not provide, at least in the desired quantity.[1] The basic mechanism is the "internal subsidy," whereby a firm (or group of firms) provides some services at a loss which it recoups by charging a price above cost for other services. Internal subsidization on a systematic basis is possible only in a regulated industry or in one, like the postal service, where the government is the provider of the service. In an unregulated private market, firms would not provide unremunerative services for any length of time.

Internal subsidies have been quite common in the communications field[2] and already have a considerable foothold in the cable television industry. Municipalities, as a condition of franchising cable television companies, commonly require that the franchisee provide one or more channels, free of charge, to the licensing authority for public purposes. The FCC insists that the larger cable companies, as a condition of being permitted to carry distant signals, provide some original programming[3]—a stipulation that would be superfluous if such programming were expected to be profitable—and is toying with the idea of requiring cable operators to remit 5 percent of their subscription revenues to noncommercial broadcasters. Additional instances of internal subsidization in the cable industry include New York City's public-access channels[4] and occasional suggestions for wiring up slum urban areas at preferential rates.

A recent paper by John McGowan, Roger Noll, and Merton Peck provides a clue to the potential importance of the practice.[5] Their procedure is to quantify the "surplus" (approximately the potential monopoly profits) from the sale of those cable communications services for which there is a market and to appraise the claims of various interests to the surplus. Such an approach assumes that internal subsidization is the crucial issue in cable television regulation.

Despite wide acceptance of the practice, I am persuaded that it would be a mistake to countenance it in the cable industry, not least

[1] See Posner [26].

[2] Some examples: Telephone rates display a uniformity at sharp variance with the structure of costs, and telephone company officials have often defended the rate structure by reference to the alleged social desirability of internal subsidization. The reader may recall that when it first appeared that communications satellites might be able to distribute network television programs at highly remunerative rates, the Ford Foundation proposed that a portion of the profits be reserved for noncommercial television—by definition a service not provided in the market at a price that covers costs. The proposal is discussed in Dirlam and Kahn [8].

[3] See First Report and Order in Docket 18397 (CATV) [32]. The requirement was recently invalidated by a federal court of appeals in a case that the Supreme Court has agreed to review: Midwest Video Corp. v. United States, 441 F. 2d 1322 (8th Cir. 1971).

[4] See New York Mayor's Advisory Committee Report [18].

[5] See [16].

from the standpoint of those who wish to see cable service rapidly attain a very high degree of market penetration. In order to obtain a fund out of which to defray the expense of unprofitable services, the industry would have to fix rates substantially above cost to subscribers (their paying customers). The McGowan, Noll, and Peck study assumes that suppliers of cable television service can exact monopoly prices from subscribers. It is the resulting monopoly profits that would be the source of the fund. Yet the study does not regard monopoly pricing as an inevitable condition of the industry. On the contrary, it assumes that regulation could be employed effectively to compress price to cost, thereby securing the entire surplus for consumers. One may have less faith in the efficacy of regulation than does the study, yet agree (for reasons discussed later) that monopoly pricing of cable service is not inevitable.

By either route, it follows that a policy of internal subsidization is likely to lead to higher subscriber rates than alternative policies.[6] This in turn will result in a reduction in the scale of the industry, for the demand for cable television cannot be completely inelastic, especially given the over-the-air alternatives. There may also be serious dynamic consequences. The McGowan, Noll, and Peck study apparently assumes that whether the surplus that remains after all internal subsidies have been paid is one dollar or one billion dollars, the expansion of the cable industry will be unaffected; but this is dubious. If the entire surplus accrues to subscribers in the form of lower prices for cable service, more households will subscribe sooner. Notice that internal subsidization does not infuse an industry with new resources for growth. It retards development in some submarkets (by compelling higher prices in them) in order to accelerate it in others. Where the burdened service is basic to the industry, as is getting the wire into the home, internal subsidization seems especially unlikely to improve the rate and direction of the industry's growth, and may retard it.[7]

Internal subsidization also erects a barrier to the displacement of old technology by new. One may illustrate with reference to the Ford Foundation proposal for the establishment of a nonprofit corporation to distribute network television programming by satellite,[8] with the profits of the corporation going to support noncommercial television. Suppose that the proposal has been adopted and several years later AT&T perfected a terrestrial laser system for distributing programs at lower cost. The networks would want to switch to AT&T. Noncommercial television, having meanwhile grown dependent on the revenues from the satellite system, could be expected to press for a rule either forbidding AT&T to offer the substitute service or compelling it to price the service at a level that would preserve a large share of the market for the satellite system.

---

[6] If monopoly pricing were inevitable, one effect of internal subsidization would be a transfer of monopoly profits from the stockholders of cable companies to the recipients of the subsidized services. But it would not be the only effect. If the subsidy were collected by a tax on costs or prices, the firm would raise price and reduce output. See Posner [23]. Proposals for internal subsidies of cable service, such as a 5-percent gross-receipts tax on cable companies for public broadcasting, are of this kind.

[7] See Coase [3].

[8] See note 2 *supra*.

The cable television industry presents an analogy. In view of the rapidity with which communications technology has been changing, one cannot assume that the cable represents the last word in the distribution of broadband communications. Satellites broadcasting directly to household television receivers may someday provide the same service as cable television systems at lower cost. Such a development would be retarded if an assumed surplus from cable service had been earmarked for specified public services, whose providers and beneficiaries would bring pressure to bear on government to prevent the erosion of the surplus by a new competitor.

At the very least, the possibility of new competition necessitates a cumbersome administrative apparatus to control entry. The last example assumed that direct satellite broadcasting might someday be a cheaper alternative to cable television. Suppose it is not cheaper; it might seem cheaper to the consumer—the price of the service might be less than the cable subscription rate—not because the cost was lower but because the subscription rate had built into it a charge for defraying a subsidy elsewhere in the system. To prevent diversion of business to the apparently cheaper but really dearer service requires public control over entry.

Let us now shift attention from efficiency to equity. Internal subsidization is a method of redistributing income. The subscriber who pays a higher rate than if the entire "surplus" were passed on to the subscribers is put in a worse position; whoever benefits from the subsidized services is put in a better position. One of the characteristics of internal subsidization as a method of redistribution is that it is likely to be regressive. It is essentially an excise tax—on a service, in this instance, that cannot be regarded as a "luxury" item. Enabling as it does the substitution of "free"[9] service for non-free sources of information and entertainment such as newspapers and motion pictures, television—cable television where over-the-air signal reception is very poor or the number of available over-the-air signals are very few—is well nigh indispensable to lower-income families.

If cable revenues are used to support public broadcasting, the result will be a redistribution of wealth from a lower to a higher income group, because noncommercial programming (with a few exceptions like "Sesame Street") is geared to highly educated, well-to-do viewers. If cable television revenues were used to finance the extension of cable service at zero or very low rates to slum neighborhoods, then the redistribution might be in the opposite direction. But even here one must be careful. The additional cost involved in complying with the requirement might retard the spread of cable service and this could delay service to all, including many lower-income people who would have been willing to pay marginal cost charges to obtain cable service.

There is a final point: The methods used in the McGowan, Noll, and Peck study to project the "surplus" of revenue over cost in the

---

[9] Over-the-air television is not strictly free: its cost is presumably reflected in the prices for the products advertised on television. But this method of financing the cost of broadcasting is highly favorable to the poor in comparison with charging viewers directly. See Lees and Yang [14]. Furthermore, as discussed *infra*, p. 105, it is not even clear that the prices of products now advertised on television would be lower were television advertising forbidden.

cable television industry permit only the crudest approximation. One cannot make accurate forecasts of aggregate nationwide consumer demand for a service that barely exists in major television markets. The resulting uncertainty, however, must greatly complicate the administration of any program of internal subsidization. Consider the FCC's proposed 5-percent cable television "dividend" for public broadcasting. If the surplus is less than at present imagined, such an exaction could have a debilitating effect on the industry's development;[10] if it is larger it could produce a revenue for public broadcasting that was in excess of the legitimate needs of that service when balanced against other claims on available sources of funds. Uncertainty as to the likely support forthcoming would retard planning by the recipients of the subsidy.

3. Regulation of cable television programming

■ Much of the sentiment for internal subsidization of cable service reflects dissatisfaction with the program policies of broadcast television and a fear that without regulatory action the program fare carried on cable television will be no more satisfactory. We consider first whether this fear has a basis.

□ **The impact of cable television on the quality or diversity of programming.** A well-functioning market may be assumed to provide the type and amount of a good that best satisfies the tastes of consumers, aggregated according to willingness to pay. In the case of over-the-air television service, however, the scarcity of channel space may appear to destroy any presumption that the market would satisfy a wide variety of tastes—and the abundance of channel space on the cable, to restore it. The matter, I believe, is more complicated.

There is a good deal of unused over-the-air television channel space in the UHF band today. Many channels allocated to UHF broadcasting by the FCC have never been assigned: no one has stepped forward to apply for a broadcasting license. Chicago, Detroit, and Philadelphia are among the many major markets where there is an unassigned commercial UHF channel. Furthermore, many independent UHF stations do not carry anywhere near a full week's programming, but come on the air in the late afternoon and go off before midnight.

A likely reason for so much unused air time is that the market for air time is thin. There are, to be sure, alternative explanations. One is that the UHF signal is weak, limiting audience and, hence advertiser, demand. In fact, UHF broadcasters are authorized to transmit as strong a signal as the VHF broadcasters (UHF channel 20 in Washington, D. C., for example, has the most powerful television transmitter in the entire country). Many UHF signals are indeed understrength, but only because the additional cost of maintaining a stronger signal is deemed to exceed the additional advertising revenues (resulting from a larger audience) that such a signal would generate. Another possibility is that the cost of

---

[10] A recent and responsible study concluded that the cost to the cable industry of complying with the various requirements imposed or proposed to be imposed by the FCC was much higher than anyone—or at least the FCC—had believed. See Comanor and Mitchell [6].

over-the-air broadcasting is very high. According to the McGowan, Noll, and Peck study, however, the cost is approximately the same as that of broadcasting on a channel of cable television.[11] The cost of transmission is, in any event, dwarfed by the talent and other costs incurred in producing a television program.

Two explanations for the large amount of unused air time that cannot be so readily rejected are, first, the fact that even today only one out of two television sets have UHF reception, and, second, the absence of click tuning for UHF, which, silly as it may seem, is widely thought to deter viewers from watching UHF stations. These are transitory problems. All new television receivers are required by law to provide UHF reception and the FCC will soon propose click tuning for the UHF channels. Perhaps when these problems are solved advertisers will purchase at remunerative rates all of the air time allocated by the FCC to commercial television. But I am skeptical, because of the nature of the market in which air time is at present sold.

Air time is sold to advertisers and what they are buying is not entertainment but an audience for their advertising. Because television is one of many advertising media and advertising only one of several business methods for promoting the sale of a product, the amount of money that an advertiser is willing to pay for broadcast time is limited. He will in fact pay only a few pennies per viewer. This means that a costly program is not feasible unless it attracts a very large audience. Therefore, multiplying the number of channels, as by licensing additional UHF stations, must soon cease to be commercially practicable as long as advertising remains the sole support of commercial television. The more channels there are, the smaller will be the audience for each and the less likely it will be that advertising revenues can cover the programming costs of all of the channels. From this it follows that cable television, insofar as it merely makes available a very large number of channels for television, is unlikely to change markedly the character and amount of programming. However, cable television does more: it facilitates the introduction of pay television, which would end the total dependence of television on advertising revenues.

One reason why the prospects of pay television on the air have remained dim is its high cost. Subscribers to Hartford's experimental pay television station were required to pay a $39 annual decoder rental to cover the cost of scrambling and unscrambling the broadcast signal (without scrambling, nonsubscribers would have received the signal free of charge), and this for only one channel of pay television.[12] Moreover, the charge to the subscriber for individual programs included substantial billing, accounting, and other operating expenses exclusive of program costs—which were in fact only about 15 percent of total costs. The nonprogram cost component would be substantially lower were pay television provided on channels of a cable television system. The cable operator who wanted to experiment with pay television would not have to buy or lease an entire broadcasting station, but could use one or more channels in

---

[11] See [16], pp. 27, 44.
[12] See Subscription Television Service [39].

his existing system. A simple filter to deny a channel to a cable subscriber who had not paid to receive that channel would replace expensive scrambling and unscrambling equipment. Billing and accounting costs would be lower because the system must bill the subscriber anyway for the basic monthly fee.

If the demand for pay television is reasonably elastic, and if the marginal cost of providing pay television on the cable is substantially less than the cost of providing the same service over the air, then we can expect the supply of, and demand for, pay television, on the cable, to be much greater than McGowan, Noll, and Peck's very modest projection of the Hartford experiment would indicate.[13] There are two additional points: Multiple channels of pay television, fully practicable on the cable, would permit a better matching of program types to viewers' preferences; and if the same pay television programs were carried by many cable systems, program costs could be spread over many more viewers than were within the broadcast radius of the Hartford station.

An important factor is the attitude of regulatory authorities toward the provision of pay television by cable operators. The development of an over-the-air pay television service has been crippled by regulatory limitations. Even the FCC's newly liberalized rules authorize the establishment of a pay television station only in markets that have at least four other broadcasting stations, and strictly limit the sports events, motion pictures, and series-type programs that a pay television station may·carry.[14]

The program ("siphoning") restrictions have been applied to cable operators wishing to institute pay television,[15] but no other restrictions have been imposed and in general the FCC seems less worried about pay television on the cable. It may feel that since cable television is a pay service to begin with, a prohibition against a charge for additional service would defy rationalization. Perhaps it recognizes that since the cable industry has a dual interest—in program revenues and in revenues from the basic subscription fee—it is unlikely to emasculate free service by bidding away all of the popular programs from advertisers for direct sale to viewers: it would lose many marginal subscribers. Whatever the precise reason, pay television on the cable may well encounter less regulatory obstruction than over-the-air pay television. Cable television may therefore provide the decisive opportunity for the establishment of a viable system of pay television.

This observation should be welcomed by those who believe that present television fare lacks richness and diversity. The essential fact is that the advertiser is not an adequate proxy for the viewer. His basic objective is to maximize audience coverage. The aversion of advertisers to supporting programs that are offensive to important groups in the community indicates that viewers will sometimes retaliate against an advertiser; perhaps there is a complementary tendency of viewers to reward advertisers whose programs please them greatly. But these tendencies are weak. They are in conflict

---

[13] See McGowan, Noll, and Peck [16], pp. 29–32. They recognize that their projection may be too low. *Ibid.*, p. 32.

[14] See Fourth Report and Order (Subscription Television) [33].

[15] See Memorandum Opinion and Order in Docket 18397 (CATV) [35].

with the individual viewer's self-interest, which is best served by separate selection of product and program. The viewer knows that his decision to buy one more (or less) box of cornflakes than he actually wants will not affect his television options.

Under a system of pay television, small audiences having strong preferences for particular types of programs would sometimes bid away time from large audiences having weak preferences for other types. This does not happen today. Even if an advertiser could measure the intensity of viewing preferences, he would not sponsor a program preferred by a smaller audience unless the viewers' program preferences fortuitously accorded with their product preferences. Direct viewer payments, moreover, might greatly increase the resources invested in television programming. Advertisers have better substitutes for television as an advertising medium than do viewers for television as a medium of entertainment and information. One can think of many programs for which viewers would probably pay much more than a few pennies and which are not broadcast today only because they cannot command a huge audience. An audience of 200,000 willing to spend $2 each can pay for an hour of expensive programming; an advertiser would insist on an audience 100 times (or more) as great.

By making the fractionation of the total audience for television programs, economically feasible, pay television would create a market for many channels, which are just what cable television can provide. The opportunity costs of providing many channels over the air would, in contrast, be extremely high because of the need to preempt spectrum space now used by other services.

Since the growth of pay television on the cable would be encouraged by repealing the "siphoning" restrictions that the FCC has imposed, we must consider whether those restrictions are justifiable. The concern that underlies them is that unregulated pay television (whether carried over the air or by cable systems) would bid away the most popular programming from the "free" broadcast service and thereby force people (some of them poor) who now watch these programs without charge to pay for them. An inadequate answer is that "free" television isn't really free because consumers of goods and services advertised on television pay for television programs in the form of higher prices for advertised products. It is not obvious, however, that such products would be cheaper if they were not advertised on television. Perhaps they would be more expensive because substitute methods of advertising or sales promotion were less efficient; or perhaps the consumer would spend more money on finding the right product. Even if not free, advertiser-supported television may be cheaper to the viewer who is a consumer of brand-name products than a system of pay television would be. Viewers might pay more for television than advertisers and might pay on top of advertisers, as in the newspaper and magazine industries, in which case it would appear to be inescapable that pay television had resulted in raising the price of television to the public.

This conclusion ignores, however, the incentive of program producers to devise substitutes for any program bought by a pay television station or network. These substitutes would be offered to advertiser-supported stations; and the pay television company would find it difficult to charge a price for seeing the original program when a substitute program was available to the viewer without charge. This of course assumes the continuation of free television, an important qualification to which we shall return.

For some television programs there may be no adequate substitute. But it is easy to exaggerate the unique and nonduplicatable in television programming. If, for example, the television revenues of professional football teams are very great, there will be more teams and greater promotion of sports such as soccer that have similar viewing characteristics. Every television viewer knows that successful formats in television entertainment are replicated endlessly.

What is likely is not that pay television will result in viewers' paying to see the identical fare that they now see for nothing, but that it will enable them to purchase television programs that they cannot obtain now on any terms (such as the opera that costs $400,000 to produce, has a potential nationwide television audience of only one million, and is not broadcast because advertisers will not pay $0.40 per viewer for television advertising time). Stated otherwise, pay television will enable viewers to substitute television programs for other goods that they value less. That is why the motion picture exhibitors are so hostile to pay television. They fear that people would rather pay $1 to see a first-run motion picture in their home, without advertising, than pay $3 to see it in a movie theatre.

The restrictions imposed by the FCC on pay television, both on the cable and over the air, may appear to let us have our cake and eat it too. They prevent the siphoning of popular television programming but leave pay television free to offer the type of program that is not carried on free television because the audience is too small. That is theory: practically, the restrictions may kill pay television in its infancy. They will certainly retard its growth.

Rather than restricting the growth of pay television, the goal of policy should be to assure competition in television distribution. As long as advertisers are able to obtain programs at cost, which are then shown to the viewer without charge, the viewer-consumer is protected, with respect to the wide range of programs that are not unique, against being forced to pay exorbitant charges. Fortunately, even the rosiest predictions of cable penetration indicate that the demise of over-the-air broadcasting is remote.[16]

□ **Monopoly regulations.** The attractive possibilities for pay television on the cable should reduce concern that cable television, as a medium of diverse and high-quality programming, is likely to founder on the same shoals as over-the-air television. But perhaps the new medium eliminates one set of programming problems only to create another—monopoly control over programming.[17]

In general, neither economic theory nor empirical study supports the belief that an unregulated monopolist will reduce the quality of his product in order to increase his profits.[18] He will provide what-

---

[16] We return to this issue in Section 5.

[17] Assuming, perhaps prematurely, that cable companies will be effective monopolists in their service areas—on which see Section 4. There we also consider the problem of cable monopoly insofar as it is assumed to lead to higher subscriber rates rather than to less program choice.

[18] See Posner [24], pp. 584–85, for a review of this question.

ever level of quality the consumer is willing to pay for. Faced with a schedule of monopoly prices for alternative levels of quality, the consumer may choose a lower (cheaper) quality level than if competitive prices were charged, but the evil in such a case is not product degradation; it is monopoly pricing. However, when the monopolist's rates are regulated—a likely outcome in the cable television industry—the analysis becomes more complicated. If price alone and not program quality were regulated, the cable monopolist would have a strong incentive to reduce the quality and hence cost of his programs in order to recapture some of the monopoly profits eliminated by the price control. The regulatory agency would try to follow him down, but it is difficult to measure a regulated firm's costs, and frequent changes in those costs due to altered quality complicate the regulatory task.

Even if the refinement just introduced is disregarded, the previous analysis was too simple; it ignored the element of nonpecuniary profit. A cable monopolist doesn't have to take all of his profits in the form of money; he can take some in the form of the satisfaction or sense of power that some people derive from preaching to others. In providing a program mixture different from what his subscribers prefer, he will not be able to charge so high a price, but the reduction in pecuniary profits may be smaller than the increase in nonpecuniary satisfaction. Regulation may encourage the substitution of nonpecuniary for pecuniary satisfactions if, as seems reasonable to assume, only pecuniary profits are effectively constrained by regulation.[19]

This is not strictly a phenomenon of monopoly or even of the communications industry. A farmer can scratch his initials on every radish that he sells, and while his costs will be higher and his net money income lower than that of other radish farmers, as long as the satisfaction he obtains exceeds the reduction in his pecuniary income he is acting rationally; the communications industry is simply a more plausible field for such endeavors. Monopoly makes the consequences of a seller's indulging his preference for nonpecuniary profits more serious than they would be in a competitive setting. If there are 30 media outlets in a market and one is owned by a crank determined to propagate his opinions, the effect on the viewing audience will be minimal because they have many alternatives. Even if there are several cranks, there is no cause for alarm because they are likely to be cranky in different ways, so that the public will be exposed to conflicting points of view. Problems of a different order of magnitude are presented if the same crank controls all of the media outlets in a market.

The propensity to trade pecuniary profits for the nonpecuniary satisfactions of seeking to mold public opinion is probably related—inversely—to the absolute size of the enterprise. A large company is less likely to be owned by an individual or family than a small one, and where ownership is widely dispersed the managers of a company will find it difficult to identify public issues on which a partisan stand would not offend large numbers of shareholders. On reflection it is not surprising that charges of unfairness in broadcasting have been directed primarily against the owners of small radio stations, inde-

---

[19] See Alchian and Kessel [1].

pendent television stations, and family-owned communications companies.

One partially offsetting factor should be noted. The larger an enterprise, the more likely that some of its activities will themselves be newsworthy, and these activities may not be fully and fairly reported by a media outlet owned by the enterprise. This was a major consideration that led the Department of Justice to oppose the merger of ABC and ITT before the Federal Communications Commission.[20] The Department pointed out that ITT's position as a major defense contractor and owner of telephone companies and other telecommunications interests in Latin America might prejudice ABC's reporting of defense and Latin-American affairs.

What are the implications of this analysis for cable television? Much of the programming carried by cable companies is beyond the power of the companies to alter or influence, for it consists of the programs of television stations whose signals are carried on the cable. Moreover, even with general rate regulation, the rates charged subscribers for special channels (or programs) are likely to remain unregulated, so that cable systems will retain a strong incentive to provide optimum service at least on those channels. Degradation of quality does not seem a serious danger.

The danger of local monopolies of the sources of opinion may well diminish rather than increase as cable television grows. By increasing the number of signals available in the home, cable television multiplies the subscriber's independent sources of news and opinion. This is an especially important factor in smaller markets, where in the absence of cable television households would receive only one or two signals; and it is in the smaller markets that the FCC has been most liberal about allowing cable systems to carry distant signals. Insofar as a cable system also originates programs on one or more channels, it creates an additional independent source (or sources) of news and opinion in the market.

Yet it is precisely the ability of a cable operator to originate on more than one channel that has led to proposals to restrict his control of channels on which he originates.[21] The cable operator who originates on two channels has been likened to a company that owns two television stations in the same market, a type of ownership forbidden by the FCC's misnamed "duopoly" rule.[22] The analogy is strained. The owner of a television station who purchases another such station in the same market thereby reduces the number of independent sources of news and opinion by one; the cable company that decides to originate on a second channel does not thereby alter the number of independent sources at all. Furthermore, the likelihood of multiple origination by the cable operator may be exaggerated. Programming and distribution on the cable are distinct functions. Distribution involves the installation, maintenance, and replacement of a grid of wires. The cable operator carries out distribution, and he also decides which broadcast signals in addition to those of the local stations (which he is required by FCC regulation to carry) to put on his cable—a programming function. If on top of this he procures the

---

[20] The story is told in Green [10], Vol. 2, pp. 853–59.

[21] See, e.g., Notice of Proposed Rulemaking and Notice of Inquiry in Docket No. 18397 (CATV) [36].

[22] This rule is described in Barnett [2], p. 251.

particular programs to be shown on one or more of "his own" channels, his operation becomes highly complex.

In these circumstances one would expect cable companies, without any prodding from government, to lease channels to firms specializing in the programming function. As the cable industry grows, we can expect the tendency toward vertical disintegration to grow too: the combination of functions observable in today's cable systems is a sign of the early stage of the industry's development.[23]

But leasing may not be a complete solution. As long as the cable operator is free to pick and choose among prospective lessees he may reject those whose programming policies do not accord with his preferences. A superficially attractive response is to forbid cable systems to discriminate among lessees of their channels. The difficulty is in defining and administering an adequate standard of nondiscrimination. The enforcing authority would perforce become deeply involved in the methods used by cable systems to price their channels and therefore in their methods of cost accounting. It would have to consider such thorny questions as whether a cable operator was justified in charging an additional price to a lessee whose unpopularity (for whatever reason) with a large segment of the viewing public was likely to impair the cable system's goodwill and revenues.

Either compulsory leasing or a rule forbidding discrimination among lessees seems too drastic, too far-reaching and, in light of experience with similar controls in the public utility and common carrier industries, too easily abused a measure to be imposed when it is as yet unclear what patterns of origination or leasing will emerge as the industry matures. Such measures might become irresistible, however, if cable systems were to affiliate with television stations, networks, newspapers, and other sources of news and opinion on a large scale. Where the only television station, newspaper, and cable system in a community are owned in common, one can still take comfort in the fact that the cable system will be importing the signals of stations not affiliated with the system; but it is small comfort, especially with regard to local news and events, in which distant stations presumably are uninterested. It is probably easier as an administrative matter to prevent concentration of a community's mass media in one set of hands than to accept the concentration and then try, through common carrier regulation, to force the monopolist to grant access to other voices on reasonable terms.

This consideration provides a practical reason for continuing (and perhaps extending to newspapers) the FCC's prohibition against common ownership of cable systems and television stations located in the same market,[24] while forgoing, at least for the present, rules governing leasing of channels. To be sure, a likely motive for the acquisition of cable systems by owners of competing media is a desire, akin to that which motivated the diversification program of the cigarette manufacturers, to move gracefully out of a declining industry. This process should be encouraged in the present context as in that of the cigarette industry in order to reduce the pressure exerted by the industry for protection against the causes of its decline. Furthermore, cross-media ownership, by increasing the size of cable

---

[23] Cf. Stigler [28], pp. 135–36.
[24] See Second Report and Order in Docket 18397 (CATV) [38].

enterprises, reduces, according to the earlier analysis, the likelihood that systematic influence molding will be attempted. On balance, even the case for ownership regulations is only marginally persuasive, albeit restrictions on cross-media ownership in a single market—which is all that I tentatively approve—would leave room for growth and diversification through media acquisitions across markets.

4. Regulation of subscriber rates

■ **Nature and magnitude of the monopoly problem.** A cable system's grid or network of cables is somewhat akin to that of the local water, electrical, gas, or telephone company. As with the supply of these other services, running more than one company's cable to any home would involve unnecessary duplication, for a single cable can carry all of the signals that a subscriber is likely to want and at substantially lower cost than two or more smaller cables. These characteristics raise the possibility of monopoly pricing, which leads to a reduction in output below efficient levels and, as mentioned earlier, would reduce the scale and growth of the cable television industry. However, some important qualifications must be borne in mind in the present context. To begin, the point that monopoly reduces output is strictly valid only if the monopolist is constrained to sell at a single price. Ordinarily, the assumption is justified, since if a seller sold at different prices to different purchasers those who bought at lower prices would resell to those charged the higher prices, and the monopolist's attempt to discriminate would fail. For sellers of non-transferable services such as cable television, however, arbitrage among purchasers is not much of a threat, and discrimination becomes a feasible strategy. A cable company would find it easy to discriminate. It could charge different rates in low- and high-income areas, a basic subscription fee and then separate charges for additional channels and/or programs, hourly rates, and so on.

Under perfect discrimination the monopolist's output would be identical to that of a competitively organized market. The only difference would be in the transfer of wealth from consumers to the monopolist. However, perfect discrimination is unattainable in the real world, and when less than perfect, its effect on allocation is indeterminate; in some cases it may be worse than if the monopolist charged a single price.[25] Price discrimination may also entail substantial administrative costs. Nonetheless, the existence of excellent opportunities for discrimination in the provision of cable service reduces one's confidence that unregulated cable monopolies would result in a substantially suboptimal output.

If the over-the-air service provided by local television stations is a good substitute for cable television service, cable companies will not be able to obtain excess profits. That some consumers are willing to pay for the better reception (especially of color) and greater number of signals that cable television offers is an inconclusive indication of monopoly power; the price that consumers are willing to pay for cable service may just cover the costs of the service.

No problem of monopoly need arise, furthermore, if purchasers have an adequate opportunity to solicit competing bids in advance. The winning bidder will be the supplier who undertakes to provide

[25] See Robinson [27], pp. 190–95.

the service at the lowest possible price, a price that will not include any monopoly toll.[26] As the cable television business now operates, subscribers are rarely if ever given a choice between cable companies; only one cable company solicits their patronage. The immediate cause of this, however, is not any inherent characteristic of cable television but the fact that a cable company must obtain a municipal franchise in order to be permitted to serve any part of the community. Whether it is because they assume that the cable television business is a natural monopoly, and they desire to limit the (surely minor) inconvenience to the public of having several companies using public rights of way to string or lay cable, or alternatively, because they seek a share of monopoly profits in the form of franchise fees, municipalities do not grant more than one cable franchise in any area within their jurisdiction.

Finally, even if cable operators enjoyed effective monopoly power, it would not follow that they would exercise it by raising subscriber rates above cost. They might prefer to charge very low or even zero rates in order to maximize coverage, and look to program fees or fees from networks, advertisers, or channel lessees—or some combination of such charges—as the source of their profits.[27] That would not eliminate the problem of monopoly, but it would eliminate the need for regulating subscriber rates.

The foregoing discussion may seem a bit unreal in light of widespread opinion, some of it supported by evidence, that cable operators enjoy astronomical profits.[28] Assuming there are such profits, we do not know to what extent they are due to technical monopoly and to what extent to municipal franchise policies that foster monopoly unnecessarily.

☐ **Nonregulation.** The last point raises an intriguing possibility in dealing with the problem of monopoly rates to subscribers: the elimination of all franchise regulation. To be sure, were there no franchise or other public regulation of the transactions between cable television companies and subscribers, and if only one company solicited subscribers in an area, the subscribers might be induced to pay a fee in excess of the cost of serving them. However, in the absence of regulation, more than one company might solicit in each area, since many companies are capable of building and operating cable television systems. In principle, competition among the soliciting companies would squeeze any monopoly profit out of the subscriber charge, as long as the companies were prevented from colluding.[29]

There are admittedly many problems. For one, if during the period of initial competition several companies succeeded in signing up some of the residents of an area, each company's subscribers might

---

[26] See Demsetz [7].

[27] Alternative methods of pricing cable service are discussed in Ohls [20], pp. 452–57.

[28] Such as the McGowan, Noll, and Peck study [16], discussed in Section 2.

[29] The result would be like that under a "full-requirements contract," where the purchaser agrees to buy all his requirements of a particular good from one supplier, at a specified price and for a specified period of time. During the life of the contract, there is only one seller; he has a legal monopoly. But the buyer is protected by the initial competition among potential sellers seeking to be awarded the exclusive contract.

be widely scattered. The building of a separate cable network by each company in such circumstances would involve unnecessary duplication of facilities. However, one would expect the companies to exchange subscribers in advance of construction so that each would be serving a compact group. The subscriber who found himself in the service area of a company other than the one to whose service he had subscribed would be protected by his contract with the first company. If the second company wanted to provide a different level of service from that specified in the subscriber's contract with the first, it would have to obtain the subscriber's consent.[30]

The contract solution is not free from difficulty. When the cable subscriber's contract with the cable company expired he would be at the company's mercy, for there would be no other cable company in the area to which he could turn. To be sure, the monopoly position in which the cable company found itself upon expiration of its contracts with subscribers would persist only until a competing company could move into the area and offer them a better contract. However, there would be a lag between the time the first company raised its price and a new company found out, signed up enough subscribers to justify building its own system, and either built such a system or bought the existing system of the first company.

The size of the area in which only one company can economically provide cable television service is probably the most important factor in determining the length of the lag. If that area is an entire city, it may take a long time for a new entrant to win over the existing cable system's subscribers and build a cable network to serve them. If the area is only a small neighborhood, entry could be rapid; cable companies in adjacent areas would only have to extend their lines a few blocks.

One might argue that new entry would be unlikely until the plant of the existing cable company was no longer usable and had to be replaced. Since the costs of operating an already constructed cable system are only a small proportion of the total costs of the system (most of the costs being incurred in the initial construction), it might appear that the existing cable company in an area would have a decisive cost advantage over any new firm which would have to construct (or extend) its system in order to serve the same area. But such reasoning again ignores the possibility of contractual arrangements. Before entering a new area, a cable company can be expected to seek contracts from subscribers now served by the firm (or firms) already in the area. Such a contract might provide that the subscriber, in exchange for a lower rate, would agree to take service from the new firm for a specified period. During this period, the firm would be protected by its subscriber contracts from retaliatory price cutting by the existing firms. To be sure, rather than lose this business the existing firms might offer subscribers a lower rate in order to forestall new entry. But that is all to the good. The process of threat and response would eventually compress rates to a competitive level.

Although rapidity of entry would obviously improve the subscriber's bargaining position, cable subscribers might not necessarily be subjected to monopoly prices if entry were slow. The feasibility

---

[30] Companies might not offer contracts—that is, enforceable commitments—at first, but competition would soon force them to offer such contracts were it common practice for cable companies to jack up rates once the system was built.

of contractural arrangements is again critical. Suppose that it it would take two years for a new company to enter the market of a company that has three-year cable service contracts with its subscribers. At the end of the first year of the contract, subscribers should be able to obtain either an extension of the contract or a new contract with a rival cable company for service commencing with the expiration of the original term. The subscriber has the upper hand.[31]

But we have ignored the problem of contract expense. Most transactions involving individual consumers are not handled by means of formal contracts embodying continuing obligations, probably because of the cost of such arrangements (warranties, however, are an important exception). A contractual solution to the problem of cable monopoly could turn out to be quite costly; whether it would or not is an unstudied empirical question.

□ **Franchise regulation.** The legal authority of municipalities to refuse the use of public rights of way can be used to affect a cable company's ability to exploit its monopolistic position (assuming it has one) in one of two basic ways. The first, which I shall call the "concession" approach, and which has already been employed widely, can take a number of forms. The simplest is to auction off the franchise to the bidder who offers to pay the largest lump sum for it. In bidding under such a system, an applicant will first estimate the monopoly profits (if any) that the franchise would yield were no fee imposed. He will then estimate the capitalized present value of those anticipated profits. That amount is the maximum amount that he will bid for the franchise. The bidder who expects the franchise to yield the largest monopoly profits will be the high bidder and receive the franchise.

This system captures the monopoly profits for the public (in the form of the lump-sum payment to the franchising authority) and is easy and cheap to administer, but it does nothing to alleviate the monopoly problem and may actually aggravate it. Fees to subscribers are no lower than if no attempt to regulate the cable monopoly were made. Less obviously, there is a danger that the franchising authority will be tempted to offer applicants not merely the right to wire homes in its jurisdiction but the exclusive right to do so. By adding a legal monopoly to the franchisee's natural monopoly, the franchising authority may be able to extract a larger sum from the franchisee, but at considerable social cost; for the grant of long-term exclusive franchises to cable companies may retard the process by which changes in technology can, over time, erode a natural monopoly.

An alternative approach would involve awarding the franchise to the firm that offered to pay the franchising authority the highest fee per subscriber or the largest percentage of gross revenues. This method is dubious because it could lead to even higher subscriber fees and lower output levels than the lump-sum auction method. If the fee is based on the number of subscribers, the franchisee will treat it as an additional cost per subscriber. The profit-maximizing strategy in these circumstances is to raise rates to subscribers.[32] If

[31] I do not assume that the subscribers will bargain collectively with the company that serves them. It is only necessary that there be potential entrants to whom individual subscribers can turn for a better deal.

[32] For an explanation of why this is so, see Posner [23], p. 16.

the payment to the franchising authority is a percentage of gross revenue, the cable operator will treat it as reducing the demand for his product; and again one can demonstrate that as long as the cable operator seeks to maximize profits he will raise his subscriber rates. Thus we end up with subscriber rates even higher than those of either an unregulated monopolist or a monopolist franchised under the lump-sum auction method outlined previously.[33]

Another alternative would be to award the franchise to the firm that offered the most service—for example, the firm that promised to dedicate the greatest number of channels, free of charge, to the use of the franchising authority, or to provide the greatest amount of original programming. The effects on output of this approach are more complicated but still adverse. If the response of applicants under such a scheme is to offer more channels or more programs, the consequences depend on the additional investment and operating cost entailed in the larger system. That cost appears to be substantial[34] and will lead to a higher price to the subscriber and to fewer subscribers being served.

The franchise applicant under pressure to offer service concessions may not respond by proposing a larger system. To illustrate, suppose he estimates that subscriber demand would warrant an eight-channel system and that a winning bid would require that he dedicate two channels to the franchising authority. He may offer to build a nine-channel rather than a ten-channel system. Since the subscriber demand for seven channels is less than the demand for eight, he will attract fewer subscribers and hence less revenue, but if the smaller system is sufficiently less expensive to build it may represent, on balance, the better bid.

The usual practice in awarding cable franchises is different from the possibilities we have been discussing. Rather than allowing the size of the concession to be determined by competitive bidding, franchising authorities typically specify a fixed percentage of gross revenues, or other specific concessions, to be provided by the franchisee. This procedure limits the undesirable effects of encouraging franchise applicants to outbid each other, but it does not eliminate them. Any franchise exaction that increases the per-subscriber cost to the cable operator will be passed on, in part at least, to the subscriber in the form of higher rates. Moreover, the fixed concession method deprives the franchise system of one of its most attractive features, ease of administration, since when the franchise is awarded to the high bidder the process of choosing among applicants involves a minimum of administrative machinery and official discretion.

The franchising power could be employed quite differently: not to compel the cable monopolist to divide monopoly profits,

---

[33] This method of awarding franchises may, indeed, be unworkable. Even when a bidder offers a fee per subscriber or a percentage of gross revenues so high that it would require him to operate at a price level where output was extremely small, he would still obtain monopoly profits. There is therefore room for a still higher bid involving a still smaller output. The tendency is for price to approach the highest point on the demand curve and for output to approach zero. The franchising authority may attempt to prevent such a result by fixing a ceiling on the rates that the franchisee may charge, but this involves a shift to another form of control, rate regulation, which has (as we shall see) severe problems of its own.

[34] See Comanor and Mitchell [6], pp. 170–72.

either in money or in service, with the franchising authority, but to induce him to charge subscribers the competitive rate. Under this approach a local agency would act as the purchasing agent of the residents in its jurisdiction for cable television service. It would conduct an auction, with the franchise awarded to the firm that offered the most attractive price-quality package from a subscriber standpoint. Each bidder would submit a plan of service and a schedule of rates. As long as there was more than one bidder and collusion among the bidders was prevented—conditions that ought not to be insuperably difficult to secure—the process of bidding subscriber rates down and quality of service up would eliminate monopoly pricing and profits.

Since bidders may offer quite different types or levels of cable service, having different costs, it may be difficult to decide which bid is best from the subscriber's standpoint. Although consumers face and overcome this problem daily in choosing among products that differ in quality as well as price, here it would not be the consumers (the cable subscribers) who determined the preferred price-quality mix but an official body that must attempt to infer the consumers' preference and, failing that, to substitute its own. The problem could be alleviated to some extent by beginning the bargaining process with an "open season" in which all franchise applicants were free to solicit the area's residents for a set period of time. This would not be a poll; the applicants would seek to obtain actual commitments from potential subscribers. At the end of the solicitation period, the commitments received by the various applicants would be compared and the franchise awarded to the applicant whose guaranteed receipts, on the basis of subscriber commitments, were largest. In this fashion the vote of each subscriber would be weighted by his willingness to pay, and the winning applicant would be the one who, in free competition with the other applicants, was preferred by subscribers in the aggregate. To keep the solicitation process honest, each applicant would be required to contract in advance that, in the event he won, he would provide the level of service, and at the rate represented, in his solicitation drive.

In some instances this method would distort consumer preference. Suppose that 30 percent of the consumers "vote" for system *A*, 30 percent for system *B*, and 40 percent for system *C*, and that *A* and *B* are almost identical but *C* is quite different: *C* will be franchised, though franchising either *A* or *B* would please more consumers. Problems of this sort are resolved automatically in a market by recontracting. One can devise methods of approximating the market result—by having a run-off solicitation campaign or by permitting subscribers to sign up with more than one system—but these may be awkward and expensive.

Another problem of the bargaining method is the duration of the franchise. If it is long, the parties may not have foreseen all of the circumstances that might require modification of its terms. Although this is a problem common to all contracts, the peculiarity here is that one of the contracting parties is not a true party in interest but a public body charged with overseeing the interest of the other parties (the subscribers). Experience with regulatory agencies suggests that one cannot assume such a body will represent the consumer interest faithfully. When the cable company asks for a modification of the contract by virtue of an unforeseen change in circumstances, the public body may react ineffectually or perversely.

It is therefore desirable to keep the term of the franchise sufficiently short so that no modification of its terms need be entertained. However, the fact that the cable company's plant normally will outlast the period of its franchise raises a question: Will not the cable company be able to outbid any new applicant, who would have to build a plant from scratch? And will not the bargaining method therefore be ineffective after the first round? Not necessarily: in bidding for the franchise on the basis of new equipment costs, new applicants need not be at a significant disadvantage in relation to the incumbent franchisee. For example, once a new applicant is franchised he could negotiate to purchase the system of the existing franchisee, who faces the loss of the unamortized portion of his investment if his successor builds a new system. Insofar as the economic life of cable plant is considered a problem when the franchise term is short, it can be solved by including in the franchise a provision requiring the franchisee, at his successor's option, to sell his plant (including improvements) to the latter at its original cost, as depreciated.

☐ **Rate regulation.** Franchise regulation (or deregulation) is only one possible approach to the problem—if there is a problem—of monopolistic subscription rates. Another is direct regulation of those rates. While there has been as yet little direct experience with attempts to regulate cable rates, there has been a good deal of experience with rate regulation in other industries, such as local gas, water, electrical, and telephone service, that resemble cable television in their supply and demand characteristics. That experience offers some guide to the likely costs and benefits of extending the principles of public utility regulation to cable television.

In principle, placing a ceiling on the rates that a monopolist may charge is a straightforward and efficacious corrective. But there is reason for concern that in practice it (1) may be ineffectual and (2) may impose substantial, if largely invisible, efficiency costs on the community.

Thus far, empirical studies have not discovered any appreciable impact of regulation on the rates of the companies regulated.[35] That is probably due in part to the paucity of resources, especially at the state level, devoted to rate regulation, and in part to the difficulty of determining a regulated firm's costs—a necessary step if its rates are to be set at a level that will limit or prevent monopoly pricing while permitting the firm to recover its legitimate expenses. Some costs can be determined easily enough if the underlying data are known, but such data are held by the regulated firms and are not always easy to extract in a trustworthy or usable form. Other costs are difficult to determine even if the underlying data are easily available. These include depreciation and the cost of equity capital. The latter depends on the rate of return that investors demand for providing capital to firms of the regulated company's risk class, and on the value of the company's capital assets against which to apply

---

[35] These studies are discussed in Posner [25]. A study not discussed there is Moore [17]. For a fuller treatment of the matters discussed in this section of the paper, refer to Posner [24].

the rate; both quantities as yet elude confident measure. Problems are also encountered in separating costs between regulated and non-regulated services provided by the company. Slight errors in the successive steps required to determine the company's relevant costs may cumulate so as to deprive regulation of any significant effect on the regulated firms' rate and profits. Furthermore, rates are reviewed periodically rather than continuously, and changing conditions of cost or demand may produce windfall profits or losses in the intervals between rate reviews.

None of these problems can be written off as trivial in the cable television context. On the contrary, with the industry in so embryonic a state of development, and demand and technology still so fluid, the determination of proper depreciation periods and of risk (and hence of the required rate of return to equity financing) is likely to be unusually difficult; periodic rate reviews may be too infrequent to permit the adjustment of rates to rapidly changing costs and demands; and since many cable companies have systems in different jurisdictions, and since some companies are subsidiaries or affiliates of non-cable enterprises, cost separation problems seem unavoidable. While present cable systems are relatively small and simple compared to many other regulated firms, the picture may change dramatically as the industry matures. And even if the difficulties in the way of effective regulation prove less pronounced with respect to cable television than with respect to some other industries, the resources devoted to its regulation are likely to be less ample as well. Legislatures often thrust additional duties on regulatory agencies faster than they appropriate additional funds, believing that the agencies can probably do more with their existing resources than they are doing.

The costs of regulation are commonly measured by the budgets of the regulatory agencies; but this procedure greatly understates the true costs. It ignores not only the legal and other expenses that are imposed upon regulated firms, which exceed by several times the expenses of the agencies,[36] but also the considerable indirect costs of regulation arising from (1) the adaptive responses that firms will make to a regulatory environment and (2) the perverse applications of regulation that are such a common and seemingly inescapable feature of public utility and common carrier regulatory schemes. This is not the place to review the depressing literature on the costs of regulation. Suffice it to say that neither in general nor in the particular circumstances of the cable television industry can it be complacently assumed that public utility controls would have a positive benefit-cost ratio.[37]

We are left, then, with a set of alternative approaches to the regulation of cable monopoly, no one of which is free from substantial difficulties. A period of experimentation would seem to be indicated.

■ The original thrust of federal regulation of cable television was to protect over-the-air broadcasters from competitive injury at the hands of the new industry. That thrust is losing momentum, in part because the prospective injury to over-the-air broadcasters,

5. Protection of broadcast television

---

[36] A case study is Gerwig [9].

[37] See Posner [24, 25].

and especially to the UHF stations that are a particular object of the FCC's solicitude, has been shown to be less severe, or at least less immediate, than originally believed;[38] but it retains a good deal of force.

☐ **The threat to broadcast television.** The subsequent subsections assume that cable television, unless restricted by the government, will make substantial inroads into the amount and quality of over-the-air television service. The assumption is probably unsound. Even if cable television were to become dominant, it does not follow that over-the-air service would decrease. If 90 percent of the country's households subscribed to cable television, the remaining 10 percent would still constitute an enormous market for advertisers. And many cable subscribers would own portable television sets. Since programming, rather than transmission, accounts for the major costs of television, the self-interest of advertisers would in all probability lead them to defray the modest costs of operating a sufficient number of transmitters to reach households not on the cable and owners of portable sets.

The principal change would be in the number of stations. The reason for having 800-odd television stations is not to maximize the amount and quality of television received in each household—a much smaller number of regional stations would permit a larger number of signals to be received by each viewer—but to preserve the curious concept of a nation of local television stations.[39] High cable penetration would make many of these local stations uneconomical and thereby foster a long overdue reorganization of the industry into a much smaller number of regional stations. Such a reorganization would confer additional social benefits by freeing up large portions of the radio spectrum for other uses.

It is sometimes argued that cable systems would buy exclusive rights to programs (and thereby deny them to the over-the-air service) in order to attract new subscribers with entertainment not available over the air. But whether this promotional device would be used extensively is conjectural. A cable system would have to pay a higher price for exclusive than for nonexclusive rights to a program, since in the former case the program owner would lose the revenues that he would have obtained by selling rights to television stations as well as to cable systems. A cable exclusive may injure broadcast competitors by making their service less attractive to viewers but it must also injure the cable system by requiring it to pay more for programs.

☐ **Arguments for protection.** Let us assume, contrary to the previous discussion, that cable television (quite apart from any pay-by-the-program feature) would lead to a reduction in the quantity and quality of over-the-air service; and let us consider, to begin, several respects in which cable television might be thought to have an unfair advantage in competition with broadcast stations as a result not of intrinsic merit but simply of unequal treatment in the eyes of the law. First, broadcast stations must pay royalties when the matter

[38] See Park [22].
[39] Discussed in Johnson [11], pp. 2-3.

they broadcast is copyrighted, while cable systems that rebroadcast those signals need not. That is the effect of the present Copyright Act as interpreted by the Supreme Court in the Fortnightly case.[40] Second, broadcast stations are expressly forbidden by Sec. 325 of the Communications Act of 1934[41] to rebroadcast any other station's signals without that station's consent; no similar provision is applicable to cable systems. Third, it is FCC policy to discourage broadcast stations from rebroadcasting another station's signals regardless of consent. A station that violated this policy would risk nonrenewal of its license.[42]

The copyright argument seems weak. A broadcast station is in effect a middleman between the owners of programs (copyright holders) and advertisers. The station buys popular programs in order to generate audience and sells time in breaks between and within programs to advertisers wanting to reach a large audience. Revenue from advertisers covers the royalties to the copyright holders. A more popular program will attract a larger audience and enable the station to charge higher rates to advertisers, and will also command a higher royalty. By carrying a station's signal beyond its ordinary range, a cable system enlarges the station's audience and thereby increases the revenue that the station is able to extract from advertisers. This in turn enables the copyright holder to extract a larger royalty. At least as a first approximation, then, both station and copyright holder benefit from cable service even though the cable system pays no royalty. Indeed, it seems anomalous to require it to pay royalties when it is not in the business of selling audience to advertisers.[43]

Since television stations located in the cable system's market must pay royalties for its programs, the question arises whether those stations will be harmed as a result of the ability of the cable system to obtain programs free of charge, even if the distant originating station and the copyright owner are adequately compensated. The local station need not suffer any harm. It is free to sell time to advertisers on the program that it buys; the cable system cannot do so unless it likewise buys the programs. What would be unfair to the local stations would be to impose more onerous conditions on them when *they* desire to carry distant signals. Here we come up against Sec. 325. If cable systems are not required to obtain the consent of the originating station, this provision should be repealed.

[40] Fortnightly Corp. v. United Artists Television, Inc., 392 U. S. 390 (1968).

[41] See [29] at 325.

[42] There is a limited exception for "translators" that extend television coverage to remote communities. See 47 C.F.R. 74.731 *et seq.*

[43] If cable systems blocked out the commercials on the station signals and sold the time to other advertisers without paying royalties to the copyright owners, they would be guilty of piracy. The cable system would be selling program time to advertisers, while refusing to buy the programs from their owners. However, instances of such substitution are apparently rare, and nothing in the Fortnightly decision suggests that cable systems could escape liability under the Copyright Act for such acts of piracy. The Court was careful to limit its decision to the situation in which the cable operator simply retransmits the signal of the distant station. In fact, the Court's holding of copyright immunity was expressly premised on the analogy of the cable system to a giant antenna erected by the set owner himself (see 392 U.S. at 399)—an analogy that collapses when the cable system does more than rebroadcast. The Court's ruling is also limited to the case in which the cable system does no original broadcasting (see *id.* at 392, note 6); inserting its own commercials would be a form of origination.

By the same token the FCC's policy against retransmission of broadcast signals by its broadcast licensees should be changed. One need not question here the Commission's preference, which appears to be at the root of the policy against retransmission, for local control of television programming. The policy against retransmission is not effective in implementing that preference. While forbidden to rebroadcast the signals of other stations, television stations can and do broadcast primarily network programs, network reruns, and other syndicated matter—none of which originates locally. What is the justification for a rule that permits broadcast stations to obtain programs from distant sources by electronic interconnection or mailed tape, and forbids them to obtain such programs only when the means of receipt is by interception of a broadcast signal?

Perhaps the answer is that a system under which both cable systems and broadcast stations were free to carry distant signals without copyright liability would not protect the legitimate interests of copyright holders. When a program is carried in a local market by a cable system, the owner of the program cannot charge the local stations in the market as much for the right to carry it, because he can no longer offer an exclusive contract. In some instances his loss will be made up by the larger royalty that he is able to extract from the originating station. But if the originating station sells time only to local advertisers who are indifferent to reaching an audience outside of the station's immediate market, carriage by the cable systems will not enhance the station's advertising revenue and enable it to pay a higher royalty.

However, this takes too static a view of the situation. A station whose signals are carried by cable systems into distant markets will market time to regional rather than local advertisers in order to capitalize on its larger, regional audience.[44] As such stations reach out for a regional market, local advertisers will switch to stations which lack regional aspirations and whose signals are not carried outside the markets in which they are located. Such a reassignment of customers would follow the pattern established in network broadcasting, whereby the network, which through its affiliates has access to national and regional audiences, sells time to national and regional advertisers while local stations sell time to local advertisers.

The more rapid the growth of the cable television industry, in fact, the better off copyright holders are likely to be. Those channels on which cable entrepreneurs plan to originate programs represent an important new market for copyrighted material. And the revenues that cable companies derive from subscriber fees represent an important potential source of augmented copyright royalties. Any rule that by limiting carriage of distant signals retards the expansion of cable television service will postpone these returns. How then to explain the opposition of the copyright interests to unrestricted carriage of distant signals? They may deem it wise strategy to oppose all attempts at limiting copyright liability. Some copyright holders, moreover, have broadcast interests. Most important, any legal hold that the copyright interests are able to establish over the

---

[44] There is evidence that stations do advertise cable carriage of their broadcasts to attract additional advertisers. See Hearings on H.R. 4347 Before Subcommittee No. 3 [30], pp. 1281–82, 1302–06.

cable companies will be worth something to those companies to remove.

The foregoing analysis lends little support to the argument that the right of cable companies to import distant signals should be limited, although it does suggest that some relatively minor legislative and administrative modifications to permit broadcast stations freely to rebroadcast the signals of other stations should be adopted. But neither does the analysis support the opposite position: that a rule limiting the right of cable systems to carry distant signals must impede the growth of the service. Where transactions are permitted and are feasible, the initial assignment of legal liability will not affect resource use.[45] The qualifications in this statement must not be ignored: The parties must be free to bargain, and transactions must not be prohibitively costly. A rule under which permission to carry distant signals depends not on the willingness of the program owner or of his proxy, the originating station, but on the leave of the Commission violates the first condition. Were the FCC to forbid the copyright and cable interests to work out clearinghouse procedures (analogous to those employed in the recorded-music field) for the wholesale granting of copyright licenses, the second condition, reasonably low transaction costs, might also be violated; haggling over every single copyrighted item might be unduly costly.

Let us now consider what the impact on the existing pattern of income distribution in our society might be if cable television continues to expand. Were over-the-air service to be wholly displaced by cable, people in remote areas, where the cost of providing cable service was prohibitive, would be cut off from any television service. However, a policy of benefiting rural inhabitants in the lump would be undiscriminating; and a method of subsidizing the wants of rural dwellers that involved a denial or limitation of service to millions of other people would impose unnecessary costs on society. If it is believed that rural inhabitants should be assured television service, that object can be secured without limiting the availability of cable television to those who want and are willing to pay for it, either by paying television stations to remain in operation or by paying cable television companies to extend service to the rural population.[46] The point need not be labored further since we have already discussed the inappropriateness of internal subsidization as a goal in the regulation of cable television.

Another effect of the displacement of over-the-air by cable service would be to impose a charge for a service that viewers now receive gratis. This might be thought to work particular hardship on lower-income groups. However, all other considerations aside, limitations on cable service could well injure rather than benefit those groups. They may rather pay $5 a month for cable service, and $1 for occasional special programs, than receive over-the-air service for nothing. The superior reception, additional signals, and an occasional first-run movie thus obtained might make cable television an acceptable substitute for more costly entertainment, information, and educational services. It is not as if the poor were especially well served by

[45] See Coase [4].

[46] The Rural Electrification Administration, with its programs of financial assistance to rural electrical and telephone cooperatives, provides a precedent for this approach.

the present system of free television service. The present system does not appear to cater to those wants or needs that are special to the poor. Geared to the tastes and interests of its predominantly middle-class audience, the television industry has offered little or no programming on child care, job opportunities, vocational training, and ethnic culture that might especially interest poor people. Accordingly, a policy of limiting the expansion of cable television service in order to assure that the poor continue to receive free television seems an impoverished, if not hypocritical, response to the problem of poverty.

There is one more ground on which to urge the protection of the broadcast industry against the competition of cable television. A firm that obtains a license from the FCC to operate a television station and succeeds in affiliating with one of the major networks will generally be able to derive a revenue from the sale of advertising time that is vastly in excess of its capital and operating costs. The government could capture these rents for itself by auctioning off broadcast licenses to the highest bidder. The amount bid would represent the bidder's estimate of the capitalized value of the anticipated rents. (When a licensee transfers his license to another, the purchase price includes just such an amount.) Instead, service in the "public interest" has been made the criterion for the initial grant and renewal of broadcast licenses.[47] In effect, the licensee is compelled to rebate a portion of his windfall profits to the public in the form of service beyond what an unfettered profit maximizer would charge. This portion may be very small, but at least some news and public-affairs programming is carried that is not remunerative. If cable television is permitted to compete away the large profits of the television stations, the public-interest programming supported by those profits may be curtailed. Because much of this programming involves the reporting of controversial political events, such as election campaigns and various governmental activities, government subsidy is not an attractive alternative.

As an argument for protecting the broadcast service from inroads by cable television, this overlooks the cost, in public-service programming foregone, that a policy of protection would impose. Cable television probably provides a better environment for the encouragement of public-interest programming than over-the-air service. With no lack of channels, such programming is not so apt to be displaced by more popular programs that can command greater advertiser support. And having subscriber as well as advertiser revenues, the cable system need not find a commercial sponsor in order to defray the cost of a program. If public-affairs and local-service programming is likely to flourish on cable television to a degree not attainable in over-the-air broadcasting, any policy of limiting the growth of cable television will curtail the public-interest programming available to cable subscribers, at the same time that it is perhaps preserving such programming for over-the-air viewers. Only if and when cable television becomes very widespread will the profits of network-owned and network-affiliated stations, the mainstays of the over-the-air service and the principal sources of the

---

[47] See Communications Act of 1934, as amended [29]; Public Service Responsibility of Broadcast Licensees [37]; and Commission Policy on Programming [31].

programming in question, be jeopardized; but at that point, by hypothesis, most viewers will be cable subscribers.

My conclusion is that a policy of protecting broadcast television from the competition of cable service cannot be justified.

■ All three levels of government—federal, state, and municipal— have become deeply involved in the regulation of cable television. The thrust of regulation, however, has been markedly different at each level.

At the municipal level, where cable regulation has usually taken the form of conditioning permission to use public rights of way upon the franchisee's agreement to rebate a portion of his gross revenues and provide free service to the city, the thrust of cable regulation has not been to limit monopoly profits, but, much more dubiously, to divert a portion of those profits to the public purse. We must inquire whether the present character of municipal regulation of cable television is accidental and easily remediable, or the result of more or less inherent conditions of local government. I suspect the latter is the case. First, municipal governments are desperate to find additional sources of revenue. Federal and state income taxation leaves little room for cities to levy their own income taxes. People who enjoy the benefits of municipal services can often escape the cost of those services by moving to the suburbs. And cities act as magnets to poor people who receive, in services and transfer payments, more than they pay in taxes. Since these factors are likely to persist, cities will continue to find cable television an attractive source of additional revenue. Among other factors, an excise tax on cable television may be more progressive than many city taxes (although it could become highly regressive if cable television ever became peculiarly responsive to the needs of the urban poor), and a tax on a new service is likely to be less disruptive of expectations, and therefore less costly politically, than a tax on an existing service.[48] The administrative costs of a tax on cable television are also low, since the municipality collects it from one or at most a few concerns, unlike a property tax or general sales tax.

Second, the traditions of monopoly regulation are very weak at the municipal level, perhaps because the conditions of local government do not favor effective monopoly regulation. Local government does not exhibit the kind of differentiation found at the state and federal levels, where there are regulatory agencies that enjoy a high degree of autonomy and specialization. Rarely will a municipal agency be sufficiently independent to subordinate municipal revenue needs to other welfare dimensions. There is also a problem of scale. It will generally not pay a city to inform itself in adequate detail of the promise and problems of cable television; the question is too large in relation to the impact of the industry on the single city in question. And there is finally a problem of freeloading. The rate at

6. Rationalizing the structure of regulation

---

[48] If a new tax is placed on barbers, they feel it in reduced demand for their services, and customers feel it in a higher price for haircuts. A tax on cable television is felt by the cable entrepreneur as an additional cost, but he is rarely a local resident. The tax enters into the fee paid by subscribers; but lacking any experience with a fee that does not include such a tax—having no basis for comparison— they are unlikely to grumble.

which the cable industry grows nationwide may affect crucially the advent of new services (such as pay televison on the cable) that could have large positive welfare effects; for many of those services, to be remunerative, require the aggregation of audience across many markets. An individual municipality knows, however, that the rate at which cable television spreads in its community will have little effect on the national scene, and that if it retards the local cable company's growth in order to squeeze badly-needed municipal revenues from cable operations, the rate of overall national growth, and the benefits such growth will bring, will not be materially affected.

Although a continuation of municipal regulation of cable television in its present form will act as a brake on the growth of cable television, it does not follow that municipal regulation should be preempted. Municipalities do need additional sources of revenue and it is not clear that on balance there are many better objects of taxation than cable television. The dilemma is particularly acute for those who believe both that urban problems are serious and that the most exciting prospects for cable television relate precisely to those problems.

The thrust of regulation at the state level has been quite different from that at the municipal level. Several states have passed statutes classifying cable systems as public utilities and regulating entry, rates, and service accordingly.[49] There has been no attempt, as at the municipal level, to derive revenue for the state government from cable television.[50] On a superficial analysis the thrust of state regulation is in the right direction, if what is desired is to encourage the growth of cable television, since the formal objective of public utility regulation is to bring about results akin to those of competition in industries not naturally competitive. Unfortunately, as discussed earlier, there is now strong reason to suspect that public utility regulation works much less well in practice than in theory, and skepticism in this regard is particularly pronounced with respect to traditionally undermanned and underfinanced state public utility commissions.

The thrust of regulation of cable television at the federal level is again different. The federal government, acting through the Federal Communications Commission, has not attempted to regulate cable television rates. The Communications Act of 1934 can perhaps be read as giving the Commission the requisite authority,[51] but it is unlikely to assume it. There are thousands of cable television companies and it would be a formidable undertaking for the Commission to regulate each one of them. It must be aware of the failure of the Federal Power Commission's attempt to regulate the thousands of independent producers of natural gas[52] and cannot desire to repeat that unhappy experience.

The Commission has manifested a dual purpose in its regulation of cable television: to shield over-the-air broadcasting from competitive injury by cable television, and to channel the development of cable television in accordance with the Commission's vaguely

---

[49] The statutes are summarized in New York State Public Service Commission Report [19].

[50] *Ibid.*, p. 112. Vermont has imposed a gross-receipts tax, but only to defray the (presumably small) expenses of the regulatory agency.

[51] See *Columbia Law Review* Note [5].

[52] See MacAvoy [15].

perceived, unarticulated, and nonetheless tenaciously maintained vision or master plan for the television industry. The second of these purposes is less well-known than the first. The Commission has long been sensitive, and rightly so, to criticisms that its management of the television industry via control of allocation of the radio spectrum has failed to develop, if indeed it has not stifled, the promise of television.[53] The allocation of spectrum to television adopted in the early 1950s gave most viewers a choice of only a few signals. They would have had a larger choice had the Commission not been wedded to a local-station concept (borrowed from its regulation of the radio industry) whereby each community, other than the smallest, was granted at least one "resident" television station. The price of having local stations was that viewers received fewer signals than if the Commission had permitted large regional stations.[54] The price has proved to be a high one; local stations do very little local programming worthy of the name.[55] The Commission expected the problem to be solved by its allocation of large sections of the UHF band for additional television stations, commercial and noncommercial, but this solution failed—most basically, I believe, because advertising, and *a fortiori* charity, cannot support so many television stations. The costs of over-the-air pay television and a general lack of interest in its potentiality seemed to close off that path to a solution also.

Against this background, cable television appears to the Commission as both danger and possible salvation. It is a danger because it jeopardizes over-the-air broadcasting, in particular the UHF service that the Commission has so assiduously nurtured (though recent scholarship may compel a reevaluation of the threat to UHF).[56] At the same time, cable television offers possible deliverance from the conditions—channel scarcity and dependence on advertiser support—that have seemed to prevent television from fulfilling its promise. The Commission is not unaware of this. But after years of master-planning the evolution of the television industry, it cannot let well enough alone. It has decided to cast free over-the-air television in the role of a medium of popular entertainment that is to be available without charge to all (including those too poor to pay for television and those who live in areas that cannot be wired at reasonable cost), and that is to be supported—necessarily if it is to be a free service—by advertisers. It has decided to cast cable television in the role of innovator. Thus, it has required the larger cable operators to originate programming, hoping that their product will be different from that presented on over-the-air television; has conspicuously permitted them to charge by the program or by the channel for original programming; and has required them to serve as an authentic voice of the local community. The distant-signal limitations that the Commission has imposed on the cable-television

---

[53] A polite but penetrating criticism is Johnson [11], pp. 2–8.

[54] The FCC's policy of encouraging a large number of stations creates lots of dead spaces in which channels cannot be utilized because to do so would cause interference with stations broadcasting on the same channel in adjacent areas. That is why many areas of the country can receive only two or three VHF television channels even though 13 such channels have been allocated to VHF television broadcasting.

[55] As indicated by a recent industry-sponsored study. See Land [13].

[56] See Park [22].

industry are also designed, in part, to push the industry away from conventional television and toward presenting more original programs. The Commission is at present mulling over additional rules similarly designed to induce cable television to play a distinctive role in the overall television scene.[57]

Thus far, however, the purpose of protecting over-the-air television from the competition of cable television has been more in evidence than the purpose of shaping cable television into a distinctive service. The limitations that the Commission has placed on the carriage of distant signals have probably retarded the development of cable television by years. Moreover, the capacity of the Commission to shape cable television in affirmative ways is extremely limited. As we have seen, to require cable companies to provide services that they cannot market remuneratively is a dubious method of promoting cable television. But this is the only method of promotion available to the Commission.

We are left with the following alternatives, which unhappily are not mutually exclusive: taxation of cable television by regulation at the municipal level; public utility controls at the state level; and a master-planning approach at the federal level that seeks to carve out a distinctive role for cable television, at the same time seeking to cushion its competitive impact on over-the-air broadcasting. None of the regulatory alternatives is terribly attractive in itself; aggregated, they become distinctly unattractive. The sheer cost of complying with three independent, overlapping, and extensive regulatory schemes could well slow the growth of cable television. And nowhere in the array of regulatory systems do we find any capability for coordinating and evaluating the various regulatory programs.

There is much to be said in these circumstances for a new federal statute defining the respective regulatory roles of federal, state, and local governments. An outline of such a statute will serve to round out our discussion of regulation and to recapitulate earlier proposals of this article.

(1) The statute would place a ceiling on the exactions that municipalities may impose on cable television systems in the form of gross-receipts taxes or free municipal channels, or in any other form, as a condition of granting a franchise. The purpose of this provision would be to accommodate the legitimate needs of the cities for additional sources of revenue with the goal of fostering the development of cable television. Municipal authorities would be permitted—and encouraged—to auction off franchises to the firm promising to provide cable service at the lowest rates to subscribers, as suggested earlier.

(2) States would be permitted, but not required, to regulate cable television companies as common carriers or public utilities. Realism would appear to dictate such a provision, whatever its wisdom, and any bad effects would be mitigated by provision (5)(a) below.

(3) The statute would embody a once-for-all legislative solution to the issues of (a) cable operators' copyright liability and (b) the

---

[57] The Commission's latest thinking is contained in a letter from Dean Burch, Chairman of the FCC, to the Chairmen of the Senate Communications Subcommittee and the House Communications and Power Subcommittee. See [34].

need (if any) to protect over-the-air broadcasting from extinction at the hands of cable television. The FCC seems incapable of resolving either issue; both will have to be resolved if cable television is to be relieved of the onerous restrictions that the Commission has placed upon it. I do not undertake here to suggest the terms of the solutions. An important object here is to facilitate the exit of the FCC from the business of regulating cable television. To this end, Congress might further wish to give permanent statutory embodiment to local-signal carriage and nonduplication rules that the Commission has promulgated and that are no longer within the arena of debate.

(4) The FCC would be forbidden to regulate cable television, with three exceptions:

    (a) The Commission would retain such authority as might be necessary to prevent purely physical interference with FCC licensees. Thus, it could regulate the frequencies used by microwave common carriers that furnish distant signals to cable companies.

    (b) It would retain authority to punish cable operators who violated the police-type regulations that have been imposed on television, such as the rule forbidding the broadcasting of obscene matter.

    (c) It would retain authority to promulgate and enforce reasonable rules limiting cross-ownership of media in the same local market.

(5) An Office of Cable Communications would be established in the federal government. It would have several functions (none regulatory):

    (a) To evaluate state and local regulation of cable television, to advise state and local governments on the uses and modes of regulating cable television, and to submit to Congress proposals for modifying state or local regulatory authority where such a course seemed indicated;

    (b) To serve as a national clearinghouse for information concerning the uses, prospects, regulation, and promotion of cable television; and

    (c) To monitor the implementation of the statute and report to Congress periodically on the progress of cable television and cable communications generally.

The statute would shift the emphasis of governmental intervention in cable communications from regulation to research and evaluation. Such a change in the focus of government activity seems more likely to foster the healthy growth of the industry than a continuation of the present emphasis on proliferating restrictions at many levels of government.

References

1. ALCHIAN, A. A. and KESSEL, R. A. "Competition, Monopoly, and the Pursuit of Pecuniary Gain," in *Aspects of Labor Economics*, a Conference Series Report by the National Bureau of Economic Research, Princeton, N. J.: Princeton Univ. Press, 1962, pp. 157–75.

2. BARNETT, S. R. "Cable Television and Media Concentration, Part I: Control of Cable Systems by Local Broadcasters." *Stanford Law Review*, Vol. 22, No. 2 (January 1970), pp. 221–329.

3. COASE, R. H. "The Economics of Uniform Pricing Systems." *Manchester School of Economics and Social Studies*, Vol. 15, No. 4 (May 1947), pp. 139–56.

4. ———. "The Problem of Social Cost." *The Journal of Law and Economics*, Vol. 3, No. 2 (October 1960), pp. 1–44.

5. COLUMBIA LAW REVIEW "Note: Regulation of Community Antenna Television." *Columbia Law Review*, Vol. 70, No. 5 (May 1970), pp. 837–75.

6. COMANOR, W. S. and MITCHELL, B. M. "Cable Television and the Impact of Regulation." *The Bell Journal of Economics and Management Science*, Vol. 2, No. 1 (Spring 1971), pp. 154–212.

7. DEMSETZ, H. "Why Regulate Utilities?" *The Journal of Law and Economics*, Vol. 11, No. 1 (April 1968), pp. 55–65.

8. DIRLAM, J. B. and KAHN, A. E. "The Merits of Reserving the Cost-Savings from Domestic Communications Satellites for Support of Educational Television." *Yale Law Journal*, Vol. 77, No. 3 (January 1968), pp. 494–519.

9. GERWIG, R. W. "Natural Gas Production: A Study of Costs of Regulation." *The Journal of Law and Economics*, Vol. 5, No. 2 (October 1962), pp. 69–92.

10. GREEN, M., ed. *The Closed Enterprise System—The Nader Study Group Report on Antitrust Enforcement*. 2 Vols. Washington, D. C.: Center for Study of Responsive Law, 1971.

11. JOHNSON, L. L. "The Future of Cable Television: Some Problems of Federal Regulation." Rand Memorandum RM-61-99FF, January 1970.

12. KITCH, E. W. "Regulation of the Field Market for Natural Gas by the Federal Power Commission." *The Journal of Law and Economics*, Vol. 11, No. 2 (October 1968), pp. 243–80.

13. LAND, HERMAN W. ASSOCIATES. *Television and the Wired City*. New York, 1968.

14. LEES, F. A. and YANG, C. Y. "The Redistributional Effect of Television Advertising." *Economic Journal*, Vol. 76, No. 298 (June 1966), pp. 328–36.

15. MACAVOY, P. "The Effectiveness of the Federal Power Commission." *The Bell Journal of Economics and Management Science*. Vol. 1, No. 2 (Autumn 1970), pp. 271–303.

16. McGOWAN, J., NOLL, R., and PECK, M. "Prospects and Policies for CATV." Mimeographed. Washington, D. C.: The Brookings Institution, March 1971.

17. MOORE, T. G. "The Effectiveness of Regulation of Electric Utility Prices." *Southern Economic Journal*, Vol. 36, No. 4 (April 1970), pp. 365–75.

18. NEW YORK MAYOR'S ADVISORY COMMITTEE ON CATV AND TELECOMMUNICATIONS. "A Report on Cable Television and Cable Telecommunications in New York City." Mimeographed. New York, September 14, 1968.

19. NEW YORK STATE PUBLIC SERVICE COMMISSION. "Regulation of Cable Television by the State of New York." Report to the Commission by Commissioner William K. Jones. Mimeographed. New York, 1970.

20. OHLS, J. C. "Marginal Cost Pricing, Investment Theory and CATV." *The Journal of Law and Economics*, Vol. 13, No. 2 (October 1970), pp. 439–60.

21. PARK, R. E. "Cable Television and UHF Broadcasting." Rand Report R-689-MF, January 1971.

22. ———. "Potential Impact of Cable Growth on Television Broadcasting." Rand Report R-587-FF, October 1970.

23. POSNER, R. A. "Cable Television: The Problem of Local Monopoly." Rand Memorandum RM-6309-FF, May 1970.

24. ———. "Natural Monopoly and Its Regulation." *Stanford Law Review*, Vol. 21, No. 3 (February 1969), pp. 548–643.

25. ———. "Natural Monopoly and Its Regulation: A Reply." *Stanford Law Review*, Vol. 22, No. 3 (February 1970), pp. 540–46.

26. ———. "Taxation by Regulation." *The Bell Journal of Economics and Management Science*, Vol. 2, No. 1 (Spring 1971), pp. 22–50.

27. ROBINSON, J. *The Economics of Imperfect Competition*. New York: The MacMillan Co., 1933.

28. STIGLER, G. *The Organization of Industry*. Homewood, Ill.: Richard D. Irwin, Inc., 1968.

29. *U. S. Code*. Communications Act of 1934, as amended. 47 U.S.C. 307 (1964).
30. U. S. CONGRESS, HOUSE, COMMITTEE ON THE JUDICIARY. *Hearings on H.R. 4347 Before Subcommittee No. 3.* 89th Cong., 1st Session, 1960.
31. U. S. FEDERAL COMMUNICATIONS COMMISSION. "Commission Policy on Programming." 25 F.R. 7291 (1960).
32. ———. *First Report and Order in Docket 18397 (CATV)*. 20 F.C.C. 2d 201 (1969).
33. ———. *Fourth Report and Order (Subscription Television)*. 15 F.C.C. 2d 446 (1968).
34. ———. *In Re Commission Proposals for Regulation of Cable Television*, 31 F.C.C. 2d 115 (1971).
35. ———. *Memorandum Opinion and Order in Docket 18397 (CATV)*. 23 F.C.C. 2d 825, 828 (1920).
36. ———. *Notice of Proposed Rulemaking and Notice of Inquiry in Docket No. 18397 (CATV)*. 15 F.C.C. 2d 417, 426–27 (1968).
37. ———. *Public Service Responsibility of Broadcast Licensees*. Washington, D. C.: U. S. Govt. Printing Office, 1947.
38. ———. *Second Report and Order in Docket 18397 (CATV)*. 23 F.C.C. 2d 816 (1970).
39. ———. *Subscription Television Service*. 3 F.C.C. 2d 1, 21 (1962).

Name index

Economists of the Twentieth Century

Monetarism and Macroeconomic
Policy
Thomas Mayer

Studies in Fiscal Federalism
Wallace E. Oates

The World Economy in Perspective
Essays in International Trade and European
Integration
Herbert Giersch

Towards a New Economics
Critical Essays on Ecology, Distribution and
Other Themes
Kenneth E. Boulding

Studies in Positive and Normative
Economics
Martin J. Bailey

The Collected Essays of Richard E.
Quandt (2 volumes)
Richard E. Quandt

International Trade Theory and Policy
Selected Essays of W. Max Corden
W. Max Corden

Organization and Technology in Capitalist
Development
William Lazonick

Studies in Human Capital
Collected Essays of Jacob Mincer, Volume 1
Jacob Mincer

Studies in Labor Supply
Collected Essays of Jacob Mincer, Volume 2
Jacob Mincer

Macroeconomics and Economic Policy
The Selected Essays of Assar Lindbeck
Volume I
Assar Lindbeck

The Welfare State
The Selected Essays of Assar Lindbeck
Volume II
Assar Lindbeck

Classical Economics, Public Expenditure
and Growth
Walter Eltis

Money, Interest Rates and Inflation
Frederic S. Mishkin

The Public Choice Approach to Politics
Dennis C. Mueller

The Liberal Economic Order
Volume I Essays on International Economics
Volume II Money, Cycles and Related Themes
Gottfried Haberler
Edited by Anthony Y.C. Koo

Economic Growth and Business Cycles
Prices and the Process of Cyclical Development
Paolo Sylos Labini

International Adjustment, Money and
Trade
Theory and Measurement for Economic Policy
Volume I
Herbert G. Grubel

International Capital and Service Flows
Theory and Measurement for Economic Policy
Volume II
Herbert G. Grubel

Unintended Effects of Government
Policies
Theory and Measurement for Economic Policy
Volume III
Herbert G. Grubel

The Economics of Competitive Enterprise
Selected Essays of P.W.S. Andrews
Edited by Frederic S. Lee
and Peter E. Earl

The Repressed Economy
Causes, Consequences, Reform
Deepak Lal

Economic Theory and Market Socialism
Selected Essays of Oskar Lange
Edited by Tadeusz Kowalik

Trade, Development and Political
Economy
Selected Essays of Ronald Findlay
Ronald Findlay

General Equilibrium Theory
The Collected Essays of Takashi Negishi
Volume I
Takashi Negishi

The History of Economics
The Collected Essays of Takashi Negishi
Volume II
Takashi Negishi

Studies in Econometric Theory
The Collected Essays of Takeshi Amemiya
Takeshi Amemiya